Handbook of Cultura and Education

CONTEXTS OF EDUCATION

Volume no. 4

Series Editor:

Michael A. Peters
University of Illinois at Urbana-Champaign, USA

Scope:

Contexts of Education is a new series of handbooks that embraces both a creative approach to educational issues focused on context and a new publishing credo.

All educational concepts and issues have a home and belong to a context. This is the starting premise for this new series. One of the big intellectual breakthroughs of post-war science and philosophy was to emphasise the theory-ladenness of observations and facts—facts and observations cannot be established independent of a theoretical context. In other words, facts and observations are radically context-dependent. We cannot just see what we like or choose to see. In the same way, scholars are argue that concepts and constructs also are relative to a context, whether this be a theory, schema, framework, perspective or network of beliefs. Background knowledge always intrudes; it is there, difficult to articulate, tacit and operates to shape and help form our perceptions. This is the central driving insight of a generation of thinkers from Ludwig Wittgenstein and Karl Popper to Thomas Kuhn and Jürgen Habermas. Increasingly, in social philosophy, hermeneutics, and literary criticism textualism has given way to contextualism, paving the way for the introduction of the notions of 'frameworks', 'paradigms' and 'networks'—concepts that emphasize a new ecology of thought.

This new series is predicated upon this insight and movement. It emphasises the importance of context in the establishment of educational facts and observations and the framing of educational hypotheses and theories. It also emphasises the relation between text and context, the discursive and the institution, the local and the global. Accordingly, it emphasizes the significance of contexts at all levels of inquiry: scientific contexts; theoretical contexts; political, social and economic contexts; local and global contexts; contexts for learning and teaching; and, cultural and interdisciplinary contexts.

Contexts of Education, as handbooks, are conceived as reference texts that also can serve as texts.

Handbook of Cultural Politics and Education

Edited by

Zeus Leonardo
University of California, Berkeley, USA

SENSE PUBLISHERS
ROTTERDAM/BOSTON/TAIPEI

A C.I.P. record for this book is available from the Library of Congress.

ISBN: 978-94-6091-175-0 (paperback)
ISBN: 978-94-6091-176-7 (hardback)
ISBN: 978-94-6091-177-4 (e-book)

Published by: Sense Publishers,
P.O. Box 21858,
3001 AW Rotterdam,
The Netherlands
http://www.sensepublishers.com

Printed on acid-free paper

EDITORIAL ADVISORY BOARD

TABLE OF CONTENTS

Affirming Ambivalence: Introduction to Cultural Politics and Education 1
Zeus Leonardo

The Cultural Politics of Neoliberalism and Education

1. Neoliberalism, Pedagogy, and Cultural Politics: Beyond the Theatre of Cruelty 49
Henry A. Giroux

2. Lessons Learned From Enron: What the Business World Really has to Teach Us 71
Greg Dimitriadis

3. Conflicts of the Education Faculty: Derrida and Democratic Cultural Politics in the Postmodern University 87
Dennis Carlson

Globalization and Culture Industries

4. Class-ifying Race: The Compassionate Racism of the Right and Why Class Still Matters 113
Peter McLaren and Valerie Scatamburlo-D'Annibale

5. A Global Standpoint?: Reification, Globalization, and Contemporary Praxis 141
Noah De Lissovoy

6. The Frankfurt School and Education: Critical Theory and Youth Alienation 161
Benjamin Frymer

7. Why Culture?: The Political Economy of Cultural Politics 175
Seehwa Cho

Subjects and Subjectivities

8. Ideology and its Modes of Existence: Toward an Althusserian Theory of Race and Racism 195
Zeus Leonardo

9. Performativity: Making the Subjects of Education 219
Deborah Youdell

10. Autism as Enemy: Metaphor and Cultural Politics 237
Alicia A. Broderick

11. Re-Reading Class, Re-Reading Cultural Studies, Re-Reading Tradition: Neo-Marxist Nostalgia and the Remorselessly Vanishing Pasts 269
Cameron McCarthy and Jennifer Logue

12. Education after the Death of the Subject: Levinas and the Pedagogy of Interruption 289
Gert Biesta

Politics of Knowledge

13. Cybernetic Capitalism, Informationalism and Cognitive Labor 303
Michael A. Peters, Rodrigo Britez and Ergin Bulut

14. A Culture of Evidence, A Politics of Objectivity: The Evidence-based Practices Movement in Educational Policy 325
Jen Sandler and Michael W. Apple

15. Education, Cultural Politics, and the New Hegemony: How Multiculturalism became a Neoconservative Weapon 341
Kristen L. Buras

16. Gender, Democracy, and Philosophy of Science 373
Sandra Harding

Social Identities

17. 'Just the Right Amount of Racism': The Cultural Politics of Race and Reform 383
David Gillborn

18. What is This 'Black' in Black Education?: Imagining a Cultural Politics without Guarantees 403
Michael J. Dumas

19. A 'Symbolic Rebirth' of the Bootstrap Guild: Applying Kenneth Burke to the Cultural Politics of the "Negro Problem" Underlying Black-White Test Score Gap Ideology 423
Sherick Hughes

20. Thinking Latina/o Education With and From Chicana/Latina Feminist Cultural Studies: Emerging Pathways – Decolonial Possibilities 451
Sofia A. Villenas

21. It's the Masculinity, Stupid: A Cultural Studies Analysis of Media, the Presidency and Pedagogy 477
Jackson Katz

Reading Formations

22. The Im-Personated and Performative Pedagogies of Social Change: Informal Education's Ever-Varying Tropes 511
Diana Silberman-Keller

23. Toward a Theory of Poemness: Cultural Politics and Transformative Pedagogies 527
Korina Jocson and Takeo Rivera

24. Space, Cultural Politics and Education 541
Kalervo N. Gulson

25. Technological Transformation, New Literacies and Democracy: Toward a Reconstruction of Education 555
Douglas Kellner

Notes on Contributors 571

ZEUS LEONARDO

AFFIRMING AMBIVALENCE

Introduction to Cultural Politics and Education

CULTURE'S TURN AND THE TRANSFORMATION OF POLITICS

In Colin Sparks' (1996) excellent introduction to Stuart Hall's corpus, Sparks characterizes the development of cultural studies as an initial intervention into orthodox Marxist studies.[1] An impasse had occurred within Marxism with respect to the superstructure's effectivity, particularly the role and status of culture. Deemed secondary and an effect of the base (sometimes referred to as infrastructure), superstructural features, like family, church, and education, became significant but not determining aspects of history and struggle. They were depicted as ideological fields where cultural processes bear the imprints of the economy. Although Marxism arguably represents within the phrase "political economy" a study of the whole rather than fragments of society, it accomplished this analysis by locating history within the economy and a necessary but insufficient politics within culture. Orthodox Marxism left undeveloped a genuine appreciation for the creative aspects of culture, even its working class version. Ambivalence toward orthodox Marxism became an opportunity for theory production, which would turn its critical eye toward the neglected process of culture.

As Sparks explains, in early cultural studies Hoggart, Williams, and Thompson offered an answer to the impasse by documenting the development of working class culture, with Thompson being its champion, Williams its believer, and Hoggart its follower. Of the three figures, Thompson represents the most direct lineage with Marxism, with Hoggart having the least umbilical relation with the previous orthodoxy. It would be inaccurate to suggest that a critical theory of culture begins with the British. Lukács, the Frankfurt School, Gramsci, and Althusser – all sensing the Marxist impasse – entered the theoretical fray decades before, with their study of working class consciousness, the culture industry, civil society, and ideological interpellation, respectively. Historical events, like the rise of European fascism also provided a thrust for theories that would speak to the exigencies of a world threatened by authoritarianism, something that Adorno took very seriously. Later, the failures of Soviet communism would become evident, leading to further questions regarding the limitations of a Marxist-Leninist project without a robust cultural component. Affirming the critical role of culture as a generative process became a revolutionary intervention within Marxism that pushed for new questions about the nature of contradiction, this time as a lived aspect of political practice.

Z. Leonardo (ed.), Handbook of Cultural Politics and Education, 1–45.

This moment crystallizes in British cultural studies, which spawned a programmatic assault at the study of culture in the Center for Contemporary Cultural Studies, in Birmingham, England. Although the CCCS occupies a small and rather insignificant physical office in the Birmingham school, as Handel Wright (1998) notes, its symbolic stature takes up as much space as the Frankfurt School within critical studies of culture. Under various leaderships from Stuart Hall to Paul Willis, the CCCS produced key and visible work that would be decisive in producing, in Kuhn's (1970) sense, a paradigm shift. In particular, Stuart Hall's early work produced key insights on the question of working class culture without falling prey to what Sparks calls a "workerist" analysis, or a romantic projection of proletarian revolutionariness. Hall's was not an anthropologically inspired take on culture, which has a long-standing tradition, but rather a *cultural materialism* (Williams, 1977) that harkens back to the early to middle Marx before the volumes of *Capital*. Hall (1996a) writes, "I like people's middle period a lot, where they have gotten over their adolescent idealism but their thought has not yet hardened into a system" (p. 146). Although Hall was inspired by Althusser – who wasn't in the 1960s? – he favored the younger Marx to the mature one. So against scientific Marxism, Hall did not accept Bachelard's notion of the "epistemological break" so dear to Althusser. Hall gave the nod to the ambivalent Marx, whose analysis was not only cultural, but less systematized and ultimately more open. With respect to culture, theory is not hopelessly tied to an idea but a set of material practices. These questions around Marxism aside, Eagleton (2003) notes that cultural theories of the 1960s and 70s were on the whole comradely rather than hostile. As we will see, this would later change.

At this point, it may be relevant to explain the difference between the relatively recent innovation of Cultural Studies and studies of culture from allied disciplines, like anthropology and sociology. In these latter disciplines, culture has been a central concern. From rituals to processes of modernization, culture is a theoretical construct that enjoys deep engagement in the disciplines. From Mauss' (1967) Melanesian ethnographies, to Bataille's (1988, 1991) studies of the sacred, to Levi-Strauss' (1963) structural anthropology, and to Weber's (1978a) disenchantment with the impersonal nature of modern bureaucracy, culture has not received short shrift. In education, anthropologists and sociologists of education are not scarce and ethnography is a methodology dedicated to the study of culture, long before Stuart Hall and Raymond Williams introduced the turn to culture. What differs in the turn from studies of culture to cultural studies is precisely a reaction to the metanarratives of Marxist science, helped along by the (re)discovery of Marx's earlier, humanist texts. The return to the anthropological Marx provided a language that allowed theorists to tap into processes associated with class consciousness, alienation, and meaning making. It shifted the attention from objective analysis of modes of production to modes of everyday class life. In terms of method, this required a shift from quantitative to qualitative, if not ethnographic, research for culture is not easily apprehensible through numbers and regressions, at least not without a good dose of violence to a proper cultural understanding. Ethnography, it seems, took over where positive science left off. The appreciation of daily life within capitalist social formations was particularly intense insofar as the rise of consumption culture (Baudrillard, 1988a, 1988b), counter or sub-cultures (Hebdige, 1996), and media and information society (Kellner, 1995; Bell, 1960) made new forms of analysis possible. It was no longer the world Marx had described and social theory slowly gave way to cultural theory. It would be inaccurate to describe this transition as evidence of a move away from politics and towards culture, but more precisely as the turn to *culture as a form of politics*: in other words, cultural politics. Moreover, the turn to cultural studies was always linked to concerns over domination and possibilities for revolutionary thought, which were not always central to mainstream uptakes of culture.

This culture-as-politics is a second difference from the already extant theories of culture. Whereas culture – from its ethnicity or tribal forms, from Balinese cock fights and Bhutanese cooking – gave the university an international flavor and extended our intellectual taste, cultural studies since the 1960s attached the problem of power with culture. This is different from Weber's (1930) earlier exposition of ethno-economic development in his book *The Protestant Ethic and the Spirit of Capitalism* and Robert Park's (1964) ethnicity paradigm in sociology. These are no doubt studies of power but inscribed by more or less traditional notions of ethnicity. The difference is captured by Hall's (1996b) invocation of "new ethnicities," or the recognition of cultural groups that are demarcated along lines of meaning rather than nations or conveniently bound geographies. Hall's rendition of culture or ethnicity aligns itself with Hebdige's legitimation of counter or sub-cultures, like punk, or what Spivak (1988) later includes in a more comprehensive study of the subaltern. Although early cultural studies shows a bias toward class – specifically working class – culture, we will see later that this culture comes with multiple inscriptions, such as race and gender. No longer disparaged as existing outside history, gender takes on greater importance as a form of social, as opposed to biological, relation. Weedon (1997) and McRobbie (1996) would insist on a full-fledged accounting of gender as a cultural system of subject positions, which relegates the feminine as a dependent sphere to the masculine. Fraser (1997) calls attention to the problem of recognition, or distribution's cultural cognate, in order to explain that a dual theory fares better than a sole focus on economic justice. People on the margins suffer from material deprivations and status differentials in a society that treats them as second class citizens while profiting from their labor. In short, social systems like gender or race are both ideological and material relations. Cultural theory as such did not evolve in isolation from other trends in thought, some of which were more committed to science, such as Althusser's structural Marxism. But even these currents could not simply return to Marx before the impasse.

Althusser's rise exemplified a great compromise for it was he who addressed the impasse between an insistence on a material struggle and the increasing importance of ideological relations and steadily developing cultural apparatuses, particularly in advanced Western societies. Although Althusser cemented Marxism into a permanent status because of the equal permanence that he established for ideology, Althusser's Lacanian-inspired theory of interpellation was a decisive moment in theory development due to its theoretical accommodations of the "culture problem."

Although he insisted on the faceless and scientific version of structural Marxism, Althusser's (1971) nod to schools as part of the Ideological State Apparatuses (ISA) gave the study of education the weight that it needed within Marxist studies, heretofore no longer merely ideological without a *proper* relation with the material. I will have more to say about Althusser below but for now it suffices to say that this *pre-poststructuralist*, even as he kicked and screamed with his fetish of science, opened the door to cultural ambivalence. His theory of interpellation, or subject-making taken to its logical extent by his former student Foucault and once collaborator Balibar, is arguably the dominant theory of cultural politics today.

As Sparks continues to survey the development of Hall and cultural studies generally, he finds that the early intervention into Marxism gives way to a Foucauldian-inspired analysis of discourse. Themes associated with Marxist materialism, such as production, commodification, and consumption, are replaced by the sign, subject, and signification. Terms so long associated with the Leftist intellectual tradition are eclipsed by a new set of concerns. Political economy becomes overshadowed by political anatomy (Foucault, 1977) and body studies (Turner, 1992), consciousness by subjectivity and subject-formation (Lather, 1991; Youdell, in press), alienation and determinisms by indeterminacy and aleatory relations (Baudrillard, 1990), teleologies with television (Kellner, 1992), and the turn from modes to movies (Giroux, 2002). In cultural theory, we have witnessed the central preoccupation with capitalist production shift to studies of Hollywood production. Eagleton (1991) laments that new students of revolutionary theory have more cant than familiarity with Kant. This is made possible by new theoretical frameworks that are introduced during these New Times, such as Habermas' (1984, 1987a) reconstruction of communication and language pragmatics, Deleuze and Guattari's (1983) rhizome alternative to the root, and Derrida's (1976) own doubts about dialectics. At times the ambivalence toward Marxism transforms into downright animosity toward the father (see Baudrillard, 1975; Leonardo, 2003a). In short, there is a theoretical falling out of love with Marxism, but we still wait to see if the break up is prelude to a make up, especially in times of economic downturn, when the bearded man's relevance is reconsidered (Hitchens, 2009).

These intellectual shifts are part of historical changes, one of which is the political melancholy following the counter-cultural movements of the 1960s. Sparks' point is that, in its current and dominant form, cultural studies exhibits a very limited relation to Marx, a tendency whose political utility about which he expresses serious reservations (see also Eagleton, 2003). Many post-grand theorists, like Foucault, Lyotard, and Derrida have paid their Marxist dues and could hardly be criticized as not possessing intimate background of the Marxist literature. But alas, as Eagleton notes, God was not a structuralist after all and it seems we have entered the beginning of the end for grand theories. As Sparks regrets, these interventions may have been necessary but remain insufficient. Many of today's dominant theorists were once students of prominent Marxists during a time when the opposition only had Marx, Freud, and Saussure upon which to rely (Foucault, 1983). The turn to Nietszche and counter-enlightenment thinkers opened new fields of possibility and political practice. This is the beginning of the "post" in social theory. In my survey of cultural politics in education, this Introduction will take its cue from Sparks' outline of early cultural Marxism, the transition to a Foucauldian analysis of discourse, and its current iterations. I will organize the chapter into themes that are central to a sweeping understanding of cultural politics. Although the chapter is admittedly not the final word on these matters, I hope it will do justice to the influential developments in cultural politics of education.

In her essay on the permutations of social theory, Seehwa Cho (2010) expertly describes the historical development of intellectual production that shifts the attention from economic to cultural production. She finds that the turn to culture is not a simple *return* to a neglected concept but a shift in problematic, this time culture as the privileged theoretical construct. Seen this way, culture is not simply the relation we enter into when we highlight rituals, meaning, and language. Rather, culture is an assemblage of themes, a whole architecture whereby social life itself finds its expression and possibilities, *including* the economy, which now takes the form of a cultural relation. In short, culture here is endowed with its full measure of radicality, a politics (Apple, 1996). With respect to education, Cho's insights bear out. In the 1970s, the educational Left witnessed a burgeoning field of studies into cultural politics, sparked in the British context by Willis' (1977) ethnography of the lads and Bernstein's (1977a, 1977b) detailed account of class-based cultural codes. Taking its cue from a newly legitimated focus on schools, Willis' study in particular has since become a classic in its appreciation of insights gained from theories of *cultural reproduction* but also introduces the importance of *cultural production*. That is, although he admits that reproduction happens by virtue of capital's imperatives and schools' place within the intellectual division of labor, Willis' study affirms the critical role that cultural insight provides for students who penetrate the social formation despite the fact that they enter contradictions within their practical consciousness. Willis (1981) remarks,

> [O]ur starting point should be in the cultural milieu, in material practices and productions, in lives in their historical context in the everyday span of existence and practical consciousness. We should investigate the form of living collective cultural productions that occur on the determinate and contradictory grounds of what is inherited and what is currently suffered through imposition, but in a way which is nevertheless creative and active (p. 49).

Still tied to a Marxist understanding of class, Willis's general findings concerning the power of cultural forms in education proved decisive. Although it would over-reach to suggest that *Learning to Labor* serves as the guiding inspiration to Giroux's (1983) theory of resistance, Apple's (1990) use of ideology as cultural mediation, and McLaren's (1991) framing of culture as a struggle over meaning, the theoretical conversation has travelled back and forth across the Atlantic. A problematization of Bowles and Gintis' (1976) economistic framework that gives short shrift to cultural struggle, the turn to culture as worldview-generating provides the neo-Marxist Left a way into schooling as part of a general capitalist production, and without the usual fear that one is being an ideologue for straying too far from economic exchange. Neither folkish in their uptake of everyday school life nor elitist in their denigration of popular culture, cultural politicians in education struck a balance that established a proper relation between the material organization of society and the ideological production of schooling.

This synthesis is most evident in Freire's (1993) concern over the "culture of silence" that is produced in a schooling experience that does not affirm students' ontological right to be free. As cultural workers (Freire, 2006), teachers work the material from nature into culture, a distinctly human form of intellectual labor. Liberated from the economy's determinisms, culture is given its autonomy that allows theorists to follow its flows without being burdened by concerns about determinisms that dogged the orthodoxy. As a cultural or humanist Marxist, Freire's work is evidence of a certain *reculturation* project in education as part of a larger social change. Although Freire was clear that the educational apparatus by itself would be an insufficient catalyst for change, he deemed it an important node in the broader search for cultural freedom (see Giroux, 2010, http://www.truthout.org/10309_Giroux_Freire). Central to Freire's analysis is the cultural process of decoding reality as a constitutive moment in dialogue. Taken as something more than mere classroom chatter, dialogue becomes the ontological property of educators and students who enter communication as incomplete subjects in search of freedom. With this admission comes the centrality of humility, which is not synonymous with humanitarian humbleness, something false at the same time that it is pretentious. On the contrary, Freire supported a form of classroom authority that admits to the openness of knowledge, not its impossibility on the left or its predetermined form on the right. Reconstructing authority, which has plagued a certain Leninist variety of Marxism, Freire's intervention is a key moment in education as a process of cultural change. Rejecting authoritarianism and vanguardism on one side but denouncing neutrality on the other, Freire reconstructs authority as a form of power sharing and does not encourage teachers to pretend that they do not have charge of a room filled with either kids or adult learners. Educators are both *in* authority to the extent that the state has given them a measure of power as well as *an* authority insofar as they possess critical amounts of training, knowledge, and skills. Abdicating their power is therefore itself an act of power, which in the end, may produce either classroom chaos at best or resorting to the subtle expression of manipulative power at worst. For Freire, reconstructing authority necessitates establishing a new culture of power, one that does not mystify it as predetermined and therefore unchangeable, and is ultimately deployed in the interest of the oppressed.

Freire was neither alone nor unpreceded by other intellectuals in the reconstruction of authority. The dissident, Antonio Gramsci, decades earlier provided insights on the nature of a passive, cultural revolution required by the development of a complex system of civil society. As Perry Anderson (1976) notes in his monograph-length essay in *New Left Review*, no Marxist thinker in the last 50 and more years has been more respected and engaged by social(ist) thinkers than Gramsci. To some the father of cultural Marxism, to others a martyr because of his imprisonment, Gramsci (1971) has generated a cottage industry of intellectual production dedicated to at least two cultural concepts: hegemony and the intellectual (see Buras, 2008; Borg, Buttigieg, and Mayo, 2003; Holst, 2001). According to Gramsci, hegemony is a process that is quite distinct from relations of domination. Whereas the first is characterized by the process of consent, the second is marked by coercion. Although Gramsci never denies the presence of coercion and its partnership with consent, it is the latter process that he pursues in light of a highly developed civil society within western nations, which ameliorates, perhaps dilutes, the coercive power of the state. According to Anderson, Lenin seems to confirm this distinction when he urges western nations to develop different strategies in their struggles against non-Czarist states, where a *war of maneuver*, or a cohesive, all out assault on the state was necessary. For highly developed states, a *war of position* requires local sensitivity to cultural processes that are not apolitical in nature, but politics in the form of meaning where the struggle over the terrain of cultural politics properly commences.

Anderson's treatment of Gramsci reminds us that in contrast to eastern socialist struggles, where the "state was everything," the state in developed, western nations is but an "outer ditch," filled in with an architecture of cultural institutions that can either work in the service of state power or become mechanisms for resistance against it. Anderson's bone of contention with Gramsci is the Italian's somewhat reformist stance on the question of force. To Anderson, power always falls back on the question of force where the state, in Weber's (1978b) terms, monopolizes its legitimate use. In other words, in times of "peace," consent is enough to convince the mass to fall in line but in times of conflict, the state reserves the right to deploy force. The elite and masses in capitalist nations are in a constant state of undeclared war. In light of this, the question of consent becomes less meaningful if it always entails the *veiled threat of force*. Consent becomes the euphemized form of coercion, its cultural cognate, its symbolic form. The ruling bloc's ability to win consent from the mass is the latter's inability to use legitimate force against the state.

These criticisms notwithstanding, Gramsci's concept of hegemony has become a household term in cultural politics. Its generative use means that resistance is built into a social system, always there as a dynamic part of the complex dance between domination and revolution. As Martin (1992) notes, this is not a "Swiss cheese theory of power" where insurgents poke holes into the fabric of domination, but rather a resistance that is already prefigured into it. For example, Martin's creative analysis of science school textbooks' cultural construction of conception extracts militarized images of sperms assaulting the passive egg waiting to be conquered. The metaphorical basis of science on which Stepan (1990) insists, is not a surrender to language and an argument for the abolition of metaphor. Rather, it engenders resistance to dominant meanings via the project of semiotic insubordination, of subverting significations that parade as truth. This is precisely why consent has to be rewon as part of the compromise into which the ruling bloc enters, in order to remain in power. In this sense, power does not ossify but is constantly reconfigured and the bloc has to recruit new elements to enter its orbit. That said, resistance does not always produce radical outcomes, as discovered by Willis' (1977) lads and MacLeod's (2008) Hallway Hangers, in whom we find a combination of good and common sense. They are realistic examples of students who possess the ability to "penetrate" the social formation and simultaneously be seduced by its machinations. Hegemony *assumes* resistance and the bloc is in no way threatened by it until the resistance matures from private, individualized expressions to cultural forms of public protest. This by no means suggests that nothing changes until this point of rupture as much as it is the confirmation that a new hegemony has been realized. This is what Laclau and Mouffe (1991) suggest when they claim that there is no revolution without hegemony, which makes the aspiration of getting *beyond* hegemony an abstraction at best and a mystification at worst. One cannot be against hegemony as much as it is useless to be against politics.

The historic bloc differs from the more orthodox concept of the ruling class. In classical Marxism, the focus falls on the singular development of the bourgeoisie. For example, as Marx and Engels (1970) note, "The ideas of the ruling class are in every epoch the ruling ideas, i.e. the class which is the ruling *material* force of society, is at the same time its ruling *intellectual* force" (p. 64; italics in original). Control of material production is key in orienting society to the will of the bourgeoisie. The concept of the bloc differs from the ruling class through the former's development as an *ideological ensemble*. No longer just the ruling class, the bloc is a combination of bourgeois and non-bourgeois elements of society. It certainly contains a material component and control of production is still key in establishing hegemony, but cultural relations become the bloc's smoking gun. Ideological hegemony is not just the process of falsifying the mass' consciousness but the way that an entire social formation functions under the alignment of disparate groups – always contingent – the result of which is to perpetuate the capitalist worldview. The ruling class no longer goes it alone and instead recruits, in both strategic and unintentional ways, a whole set of new allies from various sectors of society, compelled by both material and ideological reasons, and recrudescing into economic and identitarian-based social movements. Hegemony recruits them all for mutual benefit. This is precisely why the concept of the "bloc," rather than the more classical "ruling class," represents an advance insofar as it captures the complex power web that characterizes advanced capitalist societies and the shifting terrain of political alliances they generate.

Gramsci's study establishes the give and take that was missing in Marxist, scientific orthodoxy, where change only took place after the revolution. Gramsci illuminates the process before revolutionary periods wherein inchoate elements within the mass *prepare* an organic group for leadership and convince the mass through intellectual, moral persuasion. In this sense, Gramsci theorizes everyday life as possessing revolutionary moments, or culture in its most creative sense that would have pleased someone like Raymond Williams. In this reconstruction, the intellectual does not equate with a certain erudite version but rather its organic function of an organic relationship between a theory of society and social practice. It is less a profession and more an apprehension of the disparate levels of social analysis from media to modes of production. Revolutions in their epochal sense are hard to come by and never develop instantaneously or spontaneously. They are prepared for, through the reconstruction of common sense, the imagining of the possible, and remaking of consciousness.

The intellectual's role is key in the reconstruction of consciousness and in education this role appropriately falls on the shoulders of teachers. Functioning as potential intellectuals in Gramsci's sense, teachers have a foot in public life as workers for the state as well as a foot in cultural life as purveyors of knowledge in schools. In elementary school in particular, tens to hundreds of students pass through teachers' lives in a school day, making them second only to family in time spent with young people. Even friends rarely spend six hours a day together. With this "captive audience" in tow, teachers are in a unique position to assume the role of the organic intellectual over and beyond their role as knowledge transmitters (see Giroux, 1988). To Gramsci, the traditional intellectual is defined by his vocation, usually tied to a profession. Although they make strange bedfellows, intellectuals and the political elite often share the same room. On the other hand, the organic intellectual assumes a socio-political, rather than a technical, function. For example, intellectual by training and organic by potential, teachers have the transformative opportunity to influence young minds on questions of justice, the constitution of history, and the nature of power, as they negotiate school knowledge. Because these issues are already embedded in the creation of the curriculum, instructional practice, and assessments, they are not extra-educational themes that must be injected into the otherwise "normal" process of schooling. *They are already there* and teachers may work differently without necessarily having to working harder. It does not ask more of, but rather something different from, them (Leonardo, 2003b). Reframing teachers as cultural workers suggests that they are not custodians of the state but rather its promise keepers, of insisting that it remain accountable to them as critical citizens. As teachers build civic capacity to intervene not only on behalf of less mature students but equally on their own behalf, they affirm their autonomy as intellectuals.

IDEOLOGY

Classical social theories have been unabashedly materialist, and economistic at that. By emphasizing the base at the expense of the superstructure, social theory favored a set of concerns, such as science, history, objective relations, and the derogation of other sets of concern with subjectivity, consciousness, and meaning. The turn to culture can be linked to an equally powerful turn to studies of ideology. Turning to ideology is not simply favoring an analysis of the superstructure as an antidote to the limitations of base studies. It is an entire way of explaining social and cultural relations, including material processes. By stating this, cultural politics does not conveniently transform ideas into material forms or materiality into a mere notion. Or as an orthodox Marxist may object, this is not materialist at all but a romance with the *idea of materialism*, what Ebert (1996) calls "matterism." The uptake of ideology does not necessitate abandoning the concept within the realm of pure ideality but its direct link with modes of material existene. In other words, to affirm ideology studies is not to displace materialism but to speak from a particular point in the dialectic between ideas and the material world.

It is not far of a stone's throw to suggest that cultural politics is the fuller appreciation of ideology as a force in its own right, which, as Althusser (1969) has noted, rebounds back on economics, or is able to affect it without determining it. In fact, as a dues paying Marxist, Althusser creates the concept of "overdetermination" to suggest that the economic reigns in the final instance without being the origin in the first instance. This means that while economics does not begin the process it certainly ends it, in the final analysis. This is not only clever but represents Althusser's attempts to address the impasse in Marxist studies.[2] This point addresses the problem of determinism and teleology that has dogged Marxist theory, which demanded a response either from within or from without Marxism. Raymond Williams (1977) diagnoses the problem best when he writes,

> A Marxism without some concept of determination is in effect worthless. A Marxism with many of the concepts of determination it now has is quite radically crippled. . . The concept of overdetermination is an attempt to avoid the isolation of autonomous *categories* but at the same time to emphasize relatively autonomous yet of course interactive *practices* (p. 83; italics in original).

A Marxism that observes no conceptual limits exposes it to criticisms on the nature of a bounded analysis. It falls to the relativism of determinations that range from the economy to ear shapes. One cannot take Marxism to task for setting limits to social analysis, which is a necessary move, but a critic might hold it accountable for the choices it does make. For instance, its current forms of determination must answer to another criticism about the nature of the interconnected levels of analysis between the base and superstructure. It seems a compromise had to be struck or Marxism risks devolving from doctrine to dogma.

Economics may not be the root of social process but rather its destiny, its final resting place. It may not be the cause but an effect of social processes. For instance, where the analysis concerns gender or race, we may say that social disparities are economic in form but not in nature. Indeed race or gender discrimination includes labor exploitation but this may be one of patriarchy's effects rather than something caused (and therefore addressed) by the economy. The symptom is material, even economic, without it being determined by the economy. It is economic in the last, but not the first, instance.

Althusser's intervention reconstructs Marxist teleology insofar as the institution of communism does not rid itself of ideology, this time less of a problem for Marxist science and more of a natural progression as it matures. That is, as Marxist science becomes more rigorous (and hopefully accurate) in its understanding of social life, ideological thinking becomes a larger problem to confront. In the beginning, many Marxist strains of thought may have had legitimate claims to the status of science, much like the development of science itself. As Marxism matures, fewer iterations have bragging rights to being scientific. It becomes more selective, more refined, therefore its other, namely ideology, develops in the opposite direction alongside with common sense.[3] As ideology engulfs more of social life, it establishes itself as more or less a permanent fixture of thought and the social formation.

Taking from Lacan, Althusser then likens ideology to the unconscious, always a remainder of the day in the sense that it represents a part of experience to which subjects do not have complete access. Althusser's innovation departs from Lukács' concept of ideology, which links its development with the maturation of working class consciousness. It also goes in the opposite direction of Freire, for whom purging the ideology of the oppressed is dependent on realizing a critical, humanist, and rational consciousness, or conscientization against superstitious thought. Of course, Althusser leaves behind the utterly pejorative notion of ideology as distortion because it functions through allusion as much as illusion. It recalls the real relations, albeit in phantasmic, elusive form. In this, Althusser's appropriation of Lacan is decisive (Hirst, 1994; Apple, 1998; Aoki, 2000). Althusser shifts the theory of ideology from an exclusive attention to the real, to the real's relation with the symbolic. It allows Althusser to affirm the role of language in creating the subject, which leads to his theory of interpellation. Still concerned with capitalism, Althusser's subject is a laboring subject involved in answering to the call of class division. In all, affirming ideology reconstructs the *relationship* between the base and superstructure, not the valorization of the latter and derogation of the former.

The theory of interpellation is based on the suggestion that in order to exploit people in capitalism, a subject is already assumed. Althusser uses the analogy with the military insofar as a soldier is always assumed to be a citizen of a nation, therefore only citizens may be recruited into the army. This is made plain by the general rule that nations do not recruit other countries' citizens into its army, as it must choose from within its own ranks. This is real to the extent that there are corroborating documents regarding citizenship. However, the process is symbolic insofar as a citizen imagines him or herself as a member of the nation (see also B. Anderson, 2006). S/he participates in rituals, narratives, and symbols as part of belonging to the nation and through these performances, helps constitute the nation as well as what and who signifies a legitimate citizen. Economic classes function in similar ways, creating subjecthood for the individuals who constitute them. They participate in the cultural rituals of labor, narratives of daily class life, and establish their class identity in the process. They become subjects of labor and are subjected by it; thus "subject" takes on a double meaning. Interpellation also establishes efficiency. Although a worker can certainly be exploited in the objective sense, this is incomplete. Just as a pet answers to its name in order for the master to subjugate it, workers are more efficiently brought into the fold if they enter class interpellation. Even pets differ in our ability to interpellate them as we notice most cats' capacity to ignore their name whereas a dog is pleased as punch to hear his, and a worm is quite another story. Likewise, laborers enter the universe of the "worker," which is not a natural, pre-existing category but one created by capitalism. They may revolt against their subjugation, but this is made possible by the preceding fact of interpellation. They may not turn around to the subject hailing (it does not require this of them) and it may even miss or misfire on occasion. But once it is established, interpellation, according to Althusser, rarely fails to register a response. The subject's way out is not the absence of interpellation but the possibility of another interpellation, a counter-interpellation.

In schools, Althusser's theory of ideology transpires almost literally. Students typically answer to their name during roll call and homeroom. If the teacher fails to record a response, as an Ideological State Apparatus, the school has the power to "trace" him or her by calling the parents. These decisions have economic incentives as public school funding is tied to daily student attendance. As subjects of schooling, young people assume the position of "student" as soon as they recognize their newfound identity. They then become potential workers through the creation of dispositions and habits, skills and know-hows to master the cultural arbitrary disguised as objective and backed by science (Bowles and Gintis, 1976; Bourdieu and Passeron, 1990). The point is that interpellation here comes with economic effects as students file in line for their introduction to work life. But this destiny is also accomplished through culture by building an entire social system that functions through language and other social practices. For example, students participate in school culture by attending pep rallies and loitering next to the Pepsi machines. They sport symbols and school colors to show their loyalty. They take tests to display their school knowledge, often complaining of its lack of utility because its worth is apparently conferred through the credential earned more than the actual skills learned (Collins, 1979). These are the functional, ideological myths that integrate students into school life. At times, such as the worldwide student protests of 1968 or the East Los Angeles blow out, students refashion this interpellation and create an entirely different subject position toward schooling, a new ideological reconstitution.

Althusser rehabilitates the concept of ideology from a purely idealist and illusory status to one that has material underpinnings. Likewise, material life produces a certain worldview, which falls within the domain of ideologies. But whereas ideology itself has no history, ideologies have histories (e.g., aristocratic, capitalist, communist). Ideology continues even into communist society because it functions for subjects as it integrates them into social life. While illusory, ideology maintains its autonomy insofar as the ideology of aristocracy – for example, in the UK – continues even after it is no longer hegemonic (Poulantzas, 1994). To Althusser's collaborator, Poulantzas, this fact speaks to the effectivity of ideology that recommends it over Gramsci's concept of hegemony. Ideology's autonomy is eternal, like Freud's concept of the unconscious.

The reconstruction of ideology did not begin with Althusser. It arguably began as early as Lenin and then on to Lukács, if we do not count Marx's rescuing of its iteration as a "science of ideas" that began with Destutt de Tracy. For Lukács (1971), ideological maturity of the working class required a grasp of the totality over the fragmented and fleeting, local and specific levels of analysis. For Lenin (1963), politics was no less than a war between capitalist and socialist ideology, requiring the latter to destroy the former. Both Lukács and Lenin considered ideology as a potential weapon in class struggle, but only after a robust materialist analysis precedes it. By contrast, to Althusser no amount of materialist thinking rescues us from ideology. Ironically, he asserts the opposite: a materialist science creates an enlarged tumor called the ideological field. It is with Althusser where ideology gains its privileged status through its apparent permanence. This may not have been his intention, concerned as he was with establishing a physics of history. But it is perhaps his legacy.

Having broached the question on the status of ideology, cultural theory virtually opens the floodgates and theories of ideology explode in the 1970s and on. As a young Althusserian, Stuart Hall enters the scene and offers the worldview thesis of ideology. Pushing a little harder on Althusser's theory, Hall (1996c) culturalizes it even further and suggests a descriptive framework for ideology as the general system of meanings constituted in language: "By ideology I mean the mental frameworks – the languages, the concepts, categories, imagery of thought, and the systems of representation – which different classes and social groups deploy in order to make sense of, define, figure out and render intelligible the way society works" (p. 26). Hall's reworking of ideology is not far off from Geertz's (1994) anthropological theory of ideology as a set of linguistic tropes that make up the cultural system. It shares Ricoeur's (1986) commitment to an integrative description of ideology as a set of tools, linguistic or otherwise, which ensure that people have direction and purpose, without which society becomes ill-equipped at dealing with modern life. If this sounds a bit functionalist, then it shares Durkheim's (1933) concerns about the anomie that results when people are uncertain about the expectations placed upon them. So whereas ideology was once the antithesis of materialist thought and a source of people's estrangement or alienation from their essence, the labor process, product, and other laborers, some intellectuals have transformed ideology into the exact opposite: ideology as an unavoidable framework responsible for people's social and cultural integration. Not only do humans find ideology irresistible, they depend on it. There are several reasons for this shift in thinking.

This theoretical transformation may represent the backlash against orthodox Marxism's overreliance on science that began with the utopian socialists. Trying to provoke a theoretical break reminiscent of Althusser's radical demarcation between the ideological and scientific Marx, Aronowitz (1988) announces the conceptual dependency between science and ideology. As long as science exists as a theoretical construct, its opposing term in the dialectic, namely ideology, will continue to be a problem. As a radical solution, purging science necessitates vacating ideology. Aronowitz establishes the position that any study of ideology by default invokes the construct of science, which has been a source of another kind of problem. For example, by emphasizing rationality over myth, something of which Freire was also guilty, Marxism became vulnerable to a certain Eurocentric valuation of reason. Historical materialism was not just a science but equally a cultural apparatus that spawned a set of values that passed off as neutral and part of human nature rather than as specific and socially conditioned.

To take one instance, the notion of myth so central to European thinkers was derogated to irrational at best or reduced to falsehoods at worst. In other words, Marxism traded in truths whereas other perspectives fought over the leftover pieces called myths or falsehoods. Myth becomes a synonym for mystifications and magical thinking whereas it arguably represents the stories that bind a society (Richardson, 1994; Barthes, 1994). By demoting narratives to the status of myth,

Marxism fails to appreciate its own narrative structure, complete with its competing stories about human nature and the societies it creates. It denies its metaphorical basis, in as much as science relies on language to constitute its object of study (Stepan, 1990). It may bend the ideological stick too far to couch Marxist theory as just another story among stories, which denies its praxiological value, it does not reduce the power of Marxism to admit its situatedness, its ideology in terms of a conditioned worldview. On the contrary, it encourages a self-reflective component to Marxism that has been important to most contemporary cultural theory.

Although a purely descriptive theory of ideology contains its own limitations with respect to power relations (Larrain, 1991,1996), it avoids painting the critic into a corner of neutrality. Eagleton (1996) makes a useful distinction between neutrality and objectivity, arguing that cultural theory often problematically equates them. Whereas an intellectual (e.g. Marx) is not required to show neutrality, he may still perform an objective analysis of social processes. In other words, although Marx rejects capitalism, this does not prevent him from apprehending its objective laws. However, for some Marx's moral outrage is precisely what gets in the way of his objective social analysis (Hitchens, 2009). The upshot seems to be that while neglecting our social conditioning leads to theoretical pretensions of neutrality, reducing analysis to perspectivism imprisons the cultural critic from forming more or less accurate assessments of a situation. We may be ideological in the first instance (caught up in an unavoidable worldview) and not ideological in the second sense (caught up in falsehoods because of our worldview).

DISCOURSE

Then came poststructuralism.[4] And nothing was ever the same again. Cultural politics enters a new chapter and an epistemological break in reverse is inaugurated, critical of a science fetish. There were signs of this development evidenced by the permutations in theories of ideology and the ensuing conceptual tug-of-war so it does not pay off to conceive of recent intellectual trends as a complete break. But to underestimate the shift toward discourse does not do justice either to the innovations or the ongoing debates. Hall (1996a) is inclined to believe that something intellectually significant has occurred when he says,

> I've gone a very long way along the route of rethinking practices as functioning discursively – i.e. like languages. That metaphor has been, I think, enormously generative for me and has powerfully penetrated my thinking. If I had to put my finer on the one thing which constitutes the theoretical revolution of our time, I think it lies in that metaphor – ... it has reorganized our theoretical universe (p. 145).

Going away from science, Marxism, and centralities, and towards signs, Nietzsche, and dispersal, Foucault (1972) and company's arrival begins what Sparks considers the latest phase of cultural politics. Taking his teacher's lessons on interpellation to their logical extent, Foucault turns Althusser's structuralism into a superstructuralism in two senses.

First, the history without a subject that owes so much to Althusser's reading of Hegel becomes the mantra (see also Ashley, 1997). Not only is the subject exchanged for emphasizing the autonomy of discursive processes, the subject is outlived by such documentation and rendered largely irrelevant to it. What matters is the utterance, not the speaker. On this point, Hall (1996s) warns against a desperate effort to install a historical break by announcing it, as the high priest of postmodernism, Jean Baudrillard, has been accused of doing. Theory cannot quite do away with the subject in the absolute sense, which still makes history even as it multiplies it. It is *super*structural in the sense that an impersonal, terroristic structure goes into auto-pilot and gives rise to concepts like surveillance, docile bodies, and bodies without organs, or bodies without the imposing effect of social organization (Foucault, 1977; Deleuze and Guattari, 1983).[5] A history without a subject is precisely a history without a social being that speaks to its unified dimensions.

To some, the announcement of the death of the subject is ironic for a perspective that depends so much on themes of subjectivity and subject-formation. Although one could perform a literal reading of the announcement as the eulogy for the subject, it is more accurate to conceive of it as the *death of the liberal subject* (Biesta, 2006). The obituary for the liberal subject mourns the loss of its autonomy, rationality, and transparency, but essentially no love is lost. Of poststructuralism, Weedon (1997) writes,

> It is a theory which decentres the rational, self-present subject of humanism, seeing subjectivity and consciousness as socially produced in language, as sites of struggle and potential change. Language is not transparent as in humanist discourse, it is not expressive and does not label a 'real' world. Meanings do not exist prior to their articulation in language and language is not an abstract system, but is always socially and historically located in discourses. Discourses represent political interests and in consequence are constantly vying for status and power. The site of this battle for power is that subjectivity of the individual and it is a battle in which the individual is an active but not sovereign protagonist (p. 40).

As Jameson (2001) notes, theory and philosophy have long depended on the concept of *subjectivity*, perhaps reaching its golden age with Descartes' *cogito*.[6] By contrast, the *subject* is a relatively recent innovation, usually associated with Foucault's studies of the way discourses produce the subject it ostensibly describes. For example, in gender studies Judith Butler (2004) observes that the so-called gender stereotypes do not issue from a pre-existing patriarchal system that maps onto our language practices and confirms roles and expectations regarding men and women. These speech acts are performances that install the subjects of gender as they attempt to apprehend them through language. There is no abstract gender system behind them outside of their articulations and performances. Otherwise known as the constitutive property of language, speech performances do not just make subjects intelligible but actively invent them. . . over and over. The same can be said for racial subjects, whose "reality" is not outside the language that reflects their existence. As Derrida (1985) notes, no language, no racism; likewise, no racial discourse, no racial subjects. For the cultural critic, it necessitates knowing language in order to know race in the making (see Leonardo, in pressa). This is different from suggesting that language is a prison-house as much as it acknowledges that existing within a language opens us to the world from the inside-out rather than being "quarantined from it" (Eagleton, 2003, p. 62).

Second, recent cultural theory is also a form of superstructuralism in a more straightforward sense in that it completes the emphasis on cultural, or superstructural, features of society. Sparks is correct to announce that the late phase of cultural politics hardly resembles a relationship with Marx, a trend whose effectivity he questions. Although many critics are more sanguine than Sparks, it is worthwhile assessing the consequences resulting by moving away from Marx, what they enable and disable in terms of educational and social analysis, and to what kinds of interventions they give rise. It seems the love affair with Marx is definitely over, which does not mean that there are no social and cultural critics who carry on the torch. A theoretical legacy and insurrection that has had a long run has been all but replaced and themes about modes give way to madness, dialectics to deconstruction, and revolution to repetition.

Discourses recall ideology because they have something to do with constituting a world for the subject. Freire's insistence that a world has no meaning without minds that contemplate over it and consciousness is empty without a world to which it refers, still applies here. Discourses are about the world and cannot but be this way. The world is constituted in both the material and ideal sense because as immaterial as God is, for example, the idea alone has erected institutions worldwide. So whereas religious discourse may appeal to an ideal entity, we behave in a material way. That said, discourse is not synonymous with ideology so it is misleading to find a Foucauldian-inspired entry (p. 2) in Eagleton's (1991) definitions for ideology. Ideology assumes a deep social structure, usually but not always based on class. In race studies, this ideology is driven by whiteness, in gender studies, by patriarchy. Discourse is not the conceptual extension of ideology but rather its replacement. It does not begin with assumptions of essences, origins, and substances but shifting terrains of power configurations and cultural contestations. It departs from a different source, that of language. Whether or not it is materialist in the end is unclear but its relation with the material is indisputable. In fact, one cannot wilyy-nilly invoke ideology without recalling the avatar of Marx, at least not without conceptual consequences. As noted, there have been several attempts to rehabilitate the concept of ideology, even turning it into a positive concept that represents integration (Ricoeur, 1986; Geertz, 1994) or a modernizing outlook (Gouldner, 1976). However, these reframings were never fully successful at loosening Marxists' grip on the concept. At best, they were able to express a theoretical ambivalence toward its classical use, which is not insignificant. But the advent of discourse studies introduces a new theory rather than a remetaphorization of an existing trope.

It is in this sense that contemporary cultural theory bares little resemblance to Marx without suggesting that it owes nothing to him. It no longer represents on one side, an intellectual quarrel with, or on the other an homage to, him but a genuinely different way of analyzing social life. In Althusserian (2003) language, following Bachelard, discourse studies introduces a *new problematic*, marking a new theoretical position as radically different today as Marx's was in his time. It was made possible by initial debates around the problems within Marxism, as Sparks notes, but underestimating its newness now forgets the fact that historical changes require different intellectual tools to understand them, just as the contradictions of capitalism called on Marx to explain them. Marxism is no doubt still useful, still axiomatic to some people, especially in these times of economic instability. No doubt post-Marxism would thrive better in post-exploitation but for now, Marxism is like blue jeans refusing to fade away. That established, continuing analysis in the same vein becomes increasingly difficult to pull off because so much has been said, so much has been written. If Marxism continues its relevance, it cannot be your grandparents' Marxism.

One of the innovations of a discourse-based cultural theory is that insofar as the economy remains an important, sometimes privileged, site of analysis, it can be studied as a cultural relation. This was signalled earlier by the turn to consumptive practices, media and communication society, and popular culture. The economy is no longer only a set of material, extra-discursive arrangements in the economic sense but the circulation and control of cultural matter, such as the means of communication, as well as extra-material, discursive elements, like norms and values. The shift to discourse allows cultural politics to transition from the focus on means of production to the production of meaning. This is not altogether an idealist move to the extent that the production of meaning requires apparatuses that give texts their significance and force in the first place. That is, there is no meaning without an apparatus but no mechanism without significations that recruit subjects to constitute them.

The turn to discourse makes possible a new set of studies that before would simply have been branded as ideological in the pejorative sense. With the new appreciation of ideology turned into language-as-social practice, cultural analysis puts on equal footing with the economy, studies of Foucault and fat politics, Deleuze and people with delusions, and Lyotard on the politics of leotards. A veritable wave of research on previously silenced populations and their experiences floods the libraries, giving voice to their existence without the undue pressure to link it back to economic determinism. Of course, the economy looms largely in the new analysis but as one determination among many. An age of ambivalence about the guarantees of social and cultural analysis gives way to what Lyotard (1984) calls "slackening" as scientific and technological rationality loses its grip and metanarratives become suspect. To some, this artifice is nothing but trendy and a sign of the inability to deal with revolution in its longue durée. It must be noted again, however, that the majority of post-thinkers studied under the Marxists, modernists, and structuralists of their time: e.g., scratch Baudrillard and one finds Lefebvre, turn Foucault's stone and one finds Althusser. The hunt for theory represents not only these intellectuals' restlessness but a sincere search for liberation and all its promises and problems. Coming out of the highs and disappointments from the Bolsheviks to the Beatles, intellectuals face what Ranciere calls a profound melancholy that something has been lost. It is in this manner that theory loses its innocence and enters maturity, at least an adolescent phase of rebelling against the myths told by one's parents.[7]

In fact, there were significant pre-poststructuralists (pre-posts?) of whom we may now speak. These transitional figures represent the space of theory somewhere between Marx and Mannheim on one side, and Derrida and Deleuze on the other. Before Baudrillard and Bourdieu entered the scene, they were preceded by intellectuals who began the theoretical disobedience. We can cite at least three. When Bataille introduced Nietzsche to the French, he did more than pronounce the death of God, but decapitated a theoretical head. Arguing for an acephalic, or headless, theory of society, Bataille (1988, 1991) questions Marx's universal theory of production through an alternative theory of expenditure. Claiming that Marx was indeed radical and dialectical, Bataille faults the German for not being radical and dialectical enough. Creating the other of capitalism by imagining communism, Marx opposed the first with the second while still staying within the *logic of production*, merely substituting one private form with a public version (see also Baudrillard, 1975). He did not consider the possibility that humans were inclined to waste, or expend, rather than produce. Bataille's privileged signifier was the potlatch, not production. To be clear, following Marcel Mauss's ethnography of symbolic exchange in tribal societies, Bataille acknowledged a society's need to produce but only in order then to expend or use up what it produces, or consumption in its literal, radical sense. Consumption becomes the destiny of production, not the other way around. Bataille intervenes with a theory of expenditure, or the dialectical other of production, which was later appropriated by Derrida, Bourdieu, and Baudrillard. Bataille radicalized Mauss' notion of the *gift*, where an offering must be cancelled or exceeded by a more extravagant gift. It is guided less by a dialectical progression but rather by the drive to extremes, or more x than x (Genosko, 1989). This ethos is extended to include theory production, whose result must be regarded as a gift to be transcended. Failing to do so institutes power in the hands of the giver. In education, the gift concept has been used by McLaren, Leonardo, and Allen (2000) to argue that whiteness, for instance, not only controls the means of production but also the means of expenditure, the material process and the natural state of desiring excess. In short, whiteness hoards both.

A second transitional figure, or pre-post, is Adorno. In his sole authored *Negative Dialectics*, Adorno (1973) begins the philosophical assault on systematic thinking. Systems thinking, he would argue, undervalues the particular at best and is imperialist at worst. Theorizing at the level of systems neglects the local in favor of universal principles. As a result, specificity is given up for abstraction that subsumes the particular, here defined by Adorno (1973) as "the nonidentical" (p. 170) "which would be the thing's own identity against its identifications" (p. 161), into general explanations about social life, even when this is inappropriate. The system's code becomes imperialistic precisely at the point when all social phenomena are reduced to its precepts. Insofar as Marxism was guilty of such a reduction, it becomes a terroristic theory of society. When Adorno writes, "The innermost core of the object proves to be simultaneously extraneous to it, the phenomenon of its seclusion, the reflex of an identifying, stabilizing procedure" (p. 161), his influence on Derrida becomes clearer, a lineage that leads to the doorsteps of deconstruction's problem with interiority. This conceptual violence allows Adorno to note the suppression of difference in favor of identitarianism, which conveniently forgets its own condition of possibility through its nonidentity, its complementarity that secures the subject of whiteness, for example, with the fact of blackness (see Fanon, 1967). As Adorno (1973) puts it, "The nonidentity which determines it from within, after the criterion of identity, is at the same time the opposite of its principle, that which it vainly claims to be controlling. … Identitarian thinking is subjectivistic even when it denies being so (pp. 182–183). With Adorno's problematization of systems and identity, Foucault's uptake of localism and specificity is given context, and goes a long way to explain the origins of Derrida's celebrated critique of *logocentrism*.

The third precursor to post-theory, to whom I have made lengthy reference already, is Althusser. I will not describe *ad nauseam* his role as a transitional thinker other than focusing on his theory of interpellation. His theory of ideology-as-interpellation is perhaps the most obvious connection with Foucault's almost singular focus on the subject, subjectivity, and subject-creation. Not merely false and illusorry, ideology in the Althusserian sense calls on people, which makes possible their ultimate subjugation: subject here taking on the double meaning of subject-creation and subjection. Whereas a strictly modernist-inspired theory can speak of objective exploitation, Althusser introduces the moment of subjectification that complements objectification within capitalism. In other words, one must answer to a name given before exploitation can truly begin. In race terms, a person of color is subjected to the efficiency of discrimination only after he thinks of himself as a racialized subject; women are recruited into patriarchy once they perform the invention of womanhood as bound up with their sense of self (see Wittig, 1993). Whereas for Althusser interpellation was almost purely a phenomenon linked to exploitation, recent theorists expand the concept of interpellation to include moments of resistance through counter-interpellation, or answering a call against an existing regime. Judith Butler (1997) puts it best when she writes,

> Even the most noxious terms could be owned, that the most injurious interpellations could also be the site of radical reoccupation and resignification. But what lets us occupy the discursive site of injury? How are we animated and mobilized by that discursive site and its injury, such that our very attachment to it becomes the condition for our resignification of it? Called by an injurious name, I come into social being, and because I have an inevitable attachment to my existence, because a narcissism takes hold of any term that confers existence, I am led to embrace the terms that injure me because they constitute me socially. The self-colonizing trajectory of certain forms of identity politics is symptomatic of this paradoxical embrace of the injurious term. As a further paradox, then only by occupying – being occupied by – that injurious term can I resist and oppose it, recasting the power that constitutes me as the power I oppose. … any mobilization against subjection

> will take subjection as its resource, and that attachment to an injurious interpellation will, by way of a necessarily alienated narcissism, become the condition under which resignifying that interpellation becomes possible. This will not be an unconscious outside of power, but rather something like the unconscious of power itself, in its traumatic and productive iterability (p. 104)

Whereas Althusser focused entirely on economic interpellation, Butler and others have dispersed his theory toward multiple and competing hailings, all of which struggle with one another for supremacy over the subject as well its resistance to their molesting powers. Of course, Lyotard (1984) deems these interpellations, such as the political, ethical, economical, as incommensurable language games, further adding to the fragmentation of cultural theory and subverting its ability to explain once and for all a unified understanding of social life. Bataille, Adorno, and later Althusser provide a platform that eventually transforms the production of cultural theory and understanding of cultural politics. There are other good and possible candidates for the status of pre-posts, such as Sartre's existentialism, but suffice it to say that these three theorists represent a critical bridge between classical cultural and social thought and contemporary intellectual developments. They made it possible first to recognize the impasse within Marxism and second to address its conceptual dilemmas through alternative theories.

With respect to social transformation, the turn to cultural processes introduces ambiguity and dispersal. No longer is economic revolution the only way to go. In fact to some, Stalinism bears resemblance to Nazism over and beyond their leaders' distinctive moustache. Earlier, Weber (1994) warned sociologists about the imperialism of a centralized communist economy, which concentrates control of the means of administration in the hands of an oligarchic elite, what Dunayevskaya (1992) calls "state-capitalism." Marxist orthodoxy was unduly economic in its materialism, forsaking other nominally material relations, such as bureaucratic ones, where power does not necessarily rest in the hands of capitalists, but equally in the hands of powerful (often rich, but not the bourgeoisie), credentialed, and high status social groups and their figureheads. Fraser (1997) takes on the task of reforming theory when she recreates Weber's notions of prestige and honor into a *problem of recognition* and marries it with a nominally Marxist problem of the *politics of redistribution.* In effect, she argues that a theory of justice falls short without accounting for the dual process of dishonor and dispossession, both of which have the ability to produce the other. For instance, it is readily obvious that people of color in the US suffer from a lack of recognition (an ideological process), which then produces objective consequences (a material process). This is ultimately what Dumas (2009) finds in the case of Seattle where the Black community's demands for accountability from local schools that are already dilapidated and resource depleted, are met with casual glances from school leaders (see also North, 2006). Arguing for a post-socialist theory and against the economic reductions of Marxism as well as the relative poverty of identity politics – both deemed vulgar when acting alone – Fraser's framework forwards a two-pronged theory of distributive and political justice.

Dumas (2009) adopts Fraser's perspective and marries it with what he terms the "*Black educational imagination*" (p. 105; italics in original), an appropriation of Robin Kelley's concept of the "Black radical imagination." As the Seattle case shows, Don Alexander, leader of Seattle's *Save Our Southend Schools*, and Dr. Caprice Hollins, former director of Seattle's Office of Equity and Race Relations, found themselves at an impasse. They did not disagree over the question of justice for African Americans, and as such, were not working at cross-purposes. But through savvy, theoretical understanding, Dumas documents in convincing manner Alexander and Hollins bifurcating along distributive and recognition lines of thinking, respectively. As a result, they could not see that "there is no redistribution without recognition, and no recognition without redistribution" (p. 82). This means that focusing on racial desegregation alone does not address the fact of whiteness as an invisible, yet material force that facilitates White control over most of the valuable resources in Seattle. The differential outcome, while not always economic, is material. This leads to a condition of integration that is still inherently unequal. On the other hand, emphasizing resource allocation by itself fails to recognize the continuing assaults to dignity that African Americans suffer in schools, which rebound on distributive relations because Black students' legitimacy is always suspect. A cultural theory that decenters economic relations, while still regarding it as central to struggles over hegemony, makes room for identity-based grievances and allows for a more variegated attack on a social system from multiple nodes within the structure.

Marrying Gramsci's war of position with Foucault's dispersal of power relations and concept of discourse, Laclau and Mouffe (2001) argue for a cultural politics that is based less on a center from which everything emanates and more on multiple margins that form a collective. Finding no position outside of hegemony, the point is not to counter common sense but to reform it with as many groups' desires for justice as possible, which speaks less to Lenin's vanguard and even less to a privileged subject of revolutionary alterity, like the working class, and more about the mass, that indistinguishable desire agreeable to Deleuze and Guattari's (1983) concept of the rhizome. Having neither origin nor teleology, the reworking of hegemony is always historically specific and politically concrete since it can never be abstracted in advance by the good intentions and conceptual projection of a theorist. As a product of compromise, the alternative hegemonic bloc aspires to win the multitude's consent (see Hardt and Negri, 2001). If the world feels both post-collectivist and post-individualist, to Eagleton (2003) it may also present an opportunity. It necessitates that we would "imagine new forms of belonging, which in our kind of world are bound to be multiple rather than monolithic" (p. 21). Lost is the notion of an a priori radical class; gained is the articulation of various tendrils of politics reaching out to justice. Lost is any sense of preparing for a projected state of affair, or blueprint society; gained is the concrete working out of a practical politics based on exigent circumstances, a politics based on practice. Finally, lost is a sense of guarantees in exchange for permanent ambiguity and perpetual revolution. Contrary to the end of cultural theory, it is the opening of radical thought as always in the making.

POST-STUDIES

Perhaps nothing is more enigmatic in cultural politics than the signifier "post-modernism."[8] It represents anything from eclectic architecture and hybrid art, to anything we fail to understand. To any cultural theorist who has partaken in enough conversations about ideas, one inevitably runs into a situation where something difficult to understand is branded as "postmodern." The postmodern becomes a theoretical bin wherein anything from the unconscious to the unpresentable is stored for a later explanation. For many intellectuals, the situation can be rather frustrating or comedic, depending on the interlocutor. It represents both a pretentious appeal to high theory for someone who wants desperately to be in the know, and sometimes as a thinly veiled insult against an idea or thinker one rejects. The latter is usually followed by an uncomfortable Beavis and Butthead laughter that someone has just betrayed his or her own ignorance. In short, if we do not understand something, it must be postmodern. If it seems slightly trendy, it is postmodern too. Postmodernism becomes a term of derision. This is hardly proof of an intellectual grasp. Thus, Mary Shelley's *Frankenstein* is not postmodern but comedian and Minnesota Senator Al Franken is. It can be a bit confusing as well, as when Foucault is claimed as both as a structuralist and poststructuralist, or when Baudrillard, regarded by some as the bad boy postmodernist, denounces the idea of post-modernism altogether. But much like the "big bang" was initially a derisive phrase used against a fledgling theory of the universe before it was all but verified – since the universe was claimed to be infinitely small in origin and lacking an atmosphere to convert the explosion into sound – both "big bang" and postmodern have stuck and become household terms. The main difference is that whereas the big bang began the expansion of the universe through an outward, cataclysmic event, postmodernism can be regarded as evidence of a certain theory implosion.

Along the same lines, perhaps nothing identifies cultural politics today more than the prefix "post," known for everything post under the sun: post-Marxism, post-feminism, post-formalism, post-human, post-political, post-race, even post-contemporary (i.e., the present outruns itself). It is becoming rather post-humorous. Outside of some gratuitous usage of the "post"-script, post-theory indicates intellectual depth (against Baudrillard's 1979 position in *Seduction*) when it is specified in concrete terms. The post-nomenclature bears little agreement on what the sign actually means. For instance, the post in postmodernism may be very different from the "same" post in post-humanism. Cultural studies is replete with post-significations and if it uses them haphazardly, we may someday witness the rise of post-cultural studies.[9] As yet another attempt to delineate what the "post" signifies, the following section considers some of the elisions and edifications contained in the post-moment.

The most literal, and probably least fecund, sense of post-theory is that it is an explanatory framework for a condition that follows an era. This is Jameson's (1988) caution that theorists cannot avoid periodization and there is something about late theory as having come "after" a previous epoch that required a different intellectual apparatus to explain it. It was Saussure's students who, after all, compiled his teachings posthumously after his death. In our time, we appear to live in a post-Michael era after the fall of Jordan's highflying acrobatics, Jackson's hit after hit since "Off the Wall," and Gorbachev's memorable birth mark on the forehead. In the age of Kobe Bryant, the NBA in the US suffers apparently from a radical decentering of the concept of team in exchange for individual prowess; with the death of the man who did the moonwalk on Earth, pop has given way to hip hop and megastars are known more for sampling or producing others who know how to sample than they are for original work (to Baudrillard's delight); the Cold War having ended with frigid Russia, we apparently enter a Hot War with terrorism in the desert. We are in a decidedly new era and only nostalgia can return us to our previous selves. We are literally out of touch. Basketball shorts that stop above the knees are as outdated as heavy metal hairstyles below the shoulders.

In this sense, it is apropos to speak of the age of post-colonialism, to the chagrin of many excellent anti-colonial and decolonial scholars who insist that colonialism continues in different forms. Administrative colonialism has ended and former colonies have gained their independence. From Puerto Rico to Pilipinas, South America to South Africa, and India and Indonesia, the colonized have spoken in revolts that toppled European regimes on lands of color. While sharing in their own problems and recreation of colonialist dynamics (Fanon, 2004), these nationalist fronts accomplished something significant in ousting their masters and inaugurated a social formation after colonialism, often requiring violence. From the economic base to naval bases, anti-colonialist struggles reclaimed not only a land expropriated but also a cultural dignity radically compromised in the wake of language imposition (Memmi, 1965; Macedo, 2000), religious conversion (Spring, 2000; Dog and Erdoes, 1999), and general inferiorization (Fanon, 1967; Césaire, 2000). The colonizer's school agenda was one of cultural eradication through education. Or put simply: *cultural eraducation*. One cannot deny a transformation in cultural politics after the colonizer's departure.

Although certainly related to colonialism, the effects of race and its hirsute companion, racism, require a slightly different analytic. In the age of Obama and the reconfiguration of skin color politics, a post-race predicament has become the subject of recent discussions. Its vulgar form takes on a rather conservative tone that suggests the falling significance of race relations (see Thernstrom and Thernstrom, 1999; D'Souza, 1996; McWhorter, 2001; cf. Brown et al., 2003), which is different from implying that the racial formation (Omi and Winant, 1994) is once again shifting (Omi, 2001), or that the end of race as an organizing principle of society can be envisioned (Gilroy, 1998; Leonardo, in pressa).[10] Post-race thinking as an (after) thought falls prey to what Bonilla-Silva (2003), Gotanda (1995), and others have called "colorblind racism." It mistakes the transmutations in race as evidence of a prelude to its end. It forgets the cleverness of whiteness to shift and morph without fundamentally threatening its hegemony, its ability to compromise while maintaining general white advantage (Richardson and Villenas, 2000). It neglects the fact that race has changed before, without challenging the embeddedness of raciology. And it takes progress as a sign of the benefits of liberal democracy without considering the historical record where racism was very much part of creating the liberal nation, the US being one of them (Mills, 1997).

As a slight variation of after-theory, post-thought signals a counter-position to many established traditions. It may span iconoclastic rejections of Marxism (Baudrillard, 1990) to more or less refutations of race analysis (see Darder and Torres, 2004; Miles, 2000; Fields, 1990). In these instances, the "post" not only signals an "after" but "anti." Closely related to the designation of "after" is Jameson's (1991) notion of postmodernism as the cultural logic of late capitalism. So post-modernism announces the late phase of modernism, which suggests, with Lyotard (1984), that we are well within the modern. How late it is, however, is hard to tell. Elsewhere I (2002) have used the phrase "late whiteness" to describe something similar happening to whiteness. Finally, it is possible that the "post" signifies an intensification of the modern condition and theories to explain it. The prefix is then equitable with "super," as Foucault's (1977) studies of surveillance represent a continuity with structuralism in an overbureaucratized social life. Superstructuralism is not only anti-humanist in Althusser's sense but decisively post-humanist.

Through Said's (1979) work on the cultural relations between the Occident and Orient in modern forms of imperialism, one appreciates the textual dimensions of colonialism. In this sense, post-colonialism does not so much describe social life after the fall of major European powers in the colonies, but rather the literary enactment of power. Arguing that colonialism is as much a cultural and writing relation as it is a material or military occupation, Said excavates the constitution of the Near East through European eyes. This gaze lends credibility to Foucault's (1980) dyad of power/knowledge insofar as Europeans were able to exercise power over the Orient by controlling the knowledge produced about its peoples. In other words,

> Knowledge of the Orient, because generated out of strength, in a sense *creates* the Orient, the Oriental, and his world. In Cromer's and Balfour's language the Orient is depicted as something one judges (as in a court of law), something one studies and depicts (as in a curriculum), something one disciplines (as in a school or prison), something one illustrates (as in a zoological manual). The point is that in each of these cases the Oriental is *contained* and *represented* by dominating frameworks". (Said, 1979, p. 40; italics in original)

The modernist mantra "Speak truth to power" is replaced by "Speak power to truth." Rather than assuming a humanist ability to speak with integrity to a unified power through rigorous analysis, we have the inversion that a truth does not exist but rather truth is a function of deployments of power that invest in particular ways of seeing the world. These otherwise ideological moments are constituted through texts that frame the self and Other in a relation of power that produces material consequences as well as expressing themselves through equally material apparatuses, like education or such "innocent" exchanges like travel.

The "post" in various theories therefore signifies the turn to literature, reading, and writing as formidable moments in the articulation of power. Not only are events like colonialism examples of actual violation of human bodies but they equally transpire through the creation of bodies of knowledge, of how people are written into history, literally and figuratively. This is precisely why multiculturalism in education became a fertile battleground in the 1970s onwards (Banks, 2006). With the K-12 schools and universities completely committed to Eurocentric curricula, an insurgent student movement in the US forged what is now a hegemonic form of multiculturalism. Few self-respecting teachers today who care about their own legitimacy in public schools question the validity of multiculturalism. This struggle over hegemony was not won without fanfare as the Right did its best to reassert the rightness and whiteness of the canon (Apple, 2006; Buras, 2008). However, the dust appears to settle and the argument now is not whether or not the US should adopt multiculturalism but which version. Of course, multiculturalism may be compatible with capitalism (Zizek, 1995; San Juan, Jr., 1994), which is very happy to turn folk heroes, like Che Guevarra and Malcolm X, into commodities. Zizek (1995) observes that "the relationship between traditional imperialist colonialism and global capitalist self-colonization is exactly the same as the relationship between Western cultural imperialism and multiculturalism" (p. 44). This is true as one surveys the t-shirtization of radical thinkers, the patronizing spirit of "including" people of color into the official curriculum and tolerating their difference (see Davis, 1998). Indeed, a bourgeois form of multiculturalism is hardly threatening to global capitalism. Be that as it may, so are white supremacy and Europocentrism quite the partners-in-crime with capital.

The advent of postcolonialism opens conceptual tributaries that place language at the center of the educational debate, and not in the well-known sense of the "bilingual question." Postcolonialism treats with seriousness both the power and insufficiency of language. On one hand, it attests to the violence in language and on the other, reminds us of the incompleteness of such violence (see McLaren, Leonardo, and Allen, 1999). At stake in such an analysis is the recognition that a fundamental ambivalence lies at the heart of hegemony and this "failure" of language to achieve transparency becomes a "condition of democratic contestation itself " (Butler, Laclau, and Zizek, 2000, p. 2). The first violence of language, which Lacan clearly anticipated, becomes the source of a "way out" of semiotic brutalities and into another set of possibilities that are themselves doing violence on existing regimes of language (see Aoki, 2000; see also Leonardo and Porter, in press). Following Bataille's appropriation of Mauss' gift concept, resignifications disrupt meaning and introduce violence into an already violent regime of signs. This is accomplished through "doubling," (Bhabha, 1990), "repetition," (Butler, 1990), or in general reconfiguring what expressions or statements are made available (Goldberg, 1993).

That "post" transforms the social world into texts means that the old standby of "reading" in education takes on new importance. Reading formations introduce the power of the text to interpellate its subject, to read, i.e. position, the reader into a chain of competing sets of interest represented by the text. This is precisely Said's (1979) point when he suggests that the Orient cannot be read innocently by both the Occident and people inhabiting the Orient. As a cultural phenomenon, the economy does not evaporate and melt into the air, as the Marxist saying goes, but it is recuperated as a textual relation where meaning is the commodity being sold on the block. This meaning appears in material forms or concrete embodiments and cannot be reduced to an idea, which shares affinities with McLaren's (1992) concept of "enfleshment." As meanings descend from heaven to earth, students are able to make sense of them through educational discourses that are *available* to them (Weedon, 1997). An impoverished material condition is something to deplore but one's education may also be discursively poor; often they are connected where poverty nominally produces both conditions. Post-theory intervenes into classical theory by insisting on their bi-directional co-implication. The material is completely necessary because discourse is about something: the concrete world. Likewise, the discursive explains the material's social meaning, having none of it until the real is recruited into a symbolic system like language. No material to speak of, no discourse; no meaning, no world worth living. In all, the turn to meaning creates a materially-based discourse and a discursively-constituted materiality.

Bundled together, these iterations of the "post" indicate a break in cultural theory. This transformation has been signalled as an epistemological break, a discontinuity, or rupture. I find purchase in Lyotard's (1984) original formulation of postmodernism as essentially a filter for modern theories. By locating the postmodern as an extension of, or a protrusion from, modernism, Lyotard avoids the otherwise cynical suggestion of the postmodern project (short "o") as akin to scribbling a moustache on the portrait of modernism. As a project (long "o"), less a moustache and more a nose, postmodernism extends out from modernism as its latest phase of development characterized by ambivalence, particularly but not exclusively to metanarratives like Marxism. On projects, Hall (1996a) has this to say, "I don't think there is any such thing as *the* modernist impulse, in the singular … It was always composed of many different projects… there were often, in fact, in conflict… I don't know, analytically, what the single project was which modernism might have been" (p. 132; italics in original). Although they may share teleological and determinist assumptions, Weber, Marx, and Durkheim's modernism is more accurately described as variations of the modernist project. They each theorized the economy, but their similarity may end there as they diverged in their portrayal of the economy as a bureaucratic system, productive relation, and role differentiation, respectively.

As Lyotard (1984) suggests, the modern can still be modern but only after it becomes postmodern, after it is filtered through slackening and agonistic analysis. Or as I suggested earlier, Marxist relevance continues but only through reinvention. In my reading, Lyotard does not suggest leaving behind concerns that made Marxism a powerful intervention as much as it goes forward from them. Post-theory owes a debt without being in servitude. The dangers of excessive textualization are clear when the economy is treated as a narrative rather than a brutal experience of exploitation but so are the vulgar consequences of materialism not lost when a politics of redistribution assumes that a levelling of the politics of recognition automatically follows in due time. Cuba's socialist experiment has gone a long way to remove the material structures of racial discrimination but it has not removed the bureaucratic mechanisms that favor white, or light skin-toned, Cubans. To the Cubans' defence, forty some odd years of socialism do not cancel out longer standing racial politics. So we wait.

Hall seems to support Lyotard's point. He claims, "So 'post' means, for me, going on thinking on the ground of a set of established problems, a problematic. It doesn't mean deserting that terrain but rather, using it as one's reference point" (Hall, 1996a, p. 149). In Hall's rereading of Marxism within the postmodern moment, he does not so much abandon its main premises but proceeds "with no guarantees." As a general metaphor, a cultural politics of education that proceeds without guarantees is in line with Freire's earlier insistence on the centrality of theoretical humility, something he (1994) criticizes orthodox Marxists, in *Pedagogy of Hope*, as lacking. This remark did not make Freire less Marxist but arguably more so by being less possessively invested in it. Or as Bottomore et al. (1991) have said elsewhere, the fall of Soviet-style Marxism was a welcome setback for committed Marxists all round for as long as Soviet rigidity followed similar lines, Marxism would become anachronistic. So in this last iteration of "post," cultural theory reinvents itself, enabling it to ask new questions about its own premises and conditions of possibility. Again, Hall is helpful when he remarks, "The post-marxists use Marxist concepts while constantly demonstrating their inadequacy" (Hall, 1996c, p. 25). En route, cultural writing establishes a truly self-reflective intellectual pursuit, without which a theory has only vacuous claims to "criticality" (Leonardo, in pressb). This is the point wherein doctrine becomes dogma and position degrades into polemic. Dialogue is exchanged for diatribe and the victim is ultimately the student.

Nowhere is the post-as-filter more useful than in recent invocations of post-race analysis. Nowhere is it also more misunderstood as it is taken literally to mean "after" race relevance. Contrary to either conservative intellectuals or media analysts' hype over Obama, both of whom are not poster children for race analysis, intellectual engagements of post-race neither endorse the colorblindness of the first nor the spectacle of the second. It would seem fitting to recognize the magnitude of Obama's election to the highest office as a sign of racial slackening. It gives many young African Americans and other minority children permission to imagine themselves as potential presidents. Taken too far, this sentimentality forgets that the chances of any one them becoming president is a crap shoot; but roughly the same goes for many White children, the vast majority of whom will not aspire to such heights. The point is that, just as Reverand Al Sharpton makes the case that the late Michael Jackson made possible, against great odds, Black ascendancy into public culture, bringing Black images, musical or not, into White homes and the White House – so Obama's presidency creates a new public imagination, and not just for Blacks.[11] It would have caught the late rap artist Tupac Shakur on his heels, having declared in the 1990s in the song "Changes," that we are not likely to see a Black person for president.

That established, Obamarise is not equivalent to watching the setting of whiteness. Other events in US history, such as Emancipation and the multiple Civil Rights Movements, have instigated the audacious pronouncement that race and racism are on the wane. We only have to look at the continuing, albeit altering, structures of race relations to remark on its stubborn durability to withstand assaults, as Derrick Bell (1992) and David Gillborn (2008) are correct to remind us. It is possible to suggest that evidence exists to cite the falling **and** continuing significance of race. This is not as ludicrous as it sounds but characterizes the struggle over hegemony that is raciology. Much like the thermonuclear dynamics inside a star threatens to explode it while gravity warns of its catastrophic implosion, racial hegemony is the "tendential balance" and "unstable equilibrium" that makes it "work" (see Hall, 1996d). National and global developments petrify race at the same time that they question its validity, empirically and conceptually (Gilroy, 2000; Nayak, 2006; St. Louis, 2002). Although it is much too premature to write race's obituary, it is worthwhile asking if it is justifiable as a form of social organization in perpetuity. Post-race analysis makes it possible to pose these questions, creating dilemmas out of them that we need not fear.

Post-race analysis is a racial discourse. Just as Marxism launched class theory to transcend class (perhaps better referred to as post-class theory), so post-race theory desires getting beyond race as a mode of organizing society. It is not an attempt at colorblindness but imagines the possibility of transcending the color line, a limit situation that staples of race theory, from Du Bois to Dr. Martin Luther King Jr., have labored to expose. Just as it would sound contradictory to label Marxism classblind, charging post-race scholars with colorblindness is like pounding the square peg of sincere race engagement into the round hole of race-evasive scholarship. Post-race theorizing assumes a fundamental risk by questioning a several centuries-old concept whereas anti-race theories assume no such commitment when they question race's future. Post-race theory is a mode of analysis that goes *through* race in order to imagine going *beyond* it. It appropriates a Fanonian (1967) phenomenology and sociogenic analysis of racialized bodies before it can ponder race as a moribund social relation. In other words, it asks what we have become that we no longer want to be, mainly deposits of skin color politics and the accompanying essentialisms. Risking it all, Gilroy and company do not ask for resignifications of race but its abolition. Only twenty years ago, it was not possible to pose/post these considerations, other than Marxist depreciations of the "race problem" (see Roediger, 1991). Now, in the age of ambivalence, we have recourse to ask the unaskable. Eagleton observes, Theory of this kind comes about when we are forced into a new self-consciousness about what we are doing. It is a symptom of the fact that we can no longer take those practices for granted. On the contrary, those practices must now begin to take themselves as objects of their own inquiry. Education scholars would do well to heed these theories, for it is school where race is remade daily almost without scrutiny. Under the current pedagogical regime, racial comfort zones are favored over spaces of risk that would enable students and educators alike to become something different, which is arguably the essence of learning.

It is this ambivalence that I would like to leave the reader with, in this portion of the Introduction. Cultural politics in education owes much to Marxism's entry into the educational lexicon. It has given us the scientific knowledge that provides a radical theory of education to pose essential questions about the function and purpose of schooling. As a result, we discovered the determining effects of the economy, traced its mimetic structures in schools, and built a praxis that explains and intervenes into relations of exploitation. But as a cosmology, classical

Marxism became victim of its own conditioning and just as the bourgeoisie projects a world in its own image, Marxism painted itself into a corner. From the early writings of the Frankfurt School to the later theories of the CCCS, cultural studies as a form of praxis (Wright, 2003) and not merely a description of the world – as Marx himself warned against – enters a new threshold, which makes it nearly impossible to forge ahead in the same vein. For better or worse, Newton's age has given way to Einstein's universe. Likewise, it seems we live in the age of Foucault, a young anarchist of bad faith to some (e.g., Habermas, 1987b), the Nietszche of our time to others. Intellectuals in education proceed with no guarantees and theorize at their own risk. They flail about, much like Said's (1996) exilic intellectual, thrown into an existence for which there is no inventory, as the Gramscian lesson tells us. We sense the ambivalence because God is not only dead, but so is salvation. No theory can save us now and perhaps this is something to embrace.

THE VOLUME

This volume takes what is hopefully a structure and representation that embraces the emphasis on difference so central to cultural politics and education. Treating both education and cultural theory in the broadest sense possible, the collection takes a large slice of the politics of culture to include what is sometimes left out of more or less Eurocentric intonations of cultural politics in education. To this end, the volume excavates, in the spirit of inclusion, marginalized voices in cultural politics, such as critical studies of ability, Latino cultural studies, and analysis of Rightist formations. The authors represented here include a mixture of well-established cultural theorists and more recent voices from young scholars. An international editorial board also folds into the process a certain dialogical flavor to the chapters. Their consultation with the individual chapter authors broadens the conversation and enriches the insights. Even so, the volume does not offer the last word on these matters and the project could be more ambitious and significantly expanded in efforts to address pertinent issues in education not included here. As with all intellectual projects, this one is admittedly incomplete and begins *in medias res*. The following chapters are organized into themes with a set of essays that are grouped under them.

The first section, **The Cultural Politics of Neoliberalism**, sets up the collection by introducing the condition under which many K-12 schools and colleges of education currently function. In Henry Giroux's leading chapter, an argument for a "public pedagogy of neoliberalism" launches the collection into the material and cultural dimensions of the recent economic restructuring of social life across the globe. Here Giroux recognizes the cruel theater of neoliberalism not only as a form of economic reprioritization but equally a shift in the production of subjectivities and rearticulation of political projects where the normalization of individual consumption becomes the dominant form of citizenship. He argues that neoliberalism has to be understood within a larger crisis of vision, meaning, education, political agency, and policies of radical exclusion: in short, a powerful public pedagogy and cultural politics. However, Giroux finds interstices of hope for a resistance, at times amorphous, in the very heart of neoliberalism and its failure to commodify and co-opt everything in its wake, revealing the cracks in neoliberal hegemony. From Seattle and Davos to Genoa and Rostok, groups have mobilized to defend all those social advances that strengthen democratic public spheres and services, demand new rights and modes of power sharing, and strive for social justice adequate to creating forms of collective struggle that can imagine and sustain democracy of "another world" on a global level. Greg Dimitriadis' chapter follows Giroux's critique of neoliberalism by offering up the lessons learned from the business world with respect to its *failures*. Taking seriously the grip and role of business logic in schools, Dimitriadis takes a strategic stance toward a study of the corporatization and standardization of education, exemplified by the Bush administration's No Child Left Behind Act, which parallels an obsession with test scores with the business world's mantra of "hitting the numbers." In this, neoliberalism fails spectacularly in its efforts to deregulate both the market and schooling. The valuable lessons include an utter disregard for the lived realities in schools and the needs of the teachers and students who daily navigate them. It seems that greed isn't good, after all. The language of business has failed business itself, which progressive educators would do well to engage seriously rather than summarily dismissed.

Dennis Carlson concludes this section by documenting neoliberalism's effects on schooling as they trickle up to university settings. Using insights from Derrida, Carlson prognosticates about the "university to come." Within neoliberalism, the university's autonomy is constantly under threat of erasure. First, Carlson recalls Kant's thoughts on the historical function of university settings in determining the agenda of public discourse as well as the contradictory space that faculties occupy in them, particularly education, which for Kant has one foot in the "lower" liberal arts (e.g., philosophy) and the other in the "higher" applied disciplines. Second, Carlson segues into Derrida's more recent ruminations about the university (not to be equated with higher education per se), located within his general deconstructive philosophy, including a critique of autonomous reason. Like discourses, the university is something that the professoriate inherits and it comes with certain responsibilities as we consider ethically what and how it should serve the human striving towards democracy. This fundamentally undecidable condition is rendered fixed by neoliberalism's unabashed drive toward logos, where the university functions for certain utilitarian ends. This has translated to what Carlson considers is a dangerous current that takes away control of knowledge selection and dissemination from faculties of education or reduces them to bureaucrats of knowledge.

In the second section, **Globalization and Culture Industries**, neoliberalism's familiar partnership with globalization and capitalism is pursued. Peter McLaren and Valerie Scatamburlo-D'Annibale investigate the uses of Marxism within the study of cultural politics. Arguing for the strategic centrality of class, they insist on the usefulness of reinventing Marx for the context of an increasingly exploitative, apparently racial, predicament. They find that, with the events of the 2000 presidential elections and Hurricane Katrina, "race" becomes the language through which America's capitalist class contradictions are commonly expressed and obscured. The globalization of class is exchanged for the national focus on race, a hyper-culturalism that produces the inability to discern the roots of racial inequality in the expansion of capitalism. In particular, Katrina provides an apt example of why an exclusive focus on race must be challenged because poverty (i.e., class inequality) was the lynchpin that resulted in the masses being left behind and stranded, not race. In defence of the enduring relevance of Marxism, McLaren and Scatamburlo-D'Annibale do not argue for a flattening out of social markers in a cultural analysis of education, putting class beside other relations like race and gender, but rather the centering of class as a determining instance, the material armature or material basis for other forms of oppression within capitalist society. Here they guard against the semiotic excesses of, particularly, late cultural politics. Noah De Lissovoy's chapter follows suit in forging a language of totality, which is his conceptual equivalent to the "whole" (cf. "global"). Tracing Lukács, he reinvigorates the Hungarian's theoretical insights by marrying them to standpoint epistemology, largely gained from feminist philosophy. De Lissovoy uses the feminist concept of epistemic privilege to reiterate Lukács' analysis of the working class potential to perceive the whole (totality) despite capitalism's reifications. For De Lissovoy, working class consciousness (itself an experience rather than idea) is no more than an authentic revolutionary standpoint on the whole. But even Lukács did not witness the globalization currently sweeping across nations and any educational standpoint that claims a privileged relationship to the totality must, in the contemporary moment, speak to and from the global population of the truly dispossessed: in short, a global standpoint.

Closely related to Lukács' work is the Frankfurt School's Critical Theory programme, which Benjamin Frymer takes up in the next chapter. Taking up Marx's task, instead of merely categorizing and describing the world, dialectical theory would make possible the evaluation of history and society from the standpoint of human freedom. This required a penetrating comprehension of modern culture both within capitalist as well as socialist societies, requiring a turn to Marx's cultural, as opposed to scientific, at times positivistic, concepts. Following the Frankfurt School, Frymer privileges themes like alienation, which for Marx, he reminds us, is not only or primarily an *experience* of estrangement, but a material and ontological condition – a distorted historical being formed within the capitalist relations of production. This access to Marx's earlier manuscripts, Frymer explains, allows the Frankfurt School to tap more fully the effects of a growing culture industry that dominates a new world of standardized objects that limit people's autonomy and subjectivity even as these objects present the illusion of being freely "chosen". Ideological deception then becomes one of the main products of the culture industry. Frymer corrects what he observes is a misconception that bills the Frankfurt School, Adorno in particular, as elitist and disparaging of mass culture, when he recalls that the culture industry analysis is meant to apply to so-called "high culture" as well, which have been just as commodified and devalued as mass culture. Nowhere is modern estrangement more visible than in the Columbine school shootings, a product of youth identity in a mediatized society becoming a commodity that is bought by media conglomerates and sold back to youth themselves as part of the cultural logic of what Debord earlier termed "society of the spectacle."

Seehwa Cho completes the section by documenting the turn to culture in social theory and its arguable dominance in educational theory. One could focus on purely theoretical differences among scholars and approaches. Rather than delineate the conceptual differences between Marxism and post-al theories (poststructuralism, postmodernism, and postcolonialism) regarding the question of culture, Cho examines the historical and social contexts that provoked the emergence of a singular focus on culture. In other words, her chapter examines the political economy of cultural theories/politics, or how the changes in the mode of capitalism, from industrial to post-industrial, pushed culture to the center stage both in critical theories and Leftist politics. For Cho, the growing attention to culture is a result of the class war that was waged through cultural interventions by the cultural industries and state cultural apparatuses, shifting the focus from capitalist production to consumer creation.

In the third section, **Subjects and Subjectivities**, the set of chapters take up the concept of subject-formation and the concomitant positionalities it produces. Zeus Leonardo's chapter is an attempt to synthesize Louis Althusser's theory of ideology for the purposes of race analysis. Intervening in the debate surrounding whether or not race can be reduced to the status of an ideological concept, Leonardo offers up a reframing of race relations as having both extra-ideological as well as extra-material elements. For this he turns to Althusser, whose theory of ideology is key in appreciating the material forms that ideology takes, avoiding a radical separation between the ideality of ideology and the materiality of economic relations. In this manner, he highlights the limits of the position that reduces race to ideology since race's modes of existence, such as schools, are real while anchored to the reminder that race was a social invention, an interpellation that requires repetition and reification. Appropriating Althusser's description of ideology as fundamentally sedimented at the level of the unconscious, Leonardo argues that race common sense has firmly saturated self and social understanding, particularly in the USA.

Deborah Youdell follows with her chapter, a Butler-inspired take on subject-formation as part of a general study of performativity. Put another way, Youdell advances a theory of subjectivity against notions of essences that lurk behind them; instead, subjects of race and gender are constituted through their performance. Designations such as "boy" and "girl", "man" and "woman" are performative – they *create* the gendered subject that they name. Furthermore, these performatives do this while appearing to be just *descriptive* and create the *illusion* of gender's *prior* existence. So while it appears that the subject *expresses* a gender that is true or "proper" to it, this is actually a performative effect of gender categorizations and their use. This naming is not simply descriptive, it is, to use Butler's term, "inaugurative," and makes the subject recognizable through processes of repetition whereby the subject is consistently referred to in a ritualized manner. Discursive agency comes in many forms, one of which is to intercept these performatives in order to re-constitute discourses and subjects differently, which, while constrained are not determined in advance. Youdell then shows how performativity, from ability studies to sexuality in the classroom, has been used by educational scholars to showcase the constitutive power of discursive performances.

In the next chapter, Alicia Broderick explores the cultural politics circulating in contemporary discourses about autism, particularly the usage of metaphor therein. Writing from a Disability Studies in Education (DSE) perspective, she argues that there is currently an ongoing cultural struggle over the metaphoric constitution of autism as *disease* vs. autism as neuro*diversity*. Related to the dominant "autism as disease" metaphor, two dominant metaphors to emerge in popular cultural discourse around autism in the last several years are: (a) autism as *abductor* and (b) autism as *epidemic*. She argues that, taken together, within the organizing metaphoric construct of autism as disease, these twin metaphors serve discursively to constitute (a) an *enemy* and (b) a sense of *urgency*, each of which is necessary to constitute autism as a cultural threat significant enough to support particular approaches and postures toward both intervention (e.g., attempts at "recovery") and prevention (e.g., "curing autism"). Drawing upon Lakoff and Johnson's (2003) theories of metaphor, Broderick explores the circulation of power through metaphor in contemporary autism discourse, considering also Foucault's (1980) notions of "regimes of truth" and "subjugated knowledges." Exploring the cultural politics underlying the usage of metaphor in autism discourse illustrates the powerful ways in which broader cultural narratives about normalcy/abnormalcy become "naturalized," thus obscuring the ideological assumptions underlying decisions about educational policy and practice.

Cameron McCarthy and Jennifer Logue's chapter assesses the concept of *tradition* within the cultural studies literature on the industrial working class. They maintain that this term has been deployed within a center-periphery thesis and a field-bound ethnographic framework by cultural studies scholars pursuing a sub-cultural studies approach. Within this framework, "Britishness," for example, has been the silent organizing principle defining metropolitan working class traditions and forms of cultural resistance. British cultural studies proponents have therefore pursued the study of class and culture as a localized, nation-bound set of interests. This has placed cultural studies in tension with postcolonial subjectivities often reduced, as they have been in the classic works of Paul Willis' (1981) *Learning to Labor* and Dick Hebdige's (1979) *Subculture: The Meaning of Style*, to the metonymic "Pakis" and "Jamaicans." McCarthy and Logue write against the grain of the textual production of the working class within cultural studies scholarship insisting that recent films – such as *The Full Monty*, *Billy Eliot*, and *Bend It Like Beckham* and the literary works of Jeanette Winterson, George Orwell, George Lamming, and Kazuo Ishiguro – offer a more complex story of class identities in the age of globalization and transnationalism.

In Gert Biesta's chapter, the *subjectification function* might perhaps best be understood as the opposite of the socialization function. It is precisely *not* about the insertion of "newcomers" into existing orders, but about ways of being that hint at independence from such orders; ways of being in which the individual is not simply a "specimen" of a more encompassing order. This move was possible because Kant only allowed for *one* definition of what it meant to be human: rationally autonomous. This leads to Levinas' injunction that humanism is not sufficiently human, or not humane enough, when it specifies what it is to be human before the actual manifestations of particular humans. Levinas is not interested in the human subject as such but first and foremost in the question of the uniqueness of each individual human subject, that is, with the way in which human subjects are precisely *not* specimens of a wider order: not a *theory* of subjectivity but an *ethics* of subjectivity that does not ask what the subject is, but how he exists, how he is possible in the first place without being interchangeable. Learning from Levinas, Biesta argues, opens up the event of education rather than socialization, a pedagogy of interruption that is fundamentally not humanistic.

In the fourth section, **The Politics of Knowledge**, Michael Peters, Rodrigo Britez, and Ergin Bulut open with the idea that the most significant material change underpinning neoliberalism in the 21st century is the rize in the importance of knowledge as intellectual capital. This change, more than any, propels the neoliberal project of the "knowledge economy" that has predominated in world policy forums at the expense of alternative accounts of globalization. It is an account that universalizes policies and obscures country and regional differences. It also denies the capacity of local traditions, institutions and cultural values to mediate, negotiate, reinterpret and transmute the dominant model of globalization and the emergent form of knowledge capitalism on which it is based. This chapter traces the birth of neoliberalism and its expression in three models of economic liberalism. Finally, it provides an alternative reading of the knowledge economy based on the emergence model of social knowledge production based on peer co-production of knowledge goods and the ethics of participation and collaboration.

Jennifer Sandler and Michael Apple's chapter then begins by asking the question: "What knowledge is of most worth?" They argue that recent calls for rigor and relevance in the field of education have become increasingly unified and specific, focused and public. The critique of education research has found its voice – along with a great deal of power – within the federal educational policy sphere. This voice says not just "rigor" and "relevance," but "randomized controlled trials" and "what works." This voice suddenly seems ubiquitous in federal policy, a mantra repeated with remarkable specificity and finding its way into federal educational policy, research training programs, conferences, job postings, RFPs, and the verbiage of myriad policy organizations. It is represented in a newly coherent program of grants and fellowships on the part of the Institute of Education Sciences, as well as the over $10 million per year allocated for the What Works Clearinghouse for reviews of intervention research in education and promotion of the results of these reviews to the public. The politics of research methods in education is suddenly big news. This chapter begins to trace these politics by describing this shift – to which Sandler and Apple refer as "evidence-based policy/practices," or EBP – from what they understand to be the perspective of its advocates, creating what the authors call an *epistemological movement*. Finally, they address how the EBP movement might be understood in relation to the context of its particular constitutive outside: diverse interest groups and advocates who situate their political and educational work within subjective, lived experiences.

Kristen Buras' chapter documents and analyzes the rise of *rightist multiculturalism* as part of the new hegemony. More specifically, she refers to the propensity, especially over the past two decades, toward particular forms of compromise—namely, those building on the cultural sensibilities of and demands for recognition by marginalized groups while at the same time steering those sensibilities in dominant directions. Rightist multiculturalism represents a far more extensive effort to reconstruct the radical racial critiques of the 1960s than the inclusion of textbook sidebars on the Little Rock Nine or mainstreaming of Malcolm X through state issuance of an honorary postage stamp. Buras is referring here to the neoconservative–inspired Core Knowledge curriculum around which E. D. Hirsch and the Core Knowledge Foundation have built an entire school reform movement premised on this new hegemonic approach. Using a neo-Gramscian lens, she critically examines Hirsch's vision of education and the ways his guiding assumptions appeal to unequally empowered groups. Moreover, she traces the cultural politics and growth of the Core Knowledge movement, analyzes the allegiance of dominant and subaltern groups to Core, and underscores the tensions generated by diverse actors and interests within the movement as they strike strategic forms of compromise.

Sandra Harding rounds out the section with a report on the status of women in the sciences. It is now three decades since critics began to look at the theories and practices of science and technology (S&T) through the distinctive perspectives produced by the women's movement in the US and Europe. Yet the higher that one looks in S&T worlds, the fewer women one finds. In the last decade especially, analyses that start off from the lives of women from racial and ethnic minorities in the North and women in the Third World have added distinctive perspectives to these debates. The persistence of discrimination against women raises troubling questions. A second concern has focused on cases of sexist and androcentric applications and technologies of S&T. Third, sexist, racist, imperialist and "orientalist" results of scientific research in biology and the social sciences have justified the enforcement of women's second-class citizenship. A fourth focus has succeeded in shifting attention from the reputed deficiencies of girls and women to the documented deficiencies of S&T curricula and pedagogy. In this chapter, Harding reviews the main themes in these literatures, and then briefly turns to their implications for theories of democracy and philosophies of science.

In the fifth section, **Social Identities**, the UK's leading Critical Race Theorist, David Gillborn, introduces the main tenets of critical race theory as a form of cultural politics. Focusing specifically on interest convergence, or the way that racial progress intersects with whites' own political interests, he examines the Stephen Lawrence case in Great Britain, arguably the most famous single episode in the history of British race relations. Stephen Lawrence was 18 years old when he was murdered by a gang of White youths. His parents' fight for justice, in the face of a racist, incompetent and uncaring police force, made legal and social history. The Stephen Lawrence case led to far-reaching changes in race equality law, including the Race Relations (Amendment) Act (RRAA) that was passed in November 2000. It elevated the notion of "institutional racism" to a point in the public consciousness where the term is now frequently used and debated in politics and in the mainstream media. Despite all this, serious questions remain about the long-term impact of the case. The Lawrence case demonstrates conclusively that struggles for race equality are never complete. Landmark victories, no matter how hard won, may be the beginning, not the end, of the change process. But it would be wrong to interpret this analysis as hopeless. Rather, the chapter points to a more realistic measure of success and our chances for further change in the future. In the tradition of Derrick Bell, Gillborn's portrait of the Lawrence family's pursuit of racial justice becomes an ultimate act of defiance in a time when colorblind policies discourage such analysis.

Interpreting the work of one of the most recognized names in cultural politics – Stuart Hall – Michael Dumas' chapter asks what it means to invoke Black education in a time of intense questions regarding racial essentialism. However, just because we might agree that race is, in Hall's words, "a floating signifier," is not to say that it signifies nothing at all, or that it has no material significance. Race matters precisely because its meaning is indeterminate, thus allowing social actors to construct, dismantle, shift and then re-construct racial representations that inform how we see and "do" race in our daily lives. Documenting the intellectual and political platform of the Birmingham School, Dumas traces its Marxist roots even as it goes beyond them to account for non-class based movements and subject formations, including race. As it concerns Black identity, there is no pure blackness to which we might aspire, (re-)create or return. This is not to say that "Black" has no meaning whatsoever; nor does it suggest that there is no need for a Black cultural politics. Applying Hall's critique of racial essence, Dumas offers a *Black politics without guarantees*. This entails three pedagogical acts. First, it is important to *continually reaffirm a discourse of struggle in Black education*, indeed to struggle over the "Black" in Black education. Second, Black education *insists on the complexity of Black representation*, its multitude rather than its essence. Third, and perhaps most importantly, a critical cultural politics of Black education must *begin with an engagement of the cultural production of young people*, or their concrete acts to maintain that Black is still beautiful. In the next chapter, Sherick Hughes introduces Burke's concept of drama, an influence on major Harlem Renaissance thinkers. Dramatism is perhaps, more accurately described as Burke's *Weltanschauung* (i.e., Burke's comprehensive view of the world of human life as a stage play of and about the human symbolic condition). Dramatism is the genesis and exodus; chicken and egg of his lifelong thinking, feeling, and acting about the human symbolic condition - his, yours, and mine - with all of the conflicts and possibilities thereof. Hughes' chapter on Burke captures the theatrical in cultural politics that often blurs the already fine line between reality and performance.

Next, Sofia Villenas asks what it might mean to think critically about education with and from the knowledge and theorizing of people engaged in Chicana/Latina cultural production. She explores how Chicana literary scholarship born of the physical reality of the border serves to theorize cultural production from the epistemologies, experiences and histories of those whose lives are carved by the existence of the U.S.-Mexico/Latin American border. Specifically, Villenas outlines five tenets of Chicana/Latina feminist thought – 1) intersectionality of oppressions, 2) global solidarities, 3) breaking down dualisms, 4) embracing ambiguity, and 5) tracking decolonial agency. Together, these offer *feminista*-centered conceptualizations of methodology, identity/identifications, pedagogy and social movement – all essential considerations in the study of a critical education centered on critique and hope. In excavating a *mujerista* and feminist paradigm of cultural production from the pen of Chicana and Latina literary scholars, novelists, poets, artists, essayists, folklorists, and revisionist historians, Villenas proposes how a different yet overlooked set of theoretical perspectives and tools contribute to addressing key educational issues of local and global dimensions. Finally, she explores recent educational research that is conceptualized from the spaces of Chicana/Latina feminist cultural studies, and concludes with implications and future directions for re-thinking specific issues in critical multicultural, Latina/o and immigrant/diaspora education.

Jackson Katz's chapter shifts to a general introduction to the importance of masculinity studies in education and cultural theory. Specifically, he sketches out some of the key elements of a multiperspectival cultural studies analysis of media-driven constructions, particularly of presidential masculinity. One of the chief goals of a cultural studies approach to masculinity is to make visible some of the processes whereby white masculinity maintains its dominant social position and in doing so, to unmask and demystify it. In particular, presidential masculinity is a historical construction, and both *hegemonic masculinity* and its corollary, *emphasized femininity*, are fluid concepts that are contextual and continually negotiated in the media. Moreover, the president has arguably been the embodiment of hegemonic white masculinity in his era. Who he is and how he carries himself – and how his "manhood" is represented and constructed in media – has enormous influence in the fashioning of social norms and expectations of what it means to be a "real man." In that sense, the presidency itself can be understood as a type of public pedagogy. Through a critical political media literacy, sports discourses like "boxing" and "football" become subjects for analysis of the way that gender is learned and students are recruited into combinations of masculine and feminine roles.

Diana Silberman-Keller's chapter kicks off the last section, **Reading Formations**, by introducing the field of informal education as an ever-changing repertoire of educational, cultural, social and political activities that sometimes bridge between the deficiencies of formal and informal education and sometimes propose radical alternatives to institutionalized education. Informal learning's status as "Between Tradition and Modernity" includes the idea of sustaining idealized learning patterns from the past on the one hand, and the tendency to transport these patterns into modern public spheres where learning is not generally supposed to take place on the other. The social change orientation is the belief in informal educational activities as potentially capable of effectuating social change, that is, beyond representing an attitude toward change. Silberman-Keller surveys research on informal learning that takes place in Internet communities, video games, and traditional apprenticeship relations. As observed in the changing tropes of informal education, the future of cultural politics is captured by two main tendencies. First, the formalization and institutionalization of informal educational systems through the edification of departments, ministries and programs that foment informal education in various settings, results in the pedagogic and didactic pluralism of learning. Second and opposed to the first, the introduction of new technologies inspires the creation of new subcultures and social groups.

In Korina Jocson and Takeo Rivera's chapter, the authors introduce a theory of poetry through the works of Bakhtin. The word, for Bakhtin, is a concrete living utterance shaped by various historical moments in dialogically agitated social environments. Bakhtin, argue Jocson and Takeo, draws a parallel between the novel and the body as a living entity, as becoming, as grotesque, as different, and as continually created or re-created by the world, like the novel, which is intertextual and conceived from a web of relationships with the world. They apply specifically three of Bakhtin's concepts – polyphony (multivoicedness), chronotope (time and space), and carnival (newness and difference) – to examine empirically youth poetry and spoken word. From this, they generate the insight that the intersection of performance and poemness suggests a link between the pedagogical and ontological. If we understand performance as more than the staged act of performing a poem, but as a performance of identity, of *becoming through performing*, the importance of poemness therefore becomes far more apparent for education, both in and out of school forms of literacy.

Kalervo Gulson's chapter commences with a brief introduction to the spatial turn in education, made possible through Foucault's theoretical innnovation from temporal to spatial logics of power. Second, it highlights some of the spatial images and orderings in the cultural politics of the school, which architecturally and symbolically is replete with spatial imagery and orderings. Third, it explores some of the possibilities and limitations of spatial theories – with a focus on metaphors – in relation to issues of identity, specifically hybridity and race, where a symbiosis exists with geography. Not only is race produced by space, but so is space by race. We do not need to look further than the history of abductions of Aboriginal children in Australia or the politics of housing development and segregation in cities like Chicago, where racialization and spatialization are clearly at work. The chapter concludes with a consideration of how spatial concepts might allow for different thinking about the cultural politics of education.

Finally, Douglas Kellner completes the volume with his treatise of how digital technologies pose tremendous challenges to educators to rethink their basic tenets, to deploy the new technologies in creative and productive ways, and to restructure schooling to respond constructively and progressively to the technological and social changes currently underway and emergent forms of culture and communication. Kellner discusses the fundamental transformations in the world economy, politics, and culture in a dialectical framework that distinguishes between progressive and emancipatory features, oppressive and negative attributes, and how a radical pedagogy and new technoliteracies are essential for democratic social transformation and justice. Hence, following John Dewey and Paulo Freire, he calls for a reconstruction of education to make it more responsive to the challenges of a democratic and multicultural society.

NOTES

[1] I regard the phrase "cultural politics" as a rough equivalent of the phrase "cultural studies." That said, cultural politics is a broader descriptor for the study of cultural contestation, whereas cultural studies is a program of study and exists in a more formal space within the academy, best captured by Grossberg, Nelson, and Treichler's (1992) attempt to capture its contours in the edited collection, *Cultural Studies*. For this section, I will favor using cultural studies because of its British roots, but the remainder of the Introduction will stay with cultural politics as a more general phenomenon.

[2] I consider Althusser's attention to ideology unsurpassed in our era. This does not mean that his structural theory of ideology does not have gaps and holes, which I address in my chapter for this volume. It means that in making ideology the *defining concept of study*, Althusser has few rivals. Of current social theorists, I consider Eagleton the heir apparent to Althusser in studies of ideology.

[3] If Althusser's theory sounds elitist, it is a fair criticism. As he sees it, science and democracy develop in opposite directions. As Marxist science improves, less people have access to materialist thinking, creating a larger ideological field. It is a bit like a sports analogy wherein athletes are becoming more elite, therefore limiting access to professional sports to a narrower field of candidates. Regarding materialist thought, this narrowing is especially true in capitalist social formations, where Marxist thinking is discouraged. But to Althusser the problem does not whither away with the establishment of socialism. If this sounds like the beginning of poststructural deferral, then Fritzman (1998) is right to call Althusser a "poststructural materialist."

[4] For the moment, I am privileging poststructuralism as signifier of a general shift in cultural theory. I recognize that postmodernism in art and philosophy, postcolonialism in literature and history, as well as other post-varieties, are different discourses and react to diverse traditions. I use poststructuralism as a term that maintains a family resemblance, to borrow Wittgenstein's phrase, with other post-foundational thought. Their critiques resemble each other's spirit, if not also sharing a profound political orientation together. Some of these distinctions will be explored in the last section below on the turn to "post" in cultural politics.

[5] Foucault is commonly referred to as a poststructuralist and my use of superstructuralism is a theoretical liberty. It signifies the continuity with Althusser's structuralism taken to its height, rather than a radical break between Althusser and Foucault. It is for this reason that I consider Althusser a key predecessor of poststructuralism by calling him a pre-post thinker. Because there is no general agreement regarding the meaning of "post" in post-analysis, one possibility, which I am not championing by writing, is that it means "super." Superstructuralism takes Saussure's structuralist method of studying language without people and applies it to studying discourses without subjects.

[6] Fredric Jameson delivered a series of lectures at UCLA's Comparative Literature Department, 2001.

[7] Ranciere gave a talk for the Department of French at UC-Berkeley, March 11, 2008.

[8] Here I will privilege postmodernism as a broader cultural phenomenon. It has become a term that describes a general discomfort about new ideas as opposed to poststructuralism and postcolonialism, which remain primarily academic terms. For instance, in cycling one seatpost during the 1990s, which connects the saddle to the frame's seat tube, bears the witty marketing title of "Postmodern." There also exists a book called *Postmodernism for Dummies*. In general, the term postmodern encompasses the variety of post-discourses.

[9] In the sense of post as "after".

[10] There are two varieties of post-race thought. The first did not go by the name of "post-race" but argued for the downplaying of race structures. For this reason, it belongs in the after-race discussion in the chronological sense that we live in the aftermath of race. Conservative analysts have been tenacious with this line of thought, particularly in the US, for several decades now. They are not

normally considered as subscribing to a cultural studies persuasion but nonetheless espouse a cultural politics, albeit of the Right (see Apple, 2006; Buras, 2008). For this reason, many race scholars cringe at the suggestion of "post-race" (in any form). The second version of post-race belongs with the cultural studies movement and actually uses the phrase, "post-race," but does not strictly argue either for a time after race in which we live or the moribund status of race analysis. It may, in Gilroy's (2000) case, argue for the dispreference toward race organization but it accomplishes this move via a thorough appreciation of the awesome nature of race relations as a lived reality. I will discuss this second version of post-race below in the section on "post" as a signifier for a certain ambivalence, which I (in pressa) have argued elsewhere as a theoretical filter that changes the nature of cultural analysis and proceeds with no guarantees.

[11] The Los Angeles Staples Center, home to the Lakers, held a memorial service to honor and remember Michael Jackson on July 2009. There, Reverend Al Sharpton remarked on Michael Jackson's opening of doors for African Americans in all sectors of public life, including the nation's presidency. He spoke eloquently of Jackson's ability to create a comfort zone among the races, whose members, through their differences, came together to appreciate his music. This comfort zone, he adds, is partly responsible, for the nation's acceptance of a Black man for president. Although I am not sympathetic to an analysis that focuses on the influence of an individual, no matter the strength of presence and personality, in exchange for a fuller appreciation of the history that facilitated said events, both Jackson and President Obama are extraordinary people and not just anyone could have accomplished what they achieved. That said, one's popularity did not determine the other's success. The complete mediatization of Jackson's eccentrism may not have aided in Obama's election, but the latter may have succeeded precisely *despite* it as the electorate's overwhelming choice.

REFERENCES

Adorno, T. (1973). *Negative dialectics* (E. B. Ashton, Trans.). New York: Continuum.

Anderson, B. (2006). *Imagined communities*. New York: Verso.

Anderson, P. (1976). The antinomies of Antonio Gramsci. *New Left Review*, *I*(100), 5–65.

Althusser, L. (1969). *For Marx* (B. Brewster, Trans.). New York: Verso.

Althusser, L. (1971). *Lenin and philosophy* (B. Brewster, Trans.). New York: Monthly Review Press.

Althusser, L. (2003). *The humanist controversy and other writings*. London: Verso.

Aoki, D. (2000). The thing never speaks for itself: Lacan and the pedagogical politics of clarity. *Harvard Educational Review*, *70*(3), 345–369.

Appel, S. (1998). Jacques Lacan: Ideal-I and image, subject, and signification. In M. Peters (Ed.), *Naming the multiple: Poststructuralism and education* (pp. 25–47). Westport, CT: Bergin & Garvey.

Apple, M. (1996). *Cultural politics and education*. New York: Teachers College Press.

Apple, M. (2006). *Educating the "Right" way* (2nd ed.). New York: Routledge.

Apple, M. (1990). *Ideology and curriculum*. New York: Routledge. First published in 1979.

Aronowitz, S. (1988). Science, ideology, and Marxism. In C. Nelson & L. Grossberg (Eds.), *Marxism and the interpretation of culture* (pp. 519–541). Urbana, IL: University of Illinois Press.

Ashley, D. (1997). *History without a subject*. Boulder, CO: Westview Press.

Banks, J. (2006). *Race, culture, and education*. New York: Routledge.

Barthes, R. (1994). Myth today. In T. Eagleton (Ed.), *Ideology* (pp. 162–172). London: Longman.

Bataille, G. (1988). *The accursed share* (Vol. I, R. Hurley, Trans.). New York: Zone Books.

Bataille, G. (1991). *The accursed share* (Vols. II and III, R. Hurley, Trans.). New York: Zone Books.

Baudrillard, J. (1975). *The mirror of production*. United States: Telos Press.

Baudrillard, J. (1979). *Seduction*. New York: St. Martin's Press.

Baudrillard, J. (1988a). The system of objects. In M. Poster (Ed.), *Jean Baudrillard: Selected writings*. Stanford, CO: Stanford University Press.

Baudrillard, J. (1988b). Consumer society. In M. Poster (Ed.), *Jean Baudrillard: Selected writings*. Stanford, CA: Stanford University Press.

Baudrillard, J. (1990). *Fatal strategies*. New York: Semiotext.

Bell, D. (1960). *The end of ideology*. Urbana, IL: University of Illinois Press.

Bell, D. (1992). *Faces at the bottom of the well: The permanence of racism*. New York: Basic Books.

Bernstein, B. (1977a). Social class, language and socialization. In J. Karabel & A. H. Halsey (Eds.), *Power and ideology in education* (pp. 473–486). Oxford, UK: Oxford University Press.

Bernstein, B. (1977b). Class pedagogies: Visible and invisible. In J. Karabel & A. H. Halsey (Eds.), *Power and ideology in education* (pp. 511–534). Oxford, UK: Oxford University Press.

Bhabha, H. (1990). Interrogating identity: The postcolonial prerogative. In D. T. Goldberg (Ed.), *Anatomy of racism* (pp. 183–209). Minneapolis, MN: University of Minnesota Press.

Biesta, G. (2006). *Beyond learning*. Boulder, CO: Paradigm Publishers.

Bonilla-Silva, E. (2003). *Racism without racists: Color-blind racism and the persistence of racial inequality in the United States*. Lanham, MD: Rowman & Littlefield.

Bonilla-Silva, E. (2005). Introduction - "Racism" and "new racism": The contours of racial dynamics in contemporary America. In Z. Leonardo (Ed.), *Critical pedagogy and race* (pp. 1–36). Malden, MA: Blackwell.

Bonilla-Silva, E. (2003). *Racism without racists*. Lanham, MD: Rowman & Littlefied.

Borg, C., Buttigieg, J., & Mayo, P. (Eds.). (2003). *Gramsci and education*. Lanham, MD: Rowman & Littlefied.

Bourdieu, P., & Passeron, J. (1990). *Reproduction in education, society, and culture*. Thousand Oaks, CA: SAGE.

Bottomore, T., Harris, L., Kiernan, V. G., & Miliband, R. (1991). Introduction. In T. Bottomore, L. Harris, V. G. Kiernan, & R. Miliband (Eds.), *A dictionary of Marxist thought* (2nd ed., pp. 126–127). Oxford, UK: Blackwell.

Bowles, S., & Gintis, H. (1976). *Schooling in capitalist America*. New York: Basic Books.

Brown, M., Carnoy, M., Currie, E., Duster, T., Oppenheimer, D., Shultz, M., et al. (2003). *White-washing race*. Berkeley, CA: University of California Press.

Buras, K. (2008). *Rightist multiculturalism*. New York: London.

Butler, J. (1990). *Gender trouble*. New York: Routledge.

Butler, J. (1997). *The psychic life of power: Theories in subjection*. Stanford, CA: Stanford University Press.

Butler, J. (2004). *Undoing gender*. New York: Routledge.

Butler, J., Laclau, E., & Zizek, S. (2000). *Contingency, hegemony, universality*. London: Verso.

Césaire, A. (2000). *Discourse on colonialism*. New York: Monthly Review Press. First published in 1955.

Cho, S. (2010). Politics of critical pedagogy and new social movements. *Educational Philosophy and Theory*, *42*(3), 310–325.

Collins, R. (1979). *The credential society*. New York: Academic.

Darder, A., & Torres, R. (2004). *After race*. New York: New York University Press.

Davis, A. (1998). Afro images: Politics, fashion, and nostalgia. In J. James (Ed.), *The Angela Y. Davis reader* (pp. 273–278). Malden, MA: Wiley-Blackwell.

Deleuze, G., & Guattari, F. (1983). *Anti-Oedipus: Capitalism and schizophrenia* (R. Hurley, M. Seem, & H. Lane, Trans.). Minneapolis, MN: University of Minnesota Press.

Derrida, J. (1976). *Of grammatology* (G. Spivak, Trans.). Baltimore: The Johns Hopkins University Press.

Derrida, J. (1985). Racism's last word. *Critical Inquiry*, *12*(1), 290–299.

Dog, M., & Erdoes, R. (1999). Civilize them with a stick. In S. Ferguson (Ed.), *Mapping the social landscape* (pp. 554–562). Mountain View, CA: Mayfield Publishing Company.

D'Souza, D. (1996). *The end of racism*. New York: The Free Press.

Dumas, M. (2009). Theorizing redistribution and recognition in urban education research: "How do we get dictionaries at Cleveland?". In J. Anyon (Ed.), *Theory and educational research: Toward critical social explanation* (pp. 81–107). New York: Routledge.

Dunayevskaya, R. (1992). *The Marxist-humanist theory of state-capitalism*. Chicago: News and Letters.

Durkheim, E. (1933). *The division of labor in society*. New York: The Free Press.

Eagleton, T. (1991). *Ideology*. London: Verso.

Eagleton, T. (1996). *Postmodernism and its illusions*. Oxford: Blackwell.

Eagleton, T. (2003). *After theory*. New York: Basic Books.

Ebert, T. (1996). *Ludic feminism and after*. Ann Arbor, MI: University of Michigan Press.

Fanon, F. (1967). *Black skin White masks* (C. Markmann, Trans.). New York: Grove Weidenfeld. First published in 1952.

Fanon, F. (2004). *The wretched of the earth* (C. Farrington, Trans.). New York: Grove Press. (First published in 1963)

Fields, B. (1990, May–June). Slavery, race and ideology in the United States of America. *New Left Review*, *I*(181), 95–118.

Foucault, M. (1972). *The archaeology of knowledge* (A. M. Smith, Trans.). New York: Pantheon Books.

Foucault, M. (1977). *Discipline and punish* (A. Sheridan, Trans.). New York: Vintage Books.

Foucault, M. (1980). *Power/knowledge* (C. Gordon, Ed., C. Gordon, L. Marshall, J. Mepham, & K. Soper, Trans.). New York: Pantheon Books.

Foucault, M. (1983). Preface. In G. Deleuze & F. Guatarri (Eds.), *Anti-Oedipus* (pp. xi–xxiv). Minneapolis, MN: University of Minnesota Press.

Fraser, N. (1997). *Justice interruptus*. New York: Routledge.

Freire, P. (1993). *Pedagogy of the oppressed* (M. Ramos, Trans.). New York: Continuum. (First published in 1970)

Freire, P. (1994). *Pedagogy of hope* (R. Barr, Trans.). New York: Continuum.

Freire, P. (2006). *Teachers as cultural workers*. Boulder, CO: Westview Press.

Fritzman, J. M. (1998). Louis Althusser: Poststructural materialist. In M. Peters (Ed.), *Naming the multiple: Poststructuralism and education* (pp. 49–64). Westport, CT: Bergin & Garvey.

Genosko, G. (1989). *Baudrillard and signs: Signification ablaze*. London: Routledge.

Gillborn, D. (2008). *Racism and education: Coincidence or conspiracy?* New York: Routledge.

Gilroy, P. (1998). Race ends here. *Racial and Ethnic Studies*, *21*(5), 838–847.

Gilroy, P. (2000). *Against race*. Cambridge, MA: Belknap Press of Harvard University.

Geertz, C. (1994). Ideology as a cultural system. In T. Eagleton (Ed.), *Ideology* (pp. 279–294). London: Longman.

Giroux, H. (1983). *Theory and resistance: A pedagogy for the opposition*. Westport, CT: Bergin & Garvey.

Giroux, H. (1988). *Teachers as intellectuals*. Westport, CT: Bergin & Garvey.

Giroux, H. (2002). *Breaking in to the movies*. Malden, MA: Wiley-Blackwell.

Giroux, H. (2010). Rethinking education as the practice of freedom: Paulo Freire and the promise of critical pedagogy. *Truthout*. Retrieved January 5, 2010, from http://www.truthout.org/10309_Giroux_Freire

Goldberg, D. T. (1993). *Racist culture*. Malden, MA: Blackwell.

Gotanda, N. (1995). A critique of "Our constitution is color-blind." In K. Crenshaw, N. Gotanda, G. Peller, & K. Thomas (Eds.), *Critical race theory* (pp. 257–275). New York: The New Press.

Gouldner, A. (1976). *The dialectic of ideology and technology*. New York: The Seabury Press.

Gramsci, A. (1971). *Selections from prison notebooks* (Q. Hoare & G. Smith, Eds. & Trans.). New York: International Publishers.

Grossberg, L., Nelson, C. & Treichler, P. (Eds.) (1992). *Cultural studies*. New York: Routledge.

Habermas, J. (1984). *The theory of communicative action* (Vol. 1, T. McCarthy, Trans.). Boston: Beacon Press.

Habermas, J. (1987a). *The theory of communicative action* (Vol. 2, T. McCarthy, Trans.). Boston: Beacon Press.

Habermas, J. (1987b). *The philosophical discourse of modernity* (F. Lawrence, Trans.). Cambridge, MA: The MIT Press.

Hall, S. (1996a). On postmodernism and articulation (An interview with Lawrence Grossberg). In D. Morley & K. Chen (Eds.), *Stuart Hall* (pp. 131–150). London: Routledge.

Hall, S. (1996b). New ethnicities. In D. Morley & K. Chen (Eds.), *Stuart Hall* (pp. 441–449). London: Routledge.

Hall, S. (1996c). The problem of ideology: Marxism without guarantees. In D. Morley & K. Chen (Eds.), *Stuart Hall* (pp. 25–46). London: Routledge.

Hall, S. (1996d). Gramsci's relevance for the study of race and ethnicity. In D. Morley & K. Chen (Eds.), *Stuart Hall* (pp. 411–440). London: Routledge.

Hardt, M., & Negri, A. (2001). *Empire*. Cambridge, MA: Harvard University Press.

Hirst, P. (1994). Problems and advances in the theory of ideology. In T. Eagleton (Ed.), *Ideology* (pp. 112–125). London: Longman.

Hitchens, C. (2009, April). He's back: The current financial crisis and the enduring relevance of Marx. *The Atlantic*, 88–95.

Holst, J. (2001). *Social movements, civil society, and radical adult education*. Westport, CT: Praeger.

Jameson, F. (1991). *Postmodernism, or, the cultural logic of late capitalism*. Durham, NC: Duke University Press.

Jameson, F. (1988). *The ideologies of theory* (Vol. 2). Minneapolis, MN: University of Minnesota Press.

Kellner, D. (1995). *Media culture*. New York: Routledge.

Kellner, D. (1992). *The Persian Gulf TV war*. Boulder, CO: Westview Press.

Kuhn, T. (1970). *The structure of scientific revolutions*. Chicago: The University of Chicago Press.

Laclau, E., & Mouffe, C. (1991). *Hegemony and socialist strategy* (2nd ed.). London: Verso.

Larrain, J. (1991). Ideology. In T. Bottomore, L. Harris, V. G. Kiernan, & R. Miliband (Eds.), *Dictionary of Marxist thought* (pp. 247–252). Oxford: Blackwell.

Larrain, J. (1996). Stuart Hall and the Marxist concept of ideology. In D. Morley & K. Chen (Eds.), *Stuart Hall* (pp. 47–70). London: Routledge.

Lather, P. (1991). *Getting smart: Feminist research and pedagogy with/in the postmodern*. New York: Routledge.

Leonardo, Z. (2002). The souls of white folk: Critical pedagogy, whiteness studies, and globalization discourse. *Race Ethnicity & Education, 5*(1), 29–50.

Leonardo, Z. (2003a). Resisting capital: Simulationist and socialist strategies. *Critical Sociology, 29*(2), 211–236.

Leonardo, Z. (2003b). *Ideology, discourse, and school reform*. Westport, CT: Praeger.

Leonardo, Z. (2009). *Race, whiteness, and education*. New York: Routledge.

Leonardo, Z. (in press a). After the glow: Race ambivalence and other educational prognoses. *Educational Philosophy and Theory*.

Leonardo, Z. (in press b). Dialectics of race criticality: Studies in racial stratification and education. In A. Reid, P. Hart, M. Peters, & C. Russell (Eds.), *Companion to research in education*. Thousand Oaks, CA: SAGE.

Leonardo, Z. and Porter, R. K. (in press). Pedagogy of fear: Toward a Fanonian theory of "safety" in race dialogue. *Race Ethnicity & Education*.

Lenin, V. I. (1963). *What is to be done?* Oxford: Oxford University Press.

Levi-Strauss, C. (1963). *Structural anthropology*. New York: Basic Books.

Lukács, G. (1971). *History and class consciousness* (R. Livingstone, Trans.). Cambridge, MA: The MIT Press.

Lyotard, J. (1984). *The postmodern condition* (G. Bennington & B. Massumi, Trans.). Minneapolis, MN: University of Minnesota Press.

Macedo, D. (2000). The colonialism of the English-only movement. *Educational Researcher, 29*(3), 15–24.

MacLeod, J. (2008). *Ain't no makin' it. 3rd ed.* Boulder, CO: Westview Press.

Martin, E. (1992). Body narratives, body boundaries. In L. Grossberg, C. Nelson, & P. Treichler (Eds.), *Cultural studies* (pp. 409–423). New York: Routledge.

Marx, K., & Engels, F. (1970). *The German ideology*. New York: International Publishers.

Mauss, M. (1967). *The gift*. New York: W.W. Norton & Company.

McLaren, P. (1991). Critical pedagogy: Constructing an arch of social dreaming and a doorway to hope. *The Sociology of Education in Canada, 173*(1), 137–160.

McLaren, P. (1992). Collisions with otherness: Multiculturalism, the politics of difference, and the ethnographer as nomad. *The American Journal of Semiotics, 9*(2–3), 121–148.

McLaren, P., Leonardo, Z., & Allen, R. L. (2000). Epistemologies of whiteness: Transforming and transgressing pedagogical knowledge. In R. Mahalingam & C. McCarthy (Eds.), *Multicultural curriculum: New directions for social theory, practice, and policy* (pp. 108–123). New York: Routledge.

McLaren, P., Leonardo, Z., & Allen, R. L. (1999). The gift of si(gh)ted violence: Toward a discursive intervention into the organization of capitalism. *Discourse: Theoretical Studies in Media and Culture, 21*(2), 139–162.

McRobbie, A. (1996). Looking back at New Times and its critics. In D. Morley & K. Chen (Eds.), *Stuart Hall* (pp. 238–261). London: Routledge.

McWhorter, J. (2001). *Losing the race: Self-sabotage in Black America*. New York: Harper Perennial.

Memmi, A. (1965). *The colonizer and the colonized*. Boston: Beacon Press.

Miles, R. (2000). Apropos the idea of 'race'... again. In L. Back & J. Solomos (Eds.), *Theories of race and racism* (pp. 125–143). New York: Routledge.

Mills, C. (1997). *The racial contract*. Ithaca, NY: Cornell University Press.

Nayak, A. (2006). After race: Ethnography, race and post-race theory. *Ethnic and Racial Studies, 29*(3), 411–430.

North, C. (2006). More than words? Delving into the substantive meaning(s) of "social justice" in education. *Review of Educational Research, 76*(4), 507–535.

Omi, M. (2001). The changing meaning of race. In N. Smesler, W. J. Wilson, & F. Mitchell (Eds.), *America becoming: Racial trends and their consequences* (Vol. 1, pp. 243–263). Washington, DC: The National Academy Press.

Omi, M., & Winant, H. (1994). *Racial formation in the United States: From the 1960s to the 1990s* (2nd ed.). New York: Routledge.

Park, R. E. (1964). *Race and culture*. Glencoe, IL: Free Press.

Poulantzas, N. (1994). The capitalist state and ideologies. In T. Eagleton (Ed.), *Ideology* (pp. 126–140). London: Longman.

Richardson, M. (1994). *George Bataille*. London: Routledge.

Ricoeur, P. (1986). *Lectures on ideology and utopia* (G. Taylor, Ed.). New York: Columbia University Press.

Roediger, D. (1991). *The wages of whiteness*. New York: Verso.

Said, E. (1979). *Orientalism*. New York: Random House.

Said, E. (1996). *Representations of the intellectual*. New York: Vintage.

San Juan, E., Jr. (1994). Problematizing multiculturalism and the "common culture". *MELUS, 19*(2), 59–84.

Sparks, C. (1996). Stuart Hall, cultural studies and marxism. In D. Morley & K. Chen (Eds.), *Stuart Hall* (pp. 71–101). London: Routledge.

Spivak, G. (1988). Can the subaltern speak? In C. Nelson & L. Grossberg (Eds.), *Marxism and the interpretation of culture* (pp. 271–313). Urbana, IL: University of Illinois Press.

Spring, J. (2000). *Deculturalization and the struggle for equality* (3rd ed.). Boston: McGraw-Hill.

Stepan, N. (1990). Race and gender: The role of analogy in science. In D. T. Goldberg (Ed.), *Anatomy of racism* (pp. 38–57). Minneapolis, MN: University of Minnesota Press.

St. Louis, B. (2002). Post-race/post-politics? Activist-intellectualism and the reification of race. *Ethnic and Racial Studies, 25*(4), 652–675.

Thernstrom, S., & Thernstrom, A. (1999). *America in Black and White: One nation, indivisible*. New York: Simon and Schuster.

Turner, B. (1992). *Regulating bodies*. London: Routledge.

Richardson, T., & Villenas, S. (2000). "Other" encounters: Dances with whiteness in multicultural education. *Educational Theory, 50*(2), 255–273.

Weber, M. (1930). *The protestant ethic and the spirit of capitalism*. London: Allen and Unwin.
Weber, M. (1978a). Bureaucracy. In G. Roth & C. Wittich (Eds.), E. Fischoff, et al. (Trans.), *Economy and society* (Vol. 2, pp. 956–1005). Berkeley, CA: University of California Press.
Weber, M. (1978b). Political communities. In G. Roth & C. Wittich (Eds.), E. Fischoff, et al. (Trans.), *Economy and society* (Vol. 2, pp. 901–940). Berkeley, CA: University of California Press.
Weber, M. (1994). Bureaucracy and revolution. In J. Goldstone (Ed.), *Revolutions: Theoretical, comparative, and historical studies* (2nd ed., pp. 31–36). New York: Harcourt Brace.
Weedon, C. (1997). *Feminist practice & poststructuralist theory* (2nd ed.). Cambridge, MA: Blackwell.
Williams, R. (1977). *Marxism and literature*. Oxford: Oxford University Press.
Willis, P. (1977). *Learning to labor: How working class kids get working class jobs*. New York: Columbia University Press.
Willis, P. (1981). Cultural production is different from cultural reproduction is different from social reproduction is different from reproduction. *Interchange, 12*(2–3), 48–67.
Wittig, M. (1993). One is not born a woman. In A. Jaggar & P. Rothenberg (Eds.), *Feminist frameworks* (3rd ed., pp. 178–182). Boston: McGraw Hill.
Wright, H. (1998). Dare we de-centre Birmingham? Troubling the origin and trajectories of cultural studies. *European Journal of Cultural Studies, 1*(1), 33–56.
Wright, H. (2003). Cultural studies as praxis. *Cultural Studies, 17*(6), 805–822.
Youdell, D. (in press). *School trouble: Identity, power and politics in education*. London: Routledge.
Zizek, S. (1995). Multiculturalism, or, the cultural logic of multinational capitalism. In S. Zizek (Ed.), *Mapping ideology* (pp. 28–51). London: Verso.

Zeus Leonardo
Graduate School of Education
University of California
Berkeley

THE CULTURAL POLITICS OF NEOLIBERALISM AND EDUCATION

HENRY A. GIROUX

1. NEOLIBERALISM, PEDAGOGY, AND CULTURAL POLITICS

Beyond the Theatre of Cruelty

INTRODUCTION

As neoliberal ideology circulates around the globe inserting itself into every aspect of politics and daily life, progressive social theorists and educational critics increasingly focus their analyses on the primacy of class, economics, and the circulation of capital.[1] Unfortunately, many of the commentaries reassert the importance of class as the central axis of inequality while increasingly devaluing any notion of cultural politics and the social movements that take seriously the cultural deployment of power. Rather than acknowledging that social movements that embrace the importantce of cultural politics are about notions of freedom and equality that speak to vital issues, human needs, and desires, the economic-oriented left condemns such movements as being either merely cultural or as a species of narrow, particularistic interest. In this ongoing theoretical narrative, the challenge to repressive authority lies largely in the realm of the economic while struggles concerned with issues such as race, gender, sexuality, and disability are dismissed as either trivial or, more perniciously, a means to abet conservatives who seize upon affirmative action, gay marriage, and abortion to win over working class voters. In its most lethal form, as Eric Lott has pointed out, the purging of race from class issues not only carries "at least a tacit appeal to whiteness as the normative ground of politics" but also suggests that any political strategy that employs race [as well as gender and sexuality] also scares away white [and male] workers.[2] Rather than duelling with conservatives over the modernist divide between high and low culture, the more recent version of this "war" pits political economy warriors such as Todd Gitlin, Michael Tomasky, Michael Lind and more recently Thomas Frank, and Walter Benn Michaels[3] against all those progressives who adopt both a broad based social vision and argue that class while important "cannot be emancipatory for the whole."[4] In general terms, the strict advocates of class politics view both various species of what is reductively called identity politics as separatist cells and cultural politics more broadly as a detriment to overcoming economic equality and promoting economic justice. Four of the more important assumptions that characterize this position include: the notion that effective social movements cannot be organized by gays and lesbians, people of color, and other groups who while often recognizing that class matters, also recognize other modes of oppression

Z. Leonardo (ed.), Handbook of Cultural Politics and Education, 49–70.

as well as the diverse sites through which political struggles take place; rather than being a serious object of struggle, the cultural sphere, including mass and popular culture, is largely a site of domination controlled overwhelmingly by corporations and not susceptible to political struggle; since working class people only care about their paychecks, concerns with equality, freedom, and culture are at odds with any viable notion of politics. Finally, any political project that attempts to address either how class is lived through various social forms such as gender and race or analyze how various modes of oppression, including class domination, produce subjectivities and secure consent as part of a broader pedagogical and cultural offensive constitutes a diversion from "real" class struggles.

There is more at work here than an overdetermined emphasis on political economy and class through the disparagement of what is despairingly labeled as "cultural politics." Indeed, there is also the refusal to acknowledge that the related issues of feminism, race, immigration, and sexuality count as real issues. Similarly, there is the refusal to recognize that central to any viable notion of politics is the primacy of education, persuasion, and the dynamics of diverse cultural struggles. Lost from this economistic perspective, as theorists as diverse as Judith Butler, Ellen Willis and Robin Kelly have pointed is the insistence that domination cannot simply be explained away through a class analysis and that class politics cannot be emancipatory for all groups.[5] Moreover, a reductionist class politics and a deracinated identity politics when analyzed together do not add up to a viable notion of democratic politics. At the same time, the mass production of global poverty and inequality really matters, but it cannot be addressed by separating cultural life from material relations of power, or struggles for economic equality from other social movements. What is needed is a new political language that goes beyond the racially and gender cleansed politics of class in order to be both more inclusive and capacious in extending the boundaries of politics beyond both private life and the domain of the economic. In part, such an approach suggests a need for a new politics that takes material relations of power seriously but also calls for expanding its theoretical reach by recognizing culture as a central site in the production and struggle over power, broadening the sphere and range of experiences constituting the political, if not agency itself, and opening up new locations of resistance, struggle, alignments, experiences, and possibilities inscribed in the material contexts of every day life. Ellen Willis furthers this call for a new politics in her own critique of the old politics organized around the faulty binarism of class and cultural politics, and left politics as a zero-sum game. She writes:

> [The view that] we can do class or culture, but not both–[is] simply wrong. People's working lives, their sexual and domestic lives, their moral values are intertwined. Capitalism is not only an economic system but a pervasive social and ideological force: in its present phase, it is promoting a culture of compulsive work, social Darwinism, contempt for 'useless' artistic and intellectual pursuits, rejection of the very concept of public goods, and corporate 'efficiency' as the mode for every social activity from education to medicine.

Culture does not cancel out class as a central category of politics. On the contrary, a radical cultural politics recognizes both the strengths and limitations of a class oriented analytic paradigm and in doing so can work to address the theoretical potential for extending the reach of its possibilities by highlighting as Lawrence Grossberg argues "the specific forms in which domination and subordination are organized, about the ways they operate, about how they are lived, mobilized, and empowered, that is, questions about the actual ways in which cultural practices are deployed in relations of power and how they themselves deploy power, questions about the actual effects of culture within specific contexts, questions about culture's relations to governance." [6]

In opposition to an overly determined notion of class politics, I want to analyze how matters of culture, pedagogy, economic inequality and power intersect to construct neoliberalism as one of the most effective anti-democratic forces at work in the world today. Central to my argument is that many class-based analyses of neoliberalism fail either to critically engage how neoliberalism works to win the consent of the very populations it exploits or how the educational force of trans-national exchange dependent on the new electronic technologies of global culture works to produce those needs, values, and subjectivities that resonate with neoliberal ideology and economic relations. Equally absent from this discourse are questions about the profound appeal neoliberal ideology has in mobilizing such a large and diverse strata of people both in the United States and around the world. In what follows, I want to address these lacuna through an analysis of what I call the public pedagogy of neoliberalism and the importance of cultural politics in opposing it as a mode of economic fundamentalism, and political rationality, but also as a set of dynamic discursive practices.

NEOLIBERALISM AS A THEATRE OF CRUELTY

What is often ignored by many theorists who analyze the rise of neoliberalism in the United States is that it is not only a system of economic power relations, but also a political project of governing and persuasion intent on producing new forms of subjectivity and particular modes of conduct.[7] And while I want to develop this issue by analyzing the close link between the economic mechanisms of neo-liberalism and its cultural politics of subjectification and self-regulation, I begin with a theoretical insight provided by the British media theorist, Nick Couldry, who insists that "every system of cruelty requires its own theatre," one that draws upon the rituals of everyday life in order to legitimate its norms, values, institutions, and social practices.[8] Neoliberalism represents one such system of cruelty, a political and cultural system that is reproduced daily through a regime of commonsense and a narrow notion of political rationality that "reaches from the soul of the citizen-subject to educational policy to practices of empire."[9] What is new about neoliberalism in a post-9/11 world is that it has become normalized, serving as a powerful pedagogical force that shapes our lives, memories, and daily experiences, while attempting to erase everything critical and emancipatory about history, justice, solidarity, freedom, and democracy itself. Wedded to the belief that the market should be the organizing principle for all political, social, and economic decisions, neoliberalism wages an incessant attack on democracy, public institutions, public goods, and non-commodified values—even as it is increasingly viewed as responsible for the current global financial meltdown. Under neoliberalism everything is either for sale or is plundered for profit. Politicians willingly hand the public's airwaves over to broadcasters and large corporate interests without a dime going into the public trust; corporations drive the nation's energy policies, and the war industries give war profiteering a new meaning as the government, especially under the former Bush-Cheney regime, hands out contracts without any competitive bidding; politicians are now bouguth and sold by corporate lobbyists making a mockery out of the democratic process; the environment is polluted and despoiled in the name of profit-making just as the government passes legislation to make it easier for corporations to do so; public services are gutted in order to lower the taxes of major corporations; schools increasingly resemble malls or jails and teachers, forced to raise revenue for classroom materials, increasingly function as circus barkers hawking everything from hamburgers to pizza parties–that is, when they are not reduced to prepping students to get higher test scores. As markets are touted as the driving force of everyday life, big government is disparaged as either incompetent or a threat to individual freedom, suggesting that power should reside in markets and corporations rather than in governments and citizens. Citizenship has increasingly become a function of market values and politics has been restructured as "corporations have been increasingly freed from social control through deregulation, privatization, and other neoliberal measures."[10]

As the Obama administration bails out banks and other mega financial corporations instead of the millions of people suffering from the current economic recession, resistance is mounting to neoliberal policies. As we have seen in the last few decades, the corporate capitalist fairytale of neoliberalism is being challenged all over the globe by students, labor organizers, intellectuals, community activists, and a host of individuals and groups unwilling to allow democracy to be bought and sold by a combination of multinational corporations, corporate swindlers, international political institutions, and those government politicians who willingly align themselves with corporate interests and profits. From Seattle to Davos, people engaged in popular resistance are collectively taking up the challenge of neoliberalism and reviving both the meaning of resistance and the places where it occurs. Political culture is now global and resistance is amorphous, connecting students with workers, school teachers with parents, and intellectuals with artists. Groups protesting the attack on farmers in India whose land is being destroyed by the government in order to build dams now find themselves in alliance with young people resisting sweatshop labor in New York City. Environmental activists are joining up with key sections of organized labor as well as with groups protesting Third World debt. The collapse of the neoliberal showcase, Argentina, along with numerous corporate bankruptcies and scandals starting with Enron and more recently with Bernie Madoff, reveals the cracks in neoliberal hegemony and domination. In Latin America, a new wave of resistance to negative globalization and neoliberal structural adjustment policies has emerged among countries such as Chile, Peru, Argentina, and Venezuela.[11] In addition, the multiple forms of resistance against neoliberal capitalism are not limited by an identity politics focused on particularized rights and interests. On the contrary, new modes of popular opposition and politics have been expanded to address a broader crisis of political culture and democracy that connects the militarization and corporatization of public life with the collapse of the welfare state and the attack on civil liberties. Central to these new movements is the notion that neoliberalism has to be understood within a larger crisis of vision, meaning, education, and political agency. Democracy in this view is not limited to the struggle over economic resources and power; indeed, it also includes the creation of public spheres where individuals can be educated as political agents equipped with the skills, capacities and knowledge they need to perform as autonomous political agents. I want to expand the reaches of this debate by arguing that any form of resistance against neoliberalism must address the discourses of political agency, civic education, and cultural politics as part of a broader struggle over the relationship between democratization (the ongoing struggle for a substantive and inclusive democracy) and the global public sphere.

We live at a time when the conflation of private interests, empire building, and evangelical fundamentalism puts into question the very nature, if not existence, of the democratic process. Under the reign of neoliberalism, capital and wealth have been largely distributed upwards while civic virtue has been undermined by a slavish celebration of the free market as the model for organizing all facets of everyday life. Political culture has been increasingly emptied of democratic values as collective life is organized around the modalities of privatization, deregulation, and commercialization. When the alleged champions of neoliberalism invoke politics, they substitute "ideological certainty for reasonable doubt" and deplete "the national reserves of political intelligence" just as they endorse "the illusion that the future can be bought instead of earned."[12] Under attack is the social contract in which people were bound together, not as individuals expressing themselves only through the market place but as citizens who had obligations to one another. What neoliberalism undermines is a social contract bound to enlarging the public good, protecting the public values, and expanding social provisions–such as access to adequate health care, housing, employment, public transportation, and education – that ensure a limited though important safety net and a set of conditions upon which democracy could be experienced and critical citizenship engaged. It has been replaced with a notion of national security based on fear, surveillance, and control rather than a culture of shared responsibility. Self-reflection and collective empowerment are now reduced to self-promotion, self-interest, and legitimated by a new and ruthless economic Darwinism played out nightly on network television as a metaphor for the "naturalness" of downsizing, the celebration of hyper-masculinity, and the promotion of an unchecked notion of self-interest and individualism over even the most limited notions of solidarity and collective struggle. Neoliberalism with its celebration of markets, finance, and investors "requires a new belief in the future. … the time of investment is now. The future must be lived in the present."[13]

Under neoliberal domestic restructuring and the foreign policy initiatives of the Washington Consensus, motivated by an evangelical belief in free-market democracy at home and free trade abroad, the United States in the last thirty years has witnessed the increasing obliteration of those discourses, social forms, public institutions, and non-commercial values that are central to the language of the common good, public commitment, and democratically charged politics. Civic engagement now appears impotent as corporations privatize public space and disconnect power from issues of equity, social justice, and civic responsibility. Proceeding outside of democratic accountability, neoliberalism has allowed a handful of private interests to control as much of social life as possible in order to maximize their personal profit.

Abroad, neoliberal global policies have been used to pursue rapacious free trade agreements and expand Western financial and commercial interests through the heavy-handed policies of the World Bank, the World Trade Organization, and the International Monetary Fund in order to manage and transfer resources and wealth from the poor and less developed nations to the richest and most powerful nation states and to the wealthy, corporate defenders of capitalism.[14] Third world and semi-peripheral states of Latin America, Africa, and Asia have become client states of the wealthy nations led by the United States. Loans made to the client states by banks and other financial institutions have produced severe dislocations and consequences for "social welfare programs such as health care, education, and laws establishing labor standards."[15] For example, the restrictions that the IMF and World Bank impose on countries as a condition for granting loans not only impose capitalist values, they also undermine the very possibility of an inclusive and substantive democracy. The results have been disastrous and can be seen both in the economic collapse of countries such as Nigeria and in the fact that "one third of the world's labor force–more than a billion people–are unemployed or under-employed."[16] Tracking 26 countries that received loans from the World Bank and the IMF, *The Multinational Monitor* spelled out the conditions that accompanied such loans:

> [c]ivil service downsizing; [p]rivatization of government-owned enterprises, with layoffs required in advance of privatization and frequently following privatization; [p]romotion of labor flexibility–regulatory changes to remove restrictions on the ability of government and private employers to fire or lay off workers; [m]andated wage reductions, minimum wage reductions or containment, and spreading the wage gap between government employees and managers; and [p]ension reforms, including privatization, that cut social security benefits for workers.[17]

At home, corporations increasingly not only design the economic sphere but also shape legislation and policy affecting all levels of government, and with limited opposition. As corporate power lays siege to the political process, the benefits flow to the rich and the powerful. Included in such benefits are reform policies that shift the burden of taxes from the rich to the middle class, the working poor, and state governments as can be seen in the shift from taxes on wealth (capital gains, dividends, and estate taxes) to a tax on work, principally in the form of a regressive payroll tax. During the 2002–2004 fiscal period, tax cuts delivered $197.3 billion in tax breaks to the wealthiest 1 percent of Americans (i.e., households making more than $337,000 a year) while state governments increased taxes to fill a $200 billion budget deficit.[18] Equally alarming, a recent congressional study revealed that 63% of all corporations in 2000 paid no taxes while "[s]ix in ten corporations reported no tax liability for the five years from 1996 through 2000, even though corporate profits were growing at record-breaking levels during that period."[19] While the rich get huge tax cuts, the Pentagon is spending about "$6 billion a month on the war in Iraq or about $2 million a day."[20] Moreover, as part of an ongoing effort to destroy public entitlements, the Bush administration reduced government-provided services, income, and health care; in addition, it implemented cuts in Medicare and veterans benefits as well as trimmed back or eliminated funds for programs for children and for public housing. There is no indication that the Obama administration will significantly reverse any of these neoliberal policies.

Neoliberal global policies also further the broader cultural project of privatizing social services through appeals to "personal responsibility as the proper functions of the state are narrowed, tax and wage costs in the economy are cut, and more social costs are absorbed by civil society and the family."[21] The hard currency of human suffering permeates the social order as health care costs rise, one out of five children live beneath the poverty line, and 47 million Americans bear the burden of lacking any health insurance. In 2007, President Bush vetoed legislation that would have provided an additional and much needed $35 billion to the highly successful and popular State Children's Health Insurance Program (S-chip). Bush's justification ranged from ridiculous–as when he claimed the whole issue was a media myth–to the more transparent and ideologically driven argument that the program would expand "socialized-type medicine," interfere with private insurance, and cost too much. Actually, the costs for the bill would have come from levying a 61-cents-a-pack increase in the federal excise tax on cigarettes and other tobacco products, providing a further disincentive for smokers.[22] Moreover, the program run by insurers, doctors, and nurses who deliver the services. This bill would have provided health insurance for 3.8 million children from low-income families who are currently uninsured. Besides a veto, the Bush administration offered no alternative program to address the plight of the nine million children uninsured and the millions underinsured. What becomes clear in this egregious act of presidential incompetence and moral indifference is that Bush the unflappable neoliberal warrior was willing to sacrifice the health of millions of poor children as part of his relentless attempts to destroy all vestiges of the welfare state and promote his pro-corporate, market-based fundamentalism.[23] Draining the public treasury of funds and disparaging the social state does more than result in failed governance, it also puts people's lives at risk, as was obvious in the government's recent failure to provide decent care at Walter Reed Hospital for wounded soldiers returning from the wars in Iraq and Afghanistan. At the same time that it starves public programs and services, neoliberalism becomes complicitous with the transformation of the democratic state into a national security state that repeatedly uses its military and political power to develop a daunting police state and military-prison-education-industrial complex to punish workers, stifle dissent, and undermine the political power of labor unions and progressive social movements. Unsurprisingly, Obama's attempt to reform health care in America is unanimously opposed by the Republican Party and the debate has been largely driven by insurance and pharmaceutical companies which oppose it.

With its debased belief that profit-making is the essence of democracy, and its definition of citizenship as an energized plunge into consumerism, neoliberalism loosens or eliminates government regulation of market forces, celebrates a ruthless competitive individualism, and places the commanding political, cultural, and economic institutions of society in the hands of powerful corporate interests, the privileged, and unrepentant religious bigots. Within the discourse of neoliberalism, democracy becomes synonymous with free markets while issues of equality, social justice, and freedom are stripped of any substantive meaning and used to disparage those who suffer systemic deprivation and chronic punishment. Individual misfortune like democracy itself is now viewed either as an excess or as being in need of radical containment. The media, largely consolidated through corporate power, routinely provide a platform for high profile right-wing pundits and politicians to remind us of how degenerate the poor have become reinforcing the central neoliberal tenet that all problems are private rather than social in nature. Conservative columnist Ann Coulter captures the latter sentiment with a cruel vengeance with her comment that "[i]nstead of poor people with hope and possibility, we now have a permanent underclass of aspiring criminals knifing one another between having illegitimate children and collecting welfare checks."[24] Radio talk show host Michael Savage also exemplifies the unabashed racism and fanaticism that emerge under a neoliberal regime in which ethics and justice appear beside the point. Buttressed by a right wing media culture in which 91 percent of political talk radio is conservative,[25] Savage routinely refers to non-white countries as "turd world nations," homosexuality as a "perversion" and young children who are victims of gunfire as "ghetto slime."[26]

As Fredric Jameson argues in *The Seeds of Time*, it has now become easier to imagine the end of the world than the end of capitalism.[27] The breathless rhetoric of the global victory of free-market rationality spewed forth by the mass media, right-wing intellectuals, and governments alike, has found its material expression in both an all-out attack on democratic values and the growth of a range of social problems, including virulent and persistent poverty, joblessness, inadequate health care, racial apartheid in the inner cities, and the increasing inequalities between the rich and the poor, all of which have been made much more severe in the current economic crisis. While such issues are more visible than ever, they are rarely addressed as part of the political and ideological crisis of neoliberalism or they are factored into talk-show spectacles in which the public becomes merely a staging area for venting private outrage and emotions.

As neoliberalism takes hold of the public imagination, it becomes increasingly more difficult to talk about what is fundamental to civic life, critical citizenship, and a substantive democracy. In its dubious appeals to universal laws, neutrality, and selective scientific research, neoliberalism "eliminates the very possibility of critical thinking, without which democratic debate becomes impossible."[28] Hence, neoliberal policies that promote the cutthroat downsizing of the workforce, bleeding of social services, reduction of state governments to police precincts, the ongoing liquidation of job security, the increasing elimination of a decent social wage, the creation of a society of low-skilled workers, and the emergence of a culture of permanent insecurity and fear hide behind appeals to common sense and alleged immutable laws of nature. When and where such nakedly ideological appeals strain both reason and imagination, religious faith is invoked to silence dissension. Society is now defended as a space to nurture the most fundamental values and relations necessary to a democracy but as an ideological and political sphere "where religious fundamentalism comes together with market fundamentalism to form the ideology of American supremacy."[29] Similarly, American imperial ambitions have been legitimated by public relations intellectuals as part of the responsibilities of empire building, now celebrated as a civilizing process for the rest of the globe. As culture is increasingly militarized,civil liberties suspended, and a war is waged in Iraq and Afghanistan, shades of authoritarianism creep into the social order, lagely justified "in the service of spreading liberty and democracy."[30] Neo-conservatives join hands with neoliberals and religious fundamentalists in broadcasting to the rest of the globe an American triumphalism in which the United States is arrogantly defined as "The greatest of all great powers in world history."[31] Money, profits, and fear become powerful ideological elements in arguing for opening up new markets and closing down the possibility of dissent at home. In such a scenario, a new kind of coercive state emerges as "authorized power is [sanctioned as the only type of] credible. ... [and] state appeals to fear [become] the only effective basis for obedience."[32] This becomes clear not only in the passage of repressive laws such as the USA PATRIOT Act and the Military Commissions Act of 2006, but also in the work of prominent neoconservatives such as David Frum and Richard Pearle who without any irony intended insist that "[a] free society is not an un-policed society. A free society is self-policed society."[33] And while such flagrant violations of democracy are largely associated with the Bush-Cheney regime, they are now being carried out under the Obama administration as well. At the same time, democratic politics are increasingly derailed by the intersection of a free-market fundamentalism and an escalating militarism.[35] The consequences can be seen in the policy of anti-terrorism practiced by the Bush administration and repeated under Obama that mimics the very terrorism it wished to eliminate.

Not only does this policy of all-embracing anti-terrorism exhaust itself in a discourse of moral absolutes, militarism, revenge, and public acts of denunciation, it also strips community of democratic values by configuring politics in religious terms and defining every citizen and inhabitant of the United States as a potential terrorist. Politics becomes empty as citizens are reduced to obedient recipients of power, content to follow orders, while shaming those who make power accountable. Under the dictates of a pseudo-patriotism, dissent is stifled in the face of a growing racism that condemns Arabs and people of color as less than civilized. The ongoing refusal of the American government to address with any degree of self-criticism or humanity the torture and violation of human rights exercised by American soldiers at Abu Ghraib prison in Iraq offers a case in point.[36] In light of the revelation of the most grotesque brutality, racism, and inhumanity exhibited by American soldiers against Arab prisoners captured on camera and video, powerful right-wing politicians and pundits such as Rush Limbaugh and Cal Thomas initially defended such actions as a way for young men to either "blow some steam off," engage in a form of harmless frat hazing, or give Muslim prisoners what they deserve. It gets worse. Commentators such as Newt Gingrich and Republican Senator James Inhofe went so far as to suggest that calling attention to such crimes not only undermined troop morale in Iraq but was also unpatriotic. That argument seems to have some credibility in the highest reaches of government since as of 2010 no high ranking official has been legally charged with a crime. Defending torture and gross sexual humiliations by U.S. troops in Saddam's old jails is not merely insensitive political posturing, it is, more tellingly, indicative of how far the leadership of this country has strayed from any semblance of democracy. As a *New York Times* editorial pointed out in October 2007, the Bush administration turned the United States into a "nation that tortures human beings and then concocts legal sophistries to confuse the world and avoid accountability before American voters." The editorial goes on to state that "President Bush and his aides have not only condoned torture and abuse at secret prisons .... [whose techniques were] modelled on the dungeons of Egypt, Saudi Arabia and the Soviet Union ... but they have conducted a systematic campaign to mislead Congress, the American people and the world about those policies."[37] And while the Obama regime has softened some of these policies, it has not eliminated them.

Political culture, if not the nature of politics itself, has undergone revolutionary changes in the last two decades, reaching its most debased expression under the administration of the former imperial presidency of President George W. Bush. Within this political culture, democracy was not only subordinated to the rule of a market, but corporate decisions were also freed from territorial constraints and the demands of public obligations, just as economics was disconnected from its social consequences. Power has more and more become free from territorial constraints and politics largely nation-based. Zygmunt Bauman captures what is new about the relationship between power, politics, and the shredding of social obligations in his comment:

> The mobility acquired by 'people who invest'–those with capital, with money which the investment requires–means the new, indeed unprecedented... disconnection of power from obligations: duties towards employees, but also towards the younger and weaker, towards yet unborn generations and towards the self-reproduction of the living conditions of all; in short the freedom from the duty to contribute to daily life and the perpetuation of the community.... Shedding the responsibility for the consequences is the most coveted and cherished gain which the new mobility brings to free-floating, locally unbound capital.[38]

As corporate power increasingly frees itself from any political limitations, it uses its power through the educational force of the dominant culture to put into place an utterly privatized notion of agency in which it becomes difficult for young people and adults to imagine democracy as a public good, let alone the transformative power of collective action. Democratic politics has become ineffective, if not banal, as civic language is impoverished and genuine spaces for democratic learning, debate, and dialogue such as schools, newspapers, popular culture, television networks, and other public spheres are either underfunded, eliminated, privatized, or subject to corporate ownership. Under the politics and culture of neoliberalism, in spite of its tensions and contradictions, society is increasingly mobilized for the production of violence against the poor, immigrants, dissenters, and others marginalized because of their age, gender, race, ethnicity, and color. At the center of neoliberalism is a new form of politics in the United States, one in which radical exclusion is the order of the day, a politics in which the primary questions are no longer about equality, justice, or freedom, but about the ability to simply survive in a culture marked by fear, moral collapse, and economic deprivation. As Susan George insists, the question that now seems to define neoliberal "democracy" is "Who has a right to live or does not?"[39]

It is important to stress that neoliberalism is more than a neutral economic discourse that can be measured with the precision of a mathematical formula or defended through an appeal to the rules of a presumptively unassailable science that conveniently leaves its own history behind. On the contrary, rather than a paragon of economic rationality that offers the best "route to optimum efficiency, rapid economic growth and innovation, and rising prosperity for all who are willing to work hard and take advantage of available opportunities,"[40] it is an ideology that subordinates the art of democratic politics to the rapacious laws of a market economy, a calculating cost-benefit analysis that expands its reach to include all aspects of social life within the dictates and values of society.[41] More importantly, neoliberalism is a historical and socially constructed ideology that needs to be made visible, critically engaged, and shaken from the stranglehold of power it currently exercises over most of the commanding institutions of national and global life.[42] As an economic theory, cultural politics, and public pedagogy, neoliberalism constructs a notion of commonsense in which it becomes difficult for many people either to imagine a notion of individual and social agency necessary for reclaiming a substantive democracy or to theorize the economic, cultural, and political conditions necessary for a viable global public sphere in which public institutions, spaces, and goods become valued as part of a larger democratic struggle for a sustainable future and the downward distribution of wealth, resources, and power. Hence, it is not surprising that popular advocates of the free market such as right wing television celebrity and talk show host Glen Beck justifies his reactionary support for free market fundamentalism by an unqualified appeal to common sense.

As a public pedagogy and political ideology, the neoliberalism of Friedrich Hayek and Milton Friedman[43] is far more ruthless than the classic liberal economic theory developed by Adam Smith and David Ricardo in the eighteenth and nineteenth centuries.[44] Neoliberalism has become the present conservative revolution because it harkens back to a period in American history–the Gilded Age–that supported the sovereignty of the market over the sovereignty of the democratic state and the common good.[45] Reproducing the future in the image of the distant past, it represents a struggle designed to roll back, if not dismantle, all of the policies put into place over seventy years ago by the New Deal to curb corporate power and give substance to the liberal meaning of the social contract. The late Pierre Bourdieu captures what is distinctive about neoliberalism in his comment that it is

> a new kind of conservative revolution [which] appeals to progress, reason and science (economics in this case) to justify the restoration and so tries to write off progressive thought and action as archaic. It sets up as the norm of all practices, and therefore as ideal rules, the real regularities of the economic world abandoned to its own logic, the so-called laws of the market. It reifies and glorifies the reign of what are called the financial markets, in other words the return to a kind of radical capitalism, with no other law than that of maximum profit, an unfettered capitalism without any disguise, but rationalized, pushed to the limit of its economic efficacy by the introduction of modern forms of domination, such as 'business administration', and techniques of manipulation, such as market research and advertising.[46]

Neoliberalism has become a broad-based political and cultural movement designed to obliterate public concerns and liquidate the welfare state, and make politics everywhere an exclusively market driven project.[47] But neoliberalism does more than make the market "the informing principle of politics"[48] while allocating wealth and resources to those who are most privileged by virtue of their class, race, and power; its political culture and pedagogical practices also put into play a social universe and cultural landscape that supports a particularly barbaric notion of authoritarianism, set in motion under the combined power of a religious and market fundamentalism and anti-terrorism laws that suspend civil liberties, incarcerate disposable populations, and provide the security forces necessary for capital to destroy those spaces where democracy can be nourished. All the while the landscape and soundscape become increasingly militarized through a mass mediated spectacle of violence whose underlying purpose is to construct the public as soldiers in the 'war on terrorism' while redefining democracy as a mix of war and American idealism. As a cultural politics and form of economic domination, neoliberalism tells a very limited story, one that is antithetical to nurturing democratic identities, values, public spheres, and institutions while lacking any ethical language for recognizing politics outside of the realm of the market, controlling market excesses, or for challenging the underlying tenets of a growing authoritarianism bolstered by the pretense of religious piety.

Neoliberalism does not merely produce militarized public spheres, economic inequality, iniquitous power relations, and a corrupt political system, it also promotes rigid exclusions from national citizenship and civic participation. As Lisa Duggan points out, "Neoliberalism cannot be abstracted from race and gender relations, or other cultural aspects of the body politic. Its legitimating discourse, social relations, and ideology are saturated with race, with gender, with sex, with religion, with ethnicity, and nationality."[49] Neoliberalism comfortably aligns itself with various strands of neoconservative and religious fundamentalisms waging imperial wars abroad as well as at home against those groups and movements that threaten its authoritarian misreading of the meaning of freedom, security, and productiveness.

One controversial example of how big corporations, particularly media conglomerates, use their power to simultaneously support neoliberal values, reactionary policies, and the politicians who produce them took place in 2004 when the Sinclair Broadcast Group, a Maryland-based media company whose holdings comprise sixty-two television stations, including several ABC affiliates refused to air on its stations a special edition of *Nightline* with Ted Koppel. Sinclair was disturbed because Koppel announced that he was going to read the names and show photographs of the faces of the then 721 U.S. soldiers killed in Iraq. Sinclair's refusal to air *Nightline* on its ABC stations was based on the argument that Koppel was making a political statement that allegedly undermined the war effort by drawing attention to its most troubling consequences. And its rationale for this act of censorship was partly based on the argument that *Nightline* could have read the names of the thousands of citizens killed in terrorist attacks during and the events of September 11, 2001. The problem with this accusation, as a statement from ABC made clear shortly after the charge, is that the network did broadcast a list of the 9/11 victims, one year after the gruesome event. What Sinclair did not mention was that it has been a generous contributor to the Republican Party and that it has lobbied successfully for policies that have allowed it to own even more stations. Sinclair shares the perspective of many of its corporate allies on the Right who believe that the costs of the war should be hushed up, in favor of news that portrays the Bush administration in a favorable light. After all, censoring the news is a small price to pay for the corporate windfalls that reward such acts. Free-market fundamentalism makes it easier for corporate power and political favoritism to mutually inform each other, reinforcing the ideological and political conditions for the perpetuation of a system of profits, money, market values, and power that allows, as Bill Moyers has pointed out, big corporations and big government to scratch each others' back, while cancelling out the principles of justice and human dignity that inform a real democracy.[50]

Neoliberalism has to be understood and challenged as both an economic theory and a powerful public pedagogy and cultural politics. That is, it has to be named and critically understood before it can be critiqued. The commonsense assumptions that legitimate neoliberalism's alleged historical inevitability have to be held up to the light so as to reveal the social damage they cause at all levels of human existence. Hence, I not only attempt to identity and critically engage many of the most salient and powerful ideologies that inform and frame neoliberalism but also argue for making cultural politics and the notion of public pedagogy central to the struggle against neoliberalism, particularly since education and culture now play such a prominent political and economic role in both securing consent and producing capital. In fact, my position is similar to Susan Buck-Morss' argument that "[t]he recognition of cultural domination as just as important as, and perhaps even as the condition of possibility of, political and economic domination is a true 'advance' in our thinking."[51] Of course, this position is meant not to disavow economic and institutional struggles but rather to supplement them with a cultural politics that connects symbolic power and its pedagogical practices with material relations of power. In addition, I analyze how neoliberal policies work at the level of everyday life through the language of privatization and the lived cultural forms of class, race, gender, youth, and ethnicity. Finally, such a struggle would have to employ both a language of critique and possibility, engagement and hope as part of a broader project of viewing democracy as a site of intense struggle over matters of representation, participation, and shared power.

Central to such a political struggle is the belief, as Alain Touraine argues, that neoliberal globalization has not "dissolved our capacity for political action."[52] Such action depends on the ability of various groups–the peace movement, the anti-corporate globalization movement, the human rights movement, the environmental justice movement – within and across national boundaries to form alliances in which matters of global justice, community, and solidarity provide a common symbolic space and multiple public spheres where norms are created, debated, and engaged as part of an attempt to develop a new political language, culture, and set of relations. Such efforts must be understood as part of a broader attempt not only to resist domination, but also to defend all those social advances that strengthen democratic public spheres and services, demand new rights and modes of power sharing, and strive for social justice adequate to creating forms of collective struggle that can imagine and sustain democracy on a global level. The anti-corporate globalization struggle's slogan "Another World is Possible!" demands, as Alex Callinicos insightfully points out, a different kind of social logic, one that requires a powerful sense of unity and solidarity.

Another *world*–that is, a world based on different social logic, run according to different priorities from those that prevail today. It is easy enough to specify what the desiderata of such an alternative social logic would be–social justice, economic efficiency, environmental sustainability, and democracy–but much harder to spell out how a reproducible social system embodying these requirements could be built. And then there is the question of how to achieve it. Both these questions–What is the alternative to capitalism? What strategy can get us there?–can be answered in different ways. One thing the anti-capitalist movement is going to have to learn is how to argue through the differences that exist and will probably develop around such issues without undermining the very powerful sense of unity that has been one of the movement's most attractive qualities.[53]

Callinicos' insight suggests that any viable struggle against neoliberal capitalism will have to rethink "the entire project of politics within the changed conditions of a global public sphere, and to do this democratically, as people who speak different political languages, but whose goals are nonetheless the same: global peace, economic justice, legal equality, democratic participation, individual freedom, mutual respect."[54] Indeed, one of the most central tasks facing intellectuals, activists, educators, and others who believe in an inclusive and substantive democracy is the utilization of theory to rethink the language and possibilities of politics as a way to imagine a future outside of the powerful grip of neoliberalism. Critical reflection and social action in this discourse must acknowledge how the category of the global public sphere extends the space of politics beyond the boundaries of local resistance. Global problems need global institutions, global modes of dissent, global intellectual work, and global social movements. Moreover, any politics that is going to challenge the reach of global neoliberalism is going to have to address the formative culture that makes it possible. This suggests a politics that is capable of rethinking the relationship between culture and pedagogy.

CULTURAL POLITICS AND PUBLIC PEDAGOGY

The point is not to inculcate perfect ideas, it is to make people become self-critical, reflexive, critical of others—though not critical in an irritating sort of way—to open their eyes, especially about their own motives, and to encourage them to be autonomous. I think this is both the main aim of analysis and the prerequisite for social change.[55]

If educators, artists, parents, and others are to further their understanding of neoliberalism, educators and other cultural workers need to theorize more fully a notion of pedagogy that expands our understanding of how the educational force of the culture has become harnessed to neoliberalism as both a mode of common sense and a dangerous form of rationality. Such a recognition presents the challenge of what it means to address the pedagogical conditions at work in the reproduction of both neoliberalism and negative globalization. Engaging pedagogy as a form of cultural politics requires an analyses of the production and representation of meaning and how these practices and the practices they provoke are implicated in the dynamics of social power. Pedagogy as a form of cultural politics raises the issue of how education might be understood as a moral and political practice that takes place in a variety sites outside of schools. Pedagogy as defined here is fundamentally concerned with the relations between politics, subjectivities, and cultural and material production. As a form of cultural production, pedagogy is implicated in the construction and organization of knowledge, desires, emotional investments, values, and social practices. At stake here is developing a notion of public pedagogy, in particular, which is capable of contesting the various forms of symbolic production that secure individuals to the affective and ideological investments that produce the neoliberal subject. As Antonio Gramsci reminds us, hegemony as an educational practice is always necessarily part of a pedagogy of persuasion, one that makes a claim to "speak to vital human needs, interests, and desires, and therefore will be persuasive to many and ultimately most people."[56]

Neoliberal hegemony is partly secured as a result of the crisis of agency that now characterizes much of American politics. As neoliberal ideology successfully normalizes and depoliticizes its basic assumptions and market-based view of the world, it becomes increasingly difficult for people to recognize that neoliberal rationality is a historical and political construction, and that there are alternatives to its conceptions of democracy as an extension of market principles and citizens as hyper-consumers or unthinking patriots. Challenging neoliberal hegemony means exposing its historical character and its flimsy claims to promoting freedom through choice while making visible how it operates in the service of class and corporate power. But the ideology and structures of neoliberal domination must be analyzed not merely within economic discourses but also as an oppressive form of public pedagogy, a practice of political persuasion, actively responsible for systematic forms of misrepresentation, distortion, and a mangling of public discourse by commercial interests.[57]

The institutions and sites that constitute the machinery of persuasion are at the heart of any system of culture and thus represent crucial sites of what I have called spheres of and about public pedagogy. Recognizing this means treating conflicts of culture, power, and politics, in part, as pedagogical issues and recognizing cultural education as a project related to democracy.[58] The concern that animates this chapter is precisely to address how neoliberalism constitutes what Imre Szeman has called "a problem of and for pedagogy."[59] If neoliberalism requires a supporting political culture, it is crucial to recognize that culture is the place where deeply held meanings and values are produced, internalized, identified with, and fought over. Culture under the regulating hand of the market is not simply about texts, commodities, consumption, or the creation of the utterly privatized subject; it is also about how various people take up and invest in various symbolic representations in the ongoing and daily practices of comprehension and communication. Culture has become a form of capital for economic investment, but it has little to do with the power of self-definition or the capacities needed to expand the scope of justice and human freedom. And it is precisely the challenge of education to provide a liminal space where knowledge, values, and desires can become meaningful in order to be both critical and transformative. If neoliberalism is to be challenged as a new mode of governmentality, it will have to be engaged as both a form of cultural politics and a pedagogical force, and not merely as a political and economic theory or mode of common sense or rationality.

As democratic institutions are downsized and public goods are offered up for corporate plunder, those of us who take seriously the related issues of equality, human rights, justice, and freedom face the crucial challenge of formulating a connection between the political and pedagogical that is suitable for addressing the urgent problems facing the twenty-first century—a politics that as Bauman argues "never stops criticizing the level of justice already achieved [while] seeking more justice and better justice."[60] Part of the problem to be addressed is that neoliberal ideology and practice will have to be challenged as part of an ongoing effort to open up new national and global spaces of education—employing a vast array of old and new media including free radio stations, digital video, online magazines, the Internet, digital technologies, and cable television. This means not only making critical pedagogy central to any viable notion of politics but also struggling to expand the "spaces for public life, democratic debate and cultural expression."[61] At its best, critical pedagogy should put into place those pedagogical conditions that enable a discourse of critique and possibility, one capable of making the operations of power visible in those theories, spaces, and social relations that are often complicitous with strategies of domination.

Discursive ambivalence is an important element in a pedagogy designed to unsettle official discourses by revealing the historical and social conditions that bring them into being, interrogating them as embodiments of specific ideological interests, and disclosing how they function to actively construct particular identifications and subject positions. If civic agency is to be taken seriously, educators need a new language to both challenge and work outside of the discourse of neoliberalism in order to expose how it deploys power within its own prison-house of language. For example, "corporate crime" is more telling than "white-collar crime"; the "corporatization" of schools, water, the public airways, and highways is far more critical and revealing than "privatization" when attempting to make clear the corporate appropriation of elements of the public sphere. Similarly, a term such as "corporate welfare" reverses the script on government largesse and its most valued recipients and reveals how governance can be hijacked to serve business interests. Such a pedagogy has the potential to turn theory into a resource and reveal how power deploys culture and how culture produces power. Moreover, critical pedagogy should not only "shift the way people think about the moment but [also] potentially energize them to do something differently in that moment."[62]

It should be deeply concerned with matters of specificity and context, and demand a certain ability to listen, witness, make connections, and be open to others and the conditions that give meaning to their lives. As Nick Couldry points out, pedagogy for democracy requires more than an obsession with abstractions, rhetoric, instrumentalization, and the jargon of specialization; it demands an "engagement with the claims of others, with questions of justice [and] justice requires always an engagement with the concrete other, not merely an abstract other. For justice and, therefore, for an adequate notion of citizenship, there must be a commitment to dialogue with concrete others."[63]

We live at a time when the advocates of neoliberalism have no use for democracy except to view it as a rationale for expanding empires, opening trade barriers, and pursuing new markets. Democracy as both an ethical referent and a promise for a better future is much too important to cede to a slick new mode of authoritarianism advanced by advocates of neoliberalism and other fundamentalists. Democracy as theory, practice, and promise for a better future must be critically engaged, struggled over, and reclaimed if it is to be used in the interests of social justice and the renewal of the labor movement as well as the building of national and international social movements, the struggle for the social state, and the necessity to confront hierarchy, inequality, and power as ruling principles in an era of rampant neoliberalism.[64] Such a task necessitates a politics and pedagogy that not only expand critical awareness and promote critical modes of inquiry but also sustain public connections. As Edward Said reminds us, if such a politics is to make any difference, it must be worldly; that is, it must incorporate a critical pedagogy and an understanding of cultural politics that not only contemplates social problems but also addresses the conditions for new forms of democratic political exchange and enables new forms of agency, power, and collective struggle. This is a pedagogy that embraces a global politics in its reach and vision, in its call for the democratic sharing of power and in the elimination of those conditions that promote needless human suffering and imperil the bio-systems of the earth itself.

Part of the task of developing a new understanding of the social and a new model of democratic politics rests with the demand to make the political more pedagogical while resisting at every turn the neoliberalization of public and higher education, creating new alliances between students and faculty, and rethinking the potential connections that might be deployed between those of us who work in education and the vast array of cultural workers outside of schools. As Stanley Aronowitz, Howard Zinn, Roger Simon, Susan Giroux and others have stressed repeatedly, academics have a responsibility to view the academy as a contested site, a site where the spread of neoliberal ideas must be challenged.[65] Contesting the neoliberalization of the university must be defended as important political work[66] and viewed as a central element in theorizing the role of public intellectuals as part of a larger project in defining the meaning and purpose of the university as a democratic public sphere. In connecting the work that is done in educational institutions with the larger society, educators and academics also face the important task of supporting, as Judith Butler argues, other public spheres "where thoughtful considerations can take place."[67] There is a long legacy among educators and academics to engage in forms of criticism that appear unconnected to the discourse of possibility and hope. This approach to critique and social criticism should be modified so that while we should continue to defend critique as a democratic value and "dissent as a basis for a politics that diminishes human suffering, "[68] we have a responsibility to go beyond criticism. Transcending this space requires combining a discourse of critique and possibility, one that enables others to recast themselves as agents who can forge new democratic visions against a fractured social, racial, and economic reality while speaking in the name of a desirable democratic future. Fortunately, while neoliberalism has achieved considerable dominance over political and economic discourse, there are a number of countervailing forces both at home and abroad that are challenging the politics and commonsense assumptions that drive its rationality and practices. From Seattle and Davos to Genoa and Rostok, people are engaging in various modes of popular struggle, collectively challenging the ethos, values, and relations of neoliberalism and resuscitating the meaning of politics, resistance, and the spaces where it becomes possible and takes place. Such signs are evident in grassroots and local movements to reclaim public education, the varied movements against neoliberal globalization, various struggles on behalf of populations that are HIV positive, workers rights movements, and those diverse groups fighting for environmental justice and public goods, among other struggles. [69] Under the reign of neoliberal globalization, it is crucial for intellectuals and others to develop better theoretical frameworks for understanding how power, politics, and pedagogy as a political and moral practice work in the service of neoliberalism to secure consent, to normalize authoritarian policies and practices, and to erase a history of struggle and injustice. The stakes are too high to ignore such a task. We live in dark times and the specter of neoliberalism and other modes of authoritarianism are gaining ground throughout the globe. We need to rethink the meaning of global politics in the new millennium and part of that challenge suggests the necessity to "recognize that equality and freedom, class and culture, as ineluctably linked." Doing so offers educators and others the possibility to take new risks, develop a new vitalized sense of civic[70] struggle, and exercise the courage necessary to reclaim the pedagogical conditions, visions, and economic projects that make the promise of a democracy and a different future worth fighting for.

NOTES

1 Clearly this position ranges from very sophisticated analysis of class as in the work of David Harvey, Erik Olin Wright, Adolph Reed and the emerging discourse on disaster capitalism to the more reductive analyses put forth by a number of theorists, including Thomas Byrne Edsall and Mary D. Edsall, Michael Tomasky, Todd Gitlin, Richard Rorty, and Walter Benn Michaels. See David Harvey, *A Brief History of Neoliberalism*, (Oxford University Press, 2005); Erik Olin Wright, Approaches to Class Analysis (London: Cambridge University Press, 2005); Adolph Reed, Jr., *Class Notes: Posing as Politics and Other Thoughts on the American Scene* (New York: New Press, 2001);Thomas Byrne Edsall and Mary D. Edsall, *Chain Reaction: The Impact of Race, Rights, and Taxes on American Politics* (New York: WW. Norton, 1991); Michael Tomasky, *Left for Dead: The Life, Death and Possible Resurrection of Progressive Politics in America* (New York: Free Press, 1996); Todd Gitlin in *Twilight of our Common Dreams: What America is Wracked by Culture Wars* (New York: Owl Publishers, 1996); Walter Benn Michaels, The Trouble with Diversity (New York: Owl, 2006). Clearly, there are many approaches to economic inequality and class discrimination that do not exclude cultural politics or reify an updated version of economism. See, for example, Stanley Aronowitz, *How Class Works* (New Haven, CT: Yale University Press, 2003); Lawrence Grossberg, Grossberg, *Caught in the Crossfire: Kids, Politics, and America's Future*. (Boulder: Paradigm, 2005); Wendy Brown, *Edgework: Critical Essays on Knowledge and Politics*. (Princeton: Princeton University Press, 2005); Ken Saltman, ed. *Capitalizing on Disaster* (Boulder: Paradigm, 2007).

2 Eric Lott, "A Wrongheaded Focus on Class," *The Chronicle Review* 53:17 (December 15, 2006), p. B13.

3 Michael Tomasky, *Left for Dead: The Life, Death and Possible Resurrection of Progressive Politics in America* (New York: Free Press, 1996); Todd Gitlin in *Twilight of our Common Dreams: What America is Wracked by Culture Wars* (New York: Owl Publishers, 1996); Ted Halstead and Michael Lind, *The Radical Center* (New York: Doubleday, 2001); Thomas Frank, *What's the Matter with Kansas: How Conservatives Won the Heart of America* (New York: Metropolitan Books, 2004); Walter Benn Michaels, *The Trouble with Diversity* (New York: Owl, 2006).

4 Robin D. G. Kelley, *Yo' Mama's Disfunktional*! (Boston: Beacon Press, 1997), p. 109.

5 Kelley, Ibid.; Judith Butler, "Merely Cultural," *Social Text* 52–53, Vol 15: 3–4 (Fall\Winter, 1997), pp. 266–277; Ellen Willis, *Don't Think, Smile: Notes on a Decade of Denial* (Boston: Beacon Press, 1999).

6 Lawrence Grossberg, "Toward a Genealogy of the State of Cultural Studies," in Cary Nelson and Dilip Parameshwar Gaonkar, eds. *Disciplinarity and Dissent in Cultural Studies* (New York: Routledge, 1996), p. 142.

7 Thomas Lemke, "Foucault, Governmentality, and Critique" *Rethinking Marxism*, Volume 14, Number 3, (Fall 2002), pp. 49–64.

8 Nick Couldry, "Realty TV, or the Secret Theatre of Neoliberalism," *The Review of Education, Pedagogy, and Cultural Studies 30:1* (2008), p. 1.

9 Wendy Brown, *Edgework: Critical Essays on Knowledge and Politics*, (Princeton: Princeton University Press, 2005), p. 40.

10 William K. Tabb, "Race to the Bottom?" in Stanley Aronowitz and Heather Gautney, eds. *Implicating Empire: Globalization & Resistance in the 21 Century World Order*, (New York: Basic Books, 2003), p. 153.

11 Richard L. Harris, "Popular Resistance to Globalization and Neoliberalism in Latin America," *Journal of Developing Societies* 19:2–3(2003), pp. 365–426.

12 Lewis Lapham, "Buffalo Dances," *Harper's Magazine* (May, 2004), pp. 9, 11.

13 Randy Martin, "War, by all Means," *Social Text* 25:2 (Summer 2007), p. 17.

14 For an excellent analysis of the profound impact the world bank has on global politics and culture, see Bret Benjamin, *Invested Interest: Capital, Culture, and the World Bank* (Minneapolis: University of Minnesota Press, 2007).

15 Stanley Aronowitz and Heather Gautney, "The Debate About Globalization: An Introduction," in Stanley Aronowitz and Heather Gautney, eds. *Implicating Empire: Globalization & Resistance in the 21 Century World Order*, (New York: Basic Books, 2003), p. 3.

[16] Stanley Aronowitz, *How Class Works* (New Haven, CT: Yale University Press, 2003), p. 30.

[17] *The Multinational Monitor* (September 2001), pp. 7–8. See also, David Moberg, "Plunder and Profit," *In These Times* (March 29, 2004), pp. 20–21.

[18] Sean Gonsalves, (April 20, 2004). How to skin a rabbit. *The Cape Cod Times*. Available [Online]: www.commondreams.org/views04/0420-05.htm. Accessed on April 24, 2004.

[19] Cheryl Woodard, C.(2004, April 15). Who Really Pays Taxes in America?:Taxes and Politics in 2004. *AskQuestions.org*,. Available [On-line]: http://www.askquestions.org/articles/taxes/. Accessed on April 24, 2004.

[20] Martin Wolk, "Cost of Iraq Could Surpass $1 Trillion," *MSNBC* (March 17, 2006). Online: http://www.msnbc.msn.com/id/11880954/

[21] Lisa Duggan, *The Twilight of Equality: Neoliberalism, Cultural Politics, and the Attack on Democracy* (Boston, MA: Beacon Press, 2003), p. 16.

[22] Paul Krugman, "Children Versus Insures," *New York Times* (April 6, 2007), p. A21.

[23] For some informative commentaries on the S-chip program and Bush's veto , see Amy Goodman, "Children's Defense Fund Marian Wright Edelman Calls on Congress & Bush Administration to Help the Country's Nine Million Children Without Health Insurance," *Democracy Now* (July 24, 2007). Online: www.democracynow.org/print.p1?sid=o7/07/24/1431211; Editorial, "Misleading Spin on Children's Health," *New York Times* (October 5, 2007), p. A26; Paul Krugman, "Conservatives Are Such Jokers," *New York Times* (October 5, 2007), p. A27.

[24] Cited in Kellie Bean, "Coulter's Right-Wing Drag," The Free Press (October 29, 2003). Available online at www.freepress.org/departments/display/20/2003/441

[25] Report by the Center fr American Progress and Free Press, *The Structural Imbalance of Political Talk Radio* (Washington, D.C.: Center for American Progress and Free Press, 2007).

[26] Editorial, "Savage Anti-Semitism: Radio Hosts Targets Jewish Foes with Ethnic Derision," *Fairness and Accuracy in Reporting* (July/August 2003). Available online: http://www.fair.org/extra/0307/savage-anti-semitism.html

[27] Fredric Jameson, *The Seeds of Time* (New York: Columbia University Press, 1994), xii.

[28] Susan Buck-Morss, *Thinking Past Terror: Islamism and Critical Theory on the Left* (London: Verso, 2003), pp. 65–66.

[29] George Soros, *The Bubble of American Supremacy* (New York: Public Affairs, 2004), p. 10.

[30] Christopher Newfield, "The Culture of Force," *The South Atlantic Quarterly* 105: 1 (2006), p. 244.

[31] Here I am quoting David Frum and Richard Pearle cited in Lewis H. Lapham, "Dar al-Harb," *Harper's Magazine* (March 2004), p. 8. This fascistically inspired triumphalism can be found in a number of books churned out to gratify the demands of a much celebrated jingoism. See Joseph Farah, *Taking America Back* (New York: WND Books, 2003); Michelle Malkin, *Invasion: How America Still Welcomes Terrorists, Criminals, and Other Foreign Menaces to Our Shores* (New York: Regnery Publishing, 2002); William J. Bennett, *Why We Fight: Moral Clarity and the War on Terrorism* (New York: Regnery, 2003); John Bolton, Surrender is Not an Option: Defending America at the United Nations (New York: Threshold Editions, 2007); Norman Podhoretz, *World War IV: The Long Struggle Against Islamofascism* (New York: Doubleday, 2007). Not surprisingly, all of the Republican Party leading presidential candidates for 2008 endlessly echo the same unforgiving jingoism.

[32] Michael Foessel, "Legitimations of the State: The Weakening of Authority and the Restoration of power," *Constellations* 63:3 (2006), pp. 313–314.

[33] Cited in Lewis H. Lapham, "Dar al-Harb," *Harper's Magazine* (March 2004), p. 8. The full exposition of this position can be found in David Frum and Richard Perle, *An End to Evil: How to Win the War on Terror* (New York: Random House, 2004).

[34] For a rather vivid example of how dissent is criminalized, see the March 5, 2004, NOW with Bill Moyers transcript of "Going Undercover/Criminalizing Dissent" The program documents how undercover agents from all levels of government are infiltrating and documenting peaceful protests in America.

35 Chalmers Johnson, *Nemesis: The Last Days of the American Republic* (New York: Metropolitan Books, 2006); Andrew Bacevich, *The New American Militarism: How Americans are Seduced by War* (New York: Oxford University Press, 2005).

36 For the latest revelation about the refusal of the Bush administration to take responsibility for the abuse and torture produced at Abu Ghraib and other U.S. prisons, see Seymour M. Hersh, "The General's Report," The New Yorker (June 25, 2007), pp. 58–69. See also, Tara McKelvey, *Monstering: Inside America's Policy of Secret Interrogations and Torture in the Terror War* (New York: Carroll & Graf, 2007).

37 Editorial, "On Torture and American Values," *New York Times* (October 7, 2007), wk p. 13.

38 Zygmunt Bauman, *Globalization: The Human Consequences* (New York: Columbia University Press, 1998), pp. 9–10.

39 Susan George, Ibid., "A Short History of Neo-Liberalism: Twenty Years of Elite Economics and Emerging Opportunities for Structural Change".

40 David Kotz, "Neoliberalism and the U.S. Economic Expansion of the '90s," *Monthly Review* 54:11 (April 2003), p. 16.

41 On neoliberalism as a form of governmentality or politics of conduct, see Michael Foucault, *Society Must be Defended: Lectures at the College De France 1975–1976* (New York: Picador, 2003).

42 David Harvey, *A Brief History of Neoliberalism* (New York: Oxford University Press, 2005).

43 See for instance, Friedrich Hayek, *The Road to Serfdom* (Chicago, IL: University of Chicago Press, 1994, 50th edition); Milton Friedman, *Capitalism and Freedom*: Fortieth Anniversary Issue (Chicago, IL: University of Chicago Press, 2002).

44 See, David Harvey, *A Brief History of Neoliberalism* (New York: Oxford University Press, 2005).

45 For a comprehensive and critical analysis of The New Gilded Age, see Michael Mchugh, *The Second Gilded Age: The Great Reaction in the United States, 1973–2001* (Boulder: University Press of America, 2006).

46 Pierre Bourdieu, *Acts of Resistance* (New York: Free Press, 1989), p. 35.

47 Colin Leys, *Market Driven Politics* (London: Verso, 2001), p. 2

48 Lisa Duggan, *The Twilight of Equality: Neoliberalism, Cultural Politics, and the Attack on Democracy* (Boston, MA: Beacon Press, 2003), p. 34.

49 Lisa Duggan, Ibid., p. xvi.

50 Bill Moyers, "The Media, Politics, and Censorship," Common Dreams News Center (May 10, 2004). Available online: www.commondreams.org/cgi-bin/print.cgi?file=/viewes04/0510-10.htm. See also Eric alterman, "Is Koppel a Commie," *The Nation* (May 24, 2004), p. 10.

51 Susan Buck-Morss, *Thinking Past Terror: Islamism and Critical Theory on the Left* (London: Verso, 2003), p. 103.

52 Alain touraine, *Beyond Neoliberalism* (London; Polity press, 2001), p. 2.

53 Alex Callinicos, "The Anti-Capitalist Movement After Genoa and New York,"in Stanley Aronowitz and Heather Gautney, eds. *Implicating Empire: Globalization & Resistance in the 21 Century World Order,* (New York: Basic Books, 2003), p. 147.

54 Susan Buck-Morss, *Thinking Past Terror: Islamism and Critical Theory on the Left* (London: Verso, 2003), pp. 4–5.

55 Cornelius Castoriadis, "Imagining Society: Cornelius Castoriadis," Interview in *Variant* 15:3 (Autumn 1993), p. 41.

56 Ellen Willis, *Don't Think, Smile* (Boston: Beacon Press, 1999), p.xiv.

57 Zygmunt Bauman, "Critical Theory," in Peter Beilharz, ed., *The Bauman Reader* (Malden: Blackwell, 2001), p. 162.

58 Nick Couldry, "Dialogue in an Age of Enclosure: Exploring the Values of Cultural Studies," *Review of Education/Pedagogy/Cultural Studies* 23:1 (2001), p. 49.

59 Imre Szeman, "Introduction: Learning to Learn from Seattle," *Review of Education/Pedagogy/ Cultural Studies* 24: 1–2 (2002), pp. 3–4.

60 Zygmunt Bauman, *Society Under Siege* (Malden: Blackwell, 2002), p. 54.

[61] Lisa Duggan, *The Twilight of Equality: Neoliberalism, Cultural Politics, and the Attack on Democracy* (Boston: Beacon, Press, 2003), p. xx.

[62] A Conversation between Lani Guinier and Anna Deavere Smith, "Rethinking Power, Rethinking Theater," *Theater* 31:3 (Winter 2002), pp. 34–35.

[63] Nick Couldry, "Dialogue in an Age of Enclosure," p. 68.

[64] Mike Davis and Daniel B. Monk, eds., *Evil Paradises: Dreamworlds of Neo-Liberalism* (New York: The New Press, 2007). For an international analysis of the anti-democratic tendencies of neoliberalism, see Leslie Holmes, *Rotten States? Corruption, Post-Communism, and Neo-liberalism* (Durham: Duke University Press, 2006); Lisa Duggan, *The Twilight of Equality* (Boston: Beacon Press, 2003); Aihwa Ong, *Neoliberalism as Exception: Mutations in Citizenship and Sovereignty* (Durham: Duke University Press, 2006). Neil Smith, *The Endgame of Globalization* (New York: Routledge, 2005) and Alain Touraine, *Beyond Neoliberalism* (London: Polity Press, 2001).

[65] A variety of writers take up this issue in Henry A. Giroux and Kostas Myrsiades, eds., *Beyond the Corporate University* (Lanham: Rowman and Littlefield, 2001). See also, Henry A. Giroux, *The University in Chains: Confronting the Military-Industrial-Academic Complex* (Boulder: Paradigm, 2007); Henry A. Giroux and Susan Giroux, *Take Back Higher Education* (New York: Palgrave, 2006); Stanley Aronowitz, *The Knowledge Factory: Dismantling the Corporate University and Creating True Higher Learning* (Boston: Beacon Press, 2001); Stephen Pender, "An Interview with David Harvey," *Studies in Social Justice* 1:1 (Winter 2007), available online at http://ojs.uwindsor.ca/ojs/leddy/index.php/SSJ/article/viewFile/182/178; Stanley Aronowitz and Henry A. Giroux, *Education Still Under Siege* (New York: Bergin and Garvey, 1993); Howard Zinn, *On History* (New York: Seven Stories Press, 2001); and Edward Said, *Representations of the Intellectual* (New York: Pantheon, 1994).

[66] Stephen Pender, "An Interview with David Harvey"; Stanley Aronowitz and Henry A. Giroux, *Education Still Under Siege*.

[67] Judith Butler, *Precarious Life: The Powers of Mourning and Violence* (London: Verso Press, 2004), p. 126.

[68] Ibid., p. 104.

[69] Many excellent books and articles address the various ways in which neoliberalism is being resisted, a few examples include: Howard Zinn, *A Power Governments Cannot Suppress* (San Francisco: City Lights, 2007); Jean Comaroff, "Beyond Bare Life: AIDS, (Bio)Politics, and the Neoliberal Order," *Public Culture* 19:1 (Winter 2007), pp. 197–219; Stanley Aronowitz, *Left Turn: Forging a New Political Future* (Boulder: Paradigm Press, 2006); See David Harvey, *A Brief History of Neoliberalism* (New York: Oxford University Press, 2005), especially pp. 183–206; Lawrence Grossberg, *Caught in the Crossfire: Kids, Politics, and America's Future* (Boulder: Paradigm, 2005); Alfredo Saad-Filho and Deborah Johnston, eds. *Neoliberalism: A Critical Reader* (London: Pluto Press, 2005); Neil Smith, *The Endgame of Globalization* (New York: Routledge, 2005); Lisa Duggan, *The Twilight of Equality* (Boston: Beacon Press, 2003); and Alain Touraine, *Beyond Neoliberalism* (London: Polity Press, 2001); Aihwa Ong, *Neoliberalism as Exception: Mutations in Citizenship and Sovereignty* (Durham: Duke University Press, 2006); Alain Touraine, *Beyond Neoliberalism* (London: Polity Press, 2001);

[70] Ellen Willis, "Escape from Freedom: What's the Mater with Tom Frank (and the Lefties who Love Him)?" *Situations* 1:2 (2006), p. 20.

Henry A. Giroux
Department of English and Cultural Studies
McMaster University

GREG DIMITRIADIS

2. LESSONS LEARNED FROM ENRON

What the Business World Really has to Teach Us

For some time now, politicians, conservative critics, and other social actors have called for schools to be run like businesses—more "efficiently" (Chubb and Moe, 1990; Moe, 2002; Whittle, 2006). These tendencies have reached a devastating crescendo as of late. In particular, No Child Left Behind legislation has tied high stakes test scores to school "success" or "failure" writ large (Hess and Petrilli, 2006). This move has enabled a whole host of logics to unfold—the effort to close schools failing to meet these largely unfunded mandates, the reallocation of public funds to charter schools, the tying of teacher employment to student test scores, etc. We see, as well, moves on the part of private industry to colonize public schooling services. The most visible example here are the Edison Schools—a for-profit venture that looks to widely deliver standardized curriculum in the name of "maximized efficiency" (Saltman, 2005). While critical educators typically attack these connections wholesale (as they often do the field of administration more broadly), they often miss their specific contours. In this chapter, I argue that progressive educators in fact have much to learn from a serious look at the business world. More specifically, I argue that educators can learn much from the *failures* of business including those of the late-1990s. A close look at this moment reveals a specific striking parallel between the fields of business and education. Just as intense focus on hyped-up stock prices lead to serious aberrations in business, so does the intense focus on test scores for education. Just as inflated (and for that matter, depressed) stock prices proved a largely illusory indication of company health, so do test scores of schools. If we are to learn from big business, I argue, we must take seriously its failures as well. This chapter is an effort to learn from the business world on their own terms and in their own language.

In doing so, I hope to expand discussion among progressives about the comer-cialization and corporatization of education in the U.S. As many have argued, the language of education has been colonized by the language of business (Giroux, 2005; Grioux, 2005b; McLaren, 2005; McLaren and Farahmandpur, 2005). Schools are increasingly run as if they were corporations. Young people are increasingly trained to act as producers and consumers of commodities—not as thoughtful and deliberative social citizens. Many progressives have valiantly contested these moves, often with rhetorically strong and morally engaged arguments. I argue here that progressives might also try to understand the specifics of these claims and logics more acutely than they normally do. "Getting inside" these arguments might

Z. Leonardo (ed.), Handbook of Cultural Politics and Education, 71–86.

open unexpected vistas for critique and contestation. As I will argue here, we need not only argue against using business logics in education; we can also point out how business logics have failed business itself in some profound ways, especially in the 1990s.

THE ORIGINS OF THE CRASH

As Roger Lowenstein argues in *The Origins of the Crash: The Great Bubble and its Undoing* (2004), the roots of the late 1990's stock market collapse can be traced back to the leveraged buy out (LBO) phenomena of the 1980's. During this period, wealthy investors looked for companies they thought had an undervalued stock price. They then tried to "take over" these companies by offering attractive buy out offers to stock holders, offers supported or "leveraged" by deals with banks who supplied the necessary capital. These efforts were often unfriendly to management who often fought back with leveraged offers of their own. Perhaps the most famous such case was that of RJR Nabisco, immortalized in the best selling book *Barbarians at the Gate* (1990). The struggle over Nabisco lead to escalating offers and counter-offers, deals and counter-deals, which ultimately lead to the company's downfall.

The era is best exemplified by the fictional movie *Wall Street* and the character Gordon Gekko. Taking place in the 1980s, the film traces the relationship between a young stockbroker named Bud Fox and his older mentor, a wealthy and ruthless "takeover king" named Gordon Gekko. The film traces Gekko's seduction of Fox with his various unethical schemes, including criminal insider trading. In perhaps the film's most famous scene, Gekko confronts the management of a paper company he is attempting to acquire at a stockholder meeting. Gekko begins by drawing comparisons between the global decline of America and the global decline of American big business. He then asserts his authority—against that of "current management" as the company's largest stockholder. He charges that the management owns less than 3% of the company stock—that they have "no stake in the company," though they lost some $110,000,000 of company wealth the previous year. He calls the management "bureaucrats" running the company into the ground with their high salaries, power lunches, "hunting trips," and "golden parachutes." The real owners of the company, he asserts, are the stockholders. He implores them to support his unfriendly takeover of the company, asserting his track record of making stockholders money on previous such deals. Drawing on (seemingly) Darwinian logics, he famously concludes the speech by saying that "greed is good," that greed will save not only this failing company but "that other malfunctioning corporation called the USA."

The phrase "greed is good" crystallized the 1980s zeitgeist and became the film's most often quoted line of dialogue. The film's lesson, of course, was that greed was not always good, that it led to the kinds of unethical (at best) and criminal (at worst) excesses of the era. Yet, we see another more subtle and looming issue in this scene—that of management compensation. CEO's in the 1980s were typically compensated through high salaries and other perks. They often did not own large shares of their company's stock—hence, Gekko's charge that the 33 Vice Presidents of Teldar Paper own less than 3% of the company. The accusation was widely leveled at CEOs during the 1980s, justifying the wide prevalence of LBOs.

As Lowenstein argues, CEOs could not be complacent about the charge and faced increasing pressure to increase the stock price of their companies. CEOs were increasingly driven to deliver what came to be called "shareholder value," leading to an increasing stress on short-term stock price. Lowenstein (2004) writes,

> Takeovers had [an] . . . energizing effect on managers, in particular CEOs. Previously, theirs had been the safest jobs around; now their fortress was under siege and their pulse rate was on the rise.... To escape buyout, CEOs felt they had to raise their share price. This was a significant departure. Previously, stock prices had been seen as a long-term barometer. Prices in the short term were notoriously unreliable (this was the lesson of the Great Crash). But with a Henry Kravis [a noted "takeover king" involved in the RJR Nabisco deal] lurking, the long term might not exist. (p. 6)

Lowenstein highlights an important shift here in this focus on short-term stock prices. Short-term stock prices can reflect a range of economic, social, and psychological vicissitudes. Some of these may be just that—short-term —not reflective of the company's long-term health. This stress on daily, fluctuating stock price would have important repercussions for the business world—including in CEO compensation structures.

In a series of influential articles and books, Harvard Business School Professor Michael Jensen argued that such compensation should be tied more closely to the "health" of the companies they lead. As he wrote,

> There are serious problems with CEO compensation but "excessive" pay is not the biggest issue. The relentless focus on *how much* CEOs are paid diverts public attention from the real problem—*how* CEOs are paid. In most publicly held companies, the compensation of top executives is virtually independent of performance. On average, corporate America pays its most important leaders like bureaucrats. Is it any wonder that so many CEOs act like bureaucrats rather than the value-maximizing entrepreneurs companies need to enhance their standing in world markets (Jensen, 1998, p. 270).

Here, Jensen argues that there is a disconnect between CEO compensation and company "performance," that they are "virtually independent." Like many common sense notions, the idea that performance and compensation should be linked masks a deeper set of issues and tensions. More specifically, it begs the question—how does one measure successful "performance"? The answer for Jensen was company stock price. He continues, "The most powerful link between shareholder wealth and executive wealth is direct ownership of shares by the CEO ... By controlling a meaningful percentage of total corporate equity, senior managers experience a direct and powerful 'feedback effect' from changes in market value" (p. 275). If they own company stock, Jensen argued, CEOs have an incentive to increase its value. If they are paid through cash salary alone, they have no such incentive.

Paying CEOs through stock became increasingly pronounced in the 1990s. More specifically, CEO compensation through stock options—"options" to acquire company stock when it reaches a certain level—became increasingly popular. A CEO, therefore, might head up a company with a stock price of $80. As part of his or her compensation package, he or she might be entitled to 100,000 shares of the stock once it hit $90. Of course, the CEO here has a great incentive to push the price of the stock upward. As Michael Jensen writes, "stock options clearly provide value-increasing incentives for chief executives" (1998, p. 236).

The move to pay CEOs through stock options was set against the backdrop of new federal tax laws on compensation. In the aftermath of the 1980s, the U.S. economy went into a recession. Popular focus soon turned to the excesses of the previous decade—including outrageous CEO pay. Comparisons were drawn with Japan, which tended to pay its CEOs much less. As something of a response, President Clinton helped push a tax bill in 1993, which banned tax deductions on salaries above $1 million. But stock options were not considered a part of CEO income, strictly speaking. The plan, in large measure, backfired. As Lowenstein (2004) writes, "since stock options weren't covered under the cap, boards interpreted the rule change as an implicit encouragement to grant more options" (p. 18–19). CEOs thus had a lot of incentive to increase stock price quickly.

THE NEW ECONOMY

Emerging here was an intense, unrelenting focus on "stock price," both in and out of the company boardroom. Indeed, during the mid-to-late 1990s, a kind of popular investment fever overtook the public (Kessler, 2003; Partnoy, 2003; Shiller, 2006; Stiglitz, 2004). In *American Sucker* David Denby (2005) documents his own, highly personal seduction by the stock market, his highs and (more often) lows in amateur investing. A well-known film critic for the *New Yorker*, the book is a testament to how the rhetoric around popular wealth swept up wide and disparate groups of people from various walks of life. Lowenstein writes, "Investors … had fallen in love with stocks—with the idea of stocks. They had looked past dubious accounting, bid up multiples of earnings, and come to confuse long-term business value with the nebulous, manipulable concept of shareholder value" (2004, p. 103). This fever was fueled by new and emergent technologies, particularly the internet and its euphoric, near-religious promise of social and economic transcendence. This new technology was going to transform everything around us, from government to school to commerce—all for the better. Getting in on "the ground floor" of new, "start up" internet companies would also deliver untold wealth for investors. The fervor was compounded by news stations like MSNBC that reported on the minute-by-minute changes in stock prices and featured "rock star" stock analysts like Jack Grubman, Henry Blodget, and Mary Meeker.

The result was a net, upward surge in stock prices. This kind of market valuation, however, was often distinctly unreflective of the companies themselves which often did not have feasible business models. Millennial rhetoric, it seems, often substituted for revenue generating plans. Many investors felt they would be left behind if they did not participate. The late-nineties saw increasing numbers of non-specialists invest in the market, particularly in technology stocks. For many, the market was a risk-free way to make money. There was, to echo Alan Greenspan, an "irrational exuberance" in the stock market.

One need only look at the most spectacular such failures to see the extent of both the irrationality and the exuberance. For example, WebVan was an on-line grocer that offered great prices and doorstep delivery. It raised $375 million in four months, and was soon valued at $1.2 billion. But it had very thin profit margins and could not sustain the growth and demand. It went bankrupt soon after. Kosmo.com was another on-line company that promised free delivery for a wide range of products, from DVD rentals to ice cream to pizza, within an hour. It raised $280 million before going bankrupt, unable to make a profit on the venture. Other ideas were even more poorly conceived. For example, Flooz.com was an "on-line currency" that consumers could buy and use at select participating internet sites such as Barnes and Noble. Yet, there was nothing to distinguish using "flooze money" from a credit card—only fewer participating retailers. A seeming nonsensical idea, it raised $35 million before going bankrupt (c.net).

Perhaps the most spectacular "flame out" of all was Enron (Eichenwald, 2005; McLean and Elkind, 2003). Based in Houston, Enron began as a natural gas company under the directorship of Ken Lay. The product of a large-scale merger in the 1980s, the company was a largely traditional one—it owned miles of pipelines and sold natural gas. In 1986, Ken Lay hired into management a young consultant named Jeffrey Skilling. Skilling, who eventually became CEO, proposed turning Enron into a large "gas bank." Instead of simply selling gas, the company would "pool the resources of producers and supply them to industrial consumers" (Lowenstein, 2004, p. 130). Enron would thus coordinate a complex network of natural gas buyers and sellers—an idea clearly informed by the New Economy ethos. Enron soon went into a range of other speculative ventures and businesses, trading everything from broadband cable to futures in weather.

According to Lay, Skilling, and others, Enron's complex deals demanded more complex kinds of accounting mechanisms. In particular, management requested what was called "mark to market" accounting. This kind of accounting allowed Enron to book all projected future earnings on particular acquisitions as income for the current year. This meant that Enron could strike a deal with a company in 1999, for example, to supply its natural gas for 10 years. It could then record as revenue all its projected profits for 10 years in 1999, projecting the price of natural gas for that period as well. Perhaps the companies most decisive moment was when its accountants, Arthur Anderson, signed off on the request. This meant of course that Enron could make a series of large and perhaps shaky deals, project their revenue, and then report this as yearly earnings to their stockholders. Not surprisingly, these numbers did not represent what was happening at the company.

In an effort to increase its "bottom line," Enron also engaged in criminal activity as well. In particular, the company's Chief Financial Officer, Andrew Fastow, set up a series of companies called "limited partnerships" with names like Chewco and Death Star. In control of both these partnerships and Enron's finances themselves,

Fastow moved company debt and liability to these entities, allowing Enron to book larger and larger profits, pushing its stock price upward. As many have commented, these partnerships were part of what might be called an elaborate "shell game" of company debt and assets. Enron's Board of Directors gave Fastow permission to hold both positions, though he would eventually plead guilty to various criminal charges, including wire and securities fraud.

Of course, Enron eventually went bankrupt. Its lack of "hard assets" combined with deceptive accounting practices and fraudulent business deals created what many have called a "house of cards" that eventually fell. It was then the largest bankruptcy in U.S. history, losing over $60 billion for its stockholders. Its collapse was part of a general crash in the stock market in the late 1990s.

NEO-LIBERALISM

The spectacular failures of Enron and other such companies were not simply criminal aberrations. They emerged as the result of the massive constellation of economic and political shifts and re-alignments associated with "neo-liberalism" (Altman, 2007; Aronowitz, 2005; Fulcher, 2004; Giroux, 2005b; Harvey, 2003, 2005; Head, 2003; Klein, 2007; Piven, 2006; Reich, 1991, 2001, 2007; Stiglitz, 2003, 2006; Stiglitz & Bilmes, 2008; Weis, 2004). Commonly called "capitalism with the gloves off," neo-liberalism is an economic philosophy—largely associated with the University of Chicago's Department of Economics (generally) and Milton Friedman (specifically)—that advances the notion that an unfettered marketplace (or "free market") uses scarce resources most effectively, promoting the overall good. Thus, the common call for wholesale "deregulation" of industries such as the telephone, oil, and cable television. Neo-liberalism signalled a shift away from the kind of large-scale state spending projects often associated with "Keynesianism." Dominant throughout the middle-part of the twentieth-century, adherents to Keynesianism believed that such spending projects served to boost the entire economy and provide critical safety nets for the disenfranchised. Beginning in the latter part of the 1970s, these logics shifted. "Big government" was part of the problem, according to people such as Ronald Reagan and Margaret Thatcher. Smaller government with less regulation over business was the new dominant.

A more subtle shift registered here, one elaborated upon (among others) in Naomi Klein's *The Shock Doctrine: The Rise of Disaster Capitalism* (2007)—that is, the emergence of economics as a largely autonomous discourse disconnected from other disciplines, sciences and social concerns. As Klein shows, Friedman and others were masters of forward-looking econometric measurements—predictions about inflation, depression, employment, etc.—based on complex mathematical models disconnected from real-world vicissitudes. In this respect, "neo-liberalism" was as idealistic as any doctrine or meta-narrative. She writes,

> Like all fundamental faiths, Chicago School economics is, for its true believers, a closed loop. The starting premise is that the free market is a perfect scientific system, one in which individuals, acting on their own self-interested desires, create the maximum benefits for all. It follows ineluctably

> that if something is wrong within a free-market economy—high inflation or soaring unemployment—it has to be that the market is not truly free. There must be some interference, some distortion in the system. The Chicago solution is always the same: a stricter and more complete application of the fundamentals. (p. 51)

With the rise of neo-liberalism, economics emerged as a fully autonomous discipline—its basic premises now articles of faith. The idea that one balanced social concerns and planning with economics was totally anathema. For this reason, Klein continues, many Chicago School economists saw Keynesianism as a greater threat than Marxism (p. 52).

Neo-liberalism, however, did not serve the common good. In fact, the kinds of large-scale de-regulations advocated by Friedman, Alan Greenspan and others have allowed for wide-scale profiteering in key industries. This result has been new, massive concentrations of wealth and growing economic inequalities, prompting many to call this the new "gilded age." This kind of profiteering was at the heart of Enron's role in the noted blackouts that took place in California in 2000 and 2001. California was the first state to de-regulate the energy market, allowing companies like Enron to buy and trade energy—and seemingly compete with each other. The promise was always that such competition would be good for the consumer. Instead, traders at Enron would buy enormous amounts of energy at market price in California and then move it out of state, causing shortages and blackouts in key areas. They would then sell it back selectively for much higher prices—sometimes for five or six times what they had paid for it. The so-called "energy shortage" in California was a carefully orchestrated shell game, enabled by de-regulation and its neo-liberal logics. Predictably, Lay and others blamed the fiasco on the remaining regulations on energy in California. I will return to this idea later in the chapter.

TESTING LOGICS

So what does all this tell us about education? I want to argue here that the focus on the "bottom line" in business helped create the kinds of aberrations we saw above. Instead of focusing on the long-term health of companies, focus turned to manipulating day-to-day stock prices. I argue here that we need to look closely at these business logics and their failures, as these logics are more and more taking hold in education today. In particular, high stakes testing has created a language of "bottom lines" which largely revolve around test scores. "Performance" can be measured through test scores for many, particularly in testable subjects like Language Arts and Math. Just as these logics failed business, however, they have also failed education.

The most notable of these movements, of course, has been the No Child Left Behind legislation. The effects of this legislation have been broad and deep—including the attenuation of the curricula, both in terms of substance and pedagogical practice—though they have been particularly profound on the most vulnerable of public schools. At the most basic level, a corporate language has overtaken school discourse, a language that implies clear inputs and outputs, assessments and measurements that can be correlated and compared across disparate sites. Knowledge itself has come to be treated like a perfectly transparent commodity, one that can be treated and dispensed independent of particular actors in context.

According to federal guidelines, NCLB is "designed to change the culture of America's schools by closing the achievement gap, offering more flexibility, giving parents more options, and teaching students based on what works" (http://www.ed. gov/nclb). This seemingly objective notion of "what works" has been used to promote so-called "evidence-based" standards in federally funded research. On this model, educational research should be classically experimental and causal, relying on large-scale, randomized samples to make generalized claims. The federal guidelines go on to note,

> No Child Left Behind puts emphasis on determining which educational programs and practices have been proven effective through rigorous scientific research. Federal funding is targeted to support these programs and teaching methods that work to improve student learning and achievement. In reading, for example, No Child Left Behind supports scientifically based instruction programs in the early grades under the Reading First program and in preschool under the Early Reading First program.

A deeply positivistic approach to knowledge and understanding is embedded in these research methodologies as well as the pedagogical practices assessments that emerge from them. In particular, this approach to research has lent itself to the "drill and skill" kinds of learning favored by high stakes testing initiatives such as the Bush administrations' No Child Left Behind legislation. At the level of practice, NCLB encourages a kind of rote, short-term drill-and-skill approach to teaching, one which helps encourages a focus on lower-order skills.

Test scores also are now used to "prove" whether schools and teachers are "performing" or not. As with the stress on stock price, a whole host of "common sense" logics click into place when one assumes such test scores are representative of what students are learning. For example, one can use these test scores to measure how teachers are doing in the classroom. If they are doing well, they should be rewarded with increased salary or bonuses. If not, they should be punished. Similarly, these tests can be used to measure how efficiently schools are using their resources. Schools that are using them well should be given more resources. Schools that are using them poorly should be given less. In addition, there should be ample opportunity for private citizens and businesses to compete here. Citizens should be able to form their own charter schools. They should also be able to receive "vouchers" if they choose to opt out of the public school system. Private, for profit schools should have the chance to show they can do it better for less, of which the Edison Schools, founded by Charles Whittle, are the best example. As Kenneth Saltman (2005) demonstrates, these schools were established and later justified through their seemingly "innovative" ways of raising test scores. In doing so, they mobilized a common claim—the private sector can "do it better" without the influence and interference of bloated, public bureaucracy.

These logics have had a profound impact on everyday life in schools. In particular, we see a constant pressure to "teach to the test"—to "hit the numbers" in business terms. Recall the unrelenting stress on stock prices in our earlier discussion. Recall the uncritical connection between company health and company valuation. Recall the aberrations it produced. Indeed, both anecdotal evidence as well as current research tell us that teachers are more and more altering their pedagogical practice with a sharp eye toward these tests. On one level, this is evidenced by the amount of time now devoted to testing in school. As Gail Jones, Brett Jones, and Tracy Hargrove (2003) discuss in their recent study of North Carolina schools, 80% of elementary school teachers said they spend more than 20% of their teaching time preparing for high stakes tests; 28% said they spend more than 60% of their time on such tests; and 71% said they spend more time on these tests than they did three earlier (p. 64). On another level, this stress on tests is evidenced by the kinds of teaching practices encouraged by high-stakes tests. This includes, especially, "item teaching," or the narrow focus on teaching items identical or similar to the ones on high stakes tests. As the authors note, "the problem with item teaching is that students learn the knowledge and skills tested, but not the other knowledge and skills in the domain" (p. 66).

The effects of such testing can be seen from afar (as above) or can be seen up close. For example, Dale and Bonnie Johnson's *High Stakes: Children, Testing, and Failure in American Schools* (2002) traces the effects of high-stakes testing for one year in one poor rural school in an elementary school in Redbud, Louisiana. In this book, the authors document the crushing poverty that delimits life in the local community and in the school. "The school has no library, no playground equipment, no counselor, no art classes, no hot water (except for a faucet in the teacher's lounge), inadequate window heating and cooling units, no regular school nurse" (2002, p. xviii). In this context, high-stakes testing is one more extreme burden for the schools—its teachers, administrators, and students. They document the excessive time spent on rote, drill-and-skill practice, the constant imposition of "new programs" which will supposedly help raise the test scores, the constant tension and pressure which force many teachers to leave early. The authors also document what they don't see—including anything that seems "frivolous" and "excessive," like art or gymnastics.

In addition to the sheer time and effort spent on high-stakes tests, some schools and teachers have also resorted to deceptive reporting practices and even outright cheating. For example, as Kenneth Saltman demonstrates, Boston's Renaissance Edison School was accused of "counseling out" special education and special needs students from applying. This was a way to "raise test scores and decrease costs associated with special provisions" (2005, p. 129). In effect, we see an effort to "cook the books" when reporting gains in scores and costs to the public. Saltman notes, as well, that a Western Michigan University study contested Edison's claim that they made strong, measurable improvements in disadvantaged school. "While our findings do not suggest that Edison did less," they write, "they do not suggest that the company did more with these schools in terms of gains on standardized tests" (quoted in Saltman, 2005, p. 70). Finally, he shows that select schools were accused of cheating on tests:

> In addition to charges that Edison manipulated test reporting, it has been accused of encouraging cheating on tests in classrooms. The scandal erupted in the winter of 2002 when the *Wichita Eagle* reported that, in interviews with seven former Edison teachers, four of the seven said that they had been told by the company "to do whatever it took to make sure students succeeded on standardized tests, including ignoring time limits, reading questions from a reading comprehension test aloud and in some cases correcting answers during a test." (p. 74)

Jones, Jones, and Hargrove (2003) document, as well, numerous cases of cheating on high-stakes tests, summing up "the pressure for teachers to raise scores is enormous and comes from all sides of educational arenas" (p. 72).

Perhaps the most notable example of large-scale fraud is the so-called "Texas Miracle" that played so large a part of George W Bush's 2000 presidential campaign and largely served as the warrant for the No Child Left Behind legislation (future secretary of education Ron Paige was then Houston school superintendent). Through a number of "accountability" mechanisms as well as a range of high stakes tests, principles and administrators in Houston were made responsible for their schools' achievement though the 1990s. The results, it seems, were remarkable—including plunging dropout rates and soaring test scores. Yet, as CBS News reported in 2004, much of this was illusionary. In particular, they uncovered grave malfeasance—the kind of deceptions and manipulations associated criminal corporations like Enron. As they discovered, schools "raised average test scored by keeping low-performing kids from taking the test. And in some cases, that meant keeping kids from getting to the 10th grade at all," when they would take these exams (CBS News, Aug. 25, 2004). The Houston school system, it seemed, "cooked the books."

NCLB: A FAILED BUSINESS MODEL

Just as Chicago School economists treated economics as a science disconnected from other social concerns and issues, adherents to NCLB treat education as a science disconnected from the lives, concerns, and needs of the people who inhabit the educational system (Apple, 2006). Both tend to focus (respectively) on short-term, bottom-line indicators that are not accurate measures of economic or educational health. With the acceleration of "bottom line" thinking in business, the long-term viability of companies was ignored, leading to a "boom and bust" in the late nineties. The acceleration of "bottom line" thinking in education has led to similar disasters—though they are less spectacular. We see this in the rise of "drill and skill" pedagogies, time spent "teaching to the test," as well as the various semi-legal and illegal schemes used to "hit the numbers." We also see its effects on the psyches of youth. As is well-documented high stakes tests cause young people extraordinary amounts of stress. As Johnson and Johnson (2006) write of the Texas Assessment of Academic Skills test (TAAS), "In the Texas survey, 47 percent of students were reported to often or always develop headaches, 40 percent had upset stomachs, 38 percent showed irritability, 35 percent displayed increased aggression, 34 percent 'froze up,' and 29 percent vomited while taking the TAAS test" (p. 116).

We see this, as well, in the attenuation of a rich multi-layered curriculum. Focus has turned to the kinds of subjects that are both testable and "high stakes"—in particular Language Arts and Math. On one level, this has meant shrinking the purview of both these subjects. For example, "literacy" has come to mean a narrow, teacher-centered focus on decoding language for referential meaning. While this is important, it does not exhaust the range and kind of transactions young people can have with multiple kinds of visual and aural texts. On another level, it has meant that certain subjects have come to be seen as non-essential or subordinate to testable ones. Subjects like art or physical fitness now have to justify themselves through their supposed connections to Reading or Math. For example, many in-school creative writing interventions need now to "prove" they increase test scores in reading to remain funded.

These so-called "skills" are not even going to prepare young people for the 21st century workplace. While these impulses have of course been embedded in school life for nearly 100 years (Dimitriadis and Carlson, 2003), never before have they been so clearly pedagogically inappropriate for the long-term social and cultural reality young people face. According to Carlson and others like Andy Hargreaves, students in our so-called knowledge-society must learn to "create knowledge, apply it to unfamiliar problems, and communicate it effectively to others" (Hargreaves, 2003, p. 24). These require new modes and approaches to teaching and learning—constructivist and cooperative approaches that imply a range of learning outcomes and goals. These modes and approaches necessarily imply nuanced pedagogical practices that may only be realized in the long term. New testing regimes—in stark counter-distinction—encourage just the opposite. They encourage a kind of rote, short-term drill-and-skill approach to teaching, one which helps encourage "teachers to focus on low-level knowledge and skills, resulting in less in-depth understanding and less focus on higher-order thinking skills" (Jones, Jones, and Hargrove, 2003. p. 40). These tests encourage a narrow subjects-based approach that measures basic knowledge—not what young people can do with it. NCLB is a failed business model.

MOVING AHEAD

My point about inflated test scores and stock prices should be clear by now. Yet, I want to make a broader point here, as well, about how progressive pedagogues have responded to the ascent of business logics in education. In particular, many progressives have responded by simply dismissing such connections wholesale, mostly on moral grounds. Where some have called for an uncritical acceptance of business logics, then, others have uncritically dismissed them. Such responses lead to calcified, mutually reinforcing positions which often naturalize ideas about business itself—its effectiveness, for example. The point is important. The Right has been able to mobilize a language around education that makes sense to people. The language is seductive and idealized—a language of minimized inputs, maximized outputs, and widespread accountability. To echo Michael Apple (2004), it is the language of an "audit culture." Responses from progressives here have again been largely moralistic, that education should not be run like other kinds of businesses, that schools should prepare young people for democratic participation in public life. While this is a critical front, we should also highlight the ways in which the language of business has failed business itself. We should highlight the ways in which a focus on "the bottom line" lead to the kinds of aberrations we saw in the 1980s and 1990s (specifically) and the failures of neo-liberalism more broadly.

These failures run broad and deep. Indeed, the attendant economic fallout of the very recent collapse of the housing and mortgage market highlight another fallacy of neo-liberalism—its distain for large state intervention in economic policy noted above. As Ha-Joon Chang usefully points out in *Bad Samaritans*, "free trade free market policy claims" are largely illusionary. "Britain and the US are *not* the homes of free trade; in fact, for a long time they were the most protectionist economies in the world" (2008, p. 17). As Chang shows, the US has deployed protectionism and subsidies in selective and strategic fashion for some time now—recently, to compensate for the failed risks of wild financial speculation. Witness the recent role of the US Federal Reserve in helping to prevent the collapse of mega-bank Bear Stearns (in the form of a favorable loan to acquiring bank JP Morgan), the twelfth-hour financial bailout of mortgage guarantors Fannie Mae and Freddie Mac, as well as the federal takeover of failed bank IndyMac. In all of these cases, wild speculation in the housing market and the attendant proliferation of exotic and often "sub-prime" mortgage packages, led to the impending collapse of key financial powerhouses. In all of these cases, "big government" intervened in the name of the broader social good. More and more, neo-liberal capitalism is evidencing the claim that it is nothing more than "welfare for the rich."

In failing to take on these contradictions and discussions, again, we leave key claims unchallenged—in particular, that business logics are efficient. We do not question what is often a deep faith at the heart of neo-liberalism—the kind evidenced by Naomi Klein above—that often masks itself as a precise, mathematical science. In many respects, this allows the juggernaut of neo-liberalism and all it represents to appear immutable and inevitable. Corporate languages and logics will continue to largely overtake discussion around education in the US, particularly in the realm of public policy. While many critical pedagogues have valiantly rejected these moves, they have done so on moral grounds. I have offered perhaps another strategy here. I've looked at the ways in which business logics failed business itself. I have asked, as well, what a more expansive approach to mobilizing such discourses might look like. This discussion underscores, I hope, the importance of leaving critical discourses open to ventilation and inter-penetration. We need to ask what kinds of problems we want to solve in education—and make them matter to people. Schools are, in fact, in trouble. The Right is in fact offering an answer. And they do so with a hyper-clear language of efficiency and business. Should it be surprising that their initiatives tend to garner public support? In the end, progressives need to engage in what Gramsci calls a "war of position," challenging the Right while offering our own compelling solutions. We must get beyond cheerleading only to the converted, not remaining comfortable in and within our disciplinary and institutional homes. We must begin to think in new ways—making new connections while strengthening old alliances.

An example of such disarticulation and re-articulation comes to mind, again from the realm of economics. Eighteenth Century philosopher Adam Smith is often hailed as the forefather of neo-liberal economics. His notion of the "invisible hand" evokes the near-mystical faith many neo-liberal economists have in the market—left unfettered, it will magically sort resources more efficiently and for the common good. In his recent autobiography, *The Age of Turbulence: Adventures in a New World* (2007), Allan Greenspan notes,

> Individuals who compete for private gain, [Smith] wrote, act as if "led by an invisible hand" to promote the public good. The metaphor of the invisible hand, of course, captured the world's imagination—possibly because it seems to impute a godlike benevolence and omniscience to the market, whose workings are in reality as impersonal as natural selection, which Darwin came along and described more than half a century later. (p. 262)

Greenspan speaks in reverential tones about Smith and he certainly has been claimed as something of an intellectual patron saint for many neo-liberals. Greenspan himself, in Smith's hometown of Kirkaldy, Scotland, evoked this notion of the invisible hand," noting that Smith was "a towering contributor to the development of the modern world … of what we now term free-market capitalism" (Buchan, 2007, p. 2).

Yet, the term "invisible hand" appeared only three times in all of Smith's writings. Biographer James Buchan writes in his book *The Authentic Adam Smith: His Life and Ideas* (2007),

> The phrase "invisible hand" occurs three times in the million-odd words of Adam Smith's that have come down to us, and on not one of those occasions does it have anything to do with free-market capitalism or awesome international transactions …. A close reading of *The Wealth of Nations* and other good evidence shows that Smith was no doctrinaire free trader. He approves certain monopolies and restraints on trade, export subsidies and restrictions, sumptuary laws, penal taxation, limits on the rate of interest and the issue of bank notes, compulsory qualifications for craftsmen, [etc] … The words *laisser faire* or *laissez faire* appear nowhere in his work. (pp. 2–3)

Buchan quotes from *The Wealth of Nations*, "civil government … is in reality instituted for the defense of the rich against the poor" (p. 3). Indeed, according to Buchan and others, Smith did not see economics as existing in a vacuum. If anything, *The Wealth of Nations* (originally published in 1776) is about how to best sort wealth in society for the common good. Smith's version of economics was not disconnected from a vision of what a strong, healthy civil society would look like. In fact, his earlier book, *The Theory of Moral Sentiments* (originally published in 1759) was about the nature of morality. Many argue that these two books cannot be separated—that his version of economics presupposed notions of morality. Smith's work clearly should not provide an "alibi" for rampant, "gloves off"super-capitalism. Again, the rise of neo-liberalism near-magically wiped away such concerns, leaving only a precise science made up of mathematical models that have become articles of faith to all adherents. Economics can be thought of as an autonomous science, disconnected from all other social, political, and cultural concerns. Re-embedding our notions of economics in the everyday lives of people—getting past the failures of "bottom line" thinking—seems the question now facing economists in the wake of neo-liberal economics' excesses.

Educators, I argue, need to take up similar questions in the wake of the failed business model of NCLB and other "bottom line" approaches to education. We need to ask what a more fully and deeply holistic vision of education might look like. For starters, this means looking past the prescribed notions of education—looking towards (as in my own past research) out-of-school learning curricula and sites (Dimitriadis, 2001, 2003, 2008). But more broadly, it means looking at education as one part of a social whole—one that cannot be abstracted from and pressed down upon in isolation. I recall here the important work of Jean Anyon. In her recent book, *Radical Possibilities: Public Policy, Urban Education, and a New Social Movement* (2005), she shows how difficult and futile it is to think about education and educational policy as disconnected from other kinds of policies. She argues for the mutual imbrication of pedagogical practices and policies and macroeconomic reform.

The "bottom line" approach to education favored by NCLB assumes a strong relationship between basic skills and social mobility—e.g., if students acquire a basic understanding of math and reading, they will be able to better compete in the job marketplace and achieve higher standards of living. On this model, a "basic skills" approach to schooling puts much burden on the schools themselves. In counter-distinction, Anyon argues that "macroeconomic policies like those regulating the minimum wage, job availability, tax rates, federal transportation, and affordable housing create conditions in cities that no existing educational policy or urban school reform can transcend" (p. 2). That is to say, one needs to be sober about the power of education policy alone to ameliorate social ills—including the widening gaps between rich and poor that Greenspan himself admits is a problematic effect of neo-liberal economic policy. A wider and more expansive notion of educational policy seems necessary—one that attends to issues such as affordable housing, minimum wage policy in a growing service economy, the often lack of efficient public transportation to those who must travel to far-out suburbs for jobs, etc. As Anyon writes,

> Policies such as minimum wage statutes that yield poverty wages, affordable housing and transportation policies that segregate low-income workers of color in urban areas and industrial and other job development in far-flung suburbs where public transit does not reach, all maintain poverty in city

> neighborhoods and therefore the schools. In order to solve the systematic problems of urban education, then, we need not only school reform but the reform of these public policies. If, as I am suggesting, the macroeconomy deeply affects the quality of urban education, then perhaps we should rethink what "counts" as educational policy. (p. 3)

Educational policy, it seems, must be embedded in a broader set of economic policies.

Educators, in conclusion, must avoid the pitfalls of "bottom line" thinking. Such thinking has not put the economy in the service of the social good. Such thinking led to the aberrations of the late-nineties and beyond. We must think about education as existing in the context of young people's lives and the social whole. The key here is that we do not need only to appeal to people's sense of morality when making such arguments. We can point to the "spectacular flameouts" of Enron and other such companies that were neo-liberal darlings. We can work hard to avoid a "testing bubble" which will serve only to damage the long-term health of our school system and young people.

REFERENCES

Altman, D. (2007). *Connected: 24 hours in the global economy*. New York: Farrar, Straus, & Giroux.

Anyon, J. (2005). *Radical possibilities: Public policy, urban education, and a new social movement*. New York: Routledge.

Apple, M. (2004). Schooling, markets, and an audit culture. *Educational Policy, 18*(4), 614–621.

Apple, M. (2006). *Educating the "right" way*. New York: Routledge.

Aronowitz, S. (2005). *Just around the corner*. Philadelphia: Temple University Press.

Buchan, J. (2007). *The authentic Adam Smith: His life and ideas*. New York: WW Norton.

Burrough, B. (1990). *Barbarians at the gate: The fall of RJR Nabisco*. New York: Harper & Row.

Chang, H. (2008). *Bad samaritans: The myth of free trade and the secret history of capitalism*. New York: Bloomsbury Books.

Chubb, J., & Moe, T. (1990). *Politics, markets, and America's schools*. Washington, DC: Brookings Institute.

Denby, D. (2005). *American sucker*. Boston: Back Bay Books.

Dimitriadis, G. (2008). *Studying urban youth culture*. New York: Peter Lang.

Dimitriadis, G. (2003). *Friendship, cliques, and gangs: Young black men coming of age in urban America*. New York: Teachers College Press, Columbia University.

Dimitriadis, G. (2001). *Performing identity/performing culture: Hip hop as text, pedagogy, and lived practice*. New York: Peter Lang.

Dimitriadis, G., & Carlson, D. (2003). *Promises to keep*. New York: Routledge.

Eichenwald, K. (2005). *Conspiracy of fools: A true story*. New York: Broadway Books.

Fulcher, J. (2004). *Capitalism: A very short introduction*. New York: Oxford.

Giroux, H. (2005). *Border crossing: Cultural workers and the politics of education* (2nd ed.). New York: Routledge.

Giroux, H. (2005b). *The terror of neoliberalism*. New York: Routledge.

Greenspan, A. (2007). *The age of turbulence: Adventures in a new world*. New York: Penguin.

Hargreaves, A. (2003). *Teaching in the knowledge society*. New York: TC Press.

Harvey, D. (2003). *The new imperialism*. New York: Oxford.

Harvey, D. (2005). *A brief history of neoliberalism*. New York: Oxford.

Head, S. (2003). *The new ruthless economy*. Oxford: Oxford University Press.

Hess, F., & Petrilli, M. (2006). *No child left behind primer*. New York: Peter Lang.

Jensen, M. (1998). *Foundations of organizational strategy*. Cambridge, MA: Harvard University Press.
Johnson, D., & Johnson, B. (2002). *High stakes*. Walnut Creek, CA: Rowman and Littlefield.
Jones, G., Jones, B., & Hargrove, T. (2003). *The unintended consequences of high stakes testing*. Walnut Creek, CA: Rowman & Littlefield.
Kessler, A. (2003). *Wall street meat: Jack Grubman, Frank Quattrone, Mary Meeker, Henry Blodget, and me*. New York: Escape Velocity Press.
Klein, N. (2007). *The shock doctrine: The rise of disaster capitalism*. New York: Henry Holt.
Lowenstein, R. (2004). *Origins of the crash*. New York: Penguin Books.
McLaren, P. (2005). *Capitalists & conquerors: A critical pedagogy against empire*. Lanham, MD: Rowman & Littlefield Publishers.
McLaren, P., & Farahmandpur, R. (2005). *Teaching against global capitalism and the new imperialism*. Lanham, MD: Rowman & Littlefield Publishers.
McLean, B., & Elkind, P. (2003). *The smartest guy in the room: The amazing rise and scandalous fall of Enron*. New York: Portfolio.
Moe, L. (2002). *Schools, vouchers, and the American public*. Washington, DC: Brookings Institute.
Partnoy, F. (2003). *Infectious greed: How deceit and risk corrupted the financial markets*. New York: Henry Holt.
Piven, F. (2006). *The war at home: The domestic costs of Bush's militarism*. New York: The New Press.
Reich, R. (1991). *The work of nations : Preparing ourselves for 21st century capitalism*. New York: W.W. Knopf.
Reich, R. (2001). *The future of success*. New York: W.W. Knopf.
Reich, R. (2007). *Supercapitalism: The transformation of business, democracy, and everyday life*. New York: Knopf.
Saltman, K. (2005). *The edison schools*. New York: Routledge.
Shiller, R. (2006). *Irrational exuberance*. New York: Currency.
Smith, A. (1981). *An inquiry into the nature and causes of the wealth of nations*. Indianapolis, IN: Liberty Classics. (Originally published in 1776).
Smith, A. (1982). *The theory of moral sentiments*. Indianapolis, IN: Liberty Classics. (Originally published in 1759).
Stiglitz, J. (2004). *The roaring nineties: A new history of the world's most prosperous decade*. New York: W. W. Norton.
Stiglitz, J. (2006). *Making globalization work*. New York: W.W. Norton.
Stiglitz, J., & Bilmes, L. (2008). *The three trillion dollar war*. New York: W.W. Norton.
Weis, L. (2004). *Class reunion*. New York: Routledge.
Whitte, C. (2006). *Crash course: A radical plan for improving public education*. New York: Riverhead Trade.

Greg Dimitriadis
Graduate School of Education
The University of Buffalo
SUNY

DENNIS CARLSON

3. CONFLICTS OF THE EDUCATION FACULTY

Derrida and Democratic Cultural Politics in the Postmodern University

> Where are we? Who are we in the university where apparently we are? What do we represent? Whom do we represent? Are we responsible? For what and to whom?"
>
> Jacques Derrida (2004a, p. 83)

The contribution of Jacques Derrida to a democratic and progressive cultural politics of education is just beginning to be explored, and a number of factors stand in the way of any easy appropriation of Derrida's work (Bennington, 2000; Fagan, Glorieux, Hasimbegovic, and Suetsugu, 2007; and Mouffe, 1996). First, there is the problem of translating Derrida. I do not mean by this only the difficulty of translating from French to English, although Derrida always contended these are considerable. I mean more particularly the problem of making sense of Derrida's way of writing and speaking. He writes in a deliberately subversive rhetorical style, designed to interrupt our desire for a smooth translation of meaning from text to reader, or for words that are "pinned-down" and stable in meaning, or that claim to represent an external, "real" referent. For Derrida (1983), this disruption of what he called *logocentric* discourse is an important political project. Logocentric discourse speaks in the voice of an autonomous reason, disinterestedly dissecting arguments by pinning them down upon a table and arranging their parts in a logical sequence, so that the "body" of the argument is clearly visible, all its interrelated organs and appendages identified and marked, and all coming together in a whole, unified "body" that is knowable and intelligible. Logocentrism is also, for Derrida, inseparable from a dominant "thinking" of the world in terms of binary oppositions, in which one side of the binary is understood to totally exclude its "Other," and in which one side is privileged over the other, for example, as "reason" is privileged over "irrationality," "truth" over "myth," "objectivity" over "subjectivity," and so on. Logocentric discourse is the discourse of an authoritative "rational" voice that holds itself up against the "irrationality" of the public; and because of this Derrida viewed it as inherently undemocratic.

At the same time, Derrida never sought to champion *Mythos* over *Logos* (Carlson, 2002). Mythocentrism may be characterized as the binary opposite of logocentrism, and thus a type of narrative voice that takes for granted a common-sense mythology of the world and speaks only of personal, subjective experience. Derrida came to believe that neither *Logos* nor *Mythos* is democratic on its own;

Z. Leonardo (ed.), Handbook of Cultural Politics and Education, 87–109.

although his project, like Nietzsche's, was to restore a lost balance between the two, or more accurately disrupt the borders that separate them. For this reason he often appears to associate democratic cultural politics with a re-valuing of what has been labeled as "irrational" within normalizing, logocentric culture. In fact, he continued to call himself a philosopher, and to believe that philosophy had an important role to place in sustaining democratic traditions. He just demanded that philosophy be deconstructed and reconstructed so that it was able to call into question its own mythology of autonomous reason. For Derrida, as for those generally associated with poststructuralism and cultural studies, democratic cultural politics can only be rebuilt be disassembling the Enlightenment mythology of an autonomous reason and revealing the inseparability of reason, culture, power, and action.

Because Derrida deconstructed one of the primary groundings of liberalism—this belief in an autonomous reasoning, tied to a narrative of progress through reason—his cultural politics cannot legitimately be considered liberal, even if some of his critics have identified them as such.[1] Critical theorists influenced by the Frankfurt School of ideological critique and "demystification" have been most deeply suspicious of Derrida, who refused to be disciplined by the modernist binaries of truth production and who even dared to call into question the supposed radical politics of a critical theory that is logocentric. For these critics, deconstructionism is a postmodern, bourgeois ideology that privileges personal meaning and difference at the expense of a serious analysis of the material forces and structures of oppression in capitalist society (Eagleton, 1981; Jameson, 1991). But again, it would be a mistake to read Derrida as an anti-Marxist, or in opposition to the project of critical theory. In *Specters of Marx* (1994), he identifies Marxism as a great "inheritance," from which much can be learned that has application to contemporary democratic cultural politics. "We are inheritors," he proclaimed; but that should not mean we receive something solid, unified, and already formed as an inheritance (p. 94). The unity of an inheritance, if there is one, "can only consist in the injunction to reaffirm by choosing." To choose an inheritance is to "filter, select, criticize ... [and] to sort out among several of the possibilities which inhabit the same injunction" (p. 40). Through such a choosing, an inheritance becomes a living memory, open to being worked and reworked and stitched together with other inheritances through a form of "memory work" (Derrida, 2001b).

To choose is also to assume responsibility for an inheritance—and here Derrida's cultural politics become inseparable from what he called an "ethico-political" horizon. To speak and write of responsibility as a call to respond may seem inconsistent with the usual poststructural erasure, or at least de-centering, of human agency in the emphasis upon truth as a discursive production, and human subjects as less the producers of language than produced by it. Certainly, Derrida did not mean to imply that ethical choices and ethical responses may never be made outside of a discourse, an inheritance. But he continued to return in his work to the idea of the "calling," a call to assume responsibility for an inheritance by using it and re-working it. In a day in which progressive culture politics in the U.S. is all about identity politics and material interests, there is something at least subversive, and perhaps radical, about an appeal to ethical responsibility. At the same time, Derrida was interested in deconstructing the Kantian ethics of the Enlightenment, in which unconditional moral principles were supposedly derivable through an autonomous, philosophical reasoning. These unconditional moral and ethical principles could then be translated into law by the state and used to guide the development of public life. For Derrida, universalistic and unconditional ethical principles do have their part to play in democratic cultural politics. But no set of unconditional, universalistic ethics can account for the "singularity" of events and the radical "undecidability: of choices in a world in which much remains unknowable and unintelligible. Furthermore, ethics is inseparable from power, and a Kantian cultural politics that attempts to separate ethics and power, to let the former rule over the latter, is ultimately doomed to failure. In formulating a post-Kantian democratic ethics, Derrida was particularly indebted to Levinas (Critchley, 1999). For Levinas, ethics is performative. It is performed by calling into question the borders that constitute the Self and which regulate its relations with otherness or alterity. Ethics is what Levinas called an "exposure"—corporeal and temporal—to the Other. It is performed in the abode, or what Bourdieu terms *habitus*, of the familiar and the everyday as an exposure to that which is foreign, the Other who has crossed over the border of alterity and confronts us with a claim to be recognized. A democratic responsibility, Derrida believed, requires an exposure that cannot be contained or predetermined by linear, borders that separate Same and Absolute Other.

All of these concerns came together in Derrida's speaking and writing on the responsibility of the professoriate in the modern, public university. In what follows I want to explore Derrida's thoughts on the professoriate as they apply to an analysis of the education faculty, and more particularly those education faculty who bring critical, cultural perspectives to bear on educational issues and teacher education—which I will call the "foundational faculty of education." This faculty includes, most notably, the "social foundations of education" faculty—working within disciplines of philosophy, sociology, anthropology, and history of education, and teaching "foundations" courses in teacher licensure programs. This faculty also includes those working in diverse interpretive communities and "fields" in education—including curriculum, educational policy, educational leadership, comparative education, multicultural education, and critical pedagogy—who are influenced by the liberal arts disciplines and the cultural studies movement in the liberal arts academy. Here we might include a whole array of "post-foundational" faculty, influenced by: Critical Race Theory, post-colonialism, Gramscian theory, various strands of feminist and queer theory, and eco-justice theory, and so on. These are "gaze-switching" movements that turn a critical, deconstructive eye back on the Western, philosophical foundations of education (Mills, 1997). At the same time, they share with "foundational" faculty a common grounding in the liberal arts, and they participate in debates going on in the liberal arts having to do with the politics of "truth" and reason. All of these foundational faculties of education agree that the liberal arts—broadly defined and reconstructed in democratic ways—should be a primary grounding for teacher education; and they decry the narrowly technical and pragmatic orientation that currently guides teacher education.

If the university must be "re-thought" and reconstructed in important ways as part of a democratic cultural politics, we now approach this responsibility with some urgency. First, in post-9/11 America we have witnessed the growth of a new McCarthyism in which politically progressive professors have become the new "enemy within," and with academic freedom under attack now more now than it has been in over half a century. Since foundational faculty of education typically employ forms of pedagogy and scholarship that are critical, anti-oppressive, and socially reconstructionist, they are inevitably involved in battles over academic freedom being waged throughout the academy, the state, and civil society. Second, and related to the attack upon academic freedom, we are witnessing an intensify-cation of efforts by the neo-liberal and neo-conservative state to bring the "applied" university faculty, and particularly those in teacher education, under much greater control through accrediting agencies such as the National Council for the Accreditation of Teacher Education (NCATE). By aligning teacher education courses with performance-base certification standards, and with new forms of assessing pre-service teachers such as PRAXIS, the teacher education faculty is losing control over its own curriculum. At the same time, teacher education faculty are expected to compete for funding dollars from the federal government based on narrowly-prescriptive funding categories, linked to the test-driven reform discourse of "No Child Left Behind" (NCLB). Not only is NCLB "dumbing down" the education many young people receive to a set of basic skills, tied to a new service-industry and low-skill labor force, it is also having the effect of "dumbing down" teacher education through a narrow emphasis upon technical pedagogical knowledge and performance outcomes (Carlson, 2007).

All of this is related, in turn, to developments impacting through the university today and that lead critics such as Bill Readings (1996) to argue that the idea of the modern public university, founded upon the principle of reason and dedicated to public service, is in ruins. Henry Giroux (2007) writes that the university is in "chains," which keep it captive of elite economic, political, and military interests. For Derrida, the university is losing control of its borders so that "one no longer knows with what concept one can still rule it" (p. 89). It lacks a coherent structure and essential responsibility. Not only is the idea of a public university that serves the public being emptied of democratic meaning; so too is the idea of the university as an institutional space responsible to reason and truth. But Derrida warns against investing too much energy in re-building borders that are rupturing and hemorrhaging. For one thing this is likely to be a futile effort; and for another the old "thinking" and structuring of the university came with its own set of problems and conflicts. Derrida presents an image of a democratic university to come as neither responsible to an autonomous reason, nor to a bureaucratic and corporatist state, but rather to particular interpretive communities engaged in discourse that is also politically performative.

Derrida developed his thoughts on the cultural politics of the university and the responsibility of the faculty most extensively and systematically in "*Mochlos*: Conflict of the Faculties," originally published in 1992 and republished in a collection of essays titled *Eyes of the University: Right to Philosophy 2* (2004). The *Mochlos* essays were delivered as lectures at Columbia University in 1980, in receipt of an honorary degree; and they include a defense of leaving his own doctoral thesis uncompleted and undefended until he was 50, as a revolt against the logocentric rhetorical norms of the "standard thesis." At the heart of these essays is Derrida's deconstructive reading of Kant's last great work, *The Conflict of the Faculties* (1996) originally published in 1798. Here Derrida finds the great philosopher of the Enlightenment attempting to "think" the ground upon which the modern university might be built, although it is perhaps not coincidental (Derrida suggests) that Kant's rational "thinking" of the university turned out to look remarkably like the state university that had already begun to develop within Prussia, with the University of Berlin where Kant taught the prime example. To what extent are we inheritors of this Kantian grounding of the modern, state university in service to both reason and the public? To what extent should we question this inheritance, given that the Kantian university was designed to be consistent with rule by an enlightened despot? How might we democratically re-ground the university and the responsibility of the faculty without altogether abandoning this inheritance?

I want to turn now to address these questions specifically with regard to what I have called the foundational faculty of education, by situating that faculty and within the context of a broader discussion of Derrida's *Mochlos* essays and Kant's *Conflict of the Faculties*. My basic argument is that the foundational faculty of education occupy a contradictory location in the Kantian university, caught between liberal arts and applied faculties. To the extent that the Kantian "thinking" of the modern, public university is still very much part of a "living memory," foundational faculty of education are faced with the prospect of have to decide which side of a border they occupy. Is there responsibility to the "applied" education faculty or to the liberal arts faculty? To frame the question in an either/or manner is to stay within a binary oppositional system of limits that divides theory and practice, thinking and doing. This blocks the fuller democratic potential of the foundational faculty of education as a border-crossing faculty. To realize that potential, and respond to the call of a democratic responsibility for public education and teacher education, I argue that the foundational faculty of education will need to cross these borders within the university, and simultaneously cross the established borders between the "inside" and the "outside" of the university. But as I said, the Kantian thinking of the university is still very much with us—for good and bad. Consequently, in exploring the cultural politics of the foundational faculty of education in a post-modern age, I want to consider the foundational faculty as positioned on each side of a Kantian border within the university that separates "lower" or liberal arts faculty and "higher" or applied faculty. Then, I return at the end to develop the idea of a cultural politics of border crossing, based on a responsibility to reasoning within overlapping interpretive communities and speaking and writing in multiple voices.

THE "LOWER" FACULTY AND BATTLES OVER ACADEMIC FREEDOM

Kant recognized that German public university was a creature already, at the beginning, ridden with conflicts and contradictions, a creature that could not possibly survive unless a way could be found to logically resolve, or at least manage, these conflicts and contradictions. So he sets himself the task of doing just that, applying a philosophical reason to the problem, to bring it within the realm of a mathematic topology. He maps the university in terms of defined and identifiable borders that separate binary oppositions caught in a dialectic—although for Kant this dialectic is understood to produce merely conflict, not transformation or victory by one side. It is a conflict he felt could be managed by an enlightened state through the securing and policing of borders: those that separate an "inside" from an "outside" of the university, and those that separate "higher" or applied faculty from "lower" (and thus non-applied) liberal arts faculty. The modern, public university had to serve the public, and this was to be the responsibility of the higher faculty. But it also had to serve the principle of critical reason in its "pure," theoretical form, and this meant it needed to be governed by norms of academic freedom, of "answering" for reason and "obeying" its call, of "rendering" to reason in the sense of a debt, obligation, and imperative (Kant, 1966, p. 255). This was to be the responsibility of the "lower" or philosophical faculty, which today we would call the liberal arts or arts and sciences faculty. One might say, to begin with, that as a member of the philosophy faculty, Kant is hardly the spokesperson for an autonomous, disinterested reason—although he will claim to be. His biases against the higher faculty are hardly disguised in the text, and he often refers to them as "merchants" or "businessmen" of learning rather than real academics. So much of Kant's effort is directed to building a case for the liberal arts and sciences faculty against efforts by members of the applied faculty to claim more power and more "space" within the university, at the expense of the liberal arts. This is the central conflict that he identifies within the university, and one that puts the liberal arts faculty at a disadvantageous, for it cannot count on public support.

Kant refers to the liberal arts faculty as the "lower" faculty because it is situated deep within the protective borders of the university. He assigns to the Faculty of Philosophy the responsibility of founding the lower faculty upon reason, and dividing it into two divisions: "historical sciences" (history, geography, linguistics, and humanities) and "pure rational sciences" (mathematics, philosophy, and the natural sciences). The enlightened state, Kant argues, is to curtail its own power over this faculty and even guarantee its academic freedom because it is in its interests to see that the truth "manifests itself," even if that truth has no direct or immediate application, and even if it is unpopular. Right away, one can't help but be struck by the naiveté behind such a hope, and what a hope it is, a hope that an enlightened ruler, a philosopher king, would emerge upon the historical stage out of the Enlightenment, prepared to take on responsibility for protecting the academic freedom of the liberal arts faculty because that was the enlightened thing to do, in the long run best interests of "the people." The Platonic idea of an enlightened despot is, of course, an oxymoron, yet one that Kant never stopped believing in, and he used this idea to legitimate the absolute sovereignty of the Bavarian monarchy, believing that the monarchy would protect his academic freedom. Aside from his political naiveté, Kant's concern with making academic freedom compatible with rule by a despotic sovereign leads him to place so many restrictions on it that it ceases to pose any threat to the established order.

Given all this, it is ironic that Kant presents himself as the great champion of academic freedom in *Conflict of the Faculties*. He begins that text by quoting a letter of censure he received from the Prussian King for something he had published, followed by his own letter in defense of his academic freedom. Because these letters will play such a central role in setting out the terms and conditions of his later argument in support of the academic freedom of the lower faculty, I want to refer to them in some detail. They also suggest that behind Kant's reasoned argument lurked some very personal concerns and interests. His problems began, it seems, when he made some critical comments about the Theological faculty, which was a "higher," applied faculty engaged in preparing both ministers licensed by the state church and school teachers licensed by the state education ministry. As an applied faculty, the theological faculty placed a strong emphasis upon a curriculum that taught students the skills of organizing and delivering effective sermons and lectures. Kant had made the mistake of remarking that if the theological faculty prepared teachers the way they prepared ministers, then no students "would let themselves be converted by teachers like that" (Kant, 1966, 239). Of course, as Michel Foucault (1978) has helped us recognize, the preparation of public school teachers and church pastors and priests has been linked so closely historically because teachers have been invested with a form of pastoral authority borrowed from the clergy. As Michael Apple (2007) has observed, teacher preparation programs also have promoted the "official knowledge" contained in textbooks as the "word of god" and thus not to be questioned.

So Kant makes a good point, but one that he could have expected would get him in trouble. In 1788, King Frederick William II of Prussia, acting under pressure from the theological faculty, issued an edict of censorship that prohibited public teaching or writing in opposition to official church doctrine. Shortly thereafter, Kant published a philosophical treatise titled, *Religion Within the Boundaries of Mere Reason*, in which he had sought to put religious doctrine to the test of reason, to determine what was consistent with universalistic ethical principles and what could be dismissed as mere dogma. It is this treatise which, when brought to the attention of the king by the theological faculty, was made the cause for a royal reprimand in 1794. That reprimand, which says so much in so few words, Kant quotes in its entirety. The king begins:

> Our most high person has long observed with great displeasure how you misuse your philosophy to distort and disparage many of the cardinal and basic teachings of the Holy Scriptures and of Christianity… We expected better things of you, as you yourself must realize how irresponsibly you have acted against your duty as a teacher of youth and against our paternal purpose…. We demand that… in the future, to avoid our highest disfavor, you will be guilty of no such fault, but rather, in keeping with your duty, apply your authority, and your talents to the progressive realization of our paternal purpose (Kant, 1996, p. 240).

Does this letter, from another historical era, written by a despot, still speak to us today, if now in a softer and less obviously "paternal" state voice?

And what can we say of Kant's self-defense, if indeed that is what it is? He begins by saying that he intends to "put before your Majesty proof of my obedience." His argument will rest on the defense that he never really was a disobedient royal subject, and that he was wrongly accused of something he would never do. As to the charge that as a teacher of impressionable youth, he needed to censor in his teaching any statement or thread of argument that might lead youth astray, he responds: "As a teacher of youth... I never have and never could have mixed any evaluation of the Holy Scriptures and of Christianity into my lectures" (240). He used, after all, the standard texts and "these texts do not and cannot contain a single heading referring to the Bible or Christianity." He has always, he wrote, "censured and warned against the mistake of straying beyond the boundaries of the science at hand, or mixing one science with another" (p. 241). Kant agrees to this restriction, to not bring his thoughts about religious doctrine into his teaching of philosophy, to in effect restrict the teaching of theology to the theological faculty and the teaching of philosophy to the philosopher faculty. Kant goes further to stipulate that within each department in the lower faculty, a core curriculum of canonical texts be established designed to ensure that the nation's youth are not exposed to anything improper. Faculty members are to stick to an established body of knowledge and not interject their own views into their teaching.

By ceding ground on teaching, Kant then seeks to establish the basis for a more limited academic freedom with regard to research and scholarship, which brings us back to the treatise on religion and reason, for which he had been reprimanded. He asserts in his defense that he has done nothing to harm the established religion of the fatherland because the scholarly publication in question "is not at all suitable for the public" (p. 241). It is, first of all, "unintelligible" to the general public, a "closed book" that the masses would not care to open. It is "only a debate among scholars of the faculty," he pleads, of which the public, in its ignorance, will take no notice. Kant thus establishes academic freedom of scholarship and writing as a freedom only within the borders of the university or the academy, using an esoteric linguistic code that that only a few professors and graduate students can decode. It is an academic freedom to be grounded in the presumption that the great bulk of the public is not only illiterate but, in Kant's view, "idiots" as well, not capable of grasping the kind of complex arguments and language that academics use. The irony of Kant's "defense" of academic freedom is that he transforms an unconditional right into a "right" so constrained and so submissive that in the end it makes its peace with the power of despotism.

Derrida observes with irony that the reproductive force of authority gets along quite well with scholarly works whose encoded content presents itself as revolutionary, "provided that they respect the rights of legitimation, the rhetoric and the institutional symbolism that defuses and neutralizes everything that comes from outside the system" (2004a, p. 122). This is, of course, a recurring theme in Derrida, the argument that rhetorical style and voice come with a politics. The general rhetorical style of the academy has been what Derrida called *logocentric*, a reference to Plato's attempt to ground truth upon a formal analytic style, in a dialectical development of an argument that proceeds toward a unified, knowable, truth or *logos*.

Anyone who has ever had their writing and speaking disciplined in such a logocentric fashion in their schooling knows that part of speaking and writing in a *logocentric* manner involves taking yourself—the speaker—out of the picture and the argument. Derrida suggests that learning to "bracket" or perform a phenomenological *epoche'* on the world being studied is not just an effective way of getting at the truth. It is a way of building a rhetorical argument that is in agreement with the borders, and the border contracts, which circumscribe academic freedom and scholarship. The border between "inside" and "outside" the university is both a result of and a precondition of an epistemology of bracketing.

The system of limits within which Kant situates academic freedom ensures that bracketing is privileged as a way of research, a way of stepping outside the frame of the everyday lifeworld, and fixing a gaze on it from behind the secure borders of the university. By bracketing the everyday lifeworld, professors learn that they are outside of it, in a privileged space of reason. Brackets and borders are thus one and the same thing. They serve to remove the intellectual from the real world of cultural politics going on inside the frame of everyday life, and thus "outside" the university. In such conditions it should hardly be surprising that the idea of a public intellectual still faces much resistance within the liberal arts academy, particularly since, Derrida notes, a lack of attention has been paid in the academy to the "problem of its own phenomenological enunciation," to the necessity of using a language "that could not itself be submitted to the *epoche*," that was not apparently "in the world" (2004a, p. 118). If that was still the case when Derrida spoke at Columbia University in 1980, it is less so today, thanks in large major to cultural studies movement that Derrida championed. The result of not questioning the *epoche*, he argued, was a paradoxical transformation of a supposedly universalistic discourse into a quasi-private, insider's language based on the presumption that "to publish, popularize, or divulge it to the general public… would necessarily corrupt it" (p. 99). To speak in public would involve an action by Kant's definition, and the lower faculties are not to act. They are to think–and thereby to judge between the true and the false, the just and the unjust—but they are not to act upon this thinking in any way that impacts the public. Here we see the governing theory-practice binary is also implicated in the regulation and policing of liberal arts discourse, without any apparent recognition that all speaking and writing is an action, a performance, a way of doing something. What, then, is such a "pure" academic language performing? Derrida's answer is that it is performing its own "uselessness," its own uninvolvement in the world—which is just what the powers that be want it to perform.

There was a time in the 1960s and early 1970s (although I do not mean to over-romanticize it) when progressive professors and graduate students articulated a more expansive conception of academic freedom by reconceptualizing theory and practice as *praxis*. At that historical moment, the borders between inside and outside the university were ruptured and the Kantian topology of the university called into question. By the mid-1970s, a conservative restorational politics began to grip the U.S., forged out of a backlash politics against campus and urban "unrest" and "excesses" of the 1960s. In reaction, progressive academics—and this was true in education as in other fields—began to retreat once more to the system of limits which Kant had placed upon academic freedom, to restrict it to an intra-university discourse among other academics in one's discipline, encoded in an "insider's" language. In critical educational studies, a quite sophisticated and complex neo-Marxist theory of social and economic reproduction began to develop in this academic space; and in subsequent years other complex theories have emerged—everything from feminist theories to post-colonial theories. Somewhat ironically, while newer poststructural and cultural studies theorists, including Derrida, have recognized that the language of theory can never be separated from a social and cultural practice, and thus a politics, they have themselves been open to the charge of constructing a very esoteric, insider's language that is inaccessible across the borders of the university (Carlson & Apple, 1998). Certainly, Derrida's writing is often considered almost inaccessible to a non-specialist reader. His response to this criticism has been that while "everything must be done to come close to...accessibility," academics should "never totally renounce the demands proper to the discipline. The struggle to bring the "specialist reader" and the "non-specialist reader" into dialogue is, for Derrida, a two-way street, involving a responsibility on the part of citizens in the public as well as academic scholars (Derrida, 2004b, pp. 414–415). Once more, his response is to seek another option other than having to choose between speaking an esoteric, "bracketed" discourse or the language of everyday life, a response that calls on each to be responsible for negotiating a dialogue.

These shifts in the discourse and practice of academic freedom indicate, as Stephen Aby (2007) argues, that academic freedom has been a "contested terrain" in the U.S. The recent dismissal of Professor Ward Churchill at the University of Colorado is a good case in point, although it demonstrates just how difficult the battle is for progressives in an age of university capitulation to conservative social groups in alliance with elements in the neo-conservative state. Churchill's "sin," as you probably know, was that he wrote a short, accessible essay in the days immediately after 9/11 in which he challenged the dominant media narrative of "innocent Americans," suggesting that there were no innocent Americans to the extent that they tacitly lent their support to a system of global capitalism, military domination, and cultural hegemony that oppressed many non-Western people.[2] This was, and still is, an absolutely essential point to make. Americans need to engage and question what it means to be innocent and also who is the victim in the global "War on Terrorism," and what it might mean to respond through an openness to the Other rather than through scapegoating and demonizing. The role of education from a democratic progressive standpoint is to destroy such innocence and naivete, and to call on young people to assume responsibility for their own innocence.

Churchill got in trouble because he did not stay within the Kantian system of limits, which suggests just how much that system of limits is alive and well in the postmodern university. If Churchill had not brought his scholarship into the public, and in such an overtly political fashion, if he had only published his ideas, no matter how radical, in refereed scholarly journals in his discipline of ethnic studies, if he had only kept his views on 9/11 out of the public discourse and his teaching—then (one can imagine Kant saying) his academic freedom would have been absolute and unconditional. Still, some things have changed. Because professors in the U.S. have fought for academic freedom, and a more inclusive form of academic freedom than envisioned by Kant, Churchill could not be dismissed from the faculty for what he wrote or taught, or even where he published it. He would be tried and found guilty within the university on grounds Kant established as legitimate, concerning breeches of ethical codes of conduct in scholarship, including plagiarism and failure to adequately cite sources. None of these charges was ever substantiated in a public proceeding, but the university, under pressure from conservative social groups and state political leaders, had what it needed to revoke Churchill's tenure. Churchill's case is not alone, unfortunately, and these attacks on academic freedom, which is to say these attempts to role back academic freedom to its Kantian limits, call for an urgent response. Perhaps we too have been too innocent, rather naively believing that we have certain rights guaranteed by both law and tradition, and that political leaders and university officials are committed to protecting academic freedom in an expansive, democratic progressive sense. Derrida called on us to be less innocent about academic freedom, which also means more responsible for protecting and extending democratic discourses of academic freedom associated with speaking and writing as public intellectuals. This requires that progressive intellectuals re-think their positioning "deep" within the borders of the university, to recognize themselves as "ex-posed" subjects, constituted by borders that are also cuts and incisions, borders that bleed and contaminate both "inside" and "outside" (Kamuf, 1991, pp. xvi–xviii).[3]

The academic freedom that Derrida was concerned with preserving is thus quite different, even oppositional to, the kind of academic freedom Kant sought to construct for the liberal arts faculty. That latter discourse and practice of academic freedom has not served to advance democratic projects so much as block such an advancement. Those today who would seek to preserve the Kantian discourse of academic freedom in the liberal arts (and their forces are still considerable), exhibit a nostalgia for certain Enlightenment conceptions of autonomous reason and "thinking" as opposed to "acting," which refuses to interrogate the cultural interests served by such a discourse of reason and truth. Along with this, the "traditional" liberal arts intellectuals (as Gramsci also recognized) exhibit a fear of the "real world" which they seek to situate "outside" the university—a response that ultimately is doomed to failure, since the border that separates the university from the "real world" is an illusion. The "real world" is situated as a place of "applied" knowledge and looked-down upon with a certain disdain, from a position above; and this is the primary reason why traditional liberal arts faculty exhibit—as Kant surely did–an elitist disdain for applied faculty. At the same time, and in a contradictory fashion, the traditional liberal arts faculty becomes invested in the "idea of the university" and the idea that "ideas" can play a transformative role in society. So Kant comes to believe, naively, that "pure" reason stands outside of power and culture, capable of serving as an alternative force in organizing social institutions. Finally, Derrida faulted the traditional liberal arts faculty—as constituted by Kant's borders—for the language games it played, which performed "uselessness" outside of scholarly disciplinary communities. Traditional liberal arts faculty members publish in academic journals and speak in academic settings (such as conferences) as a form of career-building, without regard to the political implications or practical utility of their work. Or they exhibit a fear of what and who lies beyond the borders of the university. Or they are overly invested in the "idea" of the university as an autonomous space for transforming society (Martin, 1992, p. 27). All of this points, as Derrida contended, to the need to democratize the liberal arts in the process of reconstituting the idea of academic freedom.

THE "HIGHER FACULTY" AND THE CULTURAL POLITICS OF TEACHER EDUCATION

In Kant's thinking of the modern university, the applied or higher faculty is made responsible to the state and various interests groups in the public, and consequently the border that separates this faculty from the "outside" of the university is understood to be permeable—an open or porous border rather than a closed, policed one. Kant's higher faculties include law, medicine, and theology (charged with educating teachers as well as preachers), although today we could add faculties of business, engineering, social work and other fields and domains of research and teaching that are engaged in preparing professionals of one sort or another, and thus in giving-back to the state and the public a return on its investment. Kant recognizes that the state and the public cannot be expected long to support a university that is exclusively about the disinterested pursuit of truth without regard for its utility. Consequently, to secure the autonomy and academic freedom of the lower faculty, he is ready to offer up the higher faculty, to strip it of most vestiges of academic freedom and autonomy, to make it a servant of the state and of other powerful forces in civil society. He is willing to do this because he envisions a higher faculty responsible to a state ruled by an enlightened king, committed to the public good, who will listen to the advise of applied faculties and give them some autonomy to run their own "business," while always insisting that they must be obedient to the state in the last instance and respond to the demands of the people for answers to their problems (Kant, 1996, p. 256). In such an enlightened modern state, the responsibility of the higher faculty would be a duty, but one worth taking on as an ethical responsibility. One hears similar claims today, I am afraid, about the duty of teachers and teacher education faculty to serve the public through their dedicated commitment to leaving no child behind. The trouble with the Kantian "thinking" of the responsibility of the higher faculty in noblest terms, in terms of public service, is that it—once more—is naïvely hopeful. It assumes that the state will not use its power to turn responsibility into duty, and duty into compulsion by dictating what is to be taught, how it is to be taught, and what kind of research and scholarship counts for merit pay and tenure and promotion purposes.

As I have said, Kant believed that the best way to prepare teachers for the nation's new public schools would be to give them a good, well-rounded, liberal arts education, overseen by the lower faculty. Through such a preparation to teach, the teacher's duty (a duty to the state and the public) would be compatible with a responsibility to critical reason and truth, and teachers would be like philosophers, helping young people develop the capacity to reason, to recognize the difference between truth and opinion, and so on. Thus, teaching and pedagogy in the Kantian public school was to be grounded in critical reason, and in a Socratic dialogue organized around the reading and interpretation of texts. Of course, the Kantian model of teacher preparation did make some sense in an earlier time when those who went on to secondary schools were a privileged elite who studied a classical, liberal arts curriculum—as was the case throughout the 19th century, including in the U.S. This all changed during the early 20th century, when progressives argued that the education of future teachers needed to be organized around the "science" of education, by which they meant a scientific study of the curriculum, methods of instruction, and assessment of students—with an emphasis on the application of this knowledge in "normal" classrooms.

Democratic progressives such as Dewey and Counts were in agreement with the more mainstream, administrative progressives about one thing. The liberal arts could not be the basis for a democratic form of teacher education, or teaching, so long as it was grounded in a separation of "high" and "low" culture, theory and practice. What Dewey and other social reconstructionist progressives sought to develop at Columbia University Teachers College in the 1930s (with only limited success) was a new kind of teacher education program that integrated the liberal arts disciplines (through "foundations of education" courses) with applied "methods" classes in the service of a student-centered and community-centered curriculum. (Tozer, 1993). Unfortunately, the Teachers College model of teacher education, integrating theory and practice, critical reason and applied methods, did not prevail. Instead, the public debate over teacher education was framed in terms of a choice between an elitist liberal arts model and an applied model that supposedly served the public better. In fact, the applied, technical model of teacher education was more in line with the interests of a growing business-managerial, bureaucratic elite of administrative progressives, who wanted to bring the schools and teacher education under much tighter, top-down control, and make teacher education the servant of a system of schooling that was highly-bureaucratic and economically functionalist (Cuban, 1993; Tyack and Cuban, 1997). The "compromise" that emerged in teacher education the U.S. by mid-20th century was heavily weighted toward applied "methods" courses, largely devoid of theory, coupled with a few liberal arts-grounded courses (the "foundations of education") given a small, marginalized space and separated from the methods faculty by a replication of the border between higher and lower faculties. Now, even that marginalized space is a risk.

The central conflicts Kant identifies between the lower and higher faculties, a conflict replicated between "foundational" and "methods" faculty of education, is over turf. If the university is to be divided up between these two faculties, they are placed in an intractable war over the relative space each receives within the university. Kant's basic argument is that this is not a battle or war that the foundational, lower faculty can expect to win on their own. The applied faculty, after all, are aligned with powerful interest groups in civil society, and since they serve various interests groups directly, the state will be pressured by these groups to expand the role and influence of the higher faculty at the expense of the lower. This will be encouraged as well, by a widespread belief in the public that the lower faculty is "useless" and could even be eliminated in a university that truly served the public. For Kant, the public was misguided in these sentiments and could not be expected to understand the need for research and scholarship that was not aimed at applications in any direct way. He rested his hope in an enlightened despot who, like Plato's philosopher-king, would see the importance of philosophy and assume responsibility for protecting the role of the liberal arts within the public university. His fear, at the same time, was that the state would cave in to pressure from interest groups in the public who were interested only in applied, narrowly-utilitarian forms of knowledge production.

One might say that Kant's worst fears have come true. As Derrida argues, applied or technical faculties are increasingly responsible to "multinational military-industrial complexes," and "techno-economic networks" that organize through and around the state (2004a, p. 141). The "public" is, in this sense, an imagined public, constructed as a mask behind which new global interests are reshaping the university, "conquering" and "administratively dominating" it in order to secure its participation in the new global relations of power and domination (p. 93). The state, as a partner or global capitalism in this project, is advancing neo-liberal, "free" market models of competition and productivity within the academy—carried within the borders of the university through research and development programs, as "parasitic" technologies. The postmodern "public" university is fast becoming the "academic capitalism" university, privileging applied research, corporate sponsorships, global marketing of research and development efforts, and the generation of profits (Readings, 1996; Slaughter & Leslie, 1997). In this process, the applied faculty continues to grow at the expense of the liberal arts faculty, since it can best support claims to being "productive."

If we take this assessment seriously, then it has rather direct relevance in thinking about the reform movements and discourses of NCLB and NCATE, and how they impact on the education faculty. Behind the language of serving the public, and preparing teachers to be highly-trained professionals, we may identify a project of conquering and further administratively dominating teacher education to bring in into closer alignment with the interests and worldview of trans-national capitalism—interests having to do with preparing a new "world class" labor force, and interests in making public schools and teacher preparation programs more accountable to managerial technologies through what Roland Barthes (1972) has called the "quantification of quality." The new image of the intellectual—which Henry Giroux (2007) has called the "academic entrepreneur"– is based on a rejection of the images of both the traditional intellectual and the public intellectual. He observes:

> In the corporate university, academics are now expected to be "academic entrepreneurs," valuable only for the money and prestige they bring, and not for the education they can offer. Sacrificed in this transformation is any notion of higher education as a crucial public sphere in which critical citizens and democratic agents are formed.... (pp. 104–105)

These efforts at further colonizing and dominating the academy need to be appreciated within the context of a battle going on over the future of the public university, and in the face of considerable resistance by university faculty, including education faculty. The truth, of course, is that "methods" professors are really not the "Other" that liberal arts and foundations of education faculty have made them out to be. Most are progressives, appalled by what is happening to teacher education, and working to take back control of their field. Public school teachers have lost the battle over control of their work, but that battle is not yet decided at the university, where traditions of academic freedom run deep, even among applied faculty.

In spite of the fact that the battle is not yet lost in higher education, progressives cannot pretend that it is going well. Education faculty now face very powerful pressure from the state and state-sanctioned accrediting agencies like NCATE to align their teaching and scholarship with the mandates of NCLB. This means that more and more faculty lines are opening up that are technical in character, and junior faculty are expected to secure state research grants framed within the discursive parameters and of NCLB legislation. At the same time, tenure-track faculty lines are being replaced by more adjunct and instructor lines, with faculty hired to deliver a basically prepackaged course. The emergence of the internet university is only one example of this competition in higher education that is leading public universities to reduce professional preparation programs to a series of modules that can be "delivered" through the internet, and supervised by adjunct faculty. Within this environment, the number of foundational faculty of education has continued to decline as states have reduced or scaled-back the foundations of education requirement in teacher licensure programs.

The simultaneous marginalization and encapsulation of the foundational faculty of education in schools and colleges of education is also related to market forces that are forcing teacher education programs to compete with private degree-granting programs and research and development centers outside the university. If an education faculty will not compete to deliver the kind of techno-rational instruction and research mandated by the state and driven by the new competetiveness among universities and programs, then the state (and students) can always go somewhere else. The University of Oregon provides a good example of where the money is going. I do not want to single-out the University of Oregon and its College of Education unfairly, for what has been happening there in the age of NCLB has been happening elsewhere as well, if in less dramatic forms. At the University of Oregon, the educational faculty has been reorganized and partially reconstituted as a revenue-generating faculty, tied into state funds through research that directly (and narrowly) addresses the mandates of NCLB to raise achievement levels. Altogether, ten "outreach" centers connect education faculty to "evidence-based" research and development in area schools; and a strong priority is placed on grant-writing in faculty evaluation and promotion. Because of this, the University of Oregon College of Education can now boast on its webpage that it ranks first in the nation in faculty "productivity," with each faculty member bringing in, on average, over $700,000 dollars in grant monies per year. When foundational faculty of education are weighed and assessed according to their "profit"-generating potential within an NCLB discursive economy, they obviously cannot be expected to fare very well. Indeed, they lower the faculty average through their "unproductive" scholarship. At best, foundational faculty will be confined to what Derrida calls "little cells," spaces of a "growing confinement" (2004a, p. 167).

What is the responsibility of the foundational faculty of education in such times? That question has already been the basis for an extended conversation and debate within the "foundations of education"—as expressed through such groups as American Educational Studies Association (AESA), the largest group in the U.S. to represent the foundations of education faculty. Within that group the question has been framed in terms of a "seat at the table," in this case the table of NCATE as an accrediting agency. Should foundational faculty claim a seat at the table in NCATE to make sure that their interests and perspectives are represented in teacher education accreditation and licensing standards? The foundations faculty once had such a seat at the battle. But in the late 1990s, with the growing alignment of NCATE with a narrowly skill-based form of teacher education, and with NCATE raising the monetary cost of a seat at the table beyond the reach of what such a relatively small faculty could support, ties with NCATE were severed (Mueller 2006; Noblit 2002; Tozer and Miretszky 2000; Dottin, Jones, Simpson, and Watras 2005). What will be the cost of such a response? We must protest, as Derrida would say, the enclosure of the foundational faculty in a kind of "house arrest" (2004a, p. 170), a way of limiting its influence by confining it to a single class or two in an otherwise applied and technical teacher education program. But this protest cannot be expected to have much impact so long as the reign of technical rationality and corporatization continue in the university, so long as the liberal arts faculty is not seen as "productive," and so long as liberal arts teaching methods and curriculum are viewed as a more than a bit subversive and politically oppositional. Even philosophy, stripped of any overt politics, is subversive and oppositional in the context to the extent that it teaches critical rationality rather than compliance to official knowledge. Today, as cultural studies perspectives have begun to infuse the foundations of education—bringing with them a concern with cultural histories of racism, classism, patriarchy, and heteronormativity, and with counter-narratives of resistance—these politics are becoming even more overt and subversive. The irony, of course, is that this politics is contained, and thus de-radicalized, within the Kantian borders of the university.

CONCLUSION: THE UNIVERSITY TO COME

Derrida begins his concluding comments on Kant by saying he does not intent to offer any guidance as such, or suggest a way out of the conflict of the faculties. He writes: "You have wondered all along where…I was coming from, which side I was on in these conflicts: (1) to the right of the boundary or (2) to its left or (3) more probably….a tireless parasite moving in random agitation, passing over the boundary and back again" (2004a, p. 109). As I have said, each of these possible responses works within a specific system of limits that makes other options un-thinkable.

Kant chose the option of siding with the lower faculty, against the higher faculty and the "outside" of the university, and so his "solution" to the conflict of the faculties required an enlightened, protective despot to carry it out. His hope was that "[we] may indeed one day see the last become first," when an enlightened monarch might someday prefer the council of the lower, liberal arts faculty over the dutiful service of the higher, applied faculty (Kant, 1996, p. 59). That obviously cannot be the choice, or the hope, of democratic progressives in education. Nor can we afford to define our responsibility narrowly as "applied" education faculty, particularly in the age of NCLB and NCATE.

Derrida was both a visionary and a pragmatist, and he would have insisted that while we must be visionary in our effort at re-thinking the university and the responsibility of the faculty, we must be pragmatic in our response to the situation at hand. In some situations this might mean a strategy of defending borders against a looming danger on the "outside." Specifically, Derrida called upon progressives to vigorously defend academic freedom in the face of "outside" pressure from those on the political right to silence professors supposedly indoctrinating young, impressionable minds with their "politically correct" truths. In one of his last published dialogues (he died in 2004), Derrida expressed "regret that this American catchword ['politically correct'] has been imported to denounce everything that certain people don't like" (Derrida and Roudinesco, 2004, pp. 26–27). Indeed, he noted that the attempt to "put an end to all critical thought, all protest, all rebellion" by branding it "politically correct," was itself an example of a type of dogmatism and orthodoxy that could not put up with an opposition. By branding people "politically correct," the right has abused a term which has real meaning on both the orthodox right and left and turned it into a "facile technique for silencing all those who speak in the name of a just cause." He argued that progressives may legitimately acknowledge that "there are some fanatics in American Universities, as here in France...who would like to censor or exclude anything that doesn't conform to this 'political correctness,'" but that the denunciation of "political correctness" has been organized and manipulated to those on the political right (Derrida & Roudinesco, 2004, pp. 26–27).

So progressives will need to defend the border with the "outside" that provides a space of academic freedom, even as they begin to speak in the public and make their speech more performative, which involves disrupting the traditional border between the "inside" and the "outside" of the university. We must affirm a responsibility to academic freedom that is secured by defending the borders of the university and simultaneously cross over those borders by speaking and acting within public dialogues and conversations. Within the education faculty, this is, I believe, the particular responsibility of what I have called the foundational faculty of education, with closest connections to the liberal arts and to the historic memory of academic freedom. But we must also speak up for the academic freedom of "methods" and "applied" education faculty who are most at risk of losing control over what they teach and are being systematically silenced through the overlapping reform initiatives of NCLB and NCATE. I have argued, following Derrida, that as the borders of the university are being breached, the "inside" of the university is being re-assembled to more closely resemble the "outside." This translates into more closely resembling the marketplace and the neo-liberal state. As teacher education is being reorganized by the technologies of NCLB and NCATE, education faculty are reconceptualized as entrepreneurs expected to generate a "profit" by bringing in research grant monies for research that "pays off" in higher test scores for various groups of identified students.

At least in Kant's day, and in the late 19th century when universities like Columbia University were founded, it was possible, Derrida writes, "to debate together about the responsibility proper to the university," guided by a system of implicit axiomatics related to an essential calling. One could then "think the ground" on which the responsibility of various faculties was "determined, attained, or imposed" (2004a, pp. 89–90). Derrida was not certain that it was possible anymore to think the ground of the university, and so he feared that the idea of the university may become emptied of meaning. Still, he held out hope that the university might be re-grounded, for he believed passionately that the future of democracy depends on both the survival of the university and the re-grounding of the university. He returned to the Greek word *Mochlos* to refer to a type of critical, deconstructive questioning that can serve as a tool, both a lever prying loose the solid foundation under our feet and a catapult capable of lifting us to a new foundational space or grounding. A university needs a grounding; although clearly for Derrida, it does not need an originary, fixed, unshakable "foundation"—that of an autonomous reason. That foundation is crumbling now under our feet and does not represent a sufficient grounding for a democratic university to come. At the same time, to think beyond the Kantian system of limits does not mean to leave it totally behind, or dismiss it—as if that were even possible given that this is an inherited tradition. The university must be re-grounded, to be sure, but the alternative to a university grounded on the principle of autonomous reason is not a university grounded on irrationality or anti-rationality. Instead the inherited university tradition, with its liberal arts foundations, needs to "provide on its own foundational soil support for a leap toward another foundational place" (Derrida, 2004a, p. 110).

In such a re-grounding, the faculty would still be the "eyes" of the university, but now different kinds of eyes. Derrida was fascinated by the metaphor of the eye in Western metaphysics, both religious and secular, as a symbol of reason and enlightenment (Carlson, 2005). Christian religious art, as he demonstrated in his book, *Memoirs of the Blind* (1993), is full of Biblical characters—in both the "old" and "new" testaments–who were blind and now can see, or who are blinded in punishment for some sin, or who suddenly see the light.[4] Both religious and secular education in the West has been mythologized as a process of healing "blind" children by leading them toward the light—as in Plato's famous cave analogy. The eye of the Kantian Enlightenment fixed its gaze upon the world to reorder it according to a more rational, "purely" rational design. Derrida critiques Kant, and thus a certain tradition of Enlightenment thinking, for his naïve and ultimately irresponsible belief that the eye of reason can somehow ground the university—in opposition to political power and cultural heritage. Through universities responsible to reason and truth, the enlightened society was to be built, and that society would replace the age of politics. Philosophically, of course, this means that the Kantian Enlightenment followed in the political footsteps of Plato, footsteps that led to Napolean, the one who would claim the mantle of philosopher king and champion of the Enlightenment. Napolean is reported to have commented that "there are only two powers in the world, the sword and the mind. In the end, the sword is always conquered by the mind" (quoted in Camus, 1970, p. 134). How ironic, that the Napoleanic Code and the principle of reason would be brought to the people of Europe at the point of a sword. Reason, and the university upon which it is grounded, has never been separate and oppositional to political power and even the forces of domination. Progressives can no longer afford to be so naïve as to believe that the university can be founded upon these eyes. Nor can the professoriate afford to place its hope in the emergence of an "enlightened" state that will safeguard its interests.

If the professoriate is still the eyes of the university, we must now ask what kind of eyes? Derrida called for a re-valuing of perspectival eyes, inner eyes, and eyes that can weep for the unjustices of the world (memoirs of the blind). Only these counter-eyes, Derrida believed, offer the possibility of re-grounding the public university in ways that opens up its fuller democratic possibilities. This means re-valuing diverse discursive forms and rhetorical styles within the university and challenging the hegemonic power of *logocntrism* in our own speaking and writing. All of this is possible, he argued, only within a new kind of university without inflexible borders that separate binary oppositions. In *Mochlos* he calls for the re-thinking of the university in terms of overlapping and diverse "communities of thinkers" or "interpretive communities," engaged in the working and re-working of a heritage, a collective memory. Kant now exists as a set of texts in one such interpretive community called "philosophy," and Derrida does not come to overturn philosophy or Kant so much as be "unfaithful" to them. In *For What Tomorrow* Derrida writes that "the best way to be faithful to a heritage is to be unfaithful, that is, not to accept it literally, as a totality." The heir to Kant or Marx, or Derrida for that matter, is faced with a "double injunction, a contradictory assignation": we must know how to "reaffirm" that which has preceded us. But what does it mean to reaffirm? "It means not simply accepting this heritage but relaunching it otherwise and keeping it alive" (Derrida & Roudinesco, 2004, pp. 2–3).

In *Mocholos*, Derrida develops these ideas further by relating interpretive communities to the performance of language. As I have said, Derrida viewed language as performative, and the contradiction at the heart of the Kantian liberal arts heritage had to do with its presupposition that a language could be non-performative, merely a "thinking" and a "theory." In fact, language or discourse is the element common to both spheres of responsibility that Kant attempted to establish for the "higher" an "lower" faculties, and this makes it impossible to develop a rigorous and oppositional distinction between the two. Kant continuously "erases" that in language which is most essential: that it is always a performative rather than "purely constative." Language is the output of a system of production, "in that place where knowledge and power are no longer distinguished," in which language is not just a "stating, describing, saying that which is," but also productive and transformative. This also means that there is a "politics of teaching and of knowledge, a political concept of the university community." This politics, he maintained, is deeply embedded in "every sentence of a course or seminar, in every act of writing, reading, or interpretation" (2004a, pp. 100–101). The other aspect of interpretive communities that Derrida emphasizes is that they do not have borders, or at least not borders that are indivisible and unpassable, that might secure the "inside" of the "university" from a public "outside." This too Derrida attributes to language, and to "the necessarily public character of discourse (2004a, p. 98). There is absolutely no way of developing an intra-university language that is not part of a broader public discourse, since we all inherit language. Ironically, Kant claims that philosophy should be a universalistic language, yet he seeks to turn it into a "quasi-private" language and agrees not to popularize or divulge philosophical discourse to a general public that might be "corrupted" by it. Derrida's "community of interpreters" is organized and mobilized around texts not borders, and they are simultaneously part of multiple local, national, and global communities of interpreters engaged in the taking of positions regarding the institutional structures that constitute us and "regulate our practice, our competences, and our performances." In the age of NCLB and NCATE, Derrida would say that the responsibility of the education faculty is to make the "ethico-political" implications of these structures as explicit as possible within a broadening public dialogue (2004a, p. 102).

Derrida never harbored any illusions about just how difficult it would be to democratically re-ground the public university in an age in which the memory of both the heritage and the promise of the university risk being forgotten or emptied of meaning. He wrote of a "democracy to come" only as a possibility, and one which must be actively willed into existence by those who take responsibility for responding when it would be just as easy not to.[5] Furthermore, Derrida had come to believe that a "democracy to come" only exists as a possibility in the face of its alterity, its Other, which also has been constituted through the modern, Enlightenment project from the beginning. That Other was constituted in the modern era on both the political Left and Right in the form of orthodoxy, dogmatism, and the policing of borders. Derrida thus placed some democratic hope in the metaphor and the practice of crossing borders in our own teaching, writing, and speaking. One might say Derrida lived this possibility and hope. As a young Algerian French Jew during the time of the Nazi collaborationist government in WWII, he was denied the right to cross the border into France to pursue his education and escape persecution. Later, he would live his life as a nomadic border crosser, always interested in what happens when the traveler from one land crosses the border and confronts that which is "foreign." Will the traveler see in the foreigner that which he or she already expects to see, that is, the face of an Absolute Other? Or will the border crosser, the traveler, remain open to finding something unexpected, to confront the face of a difference that cannot be easily contained within the binary oppositions that the border claims to separate. It will depend upon the traveler recognizing that borders are not frontiers, that every border is perforated by a multiplicity of openings that render binary oppositions of Self and Other ungovernable, uncontrollable, and even impossible (Malabou and Derrida, 2004).

NOTES

1 Geoffrey Bennington, 2000, *Interrupting Derrida*, observes that "Derrida is, obviously and self-proclaimedly, on the Left. But on the Left, there has always been a desire for Derrida to 'come clean' about politics and a lurking suspicion that his (at least apparent) failure to do was in principle a reason for dissatisfaction." This lead to charges "from the self-appointed guardians of the 'Left" tradition in academic politics" that he was anti-Marxist and even liberal (18). Chantal Mouffe, 1996, "Deconstruction, Pragmatism, and Philosophy," writes that "Derrida should be seen as a public thinker and his work, with its growing emphasis on justice and responsibility, has important ethical and political implications" (2). Richard Rorty, 1989, in *Contingency, Irony, and Solidarity*, labels Derrida a "private ironist" whose work has no direct public policy implications. However, this is based on Rorty's attachment to a public-private binary that Derrida sought to deconstruct.

2 Churchill's op-ed essay was published in *Kersplebedeb* blog, February 10, 2005. Of the supposed "innocent victims" of the 9/11 attacks working in the World Trade Center towers, Churchill wrote: "They formed a technocratic corps at the very heart of America's global financial empire, the 'mighty engine of profit' to which the military dimension of U.S. policy has always been enslaved, and they did so both willingly and knowingly." I do not wish to defend Churchill's statement, since at best it is insensitive. But it does raise an important concern about what it might mean to feign "innocence" as an American, and how this innocence gets produced—through both schooling and popular culture.

3 Derrida develops this notion of borders as cuts, marks, and incisions, and passwords in *Sovereignties in Question: The Poetics of Paul Celan* (2005). We writes that the Hebrew word *shibboleth*, while its meaning remains open and indeterminate, implies "a password, not a word in passing, but a silent word transmitted like a... handclasp, a rallying cipher, a sign of membership and a poltical watchword" (23) A *shibboleth* makes community possible, but only by exteriorization and exclusion as well as inclusion.

4 *Memoirs of the Blind* was written as a text to accompany a series of paintings and drawings included in an exhibit Derrida helped organize for the Louve Museum in Paris in 1990 on the subject of the representation of blindness in Western art, particularly religious art. For a discussion of the metaphors of blindness and sight in Derrida's work, see Carlson, 2005.

5 Derrida refers to a "democracy to come" in *Rogues: Two Essays on Reason* (2001a). He saw a suicidal possibility inherent in the pursuit of democracy since democracy always exposes itself to the possibility that forces hostile to democracy can be elected by the people, or that anti-democratic movements can have a powerful appeal among people, as in "the rise of an Islam considered to be anti-democratic" (31).

REFERENCES

Aby, S. (Ed.). (2007). *The academic bill of rights debate: A handbook*. New York: Praeger.

Baker, B. (2001). *In perpetual motion: Theories of power, educational history, and the child*. New York: Peter Lang.

Barthes, R. (1972). *Mythologies*. New York: Hill & Wang.

Bennington, G. (2000). *Interrupting Derrida*. New York: Routledge.

Camus, A. (1970). *Lyrical and critical essays* (E. C. Kennedy, Trans.). New York: Vintage Books.

Carlson, D. (2002). *Leaving safe harbors: Towards a new progressivism in American education and public life*. New York: Routledge.

Carlson, D. (2005). The uses of spirit: Notes on derrida, spiritual politics, and educational leadership. *Journal of School Leadership, 15*, 639–655.

Carlson, D. (2007). Are we making progress? The discursive construction of achievement in the age of 'No Child Left Behind'. In D. Carlson & C. P. Gause (Eds.), *Keeping the promise: Essays on leadership, democracy, and education* (pp. 3–26). New York: Peter Lang.

Carlson, D., & Apple, M. (1998). Introduction: Critical educational theory in unsettling times. In D. Carlson & M. Apple (Eds.), *Power/Knowledge/Pedagogy: The meaning of democratic education in unsettling times* (pp. 1–40). Boulder, CO: Westview press.

Critchley, S. (1999). *The ethics of deconstruction: Derrida and Levinas*. Edinburgh, UK: Edinburgh University Press.

Cuban, L. (1993). *How teachers taught: Constancy and change in American classrooms, 1890–1990*. New York: Teachers College Press.

Derrida, J. (1983). Plato's pharmacy. In B. Johnson (Trans.), *Dissemination* (pp. 61–172). Chicago: University of Chicago Press.

Derrida, J. (1993). *Memoirs of the blind: The self-portrait and other ruins*. Chicago: University of Chicago Press.

Derrida, J. (1994). *Specters of Marx: The State of the Debt, the work of mourning, and the new international* (P. Kamuf, Trans.). New York: Routledge.

Derrida, J. (2000). *Of Hospitality: Anne Dufourmantelle Invites Jacques Derrida to Respond*. Stanford, CA: Stanford University Press.

Derrida, J. (2001a). *Rogues: Two essays on reason. (2001)* (P.-A. Brault & M. Naas, Trans.). Stanford, CA: Stanford University Press.

Derrida, J. (2001b). *The work of mourning* (P.-A. Brault & M. Nass, Trans.). Chicago: University of Chicago Press.

Derrida, J. (2004a). *Eyes of the University*. Stanford, CA: Stanford University Press.

Derrida, J. (2004b). Honoris Causa: This is extremely funny. In E. Weber (Ed.), & P. Kamuf (Trans.), *Points... Interviews, 1974–1994* (pp. 399–421). Stanford, CA: Stanford University Press.

Derrida, J., & Roudinesco, E. (2004c). *For what tomorrow? A dialogue* (J. Fort, Trans.). Stanford, CA: Stanford University Press.

Dewey, J. (1916). *Democracy and education: An introduction to the philosophy of education*. New York: Macmillan.

Dottin, E., Allan, J., Douglas, S., & Joseph, W. (2005). Representing the social foundations of education in NCATE: A chronicle of twenty-five years of effort. *Educational Studies*, *38*, 241–254.

Eagleton, T. (1981). *Walter Benjamin: Towards a revolutionary criticism*. London: New Left Boos.

Fagan, M., Ludovic, G., Hasimbegovic, I., & Suetsugu, M. (2007). *Derrida: Negotiating the legacy*. Edinburgh, UK: Edinburgh University Press.

Foucault, M. (1978). *History of sexuality volume I: An introduction*. New York: Pantheon.

Gaston, S. (2006). *Derrida and disinterest (Continuum series in continental philosophy)*. New York: Continuum.

Giroux, H. (2007). *The University in chains: Confronting the military-industrial-academic complex*. Boulder, CO: Paradigm.

Gramsci, A. (1971). *Prison notebooks*. New York: International Publishers.

Jameson, F. (1991). *Postmodernism: The cultural logic of late capitalism*. Durham, NC: Duke University Press.

Kamuf, P. (1991). Introduction: Reading between the lines. In Kamuf (Ed.), *A Derrida reader: Between the lines* (pp. xiii–xlii). New York: Harvester Wheatsheaf.

Kant, I. (1996). *The conflict of the faculties (1798), in religion and rational theology*. Cambridge, UK: Cambridge University Press.

Laclau, E. (1996). Deconstruction, pragmatism, hegemony. In C. Mouffe (Ed.), *Deconstruction and pragmatism: Critichley, Derrida, Laclau, and Rorty* (pp. 47–68). New York: Routledge.

Malabou, C., & Derrida, J. (2004). *Traveling with Jacques Derrida* (D. Wils, Trans.). Stanford, CA: Stanford University Press.

Martin, B. (1992). *Derrida and the possibilities of postmodern social theory*. Albany, NY: SUNY Press.

Mills, C. (1997). *The racial contract*. Ithaca, NY: Cornell University Press.

Mouffe, C. (1996). Deconstruction, pragmatism, and the politics of democracy. In C. Mouffe (Ed.), *Deconstruction and pragmatism: Critichley, Derrida, Laclau, and Rorty* (pp. 1–12). New York: Routledge.

Mueller, J. (2006). Does talking the talk mean walking the walk? A case for forging closer relationships between teacher education and educational foundatrions. *Educational Studies, 39*, 146–162.

National Commission on Excellence in Education. (1983). *A nation at risk*. Washington, DC: U.S. Government Printing Office.

Noblit, G. (2002). The walls of Jericho: The struggle for an American educational studies association. *Educational Studies, 33*, 6–23.

Readings, B. (1996). *The University in ruins*. Cambridge, MA: Harvard University Press. Readings, Bill.

Rorty, R. (1989). *Contingency, irony, and solidarity*. Cambridge, UK: Cambridge University Press.

Slaughter, S., & Leslie, L. (1999). *Academic capitalism: Politics, policies and the entrepreneurial University*. Baltimore: John Hopkins University Press.

Tozer, S. (1993). Toward a new consensus among social foundations educators: Draft position paper on the American educational studies association committee on academic standards and accreditation. *Educational Foundations, 7*(4).

Tozer, S., & Deborah, M. (2000). Professional teaching standards and social foundations of education. *Educational Studies, 31*, 146–162.

Tyack, D., & Larry, C. (1997). *Tinkering toward Utopia: A century of public school reform*. Cambridge, MA: Harvard University Press.

Dennis Carlson
Department of Educational Leadership
Miami University

GLOBALIZATION AND CULTURE INDUSTRIES

PETER MCLAREN AND
VALERIE SCATAMBURLO-D'ANNIBALE

4. CLASS-IFYING RACE

The Compassionate Racism of the Right and Why Class Still Matters

INTRODUCTION

Southern trees bear a strange fruit
Blood on the leaves and blood at the root
Black body swinging in the southern breeze
Strange fruit hanging from the poplar trees
Pastoral scene of the gallant south
The bulging eyes and the twisted mouth
Scent of magnolia sweet and fresh
And the sudden smell of burning flesh!
Here is a fruit for the crows to pluck
For the rain to gather, for the wind to suck
For the sun to rot, for a tree to drop
Here is a strange and bitter crop

Strange Fruit, Lewis Allan, 1938

On August 7, 1930 two young black men—Thomas Shipp and Abram Smith—were brutally lynched by the Ku Klux Klan in Marion, Indiana. The ghastly sight of their battered, lifeless bodies dangling from a tree, amidst a large crowd, was famously captured on film by studio photographer Lawrence Beitler. Thousands of copies of the photograph were eventually sold across the United States.[1] In 1937, Abel Meeropol, a Jewish schoolteacher from New York, happened upon a copy of the photograph and the horrifying images, which it hauntingly depicted, inspired him to pen the poem, *Strange Fruit*. Under the pseudonym of Lewis Allan, Meeropol (a member of the American Communist Party and union activist) eventually published the poem in the *New York Teacher* and later in the Marxist journal, *New Masses*.[2] The poem was subsequently set to a brooding melody and performed at a New York teachers' union rally in 1938. In time, it was brought to the attention of Billie Holiday whom Meeropol had seen perform at a Greenwich Village nightclub called *Café Society*. Holiday wanted to record the song but her label refused to do so. Not one to give up easily, Holiday recorded it on a specialty label instead. The song was quickly embraced as the anthem of the anti-lynching movement.[3] Despite reaching number sixteen on the charts in July 1939, the song

Z. Leonardo (ed.), Handbook of Cultural Politics and Education, 113–140.

was pusillanimously denounced by *Time Magazine* as "a prime piece of musical propaganda" for the National Association for the Advancement of Colored People (NAACP).[4] Nonetheless, it remained one of Holiday's signature songs and she performed it until her death in 1959.

The heart-wrenching lyrics of *Strange Fruit* remind us of the disturbing and deadly consequences of racism and that many of the ghosts from America's inflamed and infamous past continue to stalk the living in our contemporary cultural politics and on the national stage of American political life. While this is readily apparent in the current 2008 election campaign—a topic to which we shall return—it is also evident if one surveys some of the most provocative headlines in recent years. For example, on June 1st, 2005 the FBI had the body of Emmett Till exhumed with the hope of finding new clues in his gruesome death. In August 1955, Till's body was discovered in the Tallahatchie River. He had been shot in the head, his skull crushed, and one of his eyes had been gouged out. His "alleged" transgression was whistling at a White woman in Money, Mississippi. His presumed killers, Roy Bryant and J.W. Milian, two White men, were freed after a jury returned a "not guilty" verdict. Then on June 21st, 2005 a former Klansman, eighty-year-old, Edgar Ray Killen was convicted of manslaughter in the 1964 "Freedom Summer" killings of James Chaney, Andrew Goodman and Michael Schwerner—three civil rights activists who had been working for the Mississippi Freedom Summer initiative designed to register black voters in the state.[5]

Interestingly, only a week earlier on June 13th, 2005 the U.S. Senate formally apologized for its failure to outlaw lynchings and for repeatedly refusing to consider legislation that would have mandated investigations and punishment of such egregious crimes. Republican Senator George Allen, who was a chief sponsor of the "apology" initiative, referred to the previous "legislative inaction as a 'stain on the history of the United States Senate'" (Younge, 2005, p. 11)." However, Allen's contrite demeanor may have been a bit unexpected to some given that he used to display a Confederate flag at his home and a noose in his law office. And, of course, Allen found himself in the midst of a racially-charged controversy during his 2006 re-election campaign. While on the campaign trail, Allen referred to S.R. Sidarth, a Virginia-born American of Indian descent, as "macaca"—a racial slur against African immigrants that is commonly used in some European cultures. Sidarth, a senior at the University of Virginia, was documenting Allen's travels and speeches on behalf of James Webb—Allen's Democratic opponent in the Virginia Senate race. Webb was eventually victorious. Not so unexpected was the fact that both senators from Mississippi—Thad Cochran and Trent Lott—refused to co-sponsor the resolution (Younge, 2005). They were joined by seventeen others—all Republicans—who also voted against supporting the resolution.[6]

In July 2005, President George W. Bush (who waited almost 6 years into his presidency to adress the NAACP Annual National Convention for the first time) sent a surrogate in the form of Ken Mehlman, the chairman of the Republican National Committee, to address the annual convention of the NAACP in Milwaukee. In his speech, Mehlman apologized for the Republican Party's despicable, decades-long "Southern strategy" and confessed that "some Republicans gave up on winning the African-American vote" and had looked the "other way" while others tried to "benefit politically from racial polarization." Casting the strategy in strictly historical terms, Mehlman apologized to the gathered attendants and asserted, "I am here today as the Republican chairman to tell you we were wrong" (Herbert, 2005, p. 1). Rightfully, one might question the sincerity of the apology on behalf of the Republican Party given that nineteen Republicans had failed to support the anti-lynching resolution just weeks earlier.

Mehlman's comments elicited indignant responses from the conservative haven of talk radio. For example, Rush Limbaugh—whom president Bush himself described as a "good friend" in an August 2004 appearance on Limbaugh's show—graphically suggested that Mehlman's efforts were tantamount to Republicans bending over and grabbing their ankles.[7] Limbaugh's reaction sparked a wave of similar rants by right-wingers who were equally outraged by the "official" apology—all of which clearly demonstrated that while the symbolic gestures of George Allen and Ron Mehlman may have sought to appease certain political constituencies, conservative discourse is still rife with racial animus. Mehlman's remarks led more thoughtful observers to point out that his "apology" rang particularly hollow given the Bush administration's shameful record on "race" related matters, and the fact that the "Southern strategy" is still a powerful tool in the Republican Party's electoral arsenal (Herbert, 2005). The apology also seemed especially contrived when properly contextualized—just a year prior to the 2005 headlines, conservatives were mourning the June 2004 death of their hero, Ronald Reagan, a man who masterfully exploited the Southern strategy.

THE RACIAL LEGACY OF THE "GREAT COMMUNICATOR"

In the aftermath of Ronald Reagan's death, the American public (and indeed the world) was subjected to a week-long media orgy of propagandistic revisionism. The waypoints used by the media to make sense of Reagan's presidency were dipped in nostalgia and suffered from a knee-jerk American reflex that United States presidents could be anything less than a gift to the world, despite their failings. Journalists, pundits, and politicians mourned the passing of the "great communicator" and gushed about the "optimistic" man of "vitality" who deeply loved his country, who single-handedly revived "patriotism," and who brought hope to "the American people." In light of the mainstream media's coverage of Reagan's final hayride, which was little more than a romanticized hail-to-the-chief jamboree, one could conclude that Reagan was, indeed, beloved by all Americans. However, when we peel away the layers of the Reagan mythology promulgated by the media and the political right, a more realistic and damning portrait of the former President emerges. The "national fantasy" protecting Reagan and his divisive/dreadful legacy cannot be ignored especially since most of the 2008 Republican presidential candidates invoked the Reagan "glory years" and attempted to cast themselves as "Reagan Republicans" before John McCain (who has also donned the cloak of Reaganism) became the GOP's presumptive nominee.

Reagan's entire political career was bent towards the systematic erosion of affirmative action and other similar equity based initiatives. From his early days in the hunt for California's governorship (when he opposed the 1964 Civil Rights Act and the 1965 Voting Rights Act) to his years in office as president, Reagan served as the strong "mainstream" arm of the ultra conservative right. In 1980, Reagan was invited by Trent Lott (the disgraced former Republican Senate Majority Leader) to begin his quest for the presidency in Philadelphia, Mississippi—just sixteen years after the murders of the aforementioned civil rights activists. He was well aware that in order to garner the Southern White vote, he would have to appeal subtly (and not so subtly) to the virulent racism that at times was barely containable in Southern White enclaves. With that knowledge firmly in mind, he kicked off his general election campaign at the Neshoba County Fair, an annual gathering that was famous for diatribes given by segregationist politicians. There, he delivered a rousing speech extolling the racially coded agenda of "states rights."[8] In fact, his speech was sufficiently vitriolic that he was 'rewarded' in turn with an endorsement by the Ku Klux Klan (in fact many members of the Klan were in attendance that night). Now, the fact that Reagan launched his bid for the American presidency in Mississippi should say something quite clearly, but the fact that his speech garnered further support from the KKK should speak volumes about his candidacy and his politics.

During his tenure in office, Reagan became the Achilles of the White backlash and he deftly worked his sword arm of retributive White justice to hack to pieces affirmative action policies and programs by appointing right-wing judges to the Supreme Court and to the federal bench and by watering down the Office of Civil Rights. For example, he named William Rehnquist Chief Justice of the Supreme Court despite Rehnquist's opposition to integration in the 1960s. He also promulgated disparaging lies about "welfare queens" and tried to get tax exemptions for the racist Bob Jones University (a religious institution notorious for providing Biblical sanction for old-fashioned Southern racism) which, until 2000, enforced a ban on interracial dating. Reagan originally opposed establishing the Martin Luther King holiday before finally signing it into law but he did veto an extension of the Civil Rights Act in 1988 and undermined the US Civil Rights Commission (Jackson, 2004).

It is vital that we understand the masterful use of coded language and the manipulation of public image Reagan maintained throughout his presidency. His infamous metaphor—"welfare queens"—was a coded critique of black women who presumably rode around in pink Cadillacs while collecting food stamps. Moreover, Reagan's opposition to the establishment of Martin Luther King Day should not surprise us. After all, Terrell Bell, Reagan's Education Secretary, noted in his memoir how racial slurs were common among the Great Communicator's White House staffers, including common references to "Martin Lucifer Coon" (Wise, 2004). Reagan also supported the murderous regime of Saddam Hussein (a fact which has been conveniently brushed aside in recent years), undermined labor rights and union activity, opposed sanctions against South Africa, supported the heinous Duvalier regime in Haiti, helped to fund the brutal "death-squad governments" in Guatemala and El Salvador, and his government supported and trained the murderous Contra terrorists in Nicaragua.

With this seemingly endless stream of evidence uncovering Reagan as anything but the heroic, principled and fair-minded leader lauded in the mainstream media, one might rightfully wonder how the national fantasy surrounding the "Great Communicator" remains essentially untouched (both historically and in the present day). One might reasonably think Reagan's legacy would be tarnished given that his political "leanings" are a matter of public record. However, that is not the case—having been a Hollywood actor for many years, Reagan masterfully cultivated an "aw shucks" good natured personality that thinly veiled his racial bigotry and made it seem benign, especially when placed beside his rabid anti-communism. Greider (2004, p. 5) maintains that the structured silence of the media's fawning memorials to the "Ronald Reagan story" was a motivated amnesia that refused to acknowledge that a "chilling meanness lurked at the core of Reagan's political agenda." In perfecting the "Southern strategy," Reagan used "race" as a weapon to advance one of the most regressive and vicious social, political, and cultural agendas in American history, but that agenda was effectively maintained and concealed by Reagan's carefully crafted PR image and the conservative media machine. Indeed, under Reagan, right-wing politics were framed as respectably moderate, while anything left or liberal was portrayed as utterly fanatical. Reagan, however, was merely a link (albeit an influential link) in the chain that binds the Republican Right to its roots in the Antebellum South. After all, our latest White Achilles, George W. Bush, has a record on "race" that is arguably just as dismal and discordant as Reagan's—and that record demands brief attention as well.

THE GREAT UNITER

While the fiasco that was the 2000 election needs no introduction, it is alarming to note that the great majority of American People remain blissfully ignorant and/or skeptical of the starkly racialized and racist undertones/strategies that framed the process and the ultimate outcome. In truth, Bush's inclusionary rhetoric ("I'm a uniter not a divider") dramatically belies not only his policies but his political choices. Much like Reagan before him, Bush made a symbolically important visit to Bob Jones University during the 2000 South Carolina primary. Moreover, his success in the primary was partially enabled by a repulsive smear campaign (presumably coordinated by Bush's brain, Karl Rove) that called attention to this rival, John McCain's "black child" (actually, an adopted daughter from Bangladesh). The use of such repugnant race-baiting tactics (which represented yet another manifestation of the Southern strategy) made the "spectacle" of inclusion at the 2000 Republican National Convention all the more farcical. The event was essentially a well-choreographed, modern-day minstrel show: a theatrical production intended to stress Bush's message of racial inclusion. A seemingly endless series of black and brown performers took to the stage—the Temptations, a gospel choir, an ensemble of dancing black children, rhythm and blues and salsa singers, a black woman who sang the national anthem—and provided the entertainment to a delegation that was "over 90 percent

White, mostly male and extremely conservative" (Marable, 2000). But, of course, the major story of the 2000 election was the wholesale disenfranchisement of predominantly Black voters in the state of Florida.

Republicans have always had a rather checkered history of election shenanigans aimed at suppressing votes, but this most striking example cut at the very heart of the notion of "freedom and liberty for all." As most of the media obsessed over butterfly ballots and hanging chads, the racial disparities in the treatment of voters were, by far, the "worst scandal of the Florida 2000 election" (Marable, 2000, p. 167). And, yet, disturbingly, it somehow went largely unreported and remained generally "marginalized" in mainstream media coverage (Rampton and Stauber, 2004). In the months prior to the election, Florida Secretary of State Katherine Harris had been instructed by Governor Jeb Bush to send local election boards a list of over 40,000 names of "probable" and "possible" felons who were supposedly ineligible to vote. The "scrub list" was provided by a private firm, Database Technologies, which had strong Republican ties. An examination of the list subsequently revealed that many eligible voters had been wrongly eliminated from the voting rolls and were prevented from voting. As Palast notes in his expose, *The Best Democracy Money Can Buy*, 90.2 percent of those on the scrub list, were innocent and the purged names were both disproportionately black (54%) and overwhelmingly Democrats (2003, p. 12). The NAACP also subsequently documented widespread reports of voter irregularities and intimidation in Florida. Despite the overwhelming evidence, most Democrats and the media refused to formally acknowledge Republican malfeasance and were essentially complicit in what Kellner (2001) called "grand theft 2000."

Soon after winning the 2000 presidential race (some might say he was selected for the post by the Republican dominated Supreme Court), the new Commander-in-chief showed the nation that his rich White Christian constituency would have little to worry about over the next four years. While Bush's early nominations of Colin Powell as Secretary of State, Condoleeza Rice as National Security Adviser and Rod Paige as Secretary of Education, prompted his supporters to suggest that such gestures were indicative of Bush's commitment to "diversity" and "inclusion," Bush's actual policies have demonstrably hurt the majority of the Black population and have reinforced what many in the Black community have known for quite some time—that his administration has little regard for them despite the window-dressing provided by the likes of Powell, Paige and Rice. As Dyson (2001) has noted:

> The irony is that Powell, Paige and Rice were chosen in part to prove an inclusiveness that is meaningless if their very presence comes at the expense of representing the interests of the majority of black folk, especially those poor and working-class folk who are vulnerable and largely invisible. The lesson the Republicans would have us learn is that not all blacks think alike, that we are no ideological monolith in liberal captivity. The real lesson may be that a black face does not translate into a progressive political presence that aids the bulk of black folk. Especially when that face must put a smile on repressive policies that hurt not just most blacks but those Americans committed to radical democracy.

Dyson's remarks illustrate how the discourses of "identity politics" and "difference" politics can easily be appropriated by the Right—an observation which echoes the work of others who have aptly pointed out that historically marginalized individuals and groups can just as easily be drawn into positions on the Right as they can into progressive positions (Mercer, 1992; Hall, 1996; Wallace, 1994). Moreover, the ideology of inclusiveness merely re-inscribes the values of free market ideology and often amounts to little more than a demand for inclusion into the club of representation. That is, the mere quantitative inclusion of those historically deemed "other" (in this case, African-Americans) does not guarantee diversity of political opinions. Simply put, the Republican agenda is clearly not conducive to advancing the collective standing of peoples of color and all indicators suggest that racially marginalized peoples have lost ground under Bush's "leadership."[9] After all, along with the appointments of Rice, Powell and Paige, Bush nominated John Ashcroft—a well-known admirer of the Confederacy and an ultra-religious Christian who had been known to hold Bible Studies and prayer meetings in his office—to run the Justice Department.[10] This was the same John Ashcroft who essentially praised the institution of slavery during a 1998 interview published in the *Southern Partisan*—a leading journal of the neo-Confederacy movement that regularly publishes racist apologias and which has been known to lavish effusive praise on the likes of former KKK leader David Duke whom the magazine deemed a "Populist spokesperson for a recapturing of the American ideal" (cited in Solomon, 2001, p. 2).

Examples of Bush's troublesome racial politics come as no surprise. One need look no further than his own father's 1988 presidential campaign and his use of the overtly racist Willie Horton ads to see a glaring example of such racially motivated and manipulative strategies.[11] What we find particularly interesting is, how the sheer volume of "racially tinged" question marks that surround the Bush presidency continue to somehow escape the grasp and attention of the mainstream media. Case in point, the Lott/Thurmond debacle (that saw Trent Lott praising Strom Thurmond on the occasion of the latter's 100th birthday celebration) was another glaring public example of how the "real" politics driving the conservative agenda continues to be almost completely minimized and unaddressed in the mainstream media.[12]

At his centennial bash held in December 2002, Lott (then Senate majority leader) saw fit to laud Thurmond's segregationist past: "I want to say this about my state: When Strom Thurmond ran for President, we voted for him. We're proud of it. And if the rest of the country had followed our lead, we wouldn't have had all these problems over all these years, either" (cited in Mercurio, 2002). Unbelievably, while blogs across the nation erupted after Thurmond's incendiary remarks, it took the mainstream media five days to accord any serious attention to Lott's comments. After the story finally broke, Lott first tried to play down the controversy by claiming that his praise of Thurmond was a "light-hearted" moment and that he was just "winging it." Conservative columnists like Bob Novak leapt to his defense by suggesting that the comments were nothing more than a simple slip of the tongue. Of course, this argument was stripped of any real validity when it was revealed that Lott had made an almost identical statement at a Mississippi political rally some

20 years earlier. On this occasion in 1980, after Thurmond had made a fiery speech endorsing Ronald Reagan, then-congressman Lott told the crowd: "You know, if we had elected this man 30 years ago, we wouldn't be in the mess we are today." In short, Lott's remarks at the Thurmond celebration were hardly a 'slip of the tongue.'

As Lott's reprehensible voting record on civil rights was revealed alongside his affiliation with the White supremacist Council of Conservative Citizens (CCC), pressure mounted for Lott to resign as Senate majority leader. Such pressure did not, however, emanate from the White House as Bush was reluctant to condemn Lott's flattering and thinly disguised racist remarks about Thurmond's career.[13] Lott eventually did resign his post but retained his Senate seat. While many hailed Lott's resignation as proof that bigotry would no longer be tolerated by the political establishment (at least not publicly), it did little to challenge the structural and systemic roots of racism. Moreover, it didn't stop the Bush administration from buttressing the careers of other public officials who have openly supported racist practices and policies.

For example, Bush celebrated Martin Luther King's birthday in January 2004 by giving Charles Pickering (who has since retired from the bench) a recess appointment as an appeals court judge after he was rejected by the Senate. During his less than illustrious career, Pickering worked to support segregation, attacked civil rights advocates who sought an end to Jim Crow, and backed those who opposed national civil rights legislation and the landmark Civil Rights Act of 1964. In the world of George W. Bush and his cronies, "compassionate conservatism" often means "racism with a smile" (Blake, 2004).

ENTER KATRINA

It has been more than three years since we witnessed Hurricane Katrina ripping through the Gulf Coast with a vengeance. At the time, the media coverage of the tragedy revealed not only the bumbling incompetence of the Bush administration but also as some put it—America's dirty little secret, namely the reality of an impoverished "underclass." In the immediate aftermath of Katrina, many cultural observers and political pundits began to focus on the issues of "race" and "class" in the United States—albeit in a rather superficial way. Some, particularly those representing the right of the political spectrum, used the tragedy to further propagate their racist views—many of which employed discourses of "cultural racism" that suggested that the "moral bankruptcy" and "cultural deficiencies" of African-Americans and Black culture are largely responsible for the impoverished conditions of many African-Americans. For example, Tracinski (2005) contended that the chaos, which took hold in New Orleans after the hurricane struck, was a result of the man-made disaster of the "welfare state." While never explicitly invoking the category of race, he argued that the incidents of looting were indicative of the "psychological consequences of the welfare state" and the natural propensity of people "without values." In a similar vein, other white conservatives, including talk radio blowhard Rush Limbaugh stated that blacks in New Orleans were left behind because of "welfare state mentality." As Pitts (2005) has noted, this supposed mentality "eroded their self-reliance, inducing them to wait for government help instead of saving themselves." Of course, Pitts was quick to point out that he has seen "White folks pleading for help a hundred times in the wake of earthquakes" and the like without anyone citing such pleas as "evidence of their lack of moral fiber."

A moral panic quickly ensued as the public was fed horror stories about what it was like to be trapped in the inferno of black anarchism, stories refracted in the cesspool of racism and fear that lies deep within the structural unconscious of a nation founded upon violence, slavery, and genocide: African-American 'wildings' gang-raping women and children, looting stores of liquor and drugs, and tales of ambulances and police patrols being shot at (McLaren and Jaramillo, 2007). Over at that paragon of journalistic integrity, *Fox News*, correspondent Steve Harrington described New Orleans as the "Wild West," while his colleague Phil Keating characterized a fire visible in some news footage as being set "perhaps for no apparent reason but just for the joy of arson" (Yassin, 2005, p. 11). Right-wing journalist (and we use the term "journalist" here loosely) Jonah Goldberg described the survivors of Katrina in the *National Review Online blog* as a different species and inhuman, as a mutant breed that had infested the Superdome—what Goldberg dubbed a "Mad Max/Thunderdome/Waterworld/Lord of the Flies horror show" (Bacon, 2005, p. 14). And then there was Fox News' pugnacious posse leader, Bill O'Reilly, pontificating in the *Florida Sun-Sentinel* that

> 'the suffering' of 'the poor in New Orleans' should be a lesson: 'Connect the dots and wise up. Educate yourself, work hard and be honest ... If you don't ... the odds are that you will be desperately standing on a symbolic rooftop someday yourself. And trust me, help will not be quick in coming.' And in O'Reilly's view, help should not necessarily be offered ... 'The white American taxpayers are saying: "How much more do we have to give here?" (Bacon, 2005, p. 13).

For all the Wild West metaphors and military descriptions of New Orleans as a "war zone" where marauding hordes of malcontents and looters allegedly overturned every act of civility, it is interesting to note that subsequent reports concluded that there was no more violence in New Orleans in the aftermath of Katrina than in any other typical week (Bacon, 2005). Moreover, many tales of violence—such as snipers firing recklessly at rescue vehicles and police being attacked by mob violence—were later discredited (Bacon, 2005; Yassin, 2005).

While the tragedy of Katrina and its brutal after effects afforded some white right-wingers the opportunity to let their racism hang out, there was of course the more compassionate racism displayed by the Bush administration. Bush and Michael (you're doing a heckuva job Brownie) Brown had been warned of levee failures prior to August 29, 2005 when Katrina made landfall as a category 4 hurricane at approximately 7:00 am. On that fateful morning, just hours after the hurricane hit, Bush was mugging for the cameras in a photo-op with John McCain and the Arizona senator's 69th birthday cake at Luke Air Force Base near Phoenix. On August 30th, Bush spent the afternoon playing guitar with country singer Mark Willis before returning to his Marlboro Man ranch in Crawford, Texas for a final night of vacation. After a restful night, Bush *flew over* New Orleans on Air Force One to survey the damage on August 31 as Michael Chertoff (who would later replace Brown as head of FEMA) claimed that he was "extremely pleased" with the federal government's response to the disaster.

Later that day, Bush gave his first major address about Katrina—a speech which, according to the *New York Times*, demonstrated the President's utter inability to grasp the enormity of the situation and the depth of the crisis that had befallen the residents of the Crescent City (New York Times, 2005). On September 2, as citizens were still clinging to rooftops and wading in sewage, Bush took part in some photo-ops in the hurricane-ravaged area. Later that day, he and members of his administration launched into a blistering attack chastising local and state leaders for *their* response to the crisis.[14] Just a few days later, Bush's mother and former First Lady Barbara Bush displayed her own brand of compassionate racism. As she toured a Houston relocation site, Mama Bush declared it a success for evacuees who "were underprivileged anyway" suggesting, perhaps inadvertently, that those who had lost their homes, their belongings, who had lost contact with family members, and who had been displaced were somehow better off in an overcrowded, under-equipped stadium. In an interview on the radio program *Marketplace* she added "What I'm hearing, which is sort of scary, is they all want to stay in Texas."

After Barbara Bush's charming remarks, the liberal blogosphere erupted with charges of racism—and of course, there was certainly some truth to such allegations. However, such comments tended to conflate race and class and obscured the deeper reality that lies beneath. We agree with Reed's (2005) acute observations:

> The abstract, moralizing patter about how and whether "race matters" or "the role of race" is appealing partly because it doesn't confront the roots of the bipartisan neoliberal policy regime. It's certainly true that George W. Bush and his minions are indifferent to, or contemptuous of, black Americans in general. They're contemptuous of *anyone* who is not part of the ruling class. Although Bush and his pals are no doubt small-minded bigots in many ways, the racial dimension stands out so strikingly in part because race is now the most familiar—and apparently for many progressives the most powerful—language of social justice. For roughly a generation it seemed reasonable to expect that defining inequalities in racial terms would provoke some remedial response from the federal government. But for quite some time race's force in national politics has been as a vehicle for reassuring Whites that "public" equals some combination of "black," "poor" and "loser;" that cutting public spending is aimed at weaning a lazy black underclass off the dole or—in the supposed benign, liberal Democratic version—teaching blacks "personal responsibility." (pp. 6, 8)

Although "race" is the language through which America's capitalist class contradictions are commonly expressed, the aftermath of Katrina clearly showed, in our opinion, that it was class, more so than race, that stood as a better predictor of who was able to evacuate, who drowned, and who was left to fester. Ultimately, we assert that race alone is too blunt an analytical tool to effectively elucidate such complex social phenomena (even when such inequalities are expressed in such blatantly racial terms). Katrina provides an apt example of why an exclusive focus on "race" must be challenged because poverty (i.e. class inequality) was the lynchpin that resulted in the masses being left behind and stranded, not race.[15]

The important lesson Katrina taught us is not just to undress racism but to reveal its roots in capitalist class relations. We believe it is imperative for critical social analysts committed to the struggle against all forms of oppression to move beyond disciplinary boundaries that would have them explore equity and anti-oppression without addressing issues of class. For us, there is a primacy to class that stands as the fundamental armature for all forms of oppression. This distinction informs our work and requires further explanation.

LABOR IMPERATIVES AND 'RACIAL' FORMATIONS

> One may speak of any number of disorientations and even oppressions, but one cultivates all kinds of politeness and indirection about the structure of capitalist social relations in which those oppressions are embedded. To speak of any of that directly and simply is to be "vulgar." In this climate of Aesopian language it is absolutely essential to reiterate that most things *are* a matter of class. That kind of statement is … surprising only in a culture like that of the North American university … But is precisely in that kind of culture that people need to hear such obvious truths (Ahmad, 1997, p. 104).

> Who speaks for the poor? Who raises a voice for them when their babies are born smaller and with lead in their blood? Who makes noise on their behalf when their schools turn out illiterates and their children are diagnosed with a higher rate of developmental disorders? Who cries out in their name when violence stalks their streets and schools and living rooms? Who says, 'Wait a minute!' when their lives are reduced to caricature by media, or else ignored outright, which, in a very real sense, is the same as saying those lives do not exist. No one speaks up because we have yet to develop language to encompass the whole of the issue. Oh, we talk some about black poverty or Hispanic poverty. Less often do we speak of white poverty and even less than that do we simply talk about poverty, period … If the poor ever recognized this, got mad about it and began to coalesce irrespective of race, they could realign politics as we know it, require the nation to grapple with, and construct remedies for, their suffering. This was Martin Luther King's last dream, the one he was fighting to redeem when he was killed. Too bad we have not, since that day, found the imagination, vision, or courage to go where he led. The poor among us retreat instead to the easy comfort of tribalism, black with black, brown with brown, white with white, unable to conceive they might

> have common concerns that transcend melanin and ancestry. They divide themselves, and thus render themselves inconsequential so that those above in aeries of wealth and power can rest easy, unthreatened by demands for change (Pitts, 2008, pp. 1–2).

We have quoted Pulitzer Prize winning journalist Leonard Pitts at considerable length since the claims he makes provide an apt segue into our discussion of class. While Pitts alludes to a common language that may unite those suffering the ravages of poverty, he ultimately concludes that we have yet to find the language that would enable us to articulate that commonality. On this point, we disagree with Pitts for such language can be found in the work of Karl Marx and the concept of class. Of course, it is also the case that Ahmad's assertion rings even truer today than it did in the late 1990s when he first penned his indictment of postmodern orthodoxy and the intellectual retreat from class and analyses of capitalism. Today, talking about class is still largely "unpopular" and too "old-fashioned" for an intelligentsia seemingly more titillated by the academic eroticism of studying all forms and varieties of cultural 'difference' (including racial difference). The hyper-culturalism that permeates the post-Marxist "new times" exegesis has generally chastised Marxist theory for privileging "class" over other "differences" (i.e. race, gender, etc.). Marxism has been taken to task for its perceived lack of attention to issues of difference and while some post-al theorists fancifully adorned in avant-garde guises have suggested a wholesale dismissal of Marxism, others have tried to reconstitute Marxism as a form of radical pluralist theory in which all social axes (gender, race, class, etc.) are equally important. In such formulations, class relations are no longer privileged but rather are perceived as only one among a "diversity of semiotically constructed identities" (Dyer-Witheford, 1999, p. 9). The resistance to historical materialism is generally premised on the assertion that foregrounding capitalist social relations necessarily undermines the importance of "difference" or trivializes struggles against racism in favor of an abstractly defined class-based politics. It is argued that a politics of difference could work to further the interests of those subordinated by dominant social relations. Yet, many advocates of difference politics have neither adequately addressed the constitution of class nor have they explored the machinations of capitalist social organization. Rather, they have overemphasized the priority of language and discourse in the hegemonic processes of identity formation and cultural representation to the detriment of acknowledging how the constructions of "difference" are structurally imbricated in the antinomic configurations of capitalism. The "discourse radicalism" of "cultural radicals" has led to a situation where textual acrobatics are equated with system-shaking "revolutionary action" and where a degraded form of pluralist politics has left the unprecedented economic carnage wrought by capitalism unexamined and uncontested (Harvey, 1998). Even among the educational *Left*—comprised of self-described "progressive" critical pedagogues and radical democrats—Marxism and the concept of class have been deemed defunct and class politics is viewed as anathema to serious social progress.

In arguing for the enduring relevance of Marx, we recognize that we may be perceived as theoretical Neanderthals naively clinging to the mental furniture of a bygone era. We understand, as Ahmad suggests above, that those who argue that the concept of class still has tremendous explanatory power are routinely dismissed as "vulgar," unreconstructed Marxists who remain convinced that the fundamental relations within contemporary capitalist society are, with minor distinctions, essentially the same as they were at the dawn of the industrial revolution. Yet, while capitalism has undergone seismic shifts since its emergence, it is also the case that the violent capital relation that is rooted in the exploitation of labor has remained relatively constant. Before examining that relationship however, we need to more fully address the concept of "race."

Except in the toxic doxa of reactionary pseudo-scholars like Herrnstein and Murray—the authors of the notorious book *The Bell Curve*—and other Right-wing pundits who advance specious arguments to attack virtually all social programs designed to assist the disadvantaged, the term *race* has "no scientific referent" (San Juan, Jr., 2002). One would be hard pressed to find a competent scholar who would employ the "biology" of race as a determinant of specific social phenomena. Nonetheless, as the aforementioned examples illustrate, discussions of race continue to dominate popular political discourse. And, although some of the more nuanced scholarly perspectives on race have sought to problematize its very existence as a classificatory category, too many others (particularly in the mainstream social sciences) have succumbed to the notion that humanity exists as generally distinct "racial groups" marked by a specific combination of biologically defined or imagined phenotypical characteristics and discrete cultural practices. Even those who have sought to critically explore the complex nature of racial formation have at times unwittingly reified race in a manner that has prevented them from adequately grasping the interplay between the social relations of production and the racialization process (cf. Omi and Winant, 1986). In many ways, the use of race has become an analytical trap precisely when it has been employed in antiseptic isolation from the messy terrain of historical and material relations. This is the very reason that mainstream calls of reverse-racism and self-sabotage in minoritized communities always seem to make sense at a common-sense level—because they almost always focus on racism as a singular almost encapsulated form of oppression.

Given these limitations, we agree with Gilroy's (2000) bold call to "transcend" race. Before proceeding, we must make ourselves abundantly clear. First and foremost, we are not suggesting that the lived realities of racial oppression be ignored—that would be perilous and would undercut one of the primary aims of this work. Nor are we attempting to de-legitimize race and racism as "real," "knowable," and material phenomena. We acknowledge that misinterpretations of race's socially constructed nature can be used to downplay and mute its material reality in contemporary contexts. Moreover, we recognize that the social construction of "race" as it has developed over centuries is a basic part of social formations. Whatever race was in its origins, it is now an intrinsic part and fundamental principal of social organization and identity formation. With this clarification in mind, we believe that a deeper understanding of how 'racism' operates can only be engaged if we work to widen our lens of analysis. We agree with Pieterse (1995) who suggests that the label racism particularizes and isolates issues. If we acknowledge that 'race' is a socially constructed phenomenon, then it becomes necessary to examine the social relations that engender such constructions. As such, our call to *abandon* and *transcend* race reflects our belief in the necessity of engaging a crucial analytical shift away from more "limiting" concepts of race and towards a pluralized conceptualization of 'racisms.' This attempt to explore historical articulations of race along with other ideologies and capitalist social relations would more accurately capture the historically specific nature of racism and the variety of meanings/connotations attributed to evaluations of difference and assessments of the "superiority" and/or "inferiority" of various groups of people.

In this regard, we can take a cue from Marx who perceptively recognized the way in which European and American capitalists promoted racial divisions within the working class. In an 1870 letter Marx penned from London to two friends, he noted that

> Every industrial and commercial center in England now possesses a working class divided into two hostile camps, English proletarians and Irish proletarians. The ordinary English worker hates the Irish worker as a competitor who lowers his standard of life. In relation to the Irish worker, he regards himself as a member of the ruling nation and consequently he becomes a tool of the English aristocrats and capitalists against Ireland, thus strengthening their domination over himself. He cherishes religion, social and national prejudices against the Irish worker. His attitude towards him is much the same as that of the "poor Whites" to the Negroes in the former slave states of the U.S.A ... This antagonism is artificially kept alive and intensified by the press, the pulpit, the comic papers, in short, by all the means at the disposal of the ruling classes. This antagonism is the secret of the impotence of the English working class, despite its organization. It is the secret by which the capitalist class maintains its power. And the latter is quite aware of this.[16]

As the passage reveals, Marx was clearly attuned to the specificity of "racial" discourse and clearly acknowledged how such configurations were not necessarily constrained by actual skin "colour." But more than this, Marx's references to the cultural apparatus (i.e. the press, the pulpit, the comic papers) demonstrate that he was also aware that the exercise of domination (be it through relations of power, conquest, or colonization) was also contingent upon ideological control of the cultural apparatuses which help to buttress and stabilize the rule of the dominant class. This ideological process includes the power to control representation and construct the "other" or "others" upon whom denigrated identities are imposed. Marx was cognizant of the fact that "racialized" power relations were operationalized at both the material and the symbolic/representational levels—that it was both a political/economic relationship as well as a cultural process. Such a dialectical understanding, however, is all too often lost on post-Marxists and critical multicultural theorists who often seek to severe culture from political economy (Scatamburlo-D'Annibale and McLaren, 2003). Marx's observations about the

Irish are supported by the work of McNally who examined the experiences of the Irish in relation to the origins of racial oppression within the context of British colonialism. He is worth quoting at length:

> It was only with the emergence of agrarian capitalism in the sixteenth and seventeenth centuries that England established a new regime of colonial domination that secured its control, a regime that was to become the model for its ventures in America. This new system of control emerged tentatively in the sixteenth century when four wars were fought and a number of colonizing initiatives launched… [The] marriage of plunder with ethno-racial discrimination established the basic structures of racial oppression as it would come to be practiced in America. Violence and terror, systematic discrimination and enslavement were all employed…Of course, a regime of oppression and discrimination of this sort requires some sort of ideological justification…A key ideological move was to claim that, because they were not civilized, the Irish were not in fact Christians. Since the dominant world-view held that "savages" could not be Christians, apologists for the conquest of Ireland set about to prove Irish barbarity. To that end, a whole series of racist stereotypes were constructed depicting the Irish as licentious, incestuous, pagan and uncivilized (2002, pp. 103–104).

In a somewhat similar vein, scholars like Pieterse have illuminated the historical conditions that resulted in various groups including the Irish and the Chinese being categorized as morally inferior, backwards, savage, and childlike. Pieterse (1995) noted that the peoples of Europe both within regions and within countries were viewed as much as rungs on the racial 'ladder' as were peoples or 'races' outside Europe. For example, the British upper classes also regarded their own working class as almost a race apart.

Pieterse (1995) contends that the categorization of people as inferior and subordinate was most often tied to their positions "in the labour market" and claims that "the concept of race grew up as an *extension* of thinking in terms of class…as an alternative and additional mode of hierarchical ordering" (p. 219). While Pieterse clearly acknowledges that groups like the Irish and the Chinese do not share the same legacy of slavery with Blacks, the examples he provides point to the necessity of understanding racist formations within a broad interpretive framework. This sentiment is echoed by David McNally who maintains that the Irish experience "provides an important confirmation of the pioneering argument made by Trinidadian historian Eric Williams" who, in his "landmark book *Capitalism and Slavery* (1944)," claimed that slavery had to be understood "principally as an economic institution out of which racism" grew (McNally, 2002, p. 105). The many historical examples that illustrate the relationship between labor and the processes of racialization point to the necessity of understanding racist configurations contextually and in terms of *capitalist class relations*.

Of course, as we noted above, the very notion of class—and particularly a Marxist conception of class—has been relegated to the scrapheap of history by the sentinels of intellectual fashion. Today in the social sciences as well as in public and popular discourse, we are confronted by an iron wall whose purpose is to further ghettoize Marxist conceptions of class from less combative Weberian and neo-Weberian conceptualizations (Scatamburlo-D'Annibale and McLaren, forthcoming). As well, we are surrounded, especially within the discourses of critical pedagogy, by a motivated amnesia with respect to the efficacy and strategic potential of a Marxist analyses of class. Debates have ensued about whether or not critical pedagogy, as a field of study, has adequately incorporated issues of race and racism into its analyses. Some researchers have suggested that the Marxist foundations of critical pedagogy have led it to privilege issues of social class over race and other forms of "difference" (Lynn, 2004). Others have sweepingly declared that the entire enterprise of critical pedagogy is not only constrained by its "Marxist Eurocentricity" but that it is based on "White identity politics" (Allen, 2004). In such narratives, Marxian theory itself is maligned as Eurocentric and racist. This is often accomplished by invoking hackneyed academic buzzwords (i.e. universalizing, totalizing, etc.,) that have gained such currency and become so pervasive that it is no longer necessary to explain what these terms imply. Contrary to those who advocate the abandonment of critical pedagogy's Marxist roots and who have sought to marginalize the very concept of class, we believe that Marx has become even more relevant in light of current historical conditions.

CLASS MATTERS

When it comes to Marxist approaches to interrogating racism, the standard judgements can be "summed up in reflex epithets such as economistic, productivist, deterministic" (San Juan, Jr., 2003). However, we ardently assert that the insights of Marx and those working within the broad parameters of the Marxist tradition still have something to say despite proclamations to the contrary. Indeed, San Juan Jr. (2003) argues that a recent translation of Albert Memmi's magisterial book *Racism*, reminds us that any understanding of the complex network of ideas and practices classified by that term will always lead us to the foundational bedrock of class relations. Contrary to what many have claimed, Marxist theory does not relegate categories of "difference" (including those based on 'race') to the conceptual crematorium; rather, it seeks to reanimate such categories by exploring how they are refracted through material relations of power and privilege and linked to relations of production.

Contemporary Marxist explorations of race and racism emphasize a thorough understanding of the complexities inherent in the wider political and economic systems in which differences are embedded. Indeed, Marx clarified that constructions of race and ethnicity "are implicated in the circulation processes of variable capital." To the extent that they be understood as "social constructions" rather than as essentialist categories, the effect of exploring their insertion into the "circulation of variable capital (including positioning within the internal heterogeneity of collective labor and hence, within the division of labor and the class system)" must be interpreted as a "powerful force reconstructing them in distinctly capitalist ways" (Harvey, 2000, p. 106). Unlike many contemporary narratives which tend to focus on one or another form of oppression, the irrefragable power of Marx's historical materialism resides in its ability to reveal (i) how forms of oppression based on categories of difference (like those of race) do not possess relative autonomy from class relations but rather constitute the ways in which oppressions are lived/experienced within a class-based system; and (ii) how all forms of social oppression function within an overarching capitalist system.[17] While Marxism is often accused of neglecting all kinds of difference—of race, gender, and so on, it is important to acknowledge that it is capitalism—not Marxism—that recognizes no differences. Differences are "at once abolished by capitalism" by turning all people—regardless of gender, race, or ethnicity—into instruments of production (Ahmad, 1998, p. 22)

In their discussions about the importance of critical race theory to critical pedagogy and critical social theory in general, Parker & Stovall (2004:174) suggest that there are "some salient positions which undergird critical race theory in education…that in turn have implications for critical pedagogy." Included in that list is a suggestion that "the experiences of racial groups merit intellectual pursuit because of the uniqueness of the cultural, historical and contemporary experiences of persons of color." At the most basic level, we have no quarrel with such an assertion since we believe it is imperative to retain the category of lived experience as a reference point. We would, however, take issue with the uncritical fetishization of 'experience' that tends to assume that experience somehow guarantees the 'authenticity' of knowledge and which often treats experience as self-explanatory and transparent. It is important to make connections between seemingly isolated situations and/or particular experiences by exploring how they are constituted in, and circumscribed by, broader historical and social circumstances.

We shouldn't examine experience using some discrete approach reserved for formal contemplative thought that reduces experience to some internal object. Rather, we need to understand experience as dialectically constituted in and through structures of mediation that have been formed historically. Experiential understandings, in and of themselves, are suspect because, dialectically, they constitute a unity of opposites—they are at once unique, specific and personal, but also thoroughly partial, social, and the products of historical forces about which individuals may know little or nothing (Gimenez, 2001). In this sense, a rich description of immediate experience in terms of consciousness of a particular form of oppression (racial or otherwise) can be an appropriate and indispensable point of departure. Such understandings, however, can easily become isolated incidents in the prison house of "difference" unless they transcend the immediate perceived points of oppression, confront the social system in which they are rooted, and expand into a complex and multifaceted analyses that are capable of mapping out the general organization of social relations.

E. San Juan, Jr. (2003) has recently and compellingly articulated why we need to reject a market-relations approach to class analysis that locates discrimination by race in biased monopolistic practices, and why it is ill-advised to conceive of racial inequality in the sphere of unequal exchange. We reject both the notion that ideology and politics determine the labor market and that racial dynamics (as ideological formations and practices) determine class relationships. We agree with Bannerji (2000) that this requires a broad class-based approach:

> Having a concept of class helps us to see the network of social relations constituting an overall social organization which both implicates and cuts through racialization/ ethnicization and gender...[a] radical political economy [class] perspective emphasizing exploitation, dispossession and survival takes the issues of...diversity [and difference] beyond questions of conscious identity such as culture and ideology, or of a paradigm of homogeneity and heterogeneity...or of ethical imperatives with respect to the 'other.' (pp. 7, 19)

In line with San Juan, Jr. and Bannerji, we assert that the United States continues to function not as a democratic polity but as a class-divided racial polity because racial exclusion and differential entitlements to whites based on property relations is firmly at the center of the neoliberal capitalist system.

CLASS-IFYING 'RACE'

The much-vaunted race-class-gender triptych found in the "intersectionality thesis" maintains that race, class and gender mutually inform each other, producing the hybrid or mestizaje subject (subjects that are oppressed in different ways, according to where they are located within the triptych, given certain contexts or relational conditions with the social order). However, we would emphasize that class exploitation can be considered the material armature or material basis for other forms of oppression within capitalist society. We argue that when one speaks about racism and sexism, for example, it is inappropriate to talk about 'classism' in the same way since class exploitation is not simply one form of oppression among others. Rather class and class exploitation constitutes the ground upon which other 'isms' of oppression are sustained within capitalist societies (Scatamburlo-D'Annibale & McLaren, 2003).

When we claim that class antagonism or struggle is one in a series of social antagonisms – 'race', class, gender, etc. – we often forget the fact that *class sustains the conditions that produce and reproduce the other antagonisms*, which is not to say that we can simply reduce racism to class. In other words, class struggle is the specific antagonism—the generative matrix—that helps to structure and shape the particularities of the other antagonisms. It creates their conditions of possibility. While racism often does take on a life of its own, its material basis can be traced to the means and relations of production within capitalist society—to the social division of labor that occurs when workers sell their labor-power for a wage to the capitalist (i.e, to the ownership of the means of production). To ignore class exploitation when you are talking about racism is a serious mistake.

However, class exploitation is a topic that is very often ignored within schools of education. If it is discussed, it is often reduced to a discussion of unequal 'resource distribution' and this ignores the fact that exploitation is a fundamental character of capitalism, that it is constituent of the labor/capital relation. The unwillingness of many educators to understand or accept this relationship (class as a social relation) has caused even the educational Left to evacuate reference to historical structures of totality and universality. Class struggle is a determining force that structures 'in advance' the very agonistic terrain in which other political, racial and gender antagonisms take place. A politics that reduces class exploitation to one form of oppression amongst others re-narrates class struggle against economic exploitation and between exploiters and the exploited as cultural struggles against the dominant discourses of the 'haves' against those of the 'have nots' thus camouflaging continuing efforts by the capitalist state to subsidize the wealthy few at the expense of the many and, disguising in cultural garb, the reality of class as the unmet needs of the majority. This is not to say that cultural discourses are secondary to economic relations, or to maintain that symbolic production has no political significance or potential, or that resistance at the level of culture is trivial. Rather, we are suggesting that it is politically, pedagogically, and conceptually mistaken to reduce the reality of class struggle, the social division of labor, and relations of production into a terrain of unstable constellations of meaning and indeterminability and incommensurable discourses that seemingly bear little relationship to the messy terrain of capitalist social relations.

As E. San Juan, Jr. (2004) asserts, the separation of race and racism from the social relations of production, effectively treats them mainly as issues of ethnicity and the politics of 'difference." In doing so, the "multiculturalist problematic" operates effectively as a hegemonic scheme of peacefully managing the crisis of race, ethnicity, gender and labor in countries such as the United States. It effectively neutralizes the perennial conflicts in the system by containing diversity in a common grid and selling diversity in order to preserve the ethnocentric paradigm of commodity relations that structure the experience of life-worlds within globalizing capitalism. According to San Juan, Jr. (2004), an understanding of the hegemony of the United States as a racial polity must begin with a historical materialist approach grounded in the labor/capital dialectic, where class is seen as an antagonistic relation between labor and capital, and where "race" is understood historically as a manifestation of the class-conflicted structure of capitalism and its political/ ideological/judicial process of class rule.

Consequently, it is important to bring educational reform movements into conversation with movements that speak to the larger totality of capitalist social relations and which challenge capital's social universe. We need to keep our strategic focus on capitalist exploitation if we want to have effective anti-racist, struggles. We need to challenge global capitalism universally, which does not mean we ignore other social antagonisms and forms of oppression (the horizon of which capitalism functions to sustain). Jettisoning the Marxist view that class as a social relation serves as an important structural determinant of ideologies and practices sanctioning racial oppression in capitalist society, critical race theory and multiculturalism fail to foreground the fundamental importance of the social division of labor in the capitalist production process as a key factor in understanding racism. This dilemma has especially important consequences today, as capital's vampire-like drive for self-expansion is accumulating more surplus value in the unproductive sections of the labor market, and in doing so is further devastating the crumbling infrastructures left behind by previous modes of capitalist value augmentation that were declared unholy by the Thatcher and Reagan and Bush administrations.

The reason we need to focus on a critique of political economy in our anti-racist efforts is that racism in capitalist society results from the racialization of the social relations of capitalist exploitation. In San Juan, Jr.'s view (2004), multiculturalism has deliquesced into a disavowed, inverted, self-referential form of racism, a "racism with a distance." It "respects" the identity of the Other, conceiving the Other as a self-enclosed "authentic" community towards which he or she, the multiculturalist, maintains a strict distance rendered possible by his privileged universal position as White. Thus, dominant forms of liberal multiculturalism constitute in some cases a form of indirect racism in so far as the dominant imperial White subject retains the position as the privileged empty point of universality from which one is able to appreciate (and depreciate) properly other particular cultures.

The conclusion to be drawn, according to San Juan, Jr. (2004), is that the problematic of multiculturalism is the form of appearance of the totalizing presence of capitalism as universal world system. Here, in this world of ersatz revolutionary resistance, multiculturalists can fight for cultural differences while at the same time leaving the basic homogeneity of the capitalist world-system intact. While we surely must recognize the integrity and value of peoples' cultures and life-forms, and for their collective right to exist and flourish, the key issue is how to universalize this multiplicity and these autonomous singularities. This process of universalization cannot exist as long as the global logic of corporate accumulation determines the everyday life of people on this planet. The key is to abolish class divisions and to struggle for a socialist alternative to capitalism. However, we want to stress that in no way does this position ignore forms of non-class domination. We agree with Foster (2005) when he writes that the various forms of non-class domination which are so endemic to capitalist society, so much a part of its strategy of divide and conquer, must be addressed. No progress can be made in overcoming class oppression without also fighting...these other social divisions.

CONCLUSION

> ... we will take our stand against the evils [of capitalism, imperialism, and racism] with a solidarity derived from a proletarian internationalism born of socialist idealism (National Office of the Black Panther Party, February 1970).

> Experiences have taught us that understanding things holistically is difficult, and organizing around Marxist ideas and calls for solidarity have never been easy. There are so many 'identities' thought to be more important and easier to recognize and rally around than class. However, this has resulted in spotty ameliorative progress at best, improvements that were and are mostly at the mercy of what those who direct the capitalist system believe is necessary for their own advantage presently and in the future. There have been unjust

> systems before capitalism; however, this system, in all its complexities, is the most powerful secular system in the world today; furthermore, those who suffer, directly and indirectly, must understand how it works in order to oppose it. Marx and Marxists have been our most informative teachers on this subject; therefore, it is within and around the best of this intellectual-activist tradition that promises the best results (Brosio, 2008, pp. 15–16).

As we write—amidst the 2008 election campaign—the historical presidential candidacy of Barack Obama has thrust discussions of 'race' to the forefront. Speculations about whether "working-class" Whites will vote for him are rampant as are attempts to sabotage his campaign because he is Black, or according to some, not "Black" enough. And, not surprisingly, his presidential run prompted overt racists to come scurrying out of their caves. Indeed, one need only peruse any one of a number of disturbing Right-wing websites to see hate-mongers peddling rabid forms of racial hatred. Some have even implied that Obama is a covert Muslim sympathetic to terrorists. More "refined" conservatives have launched charges of "liberal elitism" to characterize the presidential hopeful as uppity and 'out of touch' with hard-working, God-fearing, 'real' [read: white] Americans from the heartland in their attempt to perpetuate divide and conquer strategies that would more readily maintain the structures of White supremacy and economic dominance.

After Obama's former pastor, Reverend Jeremiah Wright, thundered against racism and injustice, the Right-wing noise machine went into overdrive. Outrage was the order of the day as conservative commentators—frothing at the mouth—accused Wright (and by extension, Obama) of being anti-American, unpatriotic and, of course, racist. The mainstream media, particularly cable news networks that truck in sensationalism and scandal, jumped onto the proverbial bandwagon replaying segments of one of Wright's fiery orations (taken out of context) on a seemingly endless loop.[18] As a result, Obama was literally forced to deliver a speech on "race" in America that was later credited with sparking a wide-ranging conversation on the topic. While his speech and his momentous candidacy has, undoubtedly, precipitated such dialogues, most of them have largely remained at the symbolic and interpersonal level—as though racism is merely about individual "attitudes" and cultural misunderstandings—rather than a structural and institutionalized phenomenon rooted in capitalist class relations. Some have pointed, rather naively, to Obama's presidential run and his generally well-received address as evidence that America's 'racial divide' has been—if not completely—at least, partially overcome. Such narratives reinscribe the imaginary notion of "color-blindness" that not only ignores the concrete realities of racial oppression but also lends succor to the myth of the American dream where *anyone*—regardless of race, ethnicity, class, gender, etc.—can achieve *anything* if they adopt the "bootstrap" mentality of hard work and personal responsibility. Unfortunately, the "victim-blaming tough-love message" encapsulated in Obama's speech also reflected a form of cultural racism in that it focused on the "alleged behavioral pathologies in poor black communities" rather than class realities (Reed, 2008).

What these examples—along with the ones previously discussed herein—clearly demonstrate is how omnipresent discourses of "race" are in America. Yet, despite all the "race talk" surrounding Obama's campaign and the talk of "historical" change if an African-American is elected president, we agree with Marable (1995) who suggests that the problem with the prism of race is that it simultaneously clarifies and distorts reality and that it often clouds the concrete reality of class, and blurs the actual structures of power and privilege. The conversations that have been engendered thus far have failed to probe the underlying substance of racism and racial economic disparities that are firmly rooted in class formations. Moreover, any discussions of commonalities, particularly in terms of material and class interests, have been effectively undermined by the inordinate focus on race and difference.

Thus, as noted above, we contend that 'race' as a conceptual category, often hides more than it reveals. More significantly, it does not necessarily provide an adequate basis for political mobilization within a capitalist system as Brosio implies. Relations of oppression and strategies for transformative social change are best understood within the context of class rule as Bannerji, Marable, San Juan, Jr., and others have suggested. However, that would compel us to forge a conceptual shift in theorizing, which entails (among other things) moving beyond categories of 'difference' and 'race' as the dominant prisms through which we interpret social reality and envision the possibilities for substantive social change.[19]

While most working-class citizens—of all hues—have suffered immensely under the neoliberal economic policies of the last three decades, most recently promoted with extreme vigor by the Republican right and the Bush administration, it has been communities of color that have suffered disproportionately (Muhammad, 2008; Wright, 2008). Yet, this suffering cannot be adequately addressed or challenged by relying on narratives of "race;" nor can these disparities be overcome by the possibility of a "Black" president and politics as usual. For, regardless of racial and ethnic differences, it is certainly the case that we now live in what Doug Henwood (2008) has called the "second Gilded Age." Today, as in the robber baron era of runaway capitalism a century ago, the "gap between those at the top and the rest of us is simply staggering." The richest "1 percent of Americans currently hold wealth worth $168 trillion, nearly $2 trillion more than the bottom 90 percent" (Cavanagh & Collins, 2008, p. 11). Additionally, in the US, one in four jobs "pay less than a poverty-level income" and recent statistics indicate that at least 37 million residents in America are "officially poor" (Jeffery, 2006, p. 20). Concomitantly, the richest 1 percent of the American population—George W. Bush's "haves" and "have mores" base—continue to reap the benefits of his generous tax cut package which represents one of the most brazen redistributions of income to the wealthy that the nation has ever seen. Twenty-two years ago, American CEOs earned an average forty-two times more than production workers. Today, they earn 431 times more. In 2004, while "seventy-six Americans became billionaires," poverty increased and "real median earnings of full-time workers fell" (Juhasz, 2006, p. 100). These are the concrete class realities that exist—tales of desperation and despair alongside ostentatious displays of avarice.

So egregious is the class divide in the US, that the *Wall Street Journal* now dedicates a full-time beat reporter to cover what he calls "Richistan." Of course,

> Richistan did not suddenly appear on the American scene. Our top-heavy era has evolved from a heavily bankrolled effort by conservatives and corporations to instill blind faith in the market as the magic elixir that can solve any problem. This … war against common sense has preached that tax cuts for the rich help the poor, that labor unions keep workers from prospering, that regulations protecting consumers attack freedom … our elected officials have rewritten the rules that run our economy—on taxes and trade, on wage policies and public spending—the benefit wealthy asset owners and global corporations (Cavanagh and Collins, 2008, pp. 11–12).

In spite of this conservative and corporate assault, ironically, the only talk of "class" in the current election campaign has come from right-wingers who slickly suggest that any actions that might address the colossal redistribution of wealth which has taken place over the past three decades (and especially under Bush, Jr.) amount to a form of "class warfare."[20] And, yet, the true nature of class warfare was rightfully identified by billionaire Warren Buffet who recently stated that "there's class warfare all right, but it's my class, the rich class, that's making war, and we're winning" (Buffet, cited in Stein, 2006). As Cavanagh and Collins argue, it is important to recognize the concerted effort undertaken by conservatives and their corporate masters to promote unfettered capitalism and neoliberal ideology to the detriment of the many, for the benefit of the few. And, of course, part of their strategy has been to exploit difference and to marshal cultural and racial anger to achieve what are essentially economic ends (Frank, 2004). Himmelstein noted almost two decades ago, that the mobilization of big business around a conservative agenda involved an effort to influence politics and policies "in the interest not of specific firms or industries but of capitalists generally" and their *class* interests (1990, p. 9). Thus, racial antagonism and discourses of "difference" were employed so that (to paraphrase Leonard Pitts) those in the aeries of wealth and power could rest assured that a common language of class would remain unarticulated and their economic interests uncontested.

At this particular historical juncture, many (particularly those on the Right) are once again trying to use "race" to obfuscate the fundamental class structure of American society and to prevent the majority of working people from discovering that necessary common language Pitts alluded to. This has long been part and parcel of the Southern strategy as we have argued throughout this chapter. But, while the right has attempted to fan the flames of racial anomosity for economic ends, liberals and so-called "progressives" have also succumbed to "race talk"—that is, using race as the primary *lingua franca* of social justice as Reed (cited above) notes. However, we suggest that in order to get a firm grasp of the current class war being waged, we must veer from the safe path of the mainstream and what passes for radical scholarship—with its fascination with difference—to the lost highway of Marxist theory.

While the clarion cry for class struggle is often spurned by a cultural left, we would dare to remind them that such a struggle does, in fact, exist in the form of the "struggle by capital for profit," the struggle of capital to impose "its form of social relations" on all of us (Holloway, 2003, p. 233). It is a class struggle being waged by those few who continue to reap outrageous profits on the backs of the laboring classes. If Warren Buffet can readily confess that class warfare exists, we must ask ourselves why there is such reluctance on the part of "critical" educators to vigorously engage Marx, the concept of class, and capitalism itself.

Having stigmatized Marxists as criminal daredevils, as diabolical killer clowns, contemporary soi-disant culturalists—who fancy themselves as dissident intelligentsia—are foreclosing from the totality of history. These academic cultural workers who decry materialist critique only provide more pathways for the cannibalistic capitalist machine to insinuate itself into the world of pedagogy and praxis. This will only add to the narrowing to our understandings as the trauma of neoliberalism is dislocated from class to the register of cultural differences. As Brosio observes, structural realities "often remain hidden when concentration is limited to the cultural body around the structural skeleton" (2008, p. 9). Critical pedagogy must resist increasing embourgeoisement and political domestication if it is to remain relevant to the struggle to build a different world outside of capitalism's law of value. It must provide a vibrant forum where alternatives to capitalism and capitalist institutions can be discussed and debated without limiting the horizons of what *might be* to "some kind of New Deal or social democracy" (Brosio, 2008, p. 9). To this end, we agree with Brosio that Marxist thought is "still *primus inter pares* for analyzing and combating today's neoliberal capitalism" (2008, p. 1). More importantly, those committed to substantive social transformation must recognize that true "historical" change will only come about when we correctly identify the class ties that both bond us to each other and enslave us within capitalism's social form.

Of course, it is not enough to have a class-based approach, particularly if such an approach would remain in the realm of theory. We also require a philosophy of praxis. The important issue here is not just to undress racism to reveal its roots in capitalist class relations but to create a social universe in which such relations are transcended. We need, in short, to continue to explore the fertile legacy of Marx's work and the category of class. This is the impending challenge for a truly radical politics for we must remind ourselves that it was Marx who sought to develop "a form of common language for politics so that the scattered and disunited working-class people could understand their plight and make common cause in solidarity to overcome their oppression" (Brosio, 2008, p. 5). Marxism and the struggle for socialism must be resurrected by those seeking to change the world for that would genuinely be "change we can believe in." This is the impending challenge for critical pedagogy.

NOTES

1 See www.legendsofamerica.com/LA/-kynching9.html

2 See www.spartacus.schoolnet.co.uk/USACstrangefruit.htm

3 See the website for the documentary *Strange Fruit* at www.newsreel.org/films /strangefruit.htm

4 See www.spartacus.schoolnet.co.uk/USACstrangefruit.htm

5 On their way to investigate the burning of a black church, the trio's station wagon was intercepted by Deputy Sheriff Cecil Price and they were taken into custody on an alleged speeding violation.

While they were being detained, Price contacted local members of the Ku Klux Klan. And, when the trio was released later that evening, a posse of Klansmen—organized by Killen—stalked the young activists and viciously murdered them. Their bodies were discovered 44 days later, buried in an earthen dam.

6 Originally, Kent Conrad, a Democrat from North Dakota also refused to support the resolution but he later changed his mind and joined as a co-sponsor.

7 See "Limbaugh blasted Mehlman's renunciation of GOP racial tactics: "Republicans are going to go bend over and grab the ankles." http://mediamatters.org

8 "States' rights" had long been used as a code word for resistance to black advances, and it was a code clearly understood by white Southern voters in general, and the KKK most definitely.

9 See "Under President Bush's 'Leadership' African-Americans Lose Ground" August 6, 2004 http://actforvictory.org

10 Ashcroft's religious inclinations are well known. He gained some notoriety for his Pentacostal paean "Let the Eagle Soar," but his practice of anointing himself with oil (ala King David) really caught the public's attention. In an Associated Press article that ran on 01/11/2001, Ashcroft was quoted to say that he would "invite God's presence" while making crucial decisions and that he compared his political victories and defeats to resurrections and crucifixions. He also admitted to anointing himself with oil before each of his gubernatorial terms and with Crisco before he was sworn into the U.S. Senate (because no holy oil could be found) See, the Associated Press (2001) Ashcroft Invites God on Decisions. http://quest.cjonline.com/stories/011101/gen_0111017691.shtml

11 As noted by Geoff Price (2004) Bush Sr.'s 1988 campaign was the first to employ the tactic of using multiple independent organizations to blanket the media with campaign ads and news coverage of a politically biased nature. The Willie Horton ad campaign is now a textbook case for political campaign strategists to study and emulate. This strategy accomplished two key election goals by (a) getting around campaign finance laws, and by (b) keeping the "independent" messages separate and distinct from the candidate. This was important for the 1988 Bush campaign because this particular ad campaign was a racist attack on his opponent Michael Dukakis. See, G. Price (2004) "Fahrenheit 911 Just Scratches the Surface and Misses Target" in *Rational Revolution.net*. http://www.rationalrevolution.net/articles/fahrenheit_911_just_ scratches_th.htm

12 Thurmond, of course, ran on a feverishly racist Dixiecrat ticket in 1948 with the slogan "Segregation Forever."

13 Apparently, there were no hard feelings between Bush and Lott—Lott served as Master of Ceremonies at Bush's second inauguration.

14 See the Katrina timeline on www.thinkprogress.org

15 We can also point to how neoliberalism and the religion of the "free market" lent itself to the utter destruction witnessed in New Orleans. As Michael Parenti (2005) has argued, the neoliberal agenda so vigorously pursued by the Bush administration led to a devastating cut in government services, including the decision to slice $71.2 million from the New Orleans Corp of Engineers as well as decisions to let developers destroy the wetlands which once served as a natural environmental buffer all in the name of private profits.

16 Marx, Karl. (1870). "Marx to Sigfrid Meyer and August Vogt in New York." http://www.marxists.org/archive/marx/works/1870/letters/70_04_09.htm

17 Given this argument, it is necessary to be clear about how we conceptualize class and class relations. First and foremost we reject understandings of class which tend to be Weberian or neo-Weberian and which "ignore discussions of class and labour" (Munt, 2000:3) And we reject the facile notion that dynamics of class can be adequately captured by its common equation with lifestyle, voting preference, income, status, or some nominal aspect of personal identity—or that it is over-determined by racial identity. Moreover, we find that efforts—often as a result of a lack of understanding of Marxist theory rather than a lack of scruples—to reduce class to one social characteristic that "intersects" with others, such as 'race' or gender deeply problematical.

18 Amidst all the hoopla about Reverend Wright, what so many white conservatives and liberals alike failed to realize is that African-Americans (and communities of color more generally) have often

constructed "counter-discourses" in homes and, indeed, churches "in order to maintain their sense of humanity" in a profoundly racist culture (Leonardo, 2005, p. 44). They know all too well that their sanity, sense of self-worth and development as both individuals and as a collective, depend on forging alternative spaces and discourses that challenge the "official" narratives of white racial supremacy that are pervasive not only within the broader dominant culture but within what Leonardo (2005, p. 44) calls the "hidden curriculum of whiteness" that devalues their histories and experiences.

[19] An important caveat: as we have argued elsewhere (Scatamburlo-D'Annibale and McLaren, 2005), we are aware of some potential implications for white Marxist criticalists to unwittingly support racist practices in their criticism of "race-first" positions articulated in the social sciences and within some strands of critical race theory. In those instances, white criticalists wrongly go on 'high alert' in placing theorists of color under special surveillance for downplaying an analysis of capitalism and class. Such positions of the part of white criticalists must be condemned, as must efforts to stress class analysis primarily as a means of creating a *white vanguard position* in the struggle against capitalism. Rather, by drawing on the works of prominent theorists of color working in a broadly construed Marxist tradition, our own position is one that attempts to link practices of racism to the central, totalizing dynamics of class society in order to resist white supremacist capitalism more fully.

[20] While John Edwards did attempt to inject discussions of poverty and inequality into his unsuccessful run for nominee of the Democratic Party, he was, of course, ridiculed for it because of his expensive hair cuts.

REFERENCES

Ahmad, A. (1998). The communist manifesto and the problem of universality. *Monthly Review, 50*(2), 12–23.

Ahmad, A. (1997). Culture, nationalism and the role of intellectuals. In E. Meiksins-Wood & J. B. Foster (Eds.), *In defense of history: Marxism and the postmodern agenda* (pp. 51–64). New York: Monthly Review Press.

Allen, R. L. (2004). Whiteness and critical pedagogy. *Educational Philosophy and Theory, 36*(2), 121–136.

Bacon, J. (2005). Saying what they've been thinking. *Extra!, 18*(6), 13–15.

Bannerji, H. (2000). *The dark side of the nation: Essays on multiculturalism, nationalism and gender*. Toronto, Canada: Canadian Scholars' Press.

Brosio, R. (2008). Marxist thought: Still primus inter pares for understanding and opposing the capitalist system. *Journal for Critical Educational Studies, 6*(1). Retrieved May 5, 2008, from http://www.jceps.com/?pageID=article&articleID=113

Cavanagh, J., & Collins, C. (2008, June 30). The new inequality: The rich and the rest of us. *The Nation, 286*(25), 11–12.

Dyer-Witheford, N. (1999). *Cyber-Marx: Cycles and circuits of struggle in high-technology capitalism*. Urbana, IL and Chicago: University of Illinois Press.

Dyson, M. E. (2001, January 29). Bush's black faces." *The Nation*. Retrieved May 4, 2005, from http://www.thenation.com

Feagin, J., & Hernan, V. (1995). *White racism*. New York & London: Routledge.

Foster, J. B. (2005). The renewing of socialism. *Monthly Review, 57*(3), 1–18.

Gilroy, P. (2000). *Against race: Imagining politic culture beyond the color line*. Cambridge: Belknap.

Gimenez, M. (2001). Marxism and class, gender and race: Rethinking the trilogy. *Race, Gender & Class, 8*(2), 23–33.

Greider, W. (2004, June 28). The Gipper's economy. *The Nation, 278*(25), 5.

Hall, S. (1996). Gramsci's relevance for the study of race and ethnicity. In D. Morley & K. Chen (Eds.), *Stuart Hall: Critical Dialogues in Cultural studies* (pp. 411–440). London and New York: Routledge.

Harvey, D. (2000). *Spaces of hope*. Berkeley, CA: University of California Press.

Harvey, D. (1998). The practical contradictions of Marxism. *Critical Sociology, 24*(1/2), 1–36.

Herbert, B. (2005, July 18). An empty apology. *The New York Times*. Retrieved June 12, 2007, from http:// www.nytimes.com/2005/07/18/opinion/18herbert.html

Jackson, D. Z. (2004, June 11). He brought back black and white. *The Boston Globe*.

Jeffery, C. (2006). Poor losers: How the poor get dinged at every turn. *Mother Jones, 31*(4), 20–21.

Juhasz, A. (2006). *The Bush agenda: Invading the world, one economy at a time*. New York: Harper Collins.

Kellner, D. (2001). *Grand theft 2000: Media spectacle and a stolen election*. Lanham, MD: Rowman & Littefield.

Leonardo, Z. (2005). The color of supremacy: Beyond the discourse of 'white privilege.' In Z. Leonardo (Ed.), *Critical pedagogy and race* (pp. 37–52). Malden, MA: Blackwell Publishing.

Lynn, M. (2004). Inserting the 'race' into critical pedagogy: An analysis of 'race-based epistemologies. *Educational Philosophy and Theory, 36*(2), 153–165.

Marable, M. (1995). *Beyond black and white*. London and New York: Verso Press.

Marable, M. (2000, August 8&9). Bush's Blacks: Race traitors? Pt. I & II. *The Free Press*. Retrieved May 24, 2004, from http:// www.freepress.org

Martin, P. (2000, February 8). US presidential campaign: George W. Bush speaks at racist university. *World Socialist Web*. Retrieved April 18, 2005, from www.wsws.org/articles/2000/feb2000/bush-f08_prn.shtml

Marx, K. (1870). *Marx to Sigfrid Meyer and August Vogt in New York*. Retrieved May 16, 2004, from http://www.marxists.org/archive/marx/works/1870/letters/70_04_09.htm

McLaren, P., & Jaramillo, N. (2007). *Pedagogy and praxis in the age of empire*. Rotterdam and Taipei: Sense Publishers.

McNally, D. (2002). *Another world is possible: Globalization and anti-capitalism*. Winnipeg: Arbeiter Ring Publishing.

Mediamatters. *Limbaugh blasted Mehlman's renunciation of GOP racial tactics: "Republicans are going to go bend over and grab the ankles."* Retrieved June 6, 2007, from http://mediamatters.org

Mercer, K. (1992). 1968: Periodizing postmodern politics and identity. In L. Grossberg, et al. (Eds.), *Cultural studies* (pp. 422–437). New York: Routledge.

Mercurio, J. (2002, December 10). Lott Apologizes for Thurmond Comment. *CNN*. Retrieved May 2, 2005, from http://archives.cnn.com/2002/ALLPOLITICS/12/09/lott.comment

Miles, R., & Torres, R. (1999). Does 'race' matter? Transatlantic perspectives on racism after 'race relations.' In R. Torres (Ed.), *Race, identity and citizenship: A reader*. Oxford, UK: Basil Blackwell.

Muhammad, D. (2008, June 30). Race and extreme inequality. *The Nation, 286*(25), 26.

Munt, S. (Ed.). (2000). *Cultural studies and the working class*. New York: Cassell.

Omi, M., & Winant, H. (1986). *Racial formation in the United States*. New York: Routledge.

Palast, G. (2003). *The best democracy money can buy: The truth about corporate cons, globalization and high finance fraudsters*. New York: Plume Publishing.

Parenti, M. (2005, September 3). How the free market killed New Orleans. *ZNet*. Retrieved October 28, 2005, from http://www.zmag.org

Parker, L., & Stovall, D. (2004). Actions following words: Critical race theory connects to critical pedagogy. *Educational Philosophy and Theory, 36*(2), 167–182.

Pieterse, J. N. (1995). *White on Black: Images of Africa and Blacks in western popular culture*. New Haven, CT & London: Yale University Press.

Pittes, L., Jr. (2008, June 11). Cheney's joke about the poor isn't funny. *The Miami Herald*. Retrieved June 24, 2008, from www.miamiherald.com/living/columnists/leonard_pitts/story565679.html

Pitts, L., Jr. (2005, September 23). Katrina shows the poor still are a forgotten class. *The Miami Herald*. Retrieved October 27, 2005, from www.miami.com/mld/miamiherald/living/columnists/Leonard_pitts/12717769.htm?te

Price, G. (2004). Fahrenheit 911 just scratches the surface and misses target. In *Rational revolution.net*. Retrieved from http://www.rationalrevolution.net/articles/fahrenheit_911_just_scratches_th.htm

Rampton, S., & Stauber, J. (2004). *Banana republicans: How the right wing is turning America into a one-party state*. New York: Tarcher/Penguin.

Reed, A. (2005, October 3). Class-ifying the hurricane. *The Nation, 281*(10), 6, 8.

San Juan, E., Jr. (2003). Marxism and the race/class problematic: A re-articulation. *Cultural Logic*. Retrieved from http://eserver.org/clogic/2003/sanjuan.html

San Juan, E., Jr. (2004, November 13). Post-9/11 Reflections on Multiculturalism and Racism. *Axis of Logic*. Retrieved June 4, 2006, from http://www.axisoflogic.com/cgi-bin/exec/view.pl?archive=79&num=13554

San Juan, E., Jr. (2002). *Racism and cultural studies: Critiques of multiculturalist ideology and the politics of difference*. Durham, NC: Duke University Press.

Scatamburlo-D'Annibale, V., & McLaren, P. (forthcoming). The reign of capital: A pedagogy and praxis of class struggle. In M. Apple, et al. (Eds.), *The international handbook of critical education*. New York: Routledge.

Scatamburlo-D'Annibale, V., & McLaren, P. (2005). Class dismissed? Historical materialism and the politics of 'difference.' In Z. Leonardo (Ed.), *Critical pedagogy and race* (pp. 141–158). Malden, MA: Blackwell Publishing.

Scatamburlo-D'Annibale, V., & McLaren, P. (2003). The strategic centrality of class in the politics of "race" and "difference." *Cultural Studies/Critical Methodologies*, *3*(2), 148–175.

Solomon, N. (2001). *Confederate John*. Retrieved from www.workingforchange.com

Stein, B. (2006, November 26). In class warfare, guess which class is winning? *New York Times*. Retrieved June 16, 2008, from www.nytimes.com

Tracinski, R. (2005). An unnatural disaster: A hurricane exposes the man-made disaster of the welfare state. *The intellectual activist*. Retrieved October 6, 2005, from http://tiadaily.com

Wallace, M. (1994). Multiculturalism and oppositionality. In H. Giroux & P. McLaren (Eds.), *Between borders: Pedagogy and the politics of cultural studies* (pp. 180–191). New York & London: Routledge.

Wise, T. (2004, June 10). Reagan, race and remembrance. *The Black Commentator*. Retrieved June 18, 2005, from www.blackcommentator.com/94/94_wise_reagan_pf.html

Wright, K. (2008, July 14). The subprime swindle: How the mortgage industry stole black America's hard-won wealth. *The Nation*, *287*(2), 11–12,14, 17–18, 20, 22.

Yassin, J. O. (2005). Demonizing the victims of Katrina. *Extra!*, *18*(6), 9–12.

Younge, G. (2005, July 11). Racism rebooted: Philadelphia, Mississippi, then and now. *The Nation*, *281*(2), 11.

Peter McLaren
Graduate School of Education & Information Studies
University of California
Los Angeles

Valerie Scatamburlo-D'Annibale
Department of Communication, Media, and Film
The University of Windsor

NOAH DE LISSOVOY

5. A GLOBAL STANDPOINT?

Reification, Globalization, and Contemporary Praxis

Globalization makes it not only strategically necessary to think about politics beyond region or nation, but existentially necessary as well, since the structure of everyday and personal experience is increasingly reorganized at the vertiginous scale of the planetary. More and more of what we do and think is affected by events and processes elsewhere, and even "distant," though distance itself seems to disappear in the very fact of this influence. For those to whom globalization, as neoimperialism or neoliberalism, has brought sudden destruction or slow deprivation, there can be no doubting this, but even those who have been most insulated register the transformation, in however distorted a fashion, as can be seen in anxieties about economic survival and cultural identity in the global North. Furthermore, the "global" itself should not be thought of merely as a unit of analysis one step beyond the nation, but rather as the name for the re-emergence, in social life and thought in the present, of the category of the *whole*. This does not have to mean theoretical grandiosity, but rather simply that the sense and fact of the totality begin to intrude on each of our own small experiences, as well as decisively upon every collective project and fate. Persons and "communities" of all kinds, as well as social movements which seek to transform their conditions of existence, are forced up against this fact, and if they want to make sense of their experience, are forced to think at this scale. At this historical moment, for activists, educators, and cultural workers, the task of thinking through the problems and contradictions of globalization, and more generally of developing a praxis oriented toward the horizon of the social totality, is an inescapable necessity.

In this effort, the work of philosopher Georg Lukács has, I believe, special importance, and above all, his central achievement, *History and Class Consciousness* (1923/1971), one of the founding texts of Western Marxism. Lukács' redeployment within Marxism of the Hegelian emphasis on totality is crucial within the context of globalization, which makes an attention to this category especially apropos and urgent. Likewise, his foregrounding of the process of reification within capitalism anticipates the profound reorderings occasioned by neoliberalism's global "ownership society," which forces every organic process and product to find its secret soul as commodity, and thus to become a frozen and fragmented participant not only in the capitalist market, but also in the discursive economy of bourgeois law and science. Lukács' suggestion that only praxis can undo the clenched knots of thinking, and put the broken pieces of being together again, should be inspiration

Z. Leonardo (ed.), Handbook of Cultural Politics and Education, 141–160.

for a new militancy in theory and practice that takes global society as its object. Above all, his concept of a revolutionary standpoint remains a provocation to those committed to social change, since, as I describe below, the essential sense of this concept, in the global era, is open in a fundamentally new way. At the same time, it is important to think beyond Lukács' own conceptualizations, in order to renew the political charge and direction of his ideas. In this chapter, I reconsider these central Lukácsian categories in light of the situation of globalization, and suggest how they might be most usefully appropriated in the present; the implications are important, as I describe, not only for theorists, but for activists and educators as well.

UNDERSTANDING REIFICATION, STANDPOINT, AND PRAXIS IN LUKÁCS

Lukács placed the phenomenon of *reification* at the center of the historical logic of capitalism, and thus at the center of any effort to understand it and struggle against it. Reification is the generalization to all of social life of commodity fetishism, as described by Marx (1867/1976), in which real social relations between people appear as *things*—that is, as commodities, whose "phantom objectivity" disguises the processes of exploitation that produce them. Once the commodity form is dominant in society, according to Lukács, reification reaches to the heights and depths of consciousness and culture, as social life at all levels becomes fragmented into objectivities which (bourgeois) thought can only approach through a formal rationality that resembles and is rooted in the calculus of the capitalist who manages commodity production. Reification seizes upon the economy, resulting in the market, its laws of exchange, and its products, and converts human creativity itself into a thing. Reification results first of all in the commodification of human activity into labor-power, but it determines as well the whole superstructure of social and intellectual activity—for example, law, government, and science. These institutions are unable to understand and interact with the world as process and totality; instead, they can only approach it through a rationalistic process that recapitulates in form the management of a factory—a "principle of rationalization based on what is and *can be calculated* " (1971, p. 88). This is a result of the fact that the contents that these institutions are concerned with (e.g. scientific data) can only show up for them in the first place as reifications—isolated and independent facts or things—and secondly because intellectual work itself has become a detached and contemplative business, rather than an intervention into social life and history.

The contradictions and reifications of bourgeois consciousness, Lukács argues, reach their purest form in philosophy, which is unable to see past the immediate forms of social life within capitalism to their determination in history. Instead, bourgeois thought seeks to organize and make sense of these facts without intervening in them, since they appear to be objectively necessary (e.g., class divisions, the structure of the state, or human beings' relation to nature). This sense of the necessity of objective conditions exists side by side with a contrary insistence on the absolute subjective freedom of the individual. But in the universe of capitalism, this is actually no more than the freedom to calculate and predict the action of the "laws" of bourgeois life. In fact, this contemplative autonomy is the ideological result of the historical experience of "creative destruction" within which the bourgeoisie disposed of the social forms of feudalism, and subordinated all human relationships to the logic of the market. However, unable to recognize this dialectical background—the historical process of class struggle—which has created modern society as a *second nature* classical philosophy limits its efforts to producing purely formal representations of reality. In short, captured by its own reifications, bourgeois thought can only understand the living process of social life, whose meaning is actually found at the level of the totality and its unfolding contradictions, as a set of systems and sub-systems governed by increasingly formal and "purified" principles, within which the subject is no more than a point of detached contemplation.

On the other hand, *critical* theory must be able to grasp the logic of reification that traverses capitalism in all of its dimensions and which has captured bourgeois thought, and in rupturing that logic, discover a political and philosophical position, or *standpoint*, that can see past it. In this way, for Lukács, class struggle becomes as much a matter of the politics of knowledge as it is a matter of the objective consolidation of social forces. In fact, the central task for the proletariat is to transcend the immediacy within which bourgeois thought is mired, since the latter can only understand its own categories as natural and necessary. Overcoming these reifications means understanding the present as a moment within history, in relation to which the facts that appear to be given are transformed into fluid processes. This critical understanding is at the same time a kind of political practice, or *praxis*, since it proceeds from and consolidates the class consciousness of the proletariat. The class consciousness of the proletariat represents the coming to consciousness of the commodity-form itself, since workers are forced to sell their capacity to work as a commodity. While they are initially bound within the same unconscious relation to the social totality that captures the bourgeoisie, workers are nevertheless in a privileged position to overcome it, since they experience the process of reification qualitatively in their own minds and bodies at work, whereas for the bourgeoisie it always remains a matter of instrumental calculation (maximizing profit or consumption). The proletariat feels the fundamental split in bourgeois society between subject and object, and between freedom and necessity, as the contradiction between their own living human selves and the objectified and abject commodity labor-power to which these selves are necessarily reduced in capitalism.

The social and historical position of the proletariat, then, confers upon it a kind of epistemological privilege. This is more than an ability to better understand society in comparison with hegemonic knowledge; rather, it means the capacity for access to the truth of history, rather than to the distortion of this truth. In other words, the proletariat, situated at the center of the social, in coming to consciousness is able to comprehend the totality of reality, rather than only one side of it. In fact, if this class is "itself nothing but the contradictions of history that have become conscious" (1971, p. 178), then the proletariat has more than privileged access to this truth; in a way, it *is* this truth, as its own conscious formation as a class is identified with the awakening of history. As it alone is able to systematically undertake the process of unraveling the reifications of bourgeois life, the standpoint of the proletariat is the truly universal one, since "the self-understanding of the proletariat is...simultaneously the objective understanding of the nature of society" (p. 149). This understanding can begin to overcome the seemingly inescapable contradictions in bourgeois life between subject and object, freedom and necessity, and form and content. On the basis of its penetration of the objectification of its own activity as the commodity labor-power, it can then unravel the process of reification throughout society. In the process, the proletariat discovers that the truth is arrived at not through passive contemplation, but rather through active intervention, in praxis, which understands society in the process of transforming it. In praxis, and within an analysis oriented toward the social whole, the frozen forms of bourgeois life can begin to be resolved into fluid historical processes. The proletariat apprehends the truth of the totality, for Lukács, because it *becomes* and thus *accomplishes* that truth.

THE LEGACY OF LUKÁCS AND FEMINIST STANDPOINT THEORY: COMPLEXIFICATIONS AND CONTROVERSIES

Lukács' project has been criticized for being overly idealistic. Mészáros (1995, pp. 312–316) argues that the absence of a vision of a practical working through of the contradictions of capitalism leads Lukács to fall back on the fantasy of a solution at the level of consciousness; for Jay this is a "privileging of...subjective consciousness over objective matter" (1984, p. 118).[1] But it should be pointed out that Lukács has had an important influence, if indirectly, on many contemporary practical struggles. Not only did the appropriation of his analysis of reification by Frankfurt School theorists open the door to a more thoroughgoing critique of modernity, and via Marcuse in particular, of its inhuman militarism, racism, and technologism,[2] but his legacy has also made possible important interventions in the fields of ecology, feminism, and education. In particular, the critical pedagogy of Paulo Freire is deeply influenced by Lukács, drawing its notions of historical subjecthood, conscientization and praxis from the conceptual field of *History and Class Consciousness*.[3] Freire's pedagogy of liberation can be seen as a transposition of Lukács' central narrative of the world-historical coming to consciousness of the proletariat—in Freire's case the submerged object of history which achieves the status of historical subject is the "oppressed" (and the student), rather than the working class per se. This framework has had a powerful international influence on adult education, literacy work, teacher education, and political organizing.

Furthermore, the appropriation of Lukács' idea of a revolutionary philosophical standpoint has been very important in feminist theory. Nancy Hartsock (1983) has elaborated a feminist epistemology rooted in women's experience within the reproduction of both goods and human beings. She has argued that a standpoint can be struggled for, on the basis of this experience, that is not captured by the hierarchical dualities and denial of relation that characterize the dominant and masculinist worldview. Sandra Harding (1993) has described the special understandings available to such a standpoint in terms of a "strong objectivity" and has argued that this epistemological privilege, which Lukács accorded to the proletariat, should be recognized as potentially belonging, in different ways, to different marginalized groups. While the immediate effects of these proposals have been on academic scholarship, in this context they have had an important impact on the practice and methodology of social science. Revealing the inherently political character of this field, feminist standpoint theory has opened a much broader range of possible (and emancipatory) approaches for students.[4]

The development of feminist standpoint theory as well as critiques of this tradition are instructive both in revealing more clearly the important difficulties already inherent in Lukács' original challenge to the separation between politics and philosophy while at the same time exposing some of the problems in appropriating this theoretical apparatus for a different subject and context. Perhaps the most persistently critiqued aspect of standpoint theory (see Hekman, 2004; Hennessy, 1993) has been the appeal to the category of *experience* as the ground for a specifically feminist transformational epistemology. It has been argued that standpoint theorists overlook the way that experience itself is discursively constructed, which makes it difficult for this category to stand outside feminist philosophy as its non-discursive (and uninterrogated) substrate. This problem is already present in Lukács, to the extent that the proletariat's experience of the process of production is merely *assumed* to be (partly) resistant to the ideological effects of reification (and to provide the essential basis for the overcoming of these effects). Likewise, important complexifications of early feminist standpoint theory have been provided by feminists of color, in particular Collins (2000) and Sandoval (2000), who have shown the necessity of feminist standpoints constructed as much on the basis of experiences of racism and colonization as on the basis of the experience of sexism. In addition, Collins' description of the epistemological aspects of a specifically Black feminist theorizing directly challenges the essentialism inherent in the undifferentiated referent "women" that stands at the center, for instance, of Hartsock's (1983) analysis. This work should provoke us to consider the range of differences already elided by Lukács in his monolithic conceptualization of the proletariat. If a revolutionary standpoint is premised on the experience of the proletariat, how has that experience essentially varied with variations of gender, nationality, ethnicity, industrial sector, etc. even within the European proletariat that is Lukács' concern? At the same time, the development of standpoint theory offered by Collins and Sandoval points forward to the kinds of enlargement of the subject that any liberatory global standpoint must think through.

However, as standpoint theory moves further from the universalism argued for by Lukács (as well as by Hartsock in the context of gender), it becomes more difficult to distinguish this approach from a simple perspectivalism. This is an important problem since, as Harding (1993) explains, standpoint theory consistently claims to refuse a relativist or perspectivalist stance. Her own concept of "strong objectivity" seeks to preserve the principle that different propositions can be (objectively) more or less true and that different standpoints can have more or less access to the truth, while also allowing for the possibility and legitimacy of multiple standpoints. However, as standpoints do proliferate, these two claims begin to collide, or at least to result in a complicated portioning out of "objectivity" which makes it difficult to preserve the possibility of identifying those that are closer to the truth. Politically and philosophically, at any rate, this position is very different from Lukács' insistence that the standpoint of the proletariat is *uniquely* adequate to the historical moment of late capitalism, and uniquely capable of discovering universal truths and universally valid modes of practical reason in this moment. Being faithful to Lukács means holding to the possibility that a valid universalism can emerge from historical experience (rather than from the minds of the philosophers), even if this universalism must look somewhat different from the one that he describes. If this universalism can work through the differences between different groups' historical experiences and perspectives toward a common project and identification, it should be able to build on the strengths of distinct social struggles. One way to articulate the difference, then, between such a global project and the various approaches to feminist standpoint theory, is that a global standpoint would aim at an adequate conception of the coherent *union* rather than of the *intersection* of different experiences and understandings of oppression.

A NEW TERRAIN: REIFICATION AND GLOBALIZATION

Before a new coherence can be found for the notion of standpoint in the global era, however, we must first explore the extension and modulation of the process of reification in the context of globalization. In this regard, I believe that for liberatory movements in the present Lukács' account is indispensable. Its responsiveness to the implacable process of reification is unmatched, and the openings it provides for thinking about transformational praxis and agency are extraordinarily powerful. However, the terms of his argument need to be transposed to a much vaster scale than that for which they were originally designed. His account rests upon the classical Marxian axiom that the objectification of labor into the commodity labor-power is the central instance of reification, since it is from this unique moment that surplus value and profit are derived, and since it is on this process that the universe of capital and its reproduction depend.[5] It is important to stay true to an emphasis on the objective determination of a revolutionary standpoint against perspectives that construe the privilege of oppressed groups in moralistic terms. At the same time, in unfolding new dimensions and terrains, both contemporary capitalist accumulation and movements in struggle against it implicitly challenge a narrow framing of the central logic of reification.

Lukács' shift of the emphasis in Marxist theory from a productivist focus on the labor process and on simple accumulation to a focus on the commodity form and its organization of the totality of social life has turned out to be prescient. While his analysis of reification presupposed the "universalization" of the commodity form within European societies, globalization effects a more complete universalization of this form, as capitalism reaches throughout the world and transforms almost all dimensions of life. Even before the contemporary frenzy of privatization, Lukács wrote that "reification requires that a society should learn to satisfy all its needs in terms of commodity exchange" (1971, p. 91). This imperative is inescapable in the present, as capital seeks to reorganize education, basic services and subsistence, and even the reproduction of life itself, as market functions. Furthermore, the dramatic spread of advertising and high-tech media and communications generally allows capital to insinuate itself ever more profoundly into the texture of everyday lives and bodies, creating a kind of society that is hardly captured in the term "consumer culture"—since "private" communication, thought, and relationships are increasingly always already *branded* (think of the ways in which, for example, T-Mobile, Yahoo, and Apple mediate these activities). That all of this is a matter of reification, rather than simply more and more spectacular levels of accumulation, has to do with the way in which the subject is fragmented and reconstructed in the process: this subject can increasingly prove its existence to itself and others only in its identification with a series of addresses within a virtual universe of continuous consumption (Bauman, 2000). Here, the immateriality of the knowing subject which was pursued in theoretical terms by classical philosophy (and which Lukács critiques as a central instance of reification) is achieved in practical terms, for the masses, via cell phones and "social networking" internet sites. Again, the same insoluble contradiction between freedom and necessity in bourgeois life and thought remarked on by Lukács is reproduced on a much grander scale in the present, as we face a dazzling array of new choices (cable channels, for instance, for the more affluent, but also new patented seeds and organisms in agriculture foisted on the South) which nevertheless relentlessly condemn us to the same ultimate passivity before the market and its fundamental logic.[6]

At the same time, this very hypertrophy of the process of commodification in contemporary capitalism would seem to run counter, in part, to some of the aspects of reification that Lukács describes. In his account, the categories of consciousness and ideology are central, as reification produces their particular structures that reflect the fragmentation, instrumental rationality, and contradictory logic of bourgeois society.[7] However, in the era of globalization, it often appears as if reification operates most effectively and essentially both above and below this level. On the one hand, neoliberalism, which has undertaken a spectacular commodification of global sociality in its demands for the marketization of sectors previously off-limit to capital (e.g., public utilities and natural resources), has for the most part not worried so much about the *consciousness* (or consent) of the masses who have been dispossessed in the process, and who have often struggled very hard against it (Harvey, 2003). This is important, because peasants and indigenous communities globally do not always start from the default position of ideological mystification which Lukács attributes to the proletariat, whose very subjectivity he describes as objectified into the commodity labor-power. On the other hand, the fantastic reorganization and commodification of communication in cyberspace, the media, and telecommunications seems to operate almost immediately on the *body* of the subject, as an open neural network, as much as it arranges a higher order structure of logical intelligibility within the mind itself (ideology). Ideology is always potentially the space of some communicative rationality (however distorted); but rather than aiming simply to dominate this sphere, capital in the present seems to seek to foreclose its possibilities altogether, by occupying and capturing the very conditions of social being (Hardt & Negri, 2000, 2004).

In fact, the violent reduction of organic potentiality that marks the objectification of human labor into a commodity, becomes, in the neoliberal moment of globalization, an almost total colonization of life. Not only energy and activity, but also emotion and expression, are trained into productive activities for capital, as can be seen in the expanding sector of service work, as well as in the obsessive reflection and reconstruction of the intimate textures of human affectivity in the spectacles of advertising. At the same time, in another sphere, biological organisms are being transformed into patentable property, or invented wholesale as commodities, as can be seen in the appropriation of seed stocks by biotech firms and in genetic engineering (Shiva, 2005b). In Lukács' account, the domination of labor by capital constitutes only a first order objectification, upon which the crucial superstructure is built: namely, the inert categories and institutions of bourgeois life, whose insoluble contradictions stem from a one-sided rationalization that reifies the world into isolated and calculable quantities. But in the present, that first moment of brutal objectification—the capture of a living content and its forced entry, as a commodity, into the world of exchange value—has metastasized into an omnidirectional colonization which makes this zero degree level of reification the dominant one, as the properly ideological mediations of capital become secondary. The experience of violent seizure and reconstruction by capital, which has centrally affected the subjectivity and activity of workers, is now shared by almost all that lives, grows, or flows as a natural or social good.[8] Globalization is the name, for capital, of its ultimate extrapolation. The capture and reduction of all natural or social potential to a pure point of accumulation marks the outer limit of capital's ambition, and illuminates reification in the present as an unmediated physical trauma, rather than a second-order reflection of the original objectification of labor.

In addition, as the tendencies described by Lukács are more and more exaggerated, new contradictions appear even within the sphere of instrumental reason. Unable to think the totality (since this would involve the discovery of its own partiality and irrationality), bourgeois thought seeks an ever more absolute mastery of partial spheres. "On the one hand, it acquires increasing control over the details of its social existence, subjecting them to its needs. On the other hand it loses—likewise progressively—the possibility of gaining intellectual control of society as whole and with that it loses its own qualifications for leadership" (Lukács, 1971, p. 121). This tendency characterizes contemporary science, economics, and politics, which proclaim tremendous advances at the same time that they are less and less able to understand the systemic crises that rock them more frequently and profoundly. For instance, proud of its advances in intervention and treatment of once incurable diseases, medical science is helpless in the face of a public health and environmental crisis that reproduces human misery on a grand scale even in the wealthy countries. The more perfect and yet ever narrower mastery of the real that bourgeois reason seeks ends up straining its own internal coherence. For example, while they have often been described as atavistic, the Bush

Administration's legal doctrines in relation to war, detention of prisoners, and interrogation actually represent innovations which extend the bourgeois science of law to new (even if partly invented) situations. These innovations are monstrous and obscene not because they depart from the logic of bourgeois law, but rather because they extend it into a "system applicable to all possible and imaginable cases" (Lukács, 1971, p. 96). However, at the same time, the exceptionalities they create (enemy combatants, executive privilege, etc.) challenge the rational basis of the law itself. As bourgeois reason becomes more completely "operational" (Marcuse, 1991), it threatens to become nothing more than pure *operation*—namely, the operations of capture, torture, and murder. And yet law, science, and politics must start from and appeal to some form of reason. As the process of rationalization is extended, then, the rational itself is ever more terribly frayed. The quantitative increase in reification coincides, as Lukács puts it, with its "growing inability to do justice to the phenomena, even as isolated phenomena, even as the objects of reflection and calculation" (1971, p. 208).

GLOBALIZATION, CLASS, AND THE PROBLEM OF UNIVERSALISM

If the process of reification now appears to be more pervasive than even Lukács could have imagined, then the standpoint that would challenge that reification must itself be more authentically universal. The proletariat (traditionally defined) is not as hegemonic an oppositional class in the present as in the Europe of classical Marxism. But for Lukács, the proletariat is an epistemological and political position within the totality: it is no more than an authentic revolutionary standpoint on the whole. To the extent that globalization links disparate populations through processes of accumulation and communication into a more truly shared history, then the possibility of a universal revolutionary standpoint, and the class that it would consolidate, should be even more concrete in the present. And if commodification colonizes ever more dimensions of nature, social life, and the body, then an effective praxis against it is now both more urgent and potentially more transformative, in liberating that much more of the universal subject from its objectification by the logic of capital.

However, the shift to a global frame of reference doesn't necessarily reinforce universalistic accounts of history and society, even if they are critical ones. It may instead relativize them, as the *particular* cultural determinations of these universalisms are themselves thrown into relief, and as a cosmopolitan conversation reveals a range of different oppositional identities and perspectives, not to mention histories. It could be argued that one of the most important accomplishments of the global moment is the systematic critique of the very notion of the universal—as truth, history, or class—and the foregrounding of the radical power of the subaltern narratives that these universals have obscured (Guha & Spivak, 1988; Harding, 1998; Pollock, Bhabha, Breckenridge, & Chakrabarty, 2000). Furthermore, how do we know that the apparently privileged access of the working class (and its representative philosophers) to the truth of history is something other than an effect produced by the discursive regime of historical materialism itself, or that this truth is in any sense distinguishable from the fundamentally *ideological* determination, through and through, of the consciousness of the proletariat?[9] The transition to the new terrain of the global might seem to demand a break with all pre-given philosophical and political closures, which necessarily belong after all to local histories, however dynamic and dialectical they are.

On the other hand, if we translate Lukács' insights onto this new terrain, as I attempt to do here, and accept the argument that reification has been nearly universalized within the global contradiction between domination and shared struggle against it, other questions arise. First of all, in the present, if it doesn't belong to the proletariat, whose standpoint does look out upon the totality? (What is the object that, in becoming subject, undoes the knot of reification throughout society?) In a world in which capital seeks to occupy and command every domain, what class is able to survey this whole landscape and to become a praxis against it? Specifically, among diverse moments and movements of resistance, which has access to the truth of history, or what new one could be imagined that would authentically transcend these local instances? Do actually existing antiglobalization or "alterglobalization" movements begin to accomplish this? Given varied struggles within the domains of labor, gender, race, environment, culture, etc., to what extent is the category of class, as it is understood by Lukács, still useful? If it is not, is there any power still in the Marxian insistence on the search for an intelligible logic of society and history? Similar questions need to be asked on the side of the object: Is the society of the global era just a more complex form of the "old" totality, and do the facts within it have the same status? As far as nature is concerned, do the experiences of global environmental degradation as well as the ecological movements alter its meanings and possibilities in addition to those of human being? Could there be in this way a new kind of becoming subject, of nature itself, that extends Lukács' central dialectical story to the earth as a whole?

A global geographical perspective shows that vast numbers of people are either working in the informal sector, or not at all (Davis, 2006). So if the inner logic of capital is being tendentially universalized, the same cannot be said for the class structure it was supposed to progressively sediment, at least on the surface. The proletariat was never meant to name the whole population of the disenfranchised, but it was thought that in advanced capitalism, this class would constitute the majority, and that, against the bourgeoisie, it would be the hegemonic actor (Marx & Engels, 1848/1967). However, the very "advance" of capitalism has resulted in previously unimaginable quantities of wealth being concentrated in the hands of a few individuals at the same time as vast numbers of people are forced to live in shantytowns, and to make do with little or no organized employment or services of any kind. As Davis (2006) reports, according to UN researchers, more than one billion people currently live in slums. The underclasses that Marxism has traditionally disdained now threaten, in the age of structural adjustment, to move from the margins to the center of demography and history. Any perspective that claims a privileged relationship to the totality must, in the contemporary moment, speak from the standpoint of the global population of the truly dispossessed.

This is not only a political necessity; it also follows from the dialectical logic of praxis. For Lukács, the proletariat is central because it experiences internally the terrible fragmentation of reification—the split between subject and object imposed by the regime of capital accumulation. This class can measure the ideology of individual freedom against the actual ruthless consumption of the living bodies of its members by the process of production, and in this way discover the secret of exploitation and reification. But globalization shows that reification depends in turn upon a process of extended violation. The saturation of the world by capital is not a matter of smooth and seamless incorporation into the global economy and the universe of bourgeois ideology. It is rather a process of colonization and expulsion, in which some bodies are assimilated into the process of capital reproduction, others are destroyed (in imperialist war and occupation), and still others are cast out of the sphere of organized sociality altogether (i.e., the human surplus produced by economic austerity regimes). These processes reveal the continued presence of the brutal moment of what Marx (1867/1976) called "primitive accumulation" even in contemporary capitalism.[10] Global commodification and reification also accomplish a concrete murder of the very flesh of the earth (for example in the appropriation of naturally occurring compounds by pharmaceutical companies). Lukács' dialectic demands that the class that is able to appropriate a standpoint on the totality be one that has persistently known the violations I have just described in its own experience, since in knowing them it knows the heart of capital. This global class would include the proletariat, since the miseries of industrial workers internationally are produced by these processes, but it would also crucially include the permanently unemployed, underemployed, and cast-off; the sick and the homeless; the imprisoned and those maimed by wars; as well as those injured and marginalized by environmental plunder and degradation.

TOWARD A GLOBAL STANDPOINT

Whether it makes sense in fact to call this global population a class is a difficult question, and one to which there are many different responses among social movements, even among those in explicit struggle against neoliberalism and capitalism. For some, resistance to domination is also a struggle against the worn-out categories of the old left, while for others the traditional antagonism between the organized working class and the bourgeoisie remains fundamental (see Mertes, 2004). But the question is really whether there is a new meaning, in the global era, that can animate the *structure of contradictions* that defines a dialectical and Marxian understanding of class and society; it is not necessary to be tied to orthodox conceptions of what this class would look like. For Aronowitz (2003), a movement enters into a process of class formation when it "can organize and represent itself and make demands on the system" (p. 59), or simply when it makes "historical difference" (p. 38). This is a creative enlargement of familiar definitions; however, the essential dialectical logic of the concept of class, in which it is defined by its position within the relationships of contradiction that organize the social whole, is abandoned in this formulation. Instead of giving up on this view to the whole, we need to ask whether, in the context of globalization, there is any potential subject that stands in the same relation to the (global) totality as does the proletariat in relation to the totality of bourgeois society in Lukács' account.

Movements that confront the depredations of capitalist globalization have many different ideological orientations and practical aims, and understand themselves as mobilizing various different identities. For example, Latin American indigenous movements have variously conceived of themselves as working class movements, peasant movements, or indigenous movements proper; they have sought in some cases for greater autonomy from the state, and in other cases for fuller inclusion (Postero and Zamosc, 2004). While the emerging forces organizing the most dispossessed globally against their marginalization by privatization have often been celebrated as novel formations outside of the categories of the traditional left, many participants and leaders in these movements understand their work in the familiar idiom of class politics, as proletarian struggles against national bourgeoisies and bourgeois state power.[11] On the other hand, it is also the case that movements organized on the basis of social identities other than class may also, if differently, challenge capital, even at its heart. For example, in the context of an international division of labor that depends upon the exploitation of women in particular to maintain a segmented labor force and to guarantee sufficiently high rates of capital accumulation, confronting patriarchy is a central part of the struggle against global capital (Mies, 1998). But at the same time, as globalization is challenged from many different angles, these struggles reveal aspects of a whole which, it becomes increasingly clear, must itself be confronted as a totality, if it is to be fully understood. Relevant here is Jameson's (1988) caution that the proliferation of situated oppositional epistemologies that feminist standpoint theory contemplates can resist relativism only if the common condition within which they all struggle—"late capitalism"—is not overlooked. Here a decisive choice must be made between a postmodern particularism that fears the tyranny of any universal, and a Lukácsian "aspiration towards society in its totality" (1971, p. 174), even if this remains a loose, provisional, and emergent totality. I believe that such an aspiration is necessary, since struggles for regional or national goals, such as agrarian reform, come up against principles and processes of power that are fundamentally global—in this case, the neoliberal program (Stedile, 2004). Therefore, to challenge these processes properly even in the particular instance means to think and act on a global terrain.

At the same time that various struggles against capital discover the logical and strategic importance of an analysis of the whole, they also reorganize our understanding of this whole. (In the process, the specific "universal" standpoint of the *proletariat* begins to resemble the later rearticulation of the notion of standpoint by feminists—that is, as a *particular* epistemological and political perspective oriented towards the experience of a particular collective subject.[12]) In discovering not merely the necessity of the exploitation of women to capitalist accumulation, but in addition the centrality of (patriarchal) violence and domination in this history, feminism reorganizes our sense of the inner meaning of capital (Mies, 1998;

Mohanty, 2003). Likewise, the experience of imperialism and colonialism, as well as of the contemporary global apartheid produced by neoliberalism's (racialized) polarizations of wealth and life chances (Klein, 2007), gives rise to a new intuition of capital as a logic of conquest and exclusion, rather than simply incorporation. In short, a range of experiences of struggle begin, analytically, to locate historical processes of social violence at the center of capital's logic, rather than seeing them simply as secondary mediations of an abstract accumulative drive. However, we come full circle here, since it then becomes possible to more powerfully rethink capital as universal—understanding it now as a logic of expansive and exponential predation. In this regard, if the privileging of the industrial working class in Marxism does not seem as useful in the present, the "aspiration to the totality" still needs to be followed through toward an understanding of this global logic, and toward the imagination of a global antagonist to it.[13]

One of the most important political shifts in recent decades is the reframing by indigenous workers or peasants of their struggles: Instead of thinking of these as movements of workers or peasants who happen to be indigenous, they are increasingly proposed first of all as the struggles of indigenous people (Postero and Zamosc, 2004). This shift implies a new set of demands around cultural autonomy and representation, and also recasts the political and economic arenas, since the state and capital now confront a different and unfamiliar adversary. This process has important implications for the conceptualization of a global standpoint. Following Lukács' argument that reification is just as or more central to the logic of capital than the relation of exploitation in itself, capital must be thought of as a total universe rather than simply an exploitative labor process. But then familiar revolutionary class subject positions (i.e. the proletariat) may turn out to "belong" to capital as much as bourgeois ones, in that they express categories internal to its logic (Postone, 1996). We may now need to think of a truly oppositional class as being consolidated *outside of* the universe of capital, or from its most marginalized sectors, and as *intruding upon* or interrupting this universe, rather than transcending it from within (De Lissovoy, 2008). The movements of indigenous people may represent one such oppositional subject. The Zapatistas, for instance, have confounded both the Mexican ruling class as well as familiar assumptions about revolutionary movements in disavowing both the seizure of state power and the vanguardism of the old left (Marcos, 1995). After all, the illumination of capital's inner reason as persistent and omnipresent violence means that we can no longer hope to develop a truly emancipatory opposition out of this logic and history, or the social power it materializes. Nevertheless, we are faced with the problem that the emergence of capitalist globalization requires that any counter-subject be adequate to the scale of the totality toward which globalization implacably tends.

In imagining a planetary standpoint that would resolve this contradiction, we have to hold to Lukács' own emphasis on the subjective moment of class formation. In his account, the central problem is how proletarian consciousness can recognize its location in history at the crossroads of the central contradictions of bourgeois society. In the present, however, it is only a radical and collective project of the global imagination that can propose a truly revolutionary agency, since objective historical development and technical "progress" turn out to belong to capital as internal mediations, which can't be relied upon to produce the requisite revolutionary materials readymade (Horkheimer & Adorno, 2002).[14] This global oppositional class cannot yet be named, because it can only be accomplished through praxis, and not from a contemplative position; it can only be made, not scientifically deduced. That said, a few principles can be suggested here: 1) This standpoint ought to be generalized from the margins to the whole, under the leadership of indigenous movements, within a universal acknowledgment by the global populations of their collective residence and dependence on the earth, against the deterritorializing abstractions of capital. 2) Likewise, the involuntary "freedom" of the unemployed from the conditions and provisions of the formal economy must be inverted and appropriated as a general refusal of the categories of capitalist reason, now writ globally as neoliberalism. 3) Furthermore, feminism should become a project by and for everyone, against the dominative violence of a patriarchy that is indistinguishable from capitalism in its destruction of all relationships that do not repeat its own conquest of whatever differs from it. 4) In holding to and defending concrete human relationships, which ground the textures of lives and terrains, a global oppositional class and standpoint can be no simple abstract unity, even if it has to attain a kind of universality against the universality of capital. It must be filled with the qualitative diversity of experience, and find whatever common name brings it together from within that diversity. Under the hegemony of this class, and against the vampiric assimilation of all actual experience and content to the shadow life of the commodity form, global time would become the "uninterrupted outpouring of what is qualitatively new" (1971, p. 144) that Lukács saw as the concrete truth of history.

A global standpoint must reflect the historical subjecthood of this complete and complex living assemblage, or what Shiva (2005a) calls an "earth family." Indeed, the environmental crisis presses us to deepen even further the category of totality. The ecological movements have taught us that any politics that overlooks nature and the domains of space and geography are doomed to failure. Ecology itself, in correcting this conception of the totality, becomes a theory and politics of planetary relationships in general (rather than of nature by itself). Rather than consciousness lighting up the proletariat as the crucial vantage point from which the truth of this social whole is revealed, now the entire extent of reality must be illuminated by its own worth, against the contradictory totalization of capital itself. Proletarianism was thought of by Lukács as a dialectical working through of history as totality, as the crucial step toward overcoming the contradiction between subject and object. But in the ecological struggle, this narrative is more fully realized, since what is at stake is the literal whole of what is (the earth), not simply against the partiality of bourgeois reason, but rather against capital as a principle of total subsumption and destruction. At the same time, this crisis gives us the opportunity to see more powerfully through reification, and to recognize not just the historical process of class struggle that it conceals, but beyond this, the complete set of biological, cultural, and spiritual relationships that reification now also seeks to freeze and fragment, and which organize not just history, but being itself.

CONCLUSION: EDUCATION AND CULTURAL WORK FROM A GLOBAL STANDPOINT

In globalization, the ultimate consequences of the logic and process of capital are played out, even if these then end up looking somewhat different from the forms in which they were visible to Lukács. As the subjugation and petrification of life by the process of reification proceeds, we see the obverse of this process in the political and ecological destabilization produced by capital's assault on all externalities. For educators and cultural workers, this means that whatever our particular concerns, imagining a form of life not captured and governed by the commodity form becomes an urgent priority (McLaren, 2005). For instance, environmental activists and educators will need to recognize that without confronting capital in their work, the best hope available to their students will only be to defer (and deepen) systemic ecological crisis, since "green" businesses (and "lifestyles") depend on the same perpetually expanding and deepening logics of exploitation and destruction that organize capitalist enterprises generally (Kovel, 2002). On another front, feminist educators should realize that the media's recent ferocious hyper-sexualization of girls is the result of an economy that does not even let children now escape being "accessorized," and which refuses to allow sexual identity to be felt as something other than a possession, always eventually for sale; the global sex trade merely expresses the same imperatives with fewer mediations. More than ever, the pursuit of social relationships characterized by equality, solidarity, sustainability, and democracy implies a collective and general revolt against capitalism, and more specifically against the commodity form and its promiscuous predations. In teaching and activism committed to social justice, then, the laying bare of the problem and process of reification is an urgent task.

In order to think beyond reification, however, we need to do more than critique; we need to be able to think the whole. In the context of globalization, the category of totality re-emerges as central and inescapable. Capitalist globalization *materializes totality* as an encompassing set of economic, political, and cultural processes. This does not mean that conditions globally are homogenized; rather, it means that differing conditions everywhere can only be made sense of with reference to global processes that affect the totality: neoliberalism, cultural commodification and imperialism, and the proliferation of virtual networks of communication, to name a few. In this context, postmodernist valorizations of the momentary and fragmentary end up echoing capital's own social and ideological particularisms: consumerism, an ethos of self-help and self-absorption, as well as virulent ethnicism and xenophobia. This does not mean that postmodern concerns with the domains of culture, sexuality, race, and identity are misplaced; rather, these crucial domains need to be rescued, in the era of globalization, from the fragmentations and dispersals produced by capital itself. Race and racism, for instance, even for students, are now crucially articulated in relation to global political processes (McCarthy, Crichlow, Dimitriadis, & Dolby, 2005), resulting for example in antinomies of "East" and "West," Islamophobia, and anti-immigrant formations. Therefore, an "aspiration toward the totality," and the analysis it makes possible, is crucial in combating contemporary racist discourses. In this context, educators and cultural workers need to make global processes visible to those with whom they work, and should also facilitate the entry of students into a conceptual terrain that can begin to make sense of and confront this globality. "Totality" can be articulated in both reactionary and progressive ways (Jameson, 2004); if we want to have a say in regard to the direction this category takes, we must be prepared to intervene theoretically and practically on the terrain of the global.

Critical curricula in the global era will have to engage not only with the contemporary social processes mentioned above, but will have to do so in the context of a liberatory "planetary paradigm" (Dussel, 1998) that decisively wrenches teaching and learning free from a pervasive Eurocentrism that denies the violence of colonial conquest as well as the historical agency of the global South. In fact, the center of gravity of a global oppositional class and standpoint should be outside of the North, since it is the experience of marginalization or peripheralization, rather than incorporation, which decisively informs the challenge to capital in the present. For students in the U.S., this decentering will mean a fundamental reorganization of identity. The notion of "global citizenship" cannot capture the radical nature of this existential transformation, which is a process of articulation to fundamentally different meanings and sites, absolutely outside the "American" imaginary (De Lissovoy & McLaren, 2006). More generally, the uncertainty of the global era for young people everywhere is already destabilizing familiar narratives of identity; the task is to provide students with the resources for discovering and constructing meaning on this new terrain. Educators and activists will have to provoke the "multitude" (Hardt & Negri, 2004), and young people in particular, to invent themselves in fact as a new species, historically speaking, whose affiliations are not bounded by ethnos or nation, and whose dwelling is within a new shared time of the global. The familiar social collectivities to which we have belonged are in fact unraveling under the pressures of transnationalisms of both helpful and harmful kinds; this unraveling gives rise to resurgent nationalisms, ethnicisms, and a generalized paranoia, while also making possible new progressive formations and projects (Appadurai, 2006). The pedagogical challenge is to productively intervene on this terrain, and to help students invent new transnational solidarities and identities.

Approaches to critical literacy in this context should be especially creative, since the problem is not only to recognize a transformed communications and media landscape, but also to discover the new world that it is the project of literacy education to make available as a site of potential readings.[15] The world, in the era of globalization, still waits to be read; that is, as a space of shared dwelling, and as a shared moment of struggle, the world has not yet met the kind of reading in which it can truly emerge within consciousness. Approaches to a *literacy of the global* will need to invite students not only to decode dominant texts and representations, but also to build original concepts of and for global society. For instance, Freire (1997) found "culture" to be especially generative as a theme within his literacy circles, but he also understood this theme within a framework of psychoanalytic and geopolitical dependency theory that had already worked through the parameters of the problem. But what about the theme of *global culture*? If this refers to the scale of the global whole, rather than to the merely international, then this is a radically open-ended terrain, which has so far been discussed much more in terms of crises of familiar cultural processes and concepts than in terms of any coherent and recognizable new formation (see Featherstone, 1990).

In other words, a literacy of the global must be as much a writing of the global as a reading of it. In this literacy, the agency and autonomy of students will need to be greater than has been contemplated by even the most critical pedagogies, since no authority can be appealed to in order to guarantee the authenticity of a reading of this new world. In fact, "world" no longer quite works as the sign of a historical condition that unravels the coherence of the familiar mappings; the globalized *universe* that is already upon us and within us is still waiting for a language. This is more a practical fact than a methodological principle, but perhaps the uncertainties of globalization can become the ground of a more powerful ethic of collaboration and student-centeredness. After all, since it more completely deconstructs and reconstructs them, this universe belongs more completely to young people. If a global standpoint can be made coherent, young people will be the ones who will principally know it and name it. Teaching, then, should be less a process of inculcation and more a clearing of space for a collective and original act of the imagination, an imagination which can see past the shattered fragments of the present to that whole future that is already beginning to take shape around and inside of us.

NOTES

1 Eagleton (1991) argues that Lukács' understanding of consciousness and ideology is itself idealistic, since it overlooks the fact that these are messy terrains of contention between competing interests and class fractions, rather than being unified fields uniquely reflective of the historical position of the classes to which they belong.

2 See especially *One-Dimensional Man* (1991).

3 See especially *Pedagogy of the Oppressed* (1997).

4 In reconsidering the notions of reification, class, praxis, and standpoint in the context of globalization, this essay takes its inspiration in part from this tradition.

5 According to Marx (1867/1976), capital depends in its essence on a unique property of the commodity labor-power, which is its ability to produce more value (in a day's work, for example), than that required to reproduce it for the same period (in terms of basic necessities).

6 In capitalist society, according to Zizek (2002), mystification is at its height when our choices are seemingly clearest.

7 For Lukács, the ideological effects of reification are its most important ones, since on the one hand they motivate the most powerful intellectual efforts of the bourgeoisie itself to ground and justify its worldview, and because on the other hand they represent the essential obstacle that stands in the way of the proletariat's coming to proper self-consciousness as a revolutionary class.

8 This global drive toward commodification and privatization, which echoes the fantastic plunder that marked the origins of capitalism, has been called by Harvey (2003) "accumulation by dispossession."

9 Questions from a Foucauldian and Althusserian perspective, respectively.

10 Marx describes primitive accumulation as the original moment of pillage that secured, through colonial expansion and domestic enclosures, the initial fund of capital that allowed capitalist manufacturing and farming to be established on a wide scale in Europe.

[11] For example, Trevor Ngwane (2004), of South Africa's Anti-Privatization Forum, which has led a fight of the poor against cut-offs of public services, argues for a working-class politics that overcomes the division between the employed and unemployed.

[12] While Hartsock's early work claimed a universality for the revolutionary standpoint (now articulated in terms of gender), Harding's conceptualization, while still anti-relativist, is also resolutely opposed to claims of universality, emphasizing instead the experiential grounding of *different* standpoints.

[13] Hennessy's (1993) important proposal of a "global social analytic" attends to the complex determinations of the social across a range of gendered and raced subject positions, while nevertheless understanding these relations in the context of capitalism's overarching imperative of exploitation. However, my point here is to ask whether the logic of the standpoint that Lukács proposes can be extrapolated in the present to reveal a fundamentally *new* meaning and content for its basic categories: reification, class, and even capital itself.

[14] Michael Löwy (1997) argues that it is here that the Frankfurt School improves upon Lukács, in articulating a critique of industrial civilization more generally.

[15] An approach to literacy focused on reading the world as much as the word (Freire and Macedo, 1987) must in this context first acknowledge the radically transformed and open-ended nature of the global "world" itself.

REFERENCES

Appadurai, A. (2006). *Fear of small numbers: An essay on the geography of anger*. Durham, NC: Duke University Press.

Aronowitz, S. (2003). *How class works*. New Haven, CT: Yale University Press.

Bauman, Z. (2000). *Liquid modernity*. Cambridge, England: Polity.

Collins, P. H. (2000). *Black feminist thought: Knowledge, consciousness, and the politics of empowerment*. New York: Routledge.

Davis, M. (2006). *Planet of slums*. London: Verso.

De Lissovoy, N. (2008). Dialectic of emergency/emergency of the dialectic. *Capitalism, Nature, Socialism, 19*(1), 27–40.

De Lissovoy, N., & McLaren, P. (2006). Ghosts in the procedure: Notes on teaching and subjectivity in a new era. In K. Cooper & R. E. White (Eds.), *The practical critical educator* (pp. 151–163). Dordrecht: Springer.

Dussel, E. (1998). Beyond eurocentrism: The world-system and the limits of modernity. In F. Jameson & M. Miyoshi (Eds.), *The cultures of globalization* (pp. 3–31). Durham, NC: Duke University Press.

Eagleton, T. (1991). *Ideology: An introduction*. London: Verso.

Featherstone, M. (Ed.). (1990). *Global culture: Nationalism, globalization, and modernity*. Newbury Park, CA: Sage Publications.

Freire, P. (1997). *Pedagogy of the oppressed* (M. B. Ramos, Trans.). New York: Continuum.

Freire, P., & Macedo, D. (1987). *Literacy: Reading the word and the world*. South Hadley, MA: Bergin and Garvey.

Guha, R., & Spivak, G. C. (Eds.). (1988). *Selected subaltern studies*. Oxford: Oxford University Press.

Harding, S. (1993). Rethinking standpoint epistemology: What is "Strong objectivity"? In L. Alcoff & E. Potter (Eds.), *Feminist epistemologies* (pp. 49–82). New York: Routledge.

Harding, S. (1998). *Is science multicultural? Postcolonialisms, feminisms, and epistemologies*. Bloomington, IN: Indiana University Press.

Hardt, M., & Negri, A. (2000). *Empire*. Cambridge, MA: Harvard University Press.

Hardt, M., & Negri, A. (2004). *Multitude: War and democracy in the age of empire*. New York: Penguin Press.

Hartsock, N. (1983). The feminist standpoint: Developing the ground for a specifically feminist historical materialism. In S. Harding & M. B. Hintikka (Eds.), *Discovering reality: Feminist perspectives on epistemology, metaphysics, methodology, and philosophy of science* (pp. 283–310). Dordrecht: D. Reidel Publishing Company.

Harvey, D. (2003). *The new imperialism*. Oxford: Oxford University Press.

Hekman, S. (2004). Truth and method: Feminist standpoint theory revisited. In S. Harding (Ed.), *The feminist standpoint theory reader: Intellectual and political controversies* (pp. 225–241). New York: Routledge.

Hennessy, R. (1993). *Materialist feminism and the politics of discourse*. New York: Routledge.

Horkheimer, M., & Adorno, T. W. (2002). *Dialectic of enlightenment* (E. Jephcott, Trans.). Stanford, CA: Stanford University Press.

Jameson, F. (1988). *History and class consciousness* as an "Unfinished project". *Rethinking Marxism, 1*(1), 49–72.

Jameson, F. (2004). Foreword. *Critique of dialectical reason* (Vol. 1). London: Verso.

Jay, M. (1984). *Marxism and totality: The adventures of a concept from Lukács to Habermas*. Berkeley, CA: University of California Press.

Klein, N. (2007). *The shock doctrine: The rise of disaster capitalism*. New York: Metropolitan Books.

Kovel, J. (2002). *The enemy of nature: The end of capitalism or the end of the world?* New York: Zed Books.

Löwy, M., & Corredor, E. L. (1997). Interview with Michael Löwy. In E. L. Corredor (Ed.), *Lukács after communism: Interviews with contemporary intellectuals* (pp. 17–28). Durham, NC: Duke University Press.

Lukács, G. (1923/1971). *History and class consciousness*. Cambridge, MA: MIT Press.

Marcos. (1995). *Shadows of tender fury: The letters and communiqués of subcomandante Marcos and the Zapatista army of national liberation* (F. Bardacke & L. López, Trans.). New York: Monthly Review Press.

Marcuse, H. (1991). *One-dimensional man*. Boston: Beacon Press.

Marx, K. (1867/1976). *Capital* (Vol. I). London: Penguin Books.

Marx, K., & Engels, F. (1848/1967). *The communist manifesto*. London: Penguin Books.

McCarthy, C., Crichlow, W., Dimitriadis, G., & Dolby, N. (2005). Introduction: Transforming contexts, transforming identities: Race and education in the New Millenium. In C. McCarthy, W. Crichlow, G. Dimitriadis, & N. Dolby (Eds.), *Race, identity, and representation in education* (pp. xv–xxix). New York: Routledge.

McLaren, P. (2005). *Capitalists and conquerors: A critical pedagogy against empire*. Lanham, MD: Rowman & Littlefield.

Mertes, T. (Ed.). (2004). *A movement of movements: Is another world really possible?* London: Verso.

Mészáros, I. (1995). *Beyond capital*. New York: Monthly Review Press.

Mies, M. (1998). *Patriarchy and accumulation on a world scale: Women in the international division of labour*. London: Zed Books.

Mohanty, C. T. (2003). *Feminism without borders: Decolonizing theory, practicing solidarity*. Durham, NC: Duke University Press.

Ngwane, T. (2004). Sparks in the township. In T. Mertes (Ed.), *A movement of movements: Is another world really possible?* (pp. 111–134). London: Verso.

Pollock, S., Bhabha, H. K., Breckenridge, C. A., & Chakrabarty, D. (2000). Cosmopolitanisms. *Public Culture, 12*(3), 577–589.

Postero, N. G., & Zamosc, L. (2004). Indigenous movements and the Indian question in Latin America. In N. G. Postero & L. Zamosc (Eds.), *The struggle for indigenous rights in Latin America* (pp. 1–31). Brighton, England: Sussex Academic Press.

Postone, M. (1996). *Time, labor, and social domination*. Cambridge: Cambridge University Press.

Sandoval, C. (2000). *Methodology of the oppressed*. Minneapolis, MN: University of Minnesota Press.

Shiva, V. (2005a). *Earth democracy: Justice, sustainability, and peace*. Cambridge, MA: South End Press.

Shiva, V. (2005b). The Indian seed and patent act: Sowing the seeds of dictatorship [Electronic Version]. *ZNet*. Retrieved from http://www.zmag.org/content/showarticle.cfm?ItemID=7249

Stedile, J. P. (2004). Brazil's landless battalions. In T. Mertes (Ed.), *A movement of movements: Is another world really possible?* (pp. 17–48). London: Verso.
Zizek, S. (2002). *Welcome to the desert of the real*. London: Verso.

Noah De Lissovoy
Department of Curriculum and Instruction
University of Texas at Austin

BENJAMIN FRYMER

6. THE FRANKFURT SCHOOL AND EDUCATION

Critical Theory and Youth Alienation

This chapter explores the contributions and continuing relevance of the Frankfurt School's critical theory for the study and practice of education. Is the Frankfurt School's work relevant to late capitalist schooling and society? Is Critical Theory still critical? I argue that the current crises of advanced capitalism and social domination require substantial modification of the Frankfurt School's core problematics, but that many of their insights have tremendous relevance to understanding contemporary schools and broader analyses of alienation, reification and authoritarian political and cultural dynamics. I illustrate this through a brief examination of the centrality of alienation as a fundamental dynamic in the Columbine High School shootings.

The Institute for Social Research (Institut für Sozialforschung) was founded in 1923 by industrialist Felix J. Weil at the University of Frankfurt. Although the early years of the Institute under the directorship of Carl Grünberg were characterized by fairly orthodox economic Marxism, Max Horkheimer rapidly took what was to be known as the "Frankfurt School" in a much more unorthodox, penetrating, and interdisciplinary direction. Assuming the directorship of the Institute in 1930, Horkheimer announced his vision in an inaugural address entitled, "The State of Social Philosophy and the Tasks of an Institute for Social Research" (1995). For Horkheimer the superordinate task of the Institute centered upon a transformation and synthesis of both social philosophy and social science into a truly interdisciplinary, critical field of inquiry, undertaken in the interests of emancipation.

At the root of Horkheimer's call for a renewed project of social research was a recognition of the centrality of dialectical thought- the interpenetration of critical knowledge and historicity in the ever changing socioeconomic conditions of advanced capitalism. "Critical theory," the Institute's strategic euphemism for Marxism, would work to overcome the entrenched positivism of social science and philosophy and its false separation between what is and what could be. Dialectical thought, unlike positivism, would radically historicize empirical inquiry and would enable this inquiry to acquire meaning within the larger totality and within philosophical considerations of the ends of human activity. Instead of merely categorizing and describing the world, dialectical theory would make possible the evaluation of history and society from the standpoint of human freedom. In light of poststructural, postcolonial, and feminist critiques of modern totalizing conceptions such as "human freedom," and dramatically different historical conditions, the Frankfurt School's method, theory, and practice must be revisited so that it may be

Z. Leonardo (ed.), Handbook of Cultural Politics and Education, 161–174.

regenerated in analyses of new possibilities for social transformation in this age of capitalist and ecological crises. Still, we have much to learn from the original school, and many of its core ideas and modes of dialectical praxis remain invaluable tools not only for educational theory but also for challenging existing configurations of power and alienation in the present social totality.

Although membership in the Institute varied from the 1930s to the 1950s, the core Frankfurt School group is generally considered to include Horkheimer, Theodor Adorno, and Herbert Marcuse and to extend at times to Erich Fromm, Walter Benjamin, Leo Lowenthal and later Jurgen Habermas. Fromm and Benjamin, however, were largely resistant to inclusion in the group or, at times, explicitly rejected from Institute publications. Still, their work is so significant, so often connected to the school and so frequently categorized as "critical theory" that they will be included in the following discussion. Consideration of post-Habermas critical theory will be limited here to the field of Education (critical pedagogy) although the work of such figures as Axel Honneth, Stanley Aronowitz, and Jessica Benjamin, just to name a few, is worthy of sustained attention.

ALIENATION AND CULTURE: FROM MARX TO CRITICAL THEORY

Although Marx did not write about culture extensively, his concern with alienated labor in capitalist society has obvious implications for understanding contemporary estrangement and had a major impact on the Frankfurt School. Both in his early manuscripts and later economic studies, Marx is concerned with the subject-object dialectic in history. He develops his historical materialism in opposition to Hegel's attempt to reconcile subject and object in the sphere of consciousness instead of on the ground of human material praxis. For Marx, both alienation and commodity fetishism arise *in* capitalist society and describe an inverted form of species-being in which human beings become dominated by the objects they produce in capitalist relations of production.

Marx argues in the *Economic and Philosophic Manuscripts* (1964) that the worker in capitalist society is estranged in several respects: from the product and process of labor, from other workers, and from him/herself. What is common to and underlies all these aspects of estrangement is the *process* whereby the laborer is transformed into a commodity, and becomes an *object* to be bought and sold on the market like any other commodity. The laborer not only loses him or herself in the object (product), and loses the object to the capitalist, (s)he *becomes* an object and exists in a condition of objectification. Alienation for Marx is not only or primarily an *experience* of estrangement, but a material and ontological condition- of distorted historical being formed within the capitalist relations of production. Laborers can only enter into the realm of human being, of human subjectivity, by transcending the alienated labor and ownership relations of capitalism.

In the masterwork of his later years, *Das Kapital* (1967), Marx extends his earlier analysis of alienation to a thoroughgoing critique of the capitalist mode of production. His seminal critique of political economy proceeds through unraveling the answer to the central riddle of capitalist society- the true nature of the commodity. For Marx, commodification is another way to analyze the inverted subject-object world of capitalist society in which abstract exchange value takes precedence over concrete material use value and economic (market) relations come to dominate the whole of human and social life. In capitalist societies these economic relations are organized by the production, circulation, and exchange of objects to increase the private profit of capitalists, not to satisfy the needs and welfare of the producers. The production and exchange of these commodity-objects, an abstract historical artifact of capitalist ownership, thus becomes the basis and purpose of capitalist life itself, subordinating real material needs to its workings and the benefits of the capitalist class. As a result, "The increase in the quantity of objects is accompanied by an extension in the realm of the alien powers to which man is subjected" (Marx, 1978: 93).

As with the alienation of concrete labor in commodity production, Marx argues that the larger fetishism of commodities through the inversion of exchange value over use value operates according to the abstract, formal logic of the capitalist mode of production. Just as alienated labor constitutes the subordination of real human qualities and capacities to the objects they produce, exchange value transforms the different qualitative values and uses of unique products into quantitative rates of equivalent market value. Again, the concrete, here in the sense of specific use values that different products supply, is transformed into the abstract, in the form of exchange value. Thus the commodity form is analyzed by Marx as the major abstraction dominating human life in capitalist society to such an extent that only objects are endowed with value. In this inverted world, human qualities are transferred to commodities and the characteristics of objects are transferred to human beings. Marx's analysis of commodity fetishism uncovers the true source of capitalist value in the autonomous power the economy obtains over human life. With this autonomy, abstractions dominate the relationships and exchanges that once took place in local, concrete human communities and human beings are governed by the appearances of economic categories and objects rather than governing themselves. These economic forms appear to have a reality independently of the real human beings who have created them in history.

Marx's critique of commodity fetishism in Capital proved to be a major influence on the Hungarian thinker, Georg Lukács, and it was not until his publication of *History and Class Consciousness* in 1923 that the next major analysis of capitalist alienation would be conducted. Lukács had no access to Marx's early writings on alienation, yet nevertheless managed to extract Marx's concern with estrangement from his reading of *Capital*. According to Feenberg (1981), Lukács does this through serious reflection on Marx's methodology and by reconstructing Marx's metatheoretical "philosophy of praxis." Feenberg argues convincingly that both Marx and Lukács develop a philosophy of praxis based on the goal of transcending alienation at the level of human being, or ontology, which for both is always already historical being. Lukács follows Marx in emphasizing the necessity of transcending the gap between subject and object in modern society and ontology through historical praxis, rather than philosophy itself. The subject/object split that in capitalist society had taken the form of human commodification could not, as Hegel asserted, be transcended on the level of ideas, in consciousness, or through philosophy. It required revolutionary praxis in history to transform historical/ontological conditions. De Lissovoy's previous chapter performs an extended analysis of Lukács' work so I will limit myself to a couple of Lukács' assertions, particularly as they concern his synthesis of Marx and Weber.

In *History and Class Consciousness*, Lukács transforms Marx's concept of commodity fetishism into his own theory of reification by integrating Weber's theory of Western rationalization into Marx's philosophy of praxis. As with Marx, Lukács aims to uncover the inversion of ideological appearance over reality in capitalist societies through rigorous examination of the very cultural logic of capitalist life. However, Lukács generalizes Marx's conception of fetishism beyond the economic system, using Weber to analyze this cultural logic and its ideological effects in every institution of modern society. In his massive body of work, Weber had argued that formal or instrumental rationality had assumed dominance over substantive rationality leading to irrational modes of life in which continual calculation regarding efficiency overrode consideration of the ends of human actions. From science, to law, to religion, instrumental reason had transformed quality, substance, and purpose into quantity, and technical calculations for controlling society and nature.

Lukács argues that contemporary capitalist societies are pervaded by a similar type of formal rationality that dominates human beings to such an extent that they lose the ability to grasp the material and historical basis of their society's dominant cultural and institutional categories. His amalgamation of Weber's rationalization thesis and Marx's analysis of commodity fetishism comes together in a critical analysis of the "reification" of capitalist society. For Lukács, reification refers to a political-economic, scientific, and cultural phenomenon whereby relationships between historical subjects are mystified by formal rationality into the abstract appearance of those between ahistorical objects. While the capitalist economic system is ultimately the basis of this formal rationality, the reified world comes to have a relatively autonomous hold over social life, including the economy. In fact, for Lukács "What is customarily called the economy is nothing but the system of forms of objectivity of real life" (1971, pp. 152). With the development of reification he argued that not only autonomous individual reason, but also the possibility of working-class consciousness was structurally blocked without the mediation of critical theory. However by opposing the reified world of formal rationality with a critical dialectical reason, Marxism could explode the realm of objectified appearances and transcend the gap between subject and object in revolution.

Lukács was one of the primary influences on the Frankfurt School's work on alienation and ideology. In the face of fascism and the post-war spread of capitalist ideology, both Horkheimer (with Adorno in *Dialectic of Enlightenment* (1972)) and Marcuse modified Lukács into "end of reason" arguments that, if it wasn't proclaimed already, sounded the death-knell of the Enlightenment project. Marcuse's *One Dimensional Man* (1964) is a particularly powerful examination of reason's perversion into capitalist ideology. However, unlike Horkheimer, Marcuse and the Adorno of *Negative Dialectics* (1973) held out hope for the dialectical negation of the negation of reason- for Marcuse in the aesthetic dimension and student revolt, and for Adorno in the critique of identity theory in Western philosophy and social theory.

Building on the classical writings of Weber, the original program of Frankfurt School critical theory developed an extensive critique of capitalist institutions and culture for their pervasive "instrumental" or technocratic rationality. According to the Frankfurt School, instrumental rationality had become the dominant form of reason and institutional organization in advanced capitalist societies. As such, the cultural life of these capitalist societies is controlled by technocratic, means-end considerations of efficiency and planning which undermine the very possibilities for the realization of a critical-emancipatory rationality of certain Enlightenment thought. Consequently for theorists like Marcuse (1964), the modern capitalist subject was largely prevented from engaging in the critical thought necessary for emancipatory action or democratic participation. Without the development of critical reason, the modern individual finds it nearly impossible to penetrate the reified symbols and ideologies of capitalist culture. Thus, the pacified and petrified capitalist subject faces a bleak fate locked in an iron cage of administrative, spiritless culture that had subordinated the pursuit of meaningful worldly pursuits to a purposeless mundane existence. Currently, this Frankfurt School interrogation of instrumental reason would provide a trenchant critique of No Child Left Behind policy and the standards and accountability based educational system that has been imposed on America's teachers and students.

FRANKFURT SCHOOL ON MODERN CULTURE

The Culture Industry

In their signature work *Dialectic of Enlightenment* (1972), Adorno and Horkheimer entitled a key section "The Culture Industry: Enlightenment as Mass Deception." In this widely read part of their seminal work they analyze and critique the development and pervasive spread of industrial capitalist culture during which the organization and techniques of industrial production have moved beyond material production to the production of culture as well. Horkheimer and Adorno argue that at this stage of capitalism there is no longer any such thing as "mass culture" which comes from people themselves, i.e. "popular culture." Instead culture is commodified by an industrial apparatus and assumes the form of objects which come to dominate its consumers- the watchers of film, television, and theater for example. Consumers of cultural products are reduced to a passive and objectified position in their relationship to the world of meaning, belief, and value. They become dominated by a new world of standardized objects that limit their autonomy and subjectivity even as these objects present the illusion of being freely "chosen". Harkening back to Lukács, Adorno and Horkheimer claim that ideological deception is one of the main products of the culture industry.

One of the greatest and most common misconceptions of the Frankfurt School is that its key thinkers had a wholly monolithic and deterministic understanding of modern Western culture, symbolized by Adorno and Horkheimer's argument.

The culture industry thesis has been subject to much criticism for its supposed elitism and functionalism. Many have argued that Adorno, in particular, generally dismissed the value and political possibility of popular culture. While it is true that Adorno did not place much faith in the transformative possibility of mass culture, and largely ignored the divisions of race and gender which fractured it, the culture industry analysis is meant to apply to so-called "high culture" as well. Adorno's oeuvre contains numerous works on how classical music and "high" art have been just as commodified and devalued as the culture of the masses. In fact, half of all Adorno's work is on music and the fate of classical music in modernity (1976, 1984).

Although the culture industry thesis is problematic, it is also quite powerful and continues to be of major heuristic value in understanding late capitalism and the powerful forces shaping youth subjectivity in contemporary societies. Moreover, while this position does represent a major line of Frankfurt school thinking on modern culture, it by no means captures the complexity and dialectical character of the School's work on modern cultural forms. One only needs to casually peruse Benjamin and Adorno's voluminous work on the dialectical fragments of modern culture, Marcuse's aesthetic theory (1978), or Lowenthal's sociology of literature (1983, 1985), to be persuaded that their thought is nearly impossible to categorize or reject as "functionalist." Even the culture industry thesis itself must be contextualized within Horkheimer and Adorno's larger dialectical project in their *Dialectic of Enlightenment*.

Walter Benjamin's Aesthetics

Given the perceived pessimism if not outright fatalism of Adorno's work, in many respects Walter Benjamin's essay "The Work of Art in the Age of Mechanical Reproduction" (1968) has far surpassed Adorno's culture industry work in contemporary discussions of cultural politics. Benjamin and Adorno carried on a long-standing friendship and critical dialogue even though Benjamin was always a peripheral member of the Frankfurt School and a figure his contemporaries had great difficulty understanding. To simplify greatly, Adorno and Benjamin essentially came to opposite conclusions from their analyses of capitalist culture, especially on the place and possibility of art in a new consumer society. While Adorno saw art losing its critical potential amidst a world of circulating commodities and reified images, Benjamin believed the "mechanical reproduction" of art could actually have democratizing effects. Mechanical reproduction, while emptying art of its transcendent "aura" and authentic meaning within traditional community, could, as in the case of film, raise the political consciousness of the masses by making images of the world more accessible. Art and modern culture as a whole would become more politicized and part of the political process rather than held by elites above the realm of everyday life.

Critical Theory and Education

Do these critical theory arguments and debates hold relevance for contemporary education? The early work of Henry Giroux, particularly *Theory and Resistance in*

Education (1983), marked a major point of convergence between Frankfurt School critical theory and Education. Following the publication of Paul Willis's *Learning to Labor* (1977), a classic ethnographic study of student "resistance" to the "hidden curriculum" of a working-class high school and the reproduction of class relations, Giroux began to argue for the significance of theorizing resistance in educational theory. His work in the early 1980s constituted a marked challenge to what he termed "reproduction theory" in Education. Reproduction theory in the sociology of education, most notably represented by Bowles and Gintis's *Schooling in Capitalist America* (1976) and the work of Pierre Bordieu (1990), tended to posit overly functional models of the ways schools reproduced inequality and dominant social relations. As an opening attempt at what developed into "critical pedagogy," Giroux argued for the significance of more dialectical analyses of schools and students that would begin to theorize the complexity of capitalist education and the role of schooling in modes of domination. He turned to the Frankfurt School as a model of dialectical analysis for understanding such phenomena as school ideology, student subjectivity, and resistance. This early work, although not yet engaged with questions of gender, race, and popular culture, contains some of Giroux's most important contributions to theorizing domination and student resistance in American schools.

In the decades since Giroux's early work there has been surprisingly little engagement with the Frankfurt School in the field of education, either in theoretical or empirical work. Other than a small group of scholars (Brookfield, 2004; De Vitis 1974; Gur-Ze-ev, 2002, 2005; Kellner, 2003, 2006; Peters, 2003a, 2003b; Reitz, 2000; Young 1990) educational theorists have been far more preoccupied with cultural studies, postmodern theory and feminist analysis than first generation critical theory. Giroux himself turned quickly to a postmodern phase before focusing upon more cultural studies work on youth and popular culture.

CRITICAL THEORY, YOUTH ALIENATION AND COLUMBINE

> "The lonely man strikes with absolute rage." –Dylan Klebold (Columbine High School shooter)

Just as many of the Frankfurt School's core arguments, such as the critique of instrumental reason and the culture industry, remain relevant for dissecting educational ideology, policy, and practice including No Child Left Behind legislation, their problematic of alienation, pursued by Marcuse, Fromm, and Adorno can help us make sense of forms of alienation which pervade American schooling and the everyday life of students. Fromm's work in particular focused on new forms of alienation which were becoming more and more prevalent with the spread of consumer culture, pervasive advertising and media, and the commodification of leisure time (1955). Fromm and Marcuse's theories on the increasing commodification of capitalist culture are particularly useful for understanding contemporary youth identity and subjectivity in and out of schools. In fact an analysis of contemporary student alienation may help make sense of many facets of student subjectivity, relations of power, and everyday violence and oppression in

America's schools. I examine a vivid illustration of this alienation by going back to the Columbine High School Shootings of 1999.

Following the shootings, the print and television media continually *constructed* middle-class youth alienation through their fascination with suburban and rural school violence. "Alienation" -as psychopathology, as demonic rage, as absorption into the violence plagued virtual worlds of the internet, movies, and pop music, or as the dominant expression of the powerless lives of young victims- was presented as the major explanation for the violence. Paradoxically though, the media construction of youth alienation was itself a force of separation and isolation. As school shooters from Columbine to Virginia Tech were integrated into the society of the spectacle, ordinary Americans were increasingly separated from suburban and rural youth on an epistemological and existential level. The transformation of the impossibly complex lifeworlds and subjectivities of youth into abstract commodities worked to distance the population from any meaningful understanding- either of the real historical youth estrangement that school shooters symbolize or the existential, cultural, and economic conditions which also shape their own lives. The media spectacle of school violence rendered suburban and rural youth aliens in our midst. As has been the case historically in societies divided by hierarchies of power, youth were transformed into the "Other" of Western reason, development, and maturity.

In response to this spectacular reification, a new set of critical perspectives on youth alienation are needed to understand the current spirit of different youth subcultures in the face of novel cultural and economic conditions. However these new theories need not start from scratch and must not forget the seminal analyses of estrangement in earlier phases of capitalist development. As discussed above, beginning with Marx, there is a rich social-theoretical tradition that counters the popular tendency to reduce the complex phenomenon of alienation to psychopathology or "deviant" behavior. The path of Western Marxism that leads through Lukacs, the Frankfurt School and Debord (1995) provides essential insights into the alienation of labor and the modern subject in capitalist societies that continue to be relevant to contemporary conditions. While the reduction of alienation to class, labor, and production is limiting, and the humanist foundations of the tradition call for continuous reflexive critique, Frankfurt School emphases on ideology, culture, and the commodification of everyday life continue to be indispensable frameworks for critical understanding and intervention.

Popular post- WW II accounts of American youth alienation also continue to remain instructive for grasping contemporary developments. In fact beginning in the 1950s, considerations of youth delinquency, violence and disengagement have generated numerous theoretical, empirical, and popular works that remain instructive to this day. In addition to important more recent sociological works by Gaines (1991), Schwendinger and Schwendinger (1985), Foley (1990) and Larkin (1979), the popular sociology of the 1950s and 1960s, most notably in the works of Paul Goodman (1960), Kenneth Keniston (1965), Edgar Friedenberg (1959), David Riesman (1950), and Phil Slater (1970), went against the historically recurring stream of psychological thinking and saw the internal connections between youth identity, economic and cultural organization, and social estrangement. While tending to overlook the complexity of youth differences by race, class, gender, and sexuality, and failing to map alienation within the totality of capitalist relations, these examinations did expose the hollowness of social conditions for many youth. As a result, there was a brief but influential public and scholarly discussion of alienation as a cultural and economic problem, not a deficiency of immature youth. Above all these works come together in their focus on the problem of identity for youth, as youth identity was problematized as a social process upon which the phenomenon of estrangement rested.

Taking Paul Goodman's widely discussed *Growing Up Absurd* (1960) as the primary example of this concern with alienated identity allows for a consideration of the strengths and weaknesses of this approach and its potential application to current conditions, including new expressions of rage and violence. Goodman's work is in many ways a reflection his times- of the post-war shift to a service economy, the "organization society," and organized office work for a sizable portion of the American middle-class. At a time when "juvenile delinquency" was a major public concern, and youth movements such as the beats were gaining popularity all over the country, Goodman attempted to make sense of the widespread disaffection that had emerged. His main argument rests on the inability of the organized society to provide boys with the meaningful work or larger purpose in life in which they would be able to grow up. They grow up absurd in the sense that they gradually come to realize that society serves the organized system itself, not the honor and integrity of human beings.

Goodman's popular work was perhaps the clearest analysis of privileged youth alienation in late capitalist society. Although his analysis ignores the plight of young women and obscures the central differences of class and race, Goodman's work still retains significance as one of the few to see the emergence of widespread social disaffection that continues into the present. He wrote:

> Nevertheless, we see groups of boys and young men disaffected from the dominant society. The young men are Angry and Beat. The boys are Juvenile Delinquents. These groups are not small, and they will grow larger. Certainly they are suffering. Demonstrably they are not getting enough out of our wealth and civilization. They are not growing up to full capacity. (p. 11)

According to Goodman, they are not really allowed to grow up at all. There are not worthy or efficacious pursuits open to them in their worlds through which they can develop into adulthood or even aspire to become adults. Young lives become anomic under these conditions of the organized, affluent, bureaucratic society. Instead of slowly but surely forming meaningful and purposeful identities, youth dissolve into fragmented desiring machines.

Goodman's argument therefore revolves around the question of identity, and this contemporary youth dilemma is what continues to give *Growing Up Absurd*'s analysis relevance in postmodern times. The process of identity formation is also the key to Goodman's contribution to an understanding of youth alienation. He asserts that youth estrangement is systemic given the paucity of goals, authentic communication, and concrete "objects" the self can grasp and grapple with in American society. The conditions in which the young must find themselves and their purposes have become more abstract and absurd.

If Goodman had drawn on the Frankfurt School analyses of Marcuse, Adorno, Horkheimer, and Fromm he might have concluded that youth identity in a mediated society has become a commodity that is bought by media conglomerates and sold back to youth themselves. The production and circulation of mass-mediated images has become the defining ground upon which youth must locate a sense of self. Their selves are always already presented to them in different media, and these images conform to a restricted range of choices young people are allowed to integrate and express. The struggle that Friedenberg in *The Vanishing Adolescent* asserts to be the central task of adolescence is itself incorporated into this pre-selected set of images for public consumption. Youth style, rebellion, and marginality are hunted down and integrated into Marcuse's one-dimensionality before their cultural roots can spread and stable identities can form.

In another vein, Chancer and Donovan's work on the "mass psychology of punishment" may be particularly useful for developing a dialectical theory of self that could partially account for the spectacle of Columbine and other rural and suburban school shootings. Building upon such Frankfurt thinkers as Reich and Fromm, they outline an emotional dynamic operating in societies based on hierarchy and domination in which the emotional bases of crime and punishment dialectically interpenetrate to generate a cycle of crime. Chancer and Donovan argue that widespread "desires for retribution" emanate from what cultural critic Ellen Willis refers to as the "psychopolitics' of crime and punishment. Willis asserts that "Humiliation, powerlessness, violation and negation of self, hunger for revenge are common coin- as is the outrage that one's assumption of the right to dominance (I am a man! I am a white middle-class American!) has been contravened" (In Chancer and Donovan, 1994; pp. 56). Willis continues, claiming that "Crime and punishment, victimization and retribution, repression, explosion, and crackdown are an endless sadomasochistic dance" (pp. 56).

This dynamic, emotionally charged dance dialectically linking crime with punishment, and punishment with further acts of crime must, for Willis, Chancer, and Donovan, be situated within the context of social domination and hierarchy. It is within late capitalist societies saturated with relationships based on power and obedience, control and submission, dominator and dominated that these "sadomasochistic" dynamics play out. As Willis states, "power, control, and hierarchy are the air we breathe" (Chancer and Donovan, 1994; pp. 56). The thirst for control, revenge, and punishment of those deemed the Other springs forth from the hierarchical ground of inequality. Under these conditions, Chancer and Donovan argue that a cultural dynamic develops in which people become emotionally invested in representations of crime and therefore its perpetuation. Observer and observed enter into the cultural dance fueling a cycle of crime and retribution which feeds upon itself.

In the case of Columbine, the journals of Eric Harris and Dylan Klebold provide significant evidence that part of their desire to commit mass murder was fueled on the one hand by anger at the whole history of offences/ "crimes" committed against them and, on the other, by the vicarious thrill of being identified as hated, vilified, "Natural Born Killers." And sure enough, following their crimes they got what they wished for as they were in turn demonized by the media spectacle and turned into a new object of fear inspiring further resentment, anger, and criminal rage among American adults and youth.

Chancer and Donovan bring up the prospect that media spectacles are generated by unconscious investments in crime and demonization of the criminal. They state, "One needs criminals to have an (ironically) legitimate target of rage about whose seemingly intrinsic "badness" we are all in agreement….In this regard, the criminal can become an object of fascination- of love and hate, hate and love- because he or she expresses rage directly and openly, whereas observers of crime can do so only in mediated ways…. (p. 60). The media construction of youth alienation after Columbine fits this profile of this dynamic as media observers, or observers through the media came to form emotional identifications with Harris and Klebold which led to further pushes for control and domination of youth.

Therefore, the Columbine and subsequent shootings bring to the forefront the question of possible new forms of youth alienation in late capitalism and their connection to social rage and violence. There are, to be sure, numerous ways of characterizing contemporary estrangement generally, and a multiperspectival approach is in part necessitated by the material and existential differences generated by different social conditions and categories of identity by gender, class, race, sexuality, and religion. The millions of American youth who grow up poor, or part of vulnerable working class families, are materially marginalized from opportunity and possibility in this cold, new post-industrial, post-welfare neo-liberal world. For them "alienation" merely on the level of identity and subjectivity would be a luxury they cannot afford as they struggle to get by on a day-to-day basis. Gender also continues to be a major social category differentiating lives and experience across class and ethnic boundaries. Recent school shootings have been perpetrated by young males, and in many cases girls have been targeted as the victims.

Yet, from Columbine to Virginia Tech, new suburban and rural estrangement witnesses the struggle of marginalized boys to maintain the integrity of self in the face of the larger alienated society of spectacular life. The anomic detachment, anger, resentment, vulnerability and isolation of outsider youth forms in response to the perceived mediocrity, meaninglessness, and absurdity of life in the society of the spectacle. The Columbine shooters found it absurd that the most popular and highly rewarded of their peers were the least intelligent, the least intuitive and self-aware, and the greatest conformists to arbitrary standards of mediocrity. Paradoxically, the horizons of everyday life appear limited to these boys in the exact historical moment in which the opening up of new worlds of communication, knowledge and images in the age of new media has occurred. They see no future and no alternative past the momentary gratifications of violence and mediated diversions from boredom in the hollowed out world of suburbia or rural America. Cruelty, hypocrisy, and absurdity appear to them to be futile to resist, just part of the "way things are."

Critical theory exposes this perception as reification - an ideological blindness to the historically contingent alienation, domination, and commodification of late capitalist societies. The Columbine case exemplifies, above all, the power of historically specific capitalist relations to commodify everyday life and subjectivity itself. Both the quotidian practices and experiences of Klebold and Harris that led up to the shootings, and the construction of youth alienation by the mass media following them, were profoundly shaped by the overlapping, internally related estrangements of self and society in the spectacle society's abstract world of commodities. Harris and Klebold's rage and resentment leading to their decision to get revenge, and to go out as media celebrities, were always already shaped according to the cultural logic of the spectacle itself. The media construction of youth alienation and fear of alien youth continued the cycle and turned Harris and Klebold into the "natural born killers" they predicted they would become.

While their rage was authentic throughout, it stemmed from their subordination in school and larger social hierarchies in which each group had assumed their place according to the value they had been granted by spectacular society. In part, each social clique at Columbine formed from the constructed identities youth bring to school, and emerged through the complex negotiations of different individuals responding to each other and their search for themselves. Yet the dominant groups such as the "jocks" and "preps" were also organized according to the greater power, prestige, and sign-value they had attained as commodified objects. The perception by Klebold and Harris that this field of domination characterized by the oppression of those without sign-value, and the subordination of difference, was just "the way things were" points to insights that were only partial. While they do indeed appear to have had "self-awareness," they could not find a way to put it to constructive resistance. Instead they lived and died with the reified resignation that they lived in a closed world of hierarchy and inverted landscape of absurdity. Their horrific act of revenge, as in many cases of *non*-violent resistance to oppressive circumstance, only fed the cycle of spectacular society.

The preceding critical analysis of the media spectacle following the Columbine shootings provides strong evidence for a powerful continuity in Frankfurt School analyses of the dialectic of rationality and irrationality in modern life. Eric Harris and Dylan Klebold came to personify the "peril" of adolescence itself and the "secret vice" of strange new mediated youth cultures. The spectacle of their crimes re-classified youth in terms of innate pathology, or an incomprehensible culture of secret, subterranean violence. These fantastical constructions turned middle-class suburban and rural youth into alien creatures that simultaneously excited and frightened media consumers. Consequently, as new consumer objects of fear, white youth were commodified in a process that reinforced the very cultural conditions of hierarchy and estrangement from self that fueled the rage of Klebold and Harris to begin with. The Columbine spectacle represents a dynamic *cycle of alienation* that moves from objectification to anger and back to objectification. At every stage of this cycle, the spectacle society undermines the process of self-formation necessary for the transcendence of the estrangement it produces.

In this sense, intensified calls for the social control of youth are part of a continuum or cycle that represents a neglected part of a multi-dimensional contemporary youth crisis. For many good reasons, much greater attention has been given to working class and poor youth who face a crisis based on the "savage inequalities" (Kozol, 1991) they experience at a young age. Millions of economically marginalized youth face the harsh conditions of a post-industrial America which has witnessed massive job loss in the inner-cities, the decimation of the federal welfare system, the re-segregation of schooling, and an intensified legitimation crisis for children growing up without real opportunity for a decent future. However, comparatively little attention has been paid to a related crisis for economically privileged youth. For middle-class youth, particularly white suburban and rural kids who drift toward or are pushed to the margins, the problem of post-industrial life is the meaninglessness and absurdity of consumerism, suburbia, and abstract life. It is the set of conditions creating widespread undermining and fragmentation of identity within abstract mediated life. The society of the spectacle makes growing up absurd, especially when discipline attempts to reinforce the abstract identities it promotes. Thus, when identity crises are fueled or reinforced by cultural waves of hostility and punishment, the already existing separations between youth and society only grow larger. The result is depression, rage, detachment, and, for some homicide or suicide. These "hidden injuries" of alienation were examined in Frankfurt School works such as Fromm's *The Sane Society* (1955). Their continuing manifestation in the emotional underbelly of American society point to a need to return to the Frankfurt School and the type of critical theory of education and youth begun by Henry Giroux in the 1980s.

REFERENCES

Adorno, T. (1973). *Negative dialectics*. New York: Seabury.

Adorno, T. (1976). *Introduction to the sociology of music*. New York: Seabury.

Adorno, T. (1984). *Aesthetic theory*. London: Routledge and Kegan Paul.

Benjamin, W. (1968). *Illuminations*. New York: Schocken Books.

Beck, U. (1992). *Risk society: Towards a new modernity*. London: SAGE.

Bourdieu, P., & Passeron, J. C. (1990). *Reproduction in education, society, and culture*. New York: Sage Publications.

Bowles, S., & Gintis, H. (1976). *Schooling in Capitalist America: Educational reform and the contradictions of economic life*. New York: Basic Books.

Brookfield, S. D. (2004). *The power of critical theory: Liberating adult learning and Teaching*. San Francisco: Jossey-Bass.

Chancer, L., & Donovan, P. (1994). A mass psychology of punishment: Crime and the futility of rationally based approaches. *Social Justice*, *21*, 50–85.

Davis, N. (1999). *Youth crisis: Growing up in the high-risk society*. Westport, CO: Praeger.

Debord, G. (1995). *Society of the spectacle*. New York: Zone Books.

DeVitis, J. (1974). Marcuse on education: Social critique and social control. *Educational Theory*, *24*(3), 259–268.

Feenberg, A. (1981). *Lukacs, Marx and the sources of critical theory*. Totowa, NJ: Rowman & Littlefield.

Foley, D. E. (1990). *Learning capitalist culture: Deep in the heart of Tejas*. Philadelphia: University of Pennsylvania Press.

Friedenberg, E. (1959). *The vanishing adolescent*. Boston: Beacon Press.

Fromm, E. (1955). *The sane society*. New York: Reinhart and Co.
Gaines, D. (1991). *Teenage wasteland: Suburbia's dead end kids*. New York: Pantheon Books.
Gilligan, J. (2001). *Preventing violence*. London: Thames and Hudson.
Giroux, H. A. (1983). *Theory and resistance in education: A pedagogy for the opposition Critical perspectives in social theory*. South Hadley, MA: Bergin & Garvey.
Goodman, P. (1960). *Growing up absurd: Problems of youth in the organized society*. New York: Vintage.
Gur-Ze'ev, I. (2002). Bildung and critical theory facing post-modern education. *Journal of Philosophy of Education, 36*(3), 391–408.
Gur-Ze'ev, I. (2005). *Critical theory and critical pedagogy today: Toward a new critical language in education*. Haifa: University of Haifa, Faculty of Education.
Horkheimer, M., & Adorno, T. W. (1972). *Dialectic of enlightenment*. New York: Herder and Herder.
Horkheimer, M. (1995). *Between philosophy and social science: Selected early writings* (G. Frederick Hunter, M. S. Kramer, & John Torpey, Trans.). Cambridge, MA: MIT Press.
Kellner, D. (2003). Toward a critical theory of education. *Democracy and Nature, 9*(1), 51–64.
Kellner, D., Cho, D., & Lewis, T. (Eds.). (2006). Marcuse and education. *Policy Futures in Education, 4*(1), 1–95.
Keniston, K. (1965). *The uncommitted: Alienated youth in American society*. New York: Harcourt, Brace & World.
Kozol, J. (1991). *Savage inequalities: Children in America's schools*. New York: Crown.
Larkin, R. (1979). *Suburban youth in cultural crisis*. New York: Oxford University Press.
Lowenthal, L. (1983). *Literature and mass culture*. Edison, NJ: Transaction.
Lowenthal, L. (1985). *Literature, popular culture and society*. Palo Alto, CA: Pacific Books.
Lukács, G. (1971). *History and class consciousness*. London: Merlin.
Marcuse, H. (1964). *One-dimensional man*. Boston: Beacon.
Marcuse, H. (1978). *The aesthetic dimension*. Boston: Beacon.
Marx, K. (1964). *Early writings* (T. Bottomore, Ed.). New York: International Publishers.
Marx, K. (1967). *Capital: A critique of political economy*. New York: International Publishers.
McLaren, P., & Giarelli, J. M. (1995). *Critical theory and educational research*. Albany, NY: SUNY Press.
Peters, M. A., Lankshear, C., & Olssen, M. (Eds.). (2003). *Critical theory and the human condition: Past, present and future*. New York: Peter Lang.
Peters, M. A., Lankshear, C., & Olssen, M. (Eds.). (2003). *Futures of critical theory: Dreams of difference*. New York: Rowman & Littlefield.
Popkewitz, T. (1999). *Critical theories in education: Changing terrains of knowledge and politics*. New York: Routledge.
Reisman, D. (1950). *The lonely crowd: A study of the changing American character*. New Haven, CT: Yale University Press.
Reitz, C. (2000). *Art, alienation, and the humanities: A critical engagement with Herbert Marcuse*. Albany, NY: SUNY Press.
Schwendinger, H., & Schwendinger, J. R. (1985). *Adolescent subcultures and delinquency* (Research ed.). New York: Praeger.
Slater, P. (1970). *The pursuit of loneliness: American culture at the breaking point*. Boston: Beacon Press.
Spina, S. U. (Ed.). (2000). *Smoke and mirrors: The hidden context of violence in schools*. Lanham, MD: Rowman and Littlefield.
Willis, P. (1977). *Learning to labor*. Farnborough, UK: Saxon House.
Young, R. E. (1990). *Critical theory of education: Habermas and our children's future*. New York: Teachers College Press.

Benjamin Frymer
Hutchins School of Liberal Studies
Sonoma State University

SEEHWA CHO

7. WHY CULTURE?

The Political Economy of Cultural Politics

INTRODUCTION

In recent years, cultural theories have had significant influences on critical educational theories. Since the 1980s, we have witnessed an outpour of education literature from cultural theories and cultural studies. For instance, the emergence of critical pedagogy in the 1980s can be understood fundamentally as a new emphasis on culture (see Cho, 2006). The very identity of critical pedagogy centered around culture/cultural politics, thus differentiating and distancing it from the earlier materialist theories of education (e.g., Bowles & Gintis, 1976; Bourdieu & Passeron, 1977; Apple, 1979, 1982). In the same way, the revived interest in multicultural education in recent years can also be understood as the effect, or at least a signal, of the discovery and dominance of culture in educational discourses.

This phenomenon is not limited to the field of education. During the last three decades, "culture" has become dominant in the social sciences and the humanities, often used widely in cultural theories, cultural studies, cultural power, cultural resistance, and cultural politics. Moreover, cultural politics became a dominant political position in the New Social Movements (Teodori, 1969; Harvey, 1990; Sanbonmatsu, 2004). It is, Michael Denning (2004) says, as if we discovered culture, realizing suddenly that culture is everywhere, and it is culture that really matters. Furthermore, this trend is not limited to the West either. Although there are some differences and incompatibilities, cultural studies and cultural politics have become a global phenomenon within the last two decades.

Why did culture come to the forefront of academic studies and of the Left politics? How did culture become so important? What were the political economic contexts that catalyzed this move? What problems do these theories address that were not addressed before? These are the questions this chapter aims to explore. In contemplating these questions, one could focus on purely theoretical differences among scholars and approaches. For instance, one could delineate the differences between Marxism and post-al theories (poststructuralism, postmodernism, and post-colonialism) on how they conceptualize culture. This seems to be a common approach. Unlike this common approach, my aim is to examine the historical and social contexts that provoked the emergence of culture. In other words, my approach is a political economy of cultural theories/politics. As such, I will sketch the topic of "culture" with broad (and sometimes crude) strokes, since my intention is not to examine different theories or theorists of culture, but to capture the larger framework of how these cultural discourses and politics posit themselves.

Z. Leonardo (ed.), Handbook of Cultural Politics and Education, 175–192.

THE MEANING OF CULTURE QUESTION

As I will show later in this chapter, culture has been increasingly important within the critical social theories during the 20th century. However, in the 1970s, a new and full-blown form of cultural study emerged. This so-called "Contemporary Cultural Study" has changed how culture was to be understood, and presented culture at the center of social theories. This new focus on culture, they argue, is necessary because the society has changed dramatically since the 1970s (or since WWII according to Lyotard), and in this postmodern society, culture has become a critically important center (to some, *the* center).

Many agree that the social system has gone through some dramatic changes since the 1970s. However, what is not agreed upon is whether this change is a fundamental break, or a change in degree. It has been hotly debated whether the change since the 1970s has signaled a break from the previous social condition, or just a change within the system. In other words, this ongoing contention has been over, as Zeus Leonardo aptly points out, whether the "post" in postmodernity means "after" modernity, or "late" modernity (see Introduction to this volume). In this way, the question of culture is ultimately a question about the very nature of society itself. If the postmodern condition is a complete break from modernity, it means that the Marxist framework is no longer valid in analyzing society/ capitalism and presenting an alternative (roughly this is the postmodernists' position). However, if the postmodern condition is a late stage of modernity/ capitalism, then Marxism is still relevant in some fashion (roughly this is the Neo-Marxists' position). As such, it is no wonder why this question has not only divided, but also fueled disputes between the neo-Marxists and the post-al theorists.

This chapter, perhaps ambitiously, attempts to shed some light on the question of culture in lieu of its meaning for understanding the nature of society. My central argument in this chapter is that culture has become important in the course of the 20th century because of *changes in capitalism itself.* As I endeavor to outline the historical contexts of changes in capitalism through which culture studies and cultural politics have evolved, my treatment of "culture" in this chapter will inevitably be broader than that of the British Centre for Contemporary Cultural Studies, or postmodern cultural studies. I define the turn to culture more broadly, which is a move away from the material base to the superstructure in social theories. Thus, my examination of the move toward culture will ensue from the early 20th century, roughly since the 1930s, covering major cultural theories from Antonio Gramsci's import of the concept of hegemony in the 1920s–30s (Gramsci, 1971), to Frankfurt Critical Theories' attention to popular culture and mass media in the 1940s–60s (Benjamin, 1937; Adorno, 1938, 1962, 1973; Marcuse, 1969, 1972), to Louis Althusser's affective theory of ideology and Ideological State Apparatus (1971), to the Birmingham Cultural Studies (Hoggart, 1957; Thompson, 1957, 1958; Williams, 1961, 1963; Hall, 1958, 1980), to the poststructuralist and the postmodernist theories' focus on culture and knowledge since the 1970s (Foucault, 1977, 1980; Lyotard, 1984; Baudrillard, 1994). To reiterate, my focus is not to give a detailed review of these diverse theories, but to demonstrate how the fundamental changes in political economy changed the significance and meaning of culture, and how the changes in the mode of capitalism pushed culture to the center stage both in critical theories and Leftist politics. In short, mine is a material analysis of cultural studies and cultural politics.

WORKING CLASS CONSCIOUSNESS AND HEGEMONY

After World War I and inspired by the Russian Revolution, there was a surge of revolutionary struggles, which globally spread to Asia, Africa, and Latin America (Tilly, 2004). However, it was apparently clear by the 1930s that the proletarian revolutionary possibility in Europe was all but lost. Instead of joining the international workers' movement, the working class in Europe supported the nationalistic fascism that emerged between two World Wars. With that, European proletariats were successfully incorporated into the capitalist system (Arato & Gebhardt, 1978; Davis, 1999; Wallerstein, 2004). Why did the proletariats acquiesce to the capitalist system if they were aware that the very foundation of the system was built on exploitation of their own labor? In other words, why would the working class accept going against its own class interests? It is this very problem which became a central question to Marxists in the early part of the 20th century. Subsequently, this question directed Marxists' attention to the sphere of the superstructure (ideology and culture), on which Karl Marx and Friedrich Engels did not fully elaborate. Antonio Gramsci tried to answer this question with the cultural-political hegemony of the bourgeoisie, while György Lukács focused on the ideological crisis of the proletariat.

Recalling Marx, the dominant ideology of a society is the ideology of the dominant class, and the working class is brought into the dominant ideology mainly due to their false consciousness. To put it simply, the working class fails to see their own interests because they are duped, and they are duped because the ruling class dominates the very means of production of ideology. However, unlike this rather crude explanation provided by Marx, Gramsci (1971) saw the process not solely as a matter of falsity, but rather a matter of concession and compromise. For Gramsci, the crucial questions were: Why did Mussolini's fascism rise in Italy? Why did the Italian people support it? And how could the working class gain power in bourgeois dominated Europe? Gramsci saw the Italian people, including the working class, as having consented to and accepted fascism, rather than having been forced or duped, because the ruling bloc was able to establish hegemony. In this hegemony building process, Gramsci realized the crucial role the intellectuals played. According to Gramsci, it was the 'traditional intellectuals' who developed, articulated, and legitimated the ideology of the dominant class. As such, in order to counter this hegemony, he argued, the working class needs its own intellectuals (he called them the 'organic intellectuals') who would formulate counter-hegemonic ideologies. Thus, for Gramsci, the war was waged not only on the State ('war of maneuver'), but also on the level of ideology and consciousness ('war of position'). Hence, Gramsci proclaimed that the superstructure is as important as, if not more important than, the material base.

Lukács (1923/1971) also rejected the false consciousness thesis. Like Gramsci, he highlighted the importance of cultural mediation in the formation of working class consciousness. First of all, Lukács emphasized the complexity of cultural mediation. He rejected the view that culture and literary representation automatically correspond with class interests. On the one hand, cultural representation could be emancipatory, if it presents the vantage point of proletariats by signifying the totality of the social order. On the other hand, cultural representation could be a form of "reification," if it fragments and dislocates our reality and experiences. According to Lukács, with increasing commodification of cultural representations, culture became more of a form of reification than of emancipation, and thus functioned as a controlling mechanism for ensuring the passivity of the working classes (Smith, 2000). This theme was later picked up and further developed by others, particularly the Frankfurt School.

Through Gramsci and Lukács, ideology and culture were given far greater importance than before, thus emerging as crucial spheres to be closely analyzed in understanding the consciousness of the working class (Sparks, 1996). Later when the Birmingham Cultural Studies tried to explain why the British working class supported Margaret Thatcher (basically the same question as Gramsci's question of why Italian working class supported Mussolini), it is Gramsci that Birmingham centre revived, and from which they developed the hegemony theory of culture (see Sparks, 1996). Just like their British counterpart, the American working class also helped the rise of the Reagan administration in the early 1980s. Perhaps this similarity in political situation is one of the reasons why the British Cultural Studies deeply influenced the intellectual and political left of the U.S.

MASS CULTURE INDUSTRY AND THE SUBJECT

As Gramsci tried to understand the rise of fascism in Italy, the Frankfurt School wanted to explain the rise of fascism in Germany. How did the civilized German people, who inherited rich intellectual traditions, support Hitler's fascism and commit such inhumane and unimaginable atrocities against other human beings? As a way to explore this grave question, the Frankfurt Critical theorists turned their focus on the emergence of mass communication and the culture industry, and its impacts on culture and social subjects.

The emergence of mass culture industry changed the function that art and culture had played in society. Since the Enlightenment period, art, a realm of the life-world, was considered against and beyond the system-world that was dominated by rationality (Arato, 1978). Art was poised as an antidote against the destructive instrumental rationality of capitalism, against the effects of functionalism (Harvey, 1990). In addition, the rise of popular culture was considered as a progressive force, challenging the elite/bourgeois culture. By insisting that cultural representations of everyday people were art, the emergence of popular culture challenged the idea that only elite culture is worthy of embodying artistic values. Art and culture were no longer a monopoly of the aristocrats.

However, with the emergence of mass media and the culture industry, the progressive force of popular culture was severely diminished. It is this new development of mass media and the commercial production of mass culture to which the Frankfurt Critical Theory paid close attention, as Frymer's chapter rightly notes. According to the Frankfurt School, mass media and the culture industry transformed popular culture into commercialized mass culture. Just like other manufacturing goods, now culture was mass-produced, packaged, and distributed as consumer goods. Art and culture underwent what Andrew Arato (1978) has termed 'thingfication'. This change was crucial, according to the Frankfurt School, because it explained why working class culture and consciousness could no longer be independent of their own class position and interest. As subjects and consciousness were now constructed by mass commercial culture, the close relation between class and culture/consciousness was fundamentally broken. As a result, the Frankfurt School contended that popular culture no longer represented the culture of people. Instead, culture became a major mechanism of social control. This is how the Frankfurt school explained the lack of working class consciousness and their acceptance of Nazism, as they carried on media studies in the U.S. during the Nazi period (see Jay, 1973).

The study of mass media led to a new question of how mass media and culture industry impact the formation of 'the subject'. Among others, the work of Louis Althusser is significant on the topic of subject formation. His theory laid the foundation for contemporary accounts of cultural identity and the subject. Althusser attempted to overcome the failures of Marxist economic analysis in order to properly explain the role of ideology (culture being a sub-part of ideology) in the reproduction of the relations of production. The complex and sometime contradictory relations within the superstructure (this is articulation, not mediation - a point to which I will return later) defy the previous notion of the subject as a passive agent determined by class interests. Althusser (1971) contended that the Ideological State Apparatuses (such as the family, education system, political parties, trade unions, religious organizations, mass media and cultural agents) played a significant role in the formulation of the subject. The basic point of Althusser in the role of Ideological Sate Apparatuses is that superstructural institutions have become much more complex, and their role and influence have increased with the growing State intervention in the 20th century (see Smith, 2000). Althusser's identification of ideology as a representtation of the "imaginary" relationship of individuals to their material conditions, and the subjectification or the creation of subjects through discourse and interpellation became the basis of much of later cultural studies (see Leonardo, 2003a).

As most Frankfurt school scholars were Jewish who were exiled from Germany, it is quite understandable that their account of culture is quite grim, and their prospect for social change is quite pessimistic. Critical Theory in general became increasingly nihilistic from the late 1950s. The subject basically disappears and the society becomes all-powerful (Piccone, 1978). It is hard, if not impossible, to hold onto the existence of an autonomous subject. This means, the very idea of the free and autonomous subject is rendered hopeless because of the tight grip of the present Western system on the consciousness not only of the dominant, but also of the dominated (this theme is later echoed in Paulo Freire, 1970). With the death of the subject or the arrival of posthumanism (Hardt & Negri, 2000), obviously it is hard to even imagine the possibility for radical social change. This theme carried on prominently in the later development of poststructuralism and postmodernism. For instance, we see a similar description of power as disciplining subjects in the totally administered society described by Michel Foucault (1977).

STATE CAPITALISM, AND REMAKING OF WORKING CLASS

Above, I described how superstructure, ideology and mass culture emerged as significant themes in critical theories, and how cultural theories evolved to focus on subject formation through the mass media, the educational system, and the prisons, as studied by the Frankfurt School, Althusser, and later Foucault. The growing attention to culture is a result of the class war that is now waged through cultural interventions by the cultural industries and "state cultural apparatuses" (Denning, 2004: p. 161). In order to better understand how culture came to be a site of class struggle, we need to examine the change in the mode of capital accumulation in the first part of the 20th century.

In the early 20th century, capitalism in the industrialized West plunged into a severe crisis. With this crisis, it was recognized that the market could not regulate itself (the end of laissez-faire/liberal capitalism), and thus the State had to intervene and regulate the market in order to stabilize the economic crisis (the beginning of State capitalism). The emergence of totalitarian regimes in the 1930s and 1940s (not only fascism in Germany, Italy, and Japan, but also Stalinism in the USSR and the New Deal in the USA) was due to this major crisis in capitalism (Pollock, 1941; Arato, 1978; Harvey 1990; Wallerstein, 2004). In fact, Friedrich Pollock (1941), a Frankfurt School affiliated scholar, argued that Nazism was partly a response to the crisis of liberal capitalism, and he saw that Nazism was a necessary political form of a stabilized monopoly of capitalism. This change has a significant meaning for culture. The State regulation of capitalist economies and the increased role of the State within capitalism increased the importance of the political-administrative sphere. And as the axis moved from economy to politics, the sphere of culture became increasingly crucial for social reproduction and legitimation (Arato, 1978).

After the savage depression and the near-collapse of capitalism in the 1930s, a new mode of capitalism was devised. The understanding was that the crisis of liberal capitalism was due to the falling consumption of manufacturing goods that were produced in vast quantities. The underlying motive of Fordism (the five-dollar, eight-hour) was to solve this over-production and under-consumption problem. It provided enough income to workers to purchase the consumer products, driving up consumptive practices, which in turn increased production. With more income and leisure time (due to shorter working hours), workers were transformed into the much-needed consumers. After several different experiments, Fordism rose as the dominant configuration after WWII in the US. The long economic boom era from 1945 to 1973 was built on this combination of Fordist-Keynesianism (Harvey, 1990).

Postwar Fordism and the economic boom in the West had significant impacts on class structure and working-class culture. With the expanded opportunity for higher education (particularly due to the GI bill), increased residency in the new suburbs, and the increased power of mass consumption, the working class was transformed and remade during this period. The middle class life-style was comfortably adopted by the working class. This embourgeoisment of the working class inevitably altered the working class culture and the formation of their class consciousness. For instance, Stanley Aronowitz (1989) demonstrates how the development of the suburbs in the postwar US broke down the working class community and fractured working class culture. It is no coincidence that around this time working class representation largely disappeared from the mass media as well. Up until the early 1960s, the representation of working class (that is, white workers) was, though small in numbers, present in films and television. But from the mid-1970s, media representation of workers has basically disappeared. Thus, Aronowitz argues, working-class kids today have a harder time in forging a class identity, because "they confront a media complex that consistently denies their existence, or displaces working-class male identity to other, upwardly mobile occupations, for example, police work, football players, and other sites where conventional masculine roles are ubiquitous" (1989: p. 204).

The remaking of working class and transformation of working class culture further widened the gap between one's class position and one's class consciousness. The independent making of the working class culture seemed no longer feasible, not just because of the mass cultural industry, but also because the working class itself had changed. It is in this historical context that British cultural studies emerged in the 1960s, and this is why the Centre for Cultural Studies focused on the culturalist research agenda of studying working-class culture and education, beginning with E.P. Thompson and Richard Hoggart (see Sparks, 1996; Smith, 2000).

THE CULTURAL TURN AND CONTEMPORARY CULTURAL STUDIES

As stated above, culture (as a part of the superstructure) has become increasingly more significant in critical theories since the early 20th century. However, there was a crucial break in cultural theories in the late 1960s and 1970s, which has often been called the "cultural turn". This was the beginning of the "Contemporary Cultural Studies," and with that, a whole host of neo-Marxist and post-Marxist theories emerged: from Althusser, to the Birmingham Cultural Studies, to the poststructuralist and the postmodernist theories, to the postcolonial theories. It is neither possible nor my intention to review these diverse cultural theories. Instead, I will delineate some of the basic characteristics of contemporary cultural studies, especially highlighting how they are different from earlier approaches to culture. There are four closely related characteristics of the contemporary cultural theories.

The first is about how culture is to be understood. While earlier Marxist or neo-Marxist theories paid an increasing attention to the sphere of superstructure and culture, they still maintained a close relationship between culture and the economic base, ultimately in the form of the latter determining the former. In contrast, contemporary cultural studies basically abandoned the centrality of the material base in its discourse, and argued that culture bears no concrete relations with the material base, or at least is autonomous of it (e.g., Hindess and Hirst 1977; Laclau and Mouffe 1984). As such, poststructuralists and postmodernists understand culture (e.g., language and representation) to be free-floating, fractured, indeterminate, and infinitive - detached from any basis/base that can be traced to social structures and relations. This is made possible by a particular reading of Gramsci through the concept of "articulation," which suggests the conjuncture of events that arbitrarily congeal and are in no way determined by the economy.

This new view on culture as an autonomous sphere, I think, is due to the changes in social reality. With the global saturation of mass media and communication, it is more recognized and acclaimed that the reality of our time is a reality/image constructed and represented via mass media. Culture and signs now create and become our reality, as portrayed poignantly (and somewhat dreadfully) by Jean Baudrillard (1994) in his simulation theory (see also Leonardo, 2003b). Representation is now our reality, and, as Baudrillard and others argue, there is no such thing as "reality" outside of representation. Our experience is of a simulation of reality rather than reality itself (thus, Baudrillard calls it 'simulacra'), a chimerical relation with the Real. In short, culture has graduated to the status of reality (Denning, 2006).

Second, as contemporary cultural studies see culture as having much more autonomy than before, they place a greater degree of importance to culture. In contemporary cultural studies, the role of culture (along with education) has become much more expanded and significant in explaining the reproduction of capitalism as a system. The contemporary culturalists do not see culture as subservient or subordinate to the economy. Hence, Althusser's famous turn to reproduction and away from relations of production signalled the new concern with the ideological process of capitalism. In fact, Althusser's concept of "overdeterminism" allowed the superstructure to affect the base, cultural life rebounding in an unpredictable way onto economic life. As such, these theorists place a greater emphasis upon the role of political and ideological strategies, through which hegemonic projects are to be constructed. A major reason for this change is because culture itself became part of the economic realm. The production and consumption of culture has become a core industry in the global capitalism. The mass media, advertising, production and distribution of knowledge, information, and communication have become the leading sector of economy within industrialized societies, replacing the prominence of the manufacturing industry, once a leading sector of capitalism (thus, the 'post-industrial' society). This is precisely the theme that Jean-François Lyotard (1979) explored in his seminal book, *The Postmodern Condition.* According to him, the postmodern condition has to be understood in the cultural field and no longer within relations or modes of production.

Third, the new cultural theories reject the idea that cultural representation is a simple manifestation of class interest. In contemporary cultural theories, the identity/subject formation is understood as a much looser and complex process with neither determinism nor telos (undetermined, and unexpected/unintended).

Cultural representation and interpretation is viewed as more of a negotiation of meanings and "articulation," rather than as a "mediation" of class interests or the underlying economic foundation (Smith, 2000). This means, we are seeing different models of social formation. As seen for instance in Althusser, "[t]he centre of attention shifted from the relations between base and superstructure into an elaboration of the internal articulation of the superstructure itself" (Sparks, 1994: p, 82). From there, it is not difficult to see why symbols, representations, and meanings have become a major focus in contemporary cultural studies. With that, the focus of investigation also shifted from the production of culture towards the consumption of culture. As it was realized that culture has played more of an influential role in identity formation, popular culture emerged as a key topic in cultural studies.

And finally, given that cultural process and identity formation are now understood as more complex and loose, it is acknowledged that identity is not necessarily constructed according to class position and interest. Instead, other forms of social antagonism (race, gender, sexuality, for instance) are as relevant as class to identity formation and to the social formation. The thesis of the omnipresent centrality of class was severely tested and challenged. Here, as we know, there have been hotly contested debates on the relationships between class, race, and gender among Marxists, feminists, and anti-race theorists, to which McLaren and Scatamburlo-D'Annibale's chapter refers. The core of the assertions of contemporary cultural studies is that we should go beyond the class-dominance in critical theories, and acknowledge the co-centrality of gender, race, and other forms of social marginality with class. Consequently, since the 1970s, we see the rise of the New Social Movements, mainly based on identity politics, such as civil rights movements and the women's movement, followed by the gay and lesbian rights movement, green movements and critical-race/postcolonial politics (Harvey, 1990; Sanbonmatsu, 2004; Tilly, 2004).

THE NEW SOCIAL MOVEMENTS AND POSTMODERNISM

Between the global uprisings in 1968 and 1972, the dynamics of social movements changed, and new left politics emerged. The so-called New Social Movements moved away from class, and cultural politics have moved to the forefront of Left politics (see Philion, 1998; Cho, 2008). The struggle was no longer solely against capitalism, or economic inequality and exploitation, but rather against the totality of the system, "a struggle for redistribution of power at all levels" (Teodori, 1969: p. 37). From these new social movements, a variety of new critical theories surfaced in tandem with the anti-modern movement, which we often call postmodernism (Harvey, 1990).

To understand the new cultural politics, we need first to grasp what post-modernism is and how it came about. Postmodernism has two counterparts: modernism and Marxism. First, postmodernism is a reflection of critical and shaken awareness concerning modernity and modern projects of the West (Lyotard, 1984; Harvey, 1990). While the 20th century brought remarkable advances in inventions and technological breakthroughs, it also witnessed tremendous disasters and tragic inhumanities. Two world wars, Fascism and the Holocaust shattered the faith in the Enlightenment project of modernism. Although, as W. E. B. Du Bois (1947) pointed out, there was no Nazi-like atrocity which Christian civilization or Europe had not long been practicing against colonized bodies in all parts of world, it was the Holocaust that shook European and Western sensibility (see also Césaire, 1955/2000). In addition, the 20th century created colonial wars, atrocities carried out in the name of nationalism and socialism, and nuclear arms (enough to kill all human beings several hundred times over). As such, postmodernism rejects, or at least casts doubts on the Enlightenment philosophy of modernism.

On the other hand, postmodernism is also a critique of or an incredulity toward Marxism. The rise of Stalinism during the 1920s and 1930s already created doubts among the Western Left who, in one way or another, looked at the Soviet Union as a great historical alternative against the capitalist West (in fact, the Frankfurt School was internally divided regarding the Soviet question). However, following the Soviet invasion of Hungary in 1956 and the forceful intervention in the 1968 Prague Spring of Czechoslovakia, it became clear to many Western Leftists that the Soviet project had failed. Disillusioned, the New Left either saw Socialist theory to be in need of serious revision, or to be abandoned altogether.

As such, postmodernism no longer believes in "salvation," neither of the Spirit (modernism), nor of the Revolution (Marxism), thus forging, as Lyotard (1984) puts it, "incredulity toward metanarratives" (p. xxiv). It is within this context of a skeptical stance toward systemic changes and political struggles that we have to understand why the only salvation for Theodor Adorno (1978) was the arts (he was once aspired to be a professional violinist), why Michel Foucault (1988) endeavored on "the care of self" (he goes back to ancient Greece for this), and why Peter Sloterdijk (1997) presents "kynicism," the cheekiness of body functions, as an alternative against cynical reason.

The collapse of the Soviet project and the frustration with the Enlightenment of modernity marked the beginning of new critical theories and new political praxis (thus, 'New Left'). The old class-based social movements were replaced with New Social Movements. Instead of focusing on capitalism or the State, a new cohort of critical theorists after 1968 looked into new spheres (see Brennan, 2006). No longer believing that changing the system (e.g., social and political institutions) will bring genuine transformation and human liberation, the New Left turned to the body/individual/local struggles as alternatives (Cho, 2008). This is why in the last three decades we saw the rise of identity politics (civil rights movement, women's movement, gay movement), localized/ grassroots politics ('think globally, act locally'), and personal politics ('personal is political').

In short, postmodernism instituted culture as a privileged site for resistance and emancipatory politics. From this impetus, multifaceted cultural politics emerged over the last few decades. There are various dimensions to what is meant by cultural politics: culture as life-world against instrumental reason; cultural politics as popular culture against elite/institution culture; cultural politics as civil society against the State; and cultural politics as multiculturalism and subaltern/ postcolonial project against Eurocentricism. However, an underlying commonality among these various cultural politics is the idea that ultimately politics has turned to culture, or culture has become an important site for politics. In other words, the postmodern condition now had to be understood within the context of the cultural field and no longer within relations of production (Baudrillard 1975, 1994; Lyotard, 1984). For this reason, it is within this cultural field that the counter-hegemonic war must be waged and where possibilities are to be found again. While earlier social movements focused on the economy, the new social movements now focus on culture. As such, knowledge, images, representation, and identity are as important as, if not more important than, strikes, wages, and working conditions.

CULTURAL STUDIES IN EDUCATION

As stated in the beginning of this chapter, culture has become an important topic in the critical education literature during the past three decades. Various cultural theories influenced cultural studies in education, and there are diverse and different meanings and uses of culture in the educational literature. It is beyond the scope of this chapter to review the extensive literature on the disparate cultural theories in education. Instead, I will briefly lay out how the cultural politics are conceptualized and utilized in critical educational literature by teasing out multiple layers of different levels/dimensions. By utilizing and modifying Michael Denning's work (2004), I will identify five cultural theories in critical education theories: hegemonic theory of culture, commodity theory of culture, resistance theory of culture, disciplinary theory of culture, and identity/post-colonial theory of culture.

Initiated by the influential work of Bowles & Gintis (1974), critical education theorists in the 1970s and early 1980s attempted to explain the mechanisms whereby the school re/produces the hierarchical economic system. In this attempt, they were heavily influenced by the *hegemonic theory of culture* from the British Cultural Studies that had come to attention of U.S. academia of that era. These critical educational theorists employed Gramsci, Althusser, and Stuart Hall, and advanced concepts like hidden curriculum, ideology/hegemony, and schools as a State apparatus (Apple, 1979, 1982; Dale et al, 1981; Giroux, 1983, 1988; Carnoy & Levin, 1985). The main claim of these works is that the school, as a part of culture/superstructure, plays a significant role in reproducing and legitimating the hegemony of capitalist society. Schools and education accomplish this through several mechanisms: by certain knowledge they choose to include or exclude in curriculum, the norms and values they convey to students, and the social interactions and practices they utilize to sort out students for future careers. Ideology critique is the core of this hegemonic theory of culture, which is arguably still the dominant approach in cultural studies in education today.

The *commodity theory of culture* by Pierre Bourdieu also made a significant impact on the cultural studies in education. Bourdieu approached culture as a commodity form, and analyzed how culture emerged as an investment in the creation of cultural capital (Bourdieu & Passeron, 1977). As a result of the commodification of culture, culture (that is, elite culture as capital) now becomes an important mechanism to create "distinctions" (Bourdieu, 1984). Bourdieu's concepts such as habitus, cultural capital, symbolic violence, and distinctions provided powerful tools in revealing the power relations embedded in school knowledges. For instance, Bourdieu exposed the asymmetry of power through critique of how certain knowledges are considered as high-status, while others are seen as low-status. The concept of "cultural capital," in particular, has been widely utilized in analyzing not only class, but also race and gender power dynamics in school knowledge (e.g., Lareau, 1989; Delpit, 1995; Reay, 1998; Harry & Klingner, 2006; Paik, & Walberg, 2007).

Paul Willis' (1977) *Learning to Labour* is significant in that his work highlighted the loose yet active nature of culture. Unlike the hegemony and the commodity theory of culture, Willis observed cultural reproduction less as a seamless process, but rather a loose one with a contradictory mixture of penetration, rationality, distortion and final incorporation. What Willis highlighted is that first, culture inherently has points of weakness involved with contradiction and resistance, and second, culture maintains relative autonomy due to the effects of relatively autonomous meanings, such as those found in sexism and racism. Contrary to the deterministic and gloomy depiction of the role of education in hegemony and commodity theories, Willis' theory provided some potentiality for changes and possibility. Thus, it is not hard to understand why this *resistance theory of culture* was appreciatively embraced in education literature. A series of studies followed, examining the resistance dynamics of culture and exploring culture as a site for resistance, struggles, and changes (e.g., Apple, 1982; Giroux, 1983; Weis, 1990; MacLeod, 1995; Kenny, 2000).

Another theory that impacted critical education literature is the *disciplinary theory of culture* by Foucault. Unlike the commodity theory, Foucault's theory conceptualizes culture as dispersed systems of surveillance and the disciplining of desire by the state and quasi-state institutions, such as prisons, armies, hospitals, and schools (Foucault, 1977). In this scheme, schools are a powerful surveillance agency, disciplining the body and formulating the subjectivities of students. The effects of power in Foucault are all-encompassing and omnipresent, which is a very pessimistic view. Foucault's theory of culture, however, is utilized in sometimes conflicting ways in critical education: some employ Foucault's concept of power as predominantly disciplinary to expose schools as a system of surveillance, while others highlight more the rupture or fracture of power mechanism to envision schools as a site of possibility for resistance and change (e.g., Giroux, 1991; Aronowitz, & Giroux, 1991; Popkewitz & Brennan, 1997; Marshall, 1998; Popkewitz & Fendler, 1999; Palermo, 2002; Bratich, Packer, & McCarthy, 2003; Gabbard, 2006; Peters & Besley, 2007). Particularly, feminist education literature was heavily influenced by Foucault's conception of power/knowledge in the past two decades (e.g. Lather, 1991; Luke & Gore, 1992; Gore, 1993; St. Pierre, & Pillow, 2000). For one, his idea of "subjugated knowledge" (Foucault, 1980) is taken up by feminists and race theorists who challenge the class-dominated theories of culture.

The *identity/post-colonial theory of culture* is another approach that became visible only recently in cultural studies in education. In this approach, culture is seen mainly as communities of people, and this is due to the influence of Stuart Hall's focus on the national-popular, and to the place of racisms in its formation (Denning, 2004). Now cultural theories increasingly are about how culture produces people - nation, race, immigrant, diaspora, and postcolonial subject, with the aim to critically examine and challenge Eurocentricism. This identity/post-colonial theory of culture goes beyond the scope of multiculturalism in that "the culture of the subaltern is a product of a dialectic of self and other, where the self is objectified as the other and denied any reciprocity of recognition" (Denning, 2004: p. 90). Critical education literature is deeply influenced by this identity/post-colonial theory of culture. We have seen recently the revived interests in multiculturalism and an outpouring of cultural studies employing post-colonial/subaltern theories in critical education literature (e.g., Giroux, 1995; McLaren, 1997; McCarthy, 1998; Leonardo, 2002, 2004, 2005; Allen, 2004; Darder & Torres, 2004; Grande, 2004; Apple & Buras, 2006; Buras & Motter, 2006).

CONCLUDING REMARKS

In this chapter, I attempted to answer the question of why culture has moved to the forefront of critical theories and the politics of the 20th century in the West. I tried to make a case, perhaps in a somewhat functionalistic way, that the rise of cultural studies and cultural politics was due to the transition from the modern society of the 18th–19th century to the postindustrial society of the 20th century. While the transition to Fordist-Keynesian capitalism in the 1940s brought culture and superstructure more clearly into the picture, the transition to post-industrial society in the 1970s brought what we now know as full-fledged cultural studies and cultural politics.

Often cultural theories and cultural politics are posited as opposite to studies of the economy or materialist theories. The debates usually take an either-or approach: culture or economy, superstructure or base, discourse or materiality. As such, often materialists criticize cultural studies and cultural politics for neglecting the material structures of society, de-emphasizing the power and function of capital, and diminishing the centrality of class. Culturalists, in return, criticize materialist theories for having a tendency to trivialize cultural and subjective dimensions, and thus tend to devalue cultural studies and cultural politics as insignificant or secondary. My intention in this chapter was to go beyond, or go *sideways* from this binary approach. In a way, I tried to perform a material analysis on culture, because as a materialist, I wanted and needed to make sense of why culture emerged as a central focus in recent decades. My goal was to show that there are indeed material and structural bases for the emergence of cultural studies and cultural politics. I hope I have succeeded in this objective.

In conclusion, I will briefly mention some concerns we need to address which are related to culturalism and cultural politics. Firstly, the approach to culture is very diverse, complex, and sometimes confusing. On one end of the spectrum, culture is viewed as a medium of discipline and social control, while on the other end, culture is viewed as a site of resistance and possibility. However, I think the current use of culture in the critical education literature is geared more towards the resistance/ possibility notion. By amplifying the contradictory nature of culture, these studies tend to glorify the power of culture in transforming society. This is partly due to their attempt to overcome the seemingly pessimistic position of earlier Marxist theories of education (e.g., Bowles & Gintis, and Bourdieu). In a way, culture came to rescue the critical theories of education from a no-solution alternative (see Cho, 2006). Yet, I think it is somewhat dangerous to engage too romantically in talks of resistance. So much resistance and contradiction "is not the crumbling of the material and institutional structures," as R.W. Connell (1995: p. 226) rightly pointed out.

Secondly, a basic political stance of postmodern cultural politics is "hostility toward totality," and in general, cultural politics bears some incredulity toward metanarratives. In a sense, I think this is progress in our awareness and sensibility. Acknowledgement of heterogeneity can be a sensible antidote against Eurocentricism, or Eurocentric universalism. Along with that, a keen recognition of difference and 'otherness', which cultural politics promotes, advances democratic principles. On the other hand, however, cultural/postmodern politics can lead to fragmented, single issue-based praxis, which generally takes the form of anti-State strategies. Celebration of differences may not be a proper position to fight against the powerful global capitalism. Instead, as some critics warn, it actually helps in deepening neo-liberal global capitalism. Amin's critique is worth quoting here: "The suggested anti-state strategy united perfectly with capital's strategy, which is busy 'limiting public interventions' (deregulating) for its own benefit, reducing the role of the state to its police functions. In a similar way, the anti-nation discourse encourages the acceptance of the role of the US as military superpower and world policeman" (2004, p. 27). In other words, capitalism is able to make certain accommodations to culture.

And lastly, we need to be less sanguine and more cautious when applying cultural studies and cultural politics (especially postmodern culturalism) to the realities of the majority of people in the Third world. It is true that globalization has brought homogenization around the globe. We see the globalization of popular culture encompassing music, clothes, movies and other popular media (one could call it a "californiazation" or "Hollywoodization" of global culture). Yet globalization also brought fragmentation and diversification (Castells, 1996, 1999; Hardt & Negri, 2000; Harvey, 2000; Amin 2004). Heightened ethnic identity and intensified ethnic conflicts are just one example; the rise of fundamentalism (religious as well as secular) is another example. Some parts of the globe (Africa particularly) are becoming marginalized in the global network. Global capitalism has created more polarization, creating a wider gap between rich and poor countries. This is why postmodernism and cultural politics do not sit well with people in the South, where the brutalities of economic capitalism are still formidable forces. In other words, one senses that the cultural turn is a First World roundabout and crisis. Culturalism sounds more like a luxury for many people around the globe whose livelihoods are threatened by global capitalism. If cultural studies and cultural politics fail to adequately incorporate the gritty material reality of global capitalism, they could become merely a hollow intellectual exercise.

REFERENCES

Adoro, T. (1938). On the fetish-character in music and the regression of listening. In A. Arato & E. Gebhardt (Eds.), (1978). *The essential Frankfurt School reader*. New York: Urizen Books.

Adorno, T. (1962). Commitment. In A. Arato & E. Gebhardt (Eds.). (1978). *The essential Frankfurt School reader*. New York: Urizen Books.

Adorno, T. (1973). *Negative dialectics*. New York: Seabury Press.

Allen, R. L. (2004). Whiteness and critical pedagogy. *Educational Philosophy and Theory, 36*(2), 121–136.

Althusser, L. (1971). *Lenin and philosophy and other essays*. New York: Monthly Review Press.

Amin, S. (1997). *Capitalism in the age of globalization*. New York: Zed Books.

Amin, S. (2004). *The liberal virus*. New York: Monthly Review Press.

Apple, M. (1979). *Ideology and curriculum*. New York: Routledge.

Apple, M. (1982). *Education and power*. Boston: Routledge and Kegan Paul.

Apple, M., & Buras, K. (Eds.). (2006). *The subaltern speak: Curriculum, power, and educational struggles*. New York: Routledge.

Arato, A. (1978). Introduction: Esthetic theory and cultural criticism. In A. Arato & E. Gebhardt (Eds.), *The essential Frankfurt School reader*. New York: Urizen Books.

Aronowitz, S. (1989). Working-class identity and celluloid fantasies in the electronic age. In H. Giroux, R. Simon, & Contributors (Eds.), *Popular culture: Schooling & everyday life*. Granby, MA: Bergin & Garvey.

Aronowitz, S., & Giroux, H. (1991). *Postmodern education: Politics, culture, & social criticism*. Minneapolis, MN: University of Minnesota Press.

Baudrillard, J. (1975). *The mirror of production*. St. Louis, MO: Telos Press.

Baudrillard, J. (1994). *Simulacra and simulation*. Ann Arbor, MI: University of Michigan Press.

Benjamin, W. (1937). The author as producer. In A. Arato & E. Gebhardt (Eds.), (1978). *The essential Frankfurt School reader*. New York: Urizen Books.

Bourdieu, P. (1984). *Distinction: A social critique of the judgement of taste*. Cambridge, MA: Harvard University Press.

Bourdieu, P., & Passeron, J. (1977). *Reproduction in education, society and culture*. London: Sage.

Bowles, S., & Gintis, H. (1976). *Schooling in capitalist America: Educational reform and the contradictions of economic life*. New York: Basic Books.

Bratich, J., Packer, J., & McCarthy, C. (Eds.). (2003). *Foucault, cultural studies, and governmentality*. State University of New York Press.

Brennan, T. (2006). *Wars of position: The cultural politics of left and right*. New York: Columbia University Press.

Buras, K., & Motter, P. (2006). Cosmopolitan multiculturalism. In M. Apple & K. Buras (Eds.), *The subaltern speak: Curriculum, power, and educational struggles*. New York: Routledge.

Carnoy, M., & Levin, H. (1985). *Schooling and work in the democratic state*. Palo Alto, CA: Stanford University Press.

Castells, M. (1996). *The rise of the network society*. Cambridge, MA: Blackwell Publishers.

Castells, M. (1999). Flows, networks, and identities: A critical theory of the information society. In M. Castells, R. Flecha, P. Freire, H. Giroux, D. Macedo, & P. Willis (Eds.), *Critical education in the new information age*. Lanham, MD: Rowman & Littlefield.

Césaire, A. (1955/2000). *Discourse on colonialism*. New York: Monthly Review Press.

Cho, S. (2006). On language of possibility: Revisiting critical pedagogy. In C. Rossatto, R. Allen, & M. Pruyn (Eds.), *Reinventing critical pedagogy: Widening the circle of anti-oppression education*. Lanham, MD: Rowman & Littlefield Publishers.

Cho, S. (2008). Politics of critical pedagogy and new social movements. [Electronic version] *Educational Philosophy and Theory*. Retrieved from http://www.blackwell-synergy.com/toc/ EPAT/0/0/

Connell, R. W. (1995). *Masculinities*. Berkeley, CA: University of California Press.

Dale, R., Esland, G., Fergusson, R., & MacDonald, M. (Eds.). (1981). *Education and the state*. Barcombe, Sussex, UK: Falmer Press.

Darder, A., & Torres, R. (2004). *After race: Racism after multiculturalism*. New York: New York University Press.

Davis, M. (1999). *Prisoners of the American dream: Politics and economy in the history of the U. S. working class*. New York: Verso.

Delpit, L. (1995). *Other people's children: Cultural conflict in the classroom*. New York: New Press.

Denning, M. (2004). *Culture in the age of three worlds*. New York: Verso.

Du Bois, W. E. B. (1947/1975). *The world and Africa*. New York: International Publishers.

Foucault, M. (1977). *Discipline and punish: The birth of the prison*. New York: Vintage Books.

Foucault, M. (1980). *Power/Knowledge: Selected interviews & other writings 1972–1977*. New York: Pantheon Books.

Foucault, M. (1988). *Technologies of the self: A seminar with Michael Foucault*. Amherst, MA: University of Massachusetts Press.

Foucault, M. (1999). *Religion and culture*. New York: Routledge.

Freire, P. (1970). *Pedagogy of the oppressed*. New York: Continuum.

Gabbard, D. (2006). No "Coppertops" left behind: Foucault, the matrix, and the future of compulsory schooling. In A. Beaulieu & D. Gabbard (Eds.), *Michel Foucault and power today*. Lanham, MD: Lexington Books.

Giroux, H. (1983). *Theory and resistance in education: A pedagogy for the opposition*. South Hadley, MA: Bergin & Garvey.

Giroux, H. (1988). *Teachers as intellectuals: Toward a critical pedagogy of learning*. Granby, MA: Bergin & Garvey.

Giroux, H. (Ed.). (1991). *Postmodernism, feminism, and cultural studies: Redrawing educational boundaries*. New York: State University of New York Press.

Giroux, H. (1995). Insurgent multiculturalism and the promise of radical pedagogy. In D. Goldberg (Ed.), *Multiculturalism: A critical reader*. Oxford, UK: Blackwell.

Gore, J. (1993). *The struggle for pedagogies: Critical and feminist discourses as the regimes of truth*. New York: Routledge.

Gramsci, A. (1971). *Selections form the prison notebooks*. New York: International Publishers.

Grande, S. (2004). *Red pedagogy: Native American social and political thought*. Lanham, MD: Rowman & Littlefield Publishers.

Habermas, J. (1975). *Legitimation crisis*. Boston: Beacon Press.

Hall, S. (1958). A sense of classlessness. *Universities and Left Review*, *1*(5), 26–32.

Hall, S. (1980). Cultural studies: Two paradigms. *Media, Culture and Society*, *2*(1), 57–72.

Hardt, M., & Negri, A. (2000). *Empire*. Cambridge: Harvard University Press.

Harvey, D. (1990). *The condition of postmodernity*. Cambridge: Blackwell.

Hindess, B., & Hirst, P. (1977). *Mode of production and social formation*. London: Macmillan.

Hoggart, R. (1957). *The use of literacy*. London: Penguin.

Jay, M. (1973). *The dialectical imagination: A history of the Frankfurt School and the institute of social research, 1923–1950*. Boston: Little, Brown and Company.

Kenny, L. (2000). *Daughters of suburbia: Growing up white, middle class, and female*. New Brunswick, NJ: Rutgers University Press.

Laclau, E., & Moffe, C. (1984). *Hegemony and socialist strategy*. New York: Routledge.

Lareau, A. (1989). *Home advantage: Social class and parental intervention in elementary education*. New York: Falmer Press.

Lather, P. (1991). *Getting smart: Feminist research and pedagogy with/in the postmodern*. New York: Routledge.

Leonardo, Z. (2002). The souls of white folk: Critical pedagogy, whiteness studies, and globalization discourse. *Race Ethnicity & Education, 5*(1).

Leonardo, Z. (2003a). Reality on trial: Notes on ideology, education, and utopia. *Policy Futures in Education, 1*(3), 504–525.

Leonardo, Z. (2003b). Resisting capital: Simulationist and socialist strategies. *Critical Sociology, 29*(2), 211–236.

Leonardo, Z. (2004). The color of supremacy: Beyond the discourse of 'white privilege'. *Educational; Philosophy and Theory, 36*(2), 137–152.

Leonardo, Z. (Ed.). (2005). *Critical pedagogy and race*. Malden, MA: Blackwell.

Lukas, G. (1923/1971). *History and class consciousness*. Cambridge, MA: MIT Press.

Luke, C., & Gore, J. (Eds.). (1992). *Feminisms and critical pedagogy*. New York: Routledge.

Lyotard, J. (1984). *The postmodern condition: A report on knowledge*. Minneapolis, MN: University of Minnesota Press.

MacLeod, J. (1995). *Ain't no makin' it: Aspirations and attainment in a low-income neighborhood.* Boulder, CO: Westview Press.

Marcuse, H. (1964). *One dimensional man: Studies in the ideology of advanced industrial society*. Boston: Beacon Press.

Marcuse, H. (1969). *An essay on liberation*. Boston: Beacon Press.

Marcuse, H. (1972). *Counterrevolution and revolt*. Boston: Beacon Press.

Marshall, J. (1998). Michel Foucault: Philosophy, education, and freedom as an exercise upon the self. In M. Peters (Ed.), *Naming the multiple: Poststructuralism and education*. Westport, CO: Bergin & Garvey.

McCarthy, C. (1998). *The uses of culture: Education and the limits of ethnic affiliation*. New York: Routledge.

McLaren, P. (1997). *Revolutionary multiculturalism: Pedagogies of dissent for the New Millennium*. Boulder, CO: Westview Press.

Paik, S., & Walberg, H. (Eds.). (2007). *Narrowing the achievement gap: Strategies for educating Latino, Black and Asian students*. New York: Springer.

Palermo, J. (2002). *Poststructuralist readings of the pedagogical encounter*. New York: Peter Lang.

Peters, M., & Besley, T. (2007). *Subjectivity and truth: Foucault, education, and the culture of self*. New York: Peter Lang.

Philion, S. (1998). Bridging the gap between new social movement theory and class. *Rethinking Marxism, 10*(4), 79–104.

Piccone, P. (1978). General introduction. In A. Arato & E. Gebhardt (Eds.), *The essential Frankfurt School reader*. New York: Urizen Books.

Pollock, F. (1941). State capitalism: Its possibilities and limitations. In A. Arato & E. Gebhardt (Eds.), (1978). *The essential Frankfurt School reader*. New York: Urizen Books.

Popkewitz, T., & Brennan, M. (1997). *Foucault's challenge: Discourse, knowledge, and power in education*. New York: Teachers College Press.

Popkewitz, T., & Fendler, L. (Eds.). (1999). *Critical theories in education: Changing terrains of knowledge and politics*. New York: Routledge.

Reay, D. (1998). *Class work: Mothers' involvement in their children's primary schooling*. New York: Routledge.

Sanbonmatsu, J. (2004). *The postmodern prince*. New York: Monthly Review Press.

Smith, M. (2000). *Culture: Reinventing the social sciences*. Philadelphia: Open University Press.

Sloterdijk, P. (1997). *Critique of cynical reason* (M. Eldred, Trans.). Minneapolis, MN: University of Minnesota Press.

Sparks, C. (1996). Stuart Hall, cultural studies and Marxism. In D. Morley & K. Chen (Eds.), *Stuart hall: Critical dialogues in cultural studies*. New York: Routledge.

St. Pierre, E., & Pillow, W. (2000). *Working the ruins: Feminist poststructural theory and methods in education*. New York: Routledge.

Teodori, M. (Ed.). (1969). *The new left: A documentary history*. Indianapolis, IN: Bobbs-Merrill Company.

Tilly, C. (2004). *Social movements, 1768–2004*. Boulder, CO: Paradigm Publishers.
Thompson, E. P. (1957). Socialism and the intellectuals. *Universities and Left Review*, *1*(1), 31–36.
Thompson, E. P. (1958, Summer). Agency and choice: A reply to criticism. *New Reasoner*, 88–106.
Wallerstein, I. (2004). *World-systems analysis: An introduction*. Durham, NC: Duke University Press.
Weis, L. (1990). *Working class without work: High school students in a de-industrializing economy*. New York: Routledge.
Williams, R. (1961). *The long revolution*. London: Chatto & Windus.
Williams, R. (1963). *Culture and society 1780–1950*. London: Penguin.
Willis, P. (1977). *Learning to labour: How working class kids get working class jobs*. New York: Columbia University Press.
Zavarzadeh, M., & Morton, D. (1994). *Theory as resistance: Politics and culture after (post)structuralism*. New York: Guilford Press.

Seehwa Cho
School of Education
University of St. Thomas

SUBJECTS AND SUBJECTIVITIES

ZEUS LEONARDO

8. IDEOLOGY AND ITS MODES OF EXISTENCE

Toward an Althusserian Theory of Race and Racism[1]

As a concept, ideology explains the capacity of ideas, people, and social formations to represent reality as less than itself. In its orthodox sense, ideology mystifies understanding to stifle educators' accurate, if not scientific, apprehension of society and its structures, such as schools (see Thompson, 1984; Aronowitz, 1988). At the outset, to the extent that education is an attempt to represent reality through the pedagogical interaction, it is necessary for educators and students to appreciate the intricate relationship between ideology and schooling. For this we turn to Louis Althusser's generative theory of ideology. Before I begin in earnest, my interest in Althusser's work lies in a different problematic insofar as his theory allows us to illuminate race relations. Therefore, this chapter is a project of appropriation. Althusser's theory does not represent a single or unified front on the concept of ideology, but rather several strands of his ruminations over some years (McDonnell and Robins, 1980). The theory contains at least four strands and draws from several traditions, from Marx, to Comte and Durkheim (see Ranciere, 1994). As with classical Marxism, Althusser opposes theory to philosophy, the first a scientific undertaking and the second a speculative one. But to Althusser (2003), philosophy is not merely ideological, or the status of "sheer ideological illusion" (p. 257) to which the *The German Ideology* (1970) reduces it. It is ideological when it merely creates *new knowledge* based on existing scientific concepts without the development of *new theory*.

Althusser prefers theory over philosophy for the same reasons that Marx once criticized Feuerbach as merely interpreting, rather than transforming, history, but this is not meant to reduce the status of philosophy (and Althusser saw himself primarily as a Marxist philosopher). The task is to set philosophy on its feet, where politics finds its "theoretical expression," (Althusser, 1976, p. 160), and make it harmonious with science. It is in philosophy where the problematic is posed and in science where it is *realized*. Through philosophy, a new "position" is marked, a spatial metaphor that signals a new theoretical practice, the creation of new categories: the epistemological break. Althusser (2003) says, "All these [scientific] problems relative to the conditions for posing difficulties as problems deserve to be posed correctly in their turn. That task falls to philosophy" (p. 278). So here Althusser breaks the traditional opposition between philosophy and science and puts philosophy in its rightful place beside science in a sacred union.

Z. Leonardo (ed.), Handbook of Cultural Politics and Education, 195–217.

To Althusser (1969), the second moment of ideology belongs to humanism. Humanism denies the fact that class struggle is at the forefront of the debate. It substitutes humans as subjects of history for the historical and objective position of the working class in a class-divided society. Third, Althusser portrays ideology as like-the-unconscious. Taking his cue from Freud, read by his student Lacan, Althusser constructs ideology as a process of misrecognition by the subject (Hirst, 1994). The fourth moment of ideology traces its links with material forms. While certainly not material, ideology exists in modes that are themselves material. Or as Bernard-Donals (1998) puts it, Althusser found that "ideology has simultaneously a discursive/material component and an extra-discursive/material component" (p. 167). In the following, I present a theory of ideology by way of Althusser, whose work not only typifies the operationalization of ideology as pejorative but also represents a compendium for its recent theorization, especially its opposition to science (see also Aronowitz, 1988).

ALTHUSSER'S THEORY OF IDEOLOGY

Western society has experienced the advances and innovations of the Scientific Revolution both in terms of material comforts and the improvement of thought. Through the scientific method, Western thinkers from Marx to Mannheim have mapped out the objective laws of social behavior and evolution. However, their innovations attest to the double duty of producing scientific knowledge and combating the effects of ideological distortion. In short, as the criteria for scientific knowledge become ever more specific and precise, the criteria for ideological thought become ever more broad and all encompassing. Arguably the premier theorist of our time on the nature and concept of ideology, Althusser represents a rich starting point for discussing ideology as a form of negative distortion. Although ideology may be discussed beyond its negative iterations, like its more necessary or descriptive functions (see Leonardo, 2003a), as Althusser sometimes attempts, this section will focus on ideology's orthodox definition as a negative distortion of "reality." Starting with Althusser is productive because he represents the radical opposition between ideology and science, which is a frequent enough trope in the literature on ideology. Althusser's theory is generative because it attempts not only to synthesize various authors, like Lacan and Bachelard, to arrive at fresh ideas on ideology, but also represents a watershed in the debate over ideology and its status as only pure ideality. In other words, through Althusser we understand that ideology is not limited only to the realm of ideas, but has material underpinnings.

As mentioned, Althusser's theory of ideology contains at least four strands. His first and most fundamental assertion is that ideology is opposed to scientific thinking, or is pre-scientific. This first moment of his critique undergirds the following three moments. Arguing that Marx's great accomplishment is his founding of a science of history, Althusser (1971, p. 15) compares historical materialism with mathematics and physics: "Before Marx, two such continents had been opened up to scientific knowledge: the continent of Mathematics and continent of Physics. The first by the Greeks (Thales), the second by Galileo. Marx opened up a third continent to scientific knowledge: the continent of History." From the beginning, we must establish that Althusser elevates historical materialism to the status of a science, with Marx having discovered the objective laws of history, much like Thales and Galileo did before him with respect to the physical universe. Althusser uses the metaphor of "continent" not only to suggest that Marx was a great explorer, like Columbus before him, but that Marx discovered a material process, much like a continent is not an idea but a concrete place. History becomes a fertile land that opens up our scientific understanding of social evolution.

On the other hand, ideology stands in opposition to history and the battle for supremacy is waged between them, which is reminiscent of Lenin's (1963) point about the irreconcilable struggle between socialist and bourgeois ideology. To Althusser, ideology has no history because it is characterized by sameness rather than the dynamism one finds in history. In this sense, it is pre-scientific because it grasps apparitions in the form of ideas rather than real processes anchored in materialist understandings. However, Althusser makes a distinction between ideas and words. Whereas idealism claims that history takes the form of ideas, for Althusser (1976) "words are *weapons* in the class struggle in the field of theory" and that the "philosophical fight over words is part of the political fight" (pp. 38 and 22; italics in original). In other words, philosophy is the continuation of the class struggle in the realm of theory. Ideology is less the forward motor of change and more the endless recycling of ideas characteristic of philosophy before Marx. Here, Althusser opposes theory to philosophy, the first a scientific undertaking and the second a speculative one. Philosophy, like ideology, always lags behind science because discoveries in nature precede discoveries in the social world. Here we can say that Einstein's theory of relativity opened the path for much of postmodern theorizing that followed it. On the same note, Mandelbrot's fractal theory in mathematics leads to chaos theory in the social sciences. This point leads Althusser (1971, p. 42) to the conclusion that "Marxist philosophy should therefore lag behind the Marxist science of history." When one defends science, one also affirms theory as a *scientific practice of philosophy*. Ideology represents an unreality, or an inverted fountain that empties water into the earth rather than spouting it upward in a glorious display of form and beauty.

Althusser's second criterion for ideology is that it fulfills the requirements, and therefore problems, of humanism. He rejected the suggestions that Marxism is the doctrine for individual empowerment, despite the fact that it produces this tendency as an *effect* of its discourse. To Althusser, ideological interpretations of Marx's writings favor his earlier, anthropological, or "non-Marxist" production. Arguing that Marx's early writing was itself ideological, Althusser favors the mature Marx, following the epistemological break from which there is no return. The multiple volumes of *Capital* signaled a break in Marx's problematic whereby he purged his writing of humanist assumptions regarding the subject of history in exchange for a scientific understanding of history as an object of study. Ideological in this context means that any assertion of humanization, human power, or human capacity so characteristic of Marx's earlier manuscripts, and later adopted by Paulo

Freire, sacrifices a "true" understanding of history, which is less the accomplishment of the individual human and more determined by the masses and the internal dynamics of class struggle. This distinction leads Althusser to reject John Lewis' tripartite thesis that 1) It is man who makes history 2) Man makes history by transcending history 3) Man only knows what he himself does. Summed up in the following passage, Althusser (1976) rejection of Lewis' humanist Marxism takes this form,

> Against John Lewis's Thesis-it is man who makes history-Marxism-Leninism has always opposed the Thesis: it is the masses which make history. The masses can be defined. In capitalism, *the masses* does not mean "*the mass*" of aristocrats of the "intelligentsia", or of the ideologists of fascism; it means the set of exploited *classes*, strata and categories grouped around *the class* which is exploited *in large-scale production*, the only class which is capable of uniting them and directing their action against the bourgeois state: the proletariat. (p. 47)

To Althusser, humanism belongs on the side of ideology. There are several reasons why humanism is neither politically sound nor scientifically correct.

Humanism denies the fact that class struggle is at the forefront of the debate. It substitutes humans as subjects of history for the historical and objective position of the working class in a class-divided society. Indeed, the mass is not a collection of radical individuals and should not be romanticized in this manner. Far from it. Rather, it comprises a *revolutionary force* of a historically determined proportion. Its objective experience is such that it understands the nature of capitalist exploitation. However, this is not to suggest that its consciousness is already radical, let alone that its individual members have transcended the challenges of false consciousness. As Lenin (whom Althusser endorses) reminds us, members of the mass must be *educated* in order to realize the mass as a class-for-itself; capitalists and other oppressors, on the other hand, must be *revolutionized* or *ruptured.* Therefore, humanism mistakenly constructs history as a problem of (de)humanization rather than the primary and historically specific condition of class struggle. It prioritizes human ability to make sense of, construct, and in effect transcend history. But as Althusser (1976) reminds us,

> "Society is not *composed of individuals*", says Marx. He is right: society is not a "combination ", an "addition" of individuals. What constitutes society is the system of its social relations in which its individuals live, work and struggle. He is right: society is not made up of individuals in general, in the abstract, just so many copies of "man." Because each society has *its own* individuals, historically and socially determined. The slave-individual is not the serf-individual nor the proletarian-individual, and the same goes for the individual of each corresponding ruling class. In the same way, we must say that even a class is not "composed" of individuals in general: each class has *its own* individuals, fashioned in their individuality by their conditions of life, of work, of exploitation and of struggle-by relations of the class struggle. (p. 53; italics in original)

Similar to the post-humanist position later taken up by Foucault, Althusser's structural theory projects ideology as coterminous with humanism's focus on individuals as subjects of history. The emphasis, he argues, should fall on classes as objects of the scientific movement of history, whose individual members may come and go, whereas class struggle attains a certain status of permanence (that is, until the revolution). This is Marx's debt to Hegel who was "the first to conceive of history as a 'process without a subject'" (Althusser, 1971; Althusser, 2003, p. 239). In fact to Althusser, Feuerbach seems more culpable as a philosopher than Hegel, the more "scientific" of the two and to whom Marx owes a debt. On the other hand, Feuerbach's atheist humanism represents something of a philosophical impasse. Feuerbach's humanist essentialism becomes an additional problem of anthropology and not merely of speculation, the former becoming a source of an epistemological obstacle through its insistence on Man rather than social formations or structures. In the chapter on "Marxism and Humanism" in *For Marx,* Althusser (1969) interprets Marx's writing from 1845 on as having purged the discourse on essence, human freedom, and individuals: in short, a theoretical anti-humanism.

Along the lines of humanism as ideology, Althusser posits a third moment of ideology as like-the-unconscious. To the extent that humanism functions to integrate individuals into the social by misrecognizing it as "their" creation, so ideology's purpose is to represent this social through modes of understanding. Insofar as this moment is a necessity, then ideology achieves a level of permanence. If science is the progression of greater clarity and stringent criteria for truth, then ideology necessarily evolves in its opposite direction. If science is the empirical understanding of social structures, then ideology is comprised of the taken for granted aspects of this existence, which escape our materialist understanding. If the number of people who can scientifically apprehend the social formation dwindles as a result of scientific progress, the number of people engulfed by ideology increases. And finally, if more of social life falls into the abyss of the ideological field, then ideology begins to take on a certain permanence like-the-unconscious, continuing even into communist social formations. Althusser (1969) generalizes,

> *So ideology is as such an organic part of every social totality*. It is as if human societies could not survive without these *specific formations*, these systems of representations (at various levels), their ideologies. Human societies secrete ideology as the very element and atmosphere indispensable to their historical respiration and life. Only an ideological world outlook could have imagined societies *without ideology* and accepted the utopian idea of a world in which ideology (not just one of its historical forms) would disappear without trace, to be replaced by *science*. (p. 232; italics in original)

Althusser's criticism of utopian socialists, like Saint-Simon, is quite apparent here. Their projection of a future where science displaces ideology represents their naïve understandings of history. Ideology is as necessary to sustaining life as breathing. People depend on it as a way to make sense, albeit limited, of their lived experiences. Only an ideological world–in the sense of it as false–could project a world wherein ideology functions as a form of spontaneous philosophy absent of a detour of understanding through representation or imagination (Leonardo, 2003b, 2003c;

Ricoeur, 1986). Ideology is not an aberration to consciousness, which provides ideology's sense of autonomy, but rather an integral part of it embedded and unrecognized in the unconscious. As Althusser (1971) notes, whereas particular ideologies may have a history, ideology in general has no history and is eternal, like the unconscious. Its history lies outside of itself, in class struggle.

Taking from Lacan, Althusser makes use of the concept of the "imaginary" to explain people's ability to transcend ideology on the condition that they understand it, go *through* it rather than without it. If ideology is a system of representations, of images that people use to create a portrait of the social formation for their own understanding, then ideology, as an imaginary relation, also enables them to imagine an alternative possibility, which is often an alienated form. In this sense, ideology serves a function despite the fact that it may distort, rather than describe, a reality. It contains a practical dimension – the ability of people to construct a worldview – which is different from the theoretical function of producing real knowledge. Ideology's inability to produce knowledge also signals its lack of knowledge-of-itself, which leads Althusser to suggest that ideology has no outside. By this he means that because ideology works like the unconscious, the person who thinks through ideology misrecognizes it as knowledge rather than representation. The prison house of ideology prevents him from announcing, "Look at me, I'm swimming in ideology!" Ideology always refers to someone else, never about oneself: "Look at him, he's ideological!"

For Althusser, the fourth moment of ideology is related to the unconscious through our attempts to represent it in concrete terms. In order for ideology to become an object of understanding, subjects represent it outwardly in the form of institutions. Qualifying the original definition of ideology as pure ideality, Althusser (1971) proposes the notion that "Ideology has a material existence" (p. 165). It would be different to suggest that *ideology is material* as opposed to Althusser's contention that *ideology's existence is material.* Althusser does not deviate from the original thesis on ideology as a product of idealism, but adds the qualification, as Macdonell (1986) notes, that ideology's modes of existence are material. As such, Althusser's structural metaphor of "apparatus" distinguishes between several of the State's ideological mechanisms. In the long essay on "Ideology and Ideological State Apparatuses," Althusser's ideas on schooling endow great significance on the educational apparatus' function to reproduce the division of labor through the ideological, rather than repressive, process. To the extent that ideology promotes unscientific understanding in order for capitalism to recruit workers, it accomplishes this goal through an institutional apparatus that promulgates distorted know-hows rather than real know-whys. Or in Althusser's (1971) words,

> [A]n ideology always exists in an apparatus, and its practice, or practices. This existence is material … where only a single subject (such and such an individual) is concerned, the existence of the ideas of his belief is material in that *his ideas are his material actions inserted into material practices governed by material rituals which are themselves defined by the material ideological apparatus from which derive the ideas of that subject.* (pp. 166 and 169; italics in original)

In the last instance, ideology has a material basis because it becomes an object *for*, rather than *of*, scientific analysis. In order to Marxists to generate real knowledge *about* ideology, then it must be grounded in an empirical form.

Students are objects of the division of labor. While in school, they learn that their ultimate destiny is "to get a job." Of course, this is in direct opposition to Dewey's insistence that education is life and not preparation for future life. But in order for the ideological process to work, it must recognize students-as-subjects as well. This lends the schooling rituals more *personal* meaning - humanistic if you will - from which students gain a sense of selfhood. Interpellation in this case means that students must be recognized as concrete subjects in order for ideology to "call" on them for its functions. Althusser (1971) says it this way: "*[T]he individual is interpellated as a (free) subject in order that he shall submit freely to the commandments of the Subject, i.e. in order that he shall (freely) accept his subjection*, i.e. in order that he shall make the gestures and actions of his subjection 'all by himself '. There are no subjects except by and for their subjection" (p. 182; italics in original). Subjecthood is a myth that makes the ideological process possible. It is a reminder of humanism's fallacy that individuals freely make sense of conditions not of their own making. That said, it is a myth that makes this problematic function of humanism sustainable. It is a bit like training a dog to answer to his name (or any name for that matter) in order for the master to subject the dog to his control. The radical difference between a dog and human beings, however, is that the latter possesses the ability to reflect on their ideological conditions.

Althusser's theory of ideology as the philosophical opposite of science, as well as its corollary assumptions, provides a generative platform on which to base an analysis of the negative distortion of reality. The theory's four strands suggest that at its root, ideology functions to subvert a historical materalist position on the nature of reality. Although Althusser has suggested that ideology maintains a level of autonomy and will likely continue in perpetuity, he is convinced that Marxist science provides the "way out" of ideology, or at least procures a discourse to map out its contours, trace its material articulations, and devise ways to counteract it. But this way out of ideology comes with ironies insofar as one comes out of one house in order to enter another one. In this manner, ideology's autonomy is established.

At this point, I want to shift the focus to race and ideology. In 1996, an edited volume devoted to Stuart Hall's work published the essay, "Gramsci's relevance for the study of race and ethnicity." Central to Hall's analysis (1996) was Gramsci's deployment of the concept of hegemony. The rest of this chapter hopes to accomplish parallel insights on race by going through the concept of ideology as theorized by Althusser. A thoroughgoing and critical theory of ideology is currently missing from race studies in education. When ideology is invoked, it either goes through a Marxist refutation of the racial concept or it is posed as a problem that needs to be transcended rather than a constitutive part of the ideological struggle over race. Just as Hall reminds us that Gramsci's theory of hegemony must be taken in the context of Gramsci's Marxist problematic, this chapter notes that Althusser's theory of ideology must be taken in the context of his commitment to historical materialism. However, in order to analyze the relevance of Althusser's theory of ideology for the study of race (something which did not appear in Althusser's work), I appropriate his insights *sans* his problematic of historical materialism. Althusser's theory of ideology is useful for a study of race, which is as much a problem at the ideological as it is at the material level. Furthermore, Althusser's *discourse* on ideology enriches debates about race to the extent that his *general* insights on ideology are appropriate for such an analysis. This is where we turn to next.

IDEOLOGY, RACE, AND SCIENCE: A LOVE/HATE RELATIONSHIP

Race-conscious scholars have had a love/hate relationship with science and the scientific enterprise. On one hand, what passes off as science - e.g. eugenics - has been used to justify racial hierarchies (Stepan, 1990; Roberts, 1999). It would be tempting to assert that this mode of thinking is a relic of a cruel past. But Hernnstein and Murray's (1994) revisiting of eugenics-based arguments in their book, *The Bell Curve*, suggests that people, particularly Americans, are still obsessed with scientizing racial categories, especially when it is at the expense of blacks, or more accurately to the advantage of whites. Unlike other conservative scholars who discredit any study of race, Hernnstein and Murray informed the public that "race mattered" but because they accepted its consequences with little ounce of critical reflexivity, they reified the concept rather than demystified it. Despite the authors' mitigating ideas about environmental factors, they reaffirmed an old racist belief that whites (and Asians) are more genetically intelligent than blacks and they went about proving it "scientifically" or under the aegis of science. To Hernnstein and Murray, race was all too real yet their research hardly qualifies as race-conscious work. Scientific taxonomies of race have been guilty of reifying race as real based on physical characteristics (in this case genetics) rather than as social relations based on group power (see Watkins, 2001). For example, earlier the anthropological categories of Caucazoid, Negroid, and Mongoloid races made it possible to line up human remains next to each other and classify them by race based on physical traits. Critical of this development, Franz Boas (2000) and other anthropologists deemed "race" as unscientific and therefore was not the proper domain of anthropological research. This pronouncement had two consequences. First, "culture" graduated to the center of anthropology and now is co-extensive with the discipline itself (see Gonzalez, 2004). Second, Boas' decree was taken to mean that race is meaningless because it was unscientific.

In essence, science legitimated the *meaningfulness* (or lack thereof) of a concept, stigmatizing the study of race as merely ideological and made up, unlike its real counterpart: culture. Race has become an ideological concept without scientific merit, therefore not real. In Part I of a helpful film series on race, "Race: The Power of an Illusion," socio-biologists helped students conduct DNA experiments to jettison the idea that race is genetic if it could be proven that genetic variation within one race was at least as great as variation among racial groups. The analysis left the viewer craving an "ideological" perspective because a scientific one failed to account for the innerworkings of race, despite its scientific inaccuracy. That is, if the belief in race is based on spurious (i.e. ideological) notions of genetic inheritance, then it stands to reason that a critical understanding of race requires ideology to explain how it works. The metaphors of "blood," "skin," and "DNA" represent the ligature of race that compels its subjects to believe in its reality, in its solidity. Race was never literally about these things *per se*, but the ontological power to define and distort perception in this new way, of accounting for bodies and then stratifying them (Omi and Winant, 1994). In other words, a scientific discrediting of race (absent of accounting for ideology) is insufficient because the racial mind is hardly scientific; it is ideological. In multiculturalism, this means that a theory of ideology is necessary.

Over the years, white students in education courses on multiculturalism have worked hard to maintain their ideological worldview, even in the face of scientific evidence to contradict their perceptions. For example, they have asserted that it is not only reasonable to avoid ghettos and *barrios* out of fear of crime, but that it is ultimately rational to do so for self-preservation. Despite the fact that it is scientifically inaccurate and sociologically insignificant (Winant, 1997) to be victimized as visitors of these spaces, white students mobilize these critiques because they maintain that victimization remains a possibility for them. To many whites, it is not convincing to argue that people who live in ghettos and *barrios* are the main victims of crime in their own neighborhoods, not the unfortunate visitor. That is, higher crime rates are mainly an issue for people of color who live in poor areas, not for the occasional white visitor. Whites might as well play the lottery in hopes of hitting the jackpot. Countering with scientific evidence an ideological mindset that criminalizes people of color becomes an exercise in futility because it does not even touch the crux of the problem, one based in fear and loathing. There is the added irony that blacks are the real victims of ghettoization, of a systematic racial segregation in its *de jure* and *de facto* campaigns orchestrated by whites to destroy the black community and full integration into American society (Massey and Denton, 1993). Blaming people of color for problems they did not create is like blaming the colonies for being underdeveloped and reduced to conditions many people would consider "uncivilized."

The same cannot be said for the fear that people of color feel when confronted with a mainly white neighborhood, *of all class levels*. The history of lynching, both as a white supremacist practice and a form of social control, bears out in a way that victimization of whites in spaces of color does not. For African Americans, lynching is impressed into their consciousness and collective memory. Although traditional lynching occurs much less than it used to, there are many ways to lynch a person. Historical examples of race riots incited by white rage, white mobilization of what Althusser once called the "repressive state apparatuses," like the police, to stamp out even the most peaceful and constitutionally protected expressions of protest, and the subversion of what many Americans would consider basic rights, such as voting, are patterns of treatment that make it rational for people of color to respond with fear and suspicion of their white counterparts. In other words, this fear is sociological and historical, not mainly psychological. For all the science that multiculturalists have at our disposal, there does not seem to be a path around ideology. *For as much as critical theorists have critiqued the ideology of science, we also need a science of ideology.*

This development is not unlike the recent claims of scientific Marxism, which eschews the concept of "race" and opts for "racialism," "racialization," or "racism" (see Miles, 1993). This is a critical point and deserves some attention. Racism, in particular, becomes a subcategory of class exploitation, an oppression not based on race but the antagonisms found in capitalism. In this case, economics – like culture earlier – is the real relation that unseats the four letter word of race. Everything but racial structures seems to be more appropriate processes for a scientific understanding of the lives of people of color and whites. It would be reasonable to assume that the same argument applies to women when it comes to the equally reified notion of gender. To a race or gender-radical scholar, this becomes a bit of a challenge. In contrast to the Frankfurt School's critique of science as ideology's recent child (see Geuss, 1981), scientific Marxism discredits the concept (indeed the study) of race because it does not inhere objective status. Not only does historical materialism represent the way out of race, but class struggle is the trump card that will eventually make race struggle obsolete. However, it is worth noting that race scholars rarely suggest that race struggle cancels out class struggle. This silence may be explained for two reasons. One, much of race scholarship is driven by a bourgeois perspective that makes the problem of capital quite invisible. It could be asserted that race scholars are anti-racist but pro-capitalism, subverting their own claims to race liberation through an unrigorous critique of one of racism's partners-in-crime. Two, race scholars cultivate no illusions about canceling out class struggle through race struggle. In short, they do not posit the end of racism as the signal of the end of class struggle.

Concerning race, scientific Marxism invokes the terms racism, people of color, minorities, racialization, racialism, skin color without reference to the *term* race, despite the fact that it is obvious the *concept* of race is invoked. That is, avoiding the term-race does not guarantee that one is not wrapping one's argument in the concept-race. In fact, this is what Bonilla-Silva (2001) discovers when he interviews white workers about their perceptions concerning their work conditions. Although they seem to avoid any mention of blacks or other people of color, struggle to remain color-blind, and work excruciatingly to stay away from racially insensitive comments, Bonilla-Silva reports that most white respondents said something racially problematic sometime during the interviews. So it seems that scholarship from both the Left and Right share a common suspicion for the concept of race as a power structure or explanatory framework *in its own right*. In the case of the scientific Left, race does not matter either as a relatively independent social relation or a determining principle in the lives of both whites and people of color. It is explainable instead as a reflex of the capitalist mode of production.

In his book, *Althusser's Marxism*, Alex Callinicos (1976) makes the distinction between determining and dominant principles. Whereas many superstructural features, like the political or ideological fields, may be dominant and contribute to the overall complex unity of a mode of production, they are not determining principles. One could deduce that race may be dominant in the social formation but not determining, which is reserved for the economy in the last instance. Following Althusser, ideologies such as race have an autonomous and even material existence but scientifically lack the determinations that one finds in the economy. What seems to need some explaining is the presence of race in several modes of production, such as capitalist, communist, and mixed economies. Although communism certainly removes much of the brutal material basis in the racism from which people of color suffer, it has not succeeded in eradicating racism altogether. In fact, communist regimes have not guaranteed the obsolescence of race and instead intensify other forms of oppression, such as bureaucratic relations and other leadership arrangements. In the USA, Marxists may even blame the race-concept for fracturing class solidarity. It is curious to note that a concept becomes the culprit for compromising the class movement: not white working class racism, not the actions of white proletarian leaders to marginalize blacks from full participation in socialist organizations. All of these developments suggest that race does have a determining and autonomous existence that is complexified by and cuts across different economies. We may go so far with Giroux (1997), who says, "As a central form of difference, race will not disappear, be wished out of existence, or somehow become irrelevant in the United State and the larger global context" (p. 294). Said another way, despite its unscientific status, race is a structural formation that maintains an interdependent, co-determining, and heteronomous relation with the economy and other social relations.

That being established, science has been used by sociologists and other social scientists to map out the modes of existence of race despite the fact that the concept was an invention (see Lott, 1999). Countless social scientists from Allen and Farley (1989), to Oliver and Shapiro (1995), Bobo and Kluegel (1993), Snipp (1996), and Bonilla-Silva (1997) have relied on the scientific method to sketch the racial landscape, determine its features, and map out its consequences for whites and people of color. In other words, although race may not be a scientific concept, determining its effects requires the help of science. For instance, it took a racially-critical form of science to debunk eugenics and its ideological corollaries. Althusser's first and most determining moment in his theory of ideology (i.e., that it is unscientific) is an insufficient principle on which to base a theory of racial ideology because it problematically elevates science to the status of a color-blind theodicy. Critical work on race has good reasons to be suspicious of such a move, for it discounts the racial motivations of "scientific research" (Hunter, 2002).

On that note, radical work on race within multiculturalism cannot forsake ideology or an ideological critique of racial formations. Critical work on race does not only study its real manifestations and deems everything else ghosts of the real; it must critically understand its imaginative (i.e. ideological) dimensions, or how people imagine race in their daily lives. For example, no amount of scientific data will convince white supremacists that racism exists to benefit them and disadvantages people of color. Only an ideological shift makes this change possible, both at the individual and structural level. Racism is not a scientific mindset; on the contrary, it is quite irrational, which does not suggest that it is uncalculated or unpredictable (Feagin, Vera, and Batur, 2001). Racist ideology is driven by fear of, misinformation about, and distance from the other. As a result, science alone seems lacking as a conceptual apparatus to explain a very unscientific racist process. Instead, it requires a thorough ideological understanding of how whites distort certain facts about the world and history. A theory of racial ideology must come to grips with contradictions that seem to defy reason and scientific understanding. However, the discourse of science represents a common and public language that often begins the discussion about what does or does not exist. Race scholars utilize the scientific discourse to support the first premise of race analysis: that it matters in people's lives, that it unequally benefits whites, and that it is as real as its institutions. It is through science that one goes about making a case that a racist formation does exist. Based on these dynamics, race-conscious work must neither elevate nor forsake science.

RACE AND HUMANISM: "I BELONG TO ONLY ONE RACE, THE HUMAN RACE"

That race is an illusion is common to humanist interpretations of society. Race was created to impose a detour to a true understanding of a more fundamental human experience. It is a foil used to confuse people that they are humans of a particular skin color rather than human beings with the universal stamp of the species. On this point, there is agreement between humanists and race-conscious intellectuals. Likewise, ethnic affiliation creates cultural divisions between people who would otherwise share political or material interests. In this sense, humanism has been successful in pointing out the limitations in racial or ethnic classifications. However, it has also been used as an ideological tool to derail our understanding of the specificity, the particularity, or the historical nature of relations such as race. Its shortcoming comes from its failure to explain why a society looks *this way* and is organized with *these consequences*. It asserts universal human rights despite race rather than accounting for it. Like humanists, race-conscious intellectuals acknowledge the often arbitrary nature of race and ethnicity, who belongs in a said group, or what it means to be part of a group. Others may even go so far with humanists to consider race as fundamentally divisive, having been created in order to stratify the world according to skin color. In pursuit of Althusser's theory of ideology, we are warranted to ask: "If race has real effects, how can it merely be false? How is it merely illusory?" To the extent that race produces real effects, it accomplishes its task through allusion as much as illusion. It alludes to real processes that impact various groups in different and unequal ways.

Humanist ideology cannot explain why the structures of modern race evolved out of the colonial period and capitalist expansion because it regards "skin color experience" as something other than "human experience" rather than considering *skin color as an organizing principle for society as a whole*. In this sense, Althusser's second critique of humanist ideology is applicable for a study of race because it exposes humanism's inability to deal effectively with the "race question." Because it projects Man as the primary element of its problematic, humanism forsakes the valuable critique of racial formations or structures. With respect to gender relations, this humanist fallacy has been pointed out (see Weedon, 1997). *Race and racism are not at all about humans; they are struggles among racial groups.* In its rush to assert the universal human, humanism neglects the particular and racialized human, which it considers a block to accessing true human experience.

Humanism's search for an originary, or genetic, human experience, is quickly betrayed when, upon deconstruction, human experience appears cultural or racial (usually Euro-centric or white) and not universal. So what initially appears as general becomes a front for the universalization of a particular racialized experience, which is the lynchpin of humanist ideology. Transforming an event into something "human" when it is racial in nature has been a staple of white humanism's inability to come to terms with people of color's concrete experience. On the concept of origin, which has religious roots in *filiation* (i.e. tracking), Althusser (2003) has this to say,

> [O]ne has at last sighted the guilty party, the Originary Individual; he has been identified, he makes 'tools' of some unspecified sort, he lives in groups: *he's the one, all right. We've got him this time.* It is enough to 'tail'[*filer*] him, to track him, not to lose sight of him, since one is sure that at the end of this manhunt [*filature*], one will rediscover both the *1844 Manuscripts* and *Capital*! (p. 294; italics in original)

This genetic penchant in humanism makes it difficult to engage the structural conditions of a racialized society that constructs specific humans, such as whites and blacks. In fact, this is perhaps the most difficult aspect of teaching about race. Many whites as well as people of color who identify with whiteness find it difficult to accept that racism is mainly a white problem. They are either more accepting of and accustomed to the claim that racism is a human tragedy (therefore everyone's problem), or worse, that people of color impede their own social advancement. By saying this, one notices that humanist-minded students are no longer using race analysis, the first premise of which is that life looks quite different for whites compared to people of color. If we follow this line of argument, then racism is simply not a "race problem" anymore but a "human problem." Racism is redefined as any form of hatred based on race, regardless of its effects. It is assumed that structural white racism in the post-Civil Rights era has been all but erased/eraced. Martin Luther King's speech is reduced to his utopia without his critique (Toji, personal communication). Compared to the slave and Jim Crow eras, racism today has a human face (pick your group), not a white one. Forty years after the Civil Rights Movement, racist America has finally rid itself of this blemish in its history, this shameful 250 years of slavery and 100 years of Jim Crow, this embarrassing contradiction in American "democracy." Interpersonal racial attitudes have improved over time and it is time now to move on to bigger and better things: American humanization.

Cynicism aside, Althusser clearly saw the limitations of humanism and anticipated the poststructural movement that took humanism to task for its inability to explain why humans labor under specific conditions. Regarding race, race-conscious people also recognize the possibility of human experience before or after the concept of race, but they are dogged by the constant reminders of the complete racialization of daily life. Race-conscious scholars may be "against race" (Gilroy, 2000), that is, *anti*-race, but they may find it difficult to be *ante*-race. Trying to recapture a time before race after centuries of racialization is like trying to remember how a conversation *in medias res* got started in the first place. Too much has been said and too much has been done. The task is grounded less in escaping such vicissitudes of a race-based society and more in confronting their limitations, explaining why they exist, and countering their negative effects through rigorous examination. Because a misinformed humanism does not contain within its discourse a sufficient race critique, it bypasses an explanatory framework that many "humans" use to make sense of their lives. Moreover, humanism thwarts its own goals of achieving complete humanization when it fails to confront and help dismantle those structures responsible for the dehumanization of people in the first place: in this case, institutional racism.

As an organizing principle, race is the justification of an entire social edifice, from schooling, to jobs, to marriage. It is not only or mainly, according to Bonilla-Silva (2001), a relation of attitudes between individuals. This problematic sentiment is common enough and leads some people to assume that every group is an equal opportunity racist because whites do not have a monopoly on racial animosity. Rather, race is a structure in which these attitudes become meaningful, which otherwise are not meaningful in themselves; in other words, the racial structure gives them meaning. It is a process of marking, of hailing human subjects into the racial formation as subjects of its apparatuses, such as schools. The humanist ideology conveniently forgets that in a racist society, asserting humanity by default means asserting whiteness since whites seem to represent what it means to be human; the same can be said for men, heterosexuals, and the bourgeoisie. Textbooks, the media, government, and civilization in general all bear the marks of whiteness, which begin to suggest that "human" equates with "white," as Victor Lewis reminds us so eloquently in the film "Color of Fear." In fact, the humanist argument or liberal insistence on individuality becomes a form of rationalization for the way a society is racially structured since it fails to analyze social organization in terms of group interests. This does not suggest that humanists do not recognize the existence of racism, even at the structural level. But its discursive universe does not define the problematic as a question of structure but one of humanization. And as long as humanist ideology, according to Althusser, defines the goal as a perpetual search for Man's essence (filiation) rather than the continuous development of social structures, then it becomes difficult to combat the strongest investment in race via group affiliation.

Humanization is no doubt the goal, if by that we mean a more free or less oppressive society. A more humanizing education system, a more humanizing society, and approaching students' full humanity – these are all worthwhile endeavors. But these goals cannot be accomplished before the ethical imperative of "doing the right thing." That is, whites have not been able to relinquish their racial privileges because it is the humanizing thing to do for others, let alone that they also become humanized in the process. Fighting against racism is galvanized less by a humanist sentimentality and more by an ethical imperative, in Kant's sense of it. Anti-racism is not a commitment because one *gains* in human terms, although this certainly is a product of it. For whites, it actually means *losing* their position in the racial structure, of giving up their lion's share of resources. Ultimately, this is also Althusser's bone of contention with humanism: its penchant for individual improvement, whether this individual is represented by the person or as a metaphor for humanity at large. Meanwhile, in the case of race, it misrecognizes the racial formation and how it *functions*, how it subverts solidarity across races, and how humanism makes it difficult to define human experience without the qualifiers white, black, Latino, Asian American, Native American, or Arab. Althusser's second moment in his theory of ideology is quite applicable for a study of race and multiculturalism because it exposes the racial evasions in humanism. It suggests that far from being the autonomous reasoning individual, the subject of racial formations is motivated by the interpellations of its structures. Being human in a racial formation is inescapably bound up with being part of a racial group and subject to its shifting, intersecting, but determining effects.

RACIAL IDEOLOGY AND THE UNCONSCIOUS: "I DON'T HAVE A RACIST BONE IN MY BODY BUT..."

Althusser's third moment - that ideology is largely unconscious – is arguably the most resonating and most relevant portion of Althusser's theory for the study of race and racism. It has been suggested that racism (and therefore race) seems to have a permanent status (see Bell, 1992), not unlike the unconscious for Althusser. For example, if we survey American racial history, we note transmutations and transformations in race and racism but would not receive the general impression that they are about to go away. In fact, there is little to suggest that race is declining in significance, to William Julius Wilson's (1978) chagrin. In the USA, we have entered a new racial predicament since 9/11, where religious race (in conjunction with skin color race) complexifies our racial categories and meanings. In the face of all these developments, one would be hard pressed to show optimism that race and its problem of racism will one day diminish; instead they assume the guise of foreverness. Althusser (2003) writes,

> Only a 'subject presumed to exist' is ever interpellated – provided with his identity papers so that he can prove that he is indeed *the* subject who has been interpellated. Ideology functions, in the true sense of the word, the way the police function. It interpellates, and provides the interpellated subject with/asks the interpellated subject for his identity papers, without providing its identity papers in return, for it is *in the Subject-uniform* which is its very identity. (p. 55; italics in original)

The ideology of race and its concomitant discourses interpellate *every* human individual into the racial formation. She is signified and brought into the racial universe, which gives her a racial label, white or otherwise. Of course, this is not a literal process of hailing someone down the street, but an unconscious hailing that is part of self-recognition, or misrecognition to be more precise. Once the hailing begins and provides racialized subjects with their identity, it never fails to record a response, "Here I am!" This process does not yet speak to the eventual goal of eradicating race, which is a possibility, but points to the difficult task of countering racial identification.

Consistent with Althusser's theory, the more rigorous social scientists become in their systematic understanding of racial stratification and institutions, the larger the ideological field of racial common sense becomes. As the criteria for a systematic understanding of race become more precise (e.g., what it is or is not), the field of distortions becomes more comprehensive. As race, especially its commonsensical meanings, takes hold of more people, they begin to define their experience through reified notions of race, such as "it is about blood, genes, or biology." It becomes the ubiquitous but unexamined marker. Race is an intimate part of how people represent/understand themselves and others. Racial ideology may distort their scientific understanding of social life, but it also functions for people in a daily way, and not always in a positive sense. It gives them a threshold for comfort as they choose their friends, decide where they want to live, and deliberate on who is or is not moral. The *collective racial unconscious* includes even the most "enlightened" person who presumes to think "outside" of race. For *racial ideology has no outside* and the person or society immersed in race cannot think outside of it, which represents the racialization of reality and the realization of race (Leonardo, 2009). Either a society is completely racialized or it is not; there is no such thing as "a little bit racialized" or "this or that nation is more racialized than another." South Africa is not more racialized than China; Sweden is not less racialized than the United States. They are all racialized societies, but race has assumed a particular form in each of their history, Apartheid in one and Jim Crow in the other. Since racialization and white supremacy have reached global proportions (Mills, 2003), it is becoming impossible to find pockets of non-racialized societies. There is no island on which Robinson Crusoe could land.

The unconscious nature of racial ideology is especially pertinent when discussing racism. The racist is always the other, never the self; another society, never one's own. A racist, even the most rabid, rarely admits or recognizes that he is racist. It produces an ironic condition of "racism without any racists" (see Bonilla-Silva, 2003) since racism is like a flatulent that someone else always releases in the room. The first realization a race thinker confronts is that all but a few whites admit to their racism. Groups who appear as "obvious" candidates of white supremacy invert reality by claiming to be victims of "reverse racism." Rather than indict white advantage, white supremacists indict people of color for wanting too large a share of the "American pie." In this section of the chapter, I would like to discuss the role that white women play in the maintenance of racism: particularly, through discourses on affirmative action, inter-racial dating and marriage, and racial politics of sexuality. White men's racial atrocities are well-documented, but as a result, they have become alibis for a more general white supremacy. Less is known generally about white women's racism although critiques of feminists of color have made them more visible (see Mohanty, 1988; hooks, 1984; Anzaldua, 1999). In the case of white women who oppose affirmative action, they claim that it disadvantages them as white people. With respect to white mothers of mixed race children, this decision goes against their very own children's structural chances for advancement. First, this belief is belied by the fact that white women have been one of the largest beneficiaries of affirmative action policies (Tatum, 1997; Marable, 1996). When they oppose such corrective mechanisms, they subvert their own personal (immediate) interests as women while acting in accordance with (long term) racial supremacy. They are involved in a performative contradiction and in the process unwittingly show us their racial cards. Second, this dynamic dispels notions of white women's innocence from racism based on the belief that they are oppressed by patriarchy and therefore share interests with other oppressed people, that is, their oppressed status gives them epistemic privilege.

The racial interpellation of white women is a feminized form of racism that complexifies the patriarchal myth of women as protectors of the family, captured in the saying "blood is thicker than water." That is, it is assumed that women choose family first. Because racism makes sense only in the context of group interest, white mothers of mixed-race children are torn between race and family (Horton and Sykes, 2004). As split subjects, they may vacillate between the two poles. If blood is thicker than water, then sometimes *skin is thicker than blood.* At crucial junctures where white power is threatened, such as the debate over affirmative action, white mothers of mixed-race children could just as easily choose race over family, identifying with the former rather than the latter. This largely unconscious act is motivated by supra-individual desires, which does not suggest that white women do not know what they are doing. They may not know the extent of their participation in racism, but they are not dupes of it either. As investors in race, they know that their decisions matter, whether or not they understand the implications. As interpellated racial subjects, white women indeed answer the call but record different responses than white men. In other words, they occupy a different post in the racial army as whites defend the territory, real and imagined.

Because racism assumes a gendered form, white women play a distinct role in promoting their race, usually through the detour of mothering. It may appear in the form of discouraging their children away from inter-racial dating in efforts to "protect" them from the criticisms and challenges that await them. Here we note the racial unconscious at work through the detour of "caring." The critique does not suggest that white women are less caring than before, but that this caring contains racial contradictions. White mothers who discourage their children from inter-racial dating or miscegenation reassert the ideological purity of whiteness through the purity of "blood." Such forms of caring are a result of patriarchy to the extent that women have been socially constructed and have evolved as the caring gender. But because this process occurs in the context of race and racism, it contains racial dimensions. On the surface, the scenario appears like an instance of choosing family over race, of protecting one's child. But a closer look reveals some contradictions.

Choosing one's partner is one of the most important choices that adults make and, along with career choice, is definitive of a person's level of happiness. Protecting the family suggests that the child's ability to gauge with whom he will share his happiness is promoted, thereby increasing the overall happiness of the family unit with the assumption that all concerns but race are favorable. When this choice is thwarted because of race, resentment and guilt usually occur. Protecting a child from the "pain" of inter-racial dating or miscegenation overlooks the richness of two different worlds coming together, exposing the reified notion of racial coupling, a process which has different purposes for different races. Furthermore, it exposes the myth and ideology of love when race complexifies the match. It is a popular belief that people marry their "soul mate." When inter-racial dating and marriage are discouraged, a large portion of the dating world is outside the field of considerations. This condition is hardly conducive to finding one's soul mate.

Objectification is not only a matter of gender relations under patriarchy, it is also a racial problem. When white women objectify men of color, they participate in the upkeep of white supremacy. Often, they are informed by the assumption that sexual comments about men cannot be branded problematic in the context of patriarchy and existing power relations between men and women. Although this distinction is important, it also shows white women's racial consciousness. In other words, to some white women, *sexual comments only concern gender*. They fail to notice that although their comments are not sexist, they are both racial and racially problematic. That is, they are examples of feminized forms of racism and recall the centuries of sexual domination and manipulation of men *and* women of color by white men *and* women. They are evidence of white women's ability to assert their racial privilege and power through sexuality even in the face of their own sexual oppression. Moreover, white women's objectification of bodies of color represents an instance of their solidarity with one another as racialized subjects. White sisterhood shares something with white men through their unconscious collaboration in racial supremacy, but the former takes on a specific historical appearance that differs from the latter. On this point, men of color have been reticent to enter the fray over the gendered articulations of racism, perhaps out of fear of appearing gendered in the process. However, men of color's entrance into a critique of gender/race ideology is important because it represents their solidarity with women of color, as bell hooks (1984) reminds us.

Following Lacan's extension of Freud, Althusser reminds us that although we cannot directly experience the unconscious, it exists through its effects - in the discourses of everyday life, experience, and dreams. It would be too much to claim that the unconscious is real, but its effects are as real as the dream is to the dreamer. To the extent that racial ideology, like the unconscious, is not real, its modes of existence or manifestation are real (see also Macdonell, 1986). The racial unconscious produces functions, one of which Althusser (2003) calls the "subject-function" (p. 53), which produces a "subjectivity-effect" (p. 48). The ideology of race has produced racial discourses, which recruit racialized subjects who find their sense of self through them. Althusser (2003) explains, "It solves the problem evoked in the old complaint of military men – what a pity soldiers are recruited only among civilians – because the only soldiers it ever recruits are already in the army. For ideological discourse, there are no civilians, only soldiers, that is, ideological subjects" (p. 55). A racial formation only recruits from its citizens, which by default are the only candidates for racial subjects. Racial subjectivity is fundamentally unconscious because it always leaves a bit of itself unbeknownst to its subject. Racialism is always a remainder. And as the standards for a critical reading of race increase, more of the social field succumbs to racial ideology. That is, it engulfs its subjects to the point that they no longer imagine a non-racialized horizon. Even when they resist race at every turn, it betrays them in the end.

IDEOLOGY AND TRACIAL STATE APPARATUSES: "RACE IS REAL, RACE AIN'T REAL"

Ample controversy has been thrown into the caldron of race concerning its status. To the extent that race as a concept is not real, its modes of existence are real. Its racial subjects are real; likewise, schools, the workplace, and families are institutional forms of race. There is good reason to believe that race is not a scientific concept, which is not reason enough to reject its study but necessitates a multiple framework that includes ideological and materialist perspectives. As opposed to production, for which Marx found a suitable language to attach, race was an invention originating in the Occident. Unlike production, which humans did not have to create but discovered, race was invented in order to accomplish certain social goals. In order to rationalize their place in the world and then justify the treatment of others, white Europeans invented a classification system that put people of darkest skin tones at the bottom of the human hierarchy and lightest at the top. This position makes inequality central to the concept of a racial order and questions the notion that racial orders exist because of the mere presence of racial difference. Bonilla-Silva (2001) clarifies, "[W]e can speak of racial orders only when a racial discourse is accompanied by social relations of subordination and superordination among the races" (p. 42). The ideology of race was born and spurred on the development of the world in a direction that its creators could not have anticipated. It is in this sense that enables us to forward the thesis that race is not real because whites gave it an existence it did not already have. To the extent that monsters are not real, the giant we call race is likewise unreal. It is tempting to respond that the "race is real or not real" debate is energy not well spent, that it circumvents the more important work to be done describing how race functions and how racism can be subverted if not eradicated. However, defining correctly the conceptual status of race is part of unseating whiteness, depending on how race-conscious scholars set the terms of the debate over race.

That race is an ideology has led to the conclusion that it is not worthy of invoking because doing so further reifies what is already unreal. In that case, David Duke's sense-making of race is just as problematic as Cornel West's, each taking a different bite of the fruit from the same rotten tree. But just as Althusser warns against reducing philosophy to the status of mere ideological illusion, so we can say that race cannot be reduced to mere chimerical status devoid of material underpinnings. For example, as a racial state apparatus (RSA), school is a material institution where race takes place, where racial identity is bureaucratized/modernized, where people are hailed as racialized subjects of the state. In schools, teachers take roll as they hail students in homeroom as much as teachers hail them to answer when their race is called. Schools usually never fail to receive an answer for either one. It is one important place where race takes on an empirical form: from tracking practices, to resource disparities, to different rates of achievement. Therefore, race has material underpinnings and cannot be reduced only to ideological status (in the classical sense), or relegated to the realm of pure ideality.

Be that as it may, race-conscious work engages the ideological dimensions of race and links them to the material world and its racial organization. It is not based on skin color *simpliciter* but more accurately on the racialized imagination, of how *skin groups* exist and are reinvented over and over again. For example, through miscegenation and race mixing some African Americans are lighter skinned than South or South East Asians, but the American ideology of race neither constructs South and South East Asians as black nor do darker skinned Indians, for example, consider themselves black for that matter. The racial imagination, or the ideological process, is largely responsible for these group assignments. Even Bonilla-Silva (2001), whose structural model arguably approaches most closely the Althusserian paradigm of race studies, did not avoid the ideological dimension when he reports white workers' racial attitudes towards blacks, an ideology that serves practical functions. Bonilla-Silva (2001) favors a materialist examination of race relations and

> reserve[s] the term *racial ideology* for the segment of the ideological structure of a social system that crystallizes racial notions and stereotypes. Racial ideology provides the rationalization for social, political, and economic interactions among the races. (p. 43; italics in original)

Consequently, material institutions and their resources are modes of existence of an ideological process that requires a deep racial sensibility if undoing them remains a possibility.

Althusser's multi-pronged analysis of ideology is perhaps his greatest contribution to Marxist studies of society. Although not without its problems in the form of structural overdetermination and some theoretical excess, Althusser forged a discourse on ideology unmatched in recent debates. His thoughts represent a watershed in the debate between the real and ideological, representing genuine insights on their synthetical and recursive relationship with each other. Although a materialist in the last instance, Althusser always considered the ideologico-political battle as important theoretical and practical nodes in the warfare against bourgeois philosophy and capitalism. I have attempted to import his general findings for a study of race and ethnicity in order to illuminate the ideological contours of our current racial and cultural formation. I found that the third moment of Althusser's theory of ideology - a deployment of Lacan's theory of the imaginary and the unconscious – most directly intersects the racial problematic. It projects a clear picture of how racial ideology actually functions or works on a daily basis. Although we must mitigate the thesis that racial ideology is *completely* unconscious, to use Althusser's language, *racial ideology is unconscious in the last instance*. The three other moments in Althusser's theory provide supporting discourses to the third moment, lending the theory a sense of cohesion rather than unity. As the land of racial understanding becomes more solid, the sea of racial mystifications spreads. This is not meant to be a pessimistic statement about the future status of race and its hirsute companion, racism. On the contrary, it projects the importance of critical reflection over race and the strength of the ideological effort that such a process requires.

NOTES

[1] This chapter is reprinted with kind permission from *Policy Futures in Education*. It combines portions of Leonardo, Z. (2003). Reality on trial: Notes on ideology, education, and utopia. *Policy Futures in Education, 1*(3), 504–525 **and** Leonardo, Z. (2005). Through the multicultural glass: Althusser, ideology, and race relations in post-Civil Rights America. *Policy Futures in Education, 3*(4), 400–412.

REFERENCES

Allen, W., & Farley, R. (1989). *The color line and the quality of life in America*. Oxford, UK: Oxford University Press.

Althusser, L. (1969). *For Marx* (B. Brewster, Trans.). London and New York: Verso.

Althusser, L. (1971). *Lenin and philosophy* (B. Brewster, Trans.). New York: Monthly Review Press.

Althusser, L. (1976). *Essays in self-criticism* (G. Lock, Trans.). London: NLB and Atlantic Highlands: Humanities Press.

Althusser, A. (2003). *The humanist controversy and other writings*. London: Verso.

Anzaldua, G. (Ed.). (1999). *La Frontera/Borderlands* (2nd ed.). San Francisco: Aunt Lute Books.

Aronowitz, S. (1988). Science, ideology, and marxism. In C. Nelson & L. Grossberg (Eds.), *Marxism and the interpretation of culture* (pp. 519–537). Urbana, IL: University of Illinois Press.

Bell, D. (1992). *Faces at the bottom of the well: The permanence of racism*. New York: Basic Books.

Bernard-Donals, M. (1998). *The practice of theory: Rhetoric, knowledge, and pedagogy in the academy*. Cambridge, UK: Cambridge University Press.

Boas, F. (2000). Instability of human types. In R. Bernasconi & T. Lott (Eds.), *The idea of race* (pp. 84–88). Indianapolis, IN: Hackett.

Bobo, L., & Kluegel, J. (1993). Opposition to race-targeting: Self-interest, stratification ideology, or racial attitudes? *American Sociological Review, 58*(4), 443–464.

Bonilla-Silva, E. (1997). Rethinking racism: Toward a structural interpretation. *American Sociological Review, 62*(3), 465–480.

Bonilla-Silva, E. (2001). *White supremacy and racism in the post-civil rights era*. Boulder, CO: Lynne Rienner Publishers.

Bonilla-Silva, E. (2003). *Racism without racists: Color-blind racism and the persistence of racial inequality in the United States*. Lanham, MD: Rowman & Littlefield.

Callinicos, A. (1976). *Althusser's Marxism*. London: Pluto Press.

Feagin, J., Vera, H., & Batur, P. (2001). *White racism: The basics* (2nd ed.). New York: Routledge.

Geuss, R. (1981). *The idea of a critical theory*. Cambridge, UK: Cambridge University Press.

Gilroy, P. (2000). *Against race*. Cambridge, MA: Belknap.

Giroux, H. (1997). Racial politics and the pedagogy of whiteness. In M. Hill (Ed.), *Whiteness: A critical reader* (pp. 294–315). New York: NYU Press.

Gonzalez, N. (2004). Disciplining the discipline: Anthropology and the pursuit of quality education. *Educational Researcher, 33*(5), 17–25.

Hall, S. (1996). Gramsci's relevance for the study of race and ethnicity. In D. Morley & K. Chen (Eds.), *Stuart hall* (pp. 411–440). London: Routlege.

Hernnstein, R., & Murray, C. (1994). *The bell curve*. New York: Free Press.

Hirst, P. (1994). Problems and advances in the theory of ideology. In T. Eagleton (Ed.), *Ideology* (pp. 112–125). London: Longman.

hooks, b. (1984). *Feminist theory: From margin to center*. Boston: South End Press.

Horton, H. D., & Sykes, L. L. (2004). Toward a critical demography of neo-mulattoes: Structural change and diversity within the Black population. In C. Herring, V. Keith, & H. D. Horton (Eds.), *Skin/deep: How race and complexion matter in the "color-blind" era* (pp. 159–173). Urbana, IL: University of Illinois Press.

Hunter, M. (2002). Rethinking epistemology, methodology, and racism: Or, is White sociology really dead? *Race & Society, 5*(2002), 119–138.

Lenin, V. I. (1963). *What is to be done?* Oxford: Oxford University Press.

Leonardo, Z. (2003a). *Ideology, discourse, and school reform*. Westport, CT: Praeger.

Leonardo, Z. (2003b). Discourse and critique: Outlines of a post-structural theory of ideology. *Journal of Education Policy, 18*(2), 203–214.

Leonardo, Z. (2003c). Interpretation and the problem of domination: Paul Ricoeur's hermeneutics. *Studies in Philosophy and Education, 22*(5), 329–350.

Leonardo, Z. (2009). *Race, whiteness, and education*. New York: Routledge.

Lott, T. (1999). *The invention of race: Black culture and the politics of representation*. London: Blackwell.

Macdonell, D. (1986). *Theories of discourse*. London: Blackwell.

Marable, M. (1996). Staying on the path to racial equality. In G. Curry (Ed.), *The affirmative action debate* (pp. 3–15). New York: Addison-Wesley Publishing Company, Inc.

Marx, K., & Engels, F. (1970). *The German ideology*. New York: International Publishers.

Massey, D., & Denton, N. (1993). *American apartheid*. Cambridge, MA: Harvard University Press.

McDonnell, K., & Robins, K. (1980). Marxist cultural theory: The Althusserian smokescreen. In S. Clarke, V. Seidler, K. McDonnell, K. Robins, & T. Lovell (Eds.), *One-dimensional Marxism* (pp. 157–231). London: Allison & Bushby.

Miles, R. (1993). *Racism after "race relations"*. London: Routledge.

Mills, C. (1997). *The racial contract*. Ithaca, NY and London: Cornell University Press.

Mills, C. (2003). *From class to race: Essays in White Marxism and Black radicalism*. Lanham, MD: Rowman & Littlefield.

Mohanty, C. (1988). Under western eyes: Feminist scholarship and colonial discourses. *Feminist Review, 30*(Autumn), 61–88.

Oliver, M., & Shapiro, T. (1995). *Black wealth/White wealth: A new perspective on racial inequality*. New York: Routledge.

Omi, M., & Winant, H. (1994). *Racial formation in the United States: From the 1960s to the 1990s* (2nd ed.). New York: Routledge.

Ranciere, J. (1994). On the theory of ideology - Althusser's politics. In T. Eagleton (Ed.), *Ideology* (pp. 141–161). London: Longman.

Ricoeur, P. (1986). *Lectures on ideology and utopia* (G. Taylor, Ed.). New York: Columbia University Press.

Roberts, D. (1999). *Killing the black body: Race, reproduction, and the meaning of liberty*. New York: Vintage Books.

Snipp, C. M. (1996). The first Americans: American Indians. In S. Pedraza & R. Rumbaut (Eds.), *Origins and destinies: Immigration, race, and ethnicity in America* (pp. 390–403). Belmont, CA: Wadsworth.

Stepan, N. (1990). Race and gender: The role of analogy in science. In D. T. Goldberg (Ed.), *Anatomy of racism* (pp. 38–57). Minneapolis, MN: University of Minnesota Press.

Tatum, B. D. (1997). *Why are all the Black kids sitting together in the cafeteria?* New York: Basic Books.

Thompson, J. (1984). *Studies into the theory of ideology*. Berkeley, CA: University of California Press.

Watkins, W. (2001). *The White architects of Black education: Ideology and power in America, 1865–1954*. New York: Teachers College Press.

Weedon, C. (1997). *Feminist practice & poststructuralist theory* (2nd ed.). Oxford, UK: Blackwell.

Wilson, W. J. (1978). *The declining significance of race*. Chicago: University of Chicago Press.

Winant, H. (1997). Behind blue eyes. In M. Fine, L. Weis, L. Powell, & L. Wong (Eds.), *Off white* (pp. 40–53). New York: Routledge.

Zeus Leonardo
Graduate School of Education
University of California
Berkeley

DEBORAH YOUDELL

9. PERFORMATIVITY

Making the Subjects of Education

INTRODUCTION

Over the last decade or so the concepts of the *performative* and *performativity* have been taken-up increasingly in education studies. At its most straightforward, the field of linguistics understands the performative as something that is said that is the simultaneous 'doing' of that thing; an often-used example of this is the judge's pronouncement 'I sentence you....'. Yet the idea that what we say can, at least sometimes, *produce,* and not just describe, the social world has been seen as having significant potential both for understanding the world and for thinking about and enacting social change. This is why the idea of the performative has become a key area of exploration in the field of cultural politics in education.

In this chapter I explore the significance of the performative for politically engaged forms of education studies and practice. The chapter begins by setting out conceptual debates over the meanings, effects, and political potential of the performative and performativity. The chapter identifies two inter-related ways of working with the idea of the performative and performativity in education – one in relation to interrogating subjectivity that comes out of post-structural feminism in education and one in relation to interrogating policy that comes out of education policy sociology. The focus of the chapter is on the first of these two approaches; the question of what the performative offers to our understandings of the people – the students, teachers, parents, policy makers – who populate the education domain. The chapter goes on to explore examples of education studies that have used the idea of performativity to examine subjectivities in education settings and examines the take up of a *performative politics* inside education, considering the potential of performative politics to challenge 'who' 'makes sense' as what 'sort' of subject in education settings.

POST-STRUCTURAL THEORY

The uses of the performative that have been pursued in education studies are part of a wider engagement with post-structural theory. Before moving on to explore these uses of the performative in detail it is useful to locate it in this broader intellectual field.

Post-structural theory offers a range of inter-related conceptual tools for thinking about power, knowledge, the subject and agency. A key aspect of post-structural approaches, developed by French philosopher Michel Foucault (1991), is

Z. Leonardo (ed.), Handbook of Cultural Politics and Education, 219–236.

understanding **power** as *disciplinary* or *productive*, rather than seeing power as being held by those in positions of relative advantage over others. This leads to a focus on power as it *circulates* through the 'micro-circuits' of prevailing ideas and social practices, and not just on power as it is wielded or used to repress. Foucault (1991) argues that this disciplinary power works through institutionalised practices, or 'technologies', which make the person visible and knowable to others as well as to her/him self.

The post-structural theory of Foucault as well as other writers such as Jacques Derrida, Jean Baudrillard, and Jean-Francois Lyotard refutes the idea of universal knowledge and understands **knowledge** as located and partial and so inseparable from the circulation of power (See Baudrillard 1994, Derrida 2001, Foucault 2002, Lyotard 1984). Foucault (1990, 1991) moves to the idea of **discourse,** which has become a central concept in post-structural theory. Discourses are multiple and shifting systems of knowledge with varied and potentially porous status' ranging from what is taken as self-evident– a 'regime of truth' – through to what is unspeakable or ridiculous – 'disavowed' or 'subjugated' knowledges. It is important to recognise that discourse, in this sense, refers to much more than talk alone: discourses are cited by and circulate in speech and writing as well as visual representations, bodily movements and gestures, and social and institutional practices.

All of this thinking brings with it an understands the person, or **subject**, created over and over again through ongoing relational processes that are made meaningful by enduring discourses, an understanding that rejects the idea of a person who is complete and (relatively) constant over time. This is often called **subjectivation** (Foucault 1982 & 1988); referring to the productive force of circulating discourses that creates people as social subjects *at the same time* as it subjects them to relations of power. This leads to an understanding of **agency** as simultaneously made possible and reigned in and obscured by prevailing discourse and meaning, rather than seeing agency as being intrinsic to the subject who knows her/himself and her/his motivation and can to act to achieve her/his desired ends. These ideas of productive power, discourse and subjectivation all intersect with and underpin contemporary uses of the performative.

THE PERFORMATIVE AND PERFORMATIVITY

A useful starting point for understanding the performative is JL Austin's 1962 work *How to do Things with Words*. In this text Austin explores things that are said, often referred to as 'utterances' or 'speech acts', that *make something happen.* Austin makes a distinction between two forms of performative, the illocutionary and the perlocutionary. For Austin, an illocutionary performative always has the effect it names and has this effect in the moment of the speech act, for instance the sentence passed by the Judge that we saw above. In contrast, the perlocutionary performative may not have an immediate effect, may have no effect at all, or may have a different effect than the one expected, for instance, when a mother incites her child to 'be a good girl' the child's response may or may not be taken as fullfilling that invitation. Austin sees the slipperiness of perlocutionary performatives as failures that he calls 'infelicities'.

In a lecture given in 1971 Jacques Derrida (Derrida 1988) engages with Austin's assessment of performative infelicities and takes a different approach. Derrida argues that there is an inherent 'contextual break' between the intentions of a speaker and the meaning and effect of a performative. This means that it is the conventions and meanings of a situation, and not just the speaker, that influence what a performative will 'do'. With this in mind, instead of thinking about performative 'infelicities', Derrida argues that the break between intention and meaning opens up the space for a performative to 'misfire'. This is not a problem for Derrida, rather, the space for misfire is also a space in which the meaning and the effects of communication might change (see Derrida 1988). In this sense the 'performativity' of an utterance or text is also its potential to unsettle or resist dominant meanings and effects.

Jean-Francois Lyotard also engages with the idea of the performative in his 1984 work, *The Postmodern Condition,* where he explores the performativity of knowledge itself. Lyotard argues that the grand narratives of the enlightenment, scientific revolution, and modernity have been replaced by petite or small narratives whose status and meaning are contingent on the normative meanings of the communities in which they circulate. In this sense knowledge itself is seen as performative: its status and legitimacy is secured through its performative effects or through its performativity, its effectiveness in creating itself as knowledge. As it is applied in Lyotard's analysis of the university, this account of performativity suggests the restrictive and regulatory potential of the effective performative. For Lyotard these are the 'terrors of performativity' (Lyotard, 1984; cited by Ball, 2003 p. 220).

Derrida and Lyotard's engagements with the notion of the performative and its capacity to create the thing to which it refers are clearly related, but have been taken in different directions in the ways they have been used in different fields and by different authors. In sociological and philosophical work on education policy Lyotard's consideration of the performativity of knowledge has been pursued and developed in analysing contemporary *education policy tendencies* and their effects, including their effects on 'who' the teacher and student can be. Whereas feminist philosophy and literary studies, and later feminist education sociology and cultural studies, has engaged and developed Derrida's thinking about the performative for analysing *subjectivities* and thinking about *performative politics*.

PERFORMATIVE SUBJECTS

The idea of the performative has been central to recent post-structural thinking about the *subject* and the relationship between the subject, power and politics. This take up and development of the performative in relation to the subject has been led by Judith Butler, a contemporary US philosopher and political and literary theorist who has engaged and developed the ideas of Jacques Derrida and Michel Foucault.

Much of Butler's exploration of the performative has taken sex, gender and sexuality as its central concerns (Butler 1990, 1993, 1997, 2004a) and she is often thought of as a post-structural feminist or queer theorist. Sex, gender and sexuality are core issues for Butler, yet her interests are far-reaching, including concerns with race, ethnicity, nationhood, and nationality and even the question of *being human* (see Butler 1997, 2004b). Her work endeavours to make sense of these categories as 'cross-cutting modalities of life' (Butler 2007) and throughout her writing the capacity of the performative to make particular sorts of people – or subjects – is a key theoretical tool.

Butler defines the performative as being:

> [T]hat discursive practice that enacts or produces that which it names (Butler 1993, p. 13).

and suggests that:

> Discursive performativity appears to produce that which it names, to enact its own referent, to name and to do, to name and to make. ... [g]enerally speaking, a performative functions to produce that which it declares (Butler 1993, p. 107).

In thinking about how performatives make people, Butler turns to the classificatory systems, categories, and names that are used to designate, differentiate and sort people and suggests that these work *performatively* to create the people they name. Keeping the ideas of discourse and subjectivation that I described earlier in mind when thinking about these performative processes reminds us that performatives, and the subjects they constitute, are not neutral, but are situated in discourse and enduring relations of productive power.

Butler (1990, 1993, 1997, 2004a) argues that designations such as 'boy' and 'girl', 'man' and 'woman' are performative – they *create* the gendered subject that they name. Furthermore, these performatives do this while appearing to be just *descriptive*. By appearing to be descriptive they create the *illusion* of genders' *prior* existence. So while it appears that the subject *expresses* a gender that is true or 'proper' to it, this is actually a performative effect of gender categorisations and their use. This naming is not simply descriptive, it is 'inaugurative' – '[i]t seeks to introduce a reality rather than reporting an existing one' (Butler 1997:33).

Butler illustrates this with what she describes as 'an impossible scene': a 'body' that has not been named, is undefined, and so is not meaningful in discourse and cannot be made sense of by us. She suggests that it is only when this body is named in terms of the classificatory systems that are socially meaningful that we can make sense of and engage with 'it'. When the medic declares 'It's a girl!' or 'It's a boy!' the baby is performatively constituted as a gendered subject, as 'he' or 'she', as 'him' or 'her'. These are not performative constitutions that we can simply choose to opt-out of – Butler says they are 'compulsive' and 'compulsory' because they are the ground on which our subjecthood rests. She says that '[b]eing called a name is ... one of the conditions by which a subject is constituted in language' (Butler 1997:2) and is a prerequisite for being '*recognizable*' as a subject (Butler 1997:5, original emphasis) – we cannot simply reject the gendered pronoun 'he' or 'she', without one of these we simply do not make sense. For this reason these performatives also demand 'repetition' and 'citation' – we must be called 'she' and 'her', or 'he' and 'him' consistently and each time we are addressed in order to continue to make sense:

> The rules that constrain the intelligibility of the subject continue to structure the subject throughout his or her life. And this structuring is never fully complete. Acting one's place in language continues the subject's viability (Butler, 1997, p. 136).

And all of this demands a community of speakers and a set of discourses and conventional meanings in which naming and recognition takes place: the subject 'comes to "exist" by virtue of this fundamental dependency on the address of the Other' (Butler, 1997, p. 5). While a lot of debate in the field takes the performative to be spoken, Butler points out that a performative need not be spoken – it might be textual, it might be representational, it might be bodily, it might even be a silence or an omission. Performatives are a part of discourse and are effected through a range of discursive practices.

Butler (1997) also engages with the distinction between illocutionary and perlocutionary performatives that I discussed earlier. Butler notes that some utterances do appear to effect the acts they speak about as they are said: e.g., the judge's pronouncement of sentencing ('I sentence you'), the cleric's declaration of marriage ('I now pronounce you man and wife'). But Butler's main focus is the less certain perlocutionary performatives that Austin calls 'infelicitous' and whose potential 'misfire' Derrida highlights. Drawing attention to Derrida's contextual breaks and Austin's suggestion that the performative is 'ceremonial,' she stresses the performative as 'an inherited set of voices, an echo of others who speak as the "I"' (Butler 1997:25). She writes:

> If a performative provisionally succeeds ... [it is because] that action echoes prior actions, and *accumulates the force of authority through the repetition or citation of a prior and authoritative set of practices*. It is not simply that the speech act takes place *within* a practice, but that the act itself is a ritualised practice. What this means, then, is that a performative "works" to the extent that it *draws on and covers over* the constitutive conventions by which it is mobilized. In this sense, no term or statement can function performatively without the accumulating and dissimulating historicity of force (Butler, 1997, p. 51; emphasis in original).

Performatives, then, are citational, contextual, part of a chain of signification, and replete with prior uses whose meanings sediment as well as future uses in which their conventional meanings might be opened up to change. As such, Butler suggests that 'speech is always in some ways out of control' (Butler 1997:15).

PERFORMATIVE POLITICS

That performatives and the discourses they are part of might be 'out of control' opens up possibilities for engaging these in a *performative politics*. It does this by insisting that its meanings and effects are 'non-necessary'. (Butler 1997:39) and opening up the possibility of misfire. The performative might not 'do' what was expected, and this possibility of different meanings and effects offers the grounds for political practice concerned with changing meaning and changing how subjects are recognised and so 'who' they can be.

A key to this is a subject or a community of subjects who deploy the performative to political ends. Being performatively constituted as a subject makes a subject who joins the field of discourse whose discursive practices can constitute further subjects:

> [T]he one who names, who works within language to find a name for another, is presumed to be already named, positioned within language as one who is already subject to the founding or inaugurating address. This suggests that such a subject in language is positioned as both addressed and addressing, and that the very possibility of naming another requires that one first be named. The subject of speech who is named becomes, potentially, one who might well name another in time (Butler, 1997, p. 29).

The subject, then, has 'discursive agency' (Butler, p. 1997, p. 127) s/he can speak and act with intent and make things happen. *This is not the agency of a sovereign subject who exerts its will. Rather, discursive agency is derivative, an effect of discursive power*:

> Because the agency of the subject is not a property of the subject, an inherent will or freedom, but an effect of power, it is *constrained but not determined* in advance. ... As the agency of a post-sovereign subject, its discursive operation is delimited in advance but also open to a further unexpected delimitation (Butler, 1997, pp. 139–140; my emphasis).

The discursive agency of this performatively constituted subject is *enabled and constrained* through discourse at the same time. The subject cannot control discourse and its effects, what a performative can and will do is informed by meanings sedimented in context and past uses and is never guaranteed. Nevertheless, the performatively constituted subject can and does deploy discursive performatives that have the potential to be constitutive – the subject does this incessantly, without self-conscious intentions. But s/he might also do this tactically, with particular effects in mind.

Understanding subjects as being subjectivated through ongoing performative constitutions suggests that a key political challenge might be to intercept these performatives in order to re-constitute discourses, and so subjects, differently. Judith Butler insists that the sedimented meanings of enduring and prevailing discourses might be unsettled and reinscribed. And that subordinate, disavowed, or silenced discourses might be deployed in, and made meaningful in, contexts from which they have been barred. What these approaches suggest is that a post-structural political practice might invite the subjectivated subject to take up a position of 'strategic provisionality' (Butler, 2001), and attempt, albeit without a promise of finality or closure, to use her/his discursive agency to unsettle normative meanings and avoid being made a subject who stands in and acts her/his 'place' in discourse. The performative, then, is an opening for resisting normative meanings and making currently subjugated subjects intelligible in new ways. Gay, lesbian, bisexual and transgender politics' reinscription of 'queer'; disability studies' reinscription of 'crip'; and hip hop's reinscription of 'nigga' might all be understood as examples of such performative politics in action.

These ideas have massive implications for thinking critically about the subjects of education and the processes through which enduring inequalities are produced in the performative practices of institutions, teachers and, indeed, students. Using the idea of the performative insists that while 'who' we are is *constrained* it is not *determined* – either socially or biologically – and so what it means to be a teacher, a student, White, or of color, a boy or a girl, might be opened up to radical rethinking and remaking. And if 'who' these subjects are might be unsettled and re-inscribed, then there may also be the possibility of interrupting the enduring inequalities that are produced in part through the association in educational and popular discourse of particular abilities and talents, educational orientations and aspirations, and disabilities and deficits, with particular social groups (Youdell 2006a). Later in this chapter I offer examples from empirical education research that has sought to explore these performative practices as well as the possibilities of their meanings and effects being shifted. First, however, I turn to another use to which performativity has been put in education research.

PERFORMATIVE POLICY

Stephen Ball, a UK education policy sociologist, has been central to developing Lyotard's performativity – the production of knowledge as knowledge – in the field. Ball (2000, 2003) identifies performativity as a policy technology that, alongside the creation of markets and the insertion of managerialism into education, is a core part of the global policy tendency towards privatisation in education (Ball and Youdell, 2008). Moving from Foucault's understanding of disciplinary technologies, Ball writes: '[p]erformativity is a technology, a culture and a mode of regulation that employs judgments, comparisons and displays as means of incentive, control, attrition and change based on rewards and sanctions' (Ball, 2003, p. 216). Reflecting Foucault's identification of the technologies of disciplinary power, Ball maps a series of practices that are the technologies of performativity in education: 'it is the data-base, the appraisal meeting, the annual review, report writing, the regular publication of results and promotion applications, inspections and peer reviews that are mechanics of performativity' (Ball, 2003, p. 220). Ball is not alone in working with Lyotard's account of performativity to interrogate contemporary education policy; James Avis (2002), Jill Blackmore and Pat Thompson (2004), Michael Peters (2004a, 2004b), and Robin Usher (2006) are among a growing number of education scholars who are working with this idea.

Importantly, Ball's policy sociology emphasizes that *people* as well as *institutions* are impacted by performativity:

> the policy technologies of education reform are not simply vehicles for the technical and structural change of organizations but are also mechanisms for

> reforming teachers (scholars and researchers) and for changing what it means to be a teacher, the technologies of reform produce new kinds of teacher subjects (Ball, 2003, p. 217).

For Ball, then, these education policy technologies are performative in that they create education as a particular sort of activity, education institutions as particular sorts of places, *and educators and students as particular sorts of persons*. In these latter effects performative policy technologies can also be seen as subjectivating, a point at which Ball's take-up of performativity in policy sociology connects strongly with Judith Butler's use of the performative that I have already detailed.

It is noteworthy, however, that in policy sociology performativity is regularly interrogated for the ways that it remakes education by *reducing* both education and those who populate it to what is measurable, manageable, knowable. It is an account of the performative production of *constraint*. Whereas, while Butler details the way that the performative makes the particular subject intelligible in particular ways (and others not), her articulation of a performative politics underpinned by Derrida's performative misfire keeps open the potential for the performative to exceed these constraining meanings and effects and instead mean and make something different.

READING THE PERFORMATIVE SUBJECTS OF EDUCATION

The work of Judith Butler has had a significant impact in education studies where it has been used to understand and analyse a range of usually qualitative empirical data pertaining to everyday life in educational and related settings. The influence of Michel Foucault is evident in the work of these education scholars, but this is a Foucault transformed and sometimes even supplanted by Judith Butler's development of his ideas, her simultaneous engagement with other theoretical tools, and her application of these to feminist/queer concerns. Use of the performative to think about categorisations of identity has extended beyond gender and sexuality to a range of classificatory systems, for instance scholars concerned with the constraints of race, disability and class locations have thought about these as performative constitutions. Currently, a significant body of education scholarship was emerging in publication that covered concerns with the performative constitution of educational subjects made meaningful through gender, sexuality, social class, race, ethnicity, nationality, religion, ability, disability and special educational needs.

This work has tended to be located at the intersection of sociology of education and cultural studies in education and has drawn on a range of forms of data, from artefact and representations of popular culture and the media to detailed qualitative interviews, narratives and autobiographical accounts, ethnographic observations and everyday and institutional documents and representations. What is common across these forms of data is their qualitative richness, a richness and level of detail that allows an interrogation of the discourses circulating within it and the unpicking of the performative effects that these might have. In what follows I give a flavour of some of various these engagements.

In my paper *Identity Traps* I offer the following data episode generated from observation as part of a school ethnography:

BLACK AND OTHER NAMES

DY (*the researcher, mid/late twenties, woman, White*)
MARCELLA (*student, aged 15/16 girl, Black*)
MOLLY (*student aged 15/16, girl, White*)
JULIET (*student, aged 15/16, girl, Mixed-race*)
JASMINE (*student, aged 15/16 girl, Mixed-race*)

Sitting in a group around a table in the Year Base (Home Room). The discussion takes place while the rest of the tutor group is in a lesson. The group is in the process of recounting a conflict with RACHEL, *another girl in the year group, that resulted in* MARCELLA *being excluded from school for a fixed term (suspended).*

MARCELLA: I went to maths and I confronted her and I got excluded for it. She's just
something!
MOLLY: You called her 'Popadom'.
ALL: (*laugh*)
[…]
MARCELLA: I hit her a bit, buffed her out a bit, so she learned sense!
(*simultaneously*) JULIET: Duffed her up a bit.
(*simultaneously*) MOLLY: Called her a few names.
MARCELLA: And when I used to see her I pushed her a bit and called her abusive names ... I know the reasons sound silly but I have my reasons, (*trailing off*) she's just, one, a... (*agitated, with heightened 'Black' accent*) She thinks she's Black! Come on! She thinks she's Black! She thinks she's Black! She thinks she's Black!
(*simultaneously*) ALL: Yeah.
MARCELLA: (*parody of 'Black' accent*) She talks to me, she talks to me like that, what a
damn talk?
[…]
DY: What do you mean 'she thinks she's Black'?
JULIET: The way she acts.
MOLLY: The way she talks.
JULIET: Everyone knows, every one knows here that she's ... (*interrupted*)
(*simultaneously*) MOLLY: (*to* DY) Even you know.
MARCELLA: (*interrupting* JULIET) I know there's not a certain way for a Black person to present, but there *is.*
JULIET: No, but there is.
MARCELLA: Yeah, that's the thing, there *is*, that's what... I know... I have to say this, there *is*, that's what, I have to say, but there *is.*

JULIET: The hairstyles and stuff.
MARCELLA: Yeah, but there *is*, there *is*, I know there's not a Bla... (*laughs*) know what I mean!
ALL: (*laugh, someone claps*)
(*simultaneously*) MOLLY: (*quoting*) 'There is'!
MOLLY: (*imitating mature, rational tone*) That's the way it is in this kind of society.
MARCELLA: And you know Coolie right, she's *Indian*, a proper Indian right, I have Indian next door neighbours so I know what they look like, right.
(*simultaneously*) GROUP MEMBER: (*laughs*)
(*simultaneously*) GROUP MEMBER: (*a sharp intake of breath*)
MARCELLA: She, right, you know when a Black person and an Indian person makes a baby they call the baby *Coolie* because its got half Black and half Indian, she goes round saying that that's what she is because she's ashamed of what, where she comes from.
DY: So where is she from?
JULIET: She's Indian, yeah.
MARCELLA: Indian.
[…]
DY: So what are you saying? That she *acts* like she thinks she's Black?
MARCELLA: Blacker than me, I know this sounds funny but she does, she uses words that I'm not even ready for yet!
DY: What sort of words?
MARCELLA: I forgot what.
MOLLY: like 'gwarnin' or something like that, in'it?
ALL: (*laugh*)
(*simultaneously*) JASMINE: Not ready!
MARCELLA: She just, I don't know, she's just something else she is. And also cos she goes out with Black boys it gets to my head you see, so she gets a bit...
MOLLY: Do they actually *know* she's Indian?
JASMINE: No probably not.
(*simultaneously*) MARCELLA: No.
(*simultaneously*) JULIET: I don't think so you know.
MARCELLA: Cos [boy] thought that she was Coolie.
JASMINE: When she rings up [girl], she said he asked her 'What are you?' and she goes 'Coolie'.
ALL: Yeah.
DY: So she tells people that she's got a Black parent and an Indian parent?
MARCELLA: Yeah, Coolie.

(Youdell, 2003, pp. 7–8)

The analysis that I offer in the paper argues that a 'hierarchy within the Other' is created and policed through intersecting discourses of race, sex, gender, and sexuality which cite the natural-ness of race and sex-gender and the normal-ness of heterosexuality. Focussing on race, I suggest that the data offered above shows how raced subjects are performatively constituted and contested through their naming and designation. I also argue that it shows the discursive practices through which races are constituted as discrete, authentic and hierarchical. The group draws on a number of names that might be understood as race identities. Some of these are familiar – Black, Indian, White. Others are perhaps more recognisable as terms of abuse – 'Coolie', 'Popadom'. Drawing on Butler's notion of the performative I argue that in naming and asserting these race identities the group is not simply reporting fact or offering a description, they are citing an enduring discourse of race that performatively constitutes race identities. These names are not descriptive – this is a moment in the constitution of race identities and of these subjects in terms of these race identities.

I also argue in the paper that all of these names are permeated by an understanding of race as a discrete and authentic marker of identity and that a key feature of the students' discursive practices is a citation of an enduring discourse of race phenotypes or physiognomies. While there seems to be some oscillation between a discourse of essential races and a discourse of culturally constructed races, race remains self-evident and unproblematised (if problematic). I go on to suggest that at the core of the group's understanding there appears to be an implicit assertion of racial authenticity; individuals are *a* race – whether Black, Coolie, Indian or White – which is determined by the race of parents, is enduring, and can be identified. This recourse to authenticity carries with it at least a residual acceptance of race as natural and based in essences – race identity remains a biological fact (Youdell, 2003). What the analysis aims to show, then, is how the everyday practices of young people in schools are thick with performatives that are made meaningful and whose effects rest on their embeddedness in and citation of enduring discourses.

This reflects readings of the performativity of race offered by other scholars. Miron and Inda (2000) argue that, across race politics, race should be understood as a performative and Warren (2002) and Ringrose (2007) explore the performative constitution of Whiteness in the classroom. In Youdell (2006b) I show how institutional and everyday teacher practices deploy Orientalist discourses that act performatively to constitute Islamic students as a threat and so as impossible learners.

I have also offered analyses of this sort in relation to gender and sexuality. In Youdell (2004a, 2004b) I examine the minutiae of practice inside the classroom to show how performative constitutions of the homosexual subject have the potential injure these students *and* the potential to be reinscribed in new ways that allow these students to constitute themselves as legitimate and even desirable "gay" subjects inside school. Other education scholars do similar sorts of work with these conceptual tools. Mary Lou Rasmussen's (2006) book *Becoming Subjects* draws on Butler's notion of the performative alongside other aspects of post-structural theory to analyse empirical accounts and cultural artefacts and offer an extensive analysis of the constitution of sexualities in secondary schools. Emma Renold's (2005) book *Junior Sexualities* draws on ethnographic data generated in primary school to offer an analysis of the performative constitution of younger children's subjectivities, arguing that gender constitutions are simultaneously constitutions of young sexualities. Vicars (2006) demonstates the injurious effects of the performative 'queer' in school settings. Ringrose and Renold (2009) use the performative to interrogate the gendered constitution of violence in schools. And in Youdell (2005) I use ethnographic observation to demonstrate how performative constitutions of sex, gender and sexuality are inseparable in the discursive practices of young women inside school, so much so that a conceptualisation of 'sex-gender-sexuality' is suggested.

Special educational needs, disability and 'emotional and behavioural difficulties' have all been explored in terms of their performativity. Building of Roger Slee's (1996) Foucauldian analysis of the productive force of these discourses, Sue Saltmarsh and myself (Saltmarsh and Youdell, 2004) and Linda Graham (2007) have developed analyses of the performative constitution of 'special' and 'problematic' in education policy and institutional and teacher practices. And Cath Laws and Bronwyn Davies (2000) have analysed participant observation data to show how teachers can practice differently with students diagnosed in these ways in order to interrupt the performativity of normal (and abnormal) and remake this as a 'doing' rather than a 'being'.

An important development in the field has been in work that endeavours to unravel the performative constitution not of single classificatory systems eg gender, or single categorisations, eg girl, or obviously entangled subjectivities, such as sex-gender, but of *multiple and intersecting performatives* that make multi-faceted subjects and subjectivities.

For instance, Rasmussen and Harwood (2003) explore a range inter-connecting performatives, including race, gender, sexuality, size and ability, whose injurious effects work together to make schooling almost untenable for one girl, Jemma. Drawing on data generated through a series of interviews with Jemma, Rasmussen and Harwood unravel the performative force of the discourses that have, over time, come to push Jemma out of education. Here, extracts of Jemma's accounts are woven together with Rasmussen and Hardwood's analysis to create a detailed demonstration of how performatives have acted to shape both Jemma's school experience and her sense of self:

> In our reading of Jemma's story, her process of coming to understand her self as "slow" was the result of performative acts supported by "elaborate institutional structures" that are bigger than any one individual or group [...]. Jemma's construction as "slow" was supported by an educational bureaucracy that produced schools that "streamed" students, creating educational spaces for people defined as "slow". Adults supported her construction as "slow", particularly when she was told that she belonged in the "slowest class" and she was put in the English as a second language class; Jemma never understood why this occurred as, although she spoke both French and English, she considered English her first language. Jemma was told by some adults that she was dumb and stupid, her friend's mum said she had dyslexia, her doctor told her she had "depression", and her parents called her a "slut",

> "no good at anything and useless". Jemma's peers told her truths including that she was "dumb", "stupid", a "fat heifer", a "black mamma", a "slut", and teased her because she was "no good at school". The name"black mamma" was just one of the ways that Jemma said her peers included references to "the colour of my skin" (Jemma, Transcripts). Being told she was "stupid" led Jemma to form the belief that *she was stupid*, a truth that has "... just stuck with me ever since" (Jemma, Transcripts). Added to these experiences, Jemma stated, "When I was a kid I used to always get told that I was no good at anything, that I was useless" (Jemma, Transcripts). Jemma was told many truths about herself by both adults and by her peers, truths that "... made me believe that I was a good for nothing and useless child (Jemma, Transcripts).
>
> [...]
>
> For Jemma there is no questioning that the many labels she was given, including "slow", "fat heifer", "black mamma" were onerous, influencing her disengagement from the process of schooling and positing her as "other". These injurious discourses intertwined and sustained one another, and through processes of repetition they produced harmful effects. One such effect of these performatives that sought to produce Jemma as "slow" was that they led her to experience this as an ongoing subjectivity. The truth of being told she *was* stupid became the subjectivity of *being* stupid (Rasmussen and Harwood, 2003, pp. 29, 32).

This reading of the intersections of a number of performatives demonstrates both the complexity of these processes and how these intersections contribute to the sedimentation of performative effects. Indeed, in the case of Jemma, Rasmussen and Harwood demonstrate powerfully how these performatives come to *be* 'who' Jemma is educationally, socially, and psychically.

Pursuing similar lines of analysis Lewis and Fabos (2005) examine multiple performatives as they work in instant messaging to constitute multivocal subjects. And Robinson and Dias' (2005) analysis of practice within early childhood interrogates constitutions across race, class, gender, and sexuality. In *Impossible Bodies, Impossible Selves* I use the concept of the performative to work across multiple classificatory systems and analyse how the subjects of schooling are constituted through constellations of race, class, gender, sexuality, ability and disability and to examine the implications of these constellations for differently made subjects' for recognition (or impossibility) as students and learners (Youdell, 2006a).

The growing influence in education of Judith Butler's work on performativity, as well as her wider thinking, is reflected in the 2006 publication of a Special Edition of the *British Journal of Sociology of Education* dedicated to her work. Emma Renold (2006) interrogates the performative constitution of normative heterosexuality in the everyday practices of primary school children and offers empirical examples of moments of its interruption. Anoop Nayak & Mary Jane Kehily (2006) engaged the corporeality of the subject, exploring the gender performativity of embodiment in the practices of young people. Valerie Hey (2006) explored the usefulness of making the concept of performativity work in thinking about the lived lives of embodied subjects and considered the possibility of the performative to resignify subjugated subjectivities. In a similar vein my own contribution to the volume considered the performative politics of the practices of subjects constituted through orientalist, (anti-)Islamist, and nationalist performatives post-9/11 (Youdell, 2006b).

A PERFORMATIVE EDUCATION POLITICS?

These sorts of engagements with the politics of the performative – that is, the potential to use the performative to resist constraining, normative subjectivities and, potentially, make alternative subject positions possible – is an increasingly consistent theme in education scholarship informed by these ideas. This should not be surprising given the consistent commitment to social justice in much work in education studies, and the prior commitments to critical theory held by many of the education scholars who have engaged with post-structural thinking in an attempt to find ways to understand the limits of critical theory and politics and find additional political strategies.

Beavis and Charles' (2000) paper uses the performative to explore the potential for non-normative gender constitutions at the interface of real/cyber space. Kopelson (2002) explores the possibility for a queer performative pedagogy. Davies (2006) had drawn on the performative in developing her thinking about the politics of teachers' pedagogic and reflexive practices. LeCourt (2006) takes up the performative to demonstrate the spaces for working class to be constituted differently, that is, in ways that do not simultaneously exclude, in higher education settings. In Youdell (2006c) I explore the potential for a performative politics to be taken up in education in relation to policy, curriculum, pedagogy and everyday practice. And North (2007) seeks to test what performative politics can offer in anti-oppressive education.

These ideas were pursued through an action research project that I was involved with between 2006 and 2008, which worked with primary (elementary) school teachers to find ways to unsettle the heteronormative through curriculum, pedagogic and everyday interventions in primary education settings. Two of the education scholars leading the project, Elizabeth Atkinson and Renée DePalma, draw on a performative politics when they argue 'that in order to break old chains, new chains of invocation must be forged. In order to deconstruct 'gay' as an insult, it must be allowed to acquire new, positive and intelligible meanings and associations' (Atkinson and DePalma, in press, p. 20). They demonstrate this in practice by offering a reading of fieldnotes and reflections from one of the teacher-researchers in the project:

Teacher: Year 5 teacher in Andy's school
Sam: Year 5 (aged 9) pupil; also part of Andy's 'lunch time group' in the Nurture Room.
Tony: Year 5 (aged 9) pupil
Alan: Year 5 (aged 9) pupil

> In class, about ten minutes into the lesson, with no warning Sam stands up and shouts out:
> *Andy is gay and he's going out with a man!*
> The interruption is met with raised eyes from the class but no further reaction.
> Teacher: *Sam, everyone knows that.*
> Tony: *Old news, Sam.*
> Sam attempts to shift the failed insult to two of his classmates): *Alan is gay and is going out with Tony.*
> No response from either named child, both of whom continue with work.
> Teacher (to Sam) *Sam, sit down, and get on.*
> Sam does so. No further interruptions
> (Andy reflects) This is what we're looking for. Not losing gayness, but losing its potential as an insult (Atkinson & DePalma, in press, pp. 20–21).

Atkinson and DePalma suggests that this scene reflects at least the partial success of this teacher-researcher's pedagogy that seeks to embed within it a performative politics and the subsequent, again partial, resignification of the performative 'gay' inside his classroom. They write:

> 'Andy's ongoing attempts to forge a new chain, to create a new commensurability between teacher and gay may not have been taken up at this point by Sam, but it seems to have provided a new possibility for Tony and Alan: they do not recognise Sam's invocation of 'gay' as an insult even when it is directed at one of them. They find old discourses now unintelligible (gay-insult) in the light of new intelligibilities (gay-Andy)' (Atkinson & DePalma 2008, p. 21).

Atkinson and DePalma's analysis highlights how the force of a performative – whether inscribing normative meanings or signifying something new or previously disallowed – rests on the intelligibility or unintelligibility of these meanings within the specific context and moment. The resignification of 'gay' as an intelligible and acceptable teacher subjectivity that Andy has pursued does appear to have has some purchase in his classroom – this subject position is 'old news' to at least some of the students in his class. Tony and Alan's citation of the intelligible and acceptable gay teacher could be read as demonstrating that the resignification of 'gay' may have begun to sediment in this context. At the same time, however, Sam's citation of 'gay' as an injurious name whose performative force rests on its abiding meaning and constitution of the vilified homosexual subject continues to be intelligible in this classroom. The acceptable gay teacher subject who was previously unintelligible in this context may have been rendered intelligible, but the unacceptable, vilified homosexual subject remains intelligible in this setting and, in Sam's practice, might be seen to continue to assert it's sedimented meaning and threaten to undercut and recuperate the resignification that Andy's practices have sought.

Of course, Andy's resignification of 'gay' is effective at least in part because it cites prior resignifications that have already been pursued and are already intelligible elsewhere – through the Gay Rights movement and now in the liberal mainstream, for instance. Furthermore, the co-existence of incommensurable meanings in this classroom and the uncertainty over their performative effects – we cannot know for sure 'who' was constituted through which practices and whether those constitutions will endure – reflects the wider interplay and collision of discourses and performatives and the promise and risk of their misfire. Is Jean Paul Gaultier a fashion super-hero whose popularity evidences that 'gay' has been reinscribed already or is he yet another pansy who acts his place in normative discourse and makes dresses? It seems reasonable to argue that in Atkinson and DePalma's example we find a performative moment where the injury is overridden, where the teacher takes up an acceptable gay identification, and where this is recognisable to some of the students. Yet what remains open to question, perhaps permanently, is how far and how enduring the reach of these new discursive possibilities for identification will be?

The idea of the performative, and the performative politics that are developed from this, are being applied to education research and curricula, pedagogies, and everyday practices inside educational settings. This is not a revolutionary politics that promises a monumental upheaval and reordering of social (and political and economic) life. Nor is it a politics of liberal reform that looks to the legislature to enshrine particular rights, responsibilities and protections but leaves the textures and meanings of daily life unquestioned. It is a politics that places meaning, and its capacity to create and constrain as well as transform social life and social subjects, at the centre of an ongoing politics that takes seriously the constitutive force of the everyday practices of institutions, educators and students.

REFERENCES

Atkinson, E., & DePalma, R. (2008). *Un-believeing the matrix: Queering consensual hteronormativity.* Gender and Education.

Austin, J. L. (1962). *How to do things with words.* Cambridge, MA: Harvard University Press.

Avis, J. (2003). Re-thinking trust in a performative culture: The case of education. *Journal of Education Policy, 18*(3), 315–332.

Ball, S. J. (2000). Performativities and fabrications in the education economy: Towards the performative society? *Australian Educational Researcher, 27*(2), 1–23.

Baudrillard, J. (1994). *Simulacra and simulation.* Ann Arbor, MI: University of Michigan Press.

Beavis, C., & Charles, C. (2007). Would the "Real" girl Gamer please stand up? Gender, LAN cafes and the reformulation of the "Girl" Gamer. *Gender and Education, 19*(6), 691–705.

Blackmore, J., & Thomson, P. (2004). Just "Good and bad news? Disciplinary imaginaries of head teachers in Australian and English print media. *Journal of Education Policy, 19*(3), 301–320.

Britzman, D. (1998). *Lost subjects, contested objects: Towards a psychoanalytic inquiry of learning.* Albany, NY: State University of New York Press.

Butler, J. (1990). *Gender trouble: Feminism and the subversion of identity.* London: Routledge.

Butler, J. (1991). Imitation and gender insubordination. In D. Fuss (Ed.), *Inside/out: Lesbian theories, gay theories.* London: Routledge.

Butler, J. (1993). *Bodies that matter: On the discursive limits of "sex".* New York: Routledge.

Butler, J. (1997). *Excitable speech: A politics of the performative.* London: Routledge.

Butler, J. (2004). *Precarious life: The powers of mourning and violence.* London: Verso.

Davies, B. (2006). Subjectification: The relevance of Butler's analysis for education. *British Journal of Sociology of Education, 27*(4), 425–438.

Derrida, J. (1988). Signature event context. In J. Derrida (Ed.), *Limited Inc* (pp. 1–23). Evanston, IL: Northwestern University Press.

Derrida, J. (2000). *On writing and difference*. London: Routledge.

Foucault, M. (1982). The subject and power. In H. L. Dreyfus & P. Rabinow (Eds.), *Michel Foucault: Beyond hermenutics and structuralism* (pp. 208–226). Brighton, Sussex, Harvester.

Foucault, M. (1990a). *The history of sexuality: An introduction* (Vol. 1). London: Penguin.

Foucault, M. (1988b). An aesthetics of existence. In L. Kritzman (Ed.), *Michel Foucault – politics, philosophy, culture: Interviews and other writings 1977–1984* (pp. 47–56). London: Routledge.

Foucault, M. (1991). *Discipline and punish: The birth of the prison*. London: Penguin.

Foucault, M. (2002). *The order of things*. London: Routledge.

Graham, L. J. (2007). Speaking of 'disorderly' objects: A poetics of pedagogical discourse. *Discourse, 28*(1), 1–20.

Hey, V. (2006). The politics of performative resignification: translating Judith Butlers theoretical discourse and its potential for a sociology of education. *British Journal of Sociology of Education, 27*(4), 439–457.

Kopelson, K. (2002). Dis/Integrating the Gay/Queer binary: "Reconstructed identity politics" for a performative pedagogy. *College English, Special Issue: Lesbian and Gay Studies/Queer Pedagogies, 65*(1), 17–35.

Laqueur, T. (1990). *Making sex: Body and gender from the greeks to freud*. London: Harvard University Press.

LeCourt, D. (2006). Performing working-class identity in composition: Toward a pedagogy of textual practice. *College English, 69*(1), 22–51.

Lewis, C., & Fabos, B. (2005). Instant messaging, literacies, and social identities. *Reading Research Quarterly, 40*(4), 470–501.

Lyotard, J. (1984). *The postmodern condition: A report in knowledge*. Minnesota, MN: University of Minnisota Press.

Miron, L. F., & Inda, J. X. (2000). Race as a kind of speech act. *Cultural Studies: A Research Annual, 5*, 85–107.

Nayak, A., & Kehily, M. J. (2006). Gender undone: Subversion, regulation and embodiment in the work of Judith Butler. *British Journal of Sociology of Education, 27*(4), 459–472.

North, C. E. (2007). What do you mean by "Anti-oppressive education"? Student interpretations of a high school leadership program. *International Journal of Qualitative Studies in Education QSE, 20*(1), 73–97.

Peters, M. A. (2004a). Performative, performativity and the culture of performance: Knowledge management in the new economy (Part 1). *Management in Education, 18*(1), 35–38.

Peters, M. A. (2004b). Performative, performativity and the culture of performance: Knowledge management in the new economy (Part 2). *Management in Education, 18*(2), 20–24.

Rasmussen, M. L., & Harwood, V. (2003). Performativity, youth and injurious speech. *Teaching Education, 14*(1), 25–36.

Rasmussen, M. (2006). *Becoming subjects*. London: Routledge.

Renold, E. (2005). *Girls, Boys and junior sexualities: Exploring childrens' gender and sexual relations in the primary school*. London: RoutledgeFalmer.

Renold, E. (2006). "They won't let us play... unless you're going out with one of them": Girls, goys and Bulter's 'heterosexual matrix' in the primary years. *British Journal of Sociology of Education, 27*(4), 489–510.

Ringrose, J. (2007). Rethinking white resistance: Exploring the discursive practices and psychical negotiations of 'whiteness' in feminist, anti-racist education. *Race Ethnicity, Education, 10*(3), 323–344.

Ringrose, J., & Renold, E. (2009). Boys and girls performing normative violence in schools: A gendered critique of bully discourses. In C. Barter & D. Berridge (Eds.), *Children Behaving Badly? Exploring peer violence between children and young people*. John Wiley and Sons.

Robinson, K., & Diaz, C. J. (2005). *Diversity and difference in early childhood education: Issues for theory and practice*. Columbus, OH: Open University Press.

Vicars, M. (2006). Who are you calling queer? Sticks and stones can break my bones but names will always hurt me. *British Educational Research Journal, 32*(3), 347–361.

Warren, J. T. (2001). The social drama of a "Rice burner": A (Re)constitution of whiteness. *Western Journal of Communication, 65*(2), 184–205.

World Health Organisation. (2001). *International classification of functioning, disability and health*. Retrieved February 18, 2008, from http://www.who.int/classifications/icf/site/icftemplate.cfm

Youdell, D. (2003). Identity traps or how black students fail: The interactions between biographical, sub-cultural, and learner identities. *British Journal of Sociology of Education, 24*(1), 3–20.

Youdell, D. (2004). Wounds and reinscriptions: Schools, sexualities and performative subjects. *Discourse, 25*(4), 477–493.

Youdell, D. (2006a). *Impossible bodies, impossible selves: Exclusions and student subjectivities*. Dordrecht: Springer.

Youdell, D. (2006b). Subjectivation and performative politics - Butler thinking Althusser and Foucault: intelligibility, agency and the raced-nationed- religioned subjects of education. *British Journal of Sociology of Education, 27*(4), 511–528.

Youdell, D. (2006c). Diversity, inequality, and a post-structural politics for education. *Discourse, 27*(1), 33–42.

Deborah Youdell
Institute of Education
University of London

ALICIA A. BRODERICK

10. AUTISM AS ENEMY

Metaphor and Cultural Politics

In this chapter I explore the cultural politics circulating in contemporary autism discourse, particularly the usage of metaphor therein. Writing from a Disability Studies in Education (DSE) perspective, I argue that there is currently an ongoing cultural struggle over the metaphoric constitution of autism as *disease* vs. autism as neuro*diversity*. Related to the dominant "autism as disease" metaphor, two dominant metaphors to emerge in popular cultural discourse around autism in the last several years are: (a) autism as *abductor* and (b) autism as *epidemic*. I argue that, taken together, within the organizing metaphoric construct of autism as disease, these twin metaphors serve metaphorically to constitute (a) an *enemy* and (b) a sense of *urgency*, each of which is necessary to constitute autism as a cultural threat significant enough to support particular approaches and postures toward both intervention (e.g., attempts at "recovery" through early intensive behavioral intervention) and prevention (e.g., "curing autism"). Drawing upon Lakoff and Johnson's (2003) theories of metaphor, throughout this chapter I explore the circulation of power through metaphor in contemporary autism discourse, considering also Foucault's (1980) notions of "regimes of truth" and "subjugated knowledges." I argue that this exploration of the cultural politics underlying the usage of metaphor in autism discourse can illustrate the powerful ways in which broader cultural narratives about normalcy/abnormalcy become "naturalized," thus obscuring the fundamentally ideological nature of the assumptions underlying decisions about educational policy and practice.

INTRODUCTION: DISABILITY STUDIES IN EDUCATION

In this chapter, I take a disability studies (DS) perspective on the current popular cultural struggle between competing metaphors drawn upon to define and indeed constitute a particular disability label and identity—autism—and therefore, the individuals to whom it is ascribed. I argue that the cultural politics that surround the present metaphoric struggle over what autism "is" and perhaps more importantly, that inform the question "Who gets to say?" constitute an illustrative example of the ways in which broader cultural narrative tropes about ability and disability become naturalized in informing decisions of educational policy and practice.

While the field of disability studies has been burgeoning in the humanities and the social sciences for at least 30 years, in the past decade a DS perspective has also begun to have a significant impact around disability-related issues in education.

Z. Leonardo (ed.), Handbook of Cultural Politics and Education, 237–268.

Many scholars of disability studies in education (DSE) mark the 1999 formation of a DSE special interest group (SIG) of the American Educational Research Association (AERA) as "the formal beginning" (Gabel, 2005, p. 1) of what had been a longstanding trend (Taylor, 2006) in educational research and practice of extending the theoretical perspectives, frameworks, and approaches of DS in the humanities and social sciences to issues of educational policy and practice. According to Taylor (2006), what distinguishes DSE from traditional DS generally is

> a practical concern with schooling practices. In contrast to a traditional special education perspective and consistent with a Disability Studies perspective, Disability Studies in Education examines disability in social and cultural context. Constructions of disability are questioned and special education assumptions and practices are challenged. (p. xix)

Similarly, the DSE SIG describes DS and its emergent contributions to the field of education as follows:

> Disability studies is an emerging interdisciplinary field of scholarship that critically examines issues related to the dynamic interplays between disability and various aspects of culture and society. Disability studies unites critical inquiry and political advocacy by utilizing scholarly approaches from the humanities, humanistic/post-humanistic social sciences, and the arts. When specifically applied to educational issues, it promotes the importance of infusing analyses and interpretations of disability throughout all forms of educational research, teacher education, and graduate studies in education (DSE, ¶ 1, as cited in Gabel, 2005a, p. 1).

Interestingly, in taking generally criticalist stances toward inquiry, advocacy, and analysis, a number of DSE scholars actively critique the ways in which criticalist pedagogical traditions have historically, and perhaps unwittingly, contributed to the marginalization of disability-related issues in education through reification of realist ontological assumptions about the nature of disability identity and experience (Gabel, 2002; Erevelles, 2005).

Several cogent explorations of the evolution of the field of DSE scholarship have already been offered by other authors, and I refer the reader to these works for additional detail on the breadth and depth of DSE scholarship (Danforth & Gabel, 2006a, 2006b; Gabel, 2005a, 2005b; Ware, in press; Taylor, 2006). However, Ware (in press) makes a useful distinction when she refers to scholars who claim DS as their "ideological home" (p. 4), rather than their "disciplinary home" (p. 4), a distinction that she argues serves to "underscore the interdisciplinary and trans-disciplinary mission of disability studies" (p. 4). Ware delineates the broadest ideological commitments of DS and DSE perspectives as "interrogat[ing] ableism and the certainty that encloses the pursuit of 'normalcy' throughout society and its institutions" (p. 1). Nevertheless, taking a DSE approach to inquiry and analysis does not imply adopting a unitary perspective, disciplinary grounding, or analytical approach. Taylor (2006) notes that "scholarship in these areas includes social constructionist or interpretivist, materialist, postmodernist, poststructuralist, legal, and even structural-functionalist perspectives and draws on disciplines as diverse as sociology, literature, critical theory, economics, law, history, art, philosophy, and others" (p. xiii). Thus, in this chapter's analysis of autism metaphor I explicitly position my ideological home within both DS and DSE traditions, and I draw upon a variety of approaches to inquiry and analysis—including literary, linguistic, and postmodernist—in my exploration and discussion of the cultural politics of autism metaphor. In keeping with the criticalist and activist traditions of DS and DSE, I argue that this analysis has fundamental implications for future action, particularly for both educational and social policies and practices as they relate to autistic citizens.

ON METAPHOR

In 1978, Susan Sontag wrote a seminal essay entitled, "Illness as Metaphor," and in 1989, a follow-up essay entitled "AIDS and its Metaphors" (Sontag, 1990). In these companion essays, she explored the powerful and pervasive ways in which the diseases of tuberculosis, cancer, and human immunodeficiency virus (HIV)/acquired immune deficiency syndrome (AIDS) had seized the public imagination by examining the metaphors that were commonly drawn upon to describe and in many ways to constitute the experience of having tuberculosis, cancer, and HIV/AIDS. Sontag begins her 1978 essay with the remark:

> My point is that illness is *not* a metaphor, and that the most truthful way of regarding illness—and the healthiest way of being ill—is one most purified of, most resistant to, metaphoric thinking....It is toward an elucidation of those metaphors, and a liberation from them, that I dedicate this inquiry. (pp. 3–4)

I first read Sontag's work over ten years ago, and her discussion of metaphor as it relates to disease and, by extrapolation, disability has often informed my own thinking and analysis around these issues, particularly as it relates to the usage of metaphor in autism discourse. However, in exploring autism as metaphor, as I do in this chapter, I do not make the claim about autism, as Sontag does about illness, that "[autism] is *not* metaphoric." Perhaps more significantly, nor would I assert, as Sontag does, that (a) it is possible to be "purified of ", "resistant to," or "liberated from" metaphoric thinking, nor that (b) if it were possible to be free of metaphoric thinking that it would somehow be more "truthful." However, in asserting that autism is metaphoric, neither do I make the rather disingenuous claim that autism is *only* metaphoric. Indeed, as Danforth (2007) asserts, due to the material realities of discrimination and of impairment experienced by disabled people, "there would perhaps be no more offensive form of lying than to say that disabilities are metaphorical" (p. 8). As with other disability labels, autism obviously is enmeshed with particular material and cultural facets of both experience and identity, and many autistic citizens routinely experience oppression and discrimination in very material ways in their daily lives. However, I take, rather, a more postmodern ontological and epistemological turn, echoing Smith's (1999) assertion that "it's all metaphor" (p. 131), and argue that autism, as is the case with most human concepts and constructs, is profoundly metaphoric.

Other disability studies scholars have engaged in metaphoric analyses of representations of particular disability categories, including Baynton's (1997) exploration of metaphors of deafness, Danforth's (2007) exploration of metaphoric representations of emotional and behavioral disorders, Danforth and Naraian's (2007) exploration of usage of machine metaphors in autism research, Danforth and Kim's (2008) tracing of the metaphors of ADHD, and Zola's (1985) classic examination of metaphoric depictions of disability generally, among others. In his analysis of metaphors of deafness, Baynton (1997) asserts that people use metaphoric language to describe and to understand things that they have no direct experience with, arguing that, for people who are not deaf, metaphoric thinking about deafness is perhaps "inevitable" (p. 143). I would depart from Baynton's assertion by arguing that metaphor is not merely a substitute for direct experience, but rather is an integral part of making sense of any experience. The issue is not that hearing people rely upon metaphor to understand their (indirect) experience of deafness, but rather that *all* people rely upon metaphor to make sense of their own experiences, and that when experiences differ, so too will the conceptual metaphors drawn upon in making sense of those different experiences. However, Baynton gets to the crux of the issue when he argues further,

> The problem is that hearing people are in positions to make, on the basis of their metaphors—usually unaware that they are metaphors—decisions with profound and lasting effects upon the lives of deaf people....The metaphors of deafness—of isolation and foreignness, of animality, of darkness and silence—are projections reflecting the needs and standards of the dominant culture, not the experiences of most deaf people. (p. 143)

Indeed he notes that the most dominant and persistent metaphoric images of deafness "are images that are consistently rejected by deaf people" (p. 143). Given the analogous situation of non-autistic people generally being in positions to make (on the basis of their metaphors, which are grounded in their own, non-autistic experience) significant decisions about the lives of autistic people (as Baynton points out, often without awareness of the metaphoric nature of their thinking), it seems pertinent then to explore in this analysis the sources of the variety of metaphors that circulate in autism discourse, each often making "truth" claims about the nature of autism. Perhaps more importantly, it seems crucial to explore the ways in which dominant forms of metaphoric thinking about the construct of autism—which are, more often than not, grounded in non-autistic experience—inform decision-making regarding the lives of autistic people.

ON METHOD

The primary conceptual framework undergirding this analysis of metaphor in contemporary autism discourse is explicated in Lakoff and Johnson's (2003) *Metaphors We Live By*. Metaphor is understood primarily as a way of making sense of our own experiences in terms of similarities to other concepts; however, a central organizing tenet of these authors' theory of metaphor is not only that metaphor serves as a mechanism for understanding experience, but also that "our experiences may be metaphorical in nature" (p. 154). Lakoff and Johnson (2003) argue that although

> metaphor is typically viewed as characteristic of language alone, a matter of words rather than thought or action,...[w]e have found, on the contrary, that metaphor is pervasive in everyday life, not just in language but in thought and action. Our ordinary conceptual system, in terms of which we both think and act, is fundamentally metaphorical in nature. (p. 3)

Therefore, our metaphorical understandings and concepts will likely differ from culture to culture, and are often reflective of and/or constitutive of differences in points of view or experience. Thus, drawing upon this particular conceptual understanding of metaphor, the question is not one of establishing the truth or authenticity of any singular metaphor as being inherently more objective or truthful than another; rather, the question becomes one of understanding the relationships between experience and metaphor, and perhaps more crucially, of understanding the ways in which particular metaphors become dominant and the ways in which those dominant metaphors inform human action.

Lakoff and Johnson reject objectivist conceptualizations of "truth," and argue, rather, that "truth is always relative to a conceptual system" and that "any human conceptual system is mostly metaphorical in nature" (p. 185). They do not argue that there are no truths; rather, that "truth is relative to our conceptual system, which is grounded in...our experiences" (p. 193). Hearkening back to Sontag's (1990) framing of metaphor as primarily a literary, rhetorical, or poetic device, her call for "liberation" from metaphor appears to be grounded in an objectivist ontology that presumes a more "truthful" way of regarding illness, somehow outside of not only metaphoric language, but metaphoric conceptualization as well. I argue here that there is no inherently most "truthful" way of regarding autism; rather, that the linguistic metaphors we draw upon in autism discourse are both reflective and constitutive of "metaphorical concept[s]" (Lakoff & Johnson, 2003, p. 6) that are derived within the contexts of, and for the purpose of making sense of, our own experiences.

Because the very concepts and constructs that we draw upon in organizing and understanding our world and experiences are often metaphoric in nature, it becomes imperative that we critically examine these cultural metaphors, because, as Lakoff and Johnson (2003) remind us, a particular metaphor "not only gives us a very specific way of thinking about [a metaphorical concept] but also a way of acting toward it" (p. 34), and that, in an objectivist culture, "the people who get to impose their metaphors on the culture get to define what we consider to be true—absolutely and objectively true" (p. 160). Indeed it is this latter characteristic of metaphor—that it not only reflects and constitutes thought but that it also informs action—that makes an exploration of the metaphors surrounding particular disability identities so crucial. The import in studying metaphor is particularly critical when a range of competing metaphoric representations of particular constructs are grounded in differences in values, experiences, and perspectives, and when those differences fuel contention and conflict around issues of "appropriate" action, as in the case of educational decision-making for disabled students—in this case, for students labeled autistic. Lakoff and Johnson further note that in order to "explain such conflicts among values (and their metaphors), we must find the different priorities given to these values and metaphors by the subculture that uses them" (p. 23). Thus, I argue that a critical exploration of cultural metaphors around autism, particularly an exploration of the different "subcultures" that use differing metaphors may ultimately illuminate the complex dynamics of power/knowledge production (Foucault, 1980) in autism discourse and the ways in which those dynamics inform educational policy and practice.

To that end, in addition to Lakoff and Johnson's conceptual framework on metaphor, I draw upon several of Foucault's theoretical tools in this analysis, including the Foucauldian notions of "regimes of truth" and "subjugated knowledges" (1980). Foucault's conceptualization of "truth" is commensurate with Lakoff and Johnson's, in that both reject positivist, objectivist accounts of truth as ultimately being beside the point. Lakoff and Johnson assert that "what is at issue is not the truth or falsity of a metaphor but the perceptions and inferences that follow from it and the actions that are sanctioned by it" (p. 158). Similarly, in explicating what he refers to as "'political economy' of truth" (1980, p. 131), Foucault asserts:

> There is a battle "for truth," or at least "around truth"—it being understood once again that by truth I ...mean... "the ensemble of rules according to which the true and the false are separated and specific effects of power attached to the true," it being understood also that it's not a matter of a battle "on behalf" of the truth, but of a battle about the status of truth and the economic and political role it plays.... "Truth" is linked in a circular relation with systems of power which produce and sustain it, and to effects of power which it induces and which extend it. A "regime" of truth. (pp. 132–133)

Thus, in exploring the "systems of power" which "produce and sustain" truth, the Foucauldian task becomes one asking, "what are the rules according to which metaphor operates to establish what is true?" and "what are the economic and political effects of power attached to the true?"

In considering why certain metaphoric statements have emerged in the current historic and material circumstances, what correlations may exist with other metaphoric statements, and what forms of metaphoric statements might be excluded in autism discourse, I consider the metaphors of two different "subcultures" (Lakoff & Johnson, 2003, p. 23): both those metaphors that emerge as culturally "dominant" or as constitutive of a "regime of truth" through the exercise of power in concert with particular metaphoric conceptualizations, as well as those aspects of metaphoric discourse that Foucault (1980) describes as the "reemergence" or "insurrection" of "subjugated" or "disqualified" knowledges (pp. 81–82). In the spirit of analyzing the political economy of truth, then, I seek to excavate herein not only those metaphors that are most visible in dominant contemporary autism discourse, but perhaps more importantly, those that are subjugated, disqualified, obscured, or excluded, and to thereby explore the complex processes by which power circulates in the discursive field of metaphor in the "battle for truth."

AUTISM AS CULTURAL POLITICS: DISEASE OR NEURODIVERSITY?

In recent years, the label of "autism" has captured the public imagination in the United States in ways similar to our previous "obsessions" with cancer or AIDS (Sontag, 1990), or polio or Attention Deficit Hyperactivity Disorder (ADHD). Nadesan (2005) writes that autism has "captured the public imagination as a disorder that is regarded simultaneously as both threatening and fascinating" (p. 3). I would argue that autism is currently a popular cultural obsession, and that the ways in which autism is currently being (re)invented and indeed constituted metaphorically beg critical examination and scrutiny. Since 2005, autism has received a good deal of popular press, including featured cover stories in popular news magazines such as *Newsweek*, *Time*, and *People*, broadcast television and radio documentaries on a variety of networks including CNN, NBC, NPR, CBS, and coverage in major newspapers such as the *New York Times* and the *Los Angeles Times*. Indeed, it would be difficult to find a popular media venue that has not carried an autism-related story in the past several years (nor indeed in the past several months or even weeks), and much of this media coverage has served to reproduce and proliferate the metaphors that I analyze in this chapter.

Cultural Purposes of Autism Metaphor

It seems to me that chief among the variety of possible cultural purposes that autism metaphors have historically served are (a) to create a commonsensical narrative congruence between common understandings of "autism" and contemporary notions about its etiology(ies) or cause(s), and, intimately related to this purpose though perhaps more importantly, (b) to create a commonsensical narrative congruence between common understandings of autism and contemporary notions about appropriate responses to or interventions for autism. Indeed, Lakoff and Johnson (2003) note:

> Metaphors may create realities for us, especially social realities. A metaphor may thus be a guide for future action. Such actions will, of course, fit the metaphor. This will, in turn, reinforce the power of the metaphor to make experience coherent. In this sense metaphors can be self-fulfilling prophecies. (p. 156)

That is, as Lakoff and Johnson (2003) point out, "we define our reality in terms of metaphors and proceed to act on the basis of those metaphors" (p. 158). Thus, metaphors can be particularly powerful when they cease to be recognized or regarded as metaphoric, and when they come to be regarded as an accurate representation of an objective reality.

However, Fairclough (1989/2001) points out that "experience can be represented in terms of any number of metaphors," and that "different metaphors have different ideological attachments" (p. 100). He argues further that "different metaphors imply different ways of dealing with things" (p. 100). Lakoff and Johnson (2003) would seem to concur with Fairclough's assessment of metaphor, reminding us that any given metaphor is "not the only [one] available" (p. 159), and that "people in power get to impose their metaphors" (p. 159). Thus, it becomes significant to ask, "What are the ideological attachments underlying competing representational metaphors in autism discourse?" and perhaps more importantly, "what implications do these different metaphoric representations have for ways of acting in relation to autism and autistic people?"

In this chapter I briefly explore two competing metaphoric representations of autism (autism as *disease* and autism as *neurodiversity*), both of which serve to create a commonsensical narrative congruence between understandings of autism and contemporary notions about its etiology(ies) or cause(s), but each of which departs radically from the other in terms of creating commonsensical narrative congruence between understandings of autism and notions about appropriate responses to or interventions for autism.[1] The dominant metaphoric narrative about autism operating in many ways as a Foucauldian "regime of truth" can perhaps best described as "autism as *disease*," while a significant countercultural narrative or "insurrection of subjugated knowledges" (Foucault, 1980, p. 81) about autism can best be described as "autism as neuro*diversity*." In addition to the culturally dominant metaphor of autism as disease, I explore also in this chapter two additional metaphors that have recently emerged within the dominant disease discourse surrounding autism: (a) autism as abductor and (b) autism as epidemic.

Despite the fact that autism continues to be a largely behaviorally defined syndrome that is typically applied to a wide diversity of behavioral manifestations that undoubtedly represent an even wider diversity of etiologies, it can be argued that since the late 1960s, autism has come to be broadly regarded as a biologically-based syndrome. Indeed, Nadesan (2005) remarks, "The medical and scientific literatures represent autism as a biological facticity that must be explained using the positivist methods and assumptions of the natural sciences" (p. 2). And yet, as Nadesan further explicates:

> Although there is a biological aspect to this condition named autism, the social factors involved in its identification, representation, interpretation, remediation, and performance are the most important factors in the determination of what it means to be autistic, for individuals, for families and for society. (p. 2)

The present analysis focuses on the social and cultural facets of popular metaphoric representations of autism, which, perhaps even more significantly than any biological materialities associated with the label of autism, determine what autism *means* culturally, and which therefore impact the ways in which individuals may experience autistic identities.

The currently dominant cultural metaphor of autism as *disease* and its most visible countermetaphor of autism as a form of *neurodiversity* both appear to function, at least in part, to establish a conceptual congruence, or what Fairclough (1989/2001) refers to as discursive "cohesion," between cultural representations of autism and the dominant thinking that autism has a biological or neurological material basis, whether that basis be conceptualized as biological difference or deficit (autism as *disease*) or as biological diversity or variety (autism as *neurodiversity*). This particular discursive cohesion may be compared, for example, with early metaphors about autism (such as the child withdrawn into a "shell" or behind a "wall") that appeared to function, at least in part, to establish discursive cohesion between the earliest dominant cultural conceptualization of autism as having an etiology that was psychogenic in nature (Bettelheim, 1967) (cf., Broderick & Ne'eman, 2008; Broderick, 2004) and the cultural representation of autism as such. Thus, it makes sense that current metaphors would be consistent with establishing a narrative cohesion between common contemporary understandings of autism's etiology as being fundamentally biological in nature and cultural representations of autism as such. Despite this common function of both metaphors—autism as disease and autism as neurodiversity—to establish a discursive cohesion between cultural representations of autism and dominant notions of autism as being a principally *biological* phenomenon, the similarity ends there. Indeed the difference between conceptualizing autism as a form of bio*diversity* vs. as a form of biological *disease* or *deficit* is stark. It seems significant, though not at all surprising, to note at the outset that the bulk of the support for metaphorically framing autism within the disease model comes from within the non-autistic (or what people who identify as autistic often call the "neurotypical" or "NT") community, whereas the bulk of the support for metaphorically framing autism within the neurodiversity model comes from within the autistic community.

Autism Speaks: Framing Autism as Disesase

The single most visible and powerful lobbying organization that is currently pushing the disease metaphor in autism discourse is an organization that, ironically, calls itself "Autism Speaks," despite the fact that there has until very recently been no representation of persons who identify as autistic on Autism Speaks's board of directors or in other influential positions within the organization (Autism Speaks very recently announced (March 9, 2010) the appointment of its first autistic representative, Mr. John Elder Robison, to its Scientific Advisory and Scientific Treatment boards, a move that would appear to be in direct response to repeated critique from the autistic community that the organization during its first six years included no such representation.) Indeed, the organization's logo: a single, blue puzzle piece with the words, "Autism Speaks" beneath it, and the tag line, "It's time to listen" beneath that, employs several discursive strategies that may be understood to constitute a particular regime of truth around autism. For example, despite widespread disagreement over the particular nature of autism (apart from a very generalized and vague agreement that autism likely encompasses a biological basis or bases), and in light of the more common nomenclature of "autism spectrum disorders," a phrase that is intended to include a variety of different experiences under the overall umbrella of a "spectrum" of (plural) "disorders," autism is nonetheless represented as a singular subject, and indeed as an anthropomorphized entity. Whatever autism "is" (and the discursive implication here is that it is one thing), it *speaks*—yet another irony given how many people who have an autism label applied to them experience difficulty with verbal expression. The implication is that the organization, Autism Speaks, is either representative of or speaks for or on behalf of the authoritative entity, autism, and that "it's time to listen." The imperative tag, "it's time to listen," implies that the idealized reader/viewer has not been listening up to this point, that the time has come, and that the content of the texts that are endorsed with this logo constitute "that which is to be listened to." Thus, among the "ensemble of rules according to which the true and the false are separated and specific effects of power attached to the true" (Foucault, 1980, p. 132), the logo of Autism Speaks appears to draw upon a rule claiming authorial authority—establishing "Autism" as the speaking subject and source of authority, one which exercises an imperative authorial voice as that which is to be listened to, and by implication, that which is true. This personification of a non-human construct (autism) is an example of what Lakoff & Johnson (2003) refer to as an "ontological metaphor." These authors note that viewing a non-human construct as an entity enables us to "refer to it, quantify it, identify a particular aspect of it, see it as a cause, act with respect to it, and perhaps even believe that we understand it" (p. 26). This metaphoric personification of autism will be addressed in greater depth later in the chapter in my discussion of the metaphoric representation of autism as abductor.

Autism Speaks was founded in February of 2005 by Suzanne and Bob Wright, who are the grandparents of a child with a label of autism. At the time, Bob Wright was chairman of GE and NBC Universal, and in the four years since its inception, Autism Speaks has incorporated (literally, corporate-style) two other highly visible autism advocacy and lobbying organizations within its own—the National Alliance for Autism Research (NAAR) and Cure Autism Now (CAN), creating the world's largest and arguably most influential and powerful autism advocacy organization. Since its inception, Autism Speaks has maintained a steady schedule of media and P.R. events (see http://www.autismspeaks.org/about_us.php for a partial list) aimed at reaching broad audiences of the general public with the self-described goal of "raising awareness" about autism. Indeed, according to its own website, in its first year,

> Autism Speaks created a media blitz on behalf of autism awareness…through regular appearances in a variety of media venues, including *The Apprentice*, *The View*, *Access Hollywood*, *The Don Imus Show*, *The Big Idea with Donny Deutsch*, and more. Our launch in February 2005 coincided with a weeklong series devoted to autism on the NBC News networks, including segments on *The Today Show*, MSNBC, CNBC, and *NBC Nightly News with Brian Williams*. All told, these segments reached 40 million viewers (http://www.autismspeaks.org/about_us.php).

Additional popular media venues pursued by Autism Speaks subsequent to the initial "blitz" include *Newsweek* (a cover story), CNN's *Larry King Live*, *The Martha Stewart Show, Good Morning America, Good Housekeeping, Town & Country*, and countless others. It seems obvious that a comprehensive discursive analysis of this multitude of popular media discursive events is beyond the scope of this chapter;

however, I will closely analyze a few samples of texts that I argue are representtative of Autism Speaks's general usage of metaphor in its advancement of a particular regime of truth around autism, and furthermore, of a very particular regime of truth around notions of "appropriate" responses to autism, including efforts around both intervention and prevention.

According to the organization's Mission Statement, "Autism Speaks aims to bring the autism community together as one strong voice" and to "work together" to "find the missing pieces of the puzzle" (http://www.autismspeaks.org/goals.php). It is worth looking elsewhere to see exactly who is explicitly included and implicitly excluded from Autism Speaks's definition of "the autism community." The use of the definite article, "the," implies that the referent ("autism community") is a singular, unitary community, not one among several. Elsewhere on their website, in a letter posted from co-founders Suzanne and Bob Wright, they note that "Christian's [their grandson's] diagnosis brought us into the autism advocacy community—parents and relatives of children and adults with autism, scientists and researchers, doctors and therapists" (http://www.autismspeaks.org/founders. php). The syntactical construction of a series of noun phrases following a dash grammatically constructs the list as a definition of the noun preceding the dash ("the autism advocacy community"). A couple of glaring omissions in the list of groups defining "the autism advocacy community" are noteworthy—first, there is no mention whatsoever of teachers or educators, the absence of which may be read as metaphoric construction of autism as disease, as something that is therefore more appropriately responded to by doctors, scientists, researchers, and therapists than by educators. A second, and significantly more egregious, omission from this list is people who identify as autistic or who are labeled with autism themselves. Indeed, it is this implicitly excluded perspective from the "autism advocacy community" that has been the most vocal and visible in its opposition to the organization Autism Speaks and to the cultural representation of autism that it produces.

Suzanne Wright, co-founder of Autism Speaks, was interviewed by Larry King on *Larry King Live* on April 1, 2007, with the ostensible intent of raising "awareness" about autism though certainly also the implicit intent of advancing Autism Speak's agenda around intervention and prevention of autism. Below is a portion of the transcribed interview:

> Larry King: How do you explain that this [awareness about autism] isn't taught in medical school?
>
> Suzanne Wright: I don't explain that. I think it's absolutely deplorable...in the age of the autism epidemic. Polio, in the '50s when we were growing up, it was one in 3000 and it was a national health crisis. Everyone rallied around the fact that we needed to find a cause and a cure. Now we have—1 in 10,000 was 10 years ago, 1 in 166 was 3 years ago. The CDC numbers[2] are now 1 in 150, 1 in 94 boys will be diagnosed with autism. This is truly a national and a global epidemic. (04-01-07)

King's question, "How do you explain that this isn't taught in medical school?" squarely positions autism as a medical concern, as a "disease" that is appropriately constructed within the medical model and responded to with medical interventions. However, this point is not argued or asserted, but is rather tucked away into a subordinate clause, the discursive backgrounding of which serves to position the point as taken-for-granted, background information, rather than a point that needs be argued, established, or defended. Similarly, Wright's use of the medical terminology "*diagnosed* with autism" and her direct comparison of autism to poliomyelitis (polio) ("a national health crisis") similarly serve to constitute autism as a disease, to say nothing of her alaramist claims that we are currently "in the age of the autism epidemic" and that "this is truly a national and a global epidemic."

In the wake of Autism Speaks's founding in February of 2005, their agenda has been echoed by a variety of other autism-related organizations nationwide. For example, Wendy Fournier, president of the National Autism Association, asserted that a study released by the CDC summarizing prevalence data on autism diagnoses (see endnote #2) was no surprise to her and other parents of children with autism:

> Autism is a crisis. It's an epidemic. We're renewing our call to the CDC to declare that autism is a national emergency. If it were anything else, juvenile diabetes or blindness, the government would "go nuts" to find the cause (*The New York Times,* Medical News Today, February 11, 2007).

In this example, we see the metaphor of autism as epidemic (as well as its direct comparison to juvenile diabetes) being used to both constitute autism as a disease and to clearly establish a sense of urgency in response to these circumstances ("autism is a crisis," "It's an epidemic," "autism is a national emergency," the government should [by implication] "'go nuts' to find the cause").

Disability rights activists and disability studies scholars have long resisted, critiqued, and subverted the predominance of a medical, rather than a social, model of disability, within which disease metaphors are firmly entrenched. Charlton (1998) notes that an ever-growing number of disabled activists "have developed a consciousness that transforms the notion and concept of disability from a medical condition to a political and social condition" (p. 17). A noteworthy vein of this scholarship has been a collective critique of the ideology of "cure" and the ways in which it is culturally maintained and performed (including cultural rituals such as telethons), and an analysis of its significance in terms of the impact this ideology can have on the material lives of disabled people (Charlton, 1998; Fleischer & Zames, 2001; Garland-Thompson, 2006; Hershey, 1993; Hockenberry, 1995; Longmore, 1997; Russell, 1998). According to Garland-Thompson (2006), "as charity campaigns and telethons repeatedly affirm, cure rather than adjustment or accommodation is the overdetermined cultural response to disability (Longmore, 1997)" (p. 264). Further,

> The ideology of cure directed at disabled people focuses on changing bodies imagined as abnormal and dysfunctional rather than on exclusionary attitudinal, environmental and economic barriers. The emphasis on cure reduces the cultural tolerance for human variation and vulnerability by locating disability in bodies imagined as flawed rather than social systems in need of fixing. (p. 264)

This metaphoric emphasis of non-autistic or NT people on framing autism as a disease in need of curing not only serves to constitute medical intervention as an appropriate and preferred response, but also actually serves to reduce the tolerance for human neurological diversity that is the hallmark of the neurodiversity metaphor explored below.

Autistic Self-Advocates: Framing Autism as Neurodiversity

Smith (1999) asserts that "because the discourse of ability is centered through narratives of professionalized, positivist science, counter-narratives are required to inhabit marginalized territories" (p. 124). Indeed, according to Foucault (1980), there are

> a whole set of knowledges that have been disqualified as inadequate to their task or insufficiently elaborated: naïve knowledges, located low down on the hierarchy, beneath the required level of cognition or scientificity….it is through the re-emergence of these low-ranking knowledges, these unqualified, even directly disqualified knowledges…that criticism performs its work. (p. 82)

If counter-narratives about autism have been "required to inhabit marginalized territories;" "disqualified" as "naïve," "inadequate," or "insufficiently elaborated," they nevertheless constitute a pivotal mechanism through which "criticism performs its work."

There is a strong and ever-growing self-advocacy movement among individuals who identify as autistic. These individuals and a growing number of self-advocacy organizations are successfully challenging the cultural dominance of organizations such as Autism Speaks and the metaphors and cultural meanings that such organizations continually assert and impose upon the public imagination and consciousness as well as upon individuals who have been labeled with autism or who identify as autistic. These organizations include The Autistic Self Advocacy Network (http://www.autisticadvocacy.org), Autism Network International (http://ani.autistics.org), the Autism National Committee (AUTCOM) (http://www.autcom.org), The Autism Acceptance Project (http://www.taaproject.com/), and Aspies for Freedom (http://www.aspiesforfreedom.com), among others. Collectively, the continuing emergence and strengthening of these discourses of self-representation may be regarded as an example of Foucault's "insurrection of subjugated knowledges." One of the most important contributions that this self-advocacy movement has made thus far to the cultural and metaphoric war (if I may indulge in a military metaphor of my own) currently being waged over the meanings of "autism" is the construct of *neurodiversity*.

Ari Ne'eman, President of the Autistic Self-Advocacy Network, discusses the construct of neurodiversity:

> The essence of neurodiversity, or neurological diversity, is the idea that the paradigm of acceptance extended towards racial, religious and other similar differences should apply to neurology as well. A relatively new concept, the

> term originates from conversations held amongst individuals on the autism spectrum in various discussion boards, listservs and other areas of community interaction in the fledgling autistic community. Groups like Autism Network International and, more recently, the Autistic Self Advocacy Network, advocate a new conception of neurological difference along a social rather than a medical paradigm (http://www.autisticadvocacy.org/uploads/smartsection/19_Neurodiversity_and_the_Autistic_Community.doc).

Ne'eman discusses what he calls the "rhetoric of disease versus difference" in relation to autism, squarely positioning autism within social, cultural, and political discourse, and flatly rejecting the dominant discourse's positioning of autism within medical language and practices. The term "neurodiversity" is further explicated on a wikipedia page dedicated to the construct: (http://en.wikipedia.org/wiki/Neurodiversity). There, the construct of neurodiversity is defined as "an idea that asserts that atypical (neurodivergent) neurological development is a normal human difference that is to be tolerated and respected as any other human difference." Additionally, it is noted that "the concept of neurodiversity is embraced by some autistic individuals and people with related conditions, who believe that autism is not a disorder, but a part of their identity, so that curing autistic people would be the same as destroying their original personalities" (retrieved 01-11-08). The very notion of drawing upon a wikipedia page in a scholarly analysis is generally considered anathema—the dynamic, fluid, democratic, non-regulated, and populist nature of wikipedia epitomizes, in many ways, the very "naïve knowledges, located low down on the hierarchy, beneath the required level of cognition or scientificity" to which Foucault (1980, p. 82) refers. Nevertheless, I include it here as a significant venue through which these subjugated knowledges (often those of autistic citizens) emerge (as Ne'eman cites above), and through which cultural critique is performed.

A number of non-autistic allies have embraced the metaphor of neurodiversity as not only helpful or ethical or beneficial, but ultimately, perhaps, as crucial. Blume (1998) asserts that "neurodiversity may be every bit as crucial for the human race as biodiversity is for life in general. Who can say what form of wiring will prove best at any given moment? Cybernetics and computer culture, for example, may favor a somewhat autistic cast of mind" (paragraph 4, retrieved 09/27/08 http://www.theatlantic.com/doc/199809u/neurodiversity). Nevertheless, although there is an ever-increasing number of non-autistic allies that embrace and advocate for understanding autism through the metaphor of neurodiversity, it has been and continues to be autistic citizens who have led the "insurrection" of this particular form of "subjugated" knowledge in the "battle for truth" about autism.

Autistic self-advocate Jim Sinclair wrote a seminal piece in 1993 entitled "Don't mourn for us," based upon a presentation given at the 1993 International Conference on Autism in Toronto (aimed primarily at an audience of parents of children labeled with autism), and subsequently printed in the Autism Network International newsletter, *Our Voice.* Sinclair writes:

> Autism isn't something a person *has*, or a "shell" that a person is trapped inside. There's no normal child hidden behind the autism. Autism is a way of

> being. It is *pervasive*; it colors every experience, every sensation, perception, thought, emotion, and encounter, every aspect of existence. It is not possible to separate the autism from the person—and if it were possible, the person you'd have left would not be the same person you started with….Therefore, when parents say, I wish my child did not have autism, what they're really saying is, I wish the autistic child I have did not exist, and I had a different (non-autistic) child instead….This is what we hear when you mourn over our existence. This is what we hear when you pray for a cure. This is what we know, when you tell us of your fondest hopes and dreams for us: that your greatest wish is that one day we will cease to be, and strangers you can love will move in behind our faces (http://web.syr.edu/~jisincla/dontmourn.htm).

Not only does Sinclair squarely reject several dominant, NT metaphoric representations of autism, he also identifies, fairly early on, the troubling eugenic undertones to the prominent discourse on "curing" autism as disease. Fairclough's assertion that "different metaphors imply different ways of dealing with things" (p. 100) is worth reiterating here: the significance of the discursive battle for truth over whether autism is metaphorically constituted as disease or as neurodiversity lies in the implications the outcome of that battle have in relation to the issue of "dealing with" autism. If autism is metaphorically constituted as a form of neurological diversity, then the implication is that we "deal with" such diversity as we "deal with" other forms of cultural diversity—through educational, political, and economic efforts aimed at increasing understanding, acceptance, and tolerance, as well as through activist, civil-rights-based political efforts to resist both interpersonal and institutionalized manifestations of bias and discrimination against people who identify as autistic. If autism is metaphorically constituted as a disease, then the implication is that we "deal with" this disease as we deal with other diseases—through medical and other therapeutic efforts to "cure" people who currently have this particular illness, as well as genetic and other biomedical forms of research into finding ways to prevent people from "suffering from" this "disease" in future. When one experiences autism not as a disease but as a "way of being" as Sinclair describes, the implications of the disease metaphor for eugenic eradication of future generations of those like oneself are understandably threatening. And while the disease metaphor has been around for some time, two relatively recent related metaphors to emerge within disease discourse only add to the intensity of that perceived threat.

EMERGENT METAPHORS: AUTISM AS ABDUCTOR AND AS EPIDEMIC

In the past several years, concurrent with the ascendancy of Autism Speaks to its current position of cultural and political visibility and power in the autism advocacy community, the metaphors that have emerged as supplementary to the dominant disease metaphor in popular autism discourse have become far more ominous and threatening in nature. I turn now to an exploration of what I argue are two of the most dominant metaphors to emerge in popular cultural discourse around autism in the last several years: (a) autism as *abductor* and (b) autism as *epidemic*. I argue that, taken together, these twin metaphors serve to metaphorically constitute (a) an *enemy* (autism) and (b) a sense of *urgency*. Each of these are necessary elements to successfully constitute autism as a cultural threat significant enough to support particular approaches and postures toward both intervention (e.g., attempts at "recovery" through early intensive behavioral intervention) and prevention (e.g., "curing autism" through identification of genetic markers coupled with selective abortion), approaches that are themselves dominated by a proliferation of militaristic metaphors.

Autism as Abductor

On Autism Speaks's website, there is a quotation on a sidebar that reads, "This disease has taken our children away. It's time to get them back." (http://www.autismspeaks.org/founders.php, retrieved 01/27/08). The quotation is positioned beneath photographs of Suzanne and Bob Wright, on a page designated as the "founders' message." The quote, again, clearly positions autism as a disease, but further positions the subject "this disease," and by implication, "autism," as an active, personified agent, an abductor that has "taken our children." The usage of the first person plural possessive pronoun, "our," coupled with the plural "children" is a discursive device that establishes a shared perspective or common position between the authors (the Wrights) and the ideal viewer(s). Rather than asserting that "this disease has taken our grandchild away," they assert rather that "our children" have been taken away. Since the Wrights do not have more than one child (or grandchild) who experiences autism, the phrase "our children" can refer only to the Wrights' grandchild together with the collective children of the ideal viewer/reader, thus establishing a shared subjectivity between the Wrights and their audience. It also seems clear that the presumed audience is comprised of NT parents and family member of autistic children, rather than being inclusive of autistic citizens. The text also clearly draws upon the metaphor of autism as a personified abductor that has "taken our children away." By logical extension of this metaphor, the most commonsense response is metaphoric (or literal?) retrieval or recovery: "It's time to get them back."

A particularly vivid illustration of the current pervasiveness of this metaphor of abduction is the recent "Ransom Notes" public awareness campaign sponsored by New York University's Child Study Center. Scuttled on December 20th, 2007, fewer than three weeks after its launch in response to intense public outcry, the goals of the campaign, according to Harold S. Koplewicz, M.D., Founder and Director, NYU Child Study Center, ostensibly included "grab[bing] people's attention," "start[ing] a national dialogue," and serving as a "wake up call" to what they have called the "silent public health epidemic" of childhood psychiatric disorders (http://www.aboutourkids.org/about_us/public_awareness). The campaign included advertisements addressing the labels of ADHD, autism, Asperger's syndrome, bulimia, depression, and obsessive-compulsive disorder. Again, autism and its sister label of Asperger syndrome are discursively constructed not only as "disorders," but more specifically as diseases, held forth as examples of a "silent public health epidemic." According to John Osborn, President and CEO of BBDO

New York (the organization that produced the Ransom Notes campaign pro bono, as well as that produced pro bono a series of public service announcements for Autism Speaks's and the Ad Council), "Left untreated, these illnesses can hold children hostage. That's why we've chosen to deliver our message in the form of a ransom note" (http://www.medicalnewstoday.com/articles/90756.php). Each ad is in the form of a ransom note, signed by the disorder with the tag line, "Don't let a psychiatric disorder take your child." The ransom note for autism read: "We have your son. We will make sure he will no longer be able to care for himself or interact socially as long as he lives. This is only the beginning....Autism." The ransom note for Asperger's syndrome read: "We have your son. We are destroying his ability for social interaction and driving him into a life of complete isolation. It's up to you now....Asperger's Syndrome" (http://www.aboutourkids.org).

The usage of the metaphor of autism as abductor begs the question of who is being abducted, stolen, or taken, and from whom. With autism thus constituted as the metaphoric enemy—the alien abductor who has taken "your child," "your son," it seems clear that the intended audience is NT parents. The implicit subtext of this metaphoric constitution is that autism is abducting your [normal] child, your [normal] son, the child you believed or expected yourself to have prior to the labeling of your child as autistic. In addressing parents of autistic children, Sinclair (1993) incisively engages NT parents in a discussion of their "grief over a fantasized normal child":

> Much of the grieving parents do is over the non-occurrence of the expected relationship with an expected normal child. This grief is very real...but it has nothing to do with autism....You didn't lose a child to autism. You lost a child because the child you waited for never came into existence (http://web.syr.edu/%7Ejisincla/dontmourn.htm).

It is the fear of the threat of experiencing this very real grief over the perceived loss of an expected "normal" child that the Ransom Notes campaign and other metaphoric images of autism as abductor so powerfully evoke in non-autistic parents.

Just as Sinclair asserts that the grief many NT parents experience upon having a child labeled autistic is not actually about autism, but rather is grief over the loss of an expected "normal" child, an autistic blogger, in response to NYU's Child Study Center's recent Ransom Notes campaign, asserts that the identity of the metaphoric "abductor" is not autism at all:

> To the person(s) responsible for creating the grossly offensive "Ransom Notes" advertising campaign: Because it's so obvious that you did not consult with any autistic people or other neurological minority groups before trotting out that odious medieval stolen-child changeling nonsense, I'm going to take this opportunity to educate you on the actual views held by many people in the autistic community today.
>
> Many of us do indeed feel as if we're being held for ransom, but you've got the identity of the perpetrators all wrong. To find a clue, you might want to take a good look in a mirror. We—that is, America's autistic citizens and our families—have had our lives hijacked in recent years by a greedy profiteering agenda that has deliberately and viciously stigmatized autistic people as broken,

> less than human, our souls stolen from us, and similar bigoted garbage, all for the purpose of making money by selling therapies. As a result, we now face prejudice and discrimination every day, in all aspects of our lives (http://autisticbfh.blogspot.com/search/label/Ransom%20Notes, retrieved 12-20-07).

Conceptualized within an organizing metaphor of autism as disease, bolstered by the twin metaphors of autism as abductor and as epidemic, there seems to be little narrative or conceptual space for consideration of questions such as prejudice, bigotry, and discrimination; yet this is the very space that autistic citizens and their allies continue to work to carve out through their promotion of the metaphoric conceptualization of autism as neurodiversity, in the ongoing insurrection of subjugated knowledges.

In November of 2006, Alison Tepper Singer noted on an interview broadcast on NPR: "If one in 150 children in this country were being kidnapped, it would be a national crisis, a national emergency, and that's exactly what's happening with our children, they're being stolen away from us" (paraphrase, 11-27-06). This quote illustrates the metaphoric nature of Singer's claim that aims to constitute "autism as abductor," by utilizing what is clearly an analogy—"if one in 150 children in this country were being kidnapped"—although she asserts in the latter portion of her claim that it is actually not an analogy or a metaphor at all—"that's exactly what's happening." This particular statement also illustrates the ways in which the metaphor of autism as abductor serves to constitute both an *enemy* (autism) as well as a strong sense of *urgency* regarding action or response (just as the metaphor of epidemic does, which will be illustrated below). Having thus rhetorically established this "if " ("if one in 150 children in this country were being kidnapped, it would be a national crisis, a national emergency") as a fairly reasonable commonsense assertion, she follows with the claim that "that's exactly what's happening with our children, they're being stolen away from us," with the "therefore" of the metaphoric analogy left implicit for the reader to infer: therefore, since "our children" are also being abducted, this is a national crisis, a national emergency as well. The metaphor of child abduction taps into a powerful enough cultural fear to establish a clear sense of urgency in and of itself; this sense of urgency is heightened by an allusion to the "epidemic" metaphor through the citation of the numbers "one in 150 children in this country." In addition to the constitution of a clear and definable enemy (the disease autism), this sense of urgency is also necessary to rhetorically establish in order to garner widespread cultural and economic support for the war-like interventions (both "treatment" and "prevention") that must be waged against the enemy abductor known as autism.

Autism as Epidemic

Gernsbacher, Dawson and Goldsmith (2005) squarely challenge the predominance and the validity of the metaphor of an autism "epidemic" in their article, "Three reasons not to believe in an autism epidemic":

> If you have learned anything about autism lately from the popular media, you most likely have learned—erroneously—that there is "a mysterious upsurge"

> in the prevalence of autism (*New York Times,* October 20, 20002, Section 4, p. 10), creating a "baffling…outbreak" (CBSnews.com, October 18, 2002), in which new cases are "exploding in number" (*Time*, May 6, 2002, p. 48), and "no one knows why" (*USA Today*, May 17, 2004, p. 8D)….However, no sound scientific evidence indicates that the increase in number of diagnosed cases of autism arises from anything other than intentionally broadened diagnostic criteria, coupled with deliberately greater public awareness and conscientiously improved case finding. (p. 55)

Indeed, a recently published study suggests that "clusters" of autism diagnoses analysed in California are most closely correlated with levels of parental education (with parents with high levels of education being more likely to have a child identified as autistic), as well as with geographic proximity to specialized autism treatment centers, an analysis that does not lend support to the "epidemic" metaphor (Van Meter, Christiansen, Delwiche, Azari, Carpenter, Herz-Picciotto, 2010). Nevertheless, the metaphor of an autism "epidemic" continues to be a dominant trope drawn upon in popular autism discourse. Having positioned autism squarely within a disease model in dominant popular discourse, the metaphor of "epidemic" seems on its face a perfectly reasonable extension of the disease metaphor. If autism is indeed a "disease," and if its prevalence is indeed increasing at the rate that Autism Speaks suggests, then it stands to reason that such phenomena might reasonably be constructed as "epidemic." It may be argued that much of current discourse around autism, most particularly that coming from within the organization Autism Speaks, does not *metaphorically* constitute autism as an epidemic; rather, it flatly asserts as objective fact this particular truth claim. Several quotes already discussed flatly make this assertion. For example, Suzanne Wright refers to "the age of the autism epidemic," and asserts that "this is truly a national and a global epidemic." Wendy Fournier asserts that "Autism is a crisis. It's an epidemic," and Harold Koplewicz asserts that autism and Asperger syndrome, among other labels, constitute a "silent public health epidemic." An additional quote from Singer illustrates this assertion that autism *is* an epidemic, and directly links it with a militaristic posture toward response or intervention:

> Families are demanding answers, we are demanding action. It's time that the federal government recognized that autism is an epidemic. Ten years ago, 1 in 10,000 children were diagnosed, now 1 in 166 children are diagnosed. We need the Congress to declare war on autism." (11-27-06)

This particular interview from which this quote is drawn was aired in the weeks prior to the passage of the Combating Autism Act[3], which Autism Speaks played a particularly visible and vocal role in lobbying for and which President Bush signed into law on December 19, 2006.

This metaphoric constitution of autism as epidemic disease also brings with it a proliferation of militaristic metaphors that are associated with disease discourses. It is these militaristic disease metaphors that Sontag (1990) explored in such vivid detail, and that have recently seeped into common dominant conceptualizations of autism as well:

> Disease is seen as an invasion of alien organisms, to which the body responds by its own military operations, such as the mobilizing of immunological "defenses," and medicine is "aggressive," as in the language of most chemotherapies…. Disease is regularly described as invading the society, and efforts to reduce mortality from a given disease are called a fight, a struggle, a war. (pp. 97–98)

Thus, in extrapolating from Sontag's analysis and applying it to the current one, autism is metaphorically constituted as an invasion by a diseased alien entity, to which parents or society must respond by engagement in militaristic intervention operations. This intervention is conceptualized as "aggressive." Autism is also described as having invaded the society ("a national emergency," a "national and global epidemic," a "global health crisis,") and efforts to reduce occurrences of autism are called a fight, a struggle, a war. A notable difference is that Sontag was talking of diseases that are (or were) generally considered to be lethal (as people are now living with cancer and HIV/AIDS in ways that they did not 20 years ago, and such diseases are now be considered by many to be chronic rather than terminal). Autism, however, is a lifelong neurological makeup that generally does not affect mortality in any way. Yet it is interesting to note that within Autism Speaks's public discourse, autism is rarely associated with or compared to Down syndrome, cerebral palsy, or other lifelong developmental disabilities; rather, it is being compared to illnesses and diseases that have at least some potential to shorten one's life, such as cancer, polio, or juvenile diabetes. In drawing persistently upon these disease metaphors, particularly the comparisons drawn to potentially lethal illnesses, living life as an autistic person is often metaphorically constituted by Autism Speaks as being a fate as bad as, if not worse than, death.

Sontag notes, "Where once it was the physician who aged *bellum contra morbum*, the war against disease, now it's the whole society" (p. 98). She continues:

> Indeed, the transformation of war-making into an occasion for mass ideological mobilization has made the notion of war useful as a metaphor for all sorts of ameliorative campaigns whose goals are cast as the defeat of an "enemy."…. The metaphor implements the way particularly dreaded diseases are envisaged as an alien "other," as enemies are in modern war; and the move from the demonization of the illness to the attribution of fault to the patient is an inevitable one, no matter if patients are thought of as victims….Military metaphors contribute to the stigmatizing of certain illnesses and, by extension, of those who are ill. (pp. 98–99)

If a proliferation of military metaphors can be said to contribute to the cultural stigmatization of autism and, by extension, of autistic citizens, and if, as Sontag noted in her discussion of the metaphoric representation of cancer, "the disease itself is conceived as the enemy on which society wages war" (p. 66), then where does this metaphoric "war" leave autistic individuals? If the ideological mobilization against autism metaphorically constitutes autism as the enemy abductor, the epidemic illness to be defeated, how does the proliferation of such metaphors culturally position autistic individuals?

IMPLICATIONS FOR "INTERVENTION" AND "PREVENTION"

Within this particular metaphoric landscape, policy initiatives such as the Combating Autism Act conceptualize efforts at both intervention and prevention as weapons to be wielded against the enemy, autism. Additionally, the act provides funding for what Autism Speaks describes as "a multi-front war on autism." I will discuss the former "front" (intervention) first; the latter (etiology) will be addressed in the next section of the paper.

First Front: Intervention—on Militaristic Recovery Operations

Spatial metaphors abound in popular cultural discourse around autism, but intervention metaphors now commonly involve the traversing of space in militaristic operations of "rescue," "recovery," or "siege." To be sure, Park (1967) draws upon the metaphor of "storming the walls" of her daughter's autism in her seminal text, *The Siege,* but I argue that this metaphoric notion of a militaristic siege and recovery operation is far more culturally entrenched today than it was four decades ago. Metaphors of intervention often rely upon spatial images of retrieval, repossession, or recovery. I have argued elsewhere (Broderick, 2004, 2009) that what is so fervently sought to be retrieved, repossessed, or recovered is the status of "normalcy" that had previously been accorded the young child with the label of autism prior to his or her labeling. Indeed, I argue that:

> The notion of recovery to normalcy may be perceived to be particularly appealing and quite commonsensical when applied to young children labeled with autism, many of whom may have already enjoyed the status accorded to "normal" children, and for whom the emergence of particular actions and characteristics resulted in the subsequent acquisition of a label of autism and a status of disability, of abnormality. Thus, given that many children are not labeled with autism until they are 2, or 3, or even 4 years of age, the notion of recovery to normalcy in young children in many ways may resonate with the common experience of many parents that their child used to "be normal" and now somehow, suddenly, was not (Broderick, 2004, p. 164).

Because autism is constituted as the enemy abductor, retrieval, repossession, or recovery (ostensibly of the child, but I argue elsewhere [Broderick, 2004, 2009], of the child's previous status of normalcy) becomes the object of militaristic engagement. As Sontag points out in her analysis of the predominance of militaristic metaphors surrounding cancer, "With the patient's [child's] body [self] considered to be under attack ("invasion"), the only treatment is counterattack" (Sontag, 1990, p. 64).

Militaristic metaphors are by no means a new or recent phenomenon in autism discourse, as is illustrated by the use of militaristic metaphors in one parent's autobiographical account of her own two children labeled with autism. Catherine Maurice (1993) in *Let me Hear Your Voice* describes her family's experience in this way:

> My whole family had come through a war. We had been battered and torn, shattered over and over again, rocked and racked by a continuous onslaught of this enemy called autism." (pp. 265–266)

Maurice echoes Park's (1967) metaphor of "the siege," and the ways in which the meaning of that metaphor resonated with her own experience, as well as the ways in which her own experience departed from those meanings. I quote a passage from Maurice's (1993) text at length, as it is an organizing metaphor that is woven throughout her description:

> From the beginning, my idea of a 'siege' meant something more forceful and invasive than the kind of respectful, patient, waiting portrayed in that scene. Nevertheless, it was in Mrs. Park's book that I first found the germinal concept for my part in the battle. As I read on that night, two concepts fairly burst into my consciousness: the notion of Anne-Marie as being 'walled in,' and the idea of assaulting those ramparts...Beseiging Anne-Marie, not so much in the sense of waiting and wooing, beguiling and beckoning, but in the far more violent sense of storming the walls....I did not learn how to wait; I learned how to stalk and hunt, how to overpower....The violence of the imagery—the battering, the bending, the burning, the overthrowing, the final ravishing—was frightening. But no more so to me than was autism....I had felt from the beginning that something was 'taking over' my daughter, and that if she herself could know about and speak about what was happening to her she would cry out for rescue. There was a part of her that was still a lost and frightened baby girl, and if I had to batter her down, bend, break, and ravish her autistic self in order to get to that Anne-Marie spirit, I would do so....She will be dragged, kicking and screaming, into the human condition." (pp. 80–81)

Thus, we see the ways in which Park's notion of a militaristic "siege" resonates with Maurice's experience in that she conceptualized Anne-Marie as being spatially "walled in," but that her notion of siege is a more violent one, conceptualized as a "battle" involving "storming the walls," "stalk[ing]," "hunt[ing]," and "over-power[ing];" "battering," "bending," "burning," "overthrowing," and "ravishing." Indeed, Maurice explains that "it was because I had been charged up by the idea of an assault that I was able to even consider this behavior modification" (p. 89). Thus, this conceptualization of intervention (in this case, early, intensive, behavior modification) as an assault, predicated upon the metaphoric constitution of autism as enemy abductor and bolstered by the sense of urgency that such a threat necessarily embodies was integral to Maurice's decision to pursue this particular avenue of intervention, an avenue that, by implication, she may perhaps not have chosen but for being so "charged up" by the power of the metaphor of her "part in the battle" with the enemy autism.

The early intervention program to which Maurice refers is grounded in what she describes as "behavior modification" or applied behavior analysis (ABA). Singer similarly draws upon militaristic metaphors in her reference to this particular intervention methodology in her NPR interview:

> Early intervention is the best weapon that we have against autism. Studies show that 50% of children who are diagnosed with autism, who are in a good early intervention program before they're three, and who remain in that program for two years, 50% of those children gain enough skills to be able to be mainstreamed for kindergarten (*On Point*, November 26, 2006).

The studies to which Singer refers, and upon which Maurice made decisions to pursue ABA-based intervention programs with her children, are grounded in the operant behaviorist work of O. Ivar Lovaas (1987), work that Lovaas himself elsewhere (1977) describes as "trying to build individuals starting with a Tabula rasa" (p. 1). Early intervention programs grounded in an ABA approach are widely recommended as "scientifically proven" by both advocacy and governmental organizations such as Autism Speaks (http://www.autismspeaks.org/whattodo/what_is_aba.php), the U.S. Surgeon General (http://www.surgeongeneral.gov/library/mental health/chapter3/sec6.html#autism), and New York State's Department of Health (http://www.health.state.ny.us/community/infants_children/early_intervention/autism/ch4_pt2.htm). However, critique of these claims has been made on the basis of whether the available evidence meets criteria for empirical claims of "scientific proof" (Gernsbacher, 2003) of "recovery" (Gresham & MacMillan, 1997), as well as on the basis of whether the claims of "recovery" may be more powerful rhetorically and discursively than empirically and operationally (Broderick, 2004, 2009).

Maurice (1993) describes her initial distaste at the thought of using an ABA approach with her daughter:

> On the face of it, the idea was nothing short of appalling to us....Already, I didn't like behavior modification, and I had yet to go through Anne-Marie's first sessions. Nevertheless, if someone was recovering kids with behavior modification, we had better look into it seriously. (p. 63)

Maurice thus describes the idea of using ABA with her child initially as "nothing short of appalling," and yet, she persisted, "charged up by the idea of an assault" and bolstered by the claim that "someone was recovering kids with behavior modification." Perhaps most disturbing about Maurice's account of the militaristic siege she launched against the enemy autism in an attempt to "recover" her daughter is the contention that "she will be dragged, kicking and screaming, into the human condition" (p. 81). The implicit connotation of this assertion is that a child labeled with autism exists somehow *outside* of the human condition, that the metaphoric cultural space she refers to traversing in order to "recover" her is not merely the distance between "non-autistic" and "autistic," nor even "normal" and "abnormal," but rather may be the space between "human" and "inhuman."

Sontag points out that "the most terrifying illnesses are those perceived not just as lethal but as dehumanizing, literally so" (Sontag, 1990, p. 126). In dominant cultural metaphors, autism is often conceptualized as somehow being outside of, or foreign to, "the human condition." Indeed, the very personhood of individuals who are labeled or who identify as autistic is often called into question. Maurice, for example, writes: "There is something about autism that to me gave meaning to the phrase 'death in life.' Autism is an impossible condition of being there and not being there; a person without a self; a life without a soul" (p. 57). Another parent of a child labeled with autism, Martin Kotler (1994) writes that the symptoms of autism "strip the severely afflicted individual of the very core of what it is to be a person…" (p. 353). He goes on to claim that unless a very particular intervention is implemented (ABA), "these children not only will be excluded from school, but also will be excluded from the essence of human experience" (p. 353).

Smith (1999) points out that "this process of dehumanization, used by dominant cultures toward many minority groupings, allows for acceptance of their persecution (Sibley, 1995)" (p. 123). We thus see this subtext of the denial of autistic persons' humanity in dominant autism discourse on the first "front" of Autism Speaks' "multi-front war on autism"—intervention. It is also a critical subtext in the other "front" of their war on autism: research into etiology and "cure."

Second Front: Prevention—on Eugenic Eradication Operations

Although Autism Speaks does devote a considerable amount of its resources to issues related to "treatment" for children labeled with autism and their families (though very little for autistic adults), it also devotes a considerable amount to efforts to prevent and to cure autism (as disease). Indeed, in a January, 2008 article published in *Parade* magazine, Suzanne Wright, co-founded of Autism Speaks, states "We're now playing catch-up as we try to stem the tide and ultimately eradicate autism for the sake of future generations. If we continue our current trajectory, we'll get there in my lifetime" (http://www.parade.com/articles/editions/2008/edition_01-27-2008/Autism_Changes_Everything, as cited in "Whose Planet Is It Anyway?" weblog, http://autisticbfh.blogspot.com/2008/01/bigotry-on-parade.html). In May of 2005, former March of Dimes Senior Vice President Mark Roithmayr was appointed President of Autism Speaks by the Wrights, and he stated,

> If I have learned anything, it is that with a clear need, desperate urgency and the strength of volunteers and committed supporters, we can change history. The March of Dimes did it with polio and Autism Speaks can do it for autism (http://www.autismspeaks.org/press/roithmayr_appointed.php).

He thus points to the cultural import of establishing a "clear need" and "desperate urgency" in launching a successful cultural campaign aimed at curing or "eradicating" autism. In the press release of Roithmayr's appointment posted on the Autism Speaks website, the organization is characterized as "a not-for-profit, 501(c)3 organization devoted to educating the public about autism, facilitating and funding research, motivating private and governmental resources, and, ultimately to find a cure for autism" (http://www.autismspeaks.org/press/roithmayr_appointed.php). Thus, "ultimately," the goal of Autism Speaks is described alternately as to "cure" or to "eradicate" autism. Just as there are currently relatively few new cases of people contracting the polio virus (though there are certainly many people currently living post-polio), so too, it seems that the future vision of Autism Speaks is a world where very few people will experience autism. Alternately put, in another video that Autism Speaks produced, the video ends with the claim that "Autism Speaks wants a world where autism is a word in the history books" (http://www.youtube.com/watch?v=Xwq3LtPWm5k&feature=user).

Not surprisingly, the adult autistic community has not embraced this future vision of a world where people like themselves will no longer exist. Unlike polio, which—once understood as the infectious viral disease that it is—was addressed through a relatively straightforward vaccination campaign, there will be no such straightforward means of preventing autism, a much more complex and varied constellation of neurological conditions that are known to involve both genetic and environmental factors in their manifestation. It seems much more likely that the genetic research that is fueled by the fundraising efforts of Autism Speaks as well as federal funds appropriated through the Combating Autism Act will be used to produce a prenatal test to detect one or more genetic markers associated with autism. Since there are no known prenatal medical complications associated with autism that could potentially be addressed through either in-utero or immediately postnatal care (as is the case, for example, with Down syndrome, when associated heart defects must sometimes be surgically corrected in order to ensure the infant's survival), the only possible use for a prenatal test would be to identify in-utero fetuses that are likely to develop into autistic children in order that parents may selectively abort if they so choose.[4] The adult autistic community and many of their allies reads this agenda as a thinly (if at all) veiled eugenic agenda aimed at eradicating others like themselves from the future of the human genome (see, for example, "Autistics Speak about Autism Speaks," http://www.youtube.com/watch?v= qwdlof0kctw&NR=1).

As I wrote an early draft of this manuscript, a news story of disturbingly ironic relevance popped onto my screen: In Pekin, Illinois, Karen McCarron was being tried for the 2006 murder of her 3-year-old daughter, Katie, who had a label of autism. Prosecutors describe McCarron as being "obsessed with curing her daughter's autism" and assert that McCarron had both "suggested institutionalizing her and putting her up for adoption before she suffocated with her a plastic bag and then went out for ice cream" (Sampier, 01-08-08). Paul McCarron, Katie's father, testified (January 8, 2008) that Katie's autism was "not severe," but that his wife was "very consumed with Katie's condition," believing that "autism was something to be fixed" (Sampier, 01-08-08).

Coincidentally, McCarron smothered her daughter just days after the public release of Autism Speaks' film, *Autism Every Day*, in which Autism Speaks executive vice president Alison Tepper Singer is quoted as saying, "I remember that was a scary moment for me when I realized I had sat in the car for about 15 minutes and actually contemplated putting Jody [her autistic daughter] in the car and driving off the George Washington Bridge." To be fair, Singer makes this remark in the context of criticizing inadequate educational options for her daughter, and describes this horrific possibility as being "preferable" to having to place her daughter in what she considers to be grossly inadequate public school classrooms. Nevertheless, in the film, Singer contemplates killing her own child within earshot of her autistic daughter, Jody, but ultimately dismisses this act primarily because of her responsibilities to her other, non-autistic daughter, Lauren.

Apart from coincidence of timing, to my knowledge, these two matricidal examples—one merely contemplated, one horrifyingly and irrevocably carried out— have no direct relationship to one another. Yet, they are not unrelated as cultural phenomena. As Reynolds (2006) points out in his discussion of Karen McCarron's trial and the media's coverage of it:

> As has happened in other cases where children with disabilities were killed by their parents, many news articles and weblogs commenting on Katie's death have emphasized that raising a child with autism brings with it unique challenges that can be difficult for parents to deal with. Some have suggested that McCarron may have been overly stressed because she did not have the supports she needed to deal with her daughter's autism (paragraph 8).

Indeed, this is a common theme to emerge when children with disabilities are killed by their parents, and of course ensuring that families have adequate supports to meet their family members' needs is absolutely crucial. Nevertheless, there is a danger in focusing in media reports and broader public discourse on families' lack of pragmatic, social, and cultural supports. In Katie McCarron's case, for example, Katie had been living for nearly two years with her father and paternal grandparents in North Carolina, and had been with her mother in Illinois for only ten days prior to being murdered by her mother. Katie's paternal grandfather, Michael McCarron asserts that:

> This was not about autism. This was not about a lack of support....I am positively revolted when I read quotes that would imply any degree of understanding or hint at condoning the taking of my granddaughter's life. (Reynolds, 2006, paragraphs 1 and 10; http://www.inclusiondaily.com/archives/06/05/24/052406ilmccarron.htm).

Referring to media coverage of and by disability advocacy groups when horrific events such as these occur, the disability rights organization Not Dead Yet suggests:

> These groups might also ask, what will be accomplished by saying that murderous feelings toward disabled children are common? Will this increase the acceptance of children with disabilities in our schools and neighborhoods? Or will the public conclude that kids *that* horrible are better locked up? What is the end result when parents say feelings of murder or desperation are "the norm?" How will it affect the small percentage of parents struggling with the despair? Will it give them strength or help them leap off the abyss? (http://www.notdeadyet.org/docs/callforrestraintPR0606.html, paragraph #16,

June 22, 2006, Disability Advocates Call for Restraint and Responsibility in Murder Coverage).

Baker (2002), Campbell (2000) and others offer useful discussions on what are often referred to as the "new" eugenics. Whereas the "old" eugenics of the early 20th century consisted of systematic, government-sponsored efforts at both extermination of culturally devalued people (e.g., in the Nazi T4 program) and reproductive control through forced sterilizations, Campbell (2000), as cited in Baker (2002) suggests that the new eugenics are

> more covert and insidious and that what they have in common is that at root they concern ontological matters, "largely unexamined and unspoken preconceptions about who should and should not inherit the world." (p. 674)

In his discussion of the technologies and aims of the Human Genome Project, Wilson (2006) suggests that

> Unfortunately, many of the new technologies associated with genomics—such as genetic tests and genetic screening—raise the specter of an old social agenda that is still very much a part of medical science's professional and public discourse: eugenics. (p. 71)

Similarly, Garland-Thompson (2006) notes that

> Genetic testing and applications of the Human Genome Project as the key to expunging disability are often critiqued as enactments of eugenic ideology, what the feminist biologist Evelyn Fox Keller calls a "eugenics of normalcy" (1992). (p. 265)

These disability studies scholars writing about issues of genetic testing, selective abortion, and disability are careful not to conflate the technologies, science, and industry of genetic testing with an inherently eugenic agenda. Rather, as Garland-Thompson points out, "The practices of genetic and prenatal testing...become *potentially* eugenic practices within the context of a culture deeply intolerant of disability" (p. 265; emphasis added). Indeed, the discussion of this new eugenics is a nuanced one, and one that is not tied exclusively to genetic or reproductive technologies. Baker (2002) suggests that

> As Campbell notes, the new eugenics, if not effective in preventing certain kinds of conceptions, turns its attention to "perfecting technologies" that are at base indebted to a perhaps well-intended but nonetheless controlling logic of ableism that hopes to turn everyone into the one kind of being at least at some level. (p. 675)

Within this framework of the new eugenics and its variety of normalizing technologies, we can understand the ways in which both of Autism Speaks's "fronts" on the war on autism (attempts at "recovery" through early intensive behavioral intervention technologies and the pursuit of genetic markers for autism to be used as potential screening instruments for selective abortion) have the potential to become eugenic practices within the context of a cultural constitution of autism as an epidemic disease, as an abductor, and as an enemy deserving of "eradication."

Wilson (2006) reminds us the study of the human genome has enormous potential for advancing our understanding of human diversity, and indeed, "to remember that genetics *is* variation, and that variation is not only healthy but essential for the survival of a species" (p. 73). He further posits that

> If genomics, both the science and the industry, were to more effectively emphasize the normality of variation, the fact that human variation is a continuous spectrum, then surely there would be a better understanding and acceptance of disability. In turn, this acceptance could result in a commitment to accommodation rather than erasure. (p. 73)

Despite this potential, he argues that thus far the Human Genome Project has "pathologized disability and created the genetic Other" (p. 73). As the subjugated metaphor of autism as neurodiversity illustrates, there is tremendous value in seeking to understand human neurodiversity in order better to understand, accommodate for, and cease to discriminate on the basis of that diversity. The cultural struggle between metaphorically representing autism as a disease to be eradicated or as a form of neurodiversity to be better understood, valued, and celebrated is currently being waged through cultural narrative and counter-narrative, through metaphor and counter-metaphor, images and counter-images—on television, in newspapers, on YouTube, through weblogs and listservs, through popular cultural "media blitzes." And the stakes are high.

CONCLUSION

In critically examining autism as cultural politics, then, we can understand metaphor to be a powerful cultural Foucauldian practice that "systematically form[s] the objects of which [it] speak[s]" (Foucault, 1972, p. 48). If this be the case, then the metaphoric cultural constitution of autism as an invading enemy abductor, as an epidemic disease to be eradicated may very well systematically form a not-too-distant future wherein autistic people may be as uncommon as people with Down syndrome are becoming (92% of pregnancies where the fetus is identified with Down syndrome are currently aborted [Karr, 2008]). Indeed, one autistic blogger cogently points to the eugenic potential of not just genetic attempts at cure or eradication, but also of ostensibly educational or therapeutic interventions that are grounded in a relentless pursuit of normalcy when he asks: "How many autists have already been robbed of their personhood through therapies designed to teach *normalcy*. It is genocide already" (http://journalofanautist.blogspot.com/2009_05_01_archive.html; emphasis in original).

With the personified metaphorical construct of autism positioned as the clear enemy within this conceptual system, there is neither explicit engagement with nor acknowledgement of the existence of autistic citizens as active agents. As Lakoff and Johnson note, "In allowing us to focus on one aspect of a concept… a metaphorical concept can keep us from focusing on other aspects of the concept that are inconsistent with that metaphor" (p. 10). The notion of autistic citizens who do not wish to be cured or recovered, who do not conceptualize themselves as having been abducted, who do not consider themselves to be ill or diseased, and who do not wish to see potential future others like themselves eradicated from the human genome are inconsistent with the dominant cultural metaphorical conceptualizations of autism analyzed within this chapter.

Hearkening back to Baynton (1997) and Sinclair (1993), it seems clear that the current discursive regime of truth and its dominant metaphors surrounding autism (disease, enemy, abductor, epidemic) are not generally grounded in the experiences of autistic individuals. Rather, they are grounded in the experiences of non-autistic individuals, reflecting the needs, values, and standards of "normate" (Thomson, 1997, p. 8) culture, and promulgated by non-autistic people who are in positions of considerable power to make decisions about the lives of autistic citizens, and indeed about the very existence of future potential autistic citizens. It also seems evident that among their many acts of discursive and political insurrection and resistance to being constitued as abducted or diseased individuals in need of recovery or cure, autistic self-advocates have provided a powerful metaphoric and discursive tool—the countermetaphor of autism as neurodiversity—that implies and demands that substantially different courses of action be taken. Indeed, Lakoff and Johnson (2003) posit that "new metaphors" (p. 157) have the power to create new meanings and therefore to "define a new reality" (p. 211). The issue is not which metaphoric conceptualization represents the "truth" about autism. It is, rather, about exploring and exposing the ways in which particular metaphoric conceptualizations of autism exert cultural and political power—of representation and decision-making—in the political economy of truth. It is about understanding the ways in which particular ableist cultural narratives about normalcy/abnormalcy become successfully culturally naturalized as "the truth" about autism, thus obscuring the fundamentally ideological nature of the relationship between metaphor and action. And, since culturally dominant metaphors are not the only metaphors available, the question then becomes what is the potential for newly emergent metaphors—such as autism as neurodiversity—to perform the work not only of cultural critique, but also of transformative political imagining? And perhaps the metaphoric constitution of autism as a form of neurological diversity that has inherent value may yet constitute a future wherein discrimination against autistic citizens is mitigated, their educational needs are met, and wherein the relentless pursuit of the "eugenics of normalcy" (Keller, 1992) do not preclude their continued participation in and contributions to life on this planet.

NOTES

1. For a more thorough consideration of the metaphoric representations of autism as disease vs. autism within neurodiversity, please see Broderick and Ne'eman, 2008.
2. On February 8, 2007, the Centers for Disease Control & Prevention (CDC) issued a press release reporting on findings from "the first and largest summary of prevalence data from multiple U.S. communities participating in an autism spectrum disorder (ASD) surveillance project. The results showed an average of 6.7 children out of 1,000 had an ASD in the six communities assessed in

2000, and an average of 6.6 children out of 1,000 having an ASD in the 14 communities included in the 2002 study….The average finding of 6.6 and 6.7 per 1,000 eight-year-olds translates to approximately one in 150 children in these communities. This is consistent with the upper end of prevalence estimates from previously published ….The CDC studies provide information on the occurrence of ASDs in fourteen communities in the United States…. 'Our estimates are becoming better and more consistent, though we can't yet tell if there is a true increase in ASDs or if the changes are the result of our better studies,' said CDC Director Dr. Julie Gerberding….'It's important to note that these studies don't provide a national estimate, but that they do confirm that ASDs in the areas surveyed are more common in these communities studied than previously thought,' said Yeargin-Allsopp" (http://www.cdc.gov/media/pressrel/2007/r070208.htm). It is these prevalence numbers in fourteen U.S. states that have been widely cited as the basis for the claim that autism prevalence is increasing at "epidemic" proportions. For a cogent critique of the claim that autism constitutes an "epidemic," please see Gernsbacher, Dawson, & Goldsmith (2005), *Three reasons not to believe in an autism epidemic.*

3 The Combating Autism Act of 2006, P.L. 109-416, was introduced in the Senate by Senators Rick Santorum (R-PA) and Christopher Dodd (D-CT) and unanimously passed the upper chamber in August of 2006. The act authorized and provided funding for: the Centers for Disease Control to conduct epidemiological surveillance of the prevalence of autism spectrum disorders, the establishment of an Interagency Autism Coordinating Committee to coordinate all efforts concerning autism within the Department of Health and Human Services, public informational and educational efforts at screening and early identification of autism spectrum disorders, the provision of "evidence-based" interventions for autism spectrum disorders, and research into the etiology of autism spectrum disorders (a key revision to the initial Senate bill that was made in the House and approved in the Senate before being signed into law was the elimination of funding for research into environmental causes of autism spectrum disorders).

4 This is not to oversimplify and imply that prenatal tests for Down syndrome do not have eugenic implications of their own. Although there are certainly many cases in which prenatal tests for Down syndrome are used for planning and providing either prenatal or immediately postnatal medical intervention to ensure the health of the infant, these tests are perhaps more frequently used to inform parents' decisions surrounding selective abortion of fetuses that are likely to develop into babies with Down syndrome.

REFERENCES

Baynton, D. (1997). A silent exile on this earth: The metaphoric construction of deafness in the nineteenth century. In L. J. Davis (Ed.), *The disability studies reader* (pp. 128–150). New York and London: Routledge.

Bettelheim, B. (1967). *The empty fortress: Infantile autism and the birth of the self.* New York: The Free Press.

Biklen, D. (1998). Foreward. In C. Kliewer (Ed.), *Schooling children with Down syndrome.* New York: Teachers College Press.

Biklen, D. (1999). The metaphor of mental retardation: Rethinking ability and disability. In H. Bersani, Jr. (Ed.), *Responding to the challenge: Current trends and international issues in developmental disabilities: Essays in honor of Gunnar Dybwad.* Cambridge, MA: Brookline Books.

Biklen, D., & Kliewer, C. (2006). Constructing competence: Autism, voice and the 'disordered' body. *International Journal of Inclusive Education, 10*(2–3), 169–188.

Bogdan, R., & Taylor, S. (1976). The judged, not the judges: An insider's view of mental Retardation. *American Psychologist, 31*(1), 47–52.

Bogdan, R., & Taylor, S. (1994). *The social meaning of mental retardation: Two life stories.* New York: Teachers College Press.

Borthwick, C., & Crossley, R. (1999). Language and retardation. *Psycoloquy, 10*(38). Retrieved from http://cogprints.ecs.soton.ac.uk/cgi/psyc/newpsy?10.038

Broderick, A., & Ne'eman, A. (2008). Autism and metaphor: Narrative and counternarrative. *International Journal of Inclusive Education, 12*(5–6), 459–476.

Broderick, A. (2009). "Autism," "recovery [to normalcy]," and the politics of hope. *Intellectual and Developmental Disability, 47,* 263–281.

Broderick, A. (2004). *"Recovery," "science," and the politics of hope: A critical discourse analysis of applied behavior analysis for young children labeled with autism.* Ann Arbor, MI: ProQuest.

Charlton, J. (1998). *Nothing about us without us: Disability oppression and empowerment.* Berkeley, CA: University of California Press.

Danforth, S. (2007). Disability as metaphor: Examining the conceptual framing of emotional behavioral disorder in American public education. *Educational Studies, 2*(1), 8–27.

Danforth, S., & Gabel, S. (2006a). Introduction. In S. Danforth & S. Gabel (Eds.), *Vital questions facing disability studies in education.* New York: Peter Lang.

Danforth, S., & Gabel, S. (Eds.). (2006b). *Vital questions facing disability studies in education.* New York: Peter Lang.

Danforth, S., & Kim, T. (2008). Tracing the metaphors of ADHD: A preliminary analysis with implications for inclusive education. *International Journal of Inclusive Education, 12*(1), 49–64.

Danforth, S., & Naraian, K. (2007). The machine metaphor in autism research. *Journal of Developmental and Physical Disabilities, 19,* 273–290.

Erevelles, N. (2005). Rewriting critical pedagogy from the periphery: Materiality, disability and the politics of schooling. In S. Gabel (Ed.), *Disability studies in education: Readings in theory and method.* New York: Peter Lang.

Fleischer, D. Z., & Zames, F. (2001). *The disability rights movement: From charity to confrontation.* Philadelphia: Temple University Press.

Foucault, M. (1972). *The archaeology of knowledge and the discourse on language.* New York: Pantheon Books.

Foucault, M. (1980). *Power/knowledge: Selected interviews & other writings 1972–1977.* New York: Pantheon Books.

Gabel, S. (2002). Some conceptual problems with critical pedagogy. *Curriculum Inquiry, 32*(2), 177–201.

Gabel, S. (2005a). Introduction: Disability studies in education. In S. Gabel (Ed.), *Disability studies in education: Readings in theory and method* (pp. 1–20). New York: Peter Lang.

Gabel, S. (Ed.). (2005b). *Disability studies in education: Readings in theory and method.* New York: Peter Lang.

Garland-Thompson, R. (2006). Integrating disability, transforming feminist theory. In L. J. Davis (Ed.), *The disability studies reader* (2nd ed., pp. 257–273). New York & London: Routledge.

Gernsbacher, M. A., Dawson, M., & Goldsmith, H. H. (2005). Three reasons not tobelieve in an autism epidemic. *Current Directions in Psychological Science, 14,* 55–58.

Gernsbacher, M. A. (2003). Is one style of early behavioral treatment for autism "scientifically proven"? *The Journal of Developmental and Learning Disorders, 7,* 19–26.

Gresham, F., & MacMillan, D. (1997). Autistic recovery? An analysis and critique of the empirical evidence on the early intervention project. *Behavioral Disorders, 22,* 185–201.

Hershey, L. (1993). *Crip commentary: From poster child to protester.* Retrieved October 6, 2009, from http://www.cripcommentary.com/frompost.html

Hockenberry, J. (1995). *Moving violations: A memoir: War zones, wheelchairs, and declarations of independence.* New York: Hyperion.

Karr, V. (2008, July 14). Targeting the womb, Down syndrome, disabilities. *Newsday.* Retrieved July 15, 2008, from http://www.newsday.com/news/opinion/ny-opxxx5755254jul07,0,5073863.story

Kotler, M. (1994, Winter). The individuals with disabilities education act: A parent's perspective and proposal for change. *University of Michigan Journal of Law Reform, 27,* 331–397.

Lakoff, G., & Johnson, M. (2003). *Metaphors we live by.* Chicago: The University of Chicago Press.

Longmore, P. (1997). Conspicuous contribution and American cultural dilemmas: Telethon rituals of cleansing and renewal. In D. Mitchell & S. Snyder (Eds.), *The body and physical difference: Discourses of disability* (pp. 134–158). Ann Arbor, MI: University of Michigan Press.

Lovaas, O. I. (1977). *The autistic child: Language development through behavior modification*. New York: Irvington Publishers, Inc.

Lovaas, O. I. (1987). Behavioral treatment and normal educational and intellectual functioning in young autistic children. *Journal of Consulting and Clinical Psychology, 55*, 3–9.

Maurice, C. (1993). *Let me hear your voice*. New York: Knopf.

Park, C. (1967). *The siege: The first eight years of an autistic child*. Boston: Little, Brown, & Company.

Rogers, R. (2003). *A critical discourse analysis of family literacy practices: Power in and out of print*. Mahwah, NJ: Lawrence Erlbaum Associates, Publishers.

Russell, M. (1998). *Beyond ramps: Disability at the end of the social contract*. Monroe, ME: Common Courage Press.

Sinclair, J. (1993). Don't mourn for us. *Our voice, 1*(3). Retrieved from http://web.syr.edu/~jisincla/dontmourn.htm

Smith, P. (1999). Drawing new maps: A radical cartography of developmental disabilities. *Review of Educational Research, 69*(2), 117–144.

Sontag, S. (1990). *Illness as metaphor and AIDS and its metaphors*. New York: Anchor Books.

Taylor, S. (2006). Foreword: Before it had a name: Exploring the historical roots of disability studies in education. In S. Danforth & S. Gabel (Eds.), *Vital questions facing disability studies in education*. New York: Peter Lang.

Thomson, R. G. (1997). *Extraordinary bodies: Figuring physical disability in American culture and literature*. New York: Columbia University Press.

Van Meter, K., Christiansen, L., Delwiche, L., Azari, R., Carpenter, T., & Hertz-Picciotto, I. (2010). Geographic distribution of autism in California: A retrospective birth cohort analysis. *Autism Research, 3*, 1–11.

Ware, L. (in press). Disability studies in education. In S. Tozer, B. Gallegos, & A. Henry (Eds.), *The handbook of research in the social foundations of education*. New York & London: Routledge.

Alicia A. Broderick
Department of Curriculum and Teaching
Teachers College
Columbia University

CAMERON MCCARTHY AND JENNIFER LOGUE

11. RE-READING CLASS, RE-READING CULTURAL STUDIES, RE-READING TRADITION

Neo-Marxist Nostalgia and the Remorselessly Vanishing Pasts

INTRODUCTION

This chapter addresses the turbulent relationship that British cultural studies scholars have with the concepts of "class" and "tradition" and the problematic status of these key terms within the cultural studies literature. We maintain, in part, that these concepts have been deployed within a center-periphery thesis and a field-bound ethnographic framework by cultural studies scholars pursuing a sub-cultural studies approach. Within this framework, "Britishness" has been the silent organizing principle defining metropolitan working class traditions and forms of cultural resistance. British cultural studies proponents have therefore pursued the study of class and culture as a localized, nation-bound set of interests. This has placed cultural studies in tension with postcolonial subjectivities often reduced, as they have been in the classic works of Paul Willis's *Learning to Labor* (1981) and Dick Hebdige's *Subculture: The Meaning of Style* (1979), to the metonymic "Pakis" and "Jamaicans." We write against the grain of the textual production of the working class within cultural studies scholarship insisting that recent films—such as *The Full Monty*, *Billy Eliot*, and *Bend It Like Beckham* and the literary works of George Orwell, George Lamming, and Kazuo Ishiguro—offer a more complex story of class identities in the age of globalization and transnationalism.

In what follows, then, we address these concerns ultimately pointing to the specter of globalization and the way it challenges the relevance and insightfulness of the post-war cultural Marxism of British cultural studies. First, we grapple theoretically with the serviceable tradition that cultural studies draws on to authenticate and center the metropolitan working class in the discussion of class relations, understood transhistorically and universally. We point to the incommensurability of this approach with the contextual reality of present-day post-industrial society and the profoundly limiting framework of nationalism that undergirds the British cultural studies subcultural approach to class. We argue further that this ethnocentric approach to class in British cultural studies scholarship cuts at right angles to the postcolonial subjectivities and the presence of the third world in the metropolitan working class. Second, we go on to call sharp attention to the nation-bound language and claims that attend the discussion of the working class specifically in the writings of the great post-war cultural Marxists such as E.P. Thompson,

Z. Leonardo (ed.), Handbook of Cultural Politics and Education, 269–288.

Raymond Williams and Paul Willis among others. Third, we examine examples culled from popular film culture to show the complexity of the characterization of the working class that is found in contemporary film and paradoxically absent in the sociological writing of cultural studies. Fourth, complementing this we draw as well on the literature of George Orwell, particularly his essay "Shooting an Elephant" (1946/1981). In this essay, Orwell offers a complex portrayal of a British working class police officer operating on secondment overseas in the then colony of Burma. We conclude this chapter, by drawing the outlines of the new global context that has precipitated a crisis of language in the neo-Marxist scholarly efforts to grasp the central dynamics of contemporary societies. The latter has led to a depreciation of the value and insightfulness of neo-Marxist analysis in our time. Old metaphors associated with class, economy, state ("production," "reproduction," "resistance," "the labor/capital contradiction") are now all worn down by the transformations of the past decades in which the saturation of economic and political practices in aesthetic mediations has proceeded full scale (Naomi Klein, 2001). Let us first now consider the problem of class and tradition as they are conjoined in cultural studies.

THE PROBLEM OF CLASS, THE PROBLEM OF TRADITION

> Say Cockney fire shooter. We bus' gun
> Cockney say tea leaf. We just say sticks man
> You know dem have a wedge while we have corn
> Say Cockney "Be my first son' we just say Gwaan!
>
> – Paul Gilroy, 1991, There Aint No Black in the Union Jack, p. 196

> the problematic of a word or concept consists of the theoretical or ideological framework within which that word or concept can be used to establish, determine and discuss a particular range of issues and a particular kind of problem
>
> – Althusser and Balibar, 1968 quoted in Hebdige, *Subculture*, p. 142

Could a cockney translation of cultural Marxism, its overall perceptual, conceptual and linguistic apparatus, provide insight into the basis on which to imagine and build networks of affiliation across race, class, gender, and national divides? What does a conversation between aspects of contemporary popular culture and scholarly discourses of cultural Marxism reveal? And why is it important to ask?

Illuminating the way discourses of resistance function to reinforce aspects of the very power structures they aim and claim to subvert, we subject the analytic apparatus of cultural Marxism to scrutiny. Reading it contrapuntally (Logue, 2005) through the lenses of cinematic and literary representation (restoring an absently present cockney translation?), we begin to see how the units of analysis in the discourse of cultural/historical materialist revolution are incapable of encapsulating the dynamics of power at work in past and present social and global relations. Here, we juxtapose analysis of the nostalgic and unified nationalist structure of feeling with which the neo-Marxist discourse in postwar Britain is silently aligned to the problematization of tradition we see in cinematic and literary representation. This provides an opportunity to (re)examine the conceptual tensions and categorical contradictions existent within this discourse of resistance, the terms of which, as commonly deployed, seem to undermine the possibility of adequately diagnosing the dynamics of power and resistance it portends.

The tendency to at once universalize and pathologize particularity in a manner disavowed, allows terms such as "tradition," "culture," "class," "power," "privilege," etc. to be deployed as though they were not each of them riddled with complexity, contradiction, and antagonistic genealogical formation, an age old strategy in the struggle for domination. The persistent assignment of particularism and atavism to the vast wastes of the third world begins with Karl Marx himself as well as Max Weber and Emile Durkheim in their particular staged-model of historical evolution of human societies and it continues in contemporary thinking in the attribution of the same scarlet letter to the new social movements and the rejection of identity politics in the writings of Marxist scholars such as Tod Gitlin (Gitlin, 1995). This chapter bucks this trend, restoring a corrective valence to the whole enterprise of the analysis of culture. We read all of this against the troubling of tradition and the past in recent films on the working class subject such as *Billy Eliot* (2000) and *The Full Monty* (1997) as well as George Orwell's discourse on tradition, power, and privilege in his essay, "Shooting An Elephant" (1946/1981). Here, in the latter, the ear-holed working class subject now operates on colonial secondment overseas. In reading back and forth between Birmingham and Burma a new light is shed on recombinant particularism (*There Ain't No Black in the Union Jack!*) that the analytic framework of cultural Marxism seems to have foreclosed. For to understand British cultural studies is in part to understand that Mathew Arnold's project (the uses of culture in the preservation of a unitary British national ethos) still survives in the hearts and minds of men and women at home, and even overseas in the empire, as C. L. R. James (1983) argues in *Beyond a Boundary*.[1]

Examining the status of tradition and the past within cultural Marxism as a way of clearing a path to the future, looking particularly at the work of historical recuperation within Marxist cultural humanism and its tendencies towards the universalization of the particular, a sharp light of attention is focused on British Cultural Studies, its anxiety of influence, and its graven desire for plenitude and fullness of understanding of the socially and materially constructed demarcations of the modern world. One is reminded here of the definition of culture and cultural studies advanced by John Fiske in his essay "British Cultural Studies and Television." "Cultural studies," argues Fiske (1987), "is concerned with the generation and circulation of meanings in industrial societies (*the study of non-industrial societies may require a different theoretical base* ...)" (p. 254). Here, Fiske effectively tightens the arc of reference of modern cultural analysis around the metropole, keeping the "non-industrial" periphery at bay within the cabalistic frame of otherness to the emergent discipline of cultural studies. Cultural Studies' search for the vanishing point, the origins of consciousness and general mythologization and valorization of the industrial working class subject is nestled within a peculiar narrative and play of national endowment, affiliation, and ethnic and localist distinctiveness in its founding arguments and concerns. Of course, similar arguments could be made about the nationalist canalization of tradition and the localist focus of the urban sociological ethnographies coming out of the Chicago School inspired by Robert Park and his students, right down to Howard Becker and the deviance research that influenced cultural studies proponents' path breaking ethnographies as Michael Burawoy has argued (see Burawoy et al., 2003).

This valorization of the traditions of the industrial working class has had several consequences (beyond the mistaking of spitballs for revolution) not always adequately accessed or diagnosed to date—one being the disavowal of particularism no different in structure and tone than what could be found in the patterned variables and structural functionalism over all in the work of mainstream social scientists such as Talcott Parsons. Of course, an integral feature of the reverence for working class traditions is the methodological overlay of field-bound ethnographic rules and the visual culture documentary impulses that flow from Bronislaw Malinowski, Evans-Pritchard, Radcliffe Brown, and Margaret Meade and monumentalist classical anthropology into the critical sciences in education and elsewhere, paralleling the rise of visual culture as a whole in silent and sound film, television and radio broadcasting and the like. As an aside, it is to be remembered that in the 1920s and 30s it was naturalistic ethnographic research, not quantitative survey analysis, which was the dominant research paradigm in the social sciences. The dominance of survey and market research would come later when Paul Lazersfeld crossed the open seas of the Atlantic from Austria and joined Robert Merton at Columbia University in New York. But that is a matter for another time.

Interrogating the foundational assumptions and technical terms deployed in the discourses of cultural Marxism, we foreground the epistemological, ethical, and political implications of not investigating what it is these conceptual tools enable us to open up and what it is they foreclose. Does the concept of "class," for example, as deployed within cultural studies research properly capture the contradictions experienced by category members in their everyday, lived existence and their class trajectories as they intersect with the new social subjects of the modern world—the diasporic "Pakis" and "West Indians" of British urban ethnographic lore (carriers of class histories of a different order)? How are the class affiliation and performative practices of Willis's "earholes" to be understood within this paradigm particularly when these putative class members no longer seek to align themselves with the traditions that theorists of the working class describe? Is the working class concept equipped to theorize the collective formation of agents with shared interests as members of interpretive communities comprised of individuals that may or may not share the same relation to the means of production? Should it be? What follows is a critical conversation between foundational texts of cultural Marxism and forms of popular culture to illuminate some of these complexities captured on the big screen and in the ill-fated peregrinations of the working class/lower middle class subject in modern literature (our example, here, George Orwell's tale of an "uneducated" colonial police officer's fateful encounter with the "native" agro-proletariat in the Burmese context as British imperial rule there waits to exhale). An effort at (re)historicizing the "tradition" of cultural Marxism, uncovering its inherent ethnocentricism, provides the framework for a brief discourse analysis of the deployment of terms like class, power and privilege held together by notions of culture and tradition that are problematically monolingual and monotoned. Reading these discourses, texts and conceptual tools contrapuntally through the lenses of cinematic and literary representation magnifies the need to reconfigure language, perception, and desire so that the conversation and trans-national hybridity that is culture can take place and be grappled with collectively.

DEMYSTIFYING THE DESMYSTIFIERS

A central task of this chapter then is to demystify the demystifiers on the problem of tradition and particularism which the classical sociologists had assured us would diminish with the advance of capitalism. The tendency to shunt particularism off to the periphery is therefore consistent with this core form of thinking. The ethnographic impulse that underlies cultural Marxism fuses action and interpretation, experience and text, worlding the world from the metropolitan center into its visible hierarchies of class and culture. Standing at the center of this panopticon, the whole social field spreads out before the Marxist observer like a vast unscrolling map. This cartographer of the modern world, measures and weighs its social distinctions with the finality of a puritan and with the fervor of what Rey Chow calls "the protestant ethnic" (Chow, 2002; see also McLaren, Leonardo, and Allen, 2000). In the cultural Marxist's elective epiphany, the third world subject would virtually perish (*There Ain't No Black in the Union Jack*). But in this disavowal, particularism returned like a plague of innocence. Read on its own terms as a quest for scientificity, cultural Marxism, divines class from the entrails of the social present and past, and ethnicity disappears. Read against the grain as a reluctant form of autobiography, the root book of cultural Marxism reveals its protagonist dressed in his solipsistic bright suit of ethnic privilege. And here, by this strategy, ethnic particularism appears. It is this deep-bodied ethnocentrism, paradoxically attached to the generalizations and trans-historical statements about the industrial working class and human societies associated with the theorizing of critical social scientists that Horace Miner satirizes in his classic essay "Body Ritual among the Nacirema." (Nacirema spelled backwards, of course, is "American"). Here, Miner talks about the mouth rites of the Nacirema, in the process exposing the classic norms underlying the cultural description that constituted the leitmotif of culturalist scholars writing about others:

> The daily body ritual performed by everyone includes a mouth rite. Despite the fact that these people are so punctilious about the care of the mouth, this rite involves a practice which strikes the uninitiated stranger as revolting. It was reported to me that the ritual consists of inserting a small bundle of hog hairs into the mouth, along with certain magical powders, and then moving the bundle in a highly formalized series of gestures (Miner, 1956, p. 503).

The everyday practice of brushing the teeth is elevated to the realm of magic. The magician, the social observer and his besotted humanism, are defamiliarized here. And, the anthropological gaze of the West upon the third world subject is turned back on power for an evanescent moment full of illumination.

When we look also at the writings and founding motives of cultural studies, we find a similar hidden subject within the text that attaches itself to the working class and hides its own anxieties and its professional updraft. When we look at the work of Richard Hoggart, or Raymond Williams or E.P. Thompson, or later Paul Willis and Dick Hebdige, we find an ethnographic Marxism alloyed to a visceral nationalism, an ethnic particularism and wish fulfillment that it denies. How else can we read the intellectual history of Williams' *Culture and Society, 1780–1950* (1966) but as a formidable and unrelenting recuperation of the Leavisian moral sensibility and purpose of British cultural form–the dream of the whole way of life as the encoding and decoding of national ethos in the British industrial novel and literary works? Burke, Cobbett, Southey, Owen, Bentham, Coleridge, Carlyle, Gaskell, Disraeli, Dickens, Arnold, Ruskin, Richards, Leavis, Orwell!!! If ever there was an assertion of national canon, a court of appeal, the breaking out of particular cultural sensibility linked to national distinctiveness, this was one. How else is one to read Richard Hoggart's *The Uses of Literacy* (1958) with its characteristic mourning of the lost of the English working class way of life—its rampant nostalgia for a translucent past then in imminent dissolution? How else are we to read the brilliant E.P. Thompson, who at the end of *The Making of the English Working Class* (1980) makes the disclaimer that he was not competent to speak for any other working class than the English... not even the Scots or the Welsh? How else are we to read Paul Willis and his lads of Hammertown Boys who reduce the postcolonial other to the metonymic "Pakis" and "Jamaicans"? This great cauterizing reflex, this severe backward glance, was born in fact in the context of a general crisis of the relevance or irrelevance (depending on your ideological persuasion) of Western Marxism as the Soviets marched into Hungary in the 1950s and Later Czechoslovakia in the 1960s (Dworkin, 1997). In this rude awakening from methodological slumber, British Marxist historians would disconnect from the work of international socialism, the CP, and found its own distinctive theories of the origin of the British working class in the revival of working class radical traditions (Dworkin, 1997; Hall, 1980). This working class construct, for the subcultural theorists of resistance at Brimingham, was defined around a militancy of style, distinctive accoutrements and dress, argot and the like. This characteristically muscular construct, as Angela McRobbie (1997) would note, folded the working class into a singular, homogenous structure, powerful against its class adversaries, its semiotic chora set against the "ear holes" and contemptuous and disdainful of the periphery. The power within this framework almost operated like a blunt instrument that was applied onto the working classes and applied, in turn, like the clubbed foot of an elephant by the working class against its ethnic rivals and late comers from the third world; Sisyphus pushing against his enemies, all costermongers pushing rotten apples as V.S. Naipaul would say of the donned dwellers of Oxbridge.

In its radical ethnocentrism, cultural Marxism closed off the white working class from its racially minoritized other orientalizing the latter whether they were from Asia or the Caribbean as metonymic attachments—the Pakis or the Jamaicans. A deadly consequence of this is that the working class subject and the nature of power were not presented in a sufficiently complex or nuanced way. Indeed, it would be left to the filmic culture and the literary culture to present more complicated views of class power and class subjects. Films such as *Educating Rita* (1983), *The Full Monty* (1997), *Billy Eliot* (2000), *Sammy and Rosy Get Laid* (1987), and *My Beautiful Laundrette* (1985) exemplify some of this complexity. While in the literary world, Wilson Harris's *Carnival* (1985), Samuel Selvon's *The Lonely Londoners* (1956), Kazuo Ishiguro's *The Remains of the Day* (1989), George Lamming's *The Emigrants* (1954/1994) and *Water with Berries* (1971), V.S. Naipaul's *The Micmic Men* (1967) and *Half A Life* (2001) seem to do a better job at grappling with dynamics of power than the scholarly discourses we have been discussing. But before we turn to the filmic and literary culture for insight, let us try and spell out a little more thoroughly the nature of the conceptual tensions that stem from this radical ethnocentrism.

CONCEPTUAL CALAMITY AND LEXICAL LAPSE: WHO FILLS IN THE GAPS?

The lack of unity and fluidity found within different lived realities within nations and around the globe are not/can not be contained in the concepts we have with which to articulate them—concepts such as "the working class," which has been the animating and organizing category deployed in much contemporary "neo-Marxist" analysis. Crucial aspects of what it means to be a socio/discursively constructed subject differentially positioned in a nebulous network of power relations are overlooked when definitions of culture, class, and power involve a nationalist monologue at the expense of inter-cultural dialogue and exchange. Language, here, is of primary importance, for not only does it serve to articulate and delimit a set of criteria for establishing whether or not one belongs to a given tradition, or rather, where they belong in relation to it, but language often seems to reinforce the very social structures it is invoked to subvert.

Historicizing the concept of class, for example, reveals not only that common contemporary usage of the term too often fails to adequately absorb and embrace crucial distinctions and complex variations found within "it." But it is also the case that "class" is then disembedded from its proclaimed tradition thereby eliding paradoxical implications of forms of resistance achieved by revolutionary discourses past and present. How, for example, is the Marxian distinction between *Klasse en sich (class in itself)* and *Klasse fuer sich, (class for itself)* placed within the work of cultural Marxism? Marx theorized *class in itself* to signify those who share a common location with regard to their relations to the means of production and *class for itself* to pertain to members of a group who consciously recognize their shared predicament and common interests, actualizing their needs and desires through networks of communication and resistance by organizing around their shared conflict with the opposing class. The two contending classes here, for contemporary Marxism, included the proletariat, destined to become *class for itself* and the bourgeoise, incapable of formulating class consciousness beyond the pursuit of individual self-interest. What was less spelled out, however, were the dynamics, shifts, and conflicts found within *class in itself.* For when one tries to figure out how factors of race, gender, and sexuality figure into the operationalization of definition of the proletariat/ "working class" *in itself*, one may be inclined to suggest that there were numerous formations and reformations of *class for itself* within the "working class" and that these variations on the theme were of less urgency for Marx (and later neo-Marxists) to articulate. Continuing in this vein, early post-war cultural studies theorists failed to track the dynamic patterns of migration, dislocation, and rearticulation that had begun to feed into the class experience of working class subjects in England and that brought new elements, new potential conscripts, to membership within the industrial working class. They had failed to adequately assess the changing map of spatial relations and the interior realities of British urban life itself as part of a broad scale set of effects brought on by late-capital—effects that were now stalking modern industrial societies. It seems that, here, the seeds of an under-theorized dynamic involving the mis(sed)diagnosis of the impact of networks of global communication, movement and migration of economic and cultural capital and the amplification of representtations and images had been consolidated. What was nurtured instead was an ethnic and nationalist myopia planted firmly in the soil of an agrarian England transcoded onto the urban setting. The nurturing work of much of the historical recuperation of British radical traditions such as that of E.P. Thompson or Raymond Williams always, then, had a backward glance—an eternalist sense of *le temps perdu, los pasos perdidos*. Time and space essentially stood still. And, for instance, Willis (1981) would find in the Hammertown Boys School in *Learning to Labor* that the progeny of the working class grew from seedlings that were planted by their fathers on the shop floor. This backward glance—a nostalgia for the past, a nostalgia perplexed by the present—rendered problematic the entire analytical apparatus of the cultural studies discourse on class and change. In affirming the class essence of the industrial proletariat, this nostalgia has a particular methodological effect concerning class analysis as deployed within cultural studies: a tendency to gloss over contradiction, variation, and multiplicity.

Is this affirmation of traditional essence and the indivisibility of the working class in a sense what Hebdige (1979) accomplished by writing of reggae and punk as seemingly equivalent subcultures in *Subculture: The Meaning of Style*?. Rather than emphasizing these formations and modes of resistance as mutually constitutive, reggae figures in as an expression that culminates in the punks' response. Neither is reggae considered counter cultural or as more than an articulation of style, despite the fact that Hebdige cites its having created its own language, religion, and vision of the future. Are we to understand the white and black factions described herein as manifestations of *class for itself* contained within the "*working class*"? How are the lived realities and cultural achievements of the diaspora/black Britain subsumed by this move? Does it contribute to the idea that tradition and culture can be claimed as the moorings of an ethnically invisible yet distinctive group that remains forever threatened by that which it codes as deviant?

And what happens if we take seriously Michel Foucault's (2002) assertion in *Society Must be Defended* that the concept of class struggle evolved out of (was extracted/de-historicized from) the discourse of race war/race struggle? Foucault's genealogy of the discourse of history reveals that racism is imbricated in revolutionary thought coming from the moment when the discourse of race struggle was being transformed into revolutionary discourse, where the state functions no longer as an instrument that one race uses against another: the state becomes the protector of the integrity, the superiority, and the purity of the race. Foucault reminds us that the concept of class struggle is found first in the discourse of the French historians –in the works of Augustin Thierry, Guizot, John Wade, and others. Thierry is defined as the father of the "class struggle," used to replace the notion of "race struggle." The effort to recode race struggle into class struggle is read as a manifestation of the shift in focus on race as existing whenever one writes the history of two groups that do not have the same language, to the term race becoming pinned to a biological meaning. This shift in race as linguistic difference to race as biological is what will become actual racism. This racism, according to Foucault, takes over and reconverts the form and function of the discourse of history, which was hitherto a discourse on race struggle/race war. Racism is born then of the shift in historical discourse, once reporting on the theme of historical war with its battles, invasions, victories, and defeats, to the recording of history with a new post-evolutionist theme of the struggle for existence by that of a society that is biologically monist, but which is (needs to be) threatened by a certain number of heterogeneous elements it deems not essential to it. Racism, then, at its inception, becomes manifest in the idea that foreigners have infiltrated society, which is to be safeguarded from deviants, who serve to foreground class conflict by being coded as factors that complicate it.

Foreclosing examination of its own origins, disembedding the discourse of class conflict from the discourse of race struggle impairs analysis of the complex organization of hierarchical social relations and resistance to them. Not only does the term class commonly function as though it were a static category with an invisible ethnically particular tradition, but it fails to connote the actual strategies through which social subjects forge collective oppositional identities from the grounded pragmatics of cultural hybridities. Rather than attending to the centrality of sexual orientation, gender, and ethnic affiliation in cultural formations and transformations, in creating networks of communication and association, these categories are too often treated as complications contained within the already established organized relations to the means of production. And while the insights and methodological breakthroughs of cultural Marxism are important, like the emphasis on the popular imaginary, style and other forms of often overlooked resistance, might the struggles and forms of active resistance of what cultural Marxism lauds as the "working class" be better described as strategies developed by those differentially positioned in a complex web of power relations? It seems as though some of these overlooked dynamics of power and resistance are better captured in the very popular culture that cultural Marxism sought to interpret, but while cultural Marxism begins to analyze popular culture, does it really converse with it?

It is both in *The Full Monty* and *Billy Elliot* that we see the working class, the "foot soldiers of modernity" as Willis (2005, p. 461) calls them, metamorphosing in the transitional light of globalization, and the tragic programs of deindustrialization and postfordism that radically transform the labor market and labor process from hard to soft, from materiality to immateriality, from the decaying manufacture of the metropole to the export processing zones overseas in Asia, Latin America and the Caribbean, from hard industry to flexible information, from the working class cast in the center of history to the mass appearance of the proletarianized, tempt working cognitariat (Jencks, 1996; Klein, 2001). Do the terms of the cultural studies working class discourse on resistance traditions capture such complexity? And, how are these complexities of tradition, class, and power addressed in the filmic and literary culture?

LEAPING OUT OF THE LEXICON: CINEMATIC AND LITERARY REPRESENTATION

Billy Eliot's Dad: Ballet????
Billy Eliot: What's wrong with ballet?
Billy Eliot's Dad: What's wrong with BALLET????
Billy Eliot: It is perfectly normal…
Billy Eliot's Dad: Perfectly NORMAL???...For girls, not for lads.
Billy…Lads do football, or boxing or wrestling….Not Frigging Ballet!
Billy Eliot: What lads do?..Wrestling?...I don't see what's wrong with…
Billy Eliot's Dad: Yes you do!!!
Billy Eliot: No, I don't!!!
Billy Eliot's Dad: Yes you bloody do!!!....Who you think I am?
Billy Eliot: What are you trying to say dad……

–From *Billy Eliot*

Contemporary filmic representations offer complex and nuanced accounts of the transforming circumstances of working class lived and commodified existence, revealing fault lines of contradiction and multiplicity. Indeed, the vaunted traditions and the folkways of the past so celebrated in the cultural studies ethnographic portrayal of the proletariat from Hoggart to Willis and Hebdige now hang like proverbial dead weights upon the new working class subject. As Billy (Jamie Bell) of the film *Billy Elliot* (2000) demonstrates, the shop floor and the coal mines belong to a distant past and now exist as straitjackets constraining the desires of youth. Billy, instead, chooses a future in the Royal Ballet, in dance, rather than in the Victorian role of male provider of the coalmines and the deunionizing labor of North Durham, England. And in the end, when his late comer dad comes to his performance, he gets to see his son leap, soar, literally and metaphorically out of the terms of existence that fashioned his life. There is no possibility of return to the past, just the flatlining of traditions and ephemeral revision of hierarchy of cultural distance.

And while Billy's doing ballet demonstrates the falling and collapsing –the ephemerality of—tradition, as well as the ability and desire to leap out of it with passion and grace into creative self transformation, what does our youthful subject have in common with that weary and worn out working class subject featured in the spotlight of much media in the mainstream as well as with the scholarly and political discourses of the radical Left? It portrays the young white (presumably straight?) "working class" male as triumphant; the battle scars, struggles, and defeats of the racially and reproductively marginalized others (always present even in their absence) are subsumed in the spotlight of his victory over those forces that constrain and oppress *him*. We can see here how the construct of the working class constricts those who find themselves in it and casts out those who provide the other side of the boundary line, for it is not just the capitalists that constrain him and over whom he seeks to triumph, there are no many more lines drawn in the sand.

Providing for him an unnamed but central aspect of his co-authored identity, Debbie Wilkinson (Nicola Blackwell), the daughter of his dance teacher, his potential friend (or rather girlfriend) could have had a voice and purpose of life beyond becoming his worshipping subject seeking to possess him for herself at all costs. This one visible female counterpart is vanquished in the representation. Rather than being portrayed as a potential ally with agency, she is pitted against him, so they remain alienated from each other as well as the structures that define and code them. Moreover, the way whiteness functions (for anyone possessing it) as property, providing a special but spectacularly hidden ethnic particularity, cultural capital and symbolic power that translate into material profit, remains unexplored. But the depiction of the "traditional" masculinist working class subject united against an identifiable enemy with similarly positioned others is indeed challenged here, opening the door for analysis of the underground economies of national identity, sexual orientation and ethnic affiliation.

In a somewhat different way, but with similar intensity of the uprooting of the past and tradition, Gurinder Chadha's *Bend it like Beckham* (2002) is a yet another refreshing depiction of the flatlining of tradition, but this time the star of the show is young Asian girl, Jesminder. Jess is the youngest daughter in a rather orthodox Sikh family living in Britain who struggles to participate in family tradition while at the same time, pursuing her dream to "bend it like Beckham." She is a wonderful football (soccer) player who feels that she may be destined to only kick the ball around in parks when no one is looking, but manages to get picked up by Hounslow Harriers women's team, where she is soon to become a star. Until her parents find out and ban her from playing. Her mother scolds her, "Who'd want a girl who plays football all day but can't make *chapattis*?" But her father eventually comes around, preferring his daughter's happiness to the confines of "tradition" and we are presented with wonderful depictions of his daughter's ability to participate fully in seemingly separate traditions laid out side by side.

Again we see the notions of past and the "tradition" of the "working class" challenged when the six unemployed steel workers of *The Full Monty* (1997) form a male striptease act, literally defrocking and leaving nothing but their Poulantzian number plates on their back. The Full Monties of Sheffield literally search for, and then abandon, their iron-mongering past in the decayed industrial rubble of the once thriving, manufacturing city of Sheffield–shelving their overalls and dungarees for the regular beat as male strippers. Going a few years back in filmic representation, we must not forget the telling sentiment: "We're not English, We're Londoners" explains Sammy in *Sammy and Rosie Get Laid* (1987) after numerous depictions of what might have made Hoggart turn in his grave: Sammy is depicted doing several different things simultaneously, eating fast food, watching the news, listening to the radio, flipping through a porno magazine, sipping beer and indulging in a line or two of cocaine while conversing with his father trying to unwind. We have here a depiction of the shifting and fragmented nature of co-authored identities' dis-identification with the ethnic particularity of the "Nation" and its culture even as one seemingly indulges in what it has to offer. An alternative representation of desire, romantic/domestic partnerships is pursued here as well as the building of alliance across class (as conceived or portrayed in its strictly material sense) lines. The confines of compulsory heterosexuality and notions of ethnic purity and distinction are subverted as alliances and love affairs transpire between members who are differentially placed within the categories of race, class, and sexuality. Depictions of interracial and homoerotic desires are indeed a sight for sore eyes in this film and in the depictions of love and desire outside the confines of heteronormativity in *My Beautiful Laundrette*, which is, we can't forget, the space owned by "Pakis" who are white working class Jonny's employers and lovers.

And with an eye to the undertheorized pathologies of imperial domination, we get a glimpse in these films also of the perils of privilege lived out by its perpetrators. Ravi, Sammy's father, whose involvement in British imperialism leads him to commit suicide after he finds that relocating to Britain fails to drive the brutal memories from his mind of how perhaps his own involvement in maintaining his notion of tradition contributed to its demise. Notably, the wealth and riches he received from his affiliation with the colonizers provided not luxury, nor peace of mind, alienating him from his family who cried, but did they mourn his death? The very privilege promised by tradition seems to have driven him to take his own life, not celebrate it. But where is the guilt or the consciousness of the white colonialist? Though not depicted here, the film helps to demonstrate that thinking of class merely in terms of one's relationship to the mode of production, does not to allow for the building of allies outside shared relationships to the means of material production (often more a product of the abstract "in itself" formulations of neo-Marxists scholars). The film thus offers an excellent example of what networks of affiliation and interpretative communities could look like.

Oppositely privileged individuals both alienated from their assigned class/social function are portrayed in film, demonstrating once again the way in which crucial aspects of lived social relations form and reform with those who may or may not share the same relationship to the means of production. As Paulo Freire (1993, include in bib) would be inclined to point out both "oppressor/oppressed" are alienated, dehumanized in relations that prize hierarchy and cultural/traditional superiority as we see in the lives of white working class Rita of *Educating Rita* (1983) and her professor and fleeting mentor (Frank). Both are disillusioned by the promises of becoming offered in dominant ideologies, aspiring to cross over the confines of their class distinctions. We get a sense of the ways in which identity is not a finished product that one is bestowed at birth but a project always in process, an ongoing ever-changing conversation and exchange with Others. Filmic representations such as these depict the world of change driven by consumer durables. The logic of mobile privatization that made Hoggart so uncomfortable has followed a relentless line to the disembedding of the lads (all is left is resentment as Lois Weis so effectively underscores in *The Working Class Without Work* and Michelle Fine and Weis do in *The Unknown City*). And, the incursions and the blowback of Empire, cell phones or mobiles, smart TVs and remotes, the musical language of hip hop or Banghra or dance hall now course through and mark the new constantly disembedding territory of the Hammertown boys, the "lads"— a flower, an orchid, a rhizome blooms viscously in defiance of the grim reaper of urban space.

DEPICTIONS OF TRADITION IN THE LITERARY IMAGINATION

> Then he said, "On my travels I visited an Indian tribe known as the Hopi. I could not understand them, but in their company they had an old European man, Spanish, I think, though he spoke English to us. He said he had been captured by the tribe and now lived as one of them. I offered him passage home but he laughed in my face. I asked if their language had some similarity to Spanish and he laughed again and said, fantastically, that their language has no grammar in the way we recognize it. Most bizarre of all, they have no tenses for past, present and future. They do not sense time in that way. For them, time is one. The old man said it was impossible to learn their language without learning their world. I asked him how long it had taken him and he said that question had no meaning." "After this we continued in silence."
>
> – Jeanette Winterson, 1989, *Sexing the Cherry*

Like cinematic representations, the literary imagination troubles notions of tradition, power and privilege, revealing those dynamics of power and privilege that seem to be foreclosed in scholarly discourses of working class resistance. Orwell, for example, presents the working class ear hole or lower middle class actor "divided to the vein," conflicted to the bone (As Derek Walcott says of his identity struggle in "Far Cry from Africa" [Walcott, 1986, p. 17]). As Uma Kothari (2005) has told us, many of the colonial bureaucrats who went out to the colonies were often of working class or "earholed" backgrounds, sponsored up to the public school, Eton or Harrow or whatever and deployed to the imperial periphery with all their hang ups. Read against this phalanx of national assertion, George Orwell's "Shooting an Elephant" (1946/1981) presents a picture of the lower middle class subject operating overseas, confronting the periphery inhabitant on his native soil, in a different light...more internally divided, more complexly linked to England and Empire, more uncertain about self and role in the elaboration of Britishness. The ethnographic lens now puts the Western actor under the microscope. And, Orwell portrays the everyday negotiation of class and power in the Imperial outpost of Burma through the mediation of modernizing energies and subaltern subversions ("the weapons of the weak"), the anticipation of the waning of Empire and the dubiousness of civilizing missions abroad. The story draws on Orwell's experience as a colonial officer and it concerns the angst of an environmentally conscious, uncertain British police officer who, egged on by a crowd of natives to shoot a rogue elephant, compromises his own agency and his hegemonic subjectivity. The narrator/police officer does not want to shoot the elephant, but he feels compelled by the Burmese agro-proletarians and peasants, before whom he does not wish to appear indecisive or cowardly. The situation and events that Orwell describes underscore the hostility between the administrators of the British Empire and their "native" subjects. But, at another level, it is a deep examination of power. And, it foregrounds what the anthropologist, James Scott (1985), calls the "weapons of the weak." Here the native is not the butt of Paki jokes for the lads or the source of black cultural economy of symbols for the Punks.

Orwell problematizes power and the agency of so called dominant subjects, carefully depicting the colonial situation as one in which the "subjection of the ruled also involves the subjugation of the ruler," showing us how "subjects of colonies controlled rulers as much as they were controlled by them" (Nandy, 1983, p. 39). Plagued by a divided consciousness, unable to act in accordance with his own volition, the protagonist is tormented by guilt, hatred, and fear, and forced to suffer the felt contradictions of his precarious position "in the utter silence that is imposed on every Englishman in the East" (Orwell, 1946/1981, pp. 148–149). Having decided long ago that "imperialism is an evil thing," this colonial official claims to be on the side of the Burmese population but feels "stuck between the hatred of the empire" and "rage against" the villagers who try to make his job so utterly impossible. One part of the official, we are told, views British rule as "an unbreakable tyranny" clamping him down while the other part of him feels that the "greatest joy in the world would be to drive a bayonet into a Buddhist priest's guts" (Orwell, 1946/1981, p. 149). These feelings, we are told, are the "normal by-products of imperialism" (Orwell, 1946/1981, p. 149). And, while it is certain that the torment and suffering of those on the other side of the foul smelling "lock-ups" could never be equivocated, the dominant subject in Orwell's narration is clearly not enjoying the promise his "privilege" provides.

Challenging simplistic notions on the ways in which power operates and who creates and belongs to the "British" tradition, on the most telling event of the day in question we learn that the colonial official is far from being decisive, all-powerful, fully authoritarian, or in control. Rather, he feels like an "absurd puppet," a "hollow posing dummy" unable to do that which he most desires. Having been ordered to find a work elephant that was wreaking havoc about the town in which he was posted, the subject in question follows his orders, armed and ready to serve and protect. He sets off to pursue the rogue elephant but is met with resistance from the villagers who claim neither to have seen the elephant nor even to have heard of its havoc, though clearly standing right there in its midst. This non-co-operation on the part of the "helpless" unarmed Burmese population was yet another "normal" element of daily life one counts on as a colonial official, he adds. After almost giving up on his search, thinking the whole thing to be "a pack of lies," (p. 150) the narrator finally stumbles upon the large beast's most recent victim; the official spots the elephant up ahead in the distance and halts momentarily in his steps and reports, "As soon as I saw the elephant I knew with perfect certainty that I ought not to shoot him" (p. 151). Moreover, he adds, "I did not in the least want to shoot him" (p. 152). He decides that the best thing to do is to keep an eye for a while to ensure the elephant did not turn savage again, and go home for the day. But then he sees the crowd:

> I looked at the sea of yellow faces above the garish clothes–faces all happy and excited over this bit of fun, all certain that the elephant was going to be shot. They were watching me as they would watch a conjurer about to perform a trick. They did not like me, but with the magical rifle in my hands I was momentarily worth watching. And suddenly I realized that I should have to shoot the elephant after all. The people expected it of me and I had got to do it; I could feel their two thousand wills pressing me forward, irresistibly. And it was at this moment, as I stood there with the rifle in my hands, that I first grasped the hollowness, the futility of the white man's dominion in the East. Here was I, the white man with his gun, standing in front of the unarmed native crowd–seemingly the leading actor of the piece; but in reality I was only an absurd puppet pushed to and fro by the will of those yellow faces behind. I perceived in this moment that when the white man turns tyrant *it is his own freedom that he destroys*. He becomes a sort of *hollow, posing dummy*, the *conventionalized figure* of a sahib. For it is the condition of his rule that *he shall spend his life in trying to impress* the "natives," and so in every crisis he has got to do what the "natives" expect of him. *He wears a mask, and his face grows to fit it*. I had got to shoot the elephant (Orwell, 1946/1981, p. 152).

No simple matter for the official in question who repeatedly insists, "I did not want to shoot the elephant," (p. 153) and knowing with perfect certainty what he *ought* to do, he looks again at the crowd and he reflects that there "was only one alternative" (p. 154). He loads the cartridges into the rifle and fires. A slow and agonizing death tortures the struggling gasping elephant while the official is tormented by the sight and the need to keep shooting continuing to fail to put the beautiful gasping living being out of the misery he'd inflicted upon it.

The privileged subject here cast is condemned to conform to a tightly scripted code of conduct with which he does not identify. Three metaphors from the story - the gun, the gaze, and the mask (Louge, 2004) - serve as useful devices with which to depict what Césaire (1972) termed in *Discourse on Colonialism* the "boomerang effects of domination." (The gun symbolizes the moment of usurpation as one in which his imposed superiority coerces him to be what he has forced the other to see him as. Paradoxically, the instrument through which he performs his fantasy of superiority becomes the vehicle through which he suffers his own agentic demise. Unable to affirm his freedom, the dominant subject finds himself sentenced to an unending struggle for status and justification symbolized through the inescapable look of the Other. This gaze represents the instability and precariousness of his usurpation, his becoming a victim of his own unconscious—riddled with guilt, internal fears, and anxieties. In the desperate attempt to shield against this hideous onslaught of unruly emotion and external threat, he projects them onto the other who now constitutes that which he most needs to defend himself against. The mask signifies the onset of his own dehumanization, for in wearing it, he can only reach for the gun. A self-destructive vicious circle is begun. The "posture of absolute domination," (Theweleit, 1987) adopted by Orwell's "hollow, posing dummy" (p. 152) and the processes through which he brings about his own destruction, help to illuminate the way culture is a conversation not what belongs to an ethnically superior tradition. How are these tensions grappled with in neo-Marxist cultural analysis?

What do the imminent deaths of the elephant, Sammy's father (*Sammy and Rosie Get Laid*), and hopes "traditional" parents (*Billy Eliot*) have for their children signify? Could it be that with the death of the subject lies the death of tradition, an imperial tradition on the wane. Billy Elliot's Alzheimers grandma stands in her dream-like silence as the scrambled riddle of past attachments, past associations and feeling? Do our perceptual and linguistic apparatuses allow for the articulation of the complexities of lived social relations and networks of affiliation?

CONCLUSION: TRANSFORMING CONTEXTS, TRANSFORMING TRADITIONS, TRANSFORMING IDENTITIES

> Social science categories are becoming zombie categories, empty terms in the Kantian meaning. Zombie categories are living dead categories, which blind the social sciences to the rapidly changing realities inside the nation-state containers and outside as well.
>
> –Beck, 2002, p. 24

> The real Marxist must not be a good Marxist. His function is to put orthodoxy and codified certainties into crisis. His duty is to break the rules.
>
> –Pier Paolo Pasolini, quoted in Petkovic, 1997

Like the rest of the social sciences, against which it has previously revolted, it now seems fair to say that cultural studies analysis in its treatment of class has been overtaken by contemporary events. It seems the perceptual/conceptual/linguistic apparatus of socio-cultural analysis on the whole is now unable to diagnose the global predicament we are in, seemingly reinforcing the very structures we seek to subvert. Our entire perceptual, conceptual, and linguistic apparatus is in need of overhaul as we come to recognize the rise of networked societies in which traditions, affiliations, "cultures," subcultural or not, are now disembedded from the moorings of the final property of any group (Tomlinson, 2007). There has been a flattening out of cultures and traditions integrated into the global expansion of markets and flexible models of production of capital pursuing new sites of value in ever-increasing alienated contexts. We have reached a stage in this new millennium where the old "conflict" versus "consensus" metaphors, "your traditions versus mine" do not seem to apply. Instead of models based on conflict and resistance, increasingly social groups are being defined by overwhelming patterns of transnational hybridities, new forms of association and affiliation that seem to flash on the surface of life rather than to plunge deeper down into some kind of neo-Marxist substructure. This new model of power could now be called "integration." It does not have a negative pole. It is what Foucault (cite, include in bib) describes as a "productive" not "repressive" model of power. It articulates difference into ever-more extensive systems of association, flatlining the edges of culture into a pastiche of marketable identities, tastes, neuroses and needs processed through the universalization of the enterprise ethic (Klein, 2001). It lays traditions down side by side, layering them in ever new ephemeral patterns and intensities – whole elements and associations given in one place can be now instantaneously found in another. Paul Willis's nationally and geographically inscribed "lads" are now being replaced by Jenny Kelly's Afro-Canadian youth who are patching together their identities from the surfeit of signs and symbols crossing the border in the electronic relays of US television, popular music and cyber culture (Kelly, 2004). Post-apartheid South African youth now assign more value to markers of taste—Levis and Gap jeans, Nikes or Adidas, rap or rave—than ancestry and place in their elaboration of the new criteria of ethnic affiliation (Dolby, 2001). All these developments are turning the old materialism versus idealism debate on its head. It is the frenetic application of forms of existence, forms of life, the dynamic circulation of and strategic deployment of style, the application of social aesthetics that now govern political rationalities and corporate mobilization in our times. The new representational technologies are the new centers of public instruction providing the forum for the work of the imagination of the great masses of the people to order their pasts and present and plot their futures. They are creating instant traditions and nostalgias of the present in which our pasts are dis-embedded and separated out as abstract value into new semiotics systems and techniques of persuasions, new forms of ecumenical clothing that quote Che, Mao, Fidel and Marx, and "revolution" in the banality of commodified life—the publicity of one brand of dish-washing liquid as having "revolutionary" effects is just one good example of the brazen re-articulation of terms and traditions in the brave new world in which we live. Who now owns the terms that define the authentic traditions of radicalism that have informed our works all these years? Who now has final purchase on the terms "resistance," "revolution," "democracy," "participation," and "empowerment?" The massive work of textual production is blooming in a crucible of opposites–socially extended projects producing the cultural citizen in the new international division of labor, in which the state may not be a first or the final referent. Naomi Kein (2001) reminds us ultimately of this radical disembedding. Spadina Avenue, the garment district of Toronto of the 1930s is now in post-industrial limbo and a center of a masquerading consumerist heaven. Its transformation to its new millennial identity of warehouse flowering apartments, Sugar Mounting, retro candy, edible jewelry, and dispensing of London Fog coats owe its genesis to the cruel juxtaposition with Jakarta and the flight of its garment industry to Indonesia. And while there is not much need for overcoats on the equator, "increasingly," according to Klein, "Canadians get through their cold winters not with clothing manufactured by the tenacious seamstresses on Spadina Avenue but by young Asian women working in hot climates ...In 1997, Canada imported $11.7 million of its anoraks and ski jackets from Indonesia..." (Klein, 2000, p. xvi).

The outlines of this new global context has precipitated a crisis of language in neo-Marxist scholarly efforts to grasp the central dynamics of contemporary societies, bearing on the question of "tradition" and the centering term "culture." The latter developments have led to a depreciation of the value and insightfulness of neo-Marxist analysis in our time—old metaphors associated with class, economy, state ("production," "reproduction," "resistance," "the labor/ capital contradiction,") are all worn down by the transformations of the past decades in which the saturation of economic and political practices in aesthetic mediations has proceeded full scale (Klein, 2001). The scale and referent for most all of these organizing terms of analysis had been set and bounded at the nation, defined in the localist anthropological/ethnographic terms of "traditions," "ritual," and "culture" understood on the localizing plain of community, ethnic group, society, etc. The new circumstances associated with post-fordist capital—the new international division of labor, movement and migration and the amplification of images and the work of the imagination of the great masses of the people, the great masses of our times, driven forward by computerization, the internet, popular culture etc—have cut open particular traditions spilling the entrails of so much fluttering fish around the world. New working units for understanding modern life are needed. Maybe not the nation, not the state, not society but the "Globus," the "Global City," ultimately the "Globe," may be the new unit of analysis, the new referent, nodes and networks of affiliation where traditions are attenuated, even as the public sphere and the life world have become more susceptible to re-feudalization, sectarianism, and fundamentalism.

NOTES

[1] See C.L.R. James's account of the dominant influences on him as a British colonial school subject as reflected in his discussion of "The Novel as an Instrument of Reform" (an early essay of his which he published as a high school boy in Trinidad). See as well his allusion to the "Gospel according to St. Mathew [Arnold]" (1983, p. 29) as one of the framing discourses of his intellectual training and orientation.

REFERENCES

Burawoy, M., Blum, J. A., George, S., Gille, Z., Gowan, T., Haney, L., et al. (2000). *Global ethnography: Forces, connections, and imaginations in a postmodern world.* Berkeley, CA: University of California Press.

Cesaire, A. (1972). *Discourse on colonialism* (J. Pinkham, Trans.). New York: Monthly Review Press.

Chow, R. (2002). *The protestant ethnic & the spirit of capitalism.* New York: Columbia University.

Dolby, N. (2001). *Constructing race: Youth, identity, and popular culture in South*. Albany, NY: State University of New York Press.

Dworkin, D. (1997). *Cultural Marxism in postwar Britain*. Durham, NC: Duke University Press.

Fine, M., & Weis, L. (1998). *The unknown city*. Boston: Beacon Press.

Fiske, J. (1987). British cultural studies and television. In R. Allen (Ed.), *Channels of discourse*. Chapel Hill, NC: The University of North Carolina Press.

Foucault, M. (2002). *Society must be defended: Lectures at the College de France, 1975–76*. New York: Picador.

Gitlin, T. (1995). The rise of identity politics: An examination and critique. In M. Berube & C. Nelson (Eds.), *Higher education under fire* (pp. 305–325). New York: Routledge.

Hall, S. (1980). Cultural studies: Two paradigms. In *Media, culture and society* (Vol. 2, pp. 57–72).

Harris, W. (1985). *Carnival*. London: Faber and Faber.

Hebdige, D. (1979). *Subculture: The meaning of style*. London: Methuen.

Hoggart, R. (1958). *The uses of literacy*. Harmondsworth: Penguin Books.

James, C. L. R. (1983). *Beyond a boundary*. New York: Pantheon.

Jencks, C. (1996). *What is post-modernism?* (4th ed.). New York: St. Martin's Press.

Ishiguro, K. (1989). *The remains of the day*. New York: Vintage.

Kelly, J. (2004). *Borrowed identities*. New York: Peter Lang.

Klein, N. (2001). *No Logo* (Required). London: Harper and Collins.

Kothari, U. (2005). Authority and expertise: The professionalisation of international development and the ordering of dissent. *Antipode, 37*(2), 425–446. *Recruitment criteria: Character, Sport and Class*. Unpublished Essay, University of Manchester, Manchester, England.

Lamming, G. (1954/1994). *The emigrants*. Ann Arbor, MI: University of Michigan Press.

Lamming, G. (1971). *Water with berries*. London: Logman.

Logue, J. (2005). Deconstructing privilege: A contrapuntal approach. In K. R. Howe (Ed.), *Philosophy of education* (pp. 371–379). Urbana, IL: Philosophy of Education Society.

Logue, J. (2004). *Agentic ambiguity and the politics of privilege: Recognition versus re-evaluation of privilege in social justice education*. Unpublished MA Thesis, OISE/ University of Toronto.

McRobbie, A. (1997). More! New sexualities in girls and women's magazines. In A. McRobbie (Ed.), *Back to reality?—Social experience and cultural studies* (pp. 190–209). New York: Manchester University Press.

Miner, H. (1956). Body ritual among the Nacirema. In *American Anthropologist* (Vol. 58, pp. 503–507).

Naipaul, V. S. (1967). *The Mimic men*. London: André Deutsch.

Naipaul, V. S. (2001). *Half a life*. New York: Vintage.

Nandy, A (1983). *The intimate enemy: Loss and recovery of self under colonialism*. New York: Oxford University Press.

Petkovic, N. (1997). Re-writing the myth, rereading the life: The universalizing game in Pier Paolo Pasolini's Edipo Re. *American Imago, 54*(1), 39–68.

Selvon, S. (1956). *The lonely Londoners*. London: Logman.

Scott, J. (1985). *Weapons of the weak: Everyday forms of peasant resistance*. New Haven, CT: Yale University Press.

Thompson, E. P. (1980). *The making of the English working class*. Harmondsworth: Penguin Books.

Theweleit, K. (1989). *Male fantasies volume 2: Male bodies: Psychoanalyzing the White terror*. Cambridge, UK: Polity Press.

Tomlinson, J. (2007). Globalization and cultural analysis. In D. Held & A. McGrew (Eds.), *Globalization theory: Approaches and controversies* (pp. 148–168). Cambridge, UK: Polity.

Walcott, D. (1986). Far cry from Africa. In D. Walcott (Ed.), *Collected poems, 1948–1984*. New York: Noonday Press.

Weis, L. (1990). *The working class without work*. New York: Routledge.

Williams, R. (1966). *Culture and society, 1780–1950*. New York: Harper and Row.

Willis, P. (1981). *Learning to labor*. New York: Columbia University Press.

Willis, P. (2005). Foot soldiers of modernity: The dialectics of consumption and the 21st century school. In C. McCarthy, W. Crichlow, G. Dimitriadis, & N. Dolby (Eds.), *Race, identity and representation in education*. New York: Routledge.

Winterson, J. (1989). *Sexing the cherry*. New York: Grove Press.

Cameron McCarthy
Institute of Communications Research
University of Illinois at Urbana-Champaign

Jennifer Logue
Department of Educational Leadership
Southern Illinois University
Edwardsville

GERT BIESTA

12. EDUCATION AFTER THE DEATH OF THE SUBJECT

Levinas and the Pedagogy of Interruption

THE OPENING OF MODERN EDUCATION

'Education' is a complicated concept. On the one hand it is used to *describe* particular practices, most often the practice of schooling; on the other hand it is used to *judge* such practices and their outcomes. However, when we wish to make judgements about educational practices, for example when asking what 'good' or 'effective' education is, we first have to engage with another question, which is the question what education is *for*. A major purpose of education lies in its *qualification function*, that is, in the ways in which education contributes to the acquisition of knowledge, skills and dispositions that are necessary to 'do something – a 'doing' which can range from the very specific (such as training for a particular job or profession) to the much more general (such as liberal education or 'life skills' education). A second function of education has to do with the ways in which, through education, individuals become part of existing socio-cultural, political and moral 'orders.' This is the *socialization function* of education, which is often understood in terms of the acquisition of norms and values and of particular ways of doing and being (which, in a-political understandings of socialization are often depicted as 'normal' ways of doing). Schools and other educational practices partly engage in socialization deliberately, for example, in the form of values education or character education, through attempts to turn young people into 'good citizens,' or when they play a role in professional socialization. But socialization also happens in less visible ways, as has been made clear in the literature on the hidden curriculum and the role of education in the reproduction of social inequality.

Whereas some would argue that education should only focus on qualification, and others defend that education has an important role to play in the socialization of children and young people, there is a third function of education which is generally thought of as being different from qualification and socialization. This function has to do with the ways in which education contributes to the individuation or, as I prefer to call it, the *subjectification* of children and young people. As the aim of this chapter is to problematize prevailing understandings of subjectification in education, my definition at this point is deliberately vague. The *subjectification function* might perhaps best be understood as the opposite of the socialization function. It is precisely *not* about the insertion of 'newcomers' into

Z. Leonardo (ed.), Handbook of Cultural Politics and Education, 289–300.

existing orders, but about ways of being that hint at independence from such orders; ways of being in which the individual is not simply a 'specimen' of a more encompassing order.

The idea of the human subject as an independent, post-traditional 'centre' of being and action can (at least) be traced back to the Enlightenment (see Foucault 1984). Immanuel Kant defined Enlightenment as the release of the human being "from his [sic] self-incurred tutelage" and defined tutelage as the inability of the human being "to make use of his [sic] understanding without the direction from another" (Kant, 1992 [1784], p. 90). This immaturity is self-incurred, according to Kant, "when its cause lies not in lack of reason but in lack of resolution and courage" (ibid., p. 90). This is why he argued that human beings should have the courage to use their own understanding. It was the call for the courage to use one's own understanding which Kant saw as "the motto of Enlightenment" (ibid., p. 90).

Philosophically the most important aspect of Kant's conception of 'rational autonomy' – autonomy based upon reason – was that he did *not* conceive of this as a contingent historical possibility, but saw it instead as something that was an inherent part of human nature. Kant described the "propensity and vocation to free thinking" as the "ultimate destination" of the human being and as the "aim of his existence" (Kant 1982, p. 701; my translation). To block progress in enlightenment would therefore be "a crime against human nature" (Kant, 1992 [1784], p. 93). Interestingly enough, Kant also argued that the "propensity to free thinking" could *only* be brought about through education (see Kant, 1982, p. 710). Kant not only wrote that man "is the only creature that has to be educated" (Kant, 1982, p. 697; my translation); he also argued that the human being can only become human – that is, a rational autonomous being – "through education" ("Der Mensch kann nur Mensch werden durch Erziehung") (ibid., p. 699).

With Kant the rationale for education became founded on the idea "of a certain kind of subject who has the inherent potential to become self-motivated and self-directing," while the task of education became one of bringing about or releasing this potential "so that subjects become fully autonomous and capable of exercising their individual and intentional agency" (Usher & Edwards, 1994, pp. 24–25). Modern education thus became based upon a truth about the nature and ultimate destination of the human being, while the connection between rationality, autonomy and education became the 'Holy Trinity' of modern education. This was not only the case in approaches that followed on more or less directly from the Kantian framework, such as educational approaches based on the work of Piaget or Kohlberg. The idea of rational autonomy also became a cornerstone in critical approaches to education that took further inspiration from Hegel, Marx and Neo-Marxism, such as the work of Freire and Continental and North-American versions of critical pedagogy (see Biesta, 1998, 2005).

What is most significant about Kant's intervention – and this is why we can say that his work marks the transition to modern education – is that he established a link between education and human freedom. Kant made the question of human freedom the central issue for modern education by making a distinction between heteronomous determination and self-determination and by arguing that education ultimately had to do with the latter, not the former. We could say, therefore, that it is only after Kant that it became possible to distinguish between socialization and education and to claim that the proper interest of education is an interest in subjectification. In Kantian terms, this is an interest in bringing about autonomy, emancipation and freedom.

THE CLOSURE OF MODERN EDUCATION

Whereas on the one hand Kant opened up a whole new realm for educational thought and practice – and the idea that education should bring about rational autonomy has remained central to many educational theories and practices up to the present day (see, e.g, Winch, 2005) – he closed off this opening almost before it could start. This happened along two, related lines. It was first of all because Kant only allowed for *one* definition of what it meant to be human. With Kant 'rational autonomy' became the marker of humanity, which left those who were considered to be not or not-yet rational – including children – in a difficult position. It was also because for Kant rational autonomy was *not* understood as a contingent historical possibility, but as a necessity firmly rooted in the nature of the human being so that education thus became founded upon a particular *truth* about the nature and destiny of the human being.

For a long time the closure entailed in the Kantian articulation of the foundations of modern education went unnoticed. This was partly because there was widespread support for the underlying belief that human beings are ultimately rational beings who strive for autonomy. This, after all, was very much the agenda of the French, the German and the Scottish Enlightenment. Yet, and more importantly, the closure in Kant's articulation of the foundations of modern education went also unnoticed because those who were excluded by this definition of the human being – those who were deemed to be irrational or pre-rational (such as children) – lacked a voice to protest against their own exclusion, and they lacked this voice precisely because of the particular definition of what it meant to be human. They were excluded, in other words, before they could even speak or before they could even be acknowledged as capable of speaking (see also Rancière, 1995; Biesta, 2007).

Whereas Kant thought that he had moved education away from tradition and socialisation towards autonomy and freedom, we now live in a world in which the Kantian idea of rational autonomy has been moved back from the 'side' of freedom to the 'side' of tradition. There are not only important philosophical reasons why we should see rational autonomy as a contingent historical achievement rather than as a natural necessity or as the *telos* of history. I wish to claim that many of the most problematic clashes between different cultures and traditions in our time centre precisely on the question whether the modern, Western worldview is itself 'beyond' tradition or whether it should be seen as just one tradition amongst many. If we take the latter view – and I have argued elsewhere that there are compelling reasons for doing so (see particularly Biesta, 2005, 2006a) – it means, educationally speaking, that modern education becomes one more form of socialisation, viz., socialisation into a (or as some would argue: *the*) rational form of life. This does not automatically disqualify this particular form of life, but it does make clear that a choice for such a trajectory is indeed a *choice* – a choice that has to be made by someone – and not something that is self-evident or a natural necessity.

HUMANISM

Philosophically one way of exposing what is problematic about the way in which the modern educational project was inaugurated is by focusing on its humanist foundations. I use 'humanism' here in the philosophical sense of the word, i.e., as the idea that it is possible to know and express the essence or nature of the human being, and also that it is possible to use this knowledge as the foundation for subsequent action – in the sphere of education but also, for example, in the sphere of politics. Humanism, as Emmanuel Levinas has put it, entails "the recognition of an invariable essence named 'Man,' the affirmation of his central place in the economy of the Real and of his value which [engenders] all values" (Levinas, 1990, p. 227). Modern education in its Kantian form is clearly humanistic since it is founded upon a particular *truth* about the nature of the human being.

In 20th century philosophy humanism has basically been challenged for two reasons. On the one hand questions have been raised about the *possibility* of humanism, i.e., about the possibility for human beings to define their own essence and origin. Here we can think of the work of Foucault and Derrida who both have exposed the impossibility of capturing the essence and origin of the human – an impossibility which has become known as the 'death of the subject' (see Foucault, 1970; see also Derrida, 1982). On the other hand questions have been raised about the *desirability* of humanism. This line has particularly been developed by Heidegger and Levinas (see Biesta, 2006 for more detail; see also Derrida, 1982, pp.109–136). For Levinas the "crisis of humanism in our society" began with the "inhuman events of recent history" (Levinas, 1990, p. 279). Yet for Levinas the crisis of humanism is not simply located in these inhumanities as such, but first and foremost in humanism's inability to effectively counter such inhumanities and also in the fact that many of the inhumanities of the 20th century – "[t]he 1914 War, the Russian Revolution refuting itself in Stalinism, fascism, Hitlerism, the 1939–45 War, atomic bombings, genocide and uninterrupted war" (ibid.) – were actually based upon and motivated by particular definitions of what it means to be human. This is why Levinas concludes – with a phrase reminiscent of Heidegger – that "[h]umanism has to be denounced ... because it is not *sufficiently* human" (Levinas, 1981, p. 128; emphasis added).

The problem with humanism, so we might say, is that it posits a *norm* of 'humanness,' a norm of what it means to be human, and in doing so excludes all those who do not live up to or are unable to live up to this norm. At the dawn of the 21st century we know all too well that this is not simply a theoretical possibility. Many of the atrocities that have become the markers of the 20th century – such as the holocaust and the genocides in Cambodia, Rwanda, and Bosnia – were actually based upon a definition of what counts as and, more importantly, of *who* counts as human.

From an educational point of view the problem with humanism is that it specifies a norm of what it means to be human *before* the actual manifestation of 'instances' of humanity. Humanism specifies what the child, student or newcomer *must* become, before giving them an opportunity to show who they are and who they will be. Humanism thus seems to be unable to be open to the possibility that newcomers might radically alter our understandings of what it means to be human. This means that at a fundamental level humanism can indeed only think of education as socialisation because it is unable to grasp the uniqueness of each individual human being. It can only think of each 'newcomer' as an instance of a human essence that has already been specified and is already known in advance.

As long as we see education through the lens of socialization all this is, of course, not really a problem. Yet it is here that Kant remains important because he has left us with the idea that it might be – and in a sense *ought to be* – possible to make a meaningful distinction between education and socialization. If we are committed to this distinction, if we are committed to what Foucault has so aptly referred to as Enlightenment's "undefined work of freedom" (Foucault, 1984, p. 46), then it becomes important to think again about ways in which we might be able to distinguish education from socialisation, both in theory and in practice, and to do so in a way that does not bring us back to humanism.

EMMANUEL LEVINAS: AN ETHICS OF SUBJECTIVITY

One thinker who has made a crucial contribution to this discussion is Emmanuel Levinas. Levinas is uniquely concerned with the question of subjectivity and the process of subjectification. But instead of offering a new theory or truth about the human subject, Levinas provides us with a completely different 'avenue' towards the question of human subjectivity in which an ethical category – responsibility – is seen as "the essential, primary and fundamental structure of subjectivity" (Levinas, 1985, p. 95). This means that Levinas does not provide us with a new theory of subjectivity but with something that I suggest to call an *ethics* of subjectivity (see also Biesta, 2008). Moreover, Levinas is not interested in the human subject as such but first and foremost in the question of the uniqueness of each individual human subject, that is, with the way in which human subjects are precisely *not* specimens of a wider order. However, instead of looking for characteristics that make me different from everyone else – which basically is the question of identity – Levinas looks for characteristics of situations in which it matters that I am I and not someone else. He looks for situations, in other words, in which I cannot be replaced by someone else. What does Levinas's ethics of subjectivity entail?

Levinas has argued that he wishes to challenge the "wisdom of the Western tradition" in which it is assumed that human individuals "are human through consciousness" (Levinas, 1998, p. 190). He wishes to challenge the idea of the subject as a substantial centre of meaning and initiative, as a *cogito* who is first of all concerned with itself and only then, perhaps, if he or she decides to do so, with the other. Levinas argues instead that the subject is engaged in a relationship – or, to be more precise: is constituted by a relationship – that is "older than the ego, prior to principles" (Levinas, 1981, p. 117). This relationship is neither a knowledge relationship nor a wilful act of the ego. It is an *ethical* relationship, a relationship of infinite responsibility for the Other.

Levinas stresses that this responsibility for the Other is not a responsibility that we can choose to take upon us, since this would only be possible if we were an ego or a consciousness *before* we were 'inscribed' in this relationship. The responsibility which is the 'essential, primary and fundamental structure of subjectivity' is a responsibility "that is justified by no prior commitment" (Levinas, 1989, p. 92). It is "an obligation, anachronously prior to any commitment," an 'anteriority' that is "older than the a priori" (ibid., p. 90), "older than the time of consciousness that is accessible to memory" (ibid., p. 96). It is a 'passion' which is absolute, in that it takes hold "without any a priori" (ibid.). As Levinas writes: "The consciousness is affected (...) before forming an image of what is coming to it, affected in spite of itself." (ibid.). One way in which Levinas characterises this relationship is as 'obsession,' and he summarises this idea with the simple though also disturbing phrase that "a subject is a hostage" obsessed with responsibilities "which did not arise in decisions taken by a subject" (ibid., p. 101).

Along these lines Levinas tries to make clear that subjectivity should not be understood as something that is issued from one's own initiative. Subjectivity is not an 'abstract point' or the 'center of a rotation' but a point "already identified from the outside" (see Levinas, 1989, p. 95). As Lingis (1981) puts it: "Subjectivity is opened from the outside, by the contact with alterity" (p. xxi). This is why responsibility should not be understood as something that the subject can take upon itself. Responsibility is not "a simple attribute of subjectivity, as if the latter already existed in itself, before the ethical relationship" (Levinas, 1985, p. 96), since that would only make sense "if one has already supposed that the ego is concerned only with itself" (Levinas, 1989, p. 107). Responsibility is a structure that in no way resembles "the intentional relation which in knowledge attaches us to the object" Levinas, 1985, pp. 96–97). "The tie with the Other is knotted only as responsibility" (ibid., p. 97).

We can clearly see that by identifying responsibility as the 'essential, primary and fundamental structure of subjectivity,' Levinas tries to get away from the idea that the human subject has some kind of essence or nature. Levinas acknowledges that he describes subjectivity in ethical terms, but he hastens to add that "(e)thics, here, does not supplement a preceding existential base" (ibid., p. 95). This is why I suggest that Levinas does not provide us with a new theory of subjectivity – a theory that would claim that the subject is a being endowed with certain moral qualities – but rather with an *ethics* of subjectivity. He urges us to 'approach' (rather than to understand) the question of subjectivity through responsibility, through ethics, bearing in mind that the meaning of ethics itself has changed in the process. Levinas tries to respond to the problems of humanism by not asking *what* the subject is, but by asking how subjectivity is possible, how subjectivity exists. Levinas emphasises, however, that subjectivity-as-responsibility is *not* a different or other way of being, because "being otherwise is still being" (see ibid., p. 100). In order to safeguard the uniqueness of the subject, Levinas thus has to go 'beyond essence,' to a 'mode' that is *otherwise than being* (Levinas, 1981).

Going beyond essence brings one to a place – or better a non-place, a null-site (Levinas, 1981, p. 8) – where the first question is not that of the being of the subject, but where the first question is that of "my *right* to be" (Levinas, 1989, p. 86; emphasis added). Levinas's point is that it is only in the "very crisis of the being of a being" (ibid., p. 85), in the *interruption* of its being, that the uniqueness of the subject first acquires meaning (see Levinas, 1981, p. 13). This interruption constitutes the relationship of responsibility, which is a responsibility of "being-in-question" (ibid., p. 111). It is this being-in-question, this "assignation to answer without evasions" which "assigns the self to be a self" and thus constitutes me as this unique individual. This is why he writes that the 'oneself,' the unique individual, is precisely the "not-being-able-to-slip-away-from an assignation," an assignation that does not aim at any generality, because it is "I and no one else" who is a hostage (Levinas, 1989, p. 116). The oneself, therefore, "does not coincide with the identifying of truth, is not statable in terms of consciousness, discourse and intentionality" (ibid., p. 96). While the oneself can appear in an indirect language, under a proper name, as an entity, it still remains a "no one, clothed with purely borrowed being, which masks its nameless singularity by conferring on it a role" (ibid.) The oneself is a singularity "prior to the distinction between the particular and the universal," and therefore both unsayable and unjustifiable (ibid., p. 97). In this sense Levinas concludes that the oneself is not a being: it is "beyond the normal play of action and passion in which the identity of a being is maintained, in which it *is*" (ibid., p. 104). What constitutes me as this unique individual, as this singular being, is the point in time at which I no longer deny the undeniable responsibility that is waiting for me. It is the point in time when I say 'yes' to the other, keeping in mind that this 'yes' is always already a response to a 'question' and not an act of recognition that would only bring the Other into existence. The Other exists before me.

The uniqueness of the human subject is thus to be understood as something that goes precisely against what Levinas calls the 'ontological condition' of human beings. This is why he writes that to be human means "to live as if one were not a being among beings" (Levinas, 1985, p. 100). Or as Lingis puts it: "(T)he self cannot be conceived as an entity. It has dropped out of being" (Lingis, 1981, p. xxxi). What makes me unique is the fact that my responsibility is not transferable. Levinas summarises it as follows:

> Responsibility is what is incumbent on me exclusively, and what, humanly, I cannot refuse. This charge is a supreme dignity of the unique. I am I in the sole measure that I am responsible, a non-interchangeable I. I can substitute myself for everyone, but no one can substitute himself for me. (ibid., p. 101)

This is also why responsibility is not reciprocal. The Other may well be responsible for me, but Levinas emphasises that this is totally the affair of the Other. The intersubjective relation is a non-symmetrical relationship. "I am responsible for the Other without waiting for reciprocity, were I to die for it." (ibid., p. 98). It is precisely insofar as the relationship between the Other and me is *not* reciprocal that I am subjected to the Other and it is in this way that I am a subject. My subjectivity is my subjection to the other, which means, in the shortest formula, that for Levinas "the subject is subject" (Critchley, 1999, p. 63).

LEARNING FROM LEVINAS

The foregoing shows that Levinas is not offering us a new conception of subjectivity or a new truth about the human subject. Levinas, so we might say, attempts to account for the 'awakening' of the singularity of uniqueness of the human subject. The predicament here, however, is that although Levinas wants to speak about what is 'otherwise than being' – and he is aware that what 'is' otherwise than being "has no verb which would designate the event of its un-rest" (Levinas, 1985, p. 100) – he can only do so in the language of being, in the language of ontology, metaphysics and even, in a sense, the language of humanism.

One way to come to terms with this predicament is with the help of Levinas's own distinction between the saying (*dire*, literally "to-say") and the said (*dit*) (Levinas, 1981, pp. 5–7, 37–38). Levinas emphasises that the saying always precedes the said; that the said always comes after the event of saying. Yet, the saying can only be thematized and articulated, can only become manifest through the said. This is why he writes:

> (T)he subordination of the saying to the said, to the linguistic system and ontology, is the price that manifestation demands. In language qua said everything is conveyed before us, be it at the price of a betrayal. Language is ancillary and thus indispensable (Levinas, 1981, p. 6).

We shouldn't understand language, theory and thought as attesting to "some fall of the saying." They are motivated – or perhaps we should say: ought to be motivated – "by the pre-original vocation of the saying, by responsibility itself." (ibid.)

To theorize or thematize Levinas's writings – which are obviously part of the order of the said – therefore demands a "language that answers with responsibility" (ibid.). This means that we cannot simply approach Levinas's writings at the level of the said; we cannot simply approach them as a new theory or new truth about the human subject. We must find a different way of relating to his writings, a way that attempts to respond to the saying that is beyond what is said in his writings – and does so in a responsible manner. This is not only a question about how to read Levinas as a philosopher and about how to read Levinas's philosophy. It is also, and perhaps even first of all, an educational question – a question of pedagogy.

The issues surrounding how to relate to Levinas's oeuvre are expressed in a very helpful way in a distinction made by Todd (2003c) between learning *about* Levinas and learning *from* Levinas. Learning *about* Levinas assumes that Levinas has a truth to tell and it is our task, as readers, as educationalists and as educators, to apply this truth in the domain of education. Learning *from* Levinas, on the other hand, suggests the opening of a space where pedagogy can become and remain an *event*, something that is radically open to the future. Learning, in this view, is not about the acquisition of knowledge and truth. It is rather about responding in unique and unprecedented ways. Similarly, pedagogy ceases to be about handing down the established truths to the next generation; it is not an act of 'filling' but rather one of 'emptying' and opening up so that something new and unprecedented can occur.

In our attempts to learn from Levinas we should not therefore approach Levinas as a traditional teacher, as someone who knows what we do not know yet and where it is our task to come to know what we do not know yet but what the teacher already knows. Reading Levinas is like being with a teacher who asks questions and in doing so invites, summons and perhaps even forces us to respond. But it is important to emphasise that Levinas is not a Socratic teacher. He is not a teacher for whom questioning is simply a pedagogical technique utilised to bring the student to the *right* response. Socrates was not really interested in the answers his students gave, as long as they helped him to make his point. While for Socrates questioning was, in that sense, a dialectical process, with Levinas questioning becomes a truly dialogical process, a process where the teacher is really interested in the student's response and expects – or perhaps we should say: hopes – that this response might bring something new into the dialogue, into the conversation and into the world.

This is not to say that the questions that follow from reading Levinas are easy or even comforting questions. They are unsettling in many different ways. They are unsettling for the philosophical mind who, trained in the canon of Western philosophy finds ideas that simply do not fit into the schemata of that canon and thus seem to unsettle both the rationality of the canon and the rationality of the mind that was trained by this canon. They are unsettling for the humanist mind who, hoping to find a secure foundation from which to rebuild the dignity of the human being after all the atrocities of the 20th century, finds nothing more than a responsibility that doesn't seem to be grounded in anything but itself. And they are even unsettling in a very down to earth manner: they have the potential to make us hesitate since they interrupt the 'normal' flow of events.

The unsettling character of Levinas's philosophy may well be one of its most important qualities – at least, that is, if we try to listen to the saying in his writings with an educational ear. In the way in which Levinas unsettles his readers, in the way in which reading Levinas is an unsettling experience, readers may feel left empty-handed. They may feel that Levinas is not giving them anything. In a literal sense this is true: Levinas does not aim to give any-*thing* through his writings. If it literally leaves the reader empty-handed, then it means that the only thing the reader can do in response is *to respond with empty hands*, that is, *to respond as oneself* (see Biesta, 2008). In precisely this way the unsettling quality of Levinas's writings has the potential to call for a singular, unique response.

CONCLUSIONS: A PEDAGOGY OF INTERRUPTION?

The question of this chapter has been whether it is possible to make a distinction between socialization and education. What lies behind this question is whether we can only think of subjectification in terms of socialization, i.e., in terms of the insertion of 'newcomers' into existing orders, of whether subjectivity can be understood in a way that 'escapes' such determination. The traditional, i.e., modern answer to this question is that there is something inherent in human nature – a propensity for rational autonomy – which makes it possible for the human subject to escape external determination by engaging in forms of rational self-determination. Modern education is still built upon this assumption. From Heidegger onwards – but most specifically in the work of Foucault, Derrida and Levinas – this strategy has been exposed as a form of humanism, an attempt to define the essence and destiny of the human being. Moreover, these philosophers have argued that humanism is both impossible and undesirable. As soon as this is acknowledged, the modern way to distinguish between socialization and education disappears – and some have indeed argued that the critique of humanism implies the end of education.

I have shown in this chapter that Levinas offers us a way of approaching the question of human subjectivity that is *not* humanistic. He shows, in other words, that subjectivity and humanism do not necessarily have to go together and in this regard is able to overcome what Foucault (1984) has called 'the blackmail of Enlightenment.' Levinas does not provide us with a new truth about the human subject, but instead gives us a new question to approach the issue of subjectivity and subjectification. The key concept in this is the notion of 'uniqueness.' Levinas, however, does not ask the question as to what *makes* us unique. Instead he asks the question when does it matter that I am unique? When does it matter that I am I and that I cannot be replaced by someone else? For Levinas uniqueness is therefore not a question of identity, a question about the characteristics that define me as different from the other. Uniqueness is about a way of being – but not about being-for-ourselves but about being-for-the-other. Uniqueness, the fact that I am I, matters in those situations in which I cannot be replaced. It matters in those situations where it is *my* responsibility to respond to the 'call' of the other, and not just anyone's responsibility.

The obvious question from an educational point of view is what we can do with these insights. I call this an 'obvious' question because the predominant educational 'reflex' is always to ask what can be done, always to look for a 'solution' or 'way forward' in the sphere of action. Whereas there is a lot that can be done in the spheres of qualification and socialization, Levinas helps us to see that as long as we approach the question of subjectivity in similar terms – i.e., as something that requires our actions and activities as educators, as something that can be produced through our pedagogies – we miss the point. Subjectivity is not something that can be produced or made. It is rather something that can occur – from time to time – as an event that interrupts the normal way of doing and being. If we, as educators, can do anything at all in this sphere it is perhaps first and foremost not to close down opportunities for such interruptions in our classrooms and schools, not to make our students immune to what might affect and interrupt them (on immunity and immunization see Masschelein & Simons 2004). Perhaps we might also see it as our educational responsibility to interrupt our students, that is, to see education as something that should be difficult – not cognitively but existentially – and not as something that should be risk-free and just please our students and keep them happy (on this particular difficulty see Biesta, 2006).

Levinas thus provides us with an important new opening for educational thought and practice. He indicates that it is still possible to distinguish education from socialization and to do so in a way that does not require or is not based upon a particular truth about the human subject but rather hints at a way of being that lies beyond external determination. In this regard Levinas's ethics of subjectivity remains connected to the idea of freedom. This freedom is, however, *not* a liberal freedom in which the subject is the autonomous centre of action and initiative. It rather is a 'difficult freedom' (Levinas, 1990). It is the freedom "to live as if one were *not* a being among beings" (Levinas, 1985, p. 100; emphasis added). It is a way of being that has 'dropped out' of being (Lingis, 1981, p. xxxi). Yet for Levinas it is only when we take the possibility of an existence that is 'otherwise than being' and 'beyond essence' seriously that we might be able to do justice to the humanity of the human being in a way that humanism will forever be unable to do.

REFERENCES

Barlow, S. M. (2000). Living water, living conversation: Encountering the other in company with Emmanuel Levinas. *Journal of Religious Education, 48*(4), 22–27.

Biesta, G. J. J. (1998). "Say you want a revolution..." Suggestions for the impossible future of critical pedagogy. *Educational Theory, 48*(4), 499–510.

Biesta, G. J. J. (2005). What can critical pedagogy learn from postmodernism? Further reflections on the impossible future of critical pedagogy. In I. Gur Ze'ev (Ed.), *Critical theory and critical pedagogy today. Toward a new critical language in education* (pp. 143–159). Haifa: Studies in Education (University of Haifa).

Biesta, G. J. J. (2006). *Beyond learning: Democratic education for a human future*. Boulder, CO: Paradigm Publishers.

Biesta, G. J. J. (2007). "Don't count me in." Democracy, education and the question of inclusion. *Nordisk Pedagogik, 27*(1), 18–31.

Biesta, G. J. J. (2008). Pedagogy with empty hands: Levinas, education and the question of being human. In D. Egéa-Kuehne (Ed.), *Levinas and education: At the intersection of faith and reason* (pp. 198–210). London/New York: Routledge.

Blades, D. W. (2006). Levinas and an ethics for science education. *Educational Philosophy and Theory, 38*(5), 647–664.

Child, M., Williams, D. D., Birch, A. J., & Boody, R. M. (1995). Autonomy or heteronomy? Levinas's challenge to modernism and postmodernism. *Educational Theory, 45*(2), 167–189.

Cook, P. F., & Young, J. R. (2004). Face-to-face with children. *Journal of Curriculum Studies, 36*(3), 341–360.

Critchley, S. (1999). *Ethics, politics, subjectivity*. London/New York: Verso.

Derrida, J. (1982). *Margins of philosophy*. Chicago: Chicago University Press.

Egéa-Kuehne, D. (Ed.). (2008). *Levinas and education: At the intersection of faith and reason*. London/New York: Routledge.

Foucault, M. (1970). *The order of things. An archeology of the human sciences*. New York: Random House.

Foucault, M. (1984). What is enlightenment? In P. Rabinow (Ed.), *The Foucault reader* (pp. 32–50). New York: Pantheon Books.

Hardy, J. (2002). Levinas and environmental education. *Educational Philosophy and Theory, 34*(4), 459–476.

Joldersma, C. W. (2008). Beyond rational autonomy: Levinas and the incomparable worth of the student as singular other. *Interchange, 39*(1), 21–47.

Kant, I. (1982). Über Pädagogik. In I. Kant (Ed.), *Schiften zur Anthropologie, Geschichtsphilosophie, Politik und Pädagogik* (pp. 695–761). Frankfurt am Main: Insel Verlag.

Kant, I. (1992[1784]). An answer to the question 'What is Englightenment?' In P. Waugh (Ed.), *Post-modernism: A reader* (pp. 89–95). London: Edward Arnold.

Levinas, E. (1981). *Otherwise than being or beyond essence*. The Hague: Martinus Nijhoff.

Levinas, E. (1985). *Ethics and infinity*. Pittsburgh: Duquesne University Press.

Levinas, E. (1989). Ethics as first philosophy. In S. Hand (Ed.), *The Levinas reader* (pp. 75–87). Oxford: Blackwell.

Levinas, E. (1998). *Entre nous. Thinking-of-the-other*. New York: Columbia University Press.

Levinas, E. (1990). *Difficult freedom. Essays on Judaism*. Baltimore: The Johns Hopkins University Press.

Lingis, A. (1981). Translator's introduction. In E. Levinas (Ed.), *Otherwise than being or beyond essence* (pp. xi–xiii). The Hague: Martinus Nijhoff.

Masschelein, J. (2000). Can education still be critical? *British Journal of Philosophy of Education, 34*(4), 603–616.

Masschelein, J., & Simons, M. (2004). *Globale immuniteit (Global immunity)*. Leuven: Acco.

Ortega-Ruiz, P. (2004). Moral education as pedagogy of alterity. *Journal of Moral Education, 33*(3), 271–289.

Rancière, J. (1995). *La mésentente*. Paris: Gallilée.

Standish, P. (2001). Ethics before equality: Moral education after Levinas. *Journal of Moral Education, 30*(4), 339–347.

Strhan, A. (2007). "Bringing me more than I contain...": Discourse, subjectivity and the scene of teaching in "Totality and Infinity". *British Journal of Philosophy of Education, 41*(3), 411–430.

Todd, S. (Ed.). (2003a). Special issue: 'Levinas and education. The question of implication.' *Studies in Philosophy and Education, 22*(1), 1–68.

Todd, S. (2003b). *Learning from the other: Levinas, psychoanalysis and ethical possibilities in education*. Albany, NY: SUNY Press.

Todd, S. (2003c). A fine risk to be run? The ambiguity of eros and teacher responsiblity. *Studies in Philosophy and Education, 22*(1), 31–44.

Winch, C. (2005). *Education, autonomy and critical thinking*. London/New York: Routledge.

Usher, R., & Edwards, R. (1994). *Postmodernism and education*. London/New York: Routledge.

Zembylas, M., & Vrasidas, C. (2005). Levinas and the "inter-face": The ethical challenge of online education. *Educational Theory, 55*(1), 61–78.

Gert Biesta
The Stirling Institute of Education
University of Stirling

POLITICS OF KNOWLEDGE

MICHAEL A. PETERS, RODRIGO BRITEZ AND ERGIN BULUT

13. CYBERNETIC CAPITALISM, INFORMATIONALISM AND COGNITIVE LABOR

CYBERNETICS, CATASTROPHE, CHAOS AND COMPLEXITY

Modern cybernetics began with Norbert Weiner who defined the field with his 1948 book *Cybernetics: or Control and Communication in the Animal and the Machine* where he developed the science of information feedback systems linking control and communication in an understanding of the computer as 'ideal central nervous system to an apparatus for automatic control' (Wiener, 1948, p. 36) and, therefore, referring to the automatic control of animal and machine. The prehistory of the term can be traced back at least to Plato where *kybernētēs* meaning 'steersman' or 'governor' (from the Latin *gubernator*)–the same root as government—was used to refer governing of the city-state as an art based on the metaphor of the art of navigation or steering a ship. Thus, from the beginning the term was associated with politics and the art of government as well as with communication and organization. It is not surprising, then, that 'cybernetics' should be a significant theoretical term in global studies particularly with the growth of cognate terms derived from the root 'cyber' as a synonym for 'virtual' and emblematic of the global, such as 'cyberspace', 'cyberculture' and 'cyberpunk'.

In this context cybernetics has figured in global studies as a code word for global communications and media studies. As an epistemology related to systemics and systems philosophy the term has functioned as an approach for investigating a wide range of phenomena in information and communication theory, computer science and computer-based design environments, and artificial intelligence. It has also been applied in management, education, child-based psychology, human systems and consciousness studies, as well as cognitive engineering and knowledge-based systems, 'sociocybernetics', human development. More generally it has been use to analyze emergence and self-regulation, ecosystems, sustainable development, database and expert systems, and been applied to a range of phenomena including health and medicine, musical and theatre performance, musicology, and even peace studies, and personal and spiritual development. Most recently, it has been used to analyze multimedia, hyper- media and hypertext, collaborative decision-support systems, World Wide Web studies, cultural diversity, neural nets, software engineering, vision systems, global community, individual freedom and responsibility, urban revitalization, and environmental design.

'Governing' as a major root meaning has been picked up in all major definitions including A.M. Ampere, the French scientist, who used it to refer to the science of government, W. Ross Ashby who talked of the 'art of steermanship'

Z. Leonardo (ed.), Handbook of Cultural Politics and Education, 303–323.

and Stafford Beer who talked of the science of effective organization. Other modern pioneers in the field tended to emphasize a more technical aspect of the study of systems: 'systems open to energy but closed to information' (Ashby); 'problems of control, recursiveness, and information' (Gregory Bateson); 'feedback as purposeful behaviour in man-machines and living organisms' (Ludwig von Bertalanffy); 'the deep nature of control' (Stafford Beer); 'relationship between endogenous goals and the external environment' (Peter Corning); 'circularity' (Heinz von Forster); 'the theory of interconnectedness of possible dynamic self-regulated systems' (Georg Klaus); 'the art and science of human understanding' (Humberto Maturana); 'the study of justified intervention' (James Wilk).[1] Where one tradition emphasized circular causality in the design of computers and automata–and finds its intellectual expression in theories of computation, regulation and control another tradition, which emerged from human and social concerns, emphasizes epistemology–how we come to know– and explores theories of self-reference to understand such phenomena as autonomy, identity, and purpose' (ASC webpage).

Cybernetics is also broadly related to systems philosophy and theory and as Charles François (1999, p. 203) notes both function as 'a metalanguage of concepts and models for transdisciplinarian use, still now evolving and far from being stabilized'. François (1999) provides a detailed history of systemics and cybernetics in terms of a series historical stages: First, Precursors (Before 1948) - the 'Prehistory of Systemic-Cybernetic Language'- going back to the Greeks and to Descartes in the modern world and ranging across the disciplines with important work in philosophy, mathematics, biology, psychology, linguistics, physiology, chemistry and so on (Hartmann, Leibnitz, Bernard, Ampère, Poincaré, Konig, Whitehead, Saussure, Christaller, Losch, Xenopol, Bertalanffy, Prigogine). Second, 'From Precursors to Pioneers (1948–1960)' beginning with Weiner who aimed to address the problem of prediction and control and the importance of feedback for corrective steering and mentioning Shannon and Weaver's (1949) *Mathematical Theory of Communication,* Von Bertalanffy's 1950 paper 'An outline of general system theory', Kenneth Boulding's (1953) 'Spaceship Earth', von Neumann's theory of automata, Von Förster biological computer and his collaborators like Ashby (1956), Pask (1975) and Maturana who pursued questions in human learning, autopoiesis and cognition. François (1999) rightly devotes space to Prigogine (1955) on systemics and his escape from assumptions of thermodynamic models towards understanding dissipative structures in complex systems.[2] Third, 'Innovators (After 1960)' beginning with Simon's (1962) discussion of complexity, Miller's (1978) work on living systems, Maturana's work on autopoiesis, i.e. self-production, Mandelbrot's (1977) work on fractal forms, Zadeh (1965) work fuzzy sets and fuzzy logic, Thom's work on the theory of catastrophes, and the development of chaos theory. As François (1999) writes

> Chaos theory as the study of the irregular, unpredictable behaviour of deterministic non- linear systems is one of the most recent and important

> innovations in systemics. Complex systems are by nature non-linear, and accordingly they cannot be perfectly reduced to linear simplifications. (p. 214)

François also significantly details important work in ecology and economics mentioning Odum (1971), Daly (1973) on steady-state economy, Pimentel (1977) on the energy balance in agricultural production, among other works in the field. Fourth and finally, François (1999) examines 'Some Significant Recent Contributions (After 1985)' mentioning the Hungarian Csanyi's (1989) work on the 'replicative model of self-organization', Langton (1989) on AL, Sabeili's (1991) theory of processes, and McNeil (1993) on the possibility of a better synthesis between physical sciences and living systems. He ends by referencing Prat's (1964) work on the 'aura' (traces that remain after the demise of the system), Grassé on 'stigmergy'[3] (indirect communication taking place among individuals in social insect societies) and Gerard de Zeeuw (2000) on 'invisibility'.

In this full history we can see cybernetics passing through several phases: The Macy conferences that focused on the new science of cybernetics; catastrophe theory; chaos theory; and complexity theory. The Macy conferences were set up by Warren McCulloch under the auspices of the Macy Foundation from 1946–53 to develop a general science of the human mind and began in the first year studying self-regulating and neural networks moving through a variety of topics covering cybernetics, systems theory, integrative learning.[4] Heims (1993) provides an account of the Macy conferences as a set of dialogues that forged connections between wartime science and post-war social science transforming it through the centrality of the notion of circular causation and feedback and its naturalization through increased quantification. Heims demonstrates how Norbert Wiener, von Neumann, Margaret Mead, Gregory Bateson, Warren McCulloch, Kurt Lewin, Molly Harrower, and many others, shaped ideas in psychology, sociology, anthropology, and psychiatry during the war period.

If modern cybernetics was a child of the 1950s, catastrophe theory developed as a branch of bifurcation theory in the study of dynamical systems originating with the work of the French mathematician Rene Thom in the 1960s and developed by Christopher Zeeman in the 1970s. Catastrophes are bifurcations between different equilibria, or fixed point attractors and have been applied to capsizing boats at sea and bridge collapse. Chaos theory also describes certain aspects of dynamical systems i.e., systems whose state evolve over time such as the 'butterfly effect' that exhibit characteristics highly sensitive to initial conditions even though they are deterministic systems (e.g., the weather).[5] Chaos theory goes back to Poincaré's work and was taken up mainly by mathematicians who tried to characterize reiterations in natural systems in terms of simply mathematic formulae. Both Edward Lorenz and Benoît Mandelbrot studied recurring patterns in nature—Lorenz on weather simulation and Mandelbrot (1975) on fractals in nature (objects whose irregularity is constant over different scales). Chaos theory which deals with non-linear deterministic systems has been applied in many disciplines but has been very successful in ecology for explaining chaotic dynamics. Victor MacGill[6] provides a non-technical account of complexity theory:

> 'Complexity Theory and Chaos Theory studies systems that are too complex to accurately predict their future, but nevertheless exhibit underlying patterns that can help us cope in an increasingly complex world.' (p. 1)

Complexity is concerned with theoretical foundations of computer science being concerned with the study of the *intrinsic complexity of computational tasks*[7] *and rests on understanding the* central role of randomness.

Systems theory in sociology as it was introduced through Parsonian functionalism (Parsons 1951, 1977), developed in Luhmann's 'systemtheorie' (1995) and Immanuel Wallenstein's (1974) world system theory has been largely discredited and dismissed or superseded in an attempted new synthesis (Bailey, 1994; Bánáthy, 1996). Recently, scholars are rethinking systems theory (Pickel, 2006, 2007) emphasizing 'mechanism' and focusing on related concepts such as 'emergentism' (Elder-Vass, 2007), 'self-organization' (Summers-Effler, 2007), 'complexity theory' (Walby, 2007), and 'evolutionary systems theory (Hofkirchner, 2007). Introducing a special issue of *Theory Culture and Society*, John Urry (2005) commented that the social and cultural sciences over the last few decades have experienced a number of incursions including Marxism of the 1970s, the linguistic and postmodern turns of the 1980s, and the body, performative and global culture turns of the 1990s.[8] Without commenting on the simple meta-knowledge schema he introduces, he then goes on to present the latest turn—'complexity'—which he describes as follows:

> This turn derives from developments over the past two decades or so within physics, biology, mathematics, ecology, chemistry and economics, from the revival of neo-vitalism in social thought (Fraser *et al.*, 2005), and from the emergence of a more general 'complex structure of feeling' that challenges some everyday notions of social order (Maasen and Weingart, 2000; Thrift, 1999).
>
> Within these scientific disciplines, an array of transformations took place, loosely known as chaos, complexity, non-linearity and dynamical systems analysis. There is a shift from reductionist analyses to those that involve the study of complex adaptive ('vital') matter that shows ordering but which remains on 'the edge of chaos'. Self-assembly at the nanoscale is a current example of new kinds of matter seen as involving emergent complex adaptive systems. At the nanoscale the laws of physics operate in different ways, especially in the way that molecules stick together and through self-assembly can form complex nanoscale structures that could be the basis of whole new products, industries and forms of 'life' (Jones, 2004) (Urry, 2005, p. 1).

It is, he says, in the 1990s that the social sciences 'go complex,' which he dates from the 1996 Gulbenkian Commission on the Restructuring of the Social Sciences, chaired by Wallerstein and including non-linear scientist Prigogine, who together wanted to break down some of the divisions between the social and natural sciences. Complexity thought and the global spread of 'complexity practices' and its popularizations dates from the 1990s, including applications to the social and cultural sciences. The globalization of system analysis within and across the disciplines demands a complexity approach, but more importantly, it demonstrates that these complex systems operate at the level of infrastructure, code and content enabling certain freedoms while controlling others.

Complexity as an approach to knowledge and knowledge systems now recognizes both the developments of global systems architectures in (tele) communications and information with the development of *open knowledge production systems* that increasingly rest not only on the establishment of new and better platforms (sometimes called Web 2.0), the semantic web, new search algorithms and processes of digitization but also social processes and policies that foster *openness* as an overriding value as evidenced in the growth of open source, open access and open education and their convergences that characterize global knowledge communities that transcend borders of the nation-state. This seems to intimate new orders of global knowledge systems and cultures that portend a set of political and ethical values such as universal accessibility, rights to knowledge, and international knowledge rights to research results especially in the biosciences and other areas that have great potential to alleviate human suffering, disease and high infant mortality. Openness seems also to suggest political transparency and the norms of open inquiry, indeed, even *democracy* itself as both the basis of the logic of inquiry and the dissemination of its results (Peters & Roberts, 2010).

CONTEMPORARY FORMS OF CYBERNETIC CAPITALISM

Increasingly, cybernetics and its associated theories has become central in understanding the nature of networks and distributed systems in energy, politics and knowledge as well as becoming significant in conceptualizing the knowledge-based economy. Economics itself as a discipline has become to recognize the importance of understanding systems rather than rational agents acting alone and pure rationality models of economic behaviour are being supplemented by economic theories that use complexity theory to predict and model transactions. More critical accounts of globalization emphasize a new form of global capitalism, as Teeple (1995) remarks:

> Globalization can be defined as the arrival of 'self-generating capital' at the global level: that is, capital as capital, capital in the form of the transnational corporation, increasingly free of national loyalties, controls, and interests. (p. 7)

The 'financialization of capitalism' is a process that seems to have accompanied neoliberalism and globalization, representing a shift from production to financial services, proliferation of monopolistic multinational corporations and the financialization of the capital accumulation process (Foster, 2007). Nassim Taleb[9] and Benoit Mandelbrot (2004) joined forces to criticize the state of financial markets and the global economy, highlighting some of the key fallacies that have prevented the financial industry from correctly appreciating risk and anticipating the current crisis including, large and unexpected changes in dynamical systems that are difficult to predict, the difficulty of predicting risk based on historical experience of defaults and losses, the idea that consolidation and mergers of banks into larger entities makes them safer but in reality imperils whole financial system.[10]

Cybernetic capitalism is a system that has been shaped by the forces of formalization, mathematization and aestheticization beginning in the early twentieth century and associated with developments in mathematical theory, logic, physics, biology and information theory. Its new forms now exhibit themselves in finance capitalism, informationalism, knowledge capitalism and the learning economy with incipient nodal developments associated with the creative and open knowledge (and science) economies. The critical question in the wake of the collapse of the global finance system and the impending eco-crisis concerns whether capitalism can promote forms of social, ecological and economic sustainability.

'Cybernetic capitalism' is a term we use in order to distinguish a group of theories, or, better, positions, on the Left that attempt to theorize the nature of the *new* capitalism. We can group these contributions as largely sociological and Left-leaning and characterize them in terms of what they share with and differ from Marxist theory of industrial capitalism. Using kinship with Marxism we can generate the following rough groupings of recent work that we have systematically itemised as:

1. *Informational capitalism*
2. *Cultural capitalism*
3. *Cognitive capitalism*
4. *Finance capitalism*
5. *Biocapitalism*

There are strong overlaps and conceptual connections among these five broad categories and also some interesting differences within them. We will simply assert in this paper that they are systematically related phenomena that grow out of the same forces of increasing formalization, mathematicization and aestheticization that have been in operation since the beginning of the twentieth century but that began to coalesce and impact after WWII with the development of cybernetics and a group of theories that developed to explain linear and nonlinear dynamical systems (catastrophe, chaos, complexity). These relationships and particularly the way in which they profile education are to be the subject of other papers. This largely explains why we have adopted the general theoretical description of '*cybernetic capitalism*' as a means of grouping a set of recent theorizations together.

Group 1 – Informational capitalism: The nature of information/knowledge 'Informational', 'Digital', 'Virtual', 'Cyber', 'Fast', 'High-tech'

1. *Informational capitalism*: Emerges from the work of Manuel Castells on the 'networked society.' Castells sees informationalism as a new technological paradigm (he speaks of a mode of development) characterized by "information generation, processing, and transmission" that have become "the fundamental sources of productivity and power" (Castells, 2000a, p. 21). Morris-Suzuki (1997) and Schmiede (2006a,b) have used this term and Christian Fuchs (2007) also writes of an informational capitalism of *self-regulation*. Sometimes also referred to as the 'networked model' of capitalism.[11]
2. *Digital capitalism*: Emerges with Dan Schiller and Robert McChesney at the University of Illinois from the Marxist political economy tradition applied out of communication theory to questions of ownership of global communications: "networks are directly generalizing the social and cultural range of the capitalist economy as never before" (Schiller 2000: xiv). See also Peter Glotz (1999).
3. *Cyber-Capitalism:* N. Dyer-Witheford, *Cyber-Marx. Cycles and Circuits of Struggle in high Technology Capitalism* (1999).
4. *Knowledge Capitalism:* Michael A. Peters & Tina Besley, *Building Knowledge Cultures: Education and Development in the Age of Knowledge Capitalism* (2006); Sheila Slaughter & Gary Rhoades, *Academic Capitalism and the New Economy* (2004).
5. *Fast capitalism*: A term that was coined by Ben Agger (1989; 2004) – Also see the journal website of the same title.[1]
6. *Virtual capitalism*: the "combination of marketing and the new information technology will enable certain firms to obtain higher profit margins and larger market shares, and will thereby promote greater concentration and centralization of capital" (Dawson & Foster, 1998, p. 63).
7. *High-tech capitalism (Haug, 2003*), or informatic capitalism (Fitzpatrick, 2002) – to focus on the computer as a guiding technology that has transformed the productive forces of capitalism and has enabled a globalized economy.

[1] See http://www.fastcapitalism.com/.

Group 2 – Cultural capitalism: The change of culture 'new culture', 'knowing capitalism', 'new spirit', 'cultural economy'

8. *New culture of capitalism*: This strand emerges from work in the 'new geography' and sociology and is epitomized by Richard Sennett's (2007) *The Culture of New Capitalism.*
9. *Knowing Capitalism* – Epitomized by Nigel Thrift's (2006) *Knowing Capitalism.*
10. *The New Spirit of Capitalism*, Boltanski, L. and E. Chiapello (2005).
11. *Cultural economy* Michael Pryke and Paul du Gay.

Group 3 – Cognitive Capitalism: Immaterial Labor 'Cognitive capitalism', 'affective capitalism', 'immaterial labor'

12. *Cognitive Capitalism* – 'Affective Labour is a key feature of the new mode of cognitive capitalism based on immaterial labour. It is a key aspect of a strategy based on autonomous peer production.'[12] Yann Moulier Boutang *Le capitalisme cognitif : La Nouvelle Grande Transformation*, (2007); Vercellone C. (ed), *Capitalismo cognitivo*, (2006); De Angelis, M. and D. Harvie (2006) 'Cognitive Capitalism and the Rat Race: How capital measures ideas and affects in UK higher education.'
13. *Immaterial Labor*: Based on Deleuze and Guattari's *Anti-Oedipus: Schizophrenia and Capitalism* (1999); Negri & Hardt (2000: 290) argue that contemporary society is an Empire that is characterized by a singular global logic of capitalist domination that is based on immaterial labor. With the concept of immaterial labour Negri and Hardt introduce ideas of information society discourse into their Marxist account of contemporary capitalism. Immaterial labor would be labor "that creates immaterial products, such as knowledge, information, communication, a relationship, or an emotional response" (Hardt/Negri 2005, p. 108; cf. also 2000, pp. 280–303), or services, cultural products, knowledge (Hardt/Negri 2000, p. 290).
14. *Affective Capitalism* - Massumi, B. (n.d.) 'The Future Birth of the Affective Fact'[13]; *Immaterial and affective labor*, Emma Dowling, Rodrigo Nunes and Ben Trott (*Ephemera, 2007*); Juan Martín Prada, 'Economies of affectivity' [14] and Michael Hardt 'Affective Labor'.[15]
15. *Semio-capitalism - Precarious Rhapsody. Semio-capitalism and the Pathologies of the Post-Alpha Generation*, Franco Berardi (forthcoming)

Group 4 – Finance Capitalism: 'Financialization'

16. *Finance Capitalism*: John Bellamy Foster; Glyn, A. *Capitalism Unleashed: Finance Globalization and Welfare* (2006); Leyshon, A., and N. Thrift (2007) 'The Capitalization of Almost Everything: The Future of Finance and Capitalism'; Vestergaard, J. *Discipline in the Global Economy? International Finance and the End of Liberalism* (2008).

Group 5 – Biocapitalism & Biopolitics

17. *Biocapitalism*: Based lossely on Foucault's work on governmentality and biopower, and Deleuze and Guattari's *Anti-Oedipus: Schizophrenia and Capitalism* (1999); Rajan, K.S. *Biocapital: The Constitution of Postgenomic Life* (2006); Biotechnology and the Spirit of Capitalism[16]

In what follows we examine two of these groups, namely *informational capitalism* and *cognitive capitalism* and their differences and similarities in the final section.

INFORMATIONAL CAPITALISM

As Fuchs & Horak (2007) indicate the notion of informational capitalism was first introduced by Manuel Castells in his magnum opus *The Rise of the Network Society*. Castells describes contemporary processes in advanced developed capitalist countries transforming the dominant systems of social production and organization of capitalist societies (Castells, 1999; Castells, 2000a; Castells, 2000b; Castells, 2001a; Castells, 2001b, Castells, 2001c, Castells & Himanen, 2002, Castells & Ince, 2003). In other words, those are processes of change that permit the reproduction of the 'fundamental logic' implicit in the capitalist system, but under different rules, different social relations, different modalities of social organization (or morphology) and at a global scale, thus the emergence of a "different kind of capitalism" (Stalder, 2006, p. 48). This is the focus of Castells' analysis of the new economic globalization; the contemporary transformation of the capitalist system and its global expansion through new information technologies (Castells, 2000a). Hence, the assertion of the emergence of a 'new economy': an informational economy.

According to Castells, what is unique in this new economy is not merely its capitalist character, but the influence of technology, applied by economic actors to sustain social change. Technology, more precisely the integration of specific types of technologies in production processes helped to implement an alternative to the 1970's crisis of economic growth of 'profit making' in advanced capitalist societies. Nevertheless, it also provides something more pervasive, a new 'technique', a new logic that goes beyond the realm of economics or economic analysis. More precisely, those changes are interrelated with the creation of new forms of social structural organization, and patterns of institutional transformation through networks.

One of the basic characteristics of contemporary globalization is the significant acceleration of interactions enabled by technology. Technologies of communication are shaping reality and reconfiguring world connectedness with a concentration of traffic taking place between certain geographical nodes over others.

Patterns of mobility and exchanges have always been mediated by technologies of communication. But today, technologies of communication become globalizing forces through which projects of material integration of social spaces at a global scale are possible, allowing the emergence of "a new material basis for time-sharing on which the dominant social processes are reorganized and managed through flows" (Stalder, 2006, p. 146). In other words, they have made possible projects of global material and social integration. For instance, transnational strategies of integration are dominating the organization of economic activity through organizational networks (especially where corporations become transnational, finance activity becomes global, etc).

Networks based on informational technologies are complex forms of organization dominating the ways in which complex patterns of interaction are organized in the world. The understanding of these processes of interconnectedness in terms of networks has the basic advantage of enabling an analysis "based on flows, rather than isolated units, entities, and individuals" (Aneesh, 2006, p. 78) thereby allowing analysis of connectedness, of intrinsic interdependence (of economy, policy, society and culture) in terms of complex patterns of symbolic and material communication.

Precisely, Fuchs & Horak (2007) indicate that “the historical novelty is not that social relationships are networked, but that processes of production, power, hegemony, and struggles take on the form of transnational networks that are mediated by networked information- and communication technologies” (p. 12). As we observe, one of the main features of this ‘new economy’ is the increasing importance of knowledge or information production, or what Castells denominate as ‘informationalism’, implying the emergence of an economy based on new forms of production and labor. In other words, knowledge, information and communication in the globalized world - as informationalism - is manifested in the increased importance of labor involved in the production of what Hardt and Negri (2000) denominated ‘immaterial goods’ (p. 290).

Concomitantly, in those instances, the value labor changes from mechanical production to the primacy of ‘symbolic analytical services’, “data analysis, financial planning and most research and development jobs and occupations (Schirato & Webb, 2003, p. 77). Examples include the constant creation and recreation of products images through relentless marketing campaigns, the relevance of financial markets, and the increasing dependence of manufacturing and agricultural activities from services occupations.

We would like to state three initial points on the emergence of Castells' informational capitalism. First, it is important to note that there was not a one-dimensional causality on the way in which this capitalist restructuring could have been implemented. Hence, it is important to understand that the political context in which these reforms became effectively framed was dominated by market and profit oriented ideologies (e.g. neoliberalism). Second, informational technologies were used not only to ensure global networks of communication but allowed the introduction of new modes of global organization and production. In short, informational technologies enabled the creation of institutional “capacities to accumulate, store, transfer, analysed, and use massive databases to guide decisions in the global marketplace” (Harvey, 2005, p. 3). Third, this organizational paradigm affects more than the material economic activity of societies. It introduces cultural transformations that are “not just [about] the economy” (Stalder, 2006, p. 28). In other words, it introduces changes in the paradigm of organization favouring specific forms of social and cultural interactions and values in capitalist economies.

Stalder (2006) notes that in Castells' theoretical argumentation “each paradigm supports a particular argument of social organization (or morphology) in becoming dominant over others” (p. 30). Hence, the preferred form of social organization under informationalism becomes part of complex systems of interaction based on networks rather than the centralized hierarchies that characterized the industrial age, also known as Industrialism. Industrialism was a technological paradigm based on “technologies of energy generation and distribution” which “made possible the factory and the large corporation as the organizational foundation of the industrial society” (Castells, 2001c, p. 1). Industrialism favoured specific forms of organization required in territorially concentrated systems of manufacturing control. In contrast, informational technologies were making possible the existence of systems of production operating at a global scale coordinated by informational networks (Castells, 2001c). Thus, the transformations that we observe in contemporary societies towards an informational society are not merely based on the centrality of knowledge generation and information processing activities, but in the material basis that is giving knowledge and information generation and distribution its current and specific global character.

More important, this also implies the emergence of two sets of contradictory developments at the center of the social production systems emerging from informationalism: one based on a commodity economy and the other based on a gift economy (Fuchs, 2006). Fuchs indicates that the affordances facilitating new forms of collaborative knowledge production at the core of capitalist economies are enabling the emergence of a parallel and antagonistic economic logic: an "alternative economic model of a gift economy" (Fuchs, 2006, p. 1).

Basically, due to the very nature of the requirements of open knowledge production and communication in networked systems, knowledge is extremely difficult to transform into a commodity. Knowledge cannot be easily produced and consumed through close systems in the same manner than material goods. This is resulting in increasing conflicts between the forces of informational production and the still prevalent systems of capitalist accumulation and relationships (Fuchs, 2006). Therefore, it is possible to observe the contentious contemporary struggles over the nature of information as a property.

The strategies of capitalist accumulation that contemporary systems of information and communication favour are different from those observed during the industrial age. As Fuchs appears to indicate informationalism requires more *democratic* forms of participation and collaboration in the relationships of production and accumulation of wealth in informational capitalist societies in ways that require that information should not be consider as a restricted property, but an unhindered component of social interactions.

Moreover, it is crucial to understand that for Castells, the rise of the use of technological innovations, like internet in the 90s, is not merely defined by the technological innovation itself, but it is dependent in the ways that the consumer interests drive the implementation and use of those technologies. It is important to note that one of the main assumptions of Castells' theory is based on the affirmation of the existence of a "dialectical interaction of social relations and technological innovation, or, in Castells terminology modes of production and modes of development" (Stalder, 2006, p. 302). This last point needs some clarification to understand the nature of Castells' rupture with a traditional Marxian approach. For Castells there is no difference between modes of production and relations of production, in the sense that they are considered one dimension defined by the primacy of a particular type of organization of production and consumption. The emphasis is made in the organization of the relationships of production and consumption not in the system of production and the relations of production (Castells, 2000a; Castells & Ince, 2003).

Finally, this implies the emergence of a knowledge based economy, society and culture. In other words, the transition from industrial towards informational capitalism is destabilising systems of capitalist relationships thus opening possibilities for transformation of a different world, maybe a better one (Castells & Ince, 2003; Capra, 2002).

Transnational networked capitalism leading current processes of economic globalization had generated a process of accumulation not very different from those observed during the industrial age, with negative effects for many populations. And at the same time, this is generating global protests by networked civil society groups claiming for more democratic ways of conceiving globalization. It is important to remember that the expansion of information networks in the form of global systems of transaction, and capitalism restructuring were and are still implemented by centralized, authoritarian, mostly industrial working oriented styles through many nations.

The consequences of the contradictory positions of the emerging gift and the old proprietary economy are observed in the sometimes overlapping forms in which labor and education are conceived. The movement and organization of labor is profoundly affected and also the different levels of demands over the content and functions of higher education institutions, in which the learning value is now characterize by the "central role of knowledge, information, affect and communication" (Schirato & Webb, 2003, pp. 76–77) but whose main value is conceived as a potential access to venues of mobility. In other words, the potential entrée to nodes of activity and economic interaction requires the access to a specific, and changing, hierarchy of higher education institution. The access to those institutions potentially enables individuals, states, and business to participate or to exploit different flows generated by global networks. In those terms, higher education accreditation becomes a commodity to access a set of strategic positions allowing employability and interaction with transnational networks of capitalism. In those terms, higher education institutions are generating accreditations as commodities, following a logic common to a proprietary economy.

At the same time, it is of critical importance to understand that the educational demands for participating in the knowledge sectors of the global requires of the same skills needed to participate in the gift economy. This implies the cultivation of creative networking practices and dispositions, hence to openly share and produce information. These contradictions and confluences between the values that those two economies cultivate are a relevant aspect to understand today's complex capitalist system and social relationships.

COGNITIVE CAPITALISM AND IMMATERIAL LABOR

Richard Sennett's *The Corrosion of Character* describes the enormous difference between the lives of a Fordist worker Enrico and his son Rico, who works in the flexible post-Fordist version of capitalism. Upon reading the book, one comes to recognize the extent to which the nature of work has been transformed. This new flexible capitalism has been hailed by popular media and business circles as liberating and non-hierarchical. Additionally, even though the popular media remembers Karl Marx only during times of crisis, there are vibrant debates among Marxists themselves, regarding the transformation of work and labor processes.

We should definitely take Michael Hardt and Antonio Negri into account among the prominent names of this debate. Yet, we believe a historical account about this concept would be useful before more contemporary ones.

Leopoldina Fortunati gives the names of Gabriel Tarde and Werner Sombart as far as reflections on immaterial labor after Marx are concerned. Fortunati states that Tarde's writings [*Les Lois de L'imitation* (1890) and *La Logique Sociale* (1895)], "stressed the existence of other forces (or laws) acting on a socio-psychological level, such as imitation, the law of minimal effort, and innovation. In doing so he argued that the social teleology imposed by classical economists unaware of the true foothold of political economics was at fault for the omission of affections, and especially of desire, in analyses of valorization (spheres which were also neglected by subsequent Marxisms)" (Fortunati, 2007, p. 142). Sombart, on the other hand, in *Modern Capitalism*, argued that immaterial labor was becoming more central to capitalism and laid down three reasons for the technological developments of the time:

> first of all, the objectification of technical knowledge, which ensured a continued control over new ideas or inventions, their transmission and with it the diffusion of knowledge; secondly, the systematization of technical knowledge which allowed for a systematic progression of knowledge and its enlargement; thirdly, the mathematization of technical knowledge (Fortunati, 2007, p. 143).[17]

The revival of the contemporary versions of immaterial labor debates can be cohered around people including Antonio Negri, Michael Hardt and Maurizio Lazaratto, the journal *Futur Antereiur.* Nick Dyer-Witheford (2001) provides a smooth historical account of how these debates were chronologically shaped. Antonio Negri's writings (1988, 1989) on the "intellectual qualities of a post-Fordist proletariat enmeshed in the computers and communication networks of high-technology were intensified in the analysis of the general intellect (the socialized, collective, intelligence prophesied by the Marx of the *Grundrisse*) developed by the journal Futur Anterieur" (Dyer-Witheford, 2001, p. 70). As a precise definition of immaterial labor, we can refer to Lazzarato:

> Immaterial labor is defined as the labor that produces the informational and cultural content of the commodity. Informational content: related to big industry and tertiary sectors; skills involving cybernetics and computer control... Cultural content: kind of activities involved in defining and fixing cultural and artistic standards, fashions, tastes, consumer norms and more strategically public opinion (Lazzarato, 2006, p. 132).

The revival of these reflections reached its peak with the publication of Hardt and Negri's *Empire*.

Underlining the shift from an industrial economy towards an informational economy, Hardt and Negri focus on how the nature of labor has changed within the framework of Toyotist model, as opposed to the Fordist one. In this new phase of global capitalism, "factories will maintain zero stock" (Hardt & Negri, 2000,

p. 290) and immaterial labor will gain significance. Hardt and Negri define immaterial labor as one "that produces an immaterial good, such as a service, a cultural product, knowledge, or communication" (p. 290). According to Hardt and Negri, there are three types of immaterial labor:

> one is involved in an industrial production that has been informationalized and has incorporated communication technologies in a way that transforms the production process itself ... Second is immaterial labor of analytical and symbolic tasks, which itself breaks down into creative and intelligent manipulation on the one hand and routine symbolic tasks on the other. Finally, a third type of immaterial labor involves the production and manipulation of affect and requires (virtual or actual) human contact, labor in the bodily mode (Hardt & Negri, 2000, p. 293).[18]

As far as the rise of immaterial labor is concerned, Hardt and Negri (2000) stress a point of departure from a "Marxian political economy by which labor power is conceived as 'variable capital', that is, a force that is activated and made coherent only by capital" and argue that "today productivity, wealth, and the creation of social surpluses take the form of cooperative interactivity through linguistic, communicational, and affective networks" (p. 294). Thus, they argue, in this decentralized production, "the assembly line has been replaced by the network ... workers can even stay at home ... and these tendencies place labor in a weakened bargaining position" (Hardt and Negri, 2000, pp. 295–296). Hardt and Negri, when thinking about this assault on labor, maintain that production and life have become quite inseparable. That is, in this flexible accumulation regime, "life is made to work for production and production is made to work for life" (Hardt and Negri, 2000, p. 32).[19]

Presumably, Hardt & Negri and others' analyses of immaterial labor was attacked for some obvious reasons in the sense that these new circuits of capital "look a lot less immaterial and intellectual to the female and Southern workers who do so much of the grueling physical toil demanded by a capitalist general intellect whose metropolitan headquarters remain preponderantly male and Nothern" (Dyer-Witheford, 2001, p. 71; Dowling, 2007).

Despite these sound critiques, Dyer-Witherford acknowledges the increasing hegemony of immaterial labor along with other scholars, including Yann Moulier Boutang who has neatly classified certain characteristics of cognitive capitalism. Comparing cognitive capitalism with industrial capitalism, Boutang states that "in industrial capitalism, accumulation concerns mainly machines and the organization of work dealt with ... whereas accumulation in cognitive capitalism rests on management of knowledge and production of innovation, hence on immaterial investments" (Boutang, 2007, p. 12).[20] Along with that, Boutang stresses the differences with respect to different entrepreneurs of industrial capitalism and cognitive capitalism. While the former is defined by his/her greed and pride of loneliness and "exception of founding father", the latter is marked by the desire for fame and "pride of cooperation and connectivity" (Boutang, 2007, p. 22). Here, the issue of cooperation and connectivity directly takes us to the classification we have tried to accomplish within the framework of this chapter. We have argued that the different capitalisms we have underlined have a lot in common. In this respect, immaterial labor, cooperation and informational capitalism all have overlapping features. As it is argued with respect to information, for instance, it is not easy to control by a single person and based on networks (Fuchs, 2008a).[21] These features all have the potential for collaboration. However, it is exactly here that we might step back and be cautionary in terms of the 'cooperative or emancipatory' for two reasons: political economy and subjectivity. While the former is related to the fact that "the total assets of the top six knowledge corporations were 1,132,41 billion US dollars in 2007 and are larger than the total African GDP" (Fuchs, 2008a, p. 284), the second has to do with how labor is subsumed within cyberspace thanks to the discourse around collaboration, fun and participation. In other words, what the participation of immaterial labor within cyberspace means has not been endorsed by critical theorists, who have underlined this potential but at the same time pointed to various mechanisms through which subsumption of labor is realized in cyberspace (Fuchs, 2008b, 2007, 2002). This cautionary stance is relevant to the realm of education, as well.

David Harvie, for instance, argues that the war over value has spread over not only factory but there are also attempts to quantify the value produced by immaterial labor, especially within the framework higher education, by using techniques of "quantification, surveillance and standardization" (Harvie, 2008; 2000), (De Angelis & Harvie, 2007). Neoliberal restructuring of schooling in line with market demands has also resulted in the emergence of a global policy inflation around lifelong learning and educational credentials that would be commodified. As the assembly line with certain expected demands from the factory and workplace have moved elsewhere from the First World, schooling built around industrial lines would have been re-arranged to train students along the lines of the global knowledge economy and fluctuating market demands. However, the responsibility would be shared between the school and the individual. An awareness of these developments definitely takes us to the centrality of value creation to capitalism. That is, despite the changing nature of work and labor processes, value still represents "the life blood of capitalism", whether this or that (Rikowski, 2003). As it is also asserted, "the extraction of value from immaterial labor, much like that occurring at the zenith of Fordism in the automobile factories of Turin or Detroit, is not a friction-free matter" (Brophy & de Peuter, p. 179).

In this respect, one could argue that immaterial labor is quite material in terms of extraction of surplus value and exploitation and thus analyses based on the concept has to take an approach that is based on a layered and relational understanding of immaterial labor and the differential power relations among the people who exercise this kind of labor in their everyday lives, be it a creative design worker or the janitor who cleans his cutting edge PC.

CONCLUSION

This chapter provides a synoptic view of what we have called 'cybernetic capitalism' – a term that attempts to capture the leading sector developments within modern capitalism and to profile the leading accounts of these developments. 'Third capitalism' (after mercantilism and industrialism) now relies on a systems architecture that draws on cybernetics and modern computing that connects five aspects of cybernetic capitalism: informational capitalism, cultural capitalism, cognitive capitalism, finance capitalism and biocapitalism. These five elements are interrelated. In this chapter we have identified the five elements but not described or analysed the interconnections among them. Clearly, there are obvious links among information, cognitive and cultural capitalism even though we are not claiming that the theorists who articulate these separate elements offer the same descriptions or that they agree in their characterizations. Finance and biocapitalism also employs similar methods and works off the same systems architectures: where the former is based on sophisticated mathematical modelling and search algorithms, the latter makes 'nature' and biogenetics central to the production process.

In this chapter, we also have tried to underline the new features towards where global capitalism is shifting. Among the different models, there are strong overlapping characteristics which coalesce around aesthetization, design and immateriality. Yet, there is one concept that is central to all of the types, including industrial capitalism. That is value. Value creation for the sake of it is still central to contemporary capitalism. That is, the universal contradiction, which might manifest itself differently in different localities, between capital and labor is still there and has diffused to every sphere of our lives. Thus, any attempt to define any novelty to these capitalisms should bear this in mind. Along with that, spatiality is another concept we have to bear in mind in the sense that not all the globe is going through these changes simultaneously. In other words, the shiny capitalism of any global city is only possible through different mechanisms of capital accumulation, either based on forms of modern slavery in the sweatshops of the Third World or its own ghettoes.

Finally, these complex changes at central capitalist economies are affecting in different ways the modes in which social relationships, organization and values are conceived in society. Cybernetic capitalism implies forms of accumulation at the core of the productive process of the most relevant sectors of economy at times implying antithetical stances with the ways that capital accumulation and production is conceived by industrial capitalist economies and cultures. The different theories studying Cybernetic capitalism have the common purpose of beginning to understand the different dimensions that this radical change in the dominant paradigm of organization and production generates, the social dilemmas that produces for human beings and societies and the contradictions and overlapping that are observed in relation to other capitalisms.

NOTES

1. See the American Society for Cybernetics (ASC) webpage for a full set of definitions at http://www.asc-cybernetics.org/foundations/definitions.htm. It would like to acknowledge Fazal Rizvi's constructive criticisms of ideas in an earlier version of this paper.
2. Prigogine has an interest in time derived from the philosopher Bergson, and later from the physicists Boltzmann and Planck, where he developed a theorem on examples of systems which were highly

organized and irreversible and applied it to the energetics of embryological evolution. His work in irreversible phenomena theory led him also to reconsider their insertion into classical and quantum dynamics and to the problem of the foundations of statistical mechanics. See his discussion of his work at http://nobelprize.org/nobel_prizes/chemistry/laureates/1977/prigogine-autobio.html.

[3] For the literature on stigmergy and massive online collaboration see Susi & Ziemke (2001), Gregorio (2002) and Robles, Merelo & Gonzalez-Barahona (2005).

[4] See the description at http://www.asc-cybernetics.org/foundations/history/MacySummary.htm.

[5] For a brief introduction see http://www.imho.com/grae/chaos/chaos.html.

[6] See http://complexity.orconhosting.net.nz/.

[7] See Oded Goldreich's webpage at http://www.wisdom.weizmann.ac.il/~oded/cc.html.

[8] The next section is based on Peters (2008).

[9] See Taleb's homepage and publications at http://www.fooledbyrandomness.com/.

[10] See the video interview at http://financemanila.net/2009/01/taleb-and-mandelbrot/.

[11] See the website at http://ideas.repec.org/a/nos/voprec/2003-8-10.html.

[12] See the website http://p2pfoundation.net/Affective_Capitalism.

[13] See http://www.radicalempiricism.org/biotextes/textes/massumi.pdf.

[14] See http://www.vinculo-a.net/english_site/text_prada.html.

[15] See http://www.vinculo-a.net/english_site/text_hardt.html.

[16] See http://www.thenewatlantis.com/publications/biotechnology-and-the-spirit-of-capitalism.

[17] Fortunati also mentions the names of the human capital theorist Gary Becker, along with Michel Foucault (with his concepts biopower and biopolitics) and Deleuze and Guattari who considered human beings to be desiring machines (Fortunati, 2007, p. 144).

[18] Hardt and Negri's comments about this third type of labor is worth questioning, in terms of its immateriality, though, since this affective labor can be regarded as quite material in terms of reproduction of labor power. Along with that, we have to acknowledge that the authors clarified this point in *Multitude: War and Democracy in the Age of Empire* by arguing that the labour itself is not immaterial. What is immaterial is the product or affects it creates. (Hardt and Negri, 2004, p. 109).

[19] For the same issue, Lazzarato would argue the following: "what modern management techniques are looking for is for the worker's soul to become part of the factory … workers are expected to become "active subjects" in the coordination of the various functions of production, instead of being subjected to it as simple command" (p. 133).

[20] Boutang lists 22 main characteristics of cognitive capitalism, among which we can count: virtualization economy and increasing role of information, exploitation of the inventive force instead of the labor force, the fact that market precedes production, the blurring of the traditional division between capital and labor (Boutang, 2007, pp. 13–14).

[21] Available at: http://fuchs.icts.sbg.ac.at/Fuchs_CriticalTheory.pdf

REFERENCES

Aneesh, A. (2006). *Virtual migration*. Durham, NC: Duke University Press.

Ashby, W. R. (1956). *An introduction to cybernetics*. London: Chapman and Hall.

Bailey, K. D. (1994). *Sociology and the new systems theory: Toward a theoretical synthesis*. New York: State University of New York Press.

Bánáthy, B. (1996). *Designing social systems in a changing world*. New York: Plenum.

Berardi, F. (2009). Precarious rhapsody: Semio-capitalism and the pathologies of the post-alpha generation. London: Autonomedia.

Bertalanffy, L. von. (1950). An outline of general system theory. *British Journal for the Philosophy of Science, 1*(2), 134–165.

Bohm-Bawerk, E. (2006). *Karl Marx and the close of his system* London: Porcupine Press.

Boltanski, L., & Chiapello, E. (2005). *The new spirit of capitalism* (G. Elliott, Trans.). London: Verso.

Boulding, K. (1953). Toward a general theory of growth. *Canadian Journal of Economics and Political Science, 19*(3), 326–340. (Reprinted in General Systems Yearbook, Vol. 1, 1956)

Boutang, Y. M. (2007, September 28–29). *Cognitive capitalism and entrepreneurship decline in industrial entrepreneurship and the rising of collective intelligence*. Paper presented at conference on Capitalism and Entrepreneurship 141. Sage Hall Cornell University, Ithaca, New York.

Brophy, E., & de Peuter, G. (2007). Immaterial labor, precarity, and recomposition. In Catherine McKercher & Vincent Mosco (Eds.), *Knowledge workers in the information society* (pp. 177–193). City: Lexington Books.

Capra, F. (2002). *The hidden connections: Integrating the biological, cognitive, and social dimensions of life into a science of sustainability* (1st ed.). New York: Doubleday.

Castells, M. (1999). Flows, networks, and identities: A critical theory of the informational society. In M. Castells, R. Flecha, P. Freire, H. A. Giroux, D. Macedo, & P. Willis (Eds.), *Critical education in the new information age* (pp. 37–64). Lanham, MD: Rowman & Littlefield.

Castells, M. (2000a). *The rise of the network society* (2nd ed.). Malden, MA: Blackwell Publishers.

Castells, M. (2000b). Materials for an exploratory theory of the network society. *British Journal of Sociology*, *51*(1), 5–24.

Castells, M. (2001a). Universities as dynamic systems of contradictory functions. In J. Muller, N. Cloete, & S. Badat (Eds.), *Challenges of globalisation* (pp. 206–223). Pinelands: Maskew Miller Longman.

Castells, M. (2001b). Informationalism and the network society. Epilogue to P. Himanen. In *The hacker ethic and the spirit of informationalism* (pp. 155–178). New York: Random House.

Castells, M. (2001c). *The internet galaxy: Reflections on the internet, business, and society*. Oxford: Oxford University.

Castells, M., & Himanen, P. (2002). *The information society and the welfare state: The Finnish model*. Oxford: Oxford University Press.

Castells, M., & Ince, M. (2003). *Conversations with Manuel Castells*. Cambridge: Polity Press.

Csanyi, V. (1989). The replicative model of self- organization. In G. J. Dalenoort (Ed.), *The paradigm of self-organization* (pp. 73–86). New York: Gordon & Breach.

Daly, H. (1973). *Towards a steady-state economy*. San Francisco: Freeman.

De Angelis, M. (2007). *The beginning of history – Value struggles and global capital*. London: Pluto Press.

De Angelis, M., & Harvie, D. (2007). *Cognitive capitalism and the rat race: How capital measures and affects in UK higher education*. Paper presented at Immaterial Labor, Multitudes and New Social Subjects: Class Composition in Cognitive Capitalism, University of Cambridge. April 29–30 2006. Retrieved from http://www.geocities.com/immateriallabour/angelisharviepaper2006.html

Dowling, E,. Nunes, R., & Trott, B. (2007). Immaterial and affective labor. Special Issue, *Ephemera*.

Dowling, E. (2007). Producing the dining experience: Measure, subjectivity and the affective worker. *Ephemera*, *7*(1), 117–132.

Dyer-Witheford, N. (1999). *Cyber-Marx: Cycles and Ccrcuits of struggle in high technology Capitalism*. Urbana, IL: University of Illinois Press.

Dyer-Witheford, N. (2001). *Empire, immaterial labor, the new combinations, and the global worker, rethinking Marxism*, *13*(¾, Fall/Winter), (70–80).

Elder-Vass, D. (2007). Luhmann and emergentism: Competing paradigms for social systems theory? *Philosophy of the Social Sciences*, *37*(4), 408–432.

Fortunati, L. (2007). Immaterial labor and its machinization. *Ephemera*, *7*(1), 139–157.

François, C. (1999). Systemics and cybernetics in a historical perspective. *Systems Research and Behavioral Science*, *16*, 203–219.

Fraser, M., Kember, S., & Lury, C. (Eds.). (2005). Inventive life: Approaches to the new vitalism. *Special Issue of Theory Culture & Society*, *22*(1), 1–14.

Fuchs, C. (2002). Software engineering and the production of surplus value. *Cultural Logic*. Retrieved from http://clogic.eserver.org/2002/fuchs.html

Fuchs, C., & Horak, E. (2007). Informational capitalism and the digital divide in Africa. *Masaryk University of Law and Technology*, *1*(2), 11–32.

Fuchs, C. (2007). Transnational space and the network society. *21st Century Society*, *2*(1), 49–78.

Fuchs, C. (2008a). Towards a critical theory of information. In D. Nafria, J. María, & F. Salto Alemany (Eds.), *Qué es Información? (What is Information?)* Proceedings of the First Itnernational meeting of Experts in Infromation Theories. An Interdisciplinary Approach (Primer Encuentro Internactional de Expertos Teorías de la Información. Un enfoque interdisciplinar), November 6–7, León, Spain (pp. 247–316.). León: Universidad de León.

Fuchs, C. (2008b). Book review of Wikinomics: How mass collaboration changes everything. *International Journal of Communication*, (2), 1–11.

Glyn, A. (2006). *Capitalism unleashed: Finance globalization and welfare*. Oxford: Oxford University Press.

Gregorio, J. (2002). *Stigmergy and the world-wide web*. Bitworking (web log). Retrieved December 20, 2005, from http://bitworking.org/news/Stigmergy

Hardt, M., & Negri, A. (2000). *Empire*. Cambridge, MA: Harvard University Press.

Hardt, M., & Negri, A. (2004). *Multitude : War and democracy in the age of empire*. New York: Penguin Press.

Harvey, D. (2000). Time space compression and the Postmodern condition. In D. Held & A. McGrew (Eds.), *The global transformation reader: An introduction to the globalization debate* (pp. 82–91). Cambridge: Polity Press.

Harvey, D. (2005). *A brief history of neo liberalism*. New York: Oxford University Press.

Harvie, D. (2000). Alienation, class and enclosure in UK universities. *Capital & Class*, *71*(Summer), 103–132.

Harvie, D. (2008). Academic labor: Producing value and producing struggle. In T. Green, G. Rikowski, & H. Raduntz (Eds.), *Renewing dialogues in Marxism and education: Openings* (pp. 231–247). London: Palgrave Macmillan.

Heims, S. J. (1993). *Constructing a social science for postwar America. The Cybernetics Group, 1946–1953*. London: Cambridge University Press.

Hodfkirchner, W. (2007). A critical social systems view of the internet. *Philosophy of the Social Sciences*, *37*(4), 471–500.

Jones, R. (2004). *Soft machines: Nanotechnology and life*. Oxford: Oxford University Press.

Langton, C. (Ed.). (1989). *Artificial life*. Santa Fe Institute for Studies in the Sciences of Complexity. Reading, MA: Addison-Wesley.

Law, J., & Urry, J. (2004). Enacting the social. *Economy and Society*, *33*(3), 390–410.

Lazzarato, M. (2006). Immaterial labor. In P. Virno, S. Buckley, & M. Hardt (Eds.), *Radical thought in Italy* (pp. 133–151). Minneapolis, MN: University of Minnesota Press.

Leyshon, A., & cThrift, N. (2007). The capitalization of almost everything: The future of finance and capitalism. *Theory, Culture & Society*, *24*(7–8), 97–115.

Luhmann, N. (1995). *Social systems* (J. Bednarz, Jr. with D. Baecker, Trans.). Stanford, CA: Stanford University Press. (Original work published 1984)

Maasen, S., & Weingart, P. (2000). *Metaphors and the dynamics of knowledge*. London: Routledge.

Mance, E. A. (forthcoming). The network revolution. Solidarity economy as the material basis of a postcapitalist society. *Turbulence: ideas for movement*.

Mandelbrot, B. (1975). *The fractal geometry of nature*. New York: Freeman.

Mandelbrot, B. (1977). *Fractal forms, change and dimensions*. San Francisco: Freeman.

Mandelbrot, B., & Hudson, R. (2004). *The (mis)behavior of markets: A fractal view of risk, ruin, and reward*. New York: Basic Books.

Massumi, B. (ND). The future birth of the affective fact'. *Conference Proceedings: Genealogies of Biopolitics, 2*. Retrieved from http://www.radicalempiricism.org/biotextes/textes/massumi.pdf

Maturana, H., & Varela, F. (1980). *Autopoiesis and cognition*. Boston: Reidel.

McNeil, D. H. (1993). Architectural criteria for a general theory of systems. *Proceedings of the 37th ISSS Conference*. University of Western Sidney, Hawkesbury, Australia.

Mechanisms. New York: Palgrave. (author information?)

Miller, J. G. (1978). *Living systems*. New York: McGraw Hill.

Nowotny, H. (2005). The increase of complexity and its reduction emergent interfaces between the natural sciences, humanities and social sciences. *Theory, Culture & Society*, *22*(5), 15–31.

Odum, H. (1971). *Environment, power and society*. New York: Wiley.

Parsons, T. (1951). *The social system*. Glencoe, IL: Free Press.

Parsons, T. (1977). *Social systems and the evolution of action theory*.

Pask, G. (1975). *The cybernetics of human learning and performance*. London: Hutchinson.

Peters, M. A. (2008). 'Editorial: Complexity and knowledge systems. *Educational Philosophy and Theory*, *40*(1), 1–3.

Peters, M. A., & Roberts, P. (2010). *The virtues of openness: Education and scholarship in a digital world*. Boulder, CO: Paradigm.

Pickel, A. (2006). *The problem of order in the global age: Systems and mechanisms*. New York: Palgrave Macmillan.

Pickel, A. (2007). Rethinking systems theory: A programmatic introduction. *Philosophy of the Social Sciences*, *37*(4), 391–407.

Pimentel, D. (1977, September 8). *America's agricultural future*. *The Economist*.

Power, D., & Scott, A. (Eds.). (2004). *Cultural industries and the production of culture*. London: Routledge.

Prat, H. (1964). *Le champ Unitaire en Biologie*. Paris: Presses Universtaires de France.

Prigogine, I. (1955). *Introduction to thermodynamics of irreversible processes*. Springfield, IL: Thomas Press.

Rajan, K. S. (2006). *Biocapital: The constitution of postgenomic life*. Durham, NC: Duke University Press.

Rikowski, R. (2003). Value – The life blood of capitalism: Knowledge is the current key. *Policy Futures in Education*, *1*(1), 160–178.

Robles, G., Merelo, J. J., & Gonzalez-Barahona, J. M. (2005). Self-organized development in libre software: A model based on the stigmergy concept. *Proceedings of 6th International Workshop on Software Process Simulation and Modeling*.

Sabeili, H. (1991). Process theory: A biological model of open systems. In *Proceedings of the 35th ISSS Meeting*. Ostersund, Sweden.

Sennett, R. (1999). *The corrosion of character: The personal consequences of work in the new capitalism*. New York: W.W. Norton.

Shannon, C., & Weaver, W. (1949). *The mathematical theory of communication*. Urbana, IL: University of Illinois Press.

Simon, H. A. (1962). *The architecture of complexity*. *Proceedings of the American Philosophical Society*, *106*(6) (reprinted in *General Systems Yearbook*, Vol. X, 1965).

Slaughter, S., & Rhoades, G. (2004). *Academic capitalism and the new economy: Markets, states and higher education*. Baltimore: The Johns Hopkins University Press.

Stalder, F. (2006). *Manuel Castells: The theory of the network society*. Malden, MA: Polity Press.

Summers-Effler, E. (2007). Vortexes of oinvolvement: Social systems as turbulent flow. *Philosophy of the Social Sciences*, *37*(4), 433–448.

Susi, T., & Ziemke, T. (2001). Social cognition, artefacts, and stigmergy: A comparative analysis of theoretical frameworks for the understanding of artefact-mediated collaborative activity. *Cognitive Systems Research*, *2*(4), 273–290.

Teeple, G. (1995). *Globalization and the decline of social reform*. New York: Humanities Press.

Terranova, T. (2004). *Network culture: Politics for the information age*. London: Pluto Press.

Thom, R. (1975). *Structural stability and morphogenesis*. Benjamin, MA: Benjamin.

Urry, J. (2005). The complexity turn. *Theory, Culture & Society*, *22*(5), 1–14.

Vercellone, C. (Ed.). (2006). *Capitalismo cognitivo*. Roma: Manifestolibri.

Vestergaard, J. (2008). *Discipline in the global economy? International finance and the end of liberalism*. New York: Routledge.

von Förster, H. (1981). *Observing systems, intersystems*. Seaside CA: Intersystems Publications.

von Neumann, J. (1966). *Theory of self-producing automata*. Urbana, IL: University of Illinois Press.

Walby, S. (2007). Complexity theory, systems theory, and multiple intersecting social inequalities. *Philosophy of the Social Sciences*, *37*(4), 449–469.

Wallerstein, I. (1974). *The modern world system: Capitalist agriculture and the origins of the European world economy in the sixteenth century*. New York: Academic Press.

Wiener, N. (1948). *Cybernetics: Or control and communication in the animal and the machine*. New York: Wiley; Paris: Hermann.

Zadeh, L. (1965). Fuzzy sets. *Information and Control, 8*, 338–353.

Zeeuw, Gerard de (2000). ome problems in the observation of performance. In F. Parra Luna (Ed.), *The performance of social systems: Perspectives and problems*. Dordrecht: Kluwer Academic/Plenum Publishers.

Michael A. Peters, Rodrigo Britez and Ergin Bulut
Department of Educational Policy Studies
University of Illinois at Urbana-Champaign

JEN SANDLER AND MICHAEL W. APPLE

14. A CULTURE OF EVIDENCE, A POLITICS OF OBJECTIVITY

The Evidence-based Practices Movement in Educational Policy

INTRODUCTION

One of the most significant questions in the history of education has been "What knowledge is of most worth?" This is a highly contentious issue educationally, politically, and epistemologically. Indeed, if one were to point to a constitutive ideological fault line in education, the ground surrounding what counts as "official" or "legitimate" knowledge is the site where social movements, class, race, gender, religious antagonisms, and state and civil society do battle (Apple, 2000). For some, the question can be answered by simply referring to the traditions of organized knowledge found in the academic disciplines (Phenix, 1964). For others, knowledge from below must constantly challenge what now counts as official knowledge (Freire, 1970).

At the very core of the varying positions on this is the fact that it is a conceptual necessity for there to be what is best called a constitutive outside to categories such as legitimate knowledge. That is, in order for there to be official knowledge there needs to be its opposite, "popular knowledge," knowledge that does not have the imprimatur of the state or of culturally powerful groups. The existence of something that is pure knowledge requires something that is seen as a form of pollution, as not worthy. Because of this, no matter what position one takes on what counts as official knowledge, it should be clear cultural politics lie at the center of the entire enterprise of education (Apple, 1996).

But such cultural politics do not simply lie at the heart of what we should teach in schools and universities. They also are central to judging the worth of our institutions and their success and failure. Thus, they help create how we think about what counts as "good" or "bad" schooling, curricula, teaching, and educational reforms.

Through the work of Habermas and others (see, e.g, Habermas, 1971; Poovey, 1998), we have become considerably more aware of the nature of the interests that constitute particular ways of knowing and of the history of how such ways of knowing became dominant both in the state and in our commonsense. Unfortunately, many of the insights that were gained through the entire tradition of asking about the relationship between knowledge and human interests have been either forgotten or ignored, particularly in the United States.

Z. Leonardo (ed.), Handbook of Cultural Politics and Education, 325–340.

This is unfortunate in general, but even more so now. We are witnessing a resurgence of what is perhaps best seen as a cult of objectivity, with its attendant social and epistemological commitments. It is (re)establishing particular assumptions about what should be the ultimate arbiter of success and failure in social and educational policies. There is an attempt at a radical change in the mechanisms of state governance toward a culture of scientific evidence. This is perhaps best seen in the growing emphasis on evidence-based practices in educational and social research and evaluation.

While in Britain there has been a significant, cohesive effort on the part of critical scholars to interrogate the shifting role of the state with respect to evidence, accountability, and audit cultures (as evidenced in journals such as *Critical Perspectives on Accounting* as well as the work of Shore and Wright, 1997, and Strathern, 2000), in the U.S. such critiques have been erratic and fragmented. We suggest that much work is needed to understand the current conflicts over the **culture of evidence** in social policies that affect (and arguably produce) marginalized populations in the United States. Nowhere is this struggle over a culture of evidence more striking in the United States than in the emerging evidence-based practices movement in the field of education.

What critical research has been done related to evidence-based practices in education in the United States has, for the most part, been focused on alternative politics of knowledge (e.g. Fine, 2006), charges that the focus on evidence is a rhetorical mask for bald ideology on the part of the state (e.g. Santelli, 2006), and critiques revealing the devastating effects of accountability policies on students, teachers, and communities (e.g. Au, 2009; Apple, 2006; Valenzuela, 2005; Lipman, 2004). Here, we treat evidence-based practices movement as a coherent, **relatively autonomous** agenda and examine how this effort to impose a systematic "culture of evidence" on educational policy and practice has taken shape.

In interrogating this movement—and it is a movement—it is crucial to recognize that there is a larger epistemological politics at stake. Indeed, the effort to shift educational policy to be more responsive to – and productive of – scientific evidence is not merely a reaction to critical education research. For example, objective "evidence" is also called upon by scientistic advocates to evaluate the policies of neoliberal interest groups that would subordinate educational research of all types to ideologies valorizing individual choice within educational markets over more democratic ideas of the good such as equity, participation, and access (Apple, 2006). There are multiple politics of knowledge at work here. But at the same time as we interrogate the implications of the cult of objectivity, it is equally crucial to be concerned about whose voices are and are not heard in the intensely political debates over the ends and means of our educational institutions. Thus, the implications of these transformations are profound in terms of whether they will silence voices from below or marginalize other forms of evidence. They are at the very center of conflicts over the politics of voice, over what count as legitimate forms of knowledge and judgment, and ultimately over what our educational institutions are to do. Let us look at this movement in more detail.

Recent calls for rigor and relevance in the field of education have become increasingly unified and specific, focused and public. The critique of education research has found its voice – along with a great deal of power – within the federal educational policy sphere. This voice says not just "rigor" and "relevance," but "randomized controlled trials" and "what works." This voice suddenly seems ubiquitous in federal policy, a mantra repeated with remarkable specificity and finding its way into federal educational policy, research training programs, conferences, and job postings, Requests For Proposals, and the verbiage of myriad policy organizations. It is represented in a newly coherent program of grants and fellowships on the part of the Institute of Education Sciences, as well as the over $10 million per year allocated for the What Works Clearinghouse for reviews of intervention research in education and promotion of the results of these reviews to the public. The politics of research methods in education is suddenly big news.

Because the majority of the U.S. education research community (and we use the term "community" in the loosest possible sense) does not conduct randomized controlled trials, the sudden ubiquity of this focus in federal policy has provoked quite a critical response. Unfortunately, in our view, the response has not been particularly productive in an important sense. It has not brought us closer to understanding where the emphasis on randomized trials came from or where it is going. This response has not helped us to understand who is advocating for this change and why. Indeed, the critiques of this shift have in many cases obscured or distorted the self-understandings of the actual people involved. And this response – far from collective, thus all the more disappointingly uniform in its blind spots – has utterly ignored the **politics** of this shift.

This chapter begins to trace these politics. We will start by describing this shift – which we refer to as "evidence-based policy/practices," or EBP – from what we understand to be the perspective of its advocates. We then turn to EBP itself, suggesting an outline of what we find useful to think of as an **epistemological movement**. This will involve a discussion of both the EBP movement's structure and its advocates' understanding of their work and purpose. Finally, we will address how the EBP movement might be understood in relation to the context of its particular constitutive outside: diverse interest groups and advocates who situate their political and educational work within subjective, lived experiences.

ASSUMPTIONS AND METHODS

At the outset, it is important to note our assumption that scientific practice and scientific findings are produced through profoundly *social* processes, through not only rules but also norms and judgments and conditions that, together, produce what are considered at a given time by a given community of scientists to be established findings. Science, even at its most "pure," is not an isolated, objective set of practices driven by purely technical decisions, but is instead comprised of inter-subjective practices that are shaped, not merely influenced, by actors making subjective judgments within contexts (Latour and Woolgar, 1979). Indeed, there is a long history of scholarship addressing the relationships between modern knowledge production and bureaucratization, legitimacy, the state, and democratic life (e.g. Weber, 1948; Latour, 1983; Habermas, 1971; Habermas, 1988; Poovey, 1998). Our analysis is based upon this tradition. We presume that debates over what constitutes science and what influence science should have on policy cannot be understood in their **political** dimension if they are thought of simplistically, as debates over whether truth or "myth" should prevail.

This assumption is not the same as the (usually caricatured) relativistic claim that all methods of inquiry have the same value, that they are all equivalent in terms of their ability to explain empirical phenomena or in terms of their utility with respect to social problems. It is not the equivalence of all roads to truth that is often derided as the relativism of post-modern theory that we espouse here. Rather, it is the **particularity** of experimental scientific practice that we wish to highlight. The positivist scientific community is characterized by **particular** legitimization practices, particular "rules of the game," or "logics of practice" in Pierre Bourdieu's terms (1992, Part One), through which the relationship between individual beliefs and structures play out. These dynamics shape the ways scientists produce and legitimize findings, as well as the professional identities of scientific advocates and practitioners. Science is, moreover, political in its use, fraught with issues of power, positioning and status (Rabinow, 1999). Thus, in this chapter we focus not on the value or production of evidence-based findings, but on how this framework operates in the politics of education.

Our argument here is more theoretical than empirical, although it is based in part on empirical findings (see, e.g., Sandler, 2008). We argue for the importance of shifting the focus of reactions to EBP from rhetoric to investigation; from a focus on the epistemology underlying EBP itself to an examination of the **politics** of that epistemology in educational policy and practice and on the movements that embody this set of commitments. Upon such examination, we find that the EBP movement is not just a political movement; it is an effort to shift the **culture** of policy-making, the culture of science-driven governance, toward a reliance on objective evidence for decision-making. As we shall see, the cultural politics of EBP are deeply connected to its preferred methodology.

Just as EBP strives for objective knowledge, the EBP movement attempts to shift the culture of governance to privilege knowledge that is **objectively situated** with respect to racial, ethnic, and class experience, That is, the EBP movement represents an effort to marginalize all forms of what it calls "bias" from policy-making. In the process, it also marginalizes the lived experience of marginalized people from influence. Explicitly raced and classed knowledge is, by definition, non-objective and therefore less legitimate. The cultural politics of evidence are, in fact, a politics that involve the privileging of non-situated knowledge over situated knowledge – the privileging of knowledge **about** poor people and racial and ethnically marginalized people over knowledge produced **within and by** these communities.

This demonstration draws on data that is part of a larger project on EBP. Data collection for this larger project include (1) semi-structured interviews with and position statements (speeches, journalistic interviews, articles, etc.) by leading EBP advocates as well as staff of national education organizations and federal agencies who have interfaced with these advocates; (2) collection of documents from national education policy organizations, government agencies, federal records, and major education organization web sites; and (3) participant-observation at workshops and presentations on EBP topics between August 2006 and May 2007. Data collected represent all four education EBP advocate locations discussed in this article (private research organization staff, academic researchers, government agencies, and non-governmental policy agencies), major federal education policy advocates outside of EBP, and EBP advocates in other federal policy fields (chiefly prevention research in the mental health, delinquency and substance abuse areas).

DEFINING EBP

We use the term "evidence-based practices" (EBP) as a general term that includes several related initiatives. Among these initiatives, we intend for this term to be inclusive of the notion that educational practices ought to be guided by "scientifically based research," as indicated in the No Child Left Behind Act. We also include initiatives that call for evidence-based policy, scientifically-based research (SBR), and the increased use of randomized controlled trials (RCTs) and randomized field trials (RFTs) in social and educational reform efforts. In short, we use EBP to indicate all agendas that infuse a methodological bias toward applied, causal intervention questions and toward experimental methods as an ideal means to investigate these questions.[1]

Particular EBP agendas vary, but what they have in common is the focus on the potential for experimental research methods to transform society. The advocates of EBP in education are perhaps best represented by their most powerful policy advocate: Grover "Russ" Whitehurst, the director of the Institute for Education Sciences:

> The people on the front lines of education want research to help them make better decisions in those areas in which they have choices to make, such as curriculum, teacher professional development, assessment, technology, and management. These are questions of what works best for whom under what circumstances. These are questions that are best answered by randomized trials of interventions and approaches brought to scale. These are questions and methods and development efforts with which relatively few in the education research community have been engaged. (Whitehurst, 2003)

The primary contention of EBP advocates in education is that practical knowledge for schools and teachers requires research capable of distinguishing with certainty the effects of any particular educational intervention from effects that stem from other causes. The only way to make certain such a distinction, they claim, is through the random assignment of research participants to an educational intervention or to a no-intervention (or status quo) control group. Through the use of random assignment of participants to an intervention or a control group, the effects of the intervention can be isolated and measured, and statistical methods can be used to determine the strength and generalizability of findings and to analyze effects in terms of particular sub-populations of the sample. The contention of EBP advocates is that such research can transform educational practice because it provides dispassionate, "objective" information about the relative merits of different educational interventions.[2]

Beyond the production of evidence based on experimental intervention studies, EBP is also concerned with the dissemination of such evidence. EBP advocates for a new role of the federal government: to fund criterion-based reviews of evidence and to disseminate these reviews to the practice community. The What Works Clearinghouse (www.whatworks.ed.gov) is the largest initiative in education designed to review and disseminate evidence on intervention effectiveness in education. In other EBP-affected social policy fields, there are also structures for review and dissemination at the federal level, including the Office of Juvenile Justice and Delinquency Prevention's model program list (www.dsgonline.com/mpg2.5/mpg_index.htm) and the Substance Abuse and Mental Health Services Administration's National Registry of Evidence-based Programs and Practices (www.nrepp.samhsa.gov). There are also several review projects that are not government-initiated (although many are developed under federal contracts), including the Best Evidence Encyclopedia, the Social Programs that Work web site, and the Comprehensive School Reform Quality project. Although the criteria used differ fairly widely across these review structures (for a critical comparison of the diversity of inclusion criteria used by review projects that deal with education, see Slavin, 2008), each attempts to provide a structure for objective review of research that helps practitioners to make decisions free from the bias of researchers and intervention developers. Criterion-based review is a key component of EBP. This will become important later on in this chapter as we examine the attempt to build a culture around the focus on objective criteria.

EBP AS A MOVEMENT

Despite its political coherence and recent strides toward institutionalization over the past several years, EBP is not a homogeneous agenda. It is not represented by a single organization, and indeed its advocates are often engaged in debate with one another over which review criteria and dissemination structures are most appropriate in the implementation of EBP (e.g. Slavin, 2008; Dynarski, 2008). Within the EBP agenda there are what might be termed methodological "hard-liners" as well as more "pragmatic" or instrumentalist advocates of EBP principles. Indeed, such variation exists in every movement. EBP, like any movement, is not lacking for internal controversy and power struggles; nevertheless, its debates rest upon certain assumptions outlined in the earlier section defining EBP. Chief among these assumptions are that objective, unbiased research on the effects of interventions – of which well-designed randomized controlled trials remain the gold standard – is the primary research need in the field, and that the synthesis of such intervention study results is a (if not the) key to national educational improvement.

These epistemological and political convictions that bring EBP advocates together under the same umbrella – and that systematically threaten the legitimacy of other research paradigms and other ways of knowing – are handily identified throughout critiques of EBP (e.g. St. Pierre, 2006; Popkewitz, 2004; Erickson, 2004). Yet, despite our own lack of affinity with the epistemology or politics of EBP, we do not find it particularly fruitful to view EBP as an ideology. In fact, viewing EBP as an ideology has in our view made it difficult for researchers critical of claims about the type of evidence needed to transform education to understand accurately the shifting role of science in educational policy. Declaring the limitation of an ontology or epistemology by declaring it an "ideology" or by demonstrating its epistemological blind spots, important projects though these may be, is not the same as engaging in critical analysis of the politics based on such a theory of reality or knowledge. Since it is these politics we hope to plumb, we must pay attention to EBP not as a theory, epistemological framework, or ideology. Instead, we must look at the actors involved in advancing these ideas in policy and practice.

We view EBP as a **movement** within educational and social policy. Instead of immediately rushing to ask what this movement "means" for education research or practice, we begin by seeking to understand the contours of EBP: what kind of movement it is, how it works, and how it articulates with the current politics of education. While it is inappropriate to only think about EBP as a "social movement," much of the theory of social movements has helped us to develop our understanding of EBP as a contemporary movement for social and political change. Contemporary social movement literature focuses on many problems; among them the extent to which movements are based on cultural change and the assertion of new identities. Understanding social movements in terms of how they produce and are produced by the identities of their actors, actors who form more of a complex identity-based network than a unified organization, has been an extraordinarily fruitful line of research (e.g. Escobar, 1992; Melucci, 1980). We believe that a similar approach might be fruitful with respect to EBP, and might allow us to understand the politics at hand, the movement, in its political context and with respect to the people involved in moving forward – and potentially subverting – EBP.

But while studies of social and political movements might point toward fruitful approaches to EBP, neither "social" nor "political" accurately characterize EBP as a movement. EBP is distinguished neither by its location with respect to power and institutions, nor by its political or social objective (i.e. subverting a political regime or changing particular social conditions). It is distinguished, instead, in its advocacy of a particular way of understanding truth and effects. We thus ultimately view EBP as a distinctly epistemological movement: a movement that, wherever it occurs, is based on advancing not outcomes themselves but a way of understanding outcomes. The objective of this movement is to shift the epistemological basis of educational policy so that experimental science becomes the standard for legitimate knowledge. It is to create, as many EBP advocates put it, a "culture of evidence" in the field of education.

TRUE BELIEVERS

One of the things that points to EBP as a movement is the character of its movers. The individuals engaged actively in pushing the EBP agenda, both in education and in other fields, are not merely advocating for their own professional interests. They are not (as seems to have eluded many of EBP's critics) duplicitous, strategic, or (with few exceptions) motivated by bald self-interest. Quite the contrary, in fact. We have found that EBP advocates are remarkable precisely for the evangelical, conscience-driven quality of their advocacy. Their identities, both personally and professionally, are wrapped up with this movement. The success – and integrity – of the EBP agenda is, in no uncertain terms, a *mission* for many of these individuals.

The major U.S. non-governmental, non-research organization that is involved in advancing evidence-based policy in education and other fields right now is the Coalition for Evidence-Based Policy (CEBP). Much of CEBP's work revolves around technical and educational services that deal with evidence in policy-making. But the Coalition's "real" work – according both to its small staff and to many of its interlocutors – is about spreading the word that rigorous evidence could transform how government works and thereby improve the lives of millions of people, if only those in government understood how to allow this transformation to occur. Theirs is not a strategic or even functional mission to ensure privilege; it is a revolutionary mission to change the way that government works, the way that decisions are made, all by changing the role of science in the state.[3]

The Coalition for Evidence-Based Policy is explicitly engaged in the "conversion" of a variety of political actors to EBP. Although having a hand in the wording of policy, building capacity of agency staff, providing technical assistance, and other training comprises their day-to-day operations, underlying these tasks is an effort to change the culture of policy-making, to create what they call a "culture of evidence" in Washington. Changing culture in this case relies on shifting the consciousness of policy players. The CEBP staff and board members, among the leading EBP advocates in education, count conversion or enlightenment to the EBP paradigm as among their most important successes. They describe the importance of federal agency bureaucrats "catching fire," legislators and staff "really getting it," and making the "light bulb come on" for federal agency leaders. An independent evaluator of their work concluded his evaluation by likening CEBP's task to missionizing, citing an EBP advocate's declaration that the Coalition is "doing God's work." Several of their board members declare that CEBP is "spreading the word" and "creating understanding and good will" around the central tenets of EBP in federal policy circles. One attributes what he calls EBP's "golden age" in large part to particular "champions," or charismatic, passionate and articulate advocates of randomized trials. Some EBP advocates publicly cite the importance of what one calls "zealots" and another calls "true believers" to push randomized trials into policy. Yet another publicly calls for a "new generation" to "carry the torch."

Hyperbole? Rhetorical device? Perhaps. But this is the image EBP's staunchest advocates produce of themselves. "We" are the zealots, the champions, the converted, the true believers. EBP movement activists talk about themselves bringing light to various fields – education chief among them – that are stuck in what many of them refer to as the "Dark Ages" in which "politics," "myth," "ideology," and "professional guesswork" rule.[4]

EBP'S STRUCTURE FOR BUILDING A CULTURE OF EVIDENCE

Beyond its core advocates or "true believers," what does this movement look like? How does it shift and become more prominent, or less? What are the institutional strategies of the movement, and what are the shifts that have occurred as a result? While a full examination of these issues is beyond the scope of this chapter, it is important to describe at least an outline of this movement so that the reader might get a sense of how shifts in its power might be theorized and interrogated. We suggest there are four "types" of EBP advocates, four somewhat overlapping locations within which EBP advocates operate: government agencies, university-based researchers, research-based research organizations, and non-governmental organizations.

As is well known, Whitehurst has been the major public advocate for EBP in education in the United States. The head of the Institute of Education Sciences (IES) until his six-year term expired in 2008, Whitehurst has gained the respect of not only EBP advocates in education but heads of a number of educational practice and policy organizations that are unconvinced of the importance of randomized trials in transforming the field. IES has assembled teams of academic researchers from a variety of fields, both junior and senior scholars, to serve as reviewers, advisors, and board members. Academic researchers – even quite junior scholars – who have experience conducting RCTs in education have found themselves in extremely high demand both as researchers and in new capacities as reviewers, review project managers, and technical advisors.[5] By creating a variety of roles for academic contractors aside from conducting of original research, Whitehurst has, according to interviews with academic researchers involved in IES projects, "changed the culture of education research," "expanded the role of researchers in government," "created opportunities for our work to matter," and "challenged us to really build something important, something that will make a difference." If there is any group whose identities have already shifted in the short span of EBP's activity in education, it is academic education researchers who conduct randomized trials and who have been recruited to work with IES. Their discourse in many ways mirrors the "new middle class" of government efficiency workers in the managerial state in its tone of moral good and becoming part of a new form of governance (Apple, 2006).

The role of contractors in the expansion of EBP in education is more nuanced. Research organizations that are funded through contracts have historically been very important to expanding the use of randomized trials to inform policy.[6] But what is new in education is not a simple increase in funds to conduct randomized trials; research organizations have conducted RCTs in education for years (most of them funded through federal agencies other than the Department of Education).

What is new for research organizations is their role in the development of EBP *infrastructure*. The burden has fallen on contractors to produce and manage the new EBP infrastructure in education, chiefly the What Works Clearinghouse but some smaller EBP review and dissemination initiatives as well. The major research organizations, including the American Institute of Research, which was awarded the primary initial five-year contract to develop and run the WWC, and Mathematica, which was awarded the lead role for the WWC contract beginning in the summer of 2007, have been guardedly optimistic in their public as well as private characterizations of the project.

But several other contractors, both at major research organizations and at smaller shops, note in interviews that the WWC is a somewhat "dangerous" contract. Several cite the oft-repeated conventional wisdom of EBP advocates that EBP in education is in its earliest stages, and that "the field" (some, when pressed, specify that "the field" refers to the academic field of education research, while others say they are referring to the field of practice) is "far behind" or "slow to develop" in its orientation toward evidence. But other research organization staff – most notably, several prominent, career private research organization economists who have migrated to education after conducting RCTs in other fields – express a curious wariness of the singular focus on randomized trials. These research organization executives question the wisdom of IES's unwillingness to fund what one described as "what they [at IES] perceive as more speculative kind of process research," another called "careful process studies inside these trials to learn about how the intervention works and what are the issues with implementation on the ground," and what yet another referred to as "you know, if it didn't work why and in any case how did you get the answer you got kind of questions." Those of us in education research, of course, call such studies qualitative research. Our point here is that research organizations function both as a stable location from which EBP infrastructure is built in education as well as a location that, because of its history addressing instrumental social questions, includes true believers in EBP who are wary of the *strategy* of its progression in education.

Non-governmental federal educational policy organizations across the political spectrum have, for the most part, remained cool though not hostile to EBP. While a few have attempted to appropriate the rhetoric of "evidence-based" with their constituents, most policy organizations have basically ignored EBP, going about their particular agendas and quietly waiting for this trend to pass. This (non-) reaction to evidence-based policies stands in clear contrast to the far more polarized reaction of education policy organizations to the accountability and sanctioning requirements of NCLB. Our understanding is that EBP has simply not *directly* affected these organizations' constituents – state and local educational administrators, teachers, parents, or students. As has been discussed, the EBP movement positions these decision-makers as victims of a failure of government and the research community to provide guidance regarding "what works." Because local actors and organizations are not currently being attacked by the EBP movement (as they are by the high-stakes accountability movement), the federal non-governmental policy organizations that count local actors as their constituents have not paid much attention. Of course, thus far non-governmental policy organizations have not even begun to view EBP as a resource for their constituents, either.

A strong ally of Whitehurst, the aforementioned non-governmental Coalition for Evidence-Based Policy provides support to IES in its work with all of the other sectors. They provide technical assistance for the What Works Clearinghouse, assistance for researchers, broad circulation of EBP reports and recommendations throughout federal educational policy circles, and assistance in moving EBP-related legislation in Congress. CEBP has infused language stating a preference for randomized trials into legislative as well as executive-branch projects.[7] They have also begun to work the "stable middle" of federal agencies – long-term staff members who oversee programs and portfolios. These staff members are the people who develop the grant programs, write the RFPs, determine the types of evaluation required of grantees, and read and make recommendations based on these evaluations. CEBP has recently developed workshops to train these staff both to understand why randomized trials are a uniquely important evaluation strategy and to encourage and fund them among grantees.[8] CEBP is currently the major bridge moving EBP between the government, academic, and policy worlds.

An interest group we see as a wild card in the EBP movement in education is the for-profit educational product and service providers. The for-profit education industry is not currently suffering major consequences from EBP. Many have scrambled to insert "evidence-based" into their marketing materials or to increase funding for sponsored research, and the integrity of both of these moves have been publicly questioned by IES and its contractors (Manzo, 2006). But there appear to have been no direct consequences in the bottom line of companies thus far as a result of the EBP movement. Of course, in the case of Supplementary Educational Service providers, for-profit educational providers currently enjoy billions of dollars in government funding under NCLB due to their status as a required "sanction" for under-performing schools. However, individuals involved in IES's What Works Clearinghouse contracts indicate that there has been some trepidation surrounding the legality and political ramifications of directly "intervening in the market for educational services." Several contractors indicate that while they hope the What Works Clearinghouse affects this "market" in a positive way by providing unbiased information (comparing the WWC to Consumer Reports, for example), they emphasize consistently (and using quite similar language) that local decision-makers are "free to choose" what products they want. The for-profit educational services industry is thus an ambiguous player in EBP at the moment, and the EBP movement is an ambiguous player in this industry. How the EBP movement's "culture of evidence" will interact with the increased privatization of government-funded educational services is one to watch.

EBP, SCHOOLS, AND THE POLITICS OF KNOWLEDGE

The politics of knowledge – whose knowledge matters, whose knowledge counts – of the EBP movement revolve around a striving for objectivity. What EBP activists fight against is not simply bias, however, but *subjective experience*. What are untenable to the EBP movement are questions that address the experiences of affect, of meaning, of purpose, of identity, of history, and of difference on the part of students and educators. The EBP movement situates such un-controllable knowledge in a "danger zone" of undisciplined subjectivity. For EBP, such knowledge – tainted by the subjective, local, particular – leads down a dangerous path where the professional biases of teachers and administrators (toward easier or more pleasant work) meet the ideological biases of policy-makers and the wildly diverse experiences, ideas, desires, cultures, and histories of students.

The results of bias, as EBP activists point out, are not only that we cannot measure reliable and standardized achievement gains, but that even if there are gains we cannot know exactly what caused them so that the successful techniques could be replicated and disseminated effectively. It is not enough that educational practices "work" in the eyes of students, parents, or community members. They must produce standardized, reliable, and replicable – controllable – effects. The EBP movement enacts a cultural politics, indeed, in its effort to bring a culture of control and reason to bear on schools and communities perceived (or, more aptly put, constructed) as lacking both. This emphasis on control, on objectivity, on a language and a type of knowledge that is utterly detached from the lives of the very students targeted for "improvement," is far from neutral.

As the EBP movement's true believers build the infrastructure and political will for scientific production, review, and policy, we cannot forget that the ground on which they build is not empty. As there is an attempt to bring evidence to bear on practice, there are movements swirling in these very realms of practice, struggles for power and legitimacy on the part of diverse local interest and advocacy groups. Discourses of race and class, of experiences of poverty and violence, and of resistance in education have emerged under the auspices of parent involvement, youth development, community development, local participation, ethnic pride, nationalist fervor, and religious fundamentalisms. These "localist" discourses circulate and gain power in spaces where the language of rigorous causal evidence does not have as much currency, such as youth organizations, parent and neighborhood organizations, community-based collaborations, and churches.

Of course, not all of these discourses are progressive. Not all of them are particularly democratic – indeed, democratic knowledge requires dedicated and conscientious work, and is rarely a stable feature of collective local entities. Our point is not to romanticize the local but simply to recognize it as such. What such diverse local initiatives and collective identities around schools have in common is that each produces a type of knowledge, an analysis of what schools are and should be, that is subjective and inter-subjective. Whether produced in community-based organizations or independent parent groups, in hip-hop or in Bible study, these types of knowledge clash in local cultural politics that are often rich and contentious. The subjective knowledge at the core of these cultural politics – that they turn about questions of where knowledge is situated **subjectively**, within whose experiences – stands as a powerful counterweight to the cult of objectivity peddled by EBP movement activists in the federal government.

The EBP movement has not yet begun to contend with local cultural politics. Indeed, it is all this movement can handle at the moment to involve itself in the various structural locations at the federal level that are outlined in the previous section. Those efforts, too, are cultural struggles. But we contend that the epistemological core of the EBP movement – the commitment to objective knowledge – is most strongly contested in the cultural politics of marginality that occur outside the official policy contexts where EBP currently intervenes. EBP's explicit focus on generalizable – un-situated, objective – knowledge constructs a cultural and political boundary between the "inside" of science and the constitutive, dangerous "outside" of subjective, situated knowledge.

If ever the EBP movement wins its battles to transform the production and management of evidence in education, it may then begin to exert influence upon educational practice, upon teachers and students' daily lives. But such influence would require mixing in the daily lives of teachers. It would require entering arguments with parents who despise what has been scientifically vetted, with teachers who embrace practices deemed too difficult or expensive to test experimentally. What's more, in those communities – and there are more each year – where various local politics of knowledge have actively cultivated local **analyses** of school reform, powerful and damning resistance to or co-optation of EBP is inevitable.

The cultural politics of evidence has made great strides in federal policy and significant strides in educational research, but it has not even begun to approach the cultural politics that swirl below.[9] EBP movement advocates truly believe that if given a chance, science could transform educational practice, fixing one by one each of the problems that faces contemporary schools. They believe that schools are clamoring for objective truths, for "what works," for answers. Or, at least, EBP advocates believe that local actors **should** be clamoring for objective truths, that it makes sense that they would. But faith in utterly dispassionate reviews of scientific evidence, faith in a clean and clear truth produced by those with as little stake as possible in the outcome, will not come easy to schools. In communities and schools, where dominant cultural politics turn on subjective knowledge embedded in direct experiences, be they of community, of race, of religion, of political or cultural solidarity, the EBP movement will have a difficult and lonely ride.

CONCLUSION

We have shown in this chapter how the EBP movement functions as a new, federal-level player in the politics of knowledge in education. We have shown EBP as a movement that advocates in multiple ways for a culture of evidence, portraying itself as an effort to bring objectivity and reason to a field characterized by subjective biases and myth. And we have argued the importance of recognizing these EBP movement efforts as cultural politics.

EBP is not neutral: it advocates for a way of knowing based on scientific evidence, for the possibility and value of objectivity. The culture of evidence that the EBP movement wishes to usher into educational policy and practice would not simply place evidence and science where there was none. It would place a positivistic scientific method of understanding what schools should be and do up against **existing cultural politics**, be they progressive, critical, racist, or neoconservative. EBP offers yet another way of thinking about the purpose of education and how it ought to reach toward that purpose. Far from a truly objective intervention in a cultural and ideologically polluted field, as its advocates would have it, the EBP movement is simply another response to the question of whose knowledge is of most worth. Its answer – scientists' knowledge, or knowledge not situated in the particular realities of either educators or students – bodes poorly for the EBP movement's prospect of retaining its evidentiary integrity when (and if) it reaches inside the school and classroom doors. In any case, struggles over symbolic, material, and cultural control of schooling will be complicated, and certainly not resolved, by the EBP movement.

NOTES

1 In this paper, the term "experimental" refers to intervention research that attempts to isolate the effects of an intervention in order to measure these effects. The technical debates within the EBP community about what types of experiments are legitimate for what types of claims, including whether well-matched comparison groups or interrupted-time series methods can get meaningful results that might be taken into account in systematic reviews of interventions, are beyond the scope of this paper. For our purposes, EBP includes the broad agenda focused on measurement of intervention effects isolated from confounding factors, which is most often expressed as the need for more "experiments" or "randomized trials"; we do not mean to exclude from EBP those vying for the inclusion of alternative methods of isolating intervention effects. Neither do we include under EBP, for the purposes of this paper, researchers who use the term "evidence" or "evidence-based" for purposes other than to identify with this project of measuring the effects of interventions using methods capable of causal inference.

2 It is struggle to control the definition of truth and evidence that describes the politics of knowledge at issue here; "objectivity" should thus be understood here as the *cultural trope* of the evidence-based movement, not as an actual characterization of what this movement does.

3 This core mission of CEBP is apparent in an independent qualitative evaluation of the Coalition's work (http://coexgov.securesites.net/admin/FormManager/filesuploading/indep_evaln_for_WT_Grant.pdf, accessed November 22, 2007), and is corroborated by many of our interviews with individuals who have had contact with the Coalition.

4 The quoted phrases in this paragraph are drawn from interviews as well as statements from conference and presentation transcripts from twelve individuals associated with CEBP as staff, consultants, and advisory board members. Advisory board members represented are all themselves associated with leading universities and research organizations. Quotes are used here as examples that, in the context of a project still in progress, have suggested to us that "belief " (in contrast with, say, material or professional interest) may describe the motivation and self-understanding of many of EBP's core advocates. We do not suggest that any empirical case for this category has been made here, but simply posit the theory as a potential explanation of EBP warranting further exploration.

5 Of course, the rise in status, legitimacy, and funding bestowed upon researchers who conduct randomized trials in education is directly related to a systematic marginalization of educational researchers whose work does not fit into this narrow methods-driven agenda. Indeed, the result has been to marginalize not only those who use different methods, but also to financially and symbolically undermine researchers who *ask questions* that cannot fruitfully be addressed using experiments.

[6] MDRC, a major research shop out of New York, was the pioneer of randomized field trials in welfare reform. The American Institute of Research, Mathematica, and Abt, Incorporated, three of the other major research organizations that bid on large federal projects, built their capacity to conduct randomized trials of social interventions throughout the 1980s, following MDRC's lead.

[7] In education, for example, the CEBP advanced bills following the Education Sciences Reform Act of 2002, was a lead advisor to the development of the Academic Competitiveness Council, and is attempting to affect the reauthorization of No Child Left Behind.

[8] Two such workshops have been held thus far, in the winter and spring of 2006. Several more are planned. See CEBP's web site at: http://coexgov.securesites.net/index.php?keyword=a432fbc34d71c7 (accessed on November 1, 2007).

[9] Paradoxically, research methods that truly engage the cultural politics "from below," by working alongside oppressed communities and in partnership with racially and ethnically marginalized students, are thriving in the United States, despite their increasing marginalization by the federal government and mainstream funding sources. Participatory action research, community-based research, and research on youth development and community organizing as means of systemic educational change often engage participants in co-constructing research questions and participating in all stages of research design and analysis. Such approaches have become increasingly sophisticated and dynamic in recent years, serving perhaps as an implicit challenge to the claims of the EBP movement as well as the accountability movement to further structure, contain, and control local knowledge and action. The work of Fine (2006), Oakes (2004), and Warren (2005) have paved the way, and the AERA Special Interest Group on Grassroots Youth and Community Organizing is filled with young researchers and activists anxious for this type of participatory engagement.

REFERENCES

Apple, M. W. (2006). *Educating the "Right" way: Markets, standards, God, and inequality* (2nd ed.). New York: Routledge.

Apple, M. W. (2005). Education, markets, and an audit culture. *Critical Quarterly*, *7*(1–2), 11–29.

Apple, M. W. (2000). *Education and power*. New York: Routledge.

Apple, M. W. (1996). *Cultural politics and education*. New York: Teachers College Press.

Au, W. (2009). *Unequal by design*. New York: Routledge.

Bourdieu, P. (1992). *The logic of practice*. Stanford, CA: Stanford University Press.

Burch, P., Steinberg, M., & Donovan, J. (2007). Supplemental educational services and NCLB: Policy assumptions, market practices, emerging issues. *Educational Evaluation and Policy Analysis*, *29*(2), 115–133.

Escobar, A., & Alvarez, S. (1992). *The making of social movements in Latin America*. Boulder, CO: Westview Press.

Fine, M. (2006). Bearing witness: Methods for researching oppression and resistance—A textbook for critical research. *Social Justice Research*, *19*(1), 83–108.

Freire, P. (1970). *Pedagogy of the oppressed*. New York: Continuum.

Habermas, J. (1988). *On the logic of the social sciences*. Cambridge: MIT Press.

(1971). *Knowledge and human interests*. Boston: Beacon Press.

Latour, B., & Woolgar, S. (1979). *Laboratory life: The social construction of scientific facts*. Los Angeles: Sage.

Lipman, P. (2004). *High stakes education*. New York: Routledge.

Manzo, K. K. (2006). Surge in company-sponsored studies sparks concern. *Education Week*, *26*(13), 12–13.

Melucci, A. (1980). The new social movements: A theoretical approach. *Social Science Information*, *19*(2), 199–226.

Mosteller, F., & Boruch, R. (2002). *Evidence matters: Randomized trials in education research*. Washington, DC: Brookings.

Phenix, P. (1964). *Realms of meaning*. New York: McGraw-Hill.

Poovey, M. (1998). *A history of the modern fact*. Chicago: University of Chicago Press.

Popkewitz, T. S. (2004). Is the national research council committee's report on scientific research in education scientific? On trusting the manifesto. *Qualitative Inquiry*, *10*(2), 62–78.

Rabinow, P. (1999). *French DNA: Trouble in purgatory*. Chicago: University of Chicago.

Santelli, J. S. (2006). Abstinence-only education: Politics, science, and ethics. *Social Research: An International Quarterly of Social Sciences*, *73*(3), 835–858.

St. Pierre, E. A. (2006). Scientifically based research in education: Epistemology and ethics. *Adult Education Quarterly*, *56*(4), 239–266.

Sandler, J. D. (2008). *What works? Who decides?: Scientific evidence, local governance, and the politics of knowledge in social and educational reform*. Unpublished Dissertation, University of Wisconsin, Madison.

Shore, C., & Wright, S. (Eds.). (1997). *Anthropology of policy: Critical perspectives on governance and power*. London: Routledge.

Slavin, R. E. (2008). Perspectives on evidence-based research in education – What Works? Issues in synthesizing educational program evaluation. *Educational Researcher*, *37*(1), 5–14.

Strathern, M. (Ed.). (2000). *Audit cultures: Anthropological studies in accountability, ethics and the academy*. London: Routledge.

Valenzuela, A. (Ed.). (2005). *Leaving children behind*. Albany, NY: State University Press of New York.

Warren, M. (2005). Communities and schools: A new view of urban educational reform. *Harvard Educational Review*, *75*(2), 133–175.

Weber, M. (1948). *Max Weber: Essays in sociology* (H. Gerth & C. Mills, Eds.). New York: Oxford University Press.

Whitehurst, G. R. (2003, April 22). *The institute of education sciences: New wine and new bottles*. Presidential invited address at the Annual Meeting of the American Educational Research Association, delivered, Chicago.

Jen Sandler
Department of Education
Bates College

Michael W. Apple
Departments of Curriculum and Instruction and Educational Policy Studies
University of Wisconsin
Madison

KRISTEN L. BURAS

15. EDUCATION, CULTURAL POLITICS, AND THE NEW HEGEMONY

How Multiculturalism became a Neoconservative Weapon

Just a few days ago, I was listening to the radio. While changing stations, I paused to hear a short series of first–person vignettes, already in progress, which chronicled the lives and accomplishments of several African Americans. I was next informed of something else: This lesson on African American history was a commercial announcement sponsored by Coca–Cola. Upon further investigation, I came to discover that the soft drink company had indeed initiated a year–long campaign focused on black consumers, one that began on the national holiday reserved for Dr. Martin Luther King (Black Web Portal News Wire, 2008). In fact, this specific radio advertisement was only one component of a much wider media outreach effort. Another advertisement, one intended for television, featured a black history timeline with key turning points, such as "Montgomery, 1955: Woman remains seated. And stands for justice," visually noted alongside a Coca–Cola bottle, presumably from each respective period. The spot closes with two frames—the first displaying a Coca–Cola bottle next to the words "Celebrates Black History" (that is, Coca–Cola Celebrates Black History), and the second announcing "Especially Today." All of this is accompanied by a selection of music with jazz piano (Coca–Cola, 2008a). What is demonstrated powerfully as a result is the willingness of wealthy elites and corporations to embrace what began as a radical current from below—demands for cultural and historical recognition by traditionally oppressed groups—and to simultaneously redefine such a current as co–terminus with elite interests, inevitably bolstered through heightened consumption. Indeed, these commercials may be understood as a kind of "racial project" (Omi & Winant, 1994), one that seeks to advance a new common sense around understandings of racial power, civil rights, national progress, and the economy. Importantly, while it draws upon the legacy of African American resistance, it actually serves to mask the critical worldviews circulated through the racial projects that preceded it. That is, civil rights activists in the mid–twentieth century, including the "woman who remained seated but stood for justice," and Black Power activists, who, notably, are not featured by Coca–Cola, sought not "the Coke side of life," but a self–determined life free of racially–motivated violence and the limitations imposed by white supremacy. What is now bestowed is a portrayal of black history and success that links the civil rights agenda to unbridled consumption—the ultimate marker of meritocratic ascendancy and arrival. In the final analysis, this is the worldview

Z. Leonardo (ed.), Handbook of Cultural Politics and Education, 341–371.

endorsed in yet another Coca–Cola commercial, which asks the viewer, "What do you see when you look at me?" With pro–skater Kareem Campbell shown in motion on a sidewalk, it asks, "Someone ready to have a dream or a millionaire already living one?" Next pictured is entrepreneur Lisa Price, followed by the question, "Do you see the girl next door or a global businesswoman?" To complicate the politics of the campaign's production, the role of the black middle class itself in formulating it must be acknowledged. Yolanda White, an African American woman who is Assistant Vice President of African American Marketing for Coca–Cola North America and was involved in development, indicates that these individuals "truly embody what it means to overcome" (Coca–Cola, 2008b).

I open this chapter with the above discussion because Coca–Cola's black history campaign provides a powerful illustration of *rightist multiculturalism* as the new hegemony (Buras, 2008b). More specifically, I refer to the propensity, especially over the past two decades, toward particular forms of compromise—namely, those building on the cultural sensibilities of and demands for recognition by marginalized groups while at the same time steering those sensibilities in dominant directions. This new and potentially more "successful" hegemonic strategy is more sophisticated and encompassing than the additive multiculturalism (McCarthy, 1998) or curricular mentioning of "isolated elements of the history and culture of less powerful groups" (Apple, 2000, p. 53) that have often characterized conservative cultural work. Rightist multiculturalism represents a far more extensive effort to reconstruct the radical racial critiques of the 1960s than the inclusion of textbook sidebars on the Little Rock Nine or mainstreaming of Malcolm X through state issuance of an honorary postage stamp. Moreover, rightist multiculturalism has penetrated spheres beyond radio and television. Perhaps the most significant initiative has occurred in classrooms across the nation, and I am not speaking of the infamous Channel One, which infuses commercial programming into schools (Apple, 2000; Molnar, 2005). Rather I am referring to the neoconservative–inspired Core Knowledge curriculum around which E. D. Hirsch (1987, 1996) and the Core Knowledge Foundation (CKF, 2004e) have built an entire school reform movement premised on this new hegemonic approach (see Buras, 2008b).

Core Knowledge is undeniably an exemplar of rightist multiculturalism. Before examining the cultural politics that have shaped this educational reform, however, I first want to begin with a deeper exploration of the work of Antonio Gramsci, whose contributions to understanding struggles over culture and knowledge have been central to critical work in education. Second, I likewise will reveal the centrality of critical race theory to understanding the reconstitution of ideology around race, racial power, civil rights, and education, with special emphasis on the maintenance of white privilege and domination. All of this, finally, will be brought to bear on a case study of the dynamics of the Core Knowledge movement, which illuminates the complex and ongoing process of building hegemony for neoconservative school reform, and ultimately suggests the necessity of fighting an alternative "war of position" aimed at reclaiming multiculturalism as a counter–hegemonic project.

WAR OF POSITION, HEGEMONY, AND THE NEOCONSERVATIVE ASSAULT ON "RACE–CONSCIOUSNESS"

Imprisoned in Fascist Italy during the late 1920s, political activist and neo–Marxist Antonio Gramsci began writing what has come to be known as the *Prison Notebooks* (Hoare & Nowell–Smith, 1971). Although somewhat fragmentary in nature, this series of texts detailed a theory of ideology, culture, and power—one rooted in the historic struggles of subaltern groups to transform oppressive conditions. Gramsci's theory has had a profound influence in the cross–cutting arena of cultural studies and critical education. Substantively complicating more orthodox traditions within Marxism that conceptualized the relationship between base and superstructure (that is, economy and "everything else") as unidirectional and largely driven by the relations of production and needs of capital, neo–Marxist perspectives inspired by Gramsci instead centered on the mediating role of culture in both sustaining and challenging relations of unequal power—and not simply class relations alone (Apple & Buras, 2006; Au, 2006; Leonardo, 2005). At the heart of Gramsci's theory of hegemony, or the way that groups attain and maintain power, is the idea of strategic compromise. More specifically, Gramsci asserted:

> Hegemony presupposes that account be taken of the interests and the tendencies of the groups over which hegemony is to be exercised, and that a certain compromise equilibrium should be formed—in other words, that the leading group should make sacrifices. (Hoare & Nowell–Smith, 1971, p. 161)

While material compromises secured partial victories, it was equally important that the cultural tendencies and worldviews of subordinate groups be taken seriously by elites. In other words, the cultural leadership and authority of ruling groups was more "effective" in the long–term if continuously negotiated rather than imposed. With this dynamic in mind, Gramsci proposed the development of a history of subaltern classes in his *Notebooks* and actually began to author such a history with regard to the Italian Risorgimento—the period of unification between 1815 and 1871 during which the Italian national state was forged. He suggested that account be taken of not only the formation of subaltern groups, but also their "active or passive affiliation to the dominant political formations, their attempts to influence the programmes of these formations in order to press claims of their own, and the consequences of these attempts in determining processes of decomposition, renovation, and neo–formation." Equally important, Gramsci stressed, was an assessment of "the birth of new parties of the dominant groups, intended to conserve the assent of the subaltern groups and to maintain control over them" (p. 52). This give–and–take was of utter import, as Gramsci eschewed the tendency within orthodox Marxism to attribute relations of domination to the duped masses rather than the complexities of rule through the generation of assent. In seeking to understand the ascendancy of particular political parties, for example, Gramsci complains, "Economism asks the question: 'who profits directly from the initiative under consideration?'" It replies, he criticized, "with a line of reasoning which is as simplistic as it is fallacious: the ones who profit directly are a certain fraction of the ruling class." What results is an understanding of rule based purely on "duplicity and bad faith, or (in the case of the movement's followers), of naiveté and stupidity." Thus he goes on: "The political struggle is reduced to a series of personal affairs between on the one hand those with a genie in the lamp who know everything and on the other those who are fooled by their leaders but are so incurably thick that they refuse to believe it." Gramsci clearly asserts the inadequacy of such an explanation, proclaiming "it is not enough." By this he means that a more sophisticated "analysis of the balance of forces" is necessary to understand hegemony (pp. 166–167).

Indeed, Gramsci conceives the exercise of power itself as a balance between rule by coercion and rule by consent. In the first instance, which he referred to as the *war of maneuver*, ruling groups maintain power through force or the threat of it:

> In military war, when the strategic aim—destruction of the enemy's army and occupation of his territory—is achieved, peace comes. … It is enough that the strategic aim should simply be achieved potentially: it is enough in other words that there should be no doubt that an army is no longer able to fight, and that the victorious army "could" occupy the enemy's territory. (p. 229)

In the second instance, the *war of position*, the powerful maintain rule and the subaltern contest it through ongoing ideological and cultural struggle rather than military conflict. In comparison to the war of maneuver, Gramsci writes:

> Political struggle is enormously more complex: in a certain sense, it can be compared to colonial wars or to old wars of conquest—in which the victorious army occupies, or proposes to occupy, permanently all or part of the conquered territory. Then the defeated army is disarmed and dispersed, but the struggle continues on the terrain of politics. (p. 229)

The tug–of–war between unequally empowered groups, in other words, entails a constant effort to rearticulate popular sentiments in directions that ultimately support the interests of the contending group. More concretely, Gramsci references India's political struggle against British rule and delineates "three forms of war: war of movement, war of position, and underground warfare." He explains:

> Gandhi's passive resistance is a war of position, which at certain moments becomes a war of movement, and at others underground warfare. Boycotts are a form of war of position, strikes of war of movement, the secret preparation of weapons and combat troops belongs to underground warfare. (pp. 229–230)

These tools of warfare were interconnected, but at the same time differentially available to disparate class fractions. On this account, it was emphasized:

> A class which has to work fixed hours every day cannot have permanent and specialized assault organizations—as can a class which has ample financial resources and all of whose members are not tied down by fixed work. … Commando tactics cannot therefore have the same importance for some

> classes as for others. For certain classes a war of movement and manoeuvre is necessary—because it is the form of war which belongs to them. … But to fix one's mind on the military model is the mark of a fool: politics, here too, must have priority over its military aspect, and only politics creates the possibility for manoeuvre and movement. (p. 232)

It is here that one comes to appreciate the unapologetic emphasis on cultural politics, or the war of position, in which competing groups seek to win consent for their positions or worldviews. Moreover, it is cultural struggle in which subaltern groups in particular should invest—a weapon of immense power and one more readily accessible to those with limited resources. By doing so, the ground might be prepared for other forms of war and the accession to state power, underwritten by a new and more just hegemony (one that minimizes rather than maximizes unequal relations of power) produced through the redefinition of prevailing cultural understandings. Regarding precisely where such work was to occur, Gramsci suggests, "The superstructures of society are like the trench–systems of modern warfare" (p. 235). That is, the battle is to unfold on the ground in theaters, media, churches, cultural associations, schools, and other spaces throughout civil society. Before his own imprisonment Gramsci wrote for a number of socialist journals, including *L'Ordine Nuovo*—a paper he co–founded and produced. As its name implies, Gramsci aimed to facilitate the birth of a new order by reworking prevailing forms of common sense. He attended to a host of cultural forms, writing reviews of literature, art, and theater, "although not in the guise of great timeless monuments but always in the context of [their] reception … and absorption in particular cultures and histories" (Forgacs & Nowell–Smith, 1985, p. 12). He firmly grasped that the war of position was also fought by those in power, who must constantly attempt to control the meanings of pivotal themes that permeate popular consciousness, compromising with the oppressed but also absorbing and moderating the more progressive elements of subaltern claims (see also Apple, 2000; Omi & Winant, 1994). Such tensions and processes are powerfully at work in the Core Knowledge movement, as I will reveal.

While much of Gramsci's work focuses on class politics and derives from European history, for example, Michael Omi and Howard Winant (1994) refocus the lens on racial politics, the civil rights movement in the United States, and the neoconservative reaction that took shape in the 1970s and 1980s.[1] Placing race at the center of their theory of cultural formation, they advanced a Gramscian–inspired analysis of racial contestation and rejected the reductionist tendency to "treat race epiphenomenally or subsume it within a supposedly more fundamental category," such as class. They argued the dialectic relationship between the racial state and civil society, including new social movements, was fundamental to comprehending the terrain of racial representation and power in any given historical era. From across the political spectrum, groups mobilize and advance "racial projects," that is, "representations of racial dynamics" accompanied by "efforts to reorganize and redistribute resources along particular racial lines" (p. 56). This ongoing effort to consolidate rule as well as to challenge it through cultural struggle epitomizes the war of position. Along precisely these lines, Core Knowledge represents a racial project from above that draws upon impulses from below, but remains challenged by the perpetual necessity to arbitrate those impulses—a portion of which are closely tied to the legacy of civil rights and racial justice.

On the one hand, the civil rights movement meant that "new conceptions of racial identity and its meaning, new modes of political organization and confrontation, and new definitions of the state's role in promoting and achieving 'equality' were explored, debated, and contested on the battlegrounds of politics" (Omi & Winant, 1994, p. 95). Omi and Winant explain:

> Social movements create collective identity by offering their adherents a different view of themselves and their world; different, that is, from the worldview and self–concepts offered by the established social order. They do this by the process of *rearticulation*, which produces new subjectivity by making use of information and knowledge already present in the subject's mind. They take elements and themes of her/his culture and traditions and infuse them with new meaning. (p. 99)

Whether through liberation theology that demanded "rights" or race–conscious nationalism that demanded "power," the overthrow of racial oppression was at the core of this upswing. In turn, the transformations produced were met with racial projects intended to undermine the gains of the 1960s and to ensure the continuation of white supremacy. Importantly, however, Omi and Winant point out:

> In the aftermath of the 1960s, any effective challenge to the egalitarian ideals framed by the minority movements could no longer rely on the racism of the past. Racial equality had to be acknowledged as a desirable goal. But the *meaning* of equality, and the proper means for achieving it, remained matters of considerable debate. (p. 117)

Most profoundly influenced by neoconservatives, the ideology that came to reign was that of the "color–blind society," where any consideration of race was framed as a distortion of the civil rights agenda as well as a threat to equality and national stability itself.

Perhaps nowhere else has the de–radicalization and mainstreaming of the civil rights movement been more thoroughly critiqued than in the field of law, where critical race theory first emerged in the 1980s. Founding critical race theorist Derrick Bell challenged the iconic status of *Brown v. Board of Education* and questioned whether or not integrationist ideals had been prioritized over the needs of black children for a well–resourced education in their own communities, where parents could meaningfully contribute to curriculum and educational policy (Bell, 1995; see also Morris, 2006). Similarly, Kimberlé Crenshaw (1995) examined the ways in which the radical underpinnings of demands for racial reform in the 1960s have been undermined by a neoconservative assault on race–conscious initiatives, which allegedly perverted the law by politicizing it. On a related note, Gary Peller (1995) revealed how the analytics of mainstream integrationist ideology equated racism with any and all forms of race–consciousness. Black Power advocates and white segregationists were both and equally "racist," with color blindness, race neutrality, and an emphasis on individual merit deemed the hallmarks of a socially just, universal orientation. Too little attention was paid to the cultural terms of integration and the underlying presumption that black culture would be left at the schoolhouse door. It was precisely these concerns that led education scholars Gloria Ladson–Billings and William Tate (2006) to argue that "The current multicultural paradigm functions in a manner similar to civil rights law. Instead of creating radically new paradigms which ensure justice, multicultural reforms are routinely 'sucked back into the system'" (p. 25). In many ways, critical race theorists have been engaged in an elaborate war of position, challenging the wisdom of the meanings of civil rights and equality that have been asserted by the new right, particularly neoconservatives.

Although the racial project of neoliberals has been a daunting one, as evidenced by the Coca–Cola campaign that sutures consumption to African American history, the racial project undertaken by neoconservatives has been just as extensive. In discussing the centrality of cultural politics and compromise to hegemony, especially in relation to education, Nathan Glazer's (1997) pronouncement in the late 1990s that "we are all multiculturalists now" is more than a little relevant. By this, Glazer meant that the multiculturalism advocated by oppressed groups had gained enough strength that "simple denunciation … would no longer do" (p. 33). "Multiculturalism of some kind there is, and there will be," he conceded. "The fight is over how much, what kind, for whom, at what ages, under what standards" (p. 19). Regarding what kind of multiculturalism Glazer envisioned, it helps to recall his clarification that the declaration "we are all multiculturalists now" mirrors past resignations "pronounced wryly by persons who recognized that something unpleasant was nevertheless unavoidable; it [does not] indicate a whole-hearted embrace" (p. 160).

Glazer's proclamation offers a way to begin thinking about the cultural dynamics underlying the advance of Core Knowledge. The 1960s and 1970s were indeed decades of spirited social activism during which many subaltern groups—African Americans and women to name just two—struggled for a more equitable distribution of resources as well as cultural respect and recognition. Issues related to the production and legitimization of knowledge were central to these groups as they demanded that their perspectives and histories contribute to reconstructing the nation. The demands expressed by movement activists are partly responsible for inspiring the rise of refashioned rightist politics in the 1980s, including neoconservative reform efforts aimed at curtailing the influence of progressive multiculturalism in schools and society (Omi & Winant, 1994; see also Buras, 2008a, 2008b). In short, this kind of multiculturalism—focused on oppressed identities and ignored histories—was understood by neoconservatives as divisive and threatening to cultural cohesion, shared national identity, and the supremacy of Western civilization (Bennett, 1992; Leming et al., 2003).

Yet none of this meant the wholesale rejection of multiculturalism. Thus, in an effort to win the consent of Latino parents, for example, Hirsch's Core Knowledge Foundation began translating its encyclopedic *What Your K–6 Grader Needs to*

Know Series into Spanish and distributing the volumes free of charge. These translated readers are intended "to provide supplements to the original books for concerned Spanish–speaking parents, to enable them to help their children read and learn from the corresponding English–language volume" (Hirsch in Hirsch & Holdren, 2001, About Supplement). Clearly instead of eschewing multiculturalism, the Core Knowledge Foundation has instead engaged in the complex task of fashioning compromises and fostering alliances on the battlefield of culture. In fact, its effort to defend dominant cultural forms—in this case, to utilize Spanish as a bridge to both the inculcation of English and Core content—has been exceptionally successful. At the same time, it is crucial to acknowledge that while such compromises and efforts may serve to strengthen the neoconservative project, the ongoing task of building alliances is undoubtedly characterized by tension as differentially empowered groups maneuver to advance their concerns and interests. I now want to thoroughly interrogate all of this in relation to Core, with the goal of refining our sense of the complex exchanges, distinct strategies, and hegemonic processes that currently define rightist multiculturalism.

THE CULTURAL POLITICS OF THE CORE KNOWLEDGE MOVEMENT

Nearly two decades ago, Hirsch (1987) authored *Cultural Literacy: What Every American Needs to Know*. This bestseller generated a wave of debate as it declared not only the importance of common culture to national unity, but defined the relevant content of that culture and blamed multicultural education for undermining it. Deemed Eurocentric by critics (Aronowitz & Giroux, 1991), *Cultural Literacy* nonetheless metamorphosed into Core Knowledge—a pre–kindergarten through eighth grade curriculum that includes specific content guidelines in history, language arts, math, science, and the musical and visual arts (CKF, 1998), and resources such as literary collections and history textbooks aligned with those guidelines (Hirsch, 2002). The first school to implement the curriculum opened in 1990. Since that time, Hirsch's vision has shaped a nationwide movement focused on reforming education through Core Knowledge, which has been adopted by nearly 1,000 schools in a diverse array of communities (CKF, 2003e, 2004b). Why is it, we might wonder, that an educational initiative developed to mediate against the "threat" of multiculturalism has garnered support from a range of communities—some constituted by traditionally oppressed groups?

I plan to consider that question by briefly, but critically, examining Hirsch's vision of education and the ways his guiding assumptions appeal to unequally empowered groups. Moreover, I trace the cultural politics and growth of the Core Knowledge movement, analyze the allegiance of dominant and subaltern groups to Core, and underscore the tensions generated by diverse actors and interests within the movement. In turn, through an illustration focused on civil rights leaders, I assess the representations that characterize the narratives of Core history textbooks and the relationship of those narratives to strategic compromise (see also Buras, 1999, 2006, 2008b).

E. D. Hirsch's Educational Vision

Hirsch assumes that education is a cognitive–technical process through which factual content is transmitted. He complains that a major barrier to improving education has been "the politicization of educational issues that are at bottom technical rather than political" (1996, p. 66). Appropriating both cognitive psychology and neurophysiology to support his vision of schooling, Hirsch argues that educational excellence depends on an appreciation of short– and long–term memory, repetition, and the continuous chunking, assimilation, and stocking of new information in an accurate fashion. Learning, for Hirsch (1987, 1996), is the consumption of what he calls core content, relevant background knowledge, intellectual capital, traditional subject matter, shared national culture, and solid facts.

Such referents shelter Hirsch from having to discuss the political nature of knowledge and schooling. In fact, he consciously chooses not to explore the role of power in determining what and whose knowledge is considered relevant, reasoning: "Once you start down that road, where will you stop?" (1996, p. 31). Instead of exploring this political slippery slope, Hirsch emphasizes the need to reach an agreement on a common sequence in the curriculum, "at least in those areas like math and science and the basic facts of history and geography, which, unlike sex education, are not and should not be subjects of controversy" (p. 37). That the construction of knowledge is a political process and that the privileging and obliteration of culture have been central to the educational history of this nation are issues that Hirsch evades (e.g., see Adams, 1995; Woodson, 2000).

Another assumption made by Hirsch is that schools must compensate for the knowledge deficits of children from culturally impoverished backgrounds. He reasons that "students from good–home schools will always have an educational advantage over students from less–good home schools" (1996, p. 43). Drawing startling parallels between knowing and unknowing students, Hirsch praises the benefits of traditional knowledge and pedagogy for "the palace–tutored prince as well as the neglected pauper" (p. 226). He does not address why the cultural traditions, linguistic practices, or social mores of one home are considered good, while others are viewed as symptomatic of illiteracy, ignorance, and cultural deficit. Instead, he expresses guarded optimism:

> Young children who arrive at school with a very small vocabulary and a correspondingly limited knowledge base, *can* fortunately be brought to an age–adequate vocabulary by intelligent, focused help ... [but] when this language and knowledge deficit is not compensated for early, it is nearly impossible . . . in later grades. (p. 146)

Though articulated with benevolence and even declared part of the "new civil rights frontier," Hirsch's position is founded on a sort of cultural supremacy that fails to recognize itself as such. His perspective prevents him from fully recognizing that children—whether working class, of color, or Spanish–speaking—bring to the classroom lived experiences, cultural traditions, and languages that are diverse and rich sources of knowledge (e.g., see Apple & Beane, 2007; Delgado Bernal, 2002; Ladson–Billings, 1994; Michie, 1999).

Finally, Hirsch assumes that a common culture is shared by all members of society and should be promoted through a national curriculum in support of democracy. Providing a questionable reading of history, for example, he claims that the founding of the common school was based on "the goal of giving all children the shared intellectual and social capital" necessary for participation in "the economy and policy of the nation" (1996, p. 233). Such a rendering of history allows Hirsch to forget that the intellectual capital transmitted by the common school was not "shared." As Carl Kaestle (1983) has shown, common schools were built on a native, Anglo–American, Protestant, republican, capitalist ideology that left many groups alienated. Further, the underlying purpose of the common school was to promote moral, social, and cultural stability rather than genuine educational and political development. Yet such evidence is not considered by Hirsch who rejects the idea that "common culture" has long represented a selective tradition.

Hirsch's educational vision is instead built on the notion that an inclusive and shared culture—a mythic one that has never existed—is being undermined by a "retrogressive kind" of multiculturalism he calls "ethnic loyalism." Rather than allowing this "particularistic" tradition, which emphasizes allegiance to one's local or ethnic culture, to promote social divisions, Hirsch advocates a "universalistic" tradition he calls "cosmopolitanism," which stresses being "a member of humanity as a whole" (Hirsch, 1992b, p. 3). He also argues that the United States should adopt a national curriculum to defend shared culture, and promises that such a curriculum will remedy the deficiencies of culturally impoverished students. Although he acknowledges that the formation of such a curriculum may initially involve some conflict, he indicates that it should be possible to reach a consensus. This belief is bolstered by the fact that he views knowledge as relatively static and uncontested, asserting, "For most problems that require critical thought by the ordinary person … the most needed knowledge is usually rather basic, long–lived, and slow to change" (1996, p. 155). In the end, Hirsch's cosmopolitanism relies on a mythical consensus that overshadows the reality of cultural and economic inequality. His quest to settle on common curricular content also overshadows the fact that what should be shared in a democracy is an ongoing "process" of negotiation over what counts as knowledge, rather than adherence to some unchanging canon (see Apple, 1996).

Hirsch's neoconservative imaginary rests on a host of problematic assumptions (see also Buras, 1999). Still, the discourses adopted by him have resonated with the experiences, anxieties, and hopes of differently situated groups—something that partly explains why the Core Knowledge movement has attracted wide support. His call for common culture and a national curriculum appeals to prevalent fears about race, gender, and sexuality. In the midst of demands for the recognition of diverse cultural perspectives, cultural and religious conservatives tired of Latinos, gays and lesbians, women, and others "politicizing everything" conceivably find attractive the position that the school curriculum need not generate political struggles, but should rather be recognized as an avenue for transmitting "factual" content. Some may even hope that a commonly shared culture nurtured by the schools will diminish racial divisions and engender greater social cohesion, albeit without having to address the cultural domination and unequal distribution of resources and power at the center of these tensions. On multiple levels, then, Hirsch's educational vision synthesizes a plethora of racial anxieties and convictions.

In another vein, Hirsch's claim that the acquisition of intellectual capital through Core Knowledge will secure upward mobility addresses the concerns of marginalized groups. He asserts, "Wherever public schools have offered the choice of truly effective mainstream academic training ... minority families have signed up in disproportionate numbers. ... These parents clearly recognize the direct connection between economic advancement for their children and the mastery of ... mainstream culture" (1996, p. 208). While Hirsch fails to note the predicament in which many "minorities" find themselves—they must submit to cultural domination or risk economic hardship—and also ignores market realities, his assertion nonetheless manages to associate Core with greater access to material resources. It is not hard to appreciate why poor or even anxious middle–class parents would mobilize around a curriculum that provides children with the "background knowledge" needed to "succeed economically."

It is equally significant that Hirsch frames his initiative in terms of "civil rights" and "compensation." Building on this argumentation, Hirsch (1999) has inveighed, "In the wake of the *Brown* decision, at the very moment of our highest hopes for social justice, the victory of progressivism over academic content had already foreclosed the chance that school integration would equalize achievement and enhance social justice" (para. 2). Forging an even closer relationship between Core Knowledge and racial equality, he highlights: "The late James Farmer, the great civil rights activist, once honored our annual Core Knowledge conference by giving a keynote address in the tradition of Du Bois which said, in effect, that strong common content in the early grades is the new frontier of the civil rights movement" (para. 9). Interestingly, this is not what Farmer said—as I will show—yet such a bold statement powerfully connects Core to histories of struggle from below and to civil rights, a long–standing concern for communities of color and for many other subaltern groups, too.

Hirsch's educational vision thus incorporates and redirects an array of popular feelings and convictions, evidenced by the growth of the Core Knowledge movement. However, it took more than a vision to build the movement. It also took a specific curriculum, the Core Knowledge Foundation, and the alliance of school communities in a range of contexts. Let us take a look at the nationwide movement that has developed around Core over the past two decades. Only by gaining insight into the dynamics of this movement may the power of neoconservatives be potentially disrupted and the fears and desires of people reoriented in more democratic directions.

FROM CULTURAL LITERACY TO CORE KNOWLEDGE

In the late 1970s, Hirsch, a professor at the University of Virginia, began formulating his ideas on cultural literacy and circulating them at professional meetings. In 1983, he published an essay titled "Cultural Literacy" in *The American*

Scholar. He declared English and history "central to culture making," then charged:

> In English courses, diversity and pluralism now reign without challenge. . . . If we want to achieve a more literate culture than we now have, we shall need to restore the balance between [the] two equally American traditions of unity and diversity. We shall need to restore certain common contents to the humanistic side of the school curriculum. (pp. 160–161)

Professing his emergent philosophy, Hirsch captured the attention of the Exxon Education Foundation which supported his production of a tentative list of cultural literacy items (Hirsch, 1987). Meanwhile, he established the Cultural Literacy Foundation. In a maneuver to depict his educational initiative as detached from politics, Hirsch (1996) explained the decision to change the organization's name to the Core Knowledge Foundation: "The term 'Cultural' raised too many extraneous questions, whereas the term 'Core Knowledge' better described the chief aim ... to introduce solid knowledge in a coherent way into the elementary curriculum" (p. 13). Since 1986, the foundation has provided a good part of the organizational structure and resources needed to transform his vision into a national reform effort. With the publication of Hirsch's *Cultural Literacy* in 1987 and *The Dictionary of Cultural Literacy* the next year (Hirsch, Kett, & Trefil, 1988), the *Core Knowledge Sequence*—content guidelines for the various subject areas—was soon to follow (CKF, 1998).

According to the Core Knowledge Foundation, the content guidelines were "the result of a long process of research and consensus–building." Reports issued by state departments of education and professional associations were examined for recommended educational outcomes. Additionally, the organization "tabulated the knowledge and skills specified in the successful educational systems of several other countries, including France, Japan, Sweden, and West Germany." An advisory board on multiculturalism was invited to suggest "diverse cultural traditions that American children should all share." "Three independent groups of teachers, scholars, and scientists around the country" were provided the materials and asked to generate master lists. Those lists were used to create a "draft master plan" that was finalized by "some 100 educators and specialists" who formed "twenty–four working groups" at a gathering in March 1990. The *Sequence* was then piloted and refined during its first year of implementation at Three Oaks Elementary School, the first Core Knowledge school, in Florida. The foundation clarifies, however, that there has been "more stability than change in the Sequence," particularly considering the "inherent stability of the content of literate culture" (CKF, 1998, pp. 1–2).

The foundation's description may appear to render transparent the process by which Core was produced, but the issues associated with its production are more complex than acknowledged. The politics that shaped the standards advocated in state reports, for example, were not considered. These standards, along with those assumed to guide "successful" educational systems in other nations, were apparently embraced without criticism. The process is described in highly technical terms—content recommendations were "tabulated" and a "list" was developed.

The commissioning of an advisory board on multiculturalism raises a host of issues that remain unarticulated, including the issue of how its members and participants at the 1990 meeting were chosen. Reflecting several years later on the convocation that met in 1990, Hirsch explained, "I mean, we didn't have Lithuanians, but we did have 24 working groups" (Goldberg, 1997, p. 84). Such a statement hardly addresses the most fundamental questions. Who determined what should count as Core Knowledge? Did particular conflicts emerge during the process? If so, how were they resolved? If the politics of knowledge were not explicitly engaged, as suggested by the foundation's technical approach, then what implicit interests might have determined the content? Questions about *whose* knowledge is valued in schools are worthy of continuous and collective reflection, yet the politics surrounding the production of Core Knowledge have been rendered to a significant degree invisible and beyond the pale of inquiry. Instead, multicultural consultation is delicately combined with allegedly technical and consensus–driven processes to produce a presumably uncontested and stable representation of shared culture and knowledge.

The Role of the Core Knowledge Foundation

The development of local, regional, and national networks around Core Knowledge has been assisted by the Core Knowledge Foundation. The foundation's work has progressed from piloting Core in a single school in 1990, to working with some 300 schools by mid–1996 (CKF, 1996b), to coordinating a network of nearly 1,000 Core Knowledge schools in forty–six states by 2007 (CKF, 2004b, 2006, 2007). Although Core initially covered grades K–6, the curriculum for pre–kindergarten and grades 7–8 was subsequently developed (Marshall, 1997d, 1997e). Approximately half of Core Knowledge schools are public, another quarter are charter schools, and the remaining fraction are private or religious schools. In urban, suburban, and rural areas, Core has likewise captured attention; a quarter of the schools are rural, with the remaining percentage divided almost evenly between urban and suburban areas (CKF, 2004b, 2004c).

With such an array of communities on board, the foundation has mandated that schools comply with increasingly rigorous implementation and reporting standards in order to gain recognition. A school can qualify as either a "friend of Core Knowledge," an "official Core Knowledge school," or a "visitation site" deemed "model." Depending on its status, the school may need to complete an annual profile, but may also be required to participate in professional development offered by the foundation, fully implement the curriculum, host site visits by foundation representatives, and accommodate a strong push to utilize Core resources, such as Core Knowledge history textbooks, and provide achievement data through standardized, Core Knowledge–referenced tests (CKF, 2003b, 2003c, 2003d, 2004b). This heightened monitoring, I will argue, may be driven by a desire to discipline the very diversity that has enabled the movement's growth. But I will first consider the role the foundation has played in facilitating this growth and why differently situated communities have embraced Core.

The foundation has organized a National Core Knowledge Conference annually since 1992. The 1st national conference was attended by 50 people (Goldberg, 1997). In comparison, the 13th gathering in Atlanta in 2004 was attended by 2,100 administrators, teachers, and parents (Hassett, 2004). At the conference, participants attend formal addresses by invited speakers, receive awards for their school's progress in implementing Core, and even tour local Core Knowledge schools. An entire day is dedicated to teachers presenting lesson plans based on the *Sequence*. Actually, it is difficult to overstate the role such activities have played in mobilizing teachers around Core. Under conditions where teachers are generally blamed for the failures of the educational system, Core Knowledge teachers are viewed as professionals whose curricular ideas contribute to enhancing the quality of education in Core schools. At the 2004 national conference, Hirsch called teachers "the heart and soul of the movement." He continued:

> Our potential is being realized because of you great people in this room. I feel that every time I come to one of these conferences. … Even though it's hard work to do Core Knowledge and it's hard to get up and teach the knowledge that's in the *Sequence* and it's hard to convey it well to students, it's work that dedicated teachers are engaging in because they realize that it is best for children. … And it's also very rewarding for teachers. Many of you have told me that. (Buras, 2004)

The populist tenor of the movement is apparent in Hirsch's words and throughout the conference, where names are put to faces and hugs are exchanged between foundation staff and their grassroots allies. Foundation staff carefully listens to teachers, as revealed in one session during which draft *Teacher Handbooks* for Core were shared with teachers for their feedback (Buras, 2004). Though the balance between teachers' professional autonomy and the foundation's production of resources has generated tensions, the national conference is clearly a time for building community among a national network of Core Knowledge advocates.

The foundation also distributes a newsletter called *Common Knowledge*. Browsing its pages reveals a great deal about the philosophy of the foundation, and partly illuminates the composite character of the movement. Skimming *Common Knowledge*, the reader will often find essays by Hirsch that elaborate the guiding vision behind Core, such as "Why General Knowledge Should Be a Goal of Education in a Democracy" (1998b). It is also not uncommon to discover an odd convergence of "traditional" and "multicultural" elements on the page, albeit with no regard for how those elements might be critically connected. Newsletter highlights of one national conference illustrate this point:

> From the school visits … to the closing comments by foundation President E. D. Hirsch … the theme of "Content Counts" was underscored by speakers, presenters, and teachers. They talked of math and land bridges, of women's rights and classical music. Teachers shared slides of Antarctica and Japanese snacks.

One picture from the meeting shows two older, white, female teachers with huge eyeglasses performing "a ceremonial dance of the Aztecs" with an olive–complexioned, long–haired man dressed in Native American garb. Another reveals elementary students wearing bonnets and performing "songs from the Civil War" for conference attendees. Other photos portray students at a local Core Knowledge school marching "a Chinese dragon through the halls" and a charter school board member reading *Cultural Literacy* during the conference (Siler, 1998, pp. 10–11).

While the conference and newsletter attempt to define the movement's vision and foster a collective sense of mission, other foundation resources provide more tangible home and classroom support. The *What Your K–6 Grader Needs to Know Series* (e.g. Hirsch, 1998a), mentioned earlier, is a wildly popular, encyclopedic set of volumes sequenced in accordance with the Core curriculum. By title, these books summon parents based on myriad anxieties about the knowledge "required" for upward mobility. The literary *Core Classics* (Marshall & Hirsch, 1997) are child–friendly versions of works covered by Core, including *Robinson Crusoe*, *Treasure Island*, *Pollyanna*, and *Don Quixote*. Such resources exist alongside the recently published *Pearson Learning–Core Knowledge History and Geography Textbooks* on U.S. and world history (Hirsch, 2002). To pull it all together, *Teacher Handbooks* detail "what teachers need to know" to teach the curriculum (CKF, 2004d).

Curriculum resources have multiplied in recent years, but support services have also been enhanced. The foundation sponsors Core adoption seminars and professional development workshops (CKF, 1997, 2003a). It offers guidance to low–income schools that want to adopt Core, but need help applying for funds under the federal Comprehensive School Reform Program (Shields, 2003b). The foundation likewise maintains a website (CKF, 2004e) that serves as an avenue of communication, and continuously produces informational literature and books that help sustain the organization financially, assist teachers and parents pedagogically, and support the movement ideologically (e.g. CKF, 1996a, 2004f; Hirsch, 1992a, 1996).

The Making of a Movement

The foundation's work has been pivotal in advancing Core Knowledge as a reform, but it is important to look more broadly at the movement. Core has flourished due to the motivations and efforts of a variety of actors, communities, and foundations. It is essential to provide just a few highlights in order to demonstrate the complexity of the alliances and processes at work.

In several areas, Core has been adopted districtwide in the public school system. In the small district of Hobbs, New Mexico, Core is taught in every K–8 school (Rounds, 2004). Larger districts have likewise implemented Core, including Polk County, Florida, and Nashville, Tennessee (Jones, 1997a). Recalling his election campaign in Polk County, District Superintendent Glenn Reynolds explained the decision to adopt districtwide. "I kept hearing that the public schools were not competitive. … Our public schools were losing credibility and trust. The public was ready for major change" (in Marshall, 1997c, p. 1).

Though not part of a districtwide effort, there are notable concentrations of Core Knowledge schools elsewhere. Baltimore, where approximately fifteen Core Knowledge schools have developed, is home to the Baltimore Curriculum Project. Funded by the Abell Foundation which aimed to support a "promising education reform model," the project is dedicated to generating lesson plans that correspond with Core content guidelines. Several Baltimore schools are directly affiliated with the project and have piloted the lessons (Marshall, 1997a; Baltimore Curriculum Project 2004; Buras, 2004). Another effort in Baltimore has revolved around the implementation of Core in three elementary schools in the Sandtown–Winchester neighborhood. In this low–income, predominantly African American community, educator Sylvia Peters collaborated with the Enterprise Foundation to facilitate the initiative (Scherer, 1996; Enterprise Foundation, 2000). Attending the National Core Knowledge Conference, Peters addressed teachers and called them the "most important links in recivilizing our society" (in Siler, 1997, p. 1). "Core Knowledge is about the soul of our country," she declared (p. 8). Words used by Peters like "recivilizing" and "soul" capture the missionary spirit of the Core Knowledge movement, which partly seeks to effectuate the cultural conversion of poor communities, particularly those of color.

In Atlanta, there are eight Core schools, though the state of Georgia has about twenty–five (CKF, 2004b, 2007). The city of Atlanta was the site for the 2004 annual meeting, where attendees watched students from a local Core Knowledge school perform songs from the curriculum. With Hirsch sitting in the front row of a packed ballroom, a student choir from Morningside Elementary put on a well–polished show. The rapid–fire performance of a selection of songs that included the patriotic "America," country western "The Yellow Rose of Texas" (which in popular myth refers to an indentured mulatto woman), and African American spiritual "Swing Low, Sweet Chariot" revealed the awkward and uncritical relationship between the traditions of knowledge embodied in Core. Nonetheless, this parade of songs assured that there was something for everyone, which is one of the reasons for Core's popular appeal (Buras, 2004).

In Colorado there are over seventy Core Knowledge schools (CKF, 2004b, 2007). William Moloney, the former school superintendent of Calvert County, Maryland—the first system to adopt Core districtwide—was appointed Commissioner of Education in Colorado in 1997 (Siler, 1997; Jones 1997b). He became a member of the Core Knowledge Foundation's board of trustees that same year, and gave a keynote address at the national conference in Atlanta the next year. Moloney's (1998) speech resounded with concerns about the stability of tradition and nationhood:

> The odyssey of Core Knowledge is a remarkable story of the American journey in search of better schools. … I would first take us back to 1983 and the landmark report, "A Nation at Risk," which served as a springboard for the current school reform movement in general and for the Core Knowledge movement in particular. … Americans wanted answers to questions and concerns that had been building for many years. … Why did every survey of

> public opinion reveal our people's concern that the schools were failing to uphold the values, the discipline, and the work ethic that have been the foundations of our national heritage?

The reason for this decline, Moloney pronounced, was that "serious mission confusion began when schools were declared the ideal forum to resolve explosive issues of class, language, race, religion, and sexuality." Dismissing multiculturalism as mission confusion, he next invoked a racially coded discourse to explain the erosion of national order, emphasizing, "In more stable settings, it would be possible to paper over the cracks in the edifice, but in less stable settings, notably our large urban systems, it was impossible to mask the descent into educational chaos" (p. 5). For Moloney, the descent into educational chaos called for ongoing advocacy of Core, and he was not alone in this crusade. Holly Hensey, originally a Core Knowledge teacher in Texas where some fifty Core schools exist (CKF 2003e, 2007; Hitchcock, 2002), was recruited by the Core Knowledge Foundation to organize in the Colorado region. She has raised nearly $900,000 in grant money and has instituted many initiatives in the state, including a website, an annual Summer Writing Institute for Core teachers to develop lesson plans, an annual Colorado Core Knowledge Conference, and a project that aligned Core with educational standards in Colorado (Colorado Schools, 2003; National Core Knowledge Coordinator of Colorado, 2004).

A seminar intended to introduce interested groups statewide to Core Knowledge was arranged by the Minnesota Humanities Commission in 1997 (Jones 1997b, 1997c). Mae Schunk, a gifted and talented teacher at a Core Knowledge school in St. Paul, assisted in aligning Core with Minnesota standards and became Minnesota's Lieutenant Governor in 1999. In this position, Schunk introduced Core to parents and school officials across the state, explaining that "Core is just common sense" (in Marshall, 1999, p. 3). St. Paul is home to the Midwest Core Knowledge Center sponsored by the Minnesota Humanities Commission. The state has thirty–one Core Knowledge schools, and another twenty–five exist in nearby Michigan (CKF, 2004b, 2007).

In California, few Core Knowledge schools existed in the late 1990s. Perhaps most significant to increasing interest in the state was Hirsch's invitation to address the California State Board of Education. "If I were a member of your Board," Hirsch admonished, "I would begin to shift rather large resources into academically effective, very–early education" (1997, p. 7). Concluding, he stressed, "If reliable research does become your guide ... it may come to be said that this was the Board that put an end to the era of educational fad and failure" (p. 8). The exhortation to adopt an educational reform based on "reliable research," a reference that often invokes rather narrow conceptions of scientific method, evidence, and educational performance, is an approach frequently taken by Hirsch and the foundation. And it has some allure. There are presently thirty–two Core Knowledge schools in California (CKF, 2004b, 2007).

The growth of the Core Knowledge movement is indicative of the appeal this reform has secured in diverse kinds of communities. Having an even closer look at specific schools and particular associates of Core may illuminate further why certain groups are drawn to the reform, how those groups are differently positioned, and what interests are at play when alliances are formed.

Peculiar Alliances

At the predominantly European American, middle–class Washington Core Knowledge School in suburban Fort Collins, Colorado, parents' descriptions of the curriculum in non–Core public schools are "often filled with images of erosion. Many describe how the curriculum they knew as children, the one rooted in the granite truths of Western civilization, has disappeared from most schools." Concerned about cultural disintegration and loss of tradition, these parents petitioned the school district for the solution—a Core Knowledge school that would "emphasize a content–rich curriculum that would leave nothing to chance ... [and] be teacher–directed from beginning to end" (Ruenzel, 1996–1997, p. 8). In this community, it appears that Core made possible a return to "better" days before the multicultural assault on truth and the dominant order.

In contrast, Nathaniel Hawthorne Elementary School is a mostly Latino/a, low-income, urban Core Knowledge school in San Antonio, Texas. Two teachers (Mentzer & Shaughnessy, 1996) at Hawthorne reflect on the school before its adoption of Core:

> We, as teachers, were frustrated. Things were not working well. We did not know what to do. ... We were all scared about what was going to happen to our children if we couldn't find an intervention. ... We could see that if we did not do something to stop the cycle of failure our children would end up on the streets or dead. (pp. 14–16)

After a careful look at Core by teachers and parents, the teachers report, "We found our missing piece. ... What we had not had was a common content." For this school, Core was understood as contributing to renewal by providing a unifying educational vision and plan conducive to the advancement of struggling children. Though the specificity of content was deemed important, teachers underscored their partial renovation of the curriculum, stating "We then added items we thought were important for our students to learn such as Hispanic culture and traditions" (p. 20).

In the rural town of Crooksville, Ohio, the adoption of Core by Crooksville Elementary—a largely low–income, European American school—has meant that "students will get to see and understand the world beyond the mountains." For example, students will "learn the stories of Zeus and Hades and Persephone," "attend Renaissance Fairs, read *Don Quixote*, listen to Shakespearean actors, research and re-enact Civil War events," and "eat with chopsticks, and pantomime treaty agreements with Native Americans" (Vail, 1997, p. 14). Timm Mackley, the Superintendent of Crooksville, emphasizes, "We are dealing with kids who are narrowly confined to their small world. We are trying to share the wealth of human knowledge with them" (in Vail, p. 15; see also Mackley, 1999). This particular rural school thus views Core Knowledge as connecting isolated students to a wider "multicultural" world.

Aside from Core's appeal in regions throughout the United States, the curriculum has been used internationally by select schools in Canada, Honduras, Nicaragua, Switzerland, Taiwan, Thailand, United Kingdom, and elsewhere (CKF, 2007). At the Saipan International School in Saipan, a Mariana Island and U.S. territory in the Pacific, the world history portion of Core is utilized in classrooms. Saint Augustine Preparatory School, a private, bilingual, Catholic school located in Managua, Nicaragua, has also adopted Core. The school has found its English–language materials to be particularly helpful in teaching a bilingual curriculum in a predominantly Spanish–speaking country (Locke, 2002). Regarding why a school in Nicaragua would rely on a curriculum largely centered on U.S. content, one school leader stressed that "the United States is the dominant culture." "If our students are lucky, many will attend American universities, where this information will be key." Core was also perceived as a "liberal arts curriculum," which countered the degradation of the humanities in a Nicaraguan school system driven by a "careerist orientation" that most prioritized the skills needed to secure employment in a struggling domestic economy (Buras, 2004). Partly reflecting these sentiments, the Cofradia Bilingual School in Honduras, where the majority of teaching is conducted in English, has embraced the *What Your K–6 Grader Needs to Know Series* for the purposes of lesson planning and student research (Locke, 2002). Meanwhile, the American School in Switzerland (TASIS)—a college–preparatory boarding school where a majority are English as Second Language students—has opened an Elementary Day School that implements Core, a curriculum that teachers say "complements the TASIS Middle and Upper School curriculum with its emphasis on the milestones of Western civilization" (TASIS Staff, 2007). It should come as little surprise that the *Dictionary of Cultural Literacy* has been translated into Chinese, Dutch, German, Japanese, and Swedish (Hoover, 2002). In these ways, Core has been exported and imported as the curricular embodiment of "American" culture, allowing its civilizing mission to extend beyond U.S. borders. Core's adoption internationally, a testimony to the hegemony of the United States, is likely viewed by Hirsch as indicative of the cosmopolitan character of its content and the importance of English as a shared language (for a more critical conception of global relations and schooling, see Buras & Motter, 2006).

That schools in such different contexts could embrace Core reveals the complex alliances that have been forming in the movement. Hirsch is quite aware of this situation, stating, "To be liked by the Bushies [Bush allies] and by the AFT [American Federation of Teachers]—there's something peculiar going on" (in Lindsay, 2001, p. W24). The reality is that Hirsch and the foundation have worked to build such affiliations. Hirsch's relationship with former AFT president Albert Shanker goes back to the mid–1980s. It was then that Shanker began praising Hirsch's newly articulated theory of cultural literacy as the means to greater educational equity, with the union later arguing that Core was a more promising reform for school improvement than vouchers (AFT, 2003; Lindsay, 2001). The AFT granted Hirsch the QuEST (quality educational standards) Award in 1997, and Sandra Feldman, past president of the AFT, accepted a seat on the Core Knowledge Foundation's board of trustees in 1998 (Marshall, 1997b, 1998).

Moreover, scholars and members of historically marginalized groups were courted by the foundation, particularly after *Cultural Literacy* had been attacked for its Eurocentric content.

For instance, Henry Louis Gates, professor of humanities and Afro–American studies at Harvard, was invited to be on the Core Knowledge multicultural advisory committee (Hirsch, 1992b). Yet the formation of such alliances has not been without rifts. James Farmer, the well–known founder and civil rights activist of a different CORE—the Congress of Racial Equality—was invited to speak at the 1996 national conference. He underscored in his speech the idea that "we are bound together," then prompted Core Knowledge teachers and the foundation:

> What I'm asking for is something that maybe you have as a part of your curriculum. And that is a pluralistic culture. It's not difficult for a people in a society like ours to love themselves and at the same time join with others in loving their history and traditions. I ... *urge you* to come together with me and us in *celebrating ourselves* as well as *you celebrate yourselves*. It's not difficult at all if people are taught that way. *Perhaps the teaching of that should also be part of the core curriculum* [italics added]. (1996, p. 2)

While Farmer's presence at the conference might be read as an endorsement of Core Knowledge—as suggested by Hirsch—it may also be read as a challenge to more significantly incorporate the knowledge, culture, and history of oppressed groups into the curriculum rather than teaching children about the culture of more powerful groups only.

Equally telling, Richard Rodriguez, a noted Chicano author and lecturer, was welcomed to the conference the following year. In comparison to Farmer's talk, his speech emphasized that "assimilation happens." He declared to Core Knowledge advocates:

> This is not the voice I talked with in the first grade. It is not the way I sounded. This is *your* voice. This is the voice *you* shoved down my throat. ... There was a time in my life I would describe myself as a minority and because of you I am not a minority in the cultural sense. (1997, p. 12)

Relegating his own language and culture to the "private" sphere, Rodriguez stressed the necessity of minority children embracing "public" culture, meaning dominant ways of speaking, acting, and knowing. He went on:

> There are lots of teachers in this bilingual, ebonics age that simply do not get the point that the point is not mere self–expression. The point is trying to get children to be able to speak in a way that other people can understand them. That is what we mean by "public school." (p. 13)

To a much more significant degree than Farmer, Rodriguez supported accommodating dominant culture rather than demanding cross–cultural literacy. The fact that both have given addresses at the conference highlights the varying ideological commitments that inform the movement and the tensions that characterize existing alliances. The foundation's desire to build such relationships is even more interesting when one recalls the aforementioned effort to translate the *Grader Series* into Spanish for use alongside the English version. Clearly, the force behind this intervention is more aligned with the views of Rodriguez than Farmer, though both have been welcomed under the canopy of Core Knowledge.

The canopy stretches far and wide. Indeed, Hirsch has spent some time building alliances in Washington, D.C., where in April 2003 he addressed the White House Forum on Civic Literacy and was honored at a dinner by the Vice President and his wife, Lynne Cheney. A few months later Hirsch returned, only this time for a celebration sponsored by the Center for Education Reform that was attended by Secretary of Education Rod Paige, Florida Governor Jeb Bush, and John Walton of the Walton Foundation, a financial backer of Core Knowledge. Regarding these networking efforts, the Core Knowledge Foundation observes, "Hirsch continues to be our roving ambassador, promoting educational reform and seeking like–minded allies" (CKF, 2003e, p. 20).

Yet Hirsch himself has acknowledged that not all his allies are exactly like–minded. How is it, then, that privileged suburbanites and low–income urban and rural communities, assimilationists and cultural pluralists, subaltern parents and state officials, the American Federation of Teachers and conservative foundations are brought together around Core Knowledge? Why is it, to use the words of Minnesota's Lieutenant Governor, that Core is "just common sense?" As we have seen, Core Knowledge is officially framed in terms of social mobility and civil rights, concerns central to subaltern groups. Beyond this, its curricular "coherence" offers a promising horizon for urban schools facing various challenges. The association of well–known people of color with Core—some of whom have quite moderate positions on culture and schooling—also gives the reform an air of respectability in marginalized communities. Moreover, poor communities and communities of color that have adopted Core are strategically highlighted by the foundation. The message is that Core has the interests of these groups at its center. All of this serves to shield the reform from criticisms of elitism and Eurocentrism and helps to further the foundation's agenda on this front.

Additionally, cultural restorationists in the government, with right–wing foundations, or on the ground in suburban school districts may also securely advocate Core—a reform partly premised on a defense of tradition and order. Those who believe the national heritage is "at risk" and even those who forward a rightist cultural agenda under the banner of "reliable research" and science find Core Knowledge a comfortable home. In these cases, however, the foundation generally eschews directly propounding the classed and raced demands of such groups and uses instead democratically appealing language about "common" culture and national "unity" that masks the more coercive aspects of the reform.

The Remaking of a Movement: Autonomy, Discipline, and the Balance of Forces

The disparate social positioning of Core Knowledge advocates and the various interests being folded into the movement are indeed "peculiar," as Hirsch points out. The tensions generated by this balance of forces within the movement should not be overlooked. After all, these diverse investments have led the foundation to redefine its relationship with Core Knowledge schools, a reminder that hegemony is always contested, never permanently attained, and constantly under construction.

With the movement nearly a decade in the making, Hirsch (1998b) assured teachers that they were its vanguard rather than the foundation: "Core Knowledge has been from the start a *bottom-up not a top-down movement. ... You've done it without coercion* and with dedication, and with ever-increasing numbers [italics added]" (pp. 1, 14). Guided by Core content guidelines, teachers across the nation have spent countless hours searching for relevant materials and developing original lesson plans (CKF, 2004e, 2004g). In the beginning, this work was essential because the content guidelines were virtually all that existed. After the first Core school opened in 1990, its principal Connie Jones (1991) reported:

> Our teachers were pleased with the *amount of independence and autonomy* that the Core Knowledge Sequence afforded them. ... Selection and use of resources and materials were *completely at the discretion of the teachers. ...* Our faculty *would not look favorably on publication of a strict Core Knowledge textbook with teacher's guides* [italics added]. (p. 10)

This relative autonomy, in diverse hands, has led to interpretations of Core that fall outside the ambit of the official vision. Researchers (Datnow et al., 2000) solicited by the foundation to study Core's implementation across various sites interviewed students and reported:

> All Core Knowledge schools are to teach fifth graders about Thomas Jefferson. ... At a school serving a majority African–American population, the students recalled that Jefferson fathered children with one of his slaves. However, students at a majority white school in a suburban area told us that Jefferson was a hero. (p. 183)

Aside from this, researchers also found disparate implementation levels and teaching methods. It is well–known that teachers mediate educational initiatives within their classrooms (Grant, 2001; Schweber, 2004), and the lesson plans independently developed by Core Knowledge teachers indicate that a degree of diversity has historically prevailed when Core content is taught. At the same time, this kind of curricular deviance has only been encouraged by a lack of standardized resources to accompany Core content guidelines. There was indeed something to Hirsch's acknowledgement, "You've done it without coercion," but it was becoming increasingly apparent that some schools were not doing it fully or appropriately. In recent years, various disciplinary mechanisms—Core Knowledge history textbooks and teacher guides, *Teacher Handbooks*, refined foundation requirements for Core schools, Core curriculum–referenced tests (CKF, 2004a, n.d.), achievement data collection (Telling, 2003), and a nascent elementary teacher education reform initiative (CKF, 2002)—have begun to take shape.

At this point I wish to focus briefly on Core Knowledge history textbooks (Hirsch, 2002) and the cultural politics of representation within them. It is important to assess whose knowledge informs the histories officially endorsed by the foundation. It is equally important to think about how those histories might concurrently and strategically appeal to diverse groups within the movement, support teachers in Core classrooms, and potentially discipline more radically inclusive mediations of Core content guidelines.

Core Knowledge and the New Old History

The trajectory of struggle between old and new histories—meaning history from above and from below—is most pertinent here. Much of the neoconservative reaction, after all, has been driven by a desire to sustain a particular epistemological orientation to studying the past—one that centers on founding fathers and more powerful groups, and what they did to build the nation. Defending the tradition of old history against the onslaught of the new is what compelled Arthur Schlesinger (1992) to warn of "the disuniting of America." "The militants of ethnicity," he wrote, "now contend that a main objective of public education should be the protection, strengthening, celebration, and perpetuation of ethnic origins and identities." Sounding the alarm, he continued, "Separatism, however, nourishes prejudice, magnifies differences and stirs antagonisms. ... The result can only be the fragmentation, resegregation, and tribalization of American life" (pp. 17–18). New histories focused on subaltern groups, and conflict rather than consensus, were to blame. In turn, historians of long ignored pasts—those of African Americans, Asian Americans, women, immigrants, the working class, and so forth—defended such work as legitimate and overdue (Foner, 1997; Wiener, 1989).

This is the context in which Core history texts are embedded and to which they "respond." Unlike additive multiculturalism in which "one half of a page here and one half of a page there" discusses subaltern groups (McCarthy, 1998, p. 115), Core Knowledge history represents a strategic innovation that moves beyond additive multiculturalism to something that I have termed the "*new* old history."[2] By this, I mean that Core texts reflect to a *greater degree* the tendencies of *both* the old and the new histories, and that the relationship between these traditions within Core is more *complex* than the additive approach that has characterized so many school texts over past decades (e.g., see Zimmerman, 2002). Here I will only be able to highlight one Core text, but it is important to say that the illustrations provided reflect the broader patterns I found in the many Core history texts that I analyzed (see also Buras, 2006, 2008b).[3]

More to the point, the pattern that I documented is one in which both elite and subaltern groups are "recognized" within Core history texts, but their recognition is premised on two main conditions. First, reflecting the old and the new, the pasts of groups above and below are narrativized, but *not in relation* to one another; elites are powerful but they do not exercise power over any group, subalterns are oppressed but they do not live amid oppressors. Second, the pasts of groups above and below are narrativized *in relation* to one another through a frame that stresses *consensus* (the bulwark of old history) and overshadows or ignores conflict and power (pivotal to new history). Moreover, it is the major storyline that reflects the old history, while the minor storyline takes into account and echoes the new history.

Similarly, images in the texts generally respect these conditions. In sum, the *new* old history constructed through Core texts constitutes a strategy of rightist multiculturalism at the epistemological level.

In second grade, students read a Core history text dedicated to Civil Rights Leaders, particularly African Americans (Hirsch, 2002). Old and new, above and below, are conditionally incorporated into this narrative. The major storyline is that all Americans worked to ensure equal rights. In tension with this is a minor storyline that some groups did not have equal rights. More specifically, this story unfolds as utterances on black experience alternate with ones on white benevolence. Thus, the text indicates that Mary McLeod Bethune, whose parents "had been slaves," believed that "every black child should get an education." She "started a school" for African American girls with whom she is pictured. In this narrative frame, Bethune's experience is raced; she seeks to equalize educational conditions for *black* children (Hirsch, 2002, p. 4). Next appears Eleanor Roosevelt who "wanted to help others" (p. 5). Bethune and Roosevelt, finally, are shown together in a photo as they correspond with smiles. Students read that they "worked together to help all American children get a good education" (p. 6). In this frame, Bethune's racial struggle is transformed into a cooperative effort with Roosevelt to help all *American* children.

This pattern persists as the narrative continues: "White people played in the major leagues and black people played in the Negro leagues," but Branch Rickey, the white manager of the Brooklyn Dodgers, "still wanted Jackie Robinson" to play on his team (Hirsch, 2002, pp. 7–8). Martin Luther King "wanted integration," but at the Lincoln Memorial, he spoke to thousands who "wanted a better life for all Americans." Students are told that King knew Gandhi had freed his country "without violence" (pp. 12–13). These alternating discourses—one focused on unequal conditions and the other on cooperative relations and an "all–American" effort to ensure equality—are only reinforced by the textual images. Jackie Robinson and Branch Rickey are pictured together shaking hands and smiling. Martin Luther King is pictured at the Memorial with the statue of Lincoln elevated behind him—itself an image of non–violent relations as Lincoln "watches over" King.

Notably, this narrative is simultaneously non–relational and relational. Unequal conditions prevail in the minor storyline, but Africans Americans never encounter whites exercising power in direct or explicit ways. Violent southern segregationists did not work to help "all Americans." And the struggle for integration saw much violence—namely that perpetrated by whites against blacks. Yet all of this is absent within a non–relational frame that manages to convey a story from below of the black civil rights struggle, only without malevolent whites. At yet another point, the text explains: "Black people had to sit at the back of the bus. Rosa Parks broke the law in Alabama. She would not move to the back of the bus to give a white man her seat" (Hirsch, 2002, p. 10). Accompanying these words, however, is a photo that shows Parks sitting *in front* of a white man who is calmly seated and does not attend to her presence. It thus seems that Parks was able to address unequal treatment without tension, much less arrest. The "Read Aloud" in the Teacher

Guide—meant to be read by the teacher to the class—does on occasion allude to conflictual relations, for example, announcing that "Rosa Parks got arrested on the bus" and said she "was tired of being pushed around" (p. 14). But these representations are not reflected in the written or visual text that students directly engage. Instead, subaltern and dominant racial groups only meet within a consensual frame. The minor storyline on inequality, as lived from below, is subverted by a story in which blacks have cooperative relations with benevolent whites.

RIGHTIST MULTICULTURALISM AND THE WAR OF POSITION

A "return" to the old history, Glazer (1997) said, "would no longer do," though moving beyond additive history could certainly do Core Knowledge one better. This strategy might actually have the power to mobilize both dominant and subaltern groups around Core without either group feeling that its interests or history are being undercut. At the 5th National Core Knowledge Conference, Diane Ravitch (1996)—a current member of the foundation's board of trustees—declared: "You, as teachers and leaders of Core Knowledge schools, must foment a revolution. … America needs *more* Core Knowledge schools" (p. 11). Those of us dedicated to more progressive conceptions of democracy need to think about how precisely the revolution is being fomented. Groups from below may seek to redefine Core, but they are also surrounded by a network of very powerful conservative forces from above that will try, at every turn, to make and remake the movement and to write and rewrite the pages of history in ways that support dominant interests.

This is where we must begin to appreciate how Core is contributing to the reconstruction of common sense around issues of cultural diversity and political economy, the meaning of civil rights, and the shape of a just democratic order. Hirsch positions Core as the embodiment, if not the actualization, of an uncontested definition of equality. Relying on rightist multicultural strategies, Hirsch has responded to impulses above and below, positioning Core in–between discourses of cultural deficiency and civil rights, in–between "Americanism" and "ethnic loyalism," in–between the old history and the new, in–between autonomy and discipline, in–between cultural reaction and cultural recognition. In doing so, Core urges us, pushes us, to think about culture and democracy in specific ways—ways that tend to reinforce patterns of cultural disrespect and pressures to assimilate—and to overlook other understandings.

To some, the claim that Core is part of a broader project aimed at reconstructing our common sense around culture and economy may seem overblown. After all, Core is just one of many educational reforms. However, as Gramsci reminds us, every struggle is inherently an educational one and each contributes something to the legitimization or delegitmization of certain worldviews. Gramsci emphasizes that the educational relationship:

> should not be [understood as] restricted to the field of the strictly "scholastic" relationships by means of which the new generation comes into contact with the old. … This form of relationship exists throughout society as a whole and

> for every individual relative to other individuals. It exists between intellectual and non–intellectual sections of the population, between the rulers and the ruled, elites and their followers, leaders and led, the vanguard and the body of the army. Every relationship of "hegemony" is necessarily an educational relationship. (Hoare & Nowell–Smith, 1971, p. 350)

From above, the war of position is fought by building on the elements of good sense embedded in the everyday conceptions of subaltern groups, while redefining these in dominant cultural directions. Core Knowledge, it must be understood, is one front on which such a battle is being fought. In calling for schools to provide the same curriculum for all students, for example, Hirsch expresses his faith that all children can learn and that the challenge is not one of potential, as so often has been argued, but one of access to so–called literate culture. It is an understandably compelling argument and to make it is to begin to reconstruct the way we might think about equality in schools.

Recognizing that multiculturalism has been assumed and appropriated by the right is far from insignificant. Reminding us that cultural battles are complicated, ongoing, and always have many sides, some of the communities that have adopted Core have redefined it in often unanticipated ways, ones that may serve interests very different from those envisioned by Hirsch and the Core Knowledge Foundation. In turn, the disciplinary mechanisms more recently adopted by the foundation may be understood as yet another maneuver from above to remedy deviance and ideological resistance from below. The balance of forces here is crucial to understand. Core does have its progressive moments, but there are good reasons to conclude that overall the alliance serves neoconservative ends more generally, even if not in each specific instance or classroom. Even if Core is reconstituted on the ground, diverse participation in this initiative lends wider legitimacy to the definitions of equality, civil rights, and democracy that neoconservatives aim to circulate and normalize. The degree to which rightist multiculturalism ultimately will succeed is the question of the day. Rather than allowing Hirsch and his neoconservative compatriots to mainstream and colonize the meanings around keywords of culture (Williams, 1983), one of the most powerful contributions to an alternative war of position that grassroots activists, progressive educators and students, and activist scholars can make is to provide counterstories (Yosso, 2006) of educational initiatives that "truly embody what it means to overcome," which is indisputably different than coming over to Core (e.g., see Buras, 2009; Buras et al., 2010; Fisher, 2007; Ginwright et al., 2006).[4]

NOTES

1. Elsewhere I have documented that accounts which frame neoconservatism as a reaction to the 1960s fail to grasp antecedents of this period. Long before they were new rightists, many neoconservatives were actually old leftists. Here I refer to the history of the New York intellectuals, which is rooted in the 1930s and involves movement from left to right over the course of several decades (see Buras, 2008a, 2008b; see also Buras & Apple, 2008).
2. Gertrude Himmelfarb (2004) has used the terms *new* new history and *old* new history, and has written about Lawrence Stone's proposal for a new old history, but none of these usages correspond with my invocation of the term *new* old history.

[3] I can only provide select illustrations here, but interested readers should consult *Rightist Multiculturalism* (Buras, 2008b) in which I lay out more extensively the critical discourse analysis that I completed on purposefully sampled selections from the *Pearson Learning–Core Knowledge History and Geography Textbooks* (Hirsch, 2002). Readers should also see *Rightist Multiculturalism* for a detailed discussion of methodology in Appendix A.

[4] Parts of this chapter earlier appeared in *The Subaltern Speak* (Buras, 2006) and *Rightist Multiculturalism* (Buras, 2008b).

REFERENCES

Adams, D. W. (1995). *Education for extinction: American Indians and the boarding school experience, 1875–1928*. Lawrence, KS: University Press of Kansas.

American Federation of Teachers. (2003, March). *American federation of teachers on core knowledge* [bound compilation of articles]. Washington, DC: Author.

Apple, M. W. (2000). *Official knowledge: Democratic education in a conservative age* (2nd ed.). New York: Routledge.

Apple, M. W. (1996). *Cultural politics and education*. New York: Teachers College Press.

Apple, M. W., & Beane, J. (Eds.). (2007). *Democratic schools* (2nd ed.). Portsmouth, NH: Heinemann.

Apple, M. W., & Buras, K. L. (Eds.). (2006). *The subaltern speak: Curriculum, power, and educational struggles*. New York: Routledge.

Aronowitz, S., & Giroux, H. (1991). Textual authority, culture, and the politics of literacy. In M. W. Apple & L. K. Christian-Smith (Eds.), *The politics of the textbook* (pp. 213–241). New York: Routledge.

Au, W. (2006). Against economic determinism: Revisiting the roots of neo–Marxism in critical educational theory. *Journal for Critical Educational Policy Studies*, *4*(2), 1–18.

Baltimore Curriculum Project. (2004). *Baltimore curriculum project: Draft month-by-month content lesson plans based on the core knowledge sequence*. Retrieved from http://www.cstone.net/~bcp/

Bell, D. (2004). *Silent covenants: Brown v. Board of Education and the unfulfilled hopes forracial reform*. New York: Oxford University Press.

Bennett, W. J. (1992). *The de–valuing of America: The fight for our culture and our children*. New York: Simon & Schuster.

Black Web Portal News Wire. (2008, January 24). *Coca Cola kicks off 2008 with black history ad*. Retrieved from www.blacknewsportal.com/wire/DprA.cfm?ArticleID=3384

Buras, K. L. (1999). Questioning core assumptions: A critical reading of and response to E. D. Hirsch's The Schools We Need & Why We Don't Have Them. *Harvard Educational Review*, *69*(1), 67–93.

Buras, K. L. (2004, March). *Field notes*. Atlanta, GA: Core Knowledge national conference.

Buras, K. L. (2006). Tracing the Core Knowledge movement: History lessons from above and below. In M. W. Apple & K. L. Buras (Eds.), *The subaltern speak: Curriculum, power, and educational struggles* (pp. 43–74). New York: Routledge.

Buras, K. L. (2008a). Neoconservatism. In D. Gabbard (Ed.), *Knowledge and power in theglobal economy: The effects of school reform in a neoliberal/neoconservative age* (2nd ed., pp. 59–77). New York: Lawrence Erlbaum Associates.

Buras, K. L. (2008b). *Rightist multiculturalism: Core lessons on neoconservative school reform*. New York: Routledge.

Buras, K. L. (2009). *"We have to tell our story": Neo–griots, racial resistance, and schooling in the other South. Race Ethnicity and Education, 12*(4), 427–453.

Buras, K. L., & Apple, M. W. (2008). Radical disenchantments: Neoconservatives and the disciplining of desire in an anti–utopian era. *Comparative Education*, *44*(3), 291–304.

Buras, K. L., & Motter, P. (2006). Toward a subaltern cosmopolitan multiculturalism. In M. W. Apple & K. L. Buras (Eds.), *The subaltern speak: Curriculum, power, and educational struggles* (pp. 243–269). New York: Routledge.

Buras, K. L., Randels, J., Salaam, K. Y., & Students at the Center. (2010). *Pedagogy, policy, and the privatized city: Stories of dispossession and defiance from New Orleans*. New York: Teachers College Press.

Coca–Cola. (2008a). *Coca–Cola black history timeline*. Retrieved February 17, 2008, from http://youtube.com/watch?v=wgR92otjoUk&feature=related

Coca–Cola. (2008b). *The joy of being a history maker*. Retrieved February 19, 2008, from www.blackdigitalnetwork.com

Colorado Schools. (2003). Colorado schools grow through Holly Hensey's support [electronic version]. *Common Knowledge, 16*(3).

Core Knowledge Foundation. (1996a). *Common misconceptions about core knowledge*. Retrieved from www.coreknowledge.org

Core Knowledge Foundation. (1996b). *Core Knowledge in the schools as of Fall 1996 [brochure]*. Charlottesville, VA: Author.

Core Knowledge Foundation. (1997). *Core Knowledge professional development workshops [brochure]*. Charlottesville, VA: Author.

Core Knowledge Foundation. (1998). *The Core Knowledge sequence: Content guidelines forgrades K–6*. Charlottesville, VA: Author.

Core Knowledge Foundation. (2002). *What elementary teachers need to know: College course outlines for teacher preparation*. Charlottesville, VA: Author.

Core Knowledge Foundation. (2003a, March 1). *Professional development workshops*. Accessed October 22, 2003, from http://www.coreknowledge.org

Core Knowledge Foundation. (2003b, September 15). *Official Core Knowledge schools*. Retrieved October 14, 2003, from http://www.coreknowledge.org/CKproto2/schools/schllst_O.htm

Core Knowledge Foundation. (2003c, August 25). *Official Core Knowledge school application: Information for school year 2003–2004*. Retrieved October 14, 2003, from http://www.coreknowledge.org/CKproto2/schools/schllst_O_app.htm

Core Knowledge Foundation. (2003d, December 1). *Core Knowledge schools: How to get started*. Retrieved July 20, 2004, from http://www.coreknowledge.org/CKproto2/schools/start.htm

Core Knowledge Foundation. (2003e). *Annual report of the Core Knowledge Foundation*. Charlottesville, VA: Author.

Core Knowledge Foundation. (2004a, March 10). *Core Knowledge-TASA curriculum–referenced tests*. Retrieved July 29, 2004, from http://www.coreknowledge.org/CKproto2/schools/testing.htm

Core Knowledge Foundation. (2004b, May 25). *Core Knowledge K–8 schools list*. Retrieved June15, 2004, from http://www.coreknowledge.org

Core Knowledge Foundation. (2004c, July 16). *Becoming a Core Knowledge K–8 school* [breakdown of schools]. Retrieved July 20, 2004, from http://www.coreknowledge.org

Core Knowledge Foundation. (2004d). *Core Knowledge teacher handbook, grade 1*. Charlottesville, VA: Author.

Core Knowledge Foundation. (2004e). *Home page*. Retrieved from www.coreknowledge.org

Core Knowledge Foundation. (2004f). *Parent brochure*. Retrieved from March 31, 2005, from http://www.coreknowledge.org/CKproto2/schools/schools_parentbrochure.htm

Core Knowledge Foundation. (2004g). *Share the knowledge: Core Knowledge national conference units and handouts*. Charlottesville, VA: Author.

Core Knowledge Foundation. (2006). *Annual report of the Core Knowledge Foundation*. Charlottesville, VA: Author.

Core Knowledge Foundation. (2007, March 6). *Core Knowledge K–8 schools list*. Retrieved July 9, 2007, from http://www.coreknowledge.org

Core Knowledge Foundation. (n.d.). *Q&A: Core Knowledge testing program [brochure]*. Charlottesville, VA: Author.

Crenshaw, K. (1995). *Race, reform, and retrenchment: Transformation and legitimation in anti–discrimination law*. In K. Crenshaw, N. Gotanda, G. Peller, & K. Thomas (Eds.), *Critical race theory: The key writings that formed the movement* (pp. 103–122). New York: The New Press.

Datnow, A., Borman, G., & Stringfield, S. (2000). School reform through a highly specified curriculum: Implementation and effects of the Core Knowledge sequence. *The Elementary School Journal, 101*(2), 167–191.

Davis, M. (2002). Core Knowledge offers blueprint for content–rich teacher education. *Common Knowledge, 15*(3), 4.

Delgado Bernal, D. (2002). Critical race theory, Latino critical theory, and critical raced–gendered epistemologies: Recognizing students of color as holder and creators of knowledge. *Qualitative Inquiry, 8*(1), 105–126.

Dixson, A. D., & Rousseau, C. K. (Eds.). (2006). *Critical race theory in education: All god's children got a song*. New York: Routledge.

Enterprise Foundation. (2000). *Community building in partnership*. Baltimore, MD: Author. Retrieved from http://www. enterprisefoundation.org/resources/ERD/browse.asp?c=35

Farmer, J. (1996). We are bound together. *Common Knowledge, 9*(1/2), 2.

Fisher, M. T. (2007). *Writing in rhythm: Spoken word poetry in urban classrooms*. New York: Teachers College Press.

Foner, E. (Ed.). (1997). *The new American history*. Philadelphia: Temple University Press.

Forgacs, D., & Nowell–Smith, G. (Eds.). (1985). *Antonio Gramsci: Selections from cultural writings*. Cambridge, MA: Harvard University Press.

Ginwright, S., Noguera, P., & Cammarota, J. (2006). *Beyond resistance! Youth activism and community change*. New York: Routledge.

Glazer, N. (1997). *We are all multiculturalists now*. Cambridge: Harvard University Press.

Goldberg, M. F. (1997). An interview with E. D. Hirsch, Jr.: Doing what works. *Phi Delta Kappan, 79*(1), 83–85.

Grant, S. G. (2001). An uncertain lever: Exploring the influence of state–level testing in New York State on teaching social studies. *Teachers College Record, 103*(3), 398–426.

Hassett, M. K. (2004). A conference to remember [electronic version]. *Common Knowledge, 17*(2).

Himmelfarb, G. (2004). *The new history and the old*. Cambridge: Harvard University Press.

Hirsch, E. D., Jr. (1983). Cultural literacy. *The American Scholar, 52*, 159–169.

Hirsch, E. D., Jr. (1987). *Cultural literacy: What every American need to know*. New York: Vintage Books.

Hirsch, E. D., Jr. (1992a). *Fairness and Core Knowledge*. Charlottesville, VA: Core Knowledge Foundation.

Hirsch, E. D., Jr. (1992b). *Toward a centrist curriculum: Two kinds of multiculturalism in elementary school*. Charlottesville, VA: Core Knowledge Foundation.

Hirsch, E. D., Jr. (1996). *The schools we need & why we don't have them*. New York: Doubleday.

Hirsch, E. D., Jr. (1997). An address to the California State Board of Education. *CommonKnowledge, 10*(1/2), 4–8.

Hirsch, E. D., Jr. (Ed.). (1998a). *What your second grader needs to know: Fundamentals of a good second–grade education* (Rev. ed.). New York: Doubleday.

Hirsch, E. D., Jr. (1998b). Why general knowledge should be a goal of education in a democracy. *Common Knowledge, 11*(1/2), 1, 14–16.

Hirsch, E. D., Jr. (1999). Why Core Knowledge promotes social justice [electronic version]. *Common Knowledge, 12*(4).

Hirsch, E. D., Jr. (Ed.). (2002). *Pearson Learning–Core Knowledge history and geography textbooks, grades K–6*. New Jersey, NJ: Pearson Learning Group.

Hirsch, E. D., Jr., & Holdren, J. (Eds.). (2001). *Lo que su alumno de kindergarten necesita saber [field copy]*. Charlottesville, VA: Core Knowledge Foundation.

Hirsch, E. D., Jr., Kett, J. F., & Trefil, J. (1988). *The dictionary of cultural literacy: What every American needs to know*. New York: Houghton Mifflin Company.

Hitchcock, S. T. (2002). Teaching the teachers: New education school programs promise to help Core Knowledge teachers. *Common Knowledge, 15*(1), 4–6.

Hoare, Q., & Nowell–Smith, G. (Eds.). (1971). *Selections from the prison notebooks of Antonio Gramsci*. New York: International Publishers.

Hoover Institution. (2002). E. D. Hirsch, Jr. [Profile]. Retrieved November 12, 2003, from www.hoover.stanford.edu/BIOS/Hirsch.html

Jones, C. (1991). *A school's guide to core knowledge: Ideas for implementation.* Charlottesville, VA: Core Knowledge Foundation.

Jones, C. (1997a). School clips. *Common Knowledge, 10*(1/2), 10, 16.

Jones, C. (1997b). School clips. *Common Knowledge, 10*(3), 6, 12.

Jones, C. (1997c). School clips. *Common Knowledge, 10*(4), 6, 12.

Kaestle, C. F. (1983). *Pillars of the republic: Common schools and American society, 1780–1860.* New York: Hill & Wang.

Kantrowitz, B., Chideya, F., & Wingert, P. (1992, November 2). What kids need to know: Putting cultural literacy into elementary school. *Newsweek, 80.*

Ladson–Billings, G. (1994). *The dreamkeepers: Successful teachers of African American students.* San Francisco: Jossey–Bass.

Ladson–Billings, G., & Tate, W. F. (2006). Toward a critical race theory of education. In A. D. Dixson & C. K. Rousseau (Eds.), *Critical race theory in education: All god's children got a song* (pp. 11–30). New York: Routledge.

Leming, J., Ellington, L., & Porter, K. (Eds.). (2003). *Where did social studies go wrong?* Washington, DC: Thomas B. Fordham Foundation.

Leonardo, Z. (Ed.). (2005). *Critical pedagogy and race.* Malden, MA: Blackwell Publishing.

Lindsay, D. (2001, November 11). *Against the establishment: How a U–VA professor, denounced as elitist and ethnocentric, became a prophet of the school standards movement.* Washington Post, W24.

Locke, P. (2002). Core Knowledge takes root outside the United States. *Common Knowledge, 15*(3), 14–17.

Mackley, T. A. (1999). *Uncommon sense: Core Knowledge in the classroom.* Alexandria, VA: Association for Supervision and Curriculum Development.

Marshall, M. (Ed.). (1997a). Baltimore lessons are on the net. *Common Knowledge, 10*(3), 2.

Marshall, M. (Ed.). (1997b). Hirsch receives AFT's Quest Award. *Common Knowledge, 10*(3), 1.

Marshall, M. (1997c). In Polk County, Florida: Going for Core in a big way. *Common Knowledge, 10*(3), 1, 7, 11.

Marshall, M. (Ed.). (1997d). Preschool sequence now available. *Common Knowledge, 10*(3), 3.

Marshall, M. (Ed.). (1997e). Sequence for 7th and 8th finalized. *Common Knowledge, 10*(3), 4.

Marshall, M. (1998). Feldman joins Core Knowledge Foundation board of trustees. *Common Knowledge, 11*(3), 2.

Marshall, M. (Ed.). (1999). Minnesota's Lt. Governor is a core knowledge teacher. *Common Knowledge, 12*(1/2), 3.

Marshall, M., & Hirsch, E. D., Jr. (Eds.). (1997). *Core classics series.* Charlottesville, VA: Core Knowledge Foundation.

McCarthy, C. (1998). *The uses of culture.* New York: Routledge.

Mentzer, D., & Shaughnessy, T. (1996). Hawthorne elementary school: The teachers' perspective. *Journal of Education for Students Placed at Risk, 1*(1), 13–23.

Michie, G. (1999). *Holler if you hear me: The education of a teacher and his students.* New York: Teachers College Press.

Molnar, A. (2005). *School commercialism: From democratic ideal to market commodity.* New York: Routledge.

Moloney, W. (1998). The place of core knowledge in American school reform. *Common Knowledge, 11*(1/2), 5–6, 12–13.

Morris, J. E. (2006). Critical race perspectives on desegregation: The forgotten voices of black educators. In A. D. Dixson & C. K. Rousseau (Eds.), *Critical race theory in education: All god's children got a song* (pp. 129–151). New York: Routledge.

National Core Knowledge Coordinator of Colorado. (2004). *Home page.* Retrieved from http://www.ckcolorado.org

Omi, M., & Winant, H. (1994). *Racial formation in the United States from the 1960s to the 1990s* (2nd ed.). New York: Routledge.
Peller, G. (1995). Race–consciousness. In K. Crenshaw, N. Gotanda, G. Peller, & K. Thomas (Eds.), *Critical race theory: The key writings that formed the movement* (pp. 127–158). New York: The New Press.
Ravitch, D. (1996). Why we need a literate core curriculum. *Common Knowledge, 9*(1/2), 1, 6–11.
Rodriguez, R. (1997). Assimilation happens. *Common Knowledge, 10*(1/2), 12–13.
Rounds, S. (2004, February). *Hobbs Municipal Schools: Comprehensive K–12 reform programs—the Core Knowledge sequence*. Hobbs, New Mexico: Hobbs Municipal Schools.
Ruenzel, D. (1996–1997). Washington Core Knowledge School: Fort Collins, Colorado. *American Educator, 20*(4), 8, 24–26, 28–29.
Scherer, M. (1996). On better alternatives for urban students: A conversation with Sylvia Peters. *Educational Leadership, 54*(2), 47–52.
Schlesinger, A. M., Jr. (1992). *The disuniting of America: Reflections on a multicultural society*. New York: W. W. Norton.
Schweber, S. A. (2004). *Making sense of the holocaust: Lessons from classroom practice*. New York: Teachers College Press.
Shields, C. J. (2003b). Interview with CSR coordinator Yolanda Van Ness [electronic version]. *Common Knowledge, 16*(4).
Siler, J. N. (1997). Report on the sixth national core knowledge conference: Bigger is still better. *Common Knowledge, 10*(1/2), 1, 8–9.
Siler, J. N. (1998). Atlanta '98: Core content with southern hospitality. *Common Knowledge, 11*(1/2), 10–11.
Summers, M. (1999, July 26). Defining literacy upward. *Forbes*, 70, 72.
TASIS Staff. (2007). Core Knowledge hit the Alps [Electronic version]. *Common Knowledge, 20*(1).
Telling. (2003). Telling your story with test data [Electronic version]. *Common Knowledge, 16*(3).
Vail, K. (1997). Core comes to Crooksville. *The American School Board Journal, 184*(3), 14–18.
Woodson, C. G. (1933/2000). *The mis–education of the Negro*. Chicago: African American Images.
Wiener, J. M. (1989). Radical historians and the crisis in American history, 1959–1980. *The Journal of American History, 76*, 399–434.
Williams, R. (1983). *Keywords: A vocabulary of culture and society* (Rev. ed.). New York: Oxford University Press.
Yosso, T. J. (2006). *Critical race counterstories along the Chicana/Chicano educational pipeline*. New York: Routledge.
Zimmerman, J. (2002). *Whose America: Culture wars in the public schools*. Cambridge: Harvard University Press.

Kristen L. Buras
Division of Educational Studies
Emory University

SANDRA HARDING

16. GENDER, DEMOCRACY, AND PHILOSOPHY OF SCIENCE[1]

It is now three decades since critics began to look at the theories and practices of science and technology (S&T) through the distinctive perspectives produced by the women's movement in the U.S. and Europe. These critics asked to what extent do modern S&T fail to give equal attention to women's interests? How does a sexist social structure in science and society shape both modern sciences' patterns of knowledge and their patterns of ignorance? What can be done to increase the democratic effects of S&T projects? In the last decade especially, analyses that start off from the lives of women from racial and ethnic minorities in the North and women in the Third World have added distinctive perspectives to these debates.[2] In this chapter, I shall briefly review the main themes in these literatures, and then, even more briefly, turn to their implications for theories of democracy and philosophies of science.

GENDER ISSUES

Five kinds of gender issues initially attracted the attention of critics.[3] I will offer only a brief mention of major themes in the first four approaches. One focuses on the absence of gender equity in the social structure of the sciences, mathematics, and engineering. Historians have provided accounts of ways women and gender have influenced European and North American sciences, and social scientists have documented the continuing obstacles to equality confronting women. Today girls and women have largely gained access to science, math, and engineering pre-professional and professional education, teaching and lab appointments, publication in research journals, and membership in S&T societies. Yet the higher that one looks in S&T worlds, the fewer women one finds. In the North as in the South, few women direct the most prestigious laboratories, chair university science, mathematics and engineering departments, or hold top positions in international S&T policy agencies or organizations. (Harding and McGregor, 1996; MIT 1998; Schiebinger, 1989; Science, 1992, 1993, 1994.)

The persistence of this discrimination against women raises other troubling questions. Would more women's issues be addressed by S&T projects if there were more women making S&T policy in the North and in the South? Moreover, does this gender discrimination damage the objectivity of the knowledge claims and the patterns of knowledge produced by S&T? Shouldn't we always worry when those who hold economic, social, and political power and those who determine what counts as truth are the same people?

Z. Leonardo (ed.), Handbook of Cultural Politics and Education, 373–380.

A second concern has focused on cases of sexist and androcentric applications and technologies of S&T. Reproductive, household and workplace technologies, architecture, and urban landscapes have been designed with little concern for women's health, safety, or well-being. Feminist constructivist approaches to technology have developed illuminating analyses that were blocked by older conceptions of technologies as culturally neutral "hardware." These accounts show how artefacts have gender. (Cockburn, 1985; Berg and Lie, 1995; Wajcman, 1991) Critics have pointed to how so-called development practices have added sexist Northern assumptions of European and North American cultures, international agencies and transnational corporations to those of Southern societies to decrease the likelihood of women in the South receiving benefits of S&T research designed in either the North or the South. Especially egregious examples of such discrimination have been documented in work on health, agriculture, natural resources (energy, water, etc.), and environmental research (Braidotti *et al.*, 1994).

Third, sexist, racist, and imperialist and "orientalist" results of scientific research in biology and the social sciences have justified legal, economic, and social enforcement of women's second-class citizenship. While this kind of research began to flourish back in the Nineteenth Century, it is still doing well today in sociobiology, and mainstream social sciences (Fausto-Sterling, 1994). Especially powerful analyses have emerged from scholars and activitists working on issues of gender in Third World so-called development (Braidotti *et al.*, 1994; L. Smith, 1999; Visvanathan *et al.*, 1997).

A fourth focus on science, math, and engineering curricula and pedagogy has succeeded in shifting attention from the reputed deficiencies of girls and women to the documented deficiencies of S&T curricula and pedagogy. Girls and women tend to have different learning styles, research styles, and interests in S&T than do their brothers. In the South, S&T literacy projects must also contend with women's higher illiteracy rates in some cultures and with the demand on girls and women for household services (Harding and McGregor, 1996; Rosser, 1986).

FEMINIST EPISTEMOLOGY AND PHILOSOPHIES OF SCIENCE

Perhaps most potentially revolutionary have been criticisms of conventional philosophies of science. These philosophies articulate the "logic" of what they identify as the most desirable scientific practices based on their understandings of the history of science. Feminists asked how have the very standards for objectivity, rationality, good method, and good science disproportionately reflected the concerns of the institutions that use S&T as resources to make legal, health, educational, military, and economic policy? What would such standards look like if they were designed to respond also to women's interests, fears, and desires? What would S&T look like if women, South and North, were also their <u>subjects</u> rather than only their often mis-perceived objects? (Braidotti *et al.*, 1994; Harding, 1991; Keller, 1984).

The most interesting feminist responses to such epistemological issues have carefully avoided unhelpful rejections of objectivity, rationality, good method, and science itself. Women need <u>more</u> objectivity, rationality, good method, and good science for projects that originate in the needs of their lives. They don't need the excessively narrow forms of these that have long been favored in philosophies of science.

To take one example, consider feminist concerns about standard ways of thinking about objectivity (Harding 1998, chapter 8). Maximizing objectivity has required maximizing value-neutrality. According to the conventional view, it is the scientific methods specified by research designs through which the social values and interests that researchers inevitably bring to their work can be identified and eliminated. This approach certainly has its virtues. Yet it is evident that it has only been able to achieve a weak form of objectivity since so many sexist and androcentric assumptions (not to mention assumptions shaped by class, religion, culture, national, racial and imperial interests and values) have managed, in what were claimed to be the most rigorous of scientific research projects, to shape the results of research in S&T, especially in biology and the social sciences. How adequate can the conventional standards of objectivity be if again and again they sanction accounts of women's biological and social inferiority?[4]

Critics identify three problems with this kind of standard for maximizing objectivity. First, important scientific processes occur before scientific methods begin and are not controlled by conventional notions of method. In this "context of discovery," problematic natural or social conditions are identified–for example, poverty. Just what is problematic about them is conceptualized: "too many mouths to feed". Concepts and hypotheses to guide research are formulated: "overpopulation;" "population control;" "if women's reproduction is controlled, there will be fewer mouths to feed". Then research is designed to test hypotheses. In the case considered here, today even the United Nations recognizes (since the 1995 Cairo U.N. conference on population) that such purportedly objective research has failed to identify the sexist, racist, and class-based assumptions that have shaped many decades of research on population control issues. It is poverty that causes population growth in the first place, not the reverse. Poor families need children's labor and wages in order to survive, and children must provide the care for smaller children and, when they grow up, for the elderly that government, incomes, and inherited wealth provide for middle and upper classes. Increasing women's education and thus their income potential turns out to be the single most effective way to decrease fertility.

Thus feminist approaches have demanded systematic critical scrutiny of the "context of discovery" as well as of the "context of justification." Starting off research from women's lives instead of from the conceptual frameworks of the dominant social institutions and the research disciplines that service them can generate questions about "the conceptual practices of power" that are not available from the perspective of powerful institutions and their research agendas (D. Smith, 1990).

A second criticism of weak objectivity is that its way of identifying social values and interests is to repeat observations by different individuals or groups of them. That is, the methods of obtaining scientific results must be replicable. While this requirement is effective at identifying values and interests that differ between individual observers or research teams, it will not identify those that they all share.

Sexist and racist beliefs are not the inventions of individuals or research teams; they are widely-held institutional and societal assumptions that, prior to the emergence of feminisms and anti-racisms, have seemed perfectly natural to almost everyone.

In the case of these kinds of deep and widespread assumptions, it takes more than the exercise of standard notions of "good method" to identify distorting values and interests. In these cases, it has taken collective political criticism to bring into general visibility the social values and interests shaping sexist and racist assumptions. Again, starting off research from outside dominant conceptual frameworks brings fresh perspectives to bear on a culture's common assumptions. Of course no one can ever get completely outside their culture. Yet even just a small liberation from prevailing assumptions can provide a valuable critical perspective, as social scientists have emphasized in reporting the increased objectivity available to the stranger to a culture.

This brings us to a third problem with weak objectivity. It cannot distinguish between those kinds of values and interests that advance and those that retard the growth of knowledge. As long as maximizing value-neutrality has been assumed the only and always reasonable way to try to maximize objectivity, it has seemed counter-intuitive even to consider raising the question of whether and how some social values and interests might sometimes in fact advance objectivity. Jumping ahead for the moment to my final topic, we can note that here is an important challenge to be addressed by researchers who are interested in the social responsibility of S&T. A central part of the challenge is to conceptualize how what researchers observe is always both given by nature and constructed by culture–that is, to avoid both absolute naturalism and absolute relativism. To put the point another way, a kind of virtual reality is all that the sciences have ever charted for us or ever could chart.

As a start in responding to this challenge, we can think how anti-democratic values and interests block the growth of knowledge in the ways that they silence the most vigorous critical perspectives on anti-democratic and other dominant ways of thinking. Pro-democratic values and interests bring such perspectives into general visibility and so enlarge opportunities for maximizing the objectivity of research processes. Yet this perception is indeed just a beginning here, for we need to think further about what in particular we mean by democratic values and interests (do we mean those evident in the current tendencies toward global "democratization", where economic inequality is ignored and even sometimes intentionally advanced? [see Robinson, 1996]) and about specifically how scientific and technological research processes advance or retard them.

MANY FEMINISMS, MANY S&T INTERESTS

The preceding account may seem to suggest that there is one and ony one feminist position on epistemology and philosophy of science issues. Yet this could not be and is not the case. Distinctive "public agenda" feminisms have emerged during the last two centuries in Europe and the U.S. These have been shaped by the political philosophies–Liberalism, Marxism, etc.– through which women and men have made feminist demands on governments. Mary Wollstonecraft and John Stuart Mill started off their thought from the women's lives with which they were most familiar. These were the lives of women in the educated classes whose interests have remained central in more than two centuries of Liberal Feminism. Of course today, when state-mandated education continually increases the population of the "educated classes," one could argue that Liberal Feminism both has vastly expanded its concerns and that its adherents come from a far broader economic and political spectrum than was the case in the Eighteenth Century. Liberal feminists have had different concerns about S&T than have other feminist groups such as the Marxist and Socialist Feminisms that arose in the Nineteenth Century.

Thus it is not surprising to discover that thinking about S&T from the standpoint of the lives of racial and ethnic minorities in the North and of women in the South also produces distinctive concerns and themes. The account above suggests just a few ways in which the concerns of this majority of the world's women have appeared within the critical categories constructed to account for large groups of Northern women's S&T interests. Yet, starting thought from outside these Liberal and Marxist philosophic frameworks also raises entirely new issues for Northern S&T, feminist or not (see Harding, 1993, 1998; Hess, 1995).

After all, the attempts to add women's concerns to the dominant conceptual frameworks of biology, sociology, anthropology, economics, political philosophy and other fields have consistently revealed that the frameworks themselves were resistant to such additive projects. Women's lives could not be objectively grasped within frameworks that had elaborated complex systems of assumptions and categories for conceptualizing women's biology as inferior and their contributions to history and social relations as minimal or even negative. But then, neither, could men's lives be objectively grasped within such frameworks. If women, their natures and activities are not in fact inferior but merely different, then neither are men, their natures and activities superior or deserving of the distinctive mark of the ideally human. The conceptual frameworks themselves have been challenged by the attempts merely to "add women and stir." Similarly, attempts to add the lives of the majority of the worlds' women to categorical schemes designed to explain the lives of relatively privileged minorities in the modern North have also shown the limitations of those Eurocentric frameworks for objectively accounting for anyone's lives.

My point here is that we now have available multiple illuminating feminist theoretical perspectives from which to ask questions about the history and practices of S&T. And the multicultural and postcolonial feminisms have raised a number of new issues that pose challenges to Northern feminist as well as conventional philosophies of S&T. Here I identify just three such issues.

MULTICULTURAL AND POSTCOLONIAL FEMINIST PHILOSOPHIC ISSUES.[5]

First, we need new histories and geographies of the past and present distribution of human S&T knowledge. No longer is it reasonable to assume that Western modern science is uniquely capable of telling the one true story about nature's order.

New histories show the richness of the older Chinese, Islamic and other South Asian S&T traditions and innovative practices in contemporary indigenous S&T traditions around the globe today. They show the continual appropriation of these other knowledge traditions into Northern S&T. Within the expanded sense of S&T that such new accounts provide, women's contributions to the history and present store of human knowledge emerge into visibility. Moreover, these accounts reveal that at the moments marked as progressive in the standard triumphalist histories of science, women, along with other subordinate groups, frequently have lost social status and resources.

In the second place, multicultural and postcolonial science studies show how the standards for objectivity, rationality, good method, and even good science itself have been defined not only in terms of their distance from qualities and practices associated with the feminine, but also in terms of their distance from the primitive. The philosophic standards that guide modern Western S&T are also standards for certain forms of distinctively European (and North American) masculinity. They mark not inclusively human ideals, but only historically specific forms of masculinity. In both ways these standards undercut the ability of Western modern S&T both to detect valuable conceptual frameworks and practices that other cultures have developed and to achieve an objective assessment of the real strengths and limitations of Western modern S&T.

Women's and non-Western S&T traditions have been shunned by conventional philosophies of science on the grounds (among others) that the former are embedded in culturally local values and interests and therefore not trans-culturally disinterested and objective. Yet these S&T traditions have provided systematic knowledge about natural and social worlds that have enabled their cultures to survive and thrive. On the other hand, the disinterestedness of Western S&T has enabled its usefulness to the most powerful players in the inequality-increasing global political economy of today, not to mention to a long history of other militaristic, profiteering, and anti-democratic projects. Until we are ready to understand how ethics and politics shape good science and not just "bad science," we will not be effective at limiting the ways that S&T continue to serve the interests of political and economic power.

Finally, as the first two issues indicate, these feminist, multicultural and postcolonial S&T studies show how all knowledge systems, including Northern modern S&T, are historically distinctive, or "local", in important ways. These studies undercut standard triumphalist narratives of Western modern S&T's contributions to human progress. Insofar as different cultures, or women and men within a culture, are assigned different interactions with natural and social environments, have different interests, draw on different discursive resources, and organize differently the production of knowledge, they will tend to develop distinctive bodies of systematic knowledge and systematic ignorance. For example, those who are assigned infant care and those assigned care of motorcycles (to stick to stereotypes) will develop distinctive patterns of knowledge and of ignorance of nature and social relations. Thus women and men in every walk of life, and different cultures, everywhere in the world, insofar as they engage in distinctive kinds of activities, will develop and maintain distinctive patterns of knowledge (and of ignorance). Moreover, all of these are "modern sciences" insofar as they are continually put to the test of enabling their users to interact effectively with changing environments and newly arriving information and ways of thinking from other peoples and cultures.

These issues challenge the remnants of the old unity of science thesis, which held that there is one world, one "truth" (true account) about it, and one and only one (historically distinctive, though trans-cultural) science capable in principle of providing that true account. Few who reflect on the immense diversity of ontologies, epistemologies, and methods that characterize the so-called modern sciences today, let alone on the multitude of other S&T traditions that have contributed to the storehouse of human knowledge, would admit to that unity of science thesis in its most restrictive forms. (Galison & Stump, 1996). Yet most of us retain unity assumptions that make it difficult to appreciate the scientific, philosophic, and pro-democratic opportunities feminist, multicultural and postcolonial S&T studies have made available. What could a theory of human knowledge look like that would build on the insights of these distinctive contemporary movements?

NOTES

1 Reprinted from _Science, Engineering, and Global Responsibility_, International Network of Engineering and Science, 2001.

2 Many central terms in these discussions, such as Third World, postcolonialism, development, feminism, and even science itself are contested. They must remain so as the horizons of our understandings of how S&T function in local and global social relations continue to expand.

3 I have reviewed these issues in a number of places. See, e.g., Harding 1991.

4 There is by now a large literature documenting these claims for biology and the social sciences. For biology, Fausto-Sterling 1994 is a good place to start.

5 Multicultural and postcolonial S&T studies and their diverse feminist components have emerged into international visibility since the mid-1980's. Sources of and central themes in this literature may be found in Braidotti et al 1994, Harding 1998, and Hess 1995.

REFERENCES

Berg, A. J., & Merete, L. (1995). Feminism and constructivism: Do artifacts have gender? *Science, Technology, and Human Values, 20*(3), 332–351.

Braidotti, R., et al. (1994). *Women, the environment, and sustainable development*. Atlantic Highlands, NJ: Zed.

Cockburn, C. (1985). *Machinery of dominance: Women, men, and technical know-how*. London: Pluto Press.

Fausto-Sterling, A. (1994). *Myths of gender: Biological theories about women and men*. New York: Basic Books.

Galison, P., & D., (Eds.). (1996). *The disunity of science*. Stanford, CA: Stanford University Press.

Harding, S. (1991). Feminism confronts the sciences: Reform and transformation. In *Whose science? Whose knowledge? Thinking from women's lives* (Chapter 2). Ithaca, NY: Cornell University Press.

Harding, S. (Ed.). (1993). *The 'Racial' economy of science: Toward a democrtic future*. Bloomington, IN: Indiana University Press.

Harding, S. (1998). *Is science multicultural? Postcolonialisms, feminisms, and epistemologies*. Bloomington, IN: Indiana University Press.

Harding, S., & McGregor, E. (1996). The gender dimension of science and technology. In *UNESCO World Science Report 1996*. Paris: UNESCO.
Hess, D. (1995). *Science and technology in a multicultural world: The cultural politics of facts and artifacts*. New York: Columbia University Press.
Keller, E. F. (1984). *Reflections on gender and science*. New Haven, CT: Yale University Press.
MIT. (1998). "*Women scientists at MIT.*" A Report.
Robinson, W. I. (1996). *Promoting polyarchy: Globalization, U.S. intervention, and hegemony*. New York: Cambridge University Press.
Rosser, S. (1986). *Teaching science and health from a feminist perspective*. Oxford: Pergamon Press.
Schiebinger, L. (1989). *The mind has no sex? Women in the origins of modern science*. Cambridge: Harvard University Press.
Science. (1992, 1993, 1994). Women in science. *255*, *260*, 383–430, *263*, 1467–1493.
Smith, D. E. (1990). *The conceptual practices of power: A feminist sociology of knowledge*. Boston: Northeastern University Press.
Smith, L. T. (1999). *Decolonizing methodologies: Research and indigenous peopes*. New York: Zed Books.
Visvanathan, N., Duggan, L., Nisonoff, L., & Wiegersma, N. (Eds.). (1997). *The women, gender and development reader*. London: Zed Books.
Wajcman, J. (1991). *Feminism confronts technology*. University Park, PA: Pennsylvania State University.

Sandra Harding
Graduate School of Education & Information Studies
University of California
Los Angeles

SOCIAL IDENTITIES

DAVID GILLBORN

17. 'JUST THE RIGHT AMOUNT OF RACISM'

The Cultural Politics of Race and Reform

Power never takes a back step — only in the face of more power.

Malcolm X[1]

INTRODUCTION

Progress in the struggle against inequity is never simply gifted by a benign oppressor. The key driving force behind advances in the rights of minoritized groups is minoritized groups themselves.[2] In our rush to understand the cultural politics of contemporary education there is a danger that we might become overly fascinated with changes in popular discourses and representations, treating such factors as not only highly significant but possibly as all that there is (see Apple, 2006; Sivanandan, 1990). In England *every* notable development taking forward antiracist education, whether at a local or national level, has arisen in some way as a direct result of action by the subaltern group. Often the catalyst for change nationally is a major protest or public injustice, frequently involving bloodshed, even death (see Gillborn, 2008; Tomlinson, 2008). Such events – landmarks in the history of antiracist resistance – are typically presented by policymakers and media commentators as if they arise randomly, when some fluke occurrence exposes an unusual problem and so action is taken to rectify the anomaly; one more step on the steady road of incremental advance toward ever greater equity and social justice.

But the apparent victory is only a small part of the wider story. In the same way that we would be foolish to accept the official version of the events leading up to a supposed political landmark, so we should be equally sceptical about the long-term effects of the policy reforms that follow. Even when, to echo Malcolm X's phrase, "power" is forced into "a back step", it rarely misses an opportunity to counter-attack and advance once again. In this chapter I consider the cultural politics of such apparently 'revolutionary' moments. In order to examine the processes in detail I look at the single most important episode in recent race equality politics in the UK: the case of Stephen Lawrence. This is vital, not only because of the high profile of the Lawrence case (and its symbolic importance as a potential turning point in British educational politics) but also because of the wider lessons that it teaches us about the operation of power in a racist society; i.e., that exceptional breakthroughs can quickly be recolonized in ways that not only betray those involved in the initial struggle but may actually reinforce the very inequities that we are told have been addressed.

Z. Leonardo (ed.), Handbook of Cultural Politics and Education, 383–401.

I examine the Lawrence case using the tools and insights of critical race theory (CRT) a radical approach, that began in US legal studies, but is now of increasing importance in educational research inside, and beyond, the US (Gillborn 2008; Lynn & Parker 2006). Before looking at the detail of the Lawrence case, therefore, it is useful to begin by considering the concepts that shape the analysis.

INTEREST CONVERGENCE AND CONTRADICTION–CLOSING CASES

> Justice for blacks vs. racism = racism
> Racism vs. obvious perceptions of white self-interest = justice for blacks
> (Bell, 2004, p. 59)

Critical race theory has its roots in the diasporic writings and resistances of previous centuries, including actions by enslaved African peoples (see Baszile, 2008; Bell, 2004; Du Bois, 1975, 1990; Mills, 1997, 2003). Contemporary CRT is a direct outgrowth from debates within US legal scholarship in the mid-1970s and 1980s. It began as a radical alternative to the dominant perspectives of the time, both the conservative legal "mainstream" and the ostensibly radical tradition of critical legal studies (CLS) which, despite its radical rhetoric, continued to treat race inequity as a peripheral issue (Crenshaw *et al.,* 1995; Crenshaw, 2002; Delgado & Stefancic, 2001). CRT places race/racism[3] at the centre of its analysis: one of CRT's foundational elements is an understanding of racism as a pervasive, routine and powerful presence across society:

> CRT begins with a number of basic insights. One is that racism is normal, not aberrant, in American society. Because racism is an ingrained feature of our landscape, it looks ordinary and natural to persons in the culture. Formal equal opportunity – rules and laws that insist on treating blacks and whites (for example) alike – can thus remedy only the more extreme and shocking forms of injustice, the ones that do stand out. It can do little about the business-as-usual forms of racism that people of color confront every day and that account for much misery, alienation, and despair (Delgado & Stefancic 2000, p. xvi).

This view of racism as "endemic in US society, deeply ingrained legally, culturally, and even psychologically" (Tate, 1997, p. 234) is a source of some confusion to detractors of CRT, who sometimes misunderstand the perspective as viewing racism as inevitable and, therefore, rendering hopeless all attempts at change. In fact, CRT is founded upon activist principles: it is shaped by a constant commitment to resistance (see Bell, 1995; Stovall, 2006). However, CRT is characterized by what Derrick Bell (1992) has termed "racial realism", a recognition that in the real world racism is not a peripheral abnormality or misunderstanding that can be educated out of the majority, but a hugely powerful system of oppression that lies at the heart of US (and UK) politics and operates in the material interests of the White majority. This perspective underlies Bell's (1980) identification of what he termed the principle of "interest convergence":

> On a positivistic level – how the world *is* – large segments of the American people do not deem racial equality legitimate, at least to the extent it threatens to impair the societal status of whites ... The interest of blacks in achieving racial equality will be accommodated only when it converges with the interests of whites. (p. 523; original emphasis)

Put simply, this view argues that advances in race equality come about only when White elites see the changes as in *their* own interest. Interest convergence offers a counter hegemonic way of understanding the dynamics of racism and social policy at certain points, especially where a landmark event appears to have advanced the cause of race equality. The less well-known, but no less insightful, idea of "contradiction-closing cases" helps to explain what happens after the news headlines have died down and racism returns to its business-as-usual.

When reviewing the key civil rights decisions of the US Supreme Court, Bell shows how, in retrospect, these famous victories can be seen to have operated in much more complex ways than was initially imagined. Hailed as epochal victories that would change the social landscape forever, Bell (1985) argues that their progressive impact was not only uncertain and short lived but that, in the long run, their consequence may be to further protect the status quo:

> We can expect that the Court will favor civil rights litigants if the policies they attack are so blatantly discriminatory as to shock (or at least embarrass) the public conscience. This is particularly true when a ruling in favor of black litigants will not impose any costs on identifiable classes of whites ... Such cases might be seen as 'contradiction closing' cases ... These cases serve as a shield against excesses in the exercise of white power, yet they bring about no real change in the status of blacks. (p. 32)

The idea of contradiction-closing cases has been taken up and used by Richard Delgado (1998), another foundational CRT writer, who argues that they protect the status quo by offering an occasional symbolic victory to minorities that "allow business as usual to go on even more smoothly than before" (p. 445). Using the 1954 *Brown versus Board of Education* desegregation case as an exemplar, Delgado argues that a clear pattern can be seen: initially the case seems to offer a huge breakthrough – things will never be the same again. Those arguing the case rejoice in their victory and many liberals move on to other issues, assuming this one to be solved. However, lower courts may interpret the decision very narrowly; administrators and others in the system "drag their feet" over substantive changes; meanwhile conservatives redouble their resistance and mobilize to have the decision overturned in practice if not principle. Years later the case stands as a "landmark decision", used to celebrate the country's liberal values and commitment to equality, but on the ground little or nothing has really changed. Fifty years after the Brown decision it has been argued that US schools are even more segregated than they were at the time of the original case (Delgado & Stefancic, 2001, p. 33).

In the remainder of this chapter I analyse the racial politics of the Stephen Lawrence case – probably the most famous single episode in the history of British race relations. After years of the most painful campaigning and mistreatment, the Lawrence family's suffering and achievements were hailed (by the British prime minister Tony Blair) as a defining point in creating a new Britain, with repercussions across all public services, especially education. The policy changes were won at a bitter cost and resisted at every turn. The reforms looked impressive but, less than a decade after the laws were changed, the reality of educational inequity remains largely unchanged for Black (African Caribbean) young people and the world of education continues its racist business as usual.

WHAT IF THEY CHANGED THE LAW AND NO-ONE NOTICED?

> Looking back now, I am sure that if the government had realised all that would come out of the inquiry, they would not have let it take place.
>
> Doreen Lawrence (2006, p. 179)

Stephen Lawrence was 18 years old when he was murdered by a gang of White youths. His parents' fight for justice, in the face of a racist, incompetent and uncaring police force, made legal and social history. The Stephen Lawrence case led to far-reaching changes in race equality law (that touched every public body in the UK) and elevated the notion of "institutional racism" to a point in the public consciousness where the term is now frequently used and debated in politics and in the mainstream media. But for all this, serious questions remain about the long-term impact of the case.

The Murder, the Investigation, the Campaign, the Inquiry

At around 10:30 pm on 22 April 1993, Stephen Lawrence was waiting for a bus home with his friend Duwayne Brooks. Stephen walked a short distance from Duwayne to see if he could see a bus coming. The public inquiry into the case describes what happened next:

> Mr. Brooks called out to ask if Stephen saw the bus coming. One of the [five or six White youths on the opposite side of the road] must have heard something said, since he called out *"what, what nigger?"* With that the group came quickly across the road and literally engulfed Stephen. (Macpherson, 1999, p. 1: original emphasis)

Stephen was stabbed twice. His attackers ran off leaving him to struggle about 100 yards towards Duwayne before collapsing. A granite memorial stone now marks the spot where Stephen died: it is regularly defaced with racist graffiti.

Stephen was by no means the first Black young man to be murdered in an unprovoked racist attack on British streets, and he was not the last.[4] But his case was set apart by the courage and endurance of his parents, Doreen and Neville

Lawrence, who waged a campaign for justice that made national headlines and continues to this day.[5] From the beginning the police investigation was dogged by incompetence, disdain, racism and, possibly, corruption.[6] Shortly after witnessing his friend's murder Duwayne Brooks was questioned by police who thought him "very agitated" and "aggressive" (Macpherson, 1999, p. 15). The public inquiry concluded that "Mr Brooks was stereotyped as a young black man exhibiting unpleasant hostility and agitation, who could not be expected to help, and whose condition and status simply did not need further examination or understanding" (Macpherson, 1999, p. 16).

Stephen's parents were equally badly treated, seen by officers as troublesome and interfering, also labelled as aggressive. At the inquiry Doreen Lawrence recalled what happened:

> Basically, we were seen as gullible simpletons. This is best shown by Detective Chief Superintendent Ilsley's comment that I had obviously been primed to ask questions. Presumably, there is no possibility of me being an intelligent, black woman with thoughts of her own who is able to ask questions for herself. We were patronised and were fobbed off… (Macpherson, 1999, p. 11)

An internal review of the case concluded that "the investigation has been progressed satisfactorily" but that "relations were hampered by the involvement of active, politically motivated groups" and the investigation had been "undertaken with professionalism and dedication" (Lawrence, 2006, p. 121). The review's author, an extremely experienced police officer, later admitted suppressing evidence (that would have been critical of the original investigation) for fear of damaging police morale. His review was ultimately described by the public inquiry report as "misleading", "flawed" and "indefensible": the evidence of its author was considered "unconvincing and incredible in a number of important respects" (Macpherson, 1999, p. 11).

Undeterred, the Lawrences pursued their case through every legal channel open, including launching a private prosecution. At one point they felt confident that they had sufficient evidence to convince a jury, including surveillance video of the main suspects wielding knives and using violent racist language. On the tapes one of the suspects is seen saying:

> I reckon that every nigger should be chopped up, mate, and they should be left with nothing but fucking stumps.[7]

This damning evidence was never shown to the jury: the judge ruled out Duwayne Brook's identification evidence and directed the jury to return "not guilty" verdicts.

> Only later did I start to analyse the implications: bringing a private prosecution was a very rare event, yet here was a black family doing just that, in a case that threatened to show up the Conservative government, show up the Crown Prosecution Service, show up the Metropolitan Police force, show up the entire justice system – the enormous odds against us winning had not dawned

> on me before. In my mind's eye, I had believed that in the end right was on our side, but the forces lined up against us were too great. I may be wrong; but I know I was naïve to think we could succeed.
>
> Doreen Lawrence (2006, p. 161)

Despite these huge set backs, the Lawrences continued their campaign and, following a change of government in 1997, were finally granted the public inquiry that they sought.

Much of the inquiry, chaired by Sir William Macpherson of Cluny, was held in public and the nightly coverage in the news media meant that the catalogue of police errors and racism was broadcast nationally, initially to a sceptical public but eventually to a growing sense of outrage. Conscious of the wider issues that were emerging, the Inquiry report does not limit itself to the failings of the police in the Lawrence case. Indeed, the Inquiry identified changes in the education system as fundamental to the issues it had uncovered:

> the issue of education may not at first sight sit clearly within our terms of reference. Yet we cannot but conclude that to seek to address the well-founded concerns of minority communities simply by addressing the racism current and visible in the Police Services without addressing the educational system would be futile. The evidence we heard and read forces us to the conclusion that our education system must face up to the problems, real and potential, which exist. (Macpherson, 1999, p. 324)

Consequently, among its list of 70 recommendations, the Inquiry report includes direct calls for changes in the education system. Of greater significance than any of the individual recommendations, however, is the report's championing of a particular interpretation of racism that moves beyond the crude, limited and obvious notions that usually characterize official approaches.

Institutional Racism

> "Racism" in general terms consists of conduct or words or practices which advantage or disadvantage people because of their colour, culture or ethnic origin. In its more subtle form it is as damaging as in its overt form.
>
> "Institutional racism" consists of the collective failure of an organisation to provide an appropriate and professional service to people because of their colour, culture, or ethnic origin. It can be seen or detected in processes, attitudes and behaviour which amount to discrimination through unwitting prejudice, ignorance, thoughtlessness and racist stereotyping which disadvantage minority ethnic people. (Macpherson, 1999, p. 321)

This is how the Stephen Lawrence Inquiry defines racism and institutional racism. In reaching this position the Inquiry took evidence from a range of individuals and organisations, including academics and Black advocacy groups. The definition builds on existing notions of institutional racism in two important respects.

First, it condemns the actions both of *individuals* (in their "conduct", "attitudes and behaviour") and *organisations and agencies* whose "processes" work against minoritized groups. In this way the inquiry rejects the familiar official assertion that racism is limited to the actions of a few 'rotten apples'. Second, and most importantly, this approach moves away from endless debates about *intent* by explicitly focusing on the *outcomes* of actions and stating that "unwitting" and "thoughtless" acts are equally as problematic as overt racism. The definition removes intent from the equation and focuses simply on the outcomes of actions and policies. This is not to say, however, that the inquiry ignored the importance of people's perceptions. In fact, the report goes on to define a racist incident explicitly in terms of individual perceptions but, once again, it shifts the balance away from the usual locus of intent:

> *"A racist incident is any incident which is perceived to be racist by the victim or any other person"* ... this definition should be universally adopted by the Police, local Government and other relevant agencies (Macpherson, 1999, pp. 328–9; original emphasis).

This approach was in direct conflict with the views expressed by the country's most senior police officer, Sir Paul Condon (head of London's Metropolitan Police), who wanted to retain the most basic, crude understanding of racism (in his words the "normal" view) which, he argued, reflected what an "average member of the public" would understand:

> ... if this Inquiry labels my service as "institutionally racist" (pause) then the average police officer, the average member of the public will assume the normal meaning of those words. They will assume a finding of conscious, wilful, or deliberate action or an action to the detriment of ethnic minority Londoners.[8]

The Inquiry pushed ahead with the more radical approach and, initially at least, met with success in its attempt to shift public debate on the issue.

The Inquiry's Reception

On 24 February 1999, almost six years after the murder, the Stephen Lawrence Inquiry report was presented to Parliament by Jack Straw, the Home Secretary who had established the inquiry. Before that, however, the Prime Minister Tony Blair used his weekly Parliamentary question and answer session to praise the Lawrence family, condemn the failures that had been exposed, and to promise far-reaching action in the future:

> I am proud that it was this Government who set up the Lawrence inquiry. I am happy to accept its judgment ... The publication of today's report on the killing of Stephen Lawrence is a very important moment in the life of our country. It is a moment to reflect, to learn and to change. It will certainly lead to new laws but, more than that, it must lead to new attitudes, to a new era in race relations, and to a new more tolerant and more inclusive Britain. ... The test

> of our sincerity as law makers in this House is not how well we can express sympathy with the Lawrence family, but how well we implement the recommendations to make sure that such an incident never again happens in our country (*Hansard,* 1999a, column 380–381).

Placing the report before Parliament Jack Straw was even more forthright, making clear that the Inquiry's recommendations had the Government's support and, significantly, noting that Condon accepted the inquiry's findings *and* its definition of institutional racism: in the weeks before publication it had been clear that the Inquiry would make acceptance of its definition a key factor in taking forward its recommendations, prompting speculation that Condon would be forced to resign. In the event, Straw stated:

> The House will share my sense of shame that the criminal justice system, and the Metropolitan police in particular, failed the Lawrence family so badly. The Commissioner of Police of the Metropolis, Sir Paul Condon, has asked me to tell the House that he shares that sense of shame. He has also asked me to tell the House that, as head of the Metropolitan police service, he fully accepts the findings of the inquiry, including those relating to him. (…) I have asked Sir Paul to continue to lead the Metropolitan police to deliver the programme of work that is now required. He has agreed (*Hansard,* 1999b, column 390).

On its publication the report dominated the media. Most coverage focused on the Metropolitan police, the principal subject of the inquiry, but education also featured prominently. This was prompted by the last four of the inquiry's 70 recommendations, which were entitled "prevention and the role of education". Among the actions called for were changes to the National Curriculum "aimed at valuing cultural diversity and preventing racism"; a higher profile for these issues in official school inspections; and new duties on schools and local authorities to address racism. The latter included a call for all 'racist incidents' to be monitored and for the publication of these data annually and on a school-by-school basis (Macpherson, 1999, pp. 334–5). Every major daily newspaper covered the report in stories that ran across several pages and repeatedly framed the inquiry's findings in terms of national shame and the need for change:

> The Legacy of Stephen: Judge's damning report on race murder will change Britain
>
> *Daily Mail*, 25 February 1991, p. 1

> Stephen Lawrence's legacy: confronting racist Britain
>
> *The Guardian*, 25 February 1991, p. 1

> A family tragedy, a police force disgraced and a nation shamed
>
> *The Independent*, 25 February 1991, p. 1

> Nail Them: Mirror offers £50,000 to catch Lawrence killers
>
> Damning verdict that shames the nation
>
> *Daily Mirror*, 25 February 1991, p. 1 & 6

This near unanimity reflected the widespread disgust that the inquiry's evidence had engendered. The mood of agreement and a desire for change, however, did not last long.

The following day news broke that an appendix in the first copies of the report had included the names and addresses of people who had testified against the White murder-suspects. Although this information had always been available to the suspects' lawyers, the report that had been so critical of police incompetence was now an easy target for similar charges. By the weekend the tide was turning, with several Sunday papers carrying strongly worded opinion pieces attacking the report and its author. Stewart Steven, in *The Mail on Sunday*, provides an instructive example. First, he was keen to make clear his revulsion at racism (by which he meant deliberate, callous acts of race hatred) but he saw the Inquiry report as equally if not more dangerous:

> There are no grounds … for complacency, but that doesn't mean that we should allow the warped imagination of bigoted white low-lifes, whom we have inadequately educated to destroy that edifice of tolerance which the rest of us have built up over the years. I fear that may happen if Sir William Macpherson's definition of institutional racism is allowed to stand ... One can't be an unwitting racist any more than one can be an unwitting burglar and to pretend otherwise is to put back the cause of multiculturalism for years (Steven, 1999, p. 35).

In this way racism is equated with "bigoted white low-lifes" while the majority of the population and all its major institutions are safe in their well meaning "tolerance". This kind of argument is important because it challenges some of the most significant aspects of the Lawrence Inquiry and the most incisive of its criticisms. The whole point about the Inquiry's definition of racism is that it moves beyond questions of individual intent to address deep-seated inequalities that are born of "common sense" assumptions and actions which *actually* disadvantage minoritized people. It is more widespread and much harder to identify (in others and in oneself) than the simple murderous brutality of a few "bigoted white low-lifes".

This assertion of a minimalist understanding of racism was repeated in the specialist educational press which, just 48 hours after the inquiry's publication, carried critical statements by representatives of several teacher unions:

> It is too easy to be politically correct without facing teachers' pressures. As important as racism is, if teachers had to put every social concern first eight days a week, 25 hours a day wouldn't be enough.
>
> Peter Smith, Association of Teachers and Lecturers[9]

> I do not believe there is a school in the country which would not take urgent steps to stamp out racism.
>
> David Hart, National Association of HeadTeachers[10]

Within a few weeks more union leaders joined the public scepticism about the idea that schools might be institutionally racist. Doug McAvoy, leader of the National Union of Teachers (NUT), the largest and generally most progressive of the unions, echoed Condon's earlier worries about how the charge would be interpreted, again shifting the debate away from those *experiencing* the injustice (minoritized students) and focusing concern on those *responsible* for it:

> Teachers will interpret the term "institutional racism" as an attack on them. Teachers are not racist. We need to be very careful how language is used. It can alienate rather than include.[11]

The next largest union, the National Association of Schoolmasters/Union of Women Teachers (NASUWT) argued that race was being given too much emphasis (Dean 1999) and its general secretary, Nigel de Gruchy, reportedly described institutional racism as "gobbledegook" (Magowan, 1999). Over time the resistance of teaching unions was bolstered by concerted attacks on the Lawrence Inquiry in general, and its definition of racism in particular. *Civitas*, a Right-wing "think tank", was especially vitriolic; describing the inquiry as a "kangaroo court" (Green, 2000, p. 41) and claiming that the process had been hijacked by antiracist organisations (Dennis *et al.,* 2000).

Privately there were soon signs that the Education Department was not keen on pushing forward the Lawrence agenda. A couple of weeks after the Inquiry report was published an official report by the Office for Standards in Education (OFSTED: the independent schools inspectorate) focused on race inequality and at the press launch a senior inspector described the education system as "institutionally racist". *The Guardian* newspaper reported that:

> Ministers found the language of Ofsted's comments extremely unhelpful. Instead of a 'futile argument' about how to describe the problems faced by some ethnic minorities in schools, there should be more effort to improve standards… (Smithers & Carvel, 1999, p. 4).

And so, two weeks after the Lawrence Inquiry had (in the words of government and media alike) "*shamed*" a nation, the Education Department was privately equating discussion of racism with a question of semantics – as if racism were merely a *word* rather than a structured, recurrent, and deeply embedded *reality*. To consider the issue nothing more than a "futile argument" about terminology betrays a total failure to engage with the substance of the Inquiry's analysis. This suspicion was confirmed when the government published its "action plan" for taking forward the Lawrence recommendations. The Education Department's view was that most of the recommendations were already in motion and nothing new was needed. Macpherson's first education recommendation, for example, was that the National Curriculum be changed so as to ensure "valuing cultural diversity and preventing racism, in order better to reflect the needs of a diverse society" (Macpherson, 1999, p. 334). In reply the Department stated:

> The Department has taken a number of actions to date. The National Curriculum addresses and values the diverse nature of British society … all subject documents are designed to provide teachers with flexibility to tailor their teaching to stimulate and challenge all pupils, whatever their ethnic origin or social background (Home Office, 1999, p. 33).

Hence the Department formally claimed to accept the recommendation while actually asserting that things were fine already. Perhaps the most cynical example of this approach was the repackaging of citizenship education by the then Education Secretary, David Blunkett. On the same day that the Lawrence Inquiry was published, Blunkett issued a press release entitled *Ethnic Minority Pupils Must Have The Opportunity To Fulfil Their Potential"*:

> Mr Blunkett said the Department for Education and Employment would be carefully considering the Inquiry Report's recommendations.
>
> Mr Blunkett said: "The tragedy of Stephen Lawrence's death shows how much more needs to be done to promote social justice in our communities. This is about how we treat each other and, importantly, how we learn to respect ourselves and one another as citizens ... That is why we are promoting the teaching of citizenship at school, to help children learn how to grow up in a society that cares and to have real equality of opportunity for all" (DfEE, 1999).

With the ink barely dry on the Lawrence Inquiry report, therefore, the Education Department took the opportunity to repackage its already existing plans for citizenship education as if they were an answer to institutional racism in the system. Worse still, the development did nothing to advance antiracist education: it simply provided for basic civics lessons and reinforced a weak understanding of discrimination that is entirely at odds with the thrust of the Lawrence Inquiry (see Gillborn, 2006).

THE RACE RELATIONS (AMENDMENT) ACT 2000

Tony Blair's commitment to Parliament to bring forward new legislation as a result of the Lawrence Inquiry was made good when the Race Relations (Amendment) Act (RRAA) was passed in November 2000. The Act extended the existing race equality legislation to apply to more than 45,000 public bodies, including all state maintained schools and universities. The Act placed a duty on public bodies to pro-actively work towards the eradication of race discrimination and, specifically, required that every school should:

- have a written policy on race equality;
- monitor their activities for signs of bias (especially focusing on student achievement); &
- must actively plan to eradicate race inequality.

These duties are *mandatory* and, on paper, the new law looked like a major step forward. Unfortunately, signs soon emerged that the education sector in general, and schools in particular, were lagging behind other public authorities. Around a year after the new education requirements became active, for example, the Commission for Racial Equality (CRE)[12] published survey findings that highlighted the slow pace of change in education (Schneider-Ross 2003). In a survey of more than 3,000 public authorities, schools were the least likely to reply: only 20% of schools compared with an overall rate of almost 50%. Of course, nothing substantial can be read into a return rate alone. For example, among countless possible explanations, it might be thought that schools were not interested in race equality or that they were more fearful of responding to a survey sponsored by the CRE (the official body which – at that time – policed the legislation). The most obvious explanation, in the eyes of teachers with whom I've discussed this, is simply that schools are too busy to fill in questionnaires. Any or all of these views might have a grain of truth. Looking ahead, however, we might assume that since 80% of schools did not respond then at least the ones that *did* participate would be among the most committed. If that is true their responses make even gloomier reading. More than half of respondents in the education sector had not identified clear "goals" or "targets" for improvement. In relation to differences in attainment, which is especially prominent in the legislation, only one in three schools had set any clear goals for change (Schneider-Ross, 2003, p. 11).

The survey found schools to be among the least positive respondents when considering any changes that they had made: 65% of respondents in schools believed their race equality work had produced positive benefits, compared with 74% of those in criminal justice and policing, 80% in Further & Higher Education, and 89% in Central Government (Schneider-Ross, 2003, p. 8). Perhaps most worrying of all, despite the relatively poor response so far, people working in education were the *least* likely to express a need for further guidance (Schneider-Ross, 2003, p. 13). Put simply, the survey suggested that many schools were inactive on race equality: at best they might be thought to be "too busy", at worst, they appeared complacent about their legal duties and uninterested in further progress.

The national system of regular and punitive school inspections is widely recognized as one of the key mechanisms by which the UK government has pressured schools into taking certain actions (Gillborn & Youdell, 2000). OFSTED inspection reports are made public and, if the school raises serious cause for concern, inspectors have the power to trigger a series of "special measures" that include increased scrutiny and, eventually, can lead to closure if sufficient improvements are not delivered. Wisely the Lawrence Inquiry reflected the inspectorate's key role by explicitly recommending that inspections should check on the implementation of race equality work (Macpherson, 1999, p. 335). Predictably, OFSTED officially accepted this recommendation and stated that "OFSTED … will ensure that the important issues raised in the Report are addressed during inspections, and that appropriate training is put in place for inspectors" (Home Office, 1999, p. 37).

Although OFSTED has issued occasional special reports on race equality issues, its main programme of school inspection reports has been heavily criticized for failing to give race equality sufficient prominence (Osler & Morrison, 2000). In 2004, for example, a research report found that "Ofsted school inspections rarely comment on disproportionality in exclusions"[13] despite this being one of the most pressing issues for Black communities (Parsons *et al.*, 2004, p. 1). Shockingly the report notes that even where evidence of over-representation was contained *within* reports themselves, say in quoted statistics, the issue was never raised in the conclusions and recommendations for action (Parsons *et al.*, 2004, p. 50).

And it was not only schools and the inspectorate who were slow to react to their new legal duties on race equality. The entire direction of education policy was revealed as disturbingly colour-blind when a bold new "Five Year Strategy" was launched (DfES 2004). Running to 110 pages the document mentioned "standards" an impressive 65 times; "business/es" warranted 36 references; but racism, discrimination (and even the more anodyne "prejudice") were entirely absent. Just five years after Prime Minister Blair promised 'a new era in race relations ... a new more tolerant and more inclusive Britain', his government's education plans had jettisoned any concern with race equality and the fight against institutional racism.

If the failure of schools, OFSTED and policy-makers to take account of the Lawrence Inquiry could be excused as "mere" inaction, inattention, or misunderstanding, then 2005 brought unmistakeable evidence that Blair's government was actively stepping back from even the pretence of honouring its commitments to the Lawrence family and to racial justice. In September 2005 the then-home secretary Charles Clarke decided to disband the Stephen Lawrence Advisory Committee (a group established to help take forward the recommendations of the Lawrence Inquiry Report). Although the National Black Police Association (a key antiracist pressure group) was said to be "shocked and disgusted" by the decision (Black Information Link 2005), a Home Office spokesperson was quoted offering a reassurance that the decision will not affect the Home Office commitment to the race equality agenda" (ibid). One is tempted to conclude that the spokesperson was correct: the decision did not *reduce* the government's commitment, it merely *revealed* its true nature. A couple of months later, in the government's sixth progress report on the Lawrence recommendations, Clarke expressed his personal dedication to race equality, stating "[this] is the first report since I became Home Secretary and I am personally committed to the continuing delivery of this Action Plan" (Home Office 2005: 3). No further progress reports have ever been published.

A CHANGE OF MIND OR MORE OF THE SAME? THE RETREAT FROM THE LAWRENCE INQUIRY

Five years after the publication of the Lawrence Inquiry, institutional racism was increasingly a term used by critics but notably absent from official statements and formal policies. The abandonment of the Lawrence commitments, in practice if not in principle, became obvious through decisions that were highlighted by the press. First, in December 2006, the *Independent on Sunday* newspaper carried extensive quotations from an internal Education Department review of the reasons for Black over-representation in exclusions from school.[14] The newspaper quoted the review as stating that the problem was mostly the result of "largely unwitting, but systematic racial discrimination" concluding that "a compelling case can be made for the existence of 'institutional racism' in schools".[15] However, the same document warned that the term was potentially explosive:

> If we choose to use the term "institutional racism", we need to be sensitive to the likely reception by schools [but] if we choose not to use the term, we need to make sure that the tone of our message remains sufficiently challenging.
>
> Leaked text of an Education Department Review
> (*Independent on Sunday* 2006, p. 8; DfES, 2007, p. 26)

When the story broke the Education Department briefed journalists that "ministers had concluded that it would be inaccurate and counterproductive to brand the school system racist" (BBC News Online, 2006). The report remained unpublished until months later. Following the embarrassment of the leak it was quietly released (without any press notice) on a government website.

The last act in the official retreat from the Lawrence Inquiry came in mid-2007 when the Government published proposals for a Single Equality Act that would "modernise and simplify equality legislation" (Labour Party, 2005, p. 112). This was to be achieved by combining existing equalities legislation (on race, gender, and disability discrimination) into a single duty. In one of its final acts before being replaced (by a single equalities body) the Commission for Racial Equality issued a strongly worded attack on the proposals:

> the Government's proposals for a new single equality duty … regress entirely unnecessarily from the Macpherson Report [Lawrence Inquiry] and constitute a piecemeal approach to addressing discrimination and promoting equality … The CRE is concerned that the Government's proposals on equality duties will render them pretty well unenforceable (CRE, 2007, pp. 4 & 8).

A key principle of the new proposals was that:

> The duty is designed to help all public authorities to do what they do better, not stop them operating effectively or weigh them down with bureaucracy. The duty should not lead any public authority to feel it needs to take any action which might be disproportionate to the benefits the action would deliver. (Department for Communities and Local Government, 2007, p. 89)

If enacted the proposals will remove all the gains made after the Lawrence Inquiry by allowing public bodies to decide which equalities issues are relevant (they may legally decide that "race" is not a pressing concern) and whether addressing an inequality is actually worthwhile. Consequently, under the proposed new system, even if a school decides that race inequality *is* relevant, it is free to choose not to take action if it judges that the effort is disproportionate to the benefit. At a stroke the new equity proposals would legitimate the present (racist) state of the education system.[16]

The new single equalities body (the Equality & Human Rights Commission) is headed by Trevor Phillips; in 2009 he marked the tenth anniversary of the Lawrence Inquiry report by declaring that the term 'institutional racism' was no longer useful or accurate:

> ... institutional racism misses the fact that in many parts of the country, the colour of disadvantage is white as well as brown or black ... whatever its validity, the term 'institutional racism' created more misunderstanding and defensiveness than action'.[17]

CONCLUSION: "JUST THE RIGHT AMOUNT OF RACISM"

> Civil rights laws efficiently and smoothly replicate social reality, particularly black-white power relations. They are a little like the thermostat in your home or office. They assure that there is just the right amount of racism. Too much would be destabilizing – the victims would rebel. Too little would forfeit important pecuniary and psychic advantages for those in power. So, the existing system of race-remedies law does, in fact, grant minorities an occasional victory (…) Particularly in areas where concessions are not too costly… (Delgado, 1995, p. 80)

The Stephen Lawrence case is one of the single most important episodes in the history of British race relations and yet, just a decade after the Inquiry Report was published to such glowing tributes and heartfelt promises from politicians, the Lawrence legacy is more uncertain than ever. The concept of institutional racism has enjoyed an increased public profile but the evidence suggests that the majority of schools have been inactive on their new legal duties and the Department of Education appears to have dropped the term altogether (imagining it to be a question of semantics). When I speak to teachers and/or local education officials (who are usually White) it is not unusual for them to roll their eyes at the mention of "institutional racism", as if the concept (and the problem) is somehow out-dated or has "been done" already. The mere fact of the Stephen Lawrence Inquiry – and the attendant press coverage – is assumed by some observers to denote change. The case fits precisely the warning issued by Derrick Bell and Richard Delgado.

Years of campaigning against the odds (and the weight of the judicial system) finally paid off when the Lawrence family persuaded an incoming Labour government to grant a public inquiry into the circumstances surrounding the racist murder of their son. This was a major victory and highlights an aspect of interest convergence that is often misunderstood. The concept does not refer to a rational and fair negotiation between minoritized groups and White power holders: typically interest convergence happens after Whites have been pushed to seek a resolution through active community resistance that renders the status quo increasingly less viable.

The Lawrence inquiry made headline news and shattered the illusion of public services that treat everyone with respect and equal care regardless of their colour. The catalogue of racism endured by the Lawrences highlighted the gulf between the reality of institutional racism and the official narrative of Britain as a place of "tolerance" and "fair play". The contradiction between fact and façade was highlighted in media coverage that repeatedly talked of national shame and the need for change. It was clearly in the interests of White power holders to be seen to close this contradiction through apparently radical legal reforms. But, as predicted by CRT writings on the other side of the Atlantic, the changes have proven to be largely cosmetic.

The Lawrence case demonstrates conclusively that struggles for race equality are never complete. Landmark victories, no matter how hard won, may be the beginning, not the end, of the change process. But it would be wrong to interpret this analysis as hopeless. Rather, the chapter points to a more realistic measure of success and our chances for further change in the future. The Lawrence case proves the worth of what Girardeau Spann calls "*pure politics*" – a recognition that political mobilization takes numerous forms and is often most effective when it occurs outside the traditional electoral channels, such as in "the form of demonstrations, boycotts and riots" (Spann, 1990, p. 1992). The Lawrence Inquiry was not granted by a benign state that perceived a previously unknown injustice and wished to do the right thing; it was granted by an incoming Labour Government after years of Conservative refusals and high profile protests and public demonstrations, including support from Nelson Mandela (the World's most respected Black politician: a man, of course, who might have been executed decades earlier for his direct action against White oppression in his homeland). The Lawrence Inquiry has delivered considerable advances and still holds out the possibility of further progress (see Richardson, 2007), but it is a start not an end. Recognizing this reality is neither defeatist nor hopeless, it is a necessary step in understanding what we –as critical educators, parents and/or activists – are up against:

> …we can only *de*legitimate it [racism] if we can accurately pinpoint it. And racism lies at the center, not the periphery; in the permanent, not in the fleeting; in the real lives of black and white people, not in the sentimental caverns of the mind.
>
> Derrick Bell (1992, p. 198; original emphasis)

ACKNOWLEDGMENT

This chapter draws on previous work where I have explored the Lawrence case, including Gillborn (2008) and a keynote address for the Higher Education Academy: Sociology, Anthropology, Politics (C-SAP) Group *'Race(ing) Forward: transitions in theorizing "race" in education'*, University of Northampton, February 2008.

NOTES

1 Breitman (1990: 150).

2 I use the term 'minoritized' to refer to those race/ethnic groups who are rendered a power minority by the operation of White assumptions and interests, regardless of their numerical representation at a global, national, local or school level.

3 In much the same way that Foucault (1980) viewed power/knowledge as intimately connected (Youdell 2006: 37), so the social construction of 'race' difference is *always* associated with raced inequities. Consequently the notion of 'race' inevitably carries racist consequences (see Leonardo 2002).

4 In a case with striking similarities to the Lawrence murder, Black teenager Anthony Walker was killed by White racists in Liverpool in 2005.

5 See Lawrence (2006).

6 No charges have been brought but a BBC TV documentary has alleged that a key officer received money from the father of one of the prime murder suspects: BBC TV 2006b.

7 Jamie Acourt quoted from police surveillance video: see transcript of evidence for day 50, Monday 29th June 1998, page P-9742, at Black Information Link (2002).

8 Sir Paul Condon, evidence to the Stephen Lawrence Inquiry, Part 2 Hearings, 1 October 1998, page 290, at Black Information Link (2002).

9 Quoted in Ghouri (1999: 1). When subsequently challenged on this statement Smith sought to clarify his position in a letter to the paper: he stated, 'Having had an Irish mother I know quite a lot about racism. Stereotyping is a risk all of us run': Smith (1999).

10 Quoted in Ghouri (1999): 1.

11 Quoted in Smithers & Carvel (1999): 4.

12 At the time of the Lawrence Inquiry the CRE was the public body charged with major enforcement powers in relation to race equality.

13 'Exclusion' from school, also known as expulsion, is the most severe punishment available to schools. See Gillborn 2008: 60–63.

14 The review was eventually published the following year: DfES (2007).

15 *Independent on Sunday* (2006). The leaked quotes are indeed present in the published version: DfES (2007): 13.

16 For details on the scale and historical nature of race inequity in the English education system see Gillborn (2005 and 2008).

17 Phillips (2009, p. 26)

REFERENCES

Apple, M. W. (2006). Rhetoric and reality in critical educational studies in the United States. *British Journal of Sociology of Education, 27*(5), 679–687.

BBC News Online. (2006). *Expulsions 'fuelled by prejudice'*. Retrieved January 10, 2007, from http://news.bbc.co.uk/1/hi/education/6168285.stm

Baszile, D. T. (2008). Beyond all reason indeed: The pedagogical promise of critical race testimony. *Race Ethnicity & Education, 11*(3).

Bell, D. (1980). Brown v. Board of education and the interest convergence dilemma. *Harvard Law Review, 93*, 518–533.

Bell, D. (1985). Foreword: The civil rights chronicles (The Supreme Court, 1984 term). *Harvard Law Review, 99*, 4–83.

Bell, D. (1992). *Faces at the bottom of the well: The permanence of racism*. New York: Basic Books.

Bell, D. (1995). Who's afraid of critical race theory? *University of Illinois Law Review, 1995*, 893–910.

Bell, D. (2004). *Silent covenants: Brown v. Board of education and the unfulfilled hopes for racial reform*. Oxford: Oxford University Press.

Black Information Link. (2002). *Stephen Lawrence inquiry transcripts*. Retrieved May 3, 2007, from http://www.blink.org.uk/sli_transcripts.asp?grp=14

Black Information Link. (2005). *Don't axe Stephen Lawrence*. Retrieved May 3, 2007, from http://www.blink.org.uk/pdescription.asp?key=9638&grp=14

Breitman, G. (1990). *Malcolm X speaks: Selected speeches and statements*. New York: Grove Press.

Commission for Racial Equality (CRE). (2007). *CRE briefings on discrimination law review: Equality duties*. London: CRE.

Crenshaw, K. W. (2002). The first decade: Critical reflections, or 'a foot in the closing door'. *UCLA Law Review, 49*, 1343–1372.

Crenshaw, K., Gotanda, N., Peller, G., & Thomas, K. (Eds.). (1995). *Critical race theory: The key writings that formed the movement.* New York: New Press.

Dean, C. (1999, March 26). Ethnic monitoring 'too scarce'. *Times Educational Supplement.*

Delgado, R. (1995). *The Rodrigo chronicles: Conversations about America and race.* New York: New York University Press.

Delgado, R. (1998). Rodrigo's committee assignment: A skeptical look at judicial independence. *Southern California Law Review, 72*, 425–454.

Delgado, R., & Stefancic, J. (2000). Introduction. In R. Delgado & J. Stafancic (Eds.), *Critical race theory: The cutting edge* (2nd ed.). Philadelphia: Temple University Press.

Delgado, R., & Stefancic, J. (2001). *Critical race theory: An introduction.* New York: New York University Press.

Dennis, N., Erdos, G., & Al-Shahi, A. (2000). *Racist murder and pressure group politics: The macpherson report and the police.* London: Institute for the Study of Civil Society.

Department for Communities and Local Government (DCLG). (2007). *Discrimination law review: A framework for fairness: Proposals for a single equality Bill for Great Britain: A consultation paper.* London: Department for Communities & Local Government.

Department for Education & Employment (DfEE). (1999, February 24). *Press release 90/99.* London: Department for Education & Employment.

Department for Education & Skills (DfES). (2004). *Five year strategy for children and learners.* London: DfES.

Department for Education & Skills (DfES). (2007). *Getting it. Getting it right.* Exclusion of Black Pupils: Priority Review. London: DfES.

DuBois, W. E. B. (1975). *Dusk of dawn.* Millwood, NY: Kraus-Thomson Organization.

Du Bois, W. E. B. (1990). *The souls of Black folk* (1st Vintage Books/Library of America ed.). New York: Vintage Books/Library of America.

Foucault, M. (1980). *Power/knowledge: Selected interviews and other writings* (C. Gordon, Ed.). Hemel Hempstead: Harvester.

Ghouri, N. (1999, February 26). Schools ignore issue of racism. *Times Educational Supplement*, p. 1.

Gillborn, D. (2005). Education policy as an act of white supremacy: Whiteness, critical race theory and education reform. *Journal of Education Policy, 20*(4), 485–505.

Gillborn, D. (2006). Citizenship education as Placebo: 'Standards', institutional racism and education policy. *Education, Citizenship and Social Justice, 1*(1), 83–104.

Gillborn, D. (2008). *Racism and education: Coincidence or conspiracy?* London: Routledge.

Gillborn, D., & Youdell, D. (2000). *Rationing education: Policy, practice, reform and equity.* Buckingham: Open University Press.

Green, D. G. (2000). Commentary: Racial preferences are not the best way to create racial harmony. In D. G. Green (Ed.), *Institutional racism and the police: Fact or fiction?* London: Institute for the Study of Civil Society.

Hansard. (1999a). *Prime Minister's questions, 24 Feb 1999: Column 379–387.* Retrieved May 3, 2007, from http://www.publications.parliament.uk/pa/cm199899/cmhansrd/vo990224/debtext/90224-20.htm#90224-20_spmin0

Hansard. (1999b). *Stephen Lawrence inquiry, 24 Feb 1999: Column 389–403.* Retrieved from http://www.publications.parliament.uk/pa/cm199899/cmhansrd/vo990224/debtext/90224-21.htm#90224-21_head0

Home Office. (1999). *Home secretary's action plan.* London: Home Office.

Home Office. (2005). *Lawrence steering group: 6th annual report.* London: Home Office.

Independent on Sunday. (2006, December 10). Racist: Exclusive: A damning report on our schools. *Independent on Sunday*, pp. 1–2, 8–11.

Labour Party. (2005). *Britain forward not back: Labour party manifesto 2005.* London: Labour Party.

Lawrence, D. (2006). *And still I rise: Seeking justice for Stephen.* London: Faber and Faber.

Leonardo, Z. (2002). The souls of white folk: Critical pedagogy, whiteness studies, and globalization discourse. *Race Ethnicity & Education*, *5*(1), 29–50.

Lynn, M., & Parker, L. (2006). Critical race studies in education: Examining a decade of research on US schools. *The Urban Review*, *38*(4), 257–290.

Macpherson, W. (1999). *The Stephen Lawrence inquiry*. CM 4262-I. London: The Stationery Office. Retrieved May 2, 2007, from http://www.archive.official-documents.co.uk/document/cm42/4262/4262.htm

Magowan, C. (1999, March 12). Victims of 'racist' system. *Times Educational Supplement*.

Mills, C. W. (1997). *The racial contract*. London: Cornell University Press.

Mills, C. W. (2003). *From class to race: Essays in white Marxism and black radicalism*. New York: Rowman & Littlefield.

Osler, A., & Morrison, M. (2000). *Inspecting schools for racial equality: OFSTED's strengths and weaknesses*. A report for the CRE. Stoke-on-Trent: Trentham.

Parsons, C., Godfrey, R., Annan, G., Cornwall, J., Dussart, M., Hepburn, S., et al. (2004). *Minority ethnic exclusions and the race relations (Amendment) Act 2000*. Research Report 616. London: Department for Education & Skills.

Phillips, T. (2009, January 19). The death of racism? *Daily Mail*, pp. 26–7.

Richardson, B. (2007). *Tell it like it is: How our schools fail black children* (2nd ed.). London: Bookmarks.

Schneider-Ross. (2003). *Towards racial equality: An evaluation of the public duty to promote race equality and good race relations in England & Wales*. London: Commission for Racial Equality.

Sivanandan, A. (1990). All that melts into air is solid: The hokum of New Times. In A. Sivanandan (Ed.), *Communities of resistance: Writings on black struggles for socialism* (pp. 19–59). London: Verso.

Smith, P. (1999, April 2). Letter. *Times Educational Supplement*.

Smithers, R., & Carvel, J. (1999, March 11). Britain's schools dubbed racist. *The Guardian*, p. 4.

Spann, G. A. (1990). Pure politics. *Michigan Law Review*, *88*, 1971–2033.

Steven, S. (1999, February 28). Don't they know we're no longer a racist society? *The Mail on Sunday*, p. 35.

Stovall, D. (2006). Forging community in race and class: Critical race theory and the quest for social justice in education. *Race Ethnicity & Education*, *9*(3), 243–259.

Tate, W. F. (1997). Critical race theory and education: History, theory, and implications. In M. W. Apple (Ed.), *Review of research in education* (Vol. 22, pp. 195–247). Washington, DC: American Educational Research Association.

Tomlinson, S. (2008). *Race and education: Policy and politics in Britain*. Maidenhead: Open University Press.

Youdell, D. (2006). *Impossible bodies, impossible selves: Exclusions and student subjectivities*. Dordrecht, Netherlands: Springer.

David Gillborn
Institute of Education
University of London

MICHAEL J. DUMAS

18. WHAT IS THIS 'BLACK' IN BLACK EDUCATION?

Imagining a Cultural Politics without Guarantees

INTRODUCTION

Stuart Hall begins his important essay, *What is this 'black' in black popular culture?*, with a question: "What sort of moment is this in which to pose the question of black popular culture?" (1992, p. 21). By this, he means to instigate a critical inquiry into the meaning and function of Black cultural politics at this specific historical moment. Hall contends that key shifts in the global production of culture, and the dissemination (and exploitation) of difference in popular culture and public discourse have rendered racial essentialism ineffective as a political strategy and inadequate as an explanation of racial identities and experiences. In such a moment, we must ask anew: what do we mean to signify when we affirm or claim something *as* Black or *in the interest of* Black people? Hall argues that we must now advance a Black cultural politics that proceeds from an understanding of race as a matter of representation, rather than biological or social reality. In the new Black cultural politics, we recognize, and are inspired by the idea that it is possible to make and re-make race through discourse, through political and cultural contestation over meaning.

However, just because we might agree that race is, in Hall's words, "a floating signifier," (1996a) is not to say that it signifies nothing at all, or that it has no material effects. Quite to the contrary, race matters precisely because its meaning is indeterminate, thus allowing social actors to construct, dismantle, shift and then re-construct racial representations that inform how we see and 'do' race in our political, economic and cultural institutions and in our everyday lives. Hall does not mean to suggest that every social actor is situated equally in relation to power or the production of racial meaning. However, because racial meanings are not fixed, we can identify opportunities, few though they may be, to discursively intervene in such a way that hegemonic representations can no longer hold, or at least must contend with alternative representations.

In this essay, I use Hall's work on race and representation to begin to map a *cultural politics of Black education*. I use this term to denote the discursive practices through which social actors articulate blackness and education as a dialectic, and engage in struggle over Black representation in schools and other educational spaces. I hope to make a convincing argument for a *critical* cultural politics of Black education informed, at least in part, by Hall's call for attention to the diversity and fluidity of Black representation. While some scholars and activists

Z. Leonardo (ed.), Handbook of Cultural Politics and Education, 403–422.

worry that this kind of "postmodern"[1] turn endangers the cause of Black liberation (see, for example, Harris, 2005), I want to suggest, quite to the contrary, that Hall's work affirms and indeed, promises to reinvigorate the project of Black cultural politics. Following Hall, I contend that we need to reexamine our representation(s) of 'Black' in education to ensure that Black people have the freedom to imagine all that we now need (and need to *do*) at this historical moment in our struggle.

I fully acknowledge that the historical trajectories of race in the United States and Great Britain differ in several important respects. Although Hall has contributed extensively to intellectual discussions on Black popular culture and Black experience in the United States, the greater part of his body of work on race speaks to the construction of Black identities in Britain. However, I do not look to Hall to explain Black experience in the US, but for critical theoretical guidance on the concept of race itself as it operates within larger ideological and material processes. It is not important that Hall explicates what 'Black' *means* on this or that side of the Atlantic; rather, his work is invaluable because of his analysis of how 'Black' *acts* powerfully as a signifier of so many other things, and as a way in which we name ourselves and others for a host of cultural and political purposes.

I begin by situating Hall's theorizing about race within his work on ideology and signification, and within the broader political project of the University of Birmingham (UK) Centre for Contemporary Cultural Studies, of which Hall was the director throughout most of the 1970s. Then, informed by Hall's work on blackness and representation, I identify and critique some of the narrative themes that help to comprise the cultural politics of Black education, focusing on how Black cultural workers have made meaning of education in Black life and imagined the process of learning and creating knowledge for liberation. Finally, I enumerate some priorities for cultural workers interested in operationalizing a critical cultural politics of Black education.

Before I proceed, I want to offer definitions of some of the terms I use without further explanation throughout this chapter—terms that are certainly familiar to those steeped in the language of cultural studies, but less accessible to other scholars, educators and community folks I wish to include in the discussion. These definitions are by necessity brief and partial; my intent is not to engage the complexity and genealogy of each concept, but simply to give a broad range of readers entrée into the cultural-political argument I present here.

Postmodernism is perhaps the term that most defies attempt at explanation, perhaps appropriately, because it refers to the rejection of universalizing explanations of human processes and experiences—what are sometimes called "grand narratives"—in favor of more situated or local ways of understanding and engaging the world. Importantly, postmodernism embraces the multiple, hybridized and always contingent ways in which knowledge is constructed, and the simultaneous power and fragility (and the resulting ironies) in the discourses that inform human activity and decision-making.

I use *critical* here to denote a theoretical lens or praxis that offers explanation of, and challenges hegemonic relations of power. More broadly, I have in mind any politics that poses incisive questions about who benefits from certain social policies and cultural frames, and who is marginalized, exploited or rendered powerless (Leonardo, 2004- provide biblio).

Cultural workers are social actors who participate in the production and dissemination of ideas, discourses, and/or artistic products intended to inform or influence how we make sense of the human condition and our actions within relations of power. *Discourse*, following Foucault (1980), refers to the use of language to construct certain knowledge as legitimate, while delegitimizing other knowledges. For the purpose of this chapter, I am interested in exploring how cultural workers might systematically engage (in) processes of discursive formation in ways that shift the relations of power.

Finally, I often refer to *subjects* and *subjectivity*. Subjectivity is the process through which a human being becomes a person, an "I." Of course, as Foucault (1980) has argued, we are always "subject to" powerful discourses that regulate the social order and our own identities; however, as subjects, we express our own agency and desires by discursively engaging in individual and collective identity projects in ways that, in turn, inform the cultural production of our subjectivity.

Scholars continue to debate the meaning of each of these concepts, and do not even agree on the ends of the debate. For Hall and other founders of what came to be called the Birmingham School of Cultural Studies, the intellectual project—that is, the importance of understanding and employing such concepts—is to construct theory and engage in empirical inquiry that can serve as any number of radical political interventions (Hardt, 1996). I explore this project further in the next section, in an effort to situate a cultural politics of Black education within that tradition.

THE BIRMINGHAM SCHOOL AND THE CULTURAL POLITICS OF STUART HALL

Stuart Hall traces the beginnings of cultural studies to the social and cultural changes which took place in Britain after World War II, as traditional class structures and divisions between high and low culture shifted, complicating but not necessarily upending class hierarchies within British society. Scholars, including Hall, Richard Hoggart, Raymond Williams and E.P. Thompson—all primarily adult educators positioned rather marginally in relation to the traditional English academy—aimed to understand, describe, and theorize these cultural changes, and analyze their impact on the broader society. Cultural studies was defined as a decidedly interdisciplinary project, forging a space to ask critical questions about culture that had heretofore been unaddressed, or worse, dismissed, in the humanities and social sciences. Informed by Marx, cultural studies scholars were interested in how working-class culture, popular culture and mass media provided opportunities to challenge hegemonic forms of class hierarchies and meaning-making (Hall, 1990).

What I want to emphasize here is the explicit political commitment of cultural studies during this period. Hall (1996a) explains:

> It was not possible to present the work of cultural studies as if it had no political consequences and no form of political engagement.... From the start we said [to students]: What are you interested in? What really bugs you about

> questions of culture and society now? What do you really think is a problem you don't understand out there in the terrible interconnection between culture and politics? What is it about the way in which British culture is now living through its kind of postcolonial, posthegemonic crisis that really bites into your experience? And then we will find a way of studying that seriously. (1990, p. 17)

Hall intended that cultural studies illuminate a cultural *politics* by providing "ways of thinking, strategies for survival, and resources for resistance to all those who are now—in economic, political, and cultural terms—excluded from anything that could be called access to the national culture of the national community" (1990, p. 22). This becomes important to say here for two reasons: First, Hall refused the dichotomy often made between theory and practice, which absolves academics of the responsibility of engaging everyday life, and contributes to a kind of condescending anti-intellectualism among activists and other practitioners, who might be inclined to regard the interrogation of ideas as a distraction from the "real" terrain of struggle. Second, Hall's emphasis on counterhegemonic *practice*, on *resistance*, should allay concerns that simply because cultural studies offers a critique of identity, it means to displace or discredit collective social (and particularly identity-based) movements.

Let me return to Marx, because any understanding of Hall's relevance for a cultural politics of Black education must take into account the contributions of Marxian analysis to cultural studies. More specifically, in wrestling with the concept of ideology, Hall draws inspiration from Marx's critique of how the organization of consciousness becomes a force in everyday life. Hall contends that in materialist theory, ideology can be understood as "the mental frameworks—the languages, the concepts, categories, imagery of thought, and the systems of representation—which different classes and social groups deploy in order to make sense of, define, figure out and render intelligible the way society works" (Hall, 1996d, p. 26). However, Hall argues, Marx viewed ideology only *negatively*, as the reflection solely of bourgeois interests, determined "in the last instance" by the need to maintain specific class-based identities and social arrangements.

Hall wants to retain Marx's critique of the power of the market in capitalist societies, and specifically how it informs, even polices how we make sense of our everyday lives. He eschews those critics of Marx who wish to reduce everything to the "discursive" in ways that suggest that all thought is free-floating, as if there is no need to speak of ideology as a system. Following Gramsci, Hall proposes that ideology is the result of struggle between various social forces. That is, ideology does not arrive pre-packaged, issued forth along specific class lines; however, ideologies do reflect and reinforce specific class interests. What those interests are remains open, contingent upon the specific historical context in which ideological struggle occurs.

In this sense, then, Hall suggests, it might be more useful to think of ideology being determined by the economic "in the first instance." "Marxism is surely correct," he concludes, "...to insist that no social practice or set of relations float free of the determinate effects of the concrete relations in which they are located" (1996d, p. 45). However, there is no guarantee that those relations will be rooted, in any determined or unitary sense, in class struggle.

In fact, one of the major contributions of Hall's work is his challenge to Leftist thinkers and activists who have been disdainful of so-called identity politics, in which differences such as gender, race, and/or sexuality, rather than or in addition to class, form the basis of cultural practices and political engagement. Hall explains that part of the meaning of "New Times"—this historical-cultural moment at the center of cultural studies inquiry—is that we have embraced new subjectivities that are not transparently and immediately reactive to the material, the economic, but are creatively constructed through everyday cultural practices. Hall asks, "Can a socialism of the twenty-first century revive, or even survive, which is wholly cut off from the landscapes of popular pleasures, however contradictory and 'commodified' a terrain they represent?" (1996b, p. 223). No, he concludes, our politics must make space for "new forms of ethnicity…. which give the individual some sense of 'place' and position in the world, whether these be in relation to particular communities, localities, territories, languages, religions, or cultures" (p. 236, 237). To be sure, Hall is critical (as am I throughout this chapter) of the destructive and reactionary possibilities of identity politics. However, a radical politics for New Times recognizes that "everybody comes from some place—even if it is only an 'imagined community'" (p. 237).

These 'imagined communities' emerge largely through, or in response to what Hall would call *the politics of racial signification.* Signs are any texts, bodies, objects or aesthetic product that generate or hold meaning in relationship with other signs. A sign, then, comes to signify, or represent, specific concepts or ideas. This organization of signs into systems of meaning is what we denote when we refer to processes of signification. It follows that hegemonic ideologies heavily influence how signs become organized, and what those signs represent in the social world. Ideological struggle is thus a discursive struggle over meaning (or perhaps more precisely, our diverse and often divergent imaginations of meaning). Hall is clear that the discursive is not all there is, but he is equally adamant that there is no viable political struggle that does not engage the discursive. I am belaboring this point intentionally, because my aim is to convince a broader range of cultural workers to attend consciously to, and participate agentially in the production of (racial) meaning itself, rather than allow this process to go on above our heads or behind our backs, or equally problematic, to assume that meaning is beside the point or has been permanently fixed by others, before our time.

Hall's interest in race as a sign is motivated partly by his own experience as an immigrant from the former British colony of Jamaica. The postcolonial presence of Black bodies in England forever disrupted what we mean when we use the signs, 'British,' or 'European,' not to mention 'Empire.' Hall (1996c) argues that the hegemonic discourse which sought to restrict claims of 'Britishness' to those of 'English' ethnicity was rooted in a rightist, colonialist ideology intended to cast Black subjects as somehow outside of, or marginal in relation to the nation-state and the national-popular imagination. Hall contends that Black cultural workers' insistence on being simultaneously Black and British effectively shifted not only the meanings of 'Black' and 'British,' but also exposed the injustices of racist state policies and media (mis)representations of Black British life.

For Hall, we have three options in theorizing racial classification and represent-tation. First, we can take the *realist* position, in which we seek racial representations that reflect reality, or race *as it really is*. The problem here is that realist representations are based in either biological or cultural explanations. Biological classifications, which seek to locate racial difference in scientific or genetic terms, have largely been discredited. Cultural explanations, as I will explain in greater detail later, have also proven unreliable, as there are no neat racial alignments to be found in cultural practices either. A second option is to adopt a *textual* position on race. Here, race is seen purely as a linguistic field of play, in which we can construct and dismantle differences with the turn of a phrase. However, as should be clear by now, Hall rejects the idea that language occurs outside of history, outside of material relations of power.

This leads Hall to a third position, the *discursive*. The discursive attempts to analyze the interplay between racial representations, the establishment of power, and the production of knowledge (1996a). The key question here is one of difference: How do we talk about racial 'difference' once we have theoretically rejected the notion that race is real, but can readily see that the knowledge created about racial 'difference' organizes human interactions, and exacts (in)justice along those lines of 'difference?'

"There is the 'difference,'" Hall maintains, "which makes a radical and unbridge-able separation: and there is a 'difference' which is positional, conditional and conjunctural" (1996c). To engage in a politics of racial representation, Hall argues, does not mean we retreat to the 'real' of biology or culture, but that we dedicate our-selves to struggle over racial signification. The positions, conditions, or conjunctures to which Hall refers have their foundation in the interrelated working of power, capital and ideology. However, it is through our counterhegemonic discursive practices that we imagine a cultural politics that can impact these material conditions. We are now ready to more deeply interrogate this sign called 'Black.'

A BLACKNESS WITHOUT GUARANTEES

Historically, Hall argues, Black cultural politics involved assertion of the *difference* signified by naming something as 'Black.' In this sense, 'Black' came to mean the traditions of struggle sustained within Black communities, the various cultural practices out of which emerged a certain Black aesthetic, and the counternarratives which gave voice to Black experience. Black cultural politics articulated a particular Black authenticity, through which we could determine "good" Black culture—"which is ours and which is not" (1992, p. 29). However, Hall maintains, what counts as 'Black' has always been a cultural hybrid, 'Black' but also something else:

> Always these forms are the product of partial synchronization, of engagement across cultural boundaries, of the confluence of more than one cultural tradition, of the negotiations of dominant and subordinate positions, of the subterranean strategies of recoding and transcoding, of critical signification, of signifying. (p. 28)

There is no pure blackness to which we might aspire, (re-)create or return. This is not to say that 'Black' has no meaning; nor is it to suggest that there is no need for a Black cultural politics. As Hall acknowledges, "a very profound set of distinctive, historical defined black experiences" (1992, p. 30) inform and mark the difference that is found in Black cultural practices. However, he argues, even though Black essentialism—the desire to assert an inherent (racial) difference from the dominant (racial) culture—has been necessary and has served us well, "it is to the diversity, not the homogeneity, of black experience, that we must now give our undivided creative attention" (p. 30).

Why now?[2] Hall argues that the struggle has markedly changed. For the greater part of modern history, Black people were the objects and rarely the subjects of cultural representation, either absent from popular culture or stereotypically caricatured by whites with little opportunity for political rebuttal or creative response. The goals of Black cultural politics were two-fold: first, to struggle for access to the right of self-representation, and second, to contest the 'negative' representation of Black people by the "counterposition of a 'positive' black imagery" (Hall, 1996c, p. 442). As we have gained a degree of subjectivity, the struggle is no longer simply about gaining access to representation, but also and increasingly about engaging the complexity of what those representations will mean, and participating in the politics involved in the formation, articulation and dissemination of those representations.

Hall is quick to remind us that the old struggle has not gone anywhere. Prominent racist representations in state politics and popular culture attest to the continued misrepresentation (or perhaps, *mal*representation) of Black subjects. So it is not so much a substitution of one politics for another, but a realization that Black subjects—be they artists, activists or educators—must now struggle on two fronts: engaging in what Hall calls "a struggle over the relations of representation," on the one hand, and now, also taking on the struggle over "the politics of representation itself" (1996c, p. 442).

Hall makes a comparison here to Antonio Gramsci's distinction between wars of manouevre and wars of position. Cultural politics at this historical moment is less a war of manouevre, in which we assemble an army to launch a frontal assault on a clearly delineated enemy once and for all. Rather, recognizing that hegemony is developed all around us, through civil society as well as the state, we must develop tactics responsive to entrenched, ongoing struggle for cultural hegemony. Importantly, in cultural politics, we never achieve absolute victory or concede absolute domination. Rather, we continually engage in "changing the dispositions and the configurations of cultural power" (Hall, 1992, p. 24).

Ultimately, the new Black cultural politics is a "politics without guarantees." We have no guarantee that just because something is 'Black' that it is also inherently good or politically progressive. Hall notes:

> The essentializing moment is weak because it naturalizes and dehistoricizes difference....The moment the signifier 'black' is torn from its historical, cultural and political embedding and lodged in a biologically constituted racial category, we ... fix that signifier outside of history, outside of change,

> outside of political intervention. And once it is fixed, we are tempted to use 'black' as sufficient in itself to guarantee the progressive character of the politics we fight under this banner—as if we don't have any other politics to argue about except whether something's black or not. (1992, pp. 29–30)

It is not enough, it is not a viable politics of freedom simply to *be* 'Black.' As Black British filmmaker Isaac Julien has said: "What does that black subject *do*, how does it act, how does it think politically… being black isn't really good enough for me: I want to know what your cultural politics are" (quoted in Hall, 1992, p. 32; italics added).

I do not want to act as though there is not a tradition of reflective Black cultural criticism, both within and outside of the academy, among artists and on the street. There have always been Black people—most often Black women—who have acknowledged a range of Black subjectivities and have challenged various forms of essentialist cultural politics (see, for example, Cohen, 1999; Collins, 2004; Dawson, 2001; Mullings, 1997, 2000). However, many of these voices have been and continue to be marginalized, particularly in moments of uncertainty about the political and cultural survival of Black people. We are in such a moment. The temptation is to close ranks, to police the boundaries of Black expression, to look back for some authentic Black identity that will bring us back (always *back*) to our true selves. Hall suggests that these guarantees are illusive, that we have come to the "end of the innocent notion of the essential black subject" (1992, p. 32).

All that we have is "the maelstrom of a continuously contingent unguaranteed political argument, debate, and practice….a politics of criticism" (Hall, 1996a). And it is here, he claims, on this terrain, that we must wage our cultural politics, where "we discover and play with the identifications of ourselves, where we are imagined, where we are represented, not only to the audiences out there who do not get the message, but to ourselves for the first time" (1992, p. 32).

NARRATING THE 'BLACK' IN BLACK EDUCATION: DISCOURSE AS/IN CULTURAL POLITICS

In a scene from Marlon Riggs' (1995) documentary, *Black Is… Black Ain't*, two Black children, a boy and girl of about 10 years old, are having an exchange at a community center in South Central Los Angeles. At one point, the girl reflects on the strength and inspiration she draws from the life story of Black freedom fighter Harriet Tubman. The boy responds with a chuckle. "Hmmph!" he says, smiling. "What's Harriet done for you lately? You better learn that IBM computer!" A decade or so later, and not too far from that community center, Marisol Alba and Sean Strauss[3] lost their jobs at Celerity Nascent Charter School after the two teacher joined students in protesting the cancellation of a Black History Month event commemorating Emmett Till (Rivera, 2007). Student organizers had planned to read a poem in honor of the 14-year-old Black boy who was brutally lynched in Mississippi in 1955 because he allegedly dared to flirt with a white woman. In rejecting the proposed program, school leaders expressed concern about whether the story was developmentally appropriate for the younger children in the K-8 school; however, their main argument was that the Till story did not provide a *positive* example for Celerity Nascent's student body, which is about 80% Black and 19% Latino/a. The event highlighted a tragedy in Black history, not a triumph, administrators argued. More, the school principal speciously suggested, what Till did might very well amount to sexual harassment. "Our whole goal is how do we get these kids to not look at all of the bad things that could happen to them," explained the school's co-founder and executive director, Vielka McFarlane, "and instead focus on the process of how do we become the next surgeon or the next politician.... We don't want to focus on how the history of the country has been checkered but on how do we dress for success, walk proud and celebrate all the accomplishments we've made" (Rivera, 2007).

The young people in Riggs' film, like the educators and students at Celerity Nascent, are engaged in discursive practices that not only reflect certain understandings of blackness and the role of education in Black life, but also seek to position some interpretations over and against others. In the first exchange, on the relative educational merits of learning about Harriet Tubman and IBM computers, each child articulates an understanding of education in relation to Black identity and collective struggle. For the girl, learning about Harriet Tubman is liberatory in that such knowledge provides Black people with the emotional strength to persevere in the face of anti-Black racism. For the boy, education contributes to the social mobility of Black folks to the extent that it prepares us to more effectively compete in the market. Any other function is but a distraction. To be sure, this is a somewhat reductive analysis, but the point I wish to make here is that both young people are engaged in the cultural politics of Black education: their discourse informs and is informed by how Black people are imagined *and* how we (that is, Black people) imagine ourselves in relation to education.

In the contention over Emmett Till at the charter school, school leaders construct Black suffering as not only in the past, but as historical shame best forgotten (and intentionally *not taught*). More, we are offered a narrative of Black life in which Till's resistance to white supremacy is recast as willful and unfortunate insurgency, antithetical to Black academic achievement and social mobility. Or perhaps it is that acquiring dominant cultural capital (e.g., "dressing for success") and embracing high-status career aspirations are the new 'Black': the "checkered" past is no longer part of who we are, no longer a meaningful part of our identities; "positive" images must be proffered at the expense of historical memory.

As evident in both of these cases, the cultural politics of Black education is a discursive struggle. Within this struggle are a number of pervasive themes, or narratives that help to articulate the various positions we might take up in this "war" over representation at the nexus of blackness and education. In this section, I identify three such narratives, and analyze them through the lens of a critical Black cultural politics.

Education as Assertion of Black Humanity

Historian James Anderson documents a number of stories of slave literacy during the antebellum period. Thomas Jones, a slave in North Carolina suffered three beatings in order to hide his books from his master. "It seemed to me," he noted, "that if I could learn to read and write...this learning might, nay, I really thought it would point out the way to freedom, influence and real secure happiness" (Anderson, 1988, p. 16). Enoch Golden, a slave who taught countless others to read, was reported to have said on his deathbed that he had "been de death o' many a nigger 'cause he taught so many to read and write" (p. 17). And former slave Louisa Guase recalled, "White people never teach colored people nothing, but to be good to dey massa and mittie, what learnin dey would get in dem days dey been get it at night; taught demselves" (p. 17).

For Anderson, that so many Black people, both during and immediately following slavery, risked their lives for the sake of literacy, reveals "the important cultural significance" (p. 31) of education for Black people at that time. Education not only had a utilitarian, economic benefit, but also was understood as a means toward recognition as full members of the human family. Of course, part of the rationale for slavery was that "Negroids" did not possess the intellectual or creative capacity of whites because they were somehow biologically closer to primates. In this sense, education becomes a testimony to Black humanity, a way for Black people to move as far away as possible from an existence in which 'Black' signified an object, that is, the property—quite literally, the beast of burden—of white people.

The historical trajectory of this narrative extends far beyond the antebellum period. W.E.B. Du Bois, in expressing his concerns about school desegregation efforts in the 1930s, argued that the highest priority for Black people should be ensuring that their children attended schools where they were loved and cared for, that we could not make a political point at the expense of our humanity:

> [I]n the case of the education of the young, you must consider...the relation of the children to life.... I have repeatedly seen wise and loving colored parents take infinite pains to force these little children into schools where the white parents despised and resented the dark child, made mock of it, neglected or bullied it, and literally rendered its life a living hell. Such parents want their child to 'fight' this thing out,—but, dear God, at what a cost!.... We shall get a finer, better balance of spirit... by putting children in schools where they are wanted, and where they are happy and inspired, than in thrusting them into hells where they are ridiculed and hated. (1935, pp. 330, 331)

For Du Bois, schools could either serve to affirm or diminish Black humanity. Part of the reason Du Bois was so vehement in his critique of school desegregation is because he envisioned education as a site in which Black children learn to love themselves and their people, and begin to develop their "spirit," which is very much about an understanding of themselves as fully human. We see this narrative emerge repeatedly and consistently, specifically in relation to the treatment of Black students in both segregated and so-called integrated schools, throughout the 20th century and into the present (see, for example, Walker, 1996; Bell, 2004; Dumas, 2007).[4]

This narrative is consistent with a critical Black cultural politics to the extent that we understand Black humanity as a cultural process rather than a biological or cultural certainty. If we understand our humanness as an interaction between our individual and social selves, it becomes possible to then ask questions about the cultural production of our blackness, and the relations of power that shape our experiences as Black people, and our identification with Black collective struggle. If, on the other hand, the 'Black' in Black humanity is imagined as already in existence, and only in need of discovery, as if the Black body were merely the host for a pre-constructed racial self, then we have abandoned critical possibilities in favor of a static blackness. This makes a weak basis for a radical cultural politics. We need a Black humanity that can adjust for new conditions on the battlefield of discursive struggle, and one that can create new cultural expressions of blackness which are always in conversation with history but never neglectful of their own historicity.

Education as Resistance to White Supremacy

A key element of affirming Black humanity is maintaining resistance to white supremacy. As Cornel West has noted, Black cultural workers need to "examine and explain the historically specific ways in which 'Whiteness' is a politically constructed category parasitic on 'Blackness'" (1993, p. 19). Identifying these "parasitic" practices, and finding sword, shield and balm to struggle against and heal from the white supremacist assault becomes a necessary function of Black pedagogy, and thus, a prominent narrative in Black educational discourse.

In Toni Morrison's (1987) novel, *Beloved*, Baby Suggs delivers a sermon in which she urges Black people to love themselves (consistent with the narrative on Black humanity) and to do so (also) as a conscious rejection of white supremacist constructions of Black worth(lessness):

> Here… in this here place, we flesh; flesh that weeps, laughs; flesh that dances on bare feet in grass. Love it. Love it hard. Yonder, they do not love your flesh. They despise it…. Love your hands! Love them. Raise them up and kiss them. Touch others with them, pat them together, stroke them on your face 'cause they don't love that either. *You* got to love it, *you*!" (p. 88; italics in original)

What Morrison narrates here as a pedagogy of resistance is replicated in real (that is, non-fictional) Black educational contexts. Reay and Mirza (2001), for example, in their work on Black supplementary schools in the UK, describe how such spaces of "radical Blackness" are perceived as threats to the white majority because they are not simply defensive institutions, but counterpublic spheres wherein Black subjects learn how to oppose the hegemony of whiteness.

Vanessa Siddle Walker (1996), in her historical-ethnographic account of a segregated Black school in the US South, recounts that Black teachers would tell their students that they needed to be better than whites. Said music teacher Evon Reid, "There may be a time when you have to compete against [white people]. You don't want your work to be equal. You want your work to be better" (p. 152). And, as the school principal, N.L. Dillard, would insist, "You have to be better… It shouldn't be that way, but that is the way it is" (p. 152). Once again, we see education as a space of resistance against whiteness as hegemonic ideology *and* in regard to actual academic excellence. For these Black educators, Black students not only had to resist white supremacy in their minds, but defy it in their accomplishments.

Black narratives on education are replete with reminders that white people benefit from keeping Black people uneducated. In Lupe Fiasco's (2007) *Dumb it Down*, the hip-hop artist critiques Black people who insist that he should dumb down his lyrics because, as they complain in a number of choruses, "we ain't graduate from school, nigga/them big words ain't cool, nigga." However, these Black responses to his work are echoed in one chorus by a white male speaker, who also urges Lupe to "dumb it down," but for different reasons: "You been shedding too much light, Lu/ You're makin' em wanna do right, Lu..../They're trying to graduate from school, Lu/ They're starting to think that smart is cool, Lu/They're trying to get up out the hood, Lu/I'll tell you what you should do (Dumb it down)."In the live video for the song, these lyrics are delivered authoritatively by a stout, middle-aged white man in stereotypically conservative khakis and polo shirt, who is then laughed off the stage. "Thank you, Mr. White Man," Lupe says sardonically as the crowd claps.

This kind of "thank you, but no thank you" response to whiteness is invaluable in a critical cultural politics of Black education. However, since white is a constructed rather than biological category, we must retain for white social actors the same subjectivity that we allow Black social actors. That is, we understand that white social actors may choose to invest in white supremacy but this is not inherent to simply having white skin. They may also choose otherwise. At the same time, Black cultural workers must interrogate their own investments in whiteness, since, as Hall has demonstrated, the Black subject is not inherently innocent. And no Black pedagogy is so purely 'Black' that it is not informed by its historical encounter with whiteness. In fact, purging white influence is not the goal of a critical Black cultural politics. Rather, our work is to more fully understand that encounter, and learn how to use the politics of representation to shift the relations of power as we continue the struggle in our times.

The Importance of Knowing Black History and Culture as a Foundation for Black Collective Survival

Manning Marable (2000) has argued that scholarship in Black studies serves three interrelated functions. First, it is *descriptive* in that it provides a detailed account of Black life. Second, it serves a *corrective* role, offering a response to racist interpretations of Black experience in the popular and academic discourse. Third, Black studies is *prescriptive*, in that it draws on theoretical and empirical research to recommend strategies for Black empowerment and liberation.

I would argue that these three functions of Black studies scholarship also form the basis for a broader narrative on the necessary function of Black education in general. That is, Black people have historically embraced a vision of education informed by a belief that Black people must know their history and culture in order to secure the survival of the race. Of course, this was not universally the case; Black contributions to literature, arts, sciences, and civic life were systematically omitted in curricula at all levels of education. As Carter G. Woodson asserts, in *The Mis-education of the Negro*, some Black educators remained ignorant themselves, internalizing the notion that Black people were intellectually inferior, while those who knew better were largely powerless. "The education of the Negroes, then," Woodson laments, "the most important thing in the uplift of the Negroes, is almost entirely in the hands of those who have enslaved them and now segregate them" (p. 22).

Woodson's concerns are also echoed in much of the Afrocentric education tradition (see, for example, Shujaa, 1994 ; Kunjufu,1995; Pollard & Ajirotutu, 2001; Ginwright, 2004). Black children, it is believed, need an African-centered curriculum in order to understand the history of Black people, and the cultural traditions and practices that have sustained African peoples throughout the diaspora. Ultimately, Afrocentric curricula and pedagogies are intended to raise up a new generation of leaders committed to Black liberation from the chains of white supremacy.

We see this narrative in both liberal and nationalist Black cultural products. In the work of Bill Cosby, most notably *The Cosby Show* (1984–1992) and its spin-off, *A Different World* (1987–1993), Black young people are instructed that rooting themselves in knowledge of Black history and celebration of Black cultural traditions will provide them with the strength and direction to achieve academic success and social mobility within the capitalist state. Meanwhile, in the work of the Black nationalist hip-hop duo, Dead Prez (2000), a similar message: "I took a history class serious/ Front row, every day of the week, third period/Fuckin' with the teacher's head, callin' em racist/I tried to show them crackers some light, they couldn't face it....They seemed to only glorify the Europeans/Claimin' Africans were only three-fifths a human being."

I am not suggesting that Woodson would have fully embraced Afrocentrism or that Bill Cosby listens to revolutionary hip-hop. Rather, I want to emphasize the continuity of this narrative—the importance of knowing "where you come from" (as Aretha belts out in the opening theme for *A Different World*)—in Black education discourse, over time and across a range of ideological orientations.

Manning Marable and Leith Mullings (1994) suggest that a "transformative" approach to Black struggle places Black history and culture within a larger context:

> Its chief objective is the dismantling or destruction of all forms of inequality. It seeks to challenge the institutions of power, privilege and ownership patterns of the dominant society.... Often, Black people have begun with the objective of abolishing racism, but in the process of struggle have come to realize that wider power relationships must also be transformed to achieve full human equality—such as the inequalities and oppression rooted in gender and sexual orientation. (p. 69)

Consistent with Hall, Marable and Mullings emphasize the importance of recognizing the diversity of Black subjectivity, and insist on a critical Black political project that, although rooted in Black liberation, takes an expansive, dynamic view of Black experience (both past and present). Importantly, they signal the historical marginalization of Black women and lesbian, gay, bisexual and transgendered (LGBT) peoples in the collective imagination of what counts as 'Black,' and the relative silence on issues of economic exploitation and class arrogance within hegemonic Black discourses. From a critical perspective, then, the task is to learn how to embrace our history and cultural forms—our "roots"—without romanticizing or reifying that Black experience, or assuming that a racial narrative could ever fully encompass all that is worth struggling for.

TOWARD A CRITICAL (AND JOYFUL) CULTURAL POLITICS OF BLACK EDUCATION

In her introduction to *Black Popular Culture*, Gina Dent (1992) writes of Black critical consciousness as a site of pleasure and joy: "Blackness…. is still a mythic construction; and our love of it must be recognized as the fantasy that it is—which is not to say that we must now fall out of love. Nor is it to encourage us to end our romance with being black" (p. 18). For Dent, being in love with Blackness entails a constant rethinking of our politics of representation, and excitement about the new places knowledge of the 'Black' might take us, places of justice and vision "where more of us will find what we need and where some of us will find less of what we are accustomed to" (p. 18).

Joy in Blackness is a pervasive theme in all of the Black education narratives I have identified here, and a necessary element in Black cultural politics. At times the joy is tied to essential notions of Blackness, and becomes a stagnant delight in biological and/or cultural racial determinisms. However, what Dent points to is the possibility of a Black creative cultural production that is deeply in love with Blackness, more deeply than any racial essentialism can imagine, because Blackness is embraced as one might embrace a lover one has no desire to bend, and can never fully know. The cultural-political project thus becomes one of continual wonder, discovery, and experimentation.

What does this project look like in everyday practice? How do we actually engage in a critical cultural politics of Black education? In a general sense, we can do this simply by inspiring students, educators, activists and communities to more consciously and lovingly participate in the politics of Black representation. More specifically, I believe we can identify some cultural interventions that are crucial at this historical moment.

First, I think it is important to *continually reaffirm a discourse of struggle in Black education*. This might seem an obvious point. Of course, scholars and activists have consistently documented racial inequities in schools, and have outlined policies and practices to address the specific educational struggles of Black students (Ferguson, 2000; Lipman, 2003; Anyon, 2005). I am referring here to a discourse of struggle over the 'Black' in Black education. That is, what does 'Black' represent? When and why is it employed as a discursive signifier? How does it serve to legitimize or empower, to explain or explain away?

Carla O'Connor (1997) provides a compelling demonstration of the discourse of struggle in her study on the academic resilience of low-income Black students. She found that for some high-achieving students, understanding schools as a site of Black struggle motivated them to persist toward excellence. O'Connor's attention to Black agential cultural production contrasts with John Ogbu's more static notion of a "Black cultural frame of reference" (O'Connor, 1997, p. 624), which posits that Black students' low educational engagement is determined by their subjugated position in society. In his work, Black students' awareness of 'Black' as a signifier of oppression and reduced life chances prevents them from believing they could ever be successful. He suggests that Black students who do *not* identify as strongly with Black culture are more likely to achieve.

The students in O'Connor's study were "privy to social behavior and discourses that affirmed the need for struggle and its potential to produce desired change" (1997, p. 622). Significant others in their lives acknowledge racial (and gender) oppression, but also "signify through their ideology or behavior that social injustices can be actively resisted and need not be interpreted as given" (p. 623). Although O'Connor is not directly concerned with the politics of representation in this study, she provides ample examples of cultural workers—family members, neighbors, mentors—who are committed to affirming the 'Black' as a dynamic site of struggle, a struggle that can be won. Black young people who embraced this cultural politics "appeared to have not only insight into human agency at the personal and individual level but also a basis for interpreting Black individuals and collectives as agents of change" (p. 621).

My concern at this historical moment is that both liberal and conservative frames of multiculturalism have no language for 'Black' that affirms Black collective (and not simply individual) subjectivity. Liberal multiculturalism is yoked to the goal of a "post-racial" (and therefore, post-Black) diversity (Bonilla-Silva, 1997; Singh, 2004), while conservative multicultural projects seek to rescue Black people from a "culture" assumed to be inferior (McLaren, 1995). Consistent with Hall, O'Connor envisions a *critical* practice of Blackness in education, in which students engage in a politics of representation, using their own consciousness of collective struggle as a foundation to re-imagine what 'Black' looks like and what it does in schools.

A second priority for a critical cultural politics of Black education is to *insist on the complexity of Black representation.* Lance McCready (2004) has noted that in discourse on Black student experience, policymakers and practitioners are often reluctant to take into account the "multidimensionality" of Blackness. He recalls his work on a school-based team investigating the racial achievement gap. When he suggested that the team also examine the relatively lower scores of Black and Latino *males*, others concluded that the focus should remain on race and class because including other dimensions of social difference might "make things too complicated" (p. 137).

McCready uses qualitative data from interviews with two gender non-conforming Black gay male students to demonstrate how race informs and is informed by both gender and sexuality. David, for example, had been identified as a gifted student in elementary school, but by high school had come to be labeled as low-achieving. He experienced marginalization by students and school staff due to their bias against his gender performance. He also struggled to find a supportive place in the school's LGBT group, which primarily served the social needs of white female students. Ultimately, McCready concludes, David's academic status could not be attributed solely to race, class, or gender performance, but to the confluence of all these dimensions of his identity, and more precisely, the institutional and cultural response to his "complicated" presence in the school and broader community.

As Hall has contended, our cultural politics must now attend to the diversity of Black representation. In practice, this should translate into an understanding of 'Black' that takes into account the other axes of difference operating within and around that representation. We are no longer afraid that we cannot guarantee what 'Black' means simply by the utterance of that word. Nor do we deny that diverse expressions of Blackness are 'Black' simply because they do not conform to what we have historically, in all our patriarchal and heterosexist glory, deemed to fit (uncomplicatedly) within that representation. McCready argues that when we adopt a multidimensional approach, we open ourselves up to discovery about the complexity of Black students' lives, which then allow us to develop more effective educational interventions.

Third, and perhaps most importantly, I believe a critical cultural politics of Black education must *begin with an engagement of the cultural production of young people*. This point has been made numerous times by critical educators and theorists (see, for example, Ginwright, Noguera & Commarota, 2006; Andrade & Morrell, 2008; Commarota & Fine, 2008). However, often in our efforts to "empower" young people, we retreat to a banking approach (Freire, 2007). My sense is that this is particularly tempting for some Black middle-class leaders and educators, disturbed by what they interpret as a flagrant disrespect of young people for a proud Black heritage. For example, Bill Cosby, in his now (in)famous speech to the NAACP, argued that the school desegregation victories won in the 1950s were now being squandered by "lower economic and lower middle economic people" within the Black community who were "not holding their end in this deal." Some members of this group, he declared, tended to devalue education, glorify criminal behavior and teen pregnancy and engage in crass materialism, choosing to purchase "$500 sneakers" instead of, for example, *Hooked on Phonics* (Cosby, 2004).

The most prominent Black critic of Cosby's speech, undoubtedly, has been cultural studies scholar Michael Eric Dyson, who quickly published a book on the topic: *Is Bill Cosby Right?* (2005). Its subtitle posed another question: "*Or Has the Black Middle-Class Lost Its Mind?*" Dyson contends that Cosby's speech highlighted class divisions within Black communities; however, Dyson argued that it was *middle class* Black folks whose cultural values had been turned upside-down, guided more by "Afristocratic" elitism than genuine interest in addressing the political and economic needs of Black poor people. For Dyson, the Afristocracy include the upper middle-class, who commonly, he suggests, "rain down fire and brimstone upon poor blacks for their deviance and pathology, and for their lack of couth and culture" (2005, pp. xiii, xiv). In other words, in Dyson's view, the Black middle class position themselves as the protectors of "good" Black culture, failing to acknowledge how their representation of 'Black' is informed by their own class identification, and not simply a function of their presumed racial uprightness. In deriding poor Black people, and particularly poor underachieving Black youth, for making "us" *look* bad, middle-class Black folks shift our critical gaze from economic *mal*distribution to cultural differences, and more precisely, what they might describe as the embarrassment caused by the "cultural" practices of Black poor people.

It follows, then, that one response to low academic achievement in poor and working-class Black communities has been a call for Afrocentric education (Ginwright, 2004). In his study of an effort to introduce Afrocentric curricula in a struggling urban school in West Oakland (CA), Shawn Ginwright found that reformers failed to include young people from the community in the planning process, and did not adequately consult them in the implementation. Certain that an Afrocentric approach would instill pride and raise scores, policymakers and educators neglected to consider how Black youth in West Oakland made meaning of their Blackness, and discounted social class as a powerful force in shaping racial discourse in the neighborhood. Math courses drew on African traditions for inspiration, but failed to address the "mathematics" of economic exploitation in the blocks surrounding the school itself. The biggest names in Afrocentric scholarship came to speak at the school—at great expense—but the majority of the audiences were privileged older residents and faculty and students from nearby University of California at Berkeley.

Ginwright concludes that while students were certainly conscious of their own Blackness, the Afrocentric reforms were largely understood as "an arrogant attempt to teach them how to be better at being black" (2004, p. 119). He explains: "The promotion of Egyptian culture throughout the project was celebrated at the expense of young people's unique economic struggles and their own hip-hop culture. Simply stated, their day-to-day struggles and authentic identities were not central in the development of the reform strategy" (p. 119). Reflecting on his findings, Ginwright recommends that a more successful approach would include significant youth engagement, in which students learn to analyze the relations of power in their schools and neighborhoods, and begin to act collectively to address injustice in their communities. While not dismissing Afrocentric approaches altogether, Ginwright insists that they cannot dis' or displace a critical pedagogy that offers young people "the power, support, and opportunity to be heard concerning educational, community and social issues that most impact their lives" (p. 125).

When we affirm a discourse of struggle over the meaning of 'Black' as a signifier, insist on the multidimensionality of black representation, and engage the cultural production of young people, we commit ourselves to a politics without guarantees. This is perhaps more difficult in education, with its fixation on the certainties of measurement and standardization. The challenge is compounded by the vulnerability Black social actors may feel in an historical moment in which our young people are suffering so disproportionately, and our communities seem so socially and culturally fragmented that we feel tempted to find some assuredness in racial essentialisms. A critical cultural politics of Black education asks us to embrace a new kind of politics, in which Black is still beautiful—perhaps even more so—because there is so much that we have yet to discover. What we find in the discursive is the collective Black imagination to transform our conditions, again and again, in each new generation.

NOTES

[1] Some—though certainly not all—Afrocentric scholars and activists would characterize Hall as a postmodernist simply for posing the question of black identity—that is, presenting Black identity as a question rather than a simple statement of social or biological fact. In fact, Hall offers an extensive critique of postmodernism, particularly as employed in the US. Briefly, he is skeptical of the postmodernist tendency to displace concern with material and ideological relations of power in favor of celebration of difference and the discursive. To be sure, the concepts of difference and discourse are central in Hall's own work; however, unlike most postmodern theorists, he is not simply interested in "the political" or "resistance" as theoretical categories, but as constitutive of, and instructive for the development of an actual *politics of resistance*.

[2] Hall first presented his essay, "What is this 'black' in black popular culture?," as a talk at a conference on black popular culture held in New York City in December 1991. Hall's "New Times" (Hall, 1996b) corresponds roughly with the period often referred to in US Black scholarship as the post-civil rights era (see, for example, Marable & Mullings, 1994). Although Hall's case is made primarily—although not exclusively—based on the Black British experience, some of the historical shifts are diasporic in reach. For example, neoliberal policies adopted by Thatcher in the UK are echoed in Reagan's policies in the US during the same decade. They both rose to power, in part, by appealing to white racial groups' anxieties about minority rights, and by advocating that the state retreat from its role in maintaining the social welfare. Although Black identities are constructed and imagined differently in the US and the UK, I have chosen not to highlight that in that paper, since these differences do not make the *question of representation* any less salient on this side of the Atlantic.

[3] Interestingly, in this case, one of the teachers fired was a white male and the other was Latina, reminding us that even those who are not Black participate in the cultural politics of Black education. Just as it is not guaranteed which position is authentically 'black'—here some Black parents sided with the administrators and others with the students and the two teachers—we also cannot guarantee that the racial identities of the social actors will align neatly with a corresponding racial politic.

[4] This narrative also featured prominently in protests around the Jena 6 case, in which Black students at a Mississippi high school were expelled in the wake of Black-white contention after white students hung a noose from a tree designated as a whites-only gathering place in response to an inquiry from a Black student who wanted to know if Black students could also socialize there. In fact, I would argue that this narrative is present in any school situation in which the bodies or emotional and spiritual well-being of Black young people is in danger.

REFERENCES

Anderson, J. D. (1988). *The education of Blacks in the South, 1860–1935*. Chapel Hill, NC: University of North Carolina.

Anyon, J. (2005). *Radical possibilities: Public policy, urban education, and a new social movement*. New York: Routledge.

Bonilla-Silva, E. (1997). Rethinking racism: Toward a structural interpretation. *American Sociological Review*, *62*(3), 465–480.

Bell, D. (2004). *Silent covenants*. Oxford, UK: Oxford University.

Cammarota, J., & Fine, M. (2008). *Revolutionizing education*. New York: Routledge.

Cohen, C. (1999). *The boundaries of blackness: AIDS and the breakdown of black politics*. Chicago: University of Chicago.

Collins, P. H. (2004). *Black sexual politics*. New York: Routledge.

Cosby, W. (2004). *Speech to the NAACP on the 50th anniversary of Brown v. Board of Education*. Retrieved May 9, 2009, from www.americanrhetoric.com/speeches/billcosbypoundcakespeech.htm

Dawson, M. (2001). *Black visions: The roots of contemporary African-American political ideologies*. Chicago: University of Chicago.

Dead Prez. (2000). *They schools. On let's get free* [CD]. New York: Relativity.

Dent, G. (1992). Black pleaure, black joy. In G. Dent (Ed.), *Black popular culture* (pp. 1–19). New York: New Press.

DuBois, W. E. B. (1935). Does the Negro need separate schools? *The Journal of Negro Education, 4*(3), 328–335.

Dumas, M. J. (2007). *Sitting next to white children: School desegregation in the Black educational imagination*. Unpublished doctoral dissertation, The Graduate Center, The City University of New York.

Duncan, J., & Morrell, E. (2008). *The art of critical pedagogy*. New York: Peter Lang.

Dyson, M. E. (2005). *Is Bill Cosby right? (Or has the Black middle class lost its mind?)*. New York: Basic Civitas.

Ferguson, A. A. (2000). *Bad boys: Public schools in the making of Black masculinity*. Ann Arbor, MI: University of Michigan.

Fiasco, L. (2007). *Dumb it down. On Lupe Fiasco's The Cool* [CD]. New York: Atlantic.

Foucault, M. (1980). *Power/knowledge: Selected interviews and other writings, 1972–1977*. New York: Pantheon.

Freire, P. (2007). *Pedagogy of the oppressed* (30th anniversary edition). New York: Continuum.

Ginwright, S. A. (2004). *Black in school: Afrocentric reform, urban youth, and the promise of hip-hop culture*. New York: Teachers College.

Ginwright, S., Noguera, P., & Commarota, J. (2006). *Beyond resistance!* New York: Routledge.

Hall, S. (1990). The emergence of cultural studies and the crisis of the humanities. *October, 53*, pp. 11–23.

Hall, S. (1992). What is this 'black' in black popular culture? In G. Dent (Ed.), *Black popular culture* (pp. 21–33). New York: The New Press.

Hall, S. (1996a). *Race, the floating signifier*. Northampton, MA: Media Education Foundation.

Hall, S. (1996b). The meaning of New Times. In D. Morley & K. Chen (Eds.), *Stuart Hall: Critical dialogues in cultural studies* (pp. 223–237). New York: Routledge.

Hall, S. (1996c). New ethnicities. In D. Morley & K. Chen (Eds.), *Stuart Hall: Critical dialogues in cultural studies* (pp. 441–449). New York: Routledge.

Hall, S. (1996c). The problem of ideology: Marxism without guarantees. In D. Morley & K. Chen (Eds.), *Stuart Hall: Critical dialogues in cultural studies* (pp. 25–46). New York: Routledge.

Hardt, H. (1996). British cultural studies and the return of the 'critical.' In D. Morley & K. Chen (Eds.), *Stuart Hall: Critical dialogues in cultural studies* (pp. 102–111). New York: Routledge.

Harris, D. B. (2005). Postmodernist diversions in African American thought. *Journal of Black Studies, 36*(2), 209–228.

Kunjufu, J. (1995). *Countering the conspiracy to destroy black boys*. Chicago: African American Images.

Lipman, P. (2003). *High stakes education: Inequality, globalization and urban school reform*. New York: RoutledgeFalmer.

Marable, M. (2000). Introduction: Black studies and the racial mountain. In M. Marable (Ed.), *Dispatches from the ebony tower* (pp. 1–28). New York: Columbia University.

Marable, M., & Mullings, L. (1994). The divided mind of Black America: Race, ideology and politics in the post Civil Rights era. *Race & Class, 36*(1), 61–72.

McCready, L. (2004). Understanding the marginalization of gay and gender-non-conforming Black male students. *Theory into Practice, 43*(2), 136–143.

McLaren, P. (1995). *Critical pedagogy and predatory culture*. New York: Routledge.
Morrison, T. (1987). *Beloved*. New York: Knopf.
Mullings, L. (1997). *On our own terms: Race, class and gender in the lives of African American women*. New York: Routledge.
Mullings, L. (2000). Reclaiming culture: The dialectics of identity. In M. Marable (Ed.), *Dispatches from the ebony tower* (pp. 210–215). New York: Columbia University.
Pollard, D. S., & Ajirotutu, C. S. (2001). Lessons from America: The African American immersion schools experiment. In R. Majors (Ed.), *Educating our black children*. London: RoutledgeFalmer.
O'Connor, C. (1997). Dispositions toward (collective) struggle and educational resilience in the inner city: A case analysis of six African-American high school students. *American Educational Research Journal*, *34*(4), 593–629.
Reay, D., & Mirza, H. S. (2001). Black supplementary schools: Spaces of radical blackness. In R. Majors (Ed.), *Educating our black children*. London: RoutledgeFalmer.
Riggs, M. (Director). (1995). Black is... Black ain't [Film]. (Available from California Newsreel, P.O. Box 2284, South Burlington, VT 05407)
Rivera, C. (2007). Not the lesson they had intended. *Los Angeles Times* [On-line]. Retrieved from http://articles.latimes.com/2007/mar/19/local/me-newcharter19
Shujaa, M. J. (1994). *Too much schooling, too little education*. Trenton, NJ: Africa World Press.
Singh, N. P. (2004). *Black is a country: Race and the unfinished struggle for democracy*. Cambridge, MA: Harvard University.
Walker, V. S. (1996). *Their highest potential: An African American school community in the segregated South*. Chapel Hill, NC: University of North Carolina.
West, C. (1993). The new cultural politics of difference. In C. McCarthy & W. Crichlow (Eds.), *Race, identity and representation in education* (pp. 11–23). New York: Routledge.
Woodson, C. G. (1990). *The mis-education of the Negro*. Trenton, NJ: Africa World Press.

Michael J. Dumas
College of Education
California State University
Long Beach

SHERICK HUGHES

19. A 'SYMBOLIC REBIRTH' OF THE BOOTSTRAP GUILD

Applying Kenneth Burke to the Cultural Politics of the "Negro Problem" Underlying Black-White Test Score Gap Ideology

> BETWEEN me and the other world there is ever an unasked question: unasked by some through feelings of delicacy; by others through the difficulty of rightly framing it. All, nevertheless, flutter round it. They approach me in a half-hesitant sort of way, eye me curiously or compassionately, and then, instead of saying directly, How does it feel to be a problem? They say, I know an excellent colored man in my town; or, I fought at Mechanicsville; or, Do not these Southern outrages make your blood boil? At these I smile, or am interested, or reduce the boiling to a simmer, as the occasion may require. To the real question, **How does it feel to be a problem?** (Du Bois, 1903, p. 1; my emphasis)

INTRODUCTION

Since 1993, some ninety years after Du Bois (1903), I have been sensing, rehearsing, playing out, and foundering upon my part in the drama of the "Negro problem." I have digested messages about my educational performance from a participative audience, largely of White authorities, legitimized on legal and traditional grounds (Gerth & Mills, 1946). Some of these messages have proven to be quite supportive, critically constructive, and even transformative. Other messages have proven to be disconcerting micro-aggressions at best, disappointing and debilitating diatribes at worst. From this participative audience emerges an ideology from the seemingly more legitimized, meritocratic voices of the "Bootstrap Guild," whose most frequent and often *inadvertently complicit* (Gordon, 2005) messengers appear with a dramatic exceptionality narrative in the one hand, and a merit narrative in the other to explain my position in their otherwise exclusive theatre. Similar to Du Bois' (1903) contemporaries, they never ask me directly, "How does it feel to be a problem? (p. 1)? Instead, they may ask, "*You* did it – Obama did it – what's the matter with other young Black men these days?" They sometimes speak as if to comfort me, "You're the only Black person I understand," or "Look what you've done, other young Black men could learn from you." Similarly, graduate students from abroad have confided in me, "I learned that Blacks were the burden of America."

Z. Leonardo (ed.), Handbook of Cultural Politics and Education, 423–449.

Such narratives come from self-proclaimed conservative and liberal "educated" audiences who, at first glance, seem to be among the most sincere, conscientious people of my academic drama. Yet, they cannot see how responding to my so-called success story in this way, trivializes racism, masks White privilege, enables an insulting sophomoric explanation of the plight of the crowd of Black men, women, and professors who produced me, and reduces my people to scapegoats of "the Negro Problem" that Du Bois (1848) challenged America to reinterpret over 160 years ago. I open this chapter with the above discussion to position myself within a particular genealogical drama regarding the scapegoating of Black Americans. More specifically, I began by highlighting the drama of living concomitantly as Black, American, and dubiously successful—ultimately, as an individual with a mobility narrative now living somewhat closer to an American dream than at birth; while simultaneously living within an American nightmare that depicts my people too often as American's greatest educational problem. Kenneth Burke's work on drama and scapegoating, coupled with his critical race dialogues with Black Harlem Renaissance heavyweights, Jean Toomer and Ralph Ellison, situate Burke as a unique and important character to consider for understanding the role of race in the cultural politics of education that I describe.

One main goal of the chapter is to apply Kenneth Burke's "dramatism" and "unification device." Dramatism is Burke's *weltanschuung*, his holistic conceptualization of human life as a dramatic stage play governing and governed by the human symbolic condition. Therefore, another main goal of the chapter is to describe pertinent parts of the terminological foundation of Burke's dramatism, which thematically leads to comprehending his unification device. It is Burke's unification device that offers some insight into how the Bootstrap Guild engages (inborn dignity; a projection device—of scapegoating; and "symbolic rebirth") to separate themselves from the Black (Negro) problem via the Black-White test score gap. Burke also contributes to understanding the cultural politics of "commercial use" processes in education, which helps to theorize how authorities literally and figuratively capitalize on that separation. Essentially, Burke's unification device is used to analyse Black-White test score gap ideology as advancing an agenda of the Bootstrap Guild alongside a new iteration of the "Negro problem."

With these main goals in mind, the remaining text (1) introduces a brief history of Kenneth Burke: the man, his academic reputation, and his general connection to the Harlem Rennaissance and particular key links to Jean Toomer and Ralph Ellison, (2) details pertinent components of the terminological foundation of dramatism by applying an abridged version of the analytic framework of Zulick's (2008) Kenneth Burke Roadmap (KBR). The KBR begins with a discussion of Burke's foundation of dramatism and concludes with a description of his unification device with its pre- and post-processes of symbolic rebirth, and (3) considers an Ellison/Toomer corrective to Burke's unification device before applying it to the current case of the Black-White test score gap. In short, this chapter challenges readers to consider at least the following line of inquiry: How might Black-White test score gap narratives contribute to a symbolic rebirth of the Negro Problem in education? What are some possibilities of Kenneth Burke's language of transcendence for overcoming the dominant ideology of the Black-White test score gap?

A BRIEF HISTORY OF KENNETH BURKE

The Scholar

Kenneth Duva Burke (May 5, 1897-November 19, 1993) is acknowledged in most handbooks of critical theory as a 20th century North American critic whose work seemed ahead of its time (Coupe, 2001, p. 413). For Burke, the world is a stage and the script of that stage play provides language that binds and blinds us. Burke attended Peabody High School in Pittsburgh, Pennsylvania where he met his childhood friend and future literary giant, Malcolm Cowley. The two boys began to exchange letters and ideas (Feeney,1988) that would continue for over half a century. In 1919, Burke married Lily Mary Batterham, with whom he had three daughters (one of which was the mother of the late award-winning musician, Harry Chapin). Four years later, Burke became the editor, literature and music critic (1927–1929) of the literary magazine, *The Dial*. For his role in providing distinguished service to American literature, Burke received the Dial Award in 1928.

Six years later, Burke found himself again, as a music critic, but this time at *The Nation* (1934–1936). During his time at *The Nation,* Burke was awarded *a Guggenheim Fellowship* in 1935. Gaining influence among the literary circles of New York, he began to be recruited for faculty positions at various colleges in the Northeast. In 1945, Burke published the first of a 1200-page "Motivorum" trilogy of books on motives, *A Grammar of Motives* (1945/1969). The sequels, *A Rhetoric of Motives* (1950/1969) and *Essays Toward a Symbolic of Motives, 1950–1955* would solidify his place among the most recognized rhetorical and critical theorists of his generation. He was a versatile writer who at the dawn of his national appeal in 1951, released a highly acclaimed essay on *Othello*, which also highlighted the bredth and depth of his knowledge regarding Shakespeare, as well as his thirst for understanding life via drama. Bruster (2008) elaborates in his review of this highly acclaimed text:

> *Kenneth Burke on Shakespeare* works as a crystallizing force upon the Burke canon. The crown jewel in this collection, however, is its more difficult but tremendously rewarding sixth chapter, "*Othello*: An Essay to Illustrate a Method" (pp. 65–100). Originally published in 1951, Burke's essay contains what seems like a lifetime's worth of sensitivity to Shakespeare, with nearly every page bearing a profound insight into Shakespeare's craft. Burke's implication is that the tragic scene of *Othello* plays out a kind of *fort-da* game by which the theatre audience comes to understand the human costs of private property and possessiveness. Burke sees *Othello* as offering a ritualistic solution to a public problem (that of appropriation and engrossment), and goes on to map the structure of this ritual with a sequence-template that holds for the five acts of Shakespearean tragedy in general: (I) "the way in;" (II) "the definite pushing-off from shore;" (III) "the

> withinness-of-withinness;" (IV) the "pity act;" and (V) the "separating out" (Bruster, 2008, pp. 75–77).

A somewhat puzzled reporter at the home of an 86-year-old Burke, once observed his frantic search on and around a kitchen table for a misplaced manuscript. The reporter soon learned that "somewhere on it lies that 'dull' paper about him, the one he plans to savage at the three-day Burke conference in Philadelphia..." (*Ramano, 1984*). The consummate critic's critic, Burke is also known to have rejected a "model of transcendence," that emerged from his "language of transcendence" (Coupe, 2001) as he continued to fight and indeed won the battle against being constrained by the success of the movitorum trilogy. In fact, *Essays* were followed by more Burkean theorizing and illustrations of the essential methods for understanding what he called "dramatism" and language as "symbolic action." Ever-ready to push the envelope on writing and critical contemplation, Burke then wrote the novel, *Towards a Better Life,* winner of the National Medal for Literature in 1980 (Bloom, 1981). Bruster (2008) concurs with Burke's versatility beyond the Motivorum trilogy:

> Were Burke's theories confined to this trilogy, a reader might be able to express confidence in somehow "knowing" Burke. But the scattered nature of Burke's writings makes it nearly impossible for the non-specialist to feel any such mastery. (pp. 6–8)

At age 91, Burke lectured on his "Approaches to Language as Power" on March 17, 1984 (de Yonge 1989 A11). After a remarkable life of adding complexity and clarity to rhetoric, critical theory, and the cultural politics of race, Burke died of heart failure on his family farm in Andover, NJ at the age of 96. Much of his work, including personal papers and correspondence is housed at Penn State's *Special Collections Library*. Kenneth Burke's meticulous exploration and creative drive to critique rhetoric and aesthetics led to many publications in diverse venues, which made it difficult to confine his work to one discipline (Coupe, 2001). This diversity and range of applicability may have also contributed to the relatively limited recognition of Burke's insight (Coupe, 2001) in the multicultural and classic readings of Education. He also remains an untapped source of insight for the general study of cultural politics. Burke's death marked the end of the life of a vibrant pioneer who helped to pave the way for critical social theory and whose reputation of multidisciplinary, and yet anti-disciplinary responses to the human symbolic condition was exemplary.

His Academic Reputation

Burke never completed college, yet his critical theoretical work is studied today by scholars in English, communication studies (i.e., Zulick, 2008; Watts, 2004; and Hyde, 2004), political science, psychology, American studies, Queer Theory (Goltz, 2007) and sociology, among others. His original terminology, like "trained incapacity" is frequently used and misused without citation in educational studies. Burke's work has been used in writing courses to help students understand how language helps create what is to be considered knowledge (Fox, 2002). It has been used to examine the social construction of texts and narratives (Manning, 1999). It has been used to consider the scapegoating of racial groups (Hughes, 2003).

Burke resisted the label of one particular intellectual camp or school, preferring "Neo-Stoic, Agro-Bohemian" (Burks, 1991; and Giamo, 2004). He was known to have been influenced by Marx, Freud, Shakespeare, and Nietzsche. Burke publicly separated his work from classical Marxism by centering the symbolic in what some consider his first seminal text, *Permanence and Change* (Wolfe, 1991, p. 43). Burke finds the Marxian ontological "perspective is partially outside" "...the accepted circle of contingencies..." "...outside as regards to the basic tenets of capitalistic enterprise...inside as regards the belief in the ultimate values of industrialism" (Burke, 1954, p. 224).

It is not the Marxist take on modes of production, but its overemphasis on the means of production, and its dependence "by definition on the agency of the industrial" (Wolfe, 1991, p. 43) that troubles Burke. *Permanance and Change* highlights another fundamental difference between Burke and Marx, whereby Burke alludes to the point that "the full critical act must take into account a double dialectical relationship that roughly corresponds to the two vectors of symbolicity" (Wolfe, 1991, p. 42). For Burke, (1954), "A philosophy of being may commit one to open conflict with any persons or class of persons who would use their power to uphold instititions serving an anti-social function" (p. 272). Hence, an engaged critic must doubly "confront the dialectic of human history and sociality, as well as the dialectic between that realm and the enviroment which gets its nature of meaning from the demands we make of it" (Wolfe, 1991, p. 42).

Other recognized scholars can trace their influential terminology back to Burke. Some of the terminology Burke introduced and new syntheses of ideas he posited may feel strangely familiar to readers, because these critical thoughts have been too often applied in Education without acknowledging Burkean origins, albeit with inadvertent omissions. For example, one can trace back to Burke, the phrases "the order of words" (Frye); "the rhetoric of fiction" (Booth); "blindness and insight" (De Man); "narrative as socially symbolic act" (Jameson); "the anxiety of influence" (Bloom) (see Coupe, 2001, p. 413). Some acclaimed rhetorical-critical thinkers and writers like Edward Said, Fredric Jameson, Clifford Geertz, Ralph Ellison, Jean Toomer, and critical feminist, Susan Sontag (Burke's student at the University of Chicago), have publicly acknowledged Burke's influence. However, Kenneth Burke's work has received limited acknowledgment among critical theorists in educational studies who benefit inadvertently from it. It is not within the scope of this chapter to discuss Burke's connection to each of these scholars. However, his influence on African American writers, particularly, Harlem Rennaissance heavyweights, Jean Toomer and Ralph Ellison, is a crucial starting point to any dialogue regarding Burke's current and potential contributions to the cultural politics of race and education.

THE HARLEM RENNAISSANCE

While in New York 1930s–1940s, Burke worked as a prose writer, a poet, and literary critic. He studied for a brief stint at Columbia and lectured at places like

The New School. During this time, Burke corresponded regularly with a number of notable writers and literary-social critics like his childhood friend, Malcolm Cowley, and William Carlos Williams in Greenich Village. It was during this time, that Burke also corresponded with and in at least two cases befriended "Negro" writers and literary-social critics of Harlem Rennaissance fame, including Jean Toomer and Ralph Ellison. Burke "makes some explicit references to race in his discussion of rhetorical interations" that undoubtedly reflect his time with Toomer and Ellison (McPhail, 2002, p. 13).

Burke Meets Toomer

There are new contributions to critical and cultural theory that highlight the relationship between Kenneth Burke and African American novelist Ralph Ellison (Crable, 2003; Genter, 2002; O'Meally, 1994). Few pieces of scholarship however, discuss his relationship with Jean Toomer whose original *Cane (1988)* is arguably a major inspirational work for launching the Harlem Renaissance Movement. Toomer would have significant influences on "a second and even a third, generation of black writers" including "Toni Morrison, Gayl Jones, and Alice Walker" (Scruggs, 2001, p. 41). It is speculated that Toomer met Burke through a former coeditor of *Secession,* Gurhan Munson, but may have been introduced to his work first by one of Toomer's early mentors, Waldo Frank. Apparently, Frank urged Toomer to read Burke's [unfavourable] reviews of his two novels because he thought it would help him (Scruggs, 2001, p. 42). This reading would begin a lifelong literary relationship of constructive criticism between the two men. Toomer is said to have influenced Burke as much as Burke influenced him (Scruggs, 2001, p. 41). The details of the correctives to Burke's dramatism that Toomer seemed to contribute are discussed in the latter part of the chapter regarding Burke's critics.

Burke Meets Ellison

Kenneth Burke was first observed by Ralph Ellison on the morning of June 5, 1935, when he "heard Burke direct a seminar on 'The Rhetoric of Hitler's Battle' at the New School for Social Research" in New York (Pease, 2003, p. 66). Both Richard Wright and Ellison were in attendence. Burke's unification device spoke to Ellison and ultimately helped develop his additional "imaginative resources to distinguish his literary practices from Wright's" (Pease, 2003, p. 66). Ellison's connection to Burke is clear in the following passage from his *Shadow and Act*:

> The anti-Negro image is thus a ritual object of which Hollywood is not the creator but the manipulator. Its role has been that of justifying the widely held myth of Negro inhumanness and inferiority by offering entertaining rituals through which that myth could be reaffirmed (Ellison, 1972, p. 276–77).

From 1937–1940, Ellison abandoned Marxian analytic frameworks for Burke's insights into his analysis of the "Negro complex underpinning the psychology of white Americans" including analyses of lynch mob mentality, social policy of segregation, Jim Crow, and Black face minstrels (Pease, 2003, p. 67–69). However, their literary relationship and some say friendship, was not without fervent critique. (Burke, 1987). The details of the correctives to Burke's dramatism that Ellison contributed are discussed in the latter part of the chapter regarding Burke's critics.

BURKE AND POST-HARLEM RENAISSANCE WRITERS TODAY

Today, Burke's work continues to influence and be influenced by African American writers (Hughes, 2003; McPhail, 2002; and Watts, 2004). His correspondence with Toomer and Ellison seemed to have a profound and evident influence on all three men and ultimately, on a significant portion of the literary world (Pease, 2003). African American writers of the new millennium appropriate Burke via correctives to engage critiques of the social world. One such writer is the acclaimed Mark McPhail (2002), a pioneer of the rhetoric of racism. McPhail (2002) has been quite explicit about Burkean terminology, its influence on his work and its connections to the cultural politics of race. McPhail (2002) respects how Burke grounds his discussion of rhethoric and the consequences of the negative in language and life using terminology like "victimage," "guilt," and "hierarchy," all terms that are prominent in the pedagogy of race today (McPhail, 2002, p. 13). McPhail (2002) also links Burke's (1969) contributions to cultural politics via an Altusserian-like connection of race to ideology as concomitantly material and metacognitive (see also Leonardo, this volume):

> if one studies the pursuasiveness of false or inadequate terms which may not be directly imposed upon us from without by some skillful speaker, but which we imposed upon ourselves in varying degrees of deliberateness and awareness through motives indetermintely self-protective and/or suicidal (Burke, 1969, p. 35).

Morever, McPhail (2002) argues convincingly that Burke links to the cultural politics of race with terminology like "trained incapacity," and "occupational psychosis" (a certain way of thinking that goes with a certain way of living), which result in "terministic screens" [like race] that we use to see the world and our place in it. As a terministic screen, race language and symbols help humans to select and deselect the reality of lived experience. African American scholars were and are clearly influenced by Burke, but their critiques also had a profound influence on the his career.

KENNETH BURKE ROADMAP (KBR): A FRAMEWORK TO AND FROM DRAMATISM

No one chapter, indeed, no one volume could adequately account for the totality of Burke's long and prolific career of critical social theorizing and correspondence regarding the cultural politics of race. Rather than attempt to account for this totality, the rest of this chapter navigates Burkean critical theory with guidance from the "Kenneth Burke Roadmap," (KBR) as constructed by Zulick (2008). I find

KBR, as analytical framework to be as an instructive today about Kenneth Burke's critical theory, as it was when its tenets were first introduced to my cohort over a decade ago. It is in essence a time-tested pedagogy of scaffolding Burke. KBR's scaffolding approach seems to enlist at least a foundational understanding of Burke's contributions to critical social theory in general and cultural politics of education in particular. While gathering materials for this chapter, I found one example of Zulick's (1998) instructional application of KBR's scaffolding approach in her assessment of my February 24, 1998 class report on Burke: "B+......improving! [However], comprehending Burke's tragic and comic frames must begin with the understanding of 'frames of acceptance'"(personal communication, 2009).

Although there are myriad ways to approach Burke, Zulick (2008) suggests that a sound roadmap emphasizes Burke's "coinage of certain key terms that for him express both formal and social aspects at once...." These key terms are integral to the foundation and cultivation of "dramatism." KBR is organized first to introduce Burke's "foundation of dramatism" and second to navigate the intellectual road to understanding the foundation and cultivation of dramatism by positioning Burke's key terms into three interdependent themes: (I) Action, Motion, and Motives, (II) Form, Identification, and Symbol, (III) Perspective, Dramatistic Pentad, and Dramaturgical Frames. KBR directs readers toward comprehension by focusing upon each term within each theme and Burke's multiple references to it in his seminal works, rather than attempting to analyse his voluminous scholarship through a more traditional chronological approach.

KENNETH BURKE'S FOUNDATION OF DRAMATISM—HIS WELTANSCHUUNG

A connection to Shakespeare, *Attitudes Toward History* was published early in the Burke (1937/1984) timeline of seminal critical theoretical scholarship. Yet, within it, he introduces what would become a central purpose of his scholarship for the rest of his life—to battle the either/or dichotomies of the human symbolic condition. For readers more familiar with Derrida's work in this area, it is important to note that similar to Derrida, Burke seeks a multifaceted approach to challenge the dualisms of Western philosophy with a strong emphasis on rhetorical criticism, signs, symbols, and logology. Unlike Derrida, however, Burke does not consistently deconstruct his own thoughts, terminology, and observations used to discuss these topics, which expose some of his more modernist tendencies. Burke also initiated his work largely to open the possibilities of a language of transcendence to counter or complement a language of critique (e.g., deconstruction). He observed this bifurcated symbolic condition as main culprit of division and antagonism in humanity. Burke further clarifies, "When approached from a certain point of view, A and B are 'opposites.' We mean by 'transcendence' the adoption of another point of view from which they cease to be opposites" (Burke, 1937/1984, p. 336). Burke seemed purposefully to avoid some of the pitfalls of transcendental thought by embracing a central principal that Zulick (2008) describes as a complementary duality among human symbolic interaction that involves a formal structure and psycho-social dynamic (Zulick, 2008). He may be considered generally among the pioneers of *both/and* critical theorists, but more specifically, as the father of embodied symbolicity (Kenneth Burke Society, 2008).

By grounding his scholarship in the necessity of symbols for human thought processes, Burke set a theoretical course to transcend the dichotomous arguments so common to Western thought. It was not the degree of transcendence that set Burke apart from his contemporaries, but the kind. It is a kind of transcendence without the mandate for the elimination of *either* one perspective, *or* one party, but a refreshing form of transcendence that anticipates and acknowledges how "the symbolic nature of perspective can" operate to move us "beyond the stagnant stalemate of reified social, political, and philosophical binaries" (Kenneth Burke Society, 2008, p. 2).

Evidence suggests that Burke sought ardently to challenge our taken-for-granted, bifurcated symbolic interaction through conceptualizing, critiquing, exposing, reframing, and coining key "ultimate" terms (Burke, 1969, pp. 186–89). For Burke, these terms express both the formal and social aspects of embodied symbolicity at once (Zulick, 2008). Moreover, Kenneth Burke (a) rigorously studied the concept-tualization and operationalization of terminology within the human symbolic condition, while he (b) relentlessly pursued a disciplined cultivation of transcendence—of transcending human conflict (human vs. human, human vs. self, and human vs. nature). These conflicts can be found "in the American 'racial divide'...and humanitarian crises of today" (Kenneth Burke Society, 2008, p. 2) as well as in the exploitation of "one little fellow named Ecology" who "teaches us that the *total* economy of the planet cannot be guided by an efficient rationale of exploitation alone, but that the exploiting part must eventually suffer if it too greatly disturbs the *balance* of the whole" (Burke, 1937/1984, p. 150). It is well documented that this rigorous observation of such conflicts and the pursuit of resolution, provided a foundation from which to build, critique, and expand Burke's most acknowledged development–dramatism. Dramatism became Burke's favorite word to describe what he observed when people attempt to communicate via the symbols they co-create (Miller, 2005).

By the 1950s, dramatism was recognized as a method for understanding the social uses of language and how to encounter the social and symbolic world of a drama (Brock et al., 1985). For some scholars, dramatism is best viewed as a logical method for understanding human motives (e.g., Fox, 2002). Crable (2000) alludes to the notion of dramatism as simplistic but not simple, because its basic dramatic form allows for the consideration of multiple points of exploration and data analyses. For other scholars, dramatism is less of a method than a clear system of ontology to view the nature of one's being as a symbol-maker, symbol-user, and symbol-misuser. Still, another group of scholars focus upon the epistemology of dramatism. In this camp, dramatism positions language as a strategic, motivated response to a specific situation (Griffin, 2006), and dramatism also positions language as a mode of symbolic action rather than a mode of knowledge (Burke, 1978). Burke would likely take a both/and approach to resolving the debate about where to compart-mentalize dramatism, and disagree with compartmentalizing it in the first place.

In Burke's lifelong writing and connections, dramatism has methodological, ontological, and epistemological characteristics. For Burke, dramatism explains that "If action, then drama; if drama, then conflict; if conflict, then victimage" (Burke, 1969, p. 415). Much more than a critical social theory, then, dramatism is perhaps, more accurately described as Burke's *weltanschauung* (i.e., Burke's comprehensive view of the world of human life as a stage play of and about the human symbolic condition). Dramatism is the genesis and exodus; chicken and egg of his lifelong thinking, feeling, and acting about the human symbolic condition—his, yours, and mine; with all of the conflicts and possibilities thereof. Given its vast applications and implications, how might one begin to navigate dramatism in relation to critical theory and cultural politics?

I. Action, Motion, and Motive

As mentioned above, Zulick (2008) developed the Kenneth Burke Roadmap (KBR) as one curricular and instructional tool to begin navigating dramatism with the muliplicity of Burke's references emerging from it and growing toward it, and to help burgeoning scholars of Burkean theory locate his contributions to critical theory and cultural politics. One key to understanding the "foundation of dramatism" is in Burke's distinction between action and motion (Zulick, 2008). Zulick explains that "while motion is the basis of 'scientism,' and assumes that change is the result of purely physical, autonomous processes, action captures the idea of 'motion with intent'" (pp. 1–2). Thus, when I refer to the Burke's current and potential contributions to the language [and action] of transcendence, I am qualifying that, for Burke, language is action, or motion with intent that selects and de-selects the problematic and the possible. Zulick (2008) further explains Burke's expression of motive involving "the duality inherent in the motion-action distinction." Burke uses the root of motion and "infuses it with intent" (Zulick, 2008). As with other components of the terminological foundation of dramatism, "motive has the double meaning of the purposes surrounding discourse (one invokes the other) as an ethical-aesthetic act, and also the motives or themes found within a discourse" (Zulick, 2008, p. 1).

II. Form, Identification, and Symbol

Form. The bulk of Burke's "ideas on form can be found in *Counter-Statement*, published in 1931 before a full-blown theory of Dramatism had been developed" (Kimberling, 1982, p. 44). For Burke, form relates to the psychology of the rhetor (i.e., person intending to be persuasive) and auditor (i.e., subject and object of persuasion) with regards to common, yet contextualized and temporal verbal and nonverbal communication patterns. For the rhetor, it involves "the creation of an appetite in the mind of the auditor, and the satisfying of the appetite" (Burke, 1931, p. 31). Form works as a tool that helps us symbolize both our experiences and emotions. Form has a "cause (the human desire to externally express inner feelings)" and it has a "purpose (as an aid in persuading us of the 'human-ness' of our" (Kimberling, 1982, p. 44) expressions and communicative behaviors. Ultimately, "form is the 'glue' that unites" (Kimberling, 1982, p. 44). Similar to Bakhtin's ideas about anticipatory dialogue, Burkean form positions rhetors and auditors as co-consumers and co-producers of the communicative acts that symbolize or reflect their lived experiences and feelings about them (personal communication, 2009). It can essentially "enable the mind to follow processes amenable to it" (Burke, 1931, pp. 142–143) and form is "correct in so far as it gratifies the needs which it creates" (Burke, 1931, p. 138) through a dialectic transaction between rhetors and auditors. Form has five aspects (syllogistic progression, qualitative progression, repetitive, conventional, and minor/incidental) in the Burkean frame, all extending from "pure form" that plays upon the capacity of rhetors and auditors to *perceive* and therefore to *anticipate* as well as *generate* and communicate patterns of both experience and emotion. The fifth form, "minor/incidental" is a style component present in all of the other forms, and it occurs "in great number in any work of art" (Kimberling, 1982, p. 47). Common examples of minor/incidental form include, contrast, comparison, metaphor, synechdoche, and series (Kimberling, 1982, p. 48), as well as, tropes, figures, and larger forms, such as story or myth (Quigley, 2007, p. 3).

Identification. Identification works through form, which according to Burke (1950/1969), "many purely formal patterns can awaken an attitude of collaborative expectancy in us" (p. 58). In other words, once we comprehend the "trend of the form, it invites participation" (Quigley, 2007, p. 3). Form is necessary, but insufficient without identification, or the common ground that exists between the speaker and audience. Without identification there is no form, and without form there is neither identification, nor persuasion (Griffin, 2006). This interdependent identification/form relationship may bring nostalgia to readers more familiar with comparable themes from the cultural political work of Bakhtin (personal communication, 2009). In *A Rhetoric of Motives* (1950/1969), Burke "selects 'identification' as the key term to distinguish his rhetorical perspective from a tradition characterized by the term persuasion" (Quigley, 2007, p. 1). He does not intend to center identification by decentering persuasion. Instead, Burke "sees that interactions in our contemporary world are, in some ways, more complicated than can be understood by viewing persuasion solely as the explicit, intentional acts which a rhetor directs to a specific, known audience" (Quigley, 2007, p. 1). Thus, he sought to explore how identification connects to and extends persuasion, rather than substituting for it.

Identification has formal transitive and intransitive social components described by Burke (1950/1969) in *Rhetoric of Motives*. For Burke (1950/1969) formal identification can be illuminated by an example from the news during:

> the "Berlin crisis" of 1948: "Who controls Berlin, controls Germany; who controls Germany controls Europe; who controls Europe controls the world." As a proposition, it may or may not be true. And even if it is true, unless people are thoroughly imperialistic, they may not want to control the world.

> But regardless of these doubts about it as a proposition, by the time you arrive at the second of its three stages, you feel how it is destined to develop—and on the level of purely formal assent you would collaborate to round out its symmetry by spontaneously willing its completion and perfection as an utterance. Add, now, the psychosis of nationalism, and assent on the formal level invites assent to the doctrine. (pp. 57–58)

Burke (1950/1969) distinguishes, but doesn't disconnect social identification through an example of tragedy:

> An imagery of slaying is to be considered merely as a special case of identification in general. Or otherwise put: the imagery of slaying is a special case of transformation, and transformation involves the ideas and imagery of identification. That is: the killing of something is the changing of it, and the statement of the thing's nature before and after the change is an identifying of it. (p. 20).

In "Ethos of Invention," Zulick (2004) clarifies Burke's point on identification as both/and:

> In the transitive, formal sense, it means to put a name to something, in the intransitive, social sense it means to identify with. Burke uses the term in both senses but the two senses are not merely interchangeable–rather, the one invokes the other. (p. 1).

Zulick (2008) later adds that formal identification regresses to repetitive form, while social identification regresses to consubstantiation and victimage (p. 1). With regard to social identification, Burke finds that we are "both joined and separate, at once a distinct substance and consubstantial with another" (Burke, 1969, p. 21). He further contends that "Identification is affirmed with earnestness precisely because there is division. Identification is compensatory to division" (Burke, 1969, p. 22). He argues that humans are so often enlisted by the centrifugal forces of hierarchy and we feel guilty about the differences that separate us, and about "our inevitable failure to always support order, authority and hierarchy" (Quigley, 2007, p. 1). In short, guilt operates as a key motive of human dramatism (Miller, 2005).

One way that we purge this guilt is to seek dyads or affinity groups through exploring "ways in which our interests, attitudes, values, experiences, perceptions, and material properties are shared with others, or could appear to be shared" (Quigley, 2007, p. 1). Burke (1969) elaborates on this point, "a speaker persuades an audience by the use of stylistic identifications; his act of persuasion may be for the purpose of causing the audience to identify itself with the speaker's interests..." (p. 46). Burke illustrates a persuasive identification tactic through an example of a politician who, when speaking to farmers says, "I was a farm boy myself," (1969, p. xiv) or the "baby kissing politician's ways [with] women [and] their babies" (Burke, 1966, p. 302).

To summarize, identification involves at least three types of processes noted by Quigley (2007): (1) the process of naming something (or someone) according to specific properties; (2) the process of associating with and disassociating from others–suggesting that persons (and ideas or things) share, or do not share, important qualities in common; (3) the product or end result of identifying–the state of being consubstantial with others. In addition, Burke tells us that identification processes operate (a) through the human semi-conscious or "not wholly deliberate yet not unconscious" parts of us (Burke, 1969, 115), (b) through self-persuasion, the process of persuasion is not complete until we act upon ourselves rhetorically (Burke, 1969), (c) through the mundane and recurring, and (d) through representation, as we identify by sharing vicariously leadership roles (Burke, 1973). It is important to also comprehend the concept of identification within the context of Burke's understanding of symbols, rhetoric, patterns of experience, and language as symbolic action as Zulick's (2008) roadmap suggests.

Symbol: rhetoric, symbol, and patterns of experience. Burke conceptualizes rhetoric as "the use of words by human agents to form attitudes or induce actions in other human agents." (Burke, 1969, p. 41). His connection of rhetoric to identification is evident when Burke states, "[O]ften we must think of rhetoric not in terms of some one particular address but as a general body of identifications that owe their convincingness much more to trivial repetition and dull daily reinforcement than to exceptional rhetorical skill" (Burke, 1969, p. 26).

Zulick (2008) notes the origins of "rhetoric as such is not rooted in any past condition of human society. It is rooted in an essential function of language itself, a function that is wholly realistic, and is continually born anew" (p. 2). Rhetoric is connected to identification and symbols in that the use of language as a symbolic means of inducing cooperation via identification in beings that by nature respond to symbols (Burke, 1969, p. 43). Burke is commonly cited in English and Communication Studies for the portion of his "definition of man" that positions man as symbol-making, symbol-using, and symbol-misusing. But, what exactly does he mean by "symbols?" For Burke, symbols are perhaps best described by what they do than by what they are. Symbols work as (a) situation/strategy (incipient dramatism), every document bequeathed to us by history must be treated as a strategy for encompassing a situation (Burke, 1973, p. 109), and (b) as patterns of experience (Burke, 1931, pp. 151) the symbol is the verbal parallel to a pattern of experience (Burke, 1931, p. 152). Through our human symbolic condition we engage in some observable, universal experiences, which include the "various kinds of moods, feelings, emotions, perceptions, sensations, and attitudes discussed in the manuals of psychology and exemplified in works of art…" (Burke, 1931, p. 149). Burke suggests that it is important to consider "patterns of experience," whereby, "any … specific environmental condition calls forth and stresses certain of the universal experiences as being more relevant to it, with a slighting of those less relevant" (Burke, 1931, p. 151). Once patterns of experience exist…they become in turn restrictively "creative." (Burke, 1931, p. 151). In other words, "as a method of adjustment to one condition, the pattern may become a method of meeting other conditions—may become a typical manner of experiencing" (Burke, 1931, p. 152).

III. Perspective, Dramatistic Pentad, Dramaturgical Frames

Perspective. Perspective by incongruity is a method for gauging situations by verbal "atom cracking" (Burke, 1937/1984, pp. 308–311). For Burke, table, chairs, and diners are congruous, since patterns of experience has made them so (Zulick, 2008), "but table, chairs, living diner, and a dining lady manikin are incongruous" (Burke, 1937/1984, pp. 308–311). Burke understands the "perspective by incongruity" as what makes for a *dramatic* vocabulary, with weighting and counter-weighting, in contrast with the liberal ideal of *neutral* naming in the characterization of processes (Zulick, 2008). The result of perspective by incongruity, by imagining opposing or competing patterns of experience is an important interpretative ingredient of the dramatic pentad.

Dramatistic pentad. Burke's *Dramatistic Pentad* analyzes how we use use the ingredients of form, symbols, and identification, and perspective to persuade other human agents to accept, select, and deselect a particular construction of reality (Griffin, 2006). His dramatistic pentad includes five elements as well as ten ratios of human drama (Benoit, 1983). Those five elements and the five most commonly referenced of Burke's ten pentadic ratios are noted below:

- Act: what was or will be done.
- Scene: generally thought of as where and when; context of act.
- Agent: entity that could be construed as performing an act.
- Agency: the methods or tools used to perform the act.
- Purpose: goal of the act; entelechy.
- Act/Agency
- Agent/Scene
- Agency/Act
- Scene/Agent
- Act/Purpose

Burke's (1945/1969) Grammar of Motives discussed four master tropes engaged by human agents: (1) metaphor > perspective, (2) metonymy > reduction, (3) synecdoche > representation, and (4) irony > dialectic (Burke, 1945/1969, pp. 503–517). Rhetors use metaphor to push audiences to perceive the drama through our lenses. Metaphor includes changes like we no longer hold "stereotypes that blacks [agents] are biologically lazy [act];" rather African Americans [agents] have a cultural pathology [act] tied to history [scene] which is the new rhetoric of racism" (Villanueva, 2006, p. 6). Metonymy is a similar tool, but it reduces one agent/scene for example to an object, that is inferred to steer perception as well. For Villanueva (2006), "to reduce the idea of race is to focus on individualism" (p. 6). He uses identity as an example. Whether he is viewed as a Latino, a Puerto Rican, a Nuyorican, or perhaps a professor [agent] is determined to some degree by the setting and the context [scene] (p. 7). Synecdoche limits or reduces the representation of an act/agency to one that we are proposing for audiences. Synecdoche is like a national identity for Villanueva (2006), where racism is replaced by "civilization." He uses this example, "the only way that Mexicans [agent] will not ruin [act] America's national identity is for them to embrace the Anglo-Protestant ethos [agency]" (Villanueva, 2006, p. 16). Irony includes descriptions of the act/purpose, for example with phrases like the common "the well-planned scheme failed miserably." It makes a value judgement to persuade the audience that obviously the scheme had not been well-planned, or it would not have failed. It can also play upon the guilt of the audience regarding the act, as well as the purpose. For Villanueva (2006), the most ironic aspect of racism is colorblindness because for all intents and purposes, "no one wants to be rendered invisible" (p. 7). Even some elite Whites who seek a colorblind ideology may not really want to be rendered invisible, or indistinguishable from other ethnic groups. What they seem to want is a way to mask White privilege, elite status privilege, and their complicity in the maintenance of White hegemony (Doane & Bonilla-Silva, 2003; and Leonardo, 2009).

Dramaturgical frames. Since the expression and receptivity of language is considered an act for Burke, it is important to understand how our word order contributes to the development of terministic screens in his theoretical framework. Zulick (2008) explains that the human symbolic condition orders words that goad us to believe or to pick some particular nomenclature, ultimately, to select (and de-select) some terministic screen. Burke used the notion of terministic screens to ponder how we may proceed to track down the kinds of observations implicit in the terminology we have chosen; whether our choice of terms was deliberate or spontaneous; and how our choice contributed to framing the acceptance of some lived experiences/ emotions and rejection of others (Burke, 1966, p. 47). The notions of word order and terministic screens lead to comprehending Burke's frames of acceptance and rejection. By "frames of acceptance," Burke means "the more or less organized system of meanings by which a thinking man gauges the historical situation and adopts a role within it." (Burke, 1937/1984, p. 5). Zulick (2008) notes the following pertinent examples of the frame of acceptance, such as "the work of Emerson," and the "genres…tragedy and comedy." Conversely, a "Rejection" frame, for Burke, is but a by-product of "acceptance." It involves primarily a matter of emphasis. It takes its color from an attitude towards some reigning symbol of authority, stressing a shift in allegiance to symbols of authority (Burke, 1937/1984, p. 5). Zulick offers the following common example of a rejection frame: the writing of Machiavelli, and of genres of rejection frames including "Elegy, Satire, and Burlesque" (Zulick, 2008). Zulick also briefly notes Burke's comments on "transitional genres" like the "Grotesque." Burke says, "the grotesque is the cult of incongruity without the laughter" (Burke, 1937/1984, p. 58). An uncritical view of the dramaturgical frames of reference that we adopt, can render us inadvertently complicit (Gordon, 2005) in the creation of our own intellectual barriers, described by Burke as trained incapacity (Burke, 1954).

The dramaturgical frames of acceptance and rejection logically lead to Burke's introduction to the merger and division aspects of scapegoating (Burke, 1945/1969, p. 406). For Burke, scapegoating involves, (a) an original state of merger in that the iniquities are shared by both the iniquitous and their chosen vessel, (b) a principle of division in that the elements shared in common are being ritualistically alienated, and (c) a new principle of merger this time in the unification of those whose purified identity is defined in dialectical opposition to the sacrificial offering. The Unification Device is arguably the most instructive tool for burgeoning scholars of Burke who long for a culminating experience of the four themes (i.e., action, motion, and motives, form, identification, and symbol, perspective, and dramaturgical frames) at the heart of dramatism.

Burke's Unification Device and its Critics

First appearing in Burke (1939) and reprinted latest in Burke (1973), "The Rhetoric of Hitler's Battle" (pp. 202–204) explains that the unification device has four interdependent parts. About six years ago, I applied this unification device to theorize the origins of the negative images of Blacks in Japan (Hughes, 2003). The unification device first involves inborn dignity, a positive universal elevating of those who identify with it. Second, it involves a projection device, the "curative" process that comes with the ability to hand over one's ills to a scapegoat. Third, it involves symbolic rebirth, or the combination of dignity/ projection that gives feeling of moving forward towards a new social goal, and fourth, it involves commercial use to name the use of some material advantage accruing to acceptance of the device. The totality of Burke's dramatism, and in particular his culminating unification device, was considered "brilliant" by some of his peers including notable literary figures such as W. H. Auden and John Crowe Ransom. However, Burke was not without critics and adaptations from current writers (e.g., Brock, 1992; Brummet, 1995; Chesebro, 1999; Condit, 1994; Crowell, 1997; and Tompkins, 1993), as well as, Burke's own contemporaries (e.g., Toomer, 1924–25; and Ellison, 1972).

It is not within the scope of this chapter to go in-depth about each of Burke's various critics. However, it will return to a discussion of Ralph Ellison and Jean Toomer, two of the most influential critics of Burke's terminology and foundation of dramatism in relation to cultural politics of race. Indeed, evidence of correspondence suggest that Burke's scholarship evolved in large part because of his critical exchange with Ellison and Toomer. Ellison and Toomer essentially offer specific correctives to the terminological foundation of dramatism and his culminating unification device. Both authors shared a lifelong debate with Burke regarding the applicability of his theoretical approach to the Negro problem.

Let us first consider the correctives of Toomer (1924–25) who reviewed Burke's first book, a collection of short-stories titled *The White Oxen (1924).* It was Toomer's review of that book that Burke confessed as enhancing his awarness of "human beings as logocentric animals" (Scruggs, 2001, p. 42). Toomer (1924) wrote:

> Mr. Burke himself has openly contributed to these opinions, and at times may believe in them...the rhetorical properties of this book are emphasized, but emphasis may be a matter of wish, being related in no way to actuality...the world he lives in [is] to forcibly [hide behind rhetoric] to eliminate the disagreeable and painful (pp. 44–45).

There is evidence that Burke spent "the rest of his life pursuing the implications of Toomer's remarks, essentially giving up his career as a creative writer to become a philosopher of language and culture (Scruggs, 2001, p. 53). He wrote of Toomer's review in an initial, reluctant acknowledgement to his accuracy, "Thus I salute you, as having, in a muddled and unconvincing manner, touched the mainspring of my volume" (Scruggs, 2001, p. 55). Their literary relationship would help to lift both men to the stratosphere.

Ellison added some different correctives to Burke's analysis. Both men were of the Emerson tradition, but Emerson's exclusion of Black interlocutors, ultimately separated the degree to which the two men were influenced by him. First, and perhaps most importantly, Burke's work in symbolic action obviously involves the symbolizable, as Pease (2003) insightfully locates. However, Ellison's *Shadow and Act* referenced how the "shadows of the White American racist order [were] related to the nonsymbolizable" (Pease, 2003, p. 73). These shadow acts were the unanticipated and unacknowledged conditions of racism, white privilege, and other race-related historical acts of inequity.

Second, In 1945, Ellison constructed "'Richard Wright's Blues' out of Burke's theory of symbolic action" (Pease, 2003, p. 74). In "Richard Wright's Blues," Ellison brilliantly adapted Burkean terms to reconstruct Richard Wright's *Black Boy, (*where at times Wright seems to position himself as a Negro problem and as alone), as a form of self-scapegoating that Ellison claimed was quinntessial to the historical Black art form, the Blues. For Ellison, "the blues fall short of tragedy…in that …they provide no resolution, they provide no scapegoat but the self" (Ellison, 1972, pp. 77, 93). Ellison (1972) wrote of *Black Boy,*

> Negro leaders have often been exasperated by this phenomena, and Booker T. Washington (who demanded far less of the Negro humanity than Richard Wright) described the Negro Community as a basket of crabs, wherein should one attempt to climb out, the others immediately pull him back. (pp. 90–91)

Burke publicly disagreed with Ellison's interpretation. He disagreed on grounds that positioned Ellison's reinterpretation of Wright and interrogation of Washington as essentially and paradoxically a literary crab mentality pulling down Wright and Washington (Pease, 2003). Breaking his own rules against outsider critics attempting to label correct vs. incorrect forms, Burke initially mistook Wright's portrayal as a more "correct" and productive reflection of the Negro problem than Ellison's portrayal. Ellison responded to Burke in a scene within his famed *Invisible Man* where he described the non-symbolizable world that Burke could not experience as a White man (the world as experienced by dehumanized/marginalized persons). This non-symbolizable world of unearned white privilege and structural racism against the Negro was what initially kept Burke from being able or willing to acknowledge the disconnect between his theory of dramatism and critique of Ellison. In 1985, Burke, seemed ashamed of his initial critique – where he literally assumed he could embody the Black experience via language – and he published a private letter in which he retracted his critique of Ellison some forty years later (Pease, 2003, p. 74).

A SYMBOLIC REBIRTH OF *THE BOOTSTRAP GUILD*:
A CORRECTIVE APPLICATION OF BURKE'S UNIFICATION DEVICE TO THE CASE OF THE BLACK-WHITE TEST SCORE GAP

From a Burkean perspective, it is through the interplay of features of his unification device that rhetorical authorities in a given affinity group establish the scapegoat. The corrective application of Burke's unification device below provides evidence of: (a) a symbolic rebirth of the Bootstrap Guild and (b) the cultural politics of the "Negro problem" underlying *Black-White test score gap ideology*.

Inborn Dignity

In Black-White test score gap ideology, the dignity of a meritocratic humanity is emphasized. Burke (1995) explains that this dignity is considered to be an attribute of all people if they earn it by "right" living and "right" thinking (p. 211). However, in American history and ancestry, only certain people are considered "dignified" today. The Bootstrap Guild finds significant dignity in the current climate. Whether self-identifying as Black, White, Latino, Native, or Asian American, the Bootstrap Guild members distance themselves and their dignity from "unsuccessful" Black folks, and their *overtly* racist White adversaries. "Unsuccessful" Black folks and overt White racists are considered symbolically as inferior. The Bootstrap Guild affords a certain kind of dignity related to capitalism and aspirations for the "American Dream," where merit-based competition, and hard work are symbolic of "dignity," at least for the "successful," winners of the system. Burke (1995) explains that this type of symbolic condition, "puts the sense of dignity upon a fighting basis, requiring the conquest of 'inferior races'" (p. 211).

After the Civil Rights Movement, there were "'strong emotional needs' that this new version of inborn dignity could satisfy" (Burke, 1995, p. 211). Blacks who made it to the middle-class or higher and their White allies were signs of America's greatness, of the triumph of the dignified, whereas those still bearing the brunt of generational poverty and racism are too often viewed as products to be managed. In education, we have the Black-White test score gap, where "unsuccessful" Black test-takers are less dignified in society, and they become the center of an educational problem to be solved. The current "Black problem" has too often been overemphazised in discussions as an inborn cultural problem of Blacks themselves, rather than a product of the historically inequitable macro-economic situation perpetuated by America's systemic White privilege and structural racism.

Projection Device

Burke explained the use of a scapegoat as "a 'curative' process that comes with the ability to hand over one's ills" (1995, p. 211). Symbols, he proposed, are used to aid society in its construction of social messages about hierarchy. He further posits that hierarchical constructions inevitably lead us to purge inner guilt through victimage and scapegoating—two key projection devices. Scapegoating is essentially the "[taking] or mistaking of an agent for agency…. perfected through the projection of a total cathartic enemy" (Wolfe, 1991, p. 82), a common foe shared by all (Brummet, 1984). The Bootstrap Guild conveys messages consciously and subconsiously about appropriate Americanness, which conveniently alienates any "misfits." In education, the Black-White test score gap is often narrowed to problems of schooling and culture. The schooling structure problem too often symbolizes the bureaucracy of anonymous Whites, who are either ill-informed, uneducated, or racist. Many White adults who lived through the Civil Rights movement claim often to "not see color," "nor to act or have a hand in reproducing racism." Racism is the product of less "dignified" Blacks (not like President Obama), who presumably do not work as hard and are constantly "pulling the race card."

In Education research, the Black mother is noted often as the key *variable* in decreasing the Black-White test score gap, as if the Black mother lives in a vacuum (Jencks & Phillips, 1998). She is a scapegoat. The Bootstrap Guild willingly hands over to the Black mother things that it doesn't want to see in itself, in its complicity. In essence, the Black mother is still a target of criticism, whereby most if not all of the test score gaps separating her child from her/his White counterparts are attributed to her. Burke (1995) describes the process of projection as "especially medicinal" for the in-group (pp. 211–212), because they can position themselves outside the problematic.

Symbolic Rebirth

The third feature of Burke's unification device is described as a combination of the first two features. He explains, "the projective device of the scapegoat, coupled with the doctrine of inborn racial superiority, provides it's followers with a 'positive' view of life" (1995, p. 212). From this newly formed positive outlook, cultures replace their collective, original selves through the unification process of symbolic rebirth. After the Civil Rights Movement, the Bootstrap Guild catalyzed such a rebirth. The Bootstrap Guild with messages like "Freedom of Choice" "Choice," "meritocracy," "work hard, play hard," and "the American way" voted themselves as the "true" American people, different from the bulk of the "unsuccessful," test-takers, the "skeptics," and the "socialists," but similar in that they became examples of how everyone could work their way up. They produce a mythical narrative where hard work, and an accountable meritocracy exists that measures Blacks and Whites not by the color of their skins, but by the height of their test scores. The Black-White test score gap was also connected to socioeconomic status and unsuccessful Blacks were pitted as problematic, while sucessful Blacks were hailed as exceptional. The technocratic belief that test score technology was progress alone, without continuing to address racial ideology became the mantra of the Bootstrap Guild. They made a list of preventable and controllable educational ills without addressing disproportionate accessibility and the racial blindspots of (mis)treatment. Burke (1931) warns us about such beliefs, "efficiency was required to develop the machine. One must accept the undeniable fact that technological defficiency has become too much like psychological inefficiency" (p. 121). The advent of standardized cognitive testing was based largely in efficiency; to find an efficient way to assess teaching, learning, and schooling. The Bootstrap Guild, albeit unintentionally, developed a well-planned and efficient psychometric testing machine that is failing too many teachers, students, and public schools miserably: particularly students of color, the impoverished, and their teachers in densely populated urban and sparcely populated rural America. Arguably, the current testing system of the Bootstrap Guild does not equate authentic learning as (a) learning for in-depth understanding and (b) learning for meaningful, informed, fulfilling, critically reflexive, and socially just application. The Boostrap Guild instead seems to promote learning for the efficient test objectives of the machine within an education industrial complex. In sum, as the efficient learning goals of the testing machine that gauges the Black-White test score gap are pursued, the machine seems to perpetuate psychologically inefficient means. If historically, the means to learning for the more comprehensive types of understanding and application mentioned above have most often been reserved in the U.S. for the children of wealthy, White land-owners, the exceptional, and those with fleeting access to the networks controlled by them, then the machine may raise test scores, and even converge Black-White test scores in some limited settings, while sustaining the gap in access.

Commercial Use

During the height of the modern Civil Rights Movement, the Bootstrap Movement was devastated by the televised violence again so-called Negroes, thereby demonstrating that working hard and doing well on standardized high stakes, multiple choice, timed tests was not always enough to lead to "success" in the United States of America. The Bootstrap Movement, however, would remain steadfast because its tenets were the very basis for the U.S. Declaration of Independence, Bill of Rights, and the Constitution. Similar to the founders who wrote those documents, the Bootstrap Guild would reserve full rights for an exclusive group of elite members that Whiteness studies scholar, Gary Howard (1999) describes as White male property owners and their allies. Today, these allies seem to include both an elite guild-selected few, as well as self-proclaiming members of color, the impoverished, and women. In education, Blacks were not able to participate fully in the G. I. Bill, and neither could they benefit fully from remnants of the New Deal to secure housing in neighborhoods with enough wealth to maintain high resource public schools. This meant continued inequities related to White privilege, racism and segregation between schools, as well as within-school segregation in desegregated schools. It constructed a Black-White test score gap between racially isolated schools, as well as a gulf between urban and suburban schools. Burke (1995) explains that the commercial renewal of capital (i.e., economic, social, political, and cultural) for the Bootstrap Guild would goad them toward a "noneconomic interpretation of economic ills" (p. 212). In other words, the Bootstrap Guild was making a come back and it needed capital. Who better to connect the Guild with that capital than an established

Black scapegoat? In Education, the Bootstrap Guild has found a billion dollar market in testing, and grants available to address the "Negro problem" of the Black-White test score gap, with a Black scapegoat to blame for the seemingly noble, but somewhat misguided, pursuit to close it.

CONSUBSTANTIATION/TRANSUBSTANTIATION AND TRAGIC/COMIC HOPE

Becoming Symbol-Wise to Conceptual Paradoxes of the Black-White Test Score Gap

Is there a way out of the bind of the unification device? With a little help from Ellison and Toomer, Burke says there is. First, in consubstantiation/transubstantiation, there lies the possibility of the conceptual paradox. Burke explains that within such a paradox, "obviously is a strategic moment, an alchemic moment, wherein momentous miracles of transformation can take place" (Burke, 1945/1969, p. 24). For Burke, the anticipation and acknowledgement of the paradox offers a moment where "the intrinsic and extrinsic can change places. To tell what a thing is, you place it in terms of something else" (Burke, 1945/1969, p. 24). These moments of paradox highlight ways in which our liberation is shared, or where our ideological overlap makes us consubstantial with others (Quigley, 2007).

Second, Burke wants us to evolve a transformative pedagogy regarding the Black-White test score gap. Similar to Giroux's language of possibility, Burke seeks a language of transcendence through critical reflection en route to becoming symbol-wise (Gibson, 2005). Jessica Enoch describes Burke's contribution to the 1955 *Yearbook of the National Society of Education*, "Linguistic Approaches to Problems of Education" (LAPE). This Burkean work is acclaimed as a must-read for educators because, it embarks upon the task of demonstrating how Burke's views can be brought into the classroom in these similar times (Gibson, 2005). In LAPE, Burke (1955) argues against the competition, efficiency model of K-12 schooling, "[the] serious student enters school hoping to increase his powers, to equip himself in the competition for 'success,' to make the 'contacts' that get him a better-paying job" (pp. 299–300). Burke contends that students should instead be about the business of "exacting in [their] own ambitiousness to cancel off the many prompter ambitions that, given the new weapons, threaten to destroy [them]" (pp. 299–300). Burke was also interested in creating courses to bridge the gap between literature and life (Gibson, 2005). Further, he apparently aspired to teach students to recognize the momentous role that terminology plays in human thought and conduct (Gibson, 2005). In another letter, written to Kaplan, Burke wrote of his goals for students to gain "skill in the chosen subject, appreciation of literary attainments, the imaginative contemplation of human foibles, and the development of equipment for living in general (Gibson, 2005). Burke even offers a glimpse into a dramatistic classroom, where "the various 'persuasions' are brought together" and the "topic [to] surely transcend them all [could be] the question of persuasion itself" (Burke, 1955, p. 299), indeed it could be a "theoretical study of the forms in all persuasion" (Burke, 1955, p. 300). Gibson's (2005) concluding thoughts resound, "Burke's work is clearly relevant to our current education system and society at large" (p. 296).

Third, Burke encourages us to look at the processes of identification for spaces to transform the ideology of the Black-White test score gap. For Burke, the human need is to identify with others and this need provides a rich resource for those interested in persuading us to seek spaces of convergence (Quigley, 2007). Burke speaks on this point, "mystery arises at the point where different kinds of beings are in communication. There is strangeness but also the possibility of communion" (Burke, 1969, p. 115). Quigley (2005) offers some clarity on this point:

> Burke's perspective suggests that we consider the impact of messages we do not fully intend to send or do not consciously intend to heed. Such opportunities to identify semi-consciously might be expected to occur, especially when there exists "mystery" resulting from hierarchical estrangement, as would happen in relations between royalty and commoners.... Burke encourages us to look at processes that are semi-conscious, less than obvious, mundane, and representative, processes that invite us to collaborate in identification and transformation. (p. 3)

To elaborate on this important point, Burke sees humans as inventor of the negative and flawed with the pang for perfection and inclusion. This represents for Burke an instability that makes available to us "the art of influence… for purposes of good or harm" (Quigley, 2007, p. 1). From this perspective, if we learn to perceive at what points we are using and abusing Black-White "language to cloud our vision, create confusion, or justify various and ever present inclinations toward conflict, war and destruction," (Quigley, 2007, p. 2) we may also tap into "our equally-present inclinations toward cooperation, peace and survival" (Quigley, 2007, p. 2). However, this point is where the Toomer and Ellison correctives regarding legitimate authority of the Negro are necessary for me to translate Burke's ideals into transcending the reproductive characteristics of Black-White thinking gaps. The "Negro problem" doesn't readily place legitimatized authorities in a position to identify with their Black counterparts. Even today, with President Obama, the child of an African immigrant father and a White American mother has simply shifted the question of the BootStrap Guild to "why can't more young Black men be like Obama?" We find a hole then in the ability of privileged Whites to find their liberation tied to underprivileged Black counterparts. Hence, dramatism may overcome racism, only when a more diverse group of actors and agents are on the stage with roles of legitimate authority and with roles of political power.

Wolfe contends that "political power in the United States lies with the middle class" (Wolfe, 1991, p. 91). If she is correct, then Burke's conception of social change via class and other forms of identification could be productive. Burke's conception involves "some ideologically conservative group" being made "functionally radical" (Wolfe, 1991, p. 92). In *Counter-Statement*, Burke (1931) argues, "there is the likelihood of 'rebellion' in America only if there is some conservative group whose interests make it the equivalent of a radical group (p. 118).

Change lies in identification in the ability to cross race, "class lines by mobilizing, for example, the discourse of 'the people' in the interests of 'the worker'" (Wolfe, 1991, p. 86). The search for untapped sites of criticism to connect identities may be the key to political possibilities. Burke helps us see the possibility of new critical categories and his work points toward new sites of criticism for social change (Wolfe, 1991, p. 87).

Fourth, comedy offers possibilities for transcending the "Negro Problem" underlying Black-White test score gap ideology in Burkean thought, but how? Comedy provides a safeguard from the human tendency toward scapegoating and victimization. Comedy warns against the dangers of pride and sin, but its emphasis shifts from crime to haphazard stupidity (Burke, 1937/1984, p. 41). In other words, comedy allows humans to view the self and others as mistaken, "all people are exposed to situations in which they must act as fools, that every insight contains its own special kind of blindness…." (Burke 1937, p. 41). It is through this process that the comic circle is completed and the lesson of humility that underlies all great tragedies proliferates. Burke (1937/1984) then reminds us that "comedy…is the most civilized form of art…the class that can produce good comedy is about as happy as can be" (p. 39).

Kastely (1996) contends that comedy produces more than happiness, but aims to "understand the particular deities that control us: capitalism, technology, and hierarchy" (p. 308). For Burke, comedy is one site where the either/or is substituted by both/and thinking. Comedy is one lead into a Burkean dialectic and hence it should be approached as a critical position, rather than being reduced to some Polyannish utopian mission (Goltz, 2007, pp. 18–19). It is through comedy that Burke takes us to his "perspective of incongruity" (Burke, 1937/1984, p. 308). Goltz (2007) explains that "perspective by incongruity is a way of clouding, problematizing, and interrogating restrictive orientations through" extended metaphors (p. 19). For Burke, comedy may allow one to begin "removing words from their constitutional setting." For example, through comedy, one may begin the reframing of "proficiency tests" underlying the Black-White test score gap as "efficiency tests:" terminology that may help to disrupt the current discourse driving the Bootstrap Guild's psychometric money machine (Burke, 1937/1984, p. 309).

CONCLUSION

In this chapter, I have argued that Kenneth Burke's Dramatism, Unification Device, and the Toomer/Ellison "Harlem" correctives help to (a) discuss how unanticipated and unacknowledged contradictions of the action of language may reproduce Black-White test score gaps, and (b) initiate the work toward a language of transcendence to adequately address the educational malpractice that such unbridled, dichotomous Black-White thinking and efficiency tests engender. As I am working to understand it today, critical social theory was with me each time I anticipated and acknowledged experiences (vicarious or more directly personal) of educational malpractice and stopped to question it with a reflective and/or reflexive posture. Burke's contributions to the cultural politics of race have been particularly useful for understanding and critiquing the power of the Bootstrap Guild and their creation of a robust, commercial test machine to project any potential guilt about the myth of meritocracy onto a Black scapegoat.

Burkean theorizing with the Harlem correctives may offer some transferable tools for teacher leaders, administrators, teacher educators, critical social theorists, educational researchers, and graduate students too, as we continue the lifelong pursuit of cultivating our abilities to "critique institutional as well as conceptual dilemmas, particularly those of domination or oppression," while also promoting a complimentary "language of transcendence…to forge alternative and less oppressive social arrangements" (Leonardo, 2004, pp. 11, 12, 15). Indeed, Kenneth Burke and his openness, albeit sometimes reluctantly toToomer and Ellison, helped to build a movement in critical social theory where Western thought was no longer untouchable; and it is upon their theoretical-critical shoulders that many of us stand. Their work also marked the commencement of refreshing interracialized interpretations, applications, and self-critiques in the U.S. This chapter intended to introduce and extend that scholarship in order to challenge the overemphasis of technology and de-emphasis of destructive racial ideology in Education and educational research; and to challenge the rote drill and kill cognitive curriculum and instruction that the Bootstrap Guild deems beneficial. This type of curriculum and instruction seems to render disproportionately my people as scapegoats of the Black-White test score gap; to trivialize structural racism and mask White privilege; and to overestimate the influence of Black parents and schooling while underestimating the influence of macro-economics and the political economy on parenting and schooling. If these challenges are wrong, then I do not want to be right, as I come to terms each day with the social and emotional cost of the battle against the symbolic rebirth of the Bootstrap Guild and the "Negro problem" they perpetuate under the guise of meritocratic Black-White test score gap ideology.

REFERENCES

Benoit, W. L. (1983). Systems of explanation: Aristotle and burke on cause. *Rhetoric Society Quarterly, 13*, 41–57.

Bloom, H. (1981, May 31). A tribute to Kenneth burke. *Book World*, p. 4.

Brock, B. L., Burke, K., Burgess, P. G., Simons, H. W. (1985). Dramatism as ontology or epistemology: A symposium. *Communication Quarterly, 33*, 17–33.

Brock, B. L. (1992, August). The limits of the Burkeian system. *The Quarterly Journal of Speech, 78*(3), 347–348.

Brummett, B. (1984). Burkean comedy and tragedy, illustrated to the arrest of John.

DeLorean. *Central States Speech Journal, 35*, 217–227.

Brummett, B. (1995, Fall). Speculations on the discovery of a Burkean Blunder. *Rhetoric Review, 14*(1), 221–225.

Bruster, D. (2008, May). Review of Kenneth Burke, *Kenneth Burke on Shakespeare. Early Modern Literary Studies, 14.1*(Special Issue 18), 9.1–9. <URL: http://purl.oclc.org/emls/14-1/revburke.htm>

Burks, D. M. (1991, Fall). Kenneth Burke: The Agro-Bohemian 'Marxoid.' *Communication Studies, 42*, 219–233.

Burke, K. (1931/1968). *Counter-statement*. Berkeley, CA: University of California Press.

Burke, K. (1937/1984). *Attitudes toward history* (Vol. 1). New York: The New Republic Press.

Burke, K. (1939). The rhetoric of Hitler's "Battle". *Southern Review, 5*, 1–21.

Burke, K. (1945/1969). *A grammar of motives*. Berkeley, CA: U of California P, 1969.

Burke, K. (1950/1969). *A rhetoric of motives*. Berkeley, CA: University of California Press.

Burke, K. (1954). *Permanence and change: An anatomy of purpose*. Los Altos, CA: Hermes Publications.

Burke, K. (1955). Linguistic approaches to problems of education (LAPE). *Yearbook of the National Society for the Study of Education, 54*(1).

Burke, K. (1966). *Language as symbolic action: Essays on life, literature, and method*. Berkeley, CA: University of California Press.

Burke, K. (1973). *The philosophy of literary form: Studies in symbolic action* (3rd ed.). Berkeley, CA: The University of California Press.

Burke, K. (1978). Questions and answers about the pentad. *College Compositions and Communication, 29*, 330–335.

Burke, K. (1978, Summer). Non-symbolic motion/symbolic action. *Critical Inquiry, 4*, 809–883.

Burke, K. (1987). Ralph Ellison's trueblooded bildungsroman. In Kimberly W. Benston (Ed.), *Speaking for you: The vision of Ralph Ellison* (p. 350). Washington, DC: Howard University Press.

Burke, K. (1995). The rhetoric of Hitler's battle. In C. R. Burgchardt (Ed.), *Readings in rhetorical criticism* (pp. 206–220). State College, PA: Strata.

Chesebro, J. W. (1999). Multiculturalism and the Burkean system: Limitations and extensions. In B. L. Brock (Ed.), *Kenneth Burke and the 21st century* (pp. 167–188). Albany, NY: State U of New York Press.

Condit, C. (1994, February). Framing Kenneth Burke: Sad tragedy or comic dance? *The Quarterly Journal of Speech, 80*(1), 77–82.

Coupe, L. (2001). Kenneth Burke: Pioneer of ecocriticism. *Journal of American Studies, 35*(3), 413–431.

Crable, B. (2000). Burke's perspective on perspectives: Grounding dramatism in the representative anecdote. *Quarterly Journal of Speech, 86*, 318–333.

Crable, B. (2003). Race and *A Rhetoric of Motives*: Kenneth Burke's dialogue with Ralph Ellison. *Rhetoric Society Quarterly, 33*, 5–25. A Charles Kneupper Award recipient for Best article of 2003 from the Rhetoric Society of America.

Crowell, L. (1997). Three sheers for Kenneth Burke. *The Quarterly Journal of Speech, 63*, 152–167.

de Yonge, J. (1989, March 1). Critics Visit Brings to Mind a Different Time. *Seattle Post-Intelligencer*, p. A11.

Doane, A. W., & Bonilla-Silva, E. (2003). *White out: The continuing significance of racism*. New York: Routledge.

Du Bois, W. E. B. (1903). *The souls of black folks*. Chicago: A.C. McClurg & Co.

Du Bois, W. E. B. (1848, January). The study of the Negro problems. *The Annals of the American Academy of Political and Social Science, XI*, 1–23. Retrieved February 21, 2009, from http://www.webdubois.org/dbStudyofnprob.html

Ellison, R. (1972). *Shadow and act*. New York: Random House, Vintage Books.

Feeney, M. (1988, December 25). Letters that celebrate the life of the mind. *The Boston Globe*.

Foss, S., Foss, K., & Trapp, R. (1991). *Contemporary perspectives on rhetoric* (2nd ed.). (Waveland).

Fox, C. (2002). Beyond the tyranny of the real: Revisiting Burke's pentad as research method for professional communication. *Technical Communication Quarterly, 11*, 365–388.

Genter, R. (2002). Toward a theory of rhetoric: Ralph Ellison, Kenneth Burke, and the problem of modernism. *Twentieth Century Literature: A Scholarly and Critical Journal, 48*, 191–214.

Giamo, B. (2004). An American original. *Harvard Review, 27*, 82–89.

Giddens, A. (1979). *Central problems in social theory: Action, structure and contradiction in social analysis*. London: Macmillan.

Gibson, K. (2005, Spring). Review of Enoch, Jessica. Becoming symbol-wise: Kenneth Burke's pedagogy of critical reflection. *College Composition and Communication, 56*(2), (2004): 279–296. *KB Journal, 1.2*.

Gerth, H., & Mills, C. W. (Eds.) and (Trans.). (1946). Politics as a vocation. In *From Max Weber-1918* (pp. 77–79). New York: Oxford University Press.

Goltz, D. B. (2007, June). Perspectives by incongruity: Kenneth Burke and queer theory. *Genders*, 1–14.

Gordon, J. (2005). Inadvertent complicity: Colorblindness in teacher education. *Educational Studies*, *38*(2), 135–153.

Griffin, E. (2006). *A first look at communication theory* (6th ed.). New York: McGraw-Hill.

Howard, G. (1999). *We can't teach what we don't know*. New York: Teachers College Press.

Hughes, S. 2003. The convenient scapegoating of Blacks in postwar Japan: Shaping the Black Experience Abroad. *Journal of Black Studies*, 33(3), 335-353.

Hyde, M. (Ed.). (2004). *The ethos of rhetoric*. Columbia, SC: University of South Carolina Press.

Jordan, J. (2005). Dell Hymes, Kenneth Burke's 'Identification,' and the birth of sociolinguistics. *Rhetoric Review*, (24), 264–279.

Jencks, C., & Phillips, M. (1998). *The Black-White test score gap*. Washington, DC: Brookings.

Kastely, J. L. (1996, March). Kenneth Burke's comic rejoinder to the cult of empire college English. *58*(3), 307–326.

Kenneth Burke Society. (2008). Conference of the Kenneth Burke Society. *K.B. Journal*. Retrieved October 28, 2009, from http://www.kbjournal.org/cfp2008

Kimberling, C. R. (1982). *Kenneth Burke's dramatism and the study of the popular arts*. Madison, WI: University of Wisconsin Press.

Jackson, L. (2002). Ralph Ellison to Kenneth Burke, November 29, 1945. *Ralph Ellison: Emergence of a Genius*. New York: John Wiley and Sons.

Leonardo, Z. (2004). Critical social theory and transformative knowledge: The functions of criticism in quality education. *Educational Researcher*, *33*(6), 11–18.

Leonardo, Z. (2009). *Race, whiteness, and education*. New York: Routledge.

Manning, P. K. (1999). High risk narratives: Textual adventures. *Qualitative Sociology*, *22*, 285–299.

McPhail, M. L. (2002). *The Rhetoric of Racism Revisited: Reparations or Separation*. Lanham, MD: Rowman and Littlefield.

Miller, K. (2005). *Communication theories: Perspectives, processes, and contexts* (2nd ed.). New York: McGraw-Hill.

O'Meally, R. G. (1994). On Burke and the vernacular: Ralph Ellison's Boomerang of history. In G. Fabre & R. O'Meally (Eds.), *History and memory in African American culture* (pp. 244–260). New York: Oxford University Press.

Pease, D. E. (2003). Ralph Ellison and Kenneth Burke: The Nonsymbolizable (Trans.). Action. *Boundary 2*, *30*(2), 65–96.

Quigley, B. L. (2007). Identification as a key term in Kenneth Burke's rhetorical theory. *American Communication Journal*, *1*(3). Retrieved March 8, 2007, from http://www.acjournal.org/holdings/vol1/iss3/burke/quigley.html

Scruggs, C. (2001). Jean Toomer and Kenneth Burke and the persistence of the past. *American Literary History*, *13*(1), 41–66.

Tompkins, P. K., & Cheney, G. (1993, May). On the limits and sub-stance of Kenneth Burke and his critics. *The Quarterly Journal of Speech*, *79*(2), 225–231.

Toomer, J. (1988). *Cane: An authoritative text, backgrounds, criticism* (D. T. Turner, Ed.). New York: Norton.

Toomer, J. (1924–1925, Autumn-Winter). Oxen cart and warfare. *Little Review*, *10*, 44–48.

Villanueva, V. (2006). Blind: Talking about the new racism. *The Writing Center Journal*, *26*(1), 3–19.

Watts, E. K. (2004). The *ethos* of a black aesthetic: An exploration of Larry Neal's *Visions of a Liberated Future*. In M. J. Hyde (Ed.), *The ethos of rhetoric* (pp. 98–113). Greenville, SC: U of South Carolina P.

Wolfe, C. (1991, Spring). Nature as critical concept: Kenneth Burke, the Frankfurt school, and "Metabiology". *Cultural Critique*, *18*, 65–96. Retrieved from http://www.jstor.org/stable/1354095 Retrieved 2/20/09

Zulick, M. (2004). The ethos of invention: The dialogue of ethics and aesthetics in Kenneth Burke and Mikhail Bakhtin. In J. Michael (Ed.), *The ethos of rhetoric* (pp. 34–55). Hyde: U of South Carolina Press.

Zulick, M. (2008). *Kenneth Burke: A roadmap*. Zulick Home Page. Wake Forest University. Retrieved October 28, 2009, from http://www.wfu.edu/~zulick/4

Sherick Hughes
College of Education
University of Maryland
College Park

SOFIA A. VILLENAS

20. THINKING LATINA/O EDUCATION WITH AND FROM CHICANA/LATINA FEMINIST CULTURAL STUDIES

Emerging Pathways – Decolonial Possibilities

INTRODUCTION

The identification of a geneology of Chicana/Latina cultural production re/articulates "culture" and the production of meaning and meaningful lives from borderlands, border feminist (Saldívar-Hull, 2000), *mestiza* (mixed race woman) and *mujerista* (Latina womanist) perspectives. This chapter focuses on contemporary Chicana/ Latina feminist cultural studies and its current and potential contributions to a critical praxis of education. I explore how Chicana/Latina feminist thought serves to theorize Latina/o education from the histories, epistemologies and knowledge production of those whose lives are carved by the existence of the U.S.-Mexico/Latin American border. Specifically, I excavate a feminist paradigm of cultural production from the pen creative work of Chicana and Latina novelists, poets, artists, essayists, folklorists, and revisionist historians to outline four tenets of Chicana/Latina feminist cultural studies. I discuss how it has influenced scholarship in education by and about Latinas. I then propose how this overlooked set of theoretical perspectives and tools contribute to addressing key themes in Latina/o diaspora/immigrant education, in particular the problematic of assimilation and Americanization.

AN "OTHER" CULTURAL STUDIES: CHICANA/LATINA CULTUAL PRODUCTION

> What might it mean to think critical theory from other places - not simply from the West and from modernity, but from what has occurred in its margins or borders, and with a need to shed light on its underside, that is on coloniality? … Finally, what might this "other" thought afford to the construction of "other" cultural studies, that is to say, a cultural studies of decolonial orientation? (Walsh, 2007, p. 225).

Speaking from the context of indigenous and Afro-Latin America, Walsh (2007) urges attention to the possibilities of constructing a critical cultural studies from "other" knowledges and epistemes. Such a project can shed light on both the continual coloniality of this hemisphere – manifested as social, economic and political marginalization – and on the decolonizing possibilities for a more just

Z. Leonardo (ed.), Handbook of Cultural Politics and Education, 451–476.

social ordering. To be sure, Chicana/o cultural studies and Chicana/Latina feminist cultural studies in particular, emerge from the geopolitical space of the border and borderlands with a decolonizing orientation that "thinks" from hybrid cultural practices, knowledges, and social movements. This thinking encompasses understandings of power involving labor and migration, border/cultural surveillance and exclusionary nationalisms built on economies of race, gender and sexuality (see Chabram-Dernersesian, 2006a, 2007; Saldívar, 1997). As one might imagine, and as Chabram-Dernersesian (2007) emphasizes, this Chicana/o cultural studies breaks with narratives of cultural studies emerging in the 1990s which offered a limited incorporation of legacies of Chicana/o cultural production. In fact, as the following discussion will highlight, Chicana/o cultural studies provides a unique homegrown understanding of globalizing power relations with a border/borderlands perspective that maintains the specificity of the local and hemispheric. Chicana feminist perspectives are thus central to interventions that draw from the "underside of modernity" (Walsh, 2007, p. 225), that is from alternative sites of knowledge production and coalition-building.

Most often, when cultural anthropologists, social theorists, and cultural studies scholars think of the genesis of "cultural production," it is in terms of its roots in British and U.S. cultural studies. In the 1960s, the Center for Contemporary Cultural Studies, founded in Birmingham, England had as its project to fill out the underdeveloped part of Marxian thought – that is, to focus on subjectivity and consciousness (Levinson and Holland, 1996; see Paul Willis, 1981). Rejecting Marx's economic determinism, the interdisciplinary field of cultural studies developed "cultural production" as a conceptual, methodological and political lens to interrogate all aspects of how people live culturally. The field understood cultural forms as producing, resisting, negotiating and articulating in the context of ideological and concrete material and social conditions (Levinson and Holland, 1996).

In the U.S., the work of the CCCS was particularly useful for Chicanas/os and other scholars of color. According to José Saldívar (1997), it "encouraged not only a Birmingham-like engagement with subcultural theory, feminism, and hegemony and its resistance, but also a 'homegrown' orientation for these interventions" (p. 11). This "homegrown orientation" (Saldívar, 1997) has carried an urgency and sensitivity to excavate and emphasize cultural production from a different space – that is, from the lived memories and spatial knowledge of *la frontera* (the border) and borderlands. These memories have been sustained, transformed and proliferated by the literary, artistic, archival/historical, academic/activist work documented as Chicana/o cultural studies (see Aldama and Quiñonez, 2002; Chabram-Dernersesian, 2006a, 2006b, 2007). For example, Saldívar looked at the theorizing about the U.S.-Mexico border zone "as a paradigm of crossings, intercultural exchanges, circulations, resistances, and negotiations as well as of militarized 'low intensity' conflict" (1997, p. ix). Moreover, la frontera as a "militarized" two-thousand mile border between the U.S. and Mexico is also the borderlands/borders experienced in Los Angeles, Chicago, Kansas City and Atlanta. It is the borderlands between El Salvador and Washington D.C., or the highlands of Guatemala and the corn fields, apple orchards and dairy farms of rural upstate New York. It is not empty of culture but is about dynamic, "postmodern" fusions, hybridities, heterogeneities, ambiguities, survivals and struggles, as Chicana theorist Gloria Anzaldúa (1987) highlights. Yet these fusions belong on the same global and "trans-frontera" (Saldívar, 1997) circuits of labor exploitation, violence, wealth, poverty, and anti-immigrant and racial ideologies. In this way, as Chabram-Dernersesian emphasizes, Chicana/o cultural production from the borderlands not only involves historic struggles for survival, political agency and representation, but is pivotal for understanding "a homegrown response to an earlier phase of U.S. expansionism and hegemony, as well as a newer global situation that has pronounced hemispheric implications" (2007, p. 6).

Likewise, reflecting on key directions in Chicana/o cultural studies, Aldama and Quiñonez (2002) insist on a consideration of how the cultural practices of the borderlands speak to the intersections of local, hemispheric and globalized power relations (see also Mignolo, 2000). In other words, Chicana/o cultural studies' theorizing from and on the border/borderlands, has much to contribute to a global understanding of power relations without losing the localized specificity of the U.S./Latin American border materiality and imaginary (Saldívar, 1997 in Aldama, 2002).

Chicana and Latina feminist voices have been at the forefront of theorizing the intersections of the local, hemispheric and global. They have centered a project of recovering and excavating previously ignored and suppressed literary and creative thought, and of creating dialogue and solidarities across diverse communities. A "multiply-positioned" Chicana/o cultural studies (Chabram-Dernersesian, 2007) could not be possible without the voices of Chicanas and Latinas who brought to the forefront other borderlands experiences about gender, sexuality, spirituality, family relations and social movement (see for example Laura Pérez, Yvonne Yarbro-Bejarano, Rosa Linda Fregoso among many other practitioners of Chicana/o feminist cultural studies). Chicanas/Latinas' particular homegrown orientation to feminist, subcultural and resistance interventions are unique and begin with an excavation of alternative, often hidden or non-sanctioned sites of theory production (see Saldívar-Hull, 2000). Saldívar-Hull (2000) explains that these sites include the archives of gossip, rumor and family stories, the female spaces of the domestic, and the hidden spaces of writing such as the prefaces to anthologies and in the interstices of autobiographies (see also Villenas, Delgado Bernal, Elenes and Godinez, 2006). Chicana/Latina cultural production thus emerges from Latinas/Chicanas' everyday lives, epistemologies and pedagogies of the body (Cruz, 2006), rather than from universalized notions of humanity. In this way, Chicanas/Latinas are changing the terms of knowledge production (Brady, 2007), creating tools to articulate borderlands living, and building solidarities in difference.

Chicana/Latina feminist cultural studies (FCS) then, has an important role to play in conversations about cultural studies in education (Elenes, 2002). For example, it can inform the production of curricular knowledge and pedagogy by illuminating how "theory" emerges from specific geographies and histories of struggle. Chicana/Latina FCS introduces different subjectivities and subjects of knowledge as in *la mestiza* (the mixed-race woman) who straddles multiple worlds, languages and sexualities. It thus contributes to a liberatory praxis of education by centering the productive tensions of difference and ambiguity and the rejection of dualistic paradigms. In the following section, I take up the question of the specifics of Chicana/Latina FCS as a de-colonizing project with implications for inquiry in Latino education.

FOUR TENETS OF CHICANA/LATINA FEMINIST CULTURAL STUDIES

What then are the characterizations and contributions of Chicana/Latina cultural production? In the paragraphs that follow, I briefly outline what I imagine to be four tenets of Chicana/Latina FCS which include (1) intersectionality and global solidarity, (2) the dismantling of dualisms, (3) the embracing of ambiguity, and (4) the project of tracking diverse modes of decolonial agency. These tenets are not meant to contain Chicana/Latina FCS; rather they articulate as one of a multitude of ways to express and re-imagine decolonizing feminist modes of being, knowing and acting in the world.

Intersectionality and Global Solidarities: A New Consciousness at the Crossroads

In seeking to understand the complexities of Chicana/Latina subjectivities and projects of empowerment in the borderlands, Chicanas/Latinas have centered how systems of oppression such as racism, sexism, linguicism, heterosexism, immigration surveillance, and class subjugation have impacted their lives and ways of knowing (see for example Anzaldúa, 1987, 2000; Moraga, 1983; Moraga and Anzaldúa, 1983, Castillo, 1994; Cisneros, 1991; Viramontes, 2007; among many others). Like African American and other women of color feminists, Chicanas/Latinas discuss agency and meaning making in the context of simultaneous and interlocking structures of oppression. This task has not been easy under previous decades of Chicano nationalisms, nor in the context of the various feminist movements. For Chicanas, inserting gender and then sexuality in the Chicano movement when racial oppression and valorizing cultural traditions such as *la familia* (the family) took an unquestioned center-stage, has meant facing accusations of selling out (see Alma Garcia, 1997). Poems such as Lorna Dee Cervantes' "You Cramp My Style Baby" explored Chicano patriarchy and how women may be valued as sexual objects but not as thinkers, leaders and social activists (Quiñonez, 2002). On the other hand, inserting race in White radical feminisms served to marginalize and isolate Chicanas and other women of color who faced accusations of engaging in a "self-indulgent identity politics characteristic of a generic feminism" (Saldívar-Hull, 2000, p. 44). Saldívar-Hull sums up this dilemma: "While the men worried that Chicana feminism meant becoming White-influenced, leftist feminists feared that a racialized feminism could only mean indulgence in the concerns of a privatized self "(2000, p. 39). And yet, for first wave Chicana feminists, invoking "Chicana" precisely called attention to the simultaneous identities, identifications and oppressions, and their articulation as a source for social activism. Naomi

Quiñonez (2002) explained how for her and other Chicana feminist writers during the Chicano movement of the late 1960s and early 1970s, the process of decolonizing the mind necessarily involved a deep understanding of the intersecting forms of oppression. It entailed an understanding of praxis and social movement as grounded in collective history and memory, and in present experiences of race, class, gender, sexuality and nation.

Following at least two decades of first wave Chicana feminist writing, literature and art, including *This Bridge Called My Back* co-edited with Cherie Moraga and first published in 1983, Gloria Anzaldua's (1987) *Borderlands/La Frontera* burst onto the scene with the decolonizing project of *la conciencia de la mestiza* (the mestiza consciousness). This mestiza (mixed race woman) straddles cultures, races, languages, nations, sexualities and spiritualities. Every aspect of Anzaldúa's book of multilingual essays, poems, and short story – itself a performance of hybridity and mestizaje – speaks from the intersectionality of oppressions that are histories and practices of racism, sexism, heterosexism, economic exploitation, and "linguistic terrorism" (Anzaldúa, 1987). Yet it is from these spaces that a new consciousness emerges as a third element that breaks down old paradigms and participates in "the creation of yet another culture, a new story to explain the world and our participation in it, a new value system with images that connect us to each other and to the planet" (Anzaldúa, 1987, p. 81). This new consciousness calls for the hard work of "taking inventory" of our pasts, of our mixed bloods, of histories of patriarchy, of the negation of the indigenous, and of an Anglo heritage. It calls for us not to disown "the white parts, the male parts, the pathological parts, the queer parts, the vulnerable parts" and to try a different way, the way of the future, the Chicana way, the mestiza way (Anzaldúa, 1987, p. 88). Thus, while in affinity with but unlike postmodern theorizing, Anzaldúa offered a theory of intersectionality emanating from the body and from a particular geography (Mohanty 1991 cited in Yarbro-Bejarano, 2006). Chandra Mohanty explains this idea at length,

> Unlike a western, postmodernist notion of agency and consciousness, which often announces the splintering of the subject, and privileges multiplicity in the abstract, this [Anzaldúa's] is a notion of agency born of history and geography. It is a theorization of the materiality and politics of the everyday struggles of Chicanas (1991, p. 37, cited in Yarbro-Bejarano, 2006, p. 89).

In this way, the feminist cultural production of Anzaldúa and others has opened the way for Chicanas/Latinas to theorize subjectivities and agency based on a multiplicity of identifications. They have theorized in the midst of invisibility in the Chicano movement, the Women's movement and the mainstream worlds of art, literature and the academy (see Quiñonez, 2002).

Chicanas however did not create subjectivities of victimry. Quiñonez (2002) speaks to the profusion of Chicana literature that exploded in the 1980s and states that Latinas could have languished in discouragement; instead, "as she affirms her Self, the Latina writer engages in a dialectic and dynamic process, transforming those aggressions directed at her into her own strength" (Ortega and Saporta Sternbach, 1989, p. 16, cited in Quiñonez, 2002, p. 137). Quiñonez argues that it is precisely the postmodern condition and accompanying despair and confusion, that provide the fuel and tension not only for the creation of art, but for the transcendence of one's own social, political, economic, and personal limitations" (Quiñonez, 2002, p. 148). Similarly, Laura Pérez (2007a) emphasizes how post-1965 Chicana artists could not help but thematize oppressed cultural differences in their work; yet the Chicana aesthetic space was also a mode of community empowerment, transformation and healing. This theorizing of the self at the crossroads thus contributes to new paradigms for theorizing social consciousness, as Yarbro-Bejarano (2006) emphasizes. Yarbro-Bejarano (2006) states that "only theories of consciousness, such as Anzaldúa's or Sandoval's can elucidate what Richard Johnson calls 'structural shifts or major rearrangements of a sense of self, especially in adult life' (Johnson, 1986/1987, p. 68 cited in Yarbro-Bejarano, 2006, p. 86).

Finally, the project of a new consciousness at the crossroads also entails linking Chicanas/Latinas' de-colonizing struggles to other women, other people, other cultures and other struggles. Chicana/Latina feminisms articulate theory with global dimensions because it invites coalition-building among all people in recognition of our dialogic relationship and its tensions. As Aldama and Quiñonez (2002) insist, Chicana/o cultural studies practitioners have explicitly identified their work in affinity to and in dialogue with domestic, transnational and international cultural studies projects and movements. Global solidarity has meant activism and theory that have worked against political, economic, cultural, gender and homophobic violence at home and abroad. For example, Chicanas identify as "Latinas" to signal solidarity with other U.S. Latinas and as women of color in solidarity with African American, American Indian and Asian American womanists and feminists. The pathbreaking anthology, *This Bridge Called My Back* is a conversation among diverse U.S. Latinas and U.S. Women of Color who speak their "theories of the flesh" as creation, resilience and survival. The Combahee River Collective's black feminist statement in the anthology signals moreover the particular importance of the theoretical/activist work of African American feminists for Chicanas.

Reaching beyond the United States, Saldívar-Hull's (2000) "feminism on the border" is a working solidarity with Latin American women, "Third World" feminist movements, and with political and economic struggles against exploitation and social injustice around the globe. For example, while Chicanas point to the missed encounters between Chicanos/as and Mexicans across borders, they also write of the radical possibilities. In her short story, "Woman Hollering Creek," Sandra Cisneros (1991) writes of Felice, a Chicana who is helping Mexican Cleófilas escape from her abusive husband and return to her family in Mexico. While Cisneros' portrait of the two women illustrates the very different lives, cultural/linguistic practices and sensibilities between Chicanas and Mexicana nationals, it also points to mujerista (Latina womanist) collaboration and mutual learning. Other examples of solidarity across borders most poignantly include a connection with women who have struggled and continue to struggle against exploitation and human rights abuses in the economic and political aftermath of the civil wars and strife in El Salvador, Nicaragua, Guatemala, Honduras and Bolivia (see Gómez, Moraga and Romo-Carmona, 1989; Vigil, 2008). Cross-border solidarities are also created in the midst of the brutal border violence and murders of young Mexican women in Ciudad Juarez (Fregoso, 2003).

Lastly, reaching beyond Latin America, Chicana theorists also place their histories in a global women's context as well as examine global women's issues from Chicana feminist perspectives. Irene Blea's (1997) *U.S. Chicanas and Latinas in a Global Context: Women of Color at the Fourth World Women's Conference*, provides an example of the global dimensions of Chicana/Latinas' alliance-building. Likewise, the mural *Maestrapeace* covering the Women's Building in San Francisco's Latino Mission District is a collective celebration of women's global legacies and histories of struggle and courage. Pérez (2007b) explains how the seven artists of *Maestrapeace* are a group of "multicultural, multisexed" women including two Latinas, one of whom – Irene Perez – was also a founding member of Mujeres Muralistas, the first all-woman mural collective celebrating Latina and Latin American women's lives. In sum, the exploration of how knowledge and identities are produced at the intersections of race, class, gender, sexuality and nation, points to theory-making that is embodied and localized but also with global dimensions. There is specificity to intersectionality which simultaneously allows for always tenuous possibilities for solidarity across difference and borders.

One may see how this first tenet of Chicana/Latina FCS then contributes to portraits of complexity important to redefining the terms of discussion about Latino families. It provides a way to theorize Latino students' and parents' hybrid identities and identifications. It offers a theoretical lens from which to explore the multiple ways that Latina/o students and parents have created lives in response to and in spite of the contradictions of race, class, gender, sexuality, language and nation. For example, long-standing Mexican-origin communities might identify with and create identities in a myriad of social spaces including extended family gatherings across borders, evangelical churches, the U.S. armed forces, and through Mexican or U.S. patriotic activities (see Vélez-Ibañez, 1997). Finally, Chicana/ Latina FCS informs discussions about research methodology. As Latinas/os increasingly become the researchers of their own or other Latino diaspora communities, Chicana/Latina FCS helps us to explore the possibilities for active solidarities and relationships through both connectedness and difference (Villenas, 2006).

Breaking Down Dualisms

> A massive uprooting of dualistic thinking in the individual and collective consciousness is the beginning of a long struggle, but one that could, in our best hopes, bring us to the end of rape, of violence, of war (Anzaldúa, 1987, p. 80).

How we approach interlocking structures of oppression and solidarities across difference, is made possible by the second tenet of Chicana/Latina cultural production – the breaking down of dualisms. Throughout *Borderlands/La Frontera*, Anzaldúa writes and performs a new mestiza consciousness that, "though it is a source of intense pain, its energy comes from continual creative motion that keeps breaking down the unitary aspect of each new paradigm" (1987, p. 80). Pérez (2007a) explores a similar point about Chicana artists. While they thematized oppression, they did so "not by countering one ethnocentrism with another but by blowing apart stereotypes and refusing to replace them with newer ones" (Pérez, 2007a, p. 6). Likewise, Sandoval's (2000) methodology of emancipation and social movement articulated in *Methodology of the Oppressed*, breaks down dualisms and paradigms by marking affinities and contradictions or the decolonial "lines of force and affinity" with other post-humanist thinkers, and by specifically resisting theoretical and disciplinary categorization (Tapia, 2001).

Chicana/Latina writers and artists have indeed exploded dualisms that trap and continue to limit Chicana/Latinas' lives. They challenge such dichotomies as virgin/whore, man/woman, colonized/colonizer, tradition/change and citizen/illegal to name a few. For instance, with respect to the virgin/whore dichotomy, Chicana/ Latina artists such as Ester Hernández, Diane Gamboa and Yolanda Lopez, have re-imagined and reworked Mexico's "women" symbols. These include La Virgen de Guadalupe considered to be the patron saint of Greater Mexico, and Malintzín or La Malinche (also known as Doña Marina), considered whore and traitor to Mexico in her role as aid to Hernán Cortez in the conquest of Mexico. Chicana artists reject patriarchal ideologies of women's worth based on their honor, virtue and passivity by portraying La Virgen de Guadalupe as the image of strong working, athletic, sexual women. Chicana artists and writers acknowledge Malintzín for her courage and intelligence and is refused the title of traitor and whore (see Alarcón, 2006). Anzaldúa speaks of how these dualisms have split the feminine mind and body, spirit and soul: a violence towards women that disempowers them (Anzaldúa and Keating, 2000). Chicanas have thus sought to re-historicize, appropriate, humanize, and sexualize these symbols to explode dualistic categories and express the power rather than the powerlessness of women in history and presently (Villenas, 2006).

Likewise, Chicanas and Latinas have challenged dualistic thinking about *la familia* as the all-good and safe haven for women. In refusing to celebrate static and culturally oppressive notions of la familia, Chicana/Latina writers have brought to light the pain, suffering, violence and abuse that can take place within the home, while also acknowledging women's creativity and power within this same space. For example, the women and girls in Sandra Cisneros' (1985) *The House on Mango Street* encounter the home space as prisons controlled by overbearing fathers and husbands. At the same time, however, la familia is the haven for women's cultural survival and resilience as Cisneros also shows in her portrayal of women's everyday activities in the home (1985, 1991; Anzaldúa and Keating, 2000; see also the portrayal of women and family in Viramontes, 1985/1995). In short, Chicana/ Latina writers have refuted the dichotomies that imprison them as either/or (i.e., either virgins or whores) and in simplistic categories of colonizer (i.e., traitor to la familia) or colonized. Moreover, the putting back together what has been divided up – women's bodies, spiritualities, sexualities and kinships – is a way to move from victimhood to resistance, resilience and creation (Anzaldúa and Keating, 2000, p. 180). As I will explore later, the dismantling of dualisms becomes important in moving outside assimilation frameworks for articulating complex Latina/o subjectivities.

Embracing Ambiguity

> The new *mestiza* copes by developing a tolerance for contradictions, a tolerance for ambiguity . . . she learns to juggle cultures. She has a plural personality, she operates in a pluralistic mode – nothing is thrust out, the good, the bad and the ugly, nothing rejected, nothing abandoned. Not only does she sustain contradictions, she turns the ambivalence into something else (Anzaldúa, 1987, p. 79).

To reject dualisms then and to embrace wholeness requires negotiating ambiguity and ambivalence, the third tenet of Chicana/Latina cultural production. Referring to Chicana/Latina art, Laura Pérez explains how in the context of historical marginalization "subjectivity and agency in this work are complex, and desire and identity are approached through telling ambivalences rather than the pretence of control and omniscience" (2007a, p. 6). As has been discussed, Chicana/Latinas' lives lived in the interstices of oppressions produce profound ambivalences. And yet, as Pérez (2007a) asserts, the response has been one of defying paradigms and the pretence of control, while embracing and mining the power of ambiguity. Or as Anzaldúa asserts in the quote above, the new mestiza sustains contradictions and turns "the ambivalence into something else" (1987, p. 79). Chicanas/Latinas as producers of culture in the interstices are cultural interpreters who negotiate and draw strength from the ambiguities of cultural, racial, sexual and gendered crossings. Going back over 500 years, Quiñonez (2002) draws attention to Malintzín's role of cultural interpreter and mediator during the conquest as "profoundly ambiguous" with "radically divided objectives" of destruction, preservation and creation (Ashcroft, Griffins and Tiffin, 1989/2002, p. 80, cited in Quiñonez, 2002, p. 139). Yet, as Quiñonez (2002) points out, Malintzín embodied the characteristics of intelligence, initiative, adaptability, and leadership at a time of great cultural upheaval, much like first wave Chicana/Latina feminists did and how Chicanas/ Latinas and other racialized people continue to do so in the twenty-first century. In bringing together the notions of dismantling dualisms and embracing ambiguity, Chicana/Latina FCS offers a lens to consider the complex subjectivities of all peoples in their historical context. This includes attention to how Latinas/os construct complex, contradictory and ambiguous identities and identifications around middle class status, mixed-race and mixed ethnicities, hybrid language practices, and between nationalisms. In other words, in differently reading complex Latina/o subjectivities, we reject the dualisms of activist/sellout, resistor/ assimilationist, and colonizer/colonized, to name a few of the binaries. Chicana/Latina cultural production sets a precedent for exploring how Latina/o parents, youths and educators may make deep concessions as part of a response to forging life in borderlands contexts.

Tracking Decolonial Agency

Exploring Latinas/os' cultural production marking solidarity, contradictions, ambiguities and struggles that defy simplistic categorizations and dichotomies requires a theory and method for tracking this agency – a fourth tenet of Chicana/Latina FCS.

In her book *The Decolonial Imaginary: Writing Chicanas into History,* historian and creative writer Emma Pérez (1999) works to break from methods and theories rooted in dominant forms and categories of inquiry in order to trace women's agency. Pérez writes that while women are conceptualized as a background to men's activities, "they are in fact intervening interstitially while sexing the colonial imaginary ... Chicana, Mexicana, Mestiza, India actions, words spoken and unspoken, survive and persist whether acknowledged or not" (1999, p. 7). Pérez (1999) believes women's activities, words and silences have been over-determined as assimilationist rather than as persistent interstitial interventions (see Villenas, 2006).

In conversation with revisionist historian Vicki Ruiz (1998), Pérez (1999) then argues that we need to reconsider diaspora women as creative cultural survivors. In Ruiz's (1998) book, *Out of the Shadows: Mexican Women in Twentieth Century America,* Mexican American women are portrayed as using what was available to them to intervene with their own tactics as diasporic subjects claiming survival. To say yes to English, yes to an American education and yes to participation in mainstream organizations were interstitial moves for survival (Pérez, 1999). The contradictions women faced compelled them to accept existing structures and to create their subjecthood within those structures. This does not mean that women lived comfortably within a patriarchal order, whether in the old country or the new, as Pérez (1999) reminds her readers. Ruiz (2007) speaks of the aims of her book as providing "an understanding of what decisions they [Mexican origin women] could make within the parameters of their world, of considering the structural elements in their lives (deportation, repatriations, poverty) as well as their possibilities and aspirations" (p. 97). Ruiz was also interested in looking at "the ways in which their relationship with popular culture fed their dreams" (2007, p. 97).

How then do we track this agency, these interstitial moves for survival, and these subtle interventions? Pérez appropriates postcolonial theorist Homi Bhabha's notion of the "dialectics of doubling," to "refer to the manner in which women 'doubled' with men's agendas, seeming to agree, yet in actuality articulating their own position" (p. 141). With this notion of "doubling," Pérez traces these interventions or "third space feminisms" in three historical moments – Yucatan's feminist congresses between the years 1910–1920s; the Partido Liberal Mexicano, an anarchosyndicalist, transnationalist organization in the Los Angeles of the early 1900s; and Mexican community and civic organizations of Texas in the 1930s. Pérez argues that while women's politics have been subordinated under the nationalist, internationalist, and cultural agendas of these historical moments, "women as agents have always constructed their own spaces interstitially, within nationalisms" (1999, p. 33) and other agendas. This theory and method for tracking agency, that is, of excavating women's "doubling" and subtle interventions, opens up new questions for inquiry and new insights and possibilities for articulating Latina/os' lives and subjectivities. For example, how does cultural survival come into play when thinking about some Latino parents' insistence on English only or some Latina/o students' rejection of the home language and adoption of certain dominant cultural norms?

How might Latino educational research sense Latino youths' subtle interventions and how they create interstitial spaces of agency characterized by contradictions and doubling?

Similarly, Chela Sandoval (2000) brilliantly contributes to a decolonizing theory and method for tracking agency. For Pérez (1999) and Sandoval (2000, 2007), the differential consciousness, the new mestiza or the decolonial imaginary is activated within the interstices of difference and oppressions that produce ambivalent spaces of dissonance, as discussed earlier. It is from these spaces then, that it becomes possible to intervene in the slippages of meaning and to counter dominant ideologies that support unequal relations of power. For Sandoval (2007), when one deploys the differential mode of consciousness such as *la conciencia de la mestiza*, "You have entered the place where signs are made and linked, you become aware of moving around in that realm where normalizing systems are challenged" (p. 73). Sandoval (2000) describes the resulting mobile and tactical subjectivities and their potential for alliance-building and social movement as not true or false, "only possible, active, and present" (pp. 179–180). In working the affinities and exchanges between liberatory post-humanist, postcolonial and third world feminist thought, Sandoval describes a methodology "developed by the oppressed under previous social formations and which is now re-emerging as useful to all citizen-subjects who must learn to negotiate, survive, and transform present social conditions into better worlds come to life" (2000, p. 179). In this way, Sandoval elevates the differential consciousness (such as la conciencia de la mestiza) to the level of a methodology applicable to all human beings who are struggling to create a more just world. Undoubtedly, the tracking of decolonial agency as a fourth tenet of Chicana/Latina cultural production is at the heart of theory and methods for thinking Latino education with and from Chicana/Latina feminist cultural studies.

THINKING LATINA/O EDUCATION WITH AND FROM CHICANA/LATINA FEMINIST CULTURAL STUDIES

I have described what I imagine to be four tenets of Chicana/Latina feminist cultural studies. I highlighted intersectionality with an emphasis on the emergence of self at the crossroads and always tenuous solidarities across difference, second, the dismantling of dualisms, third, the embracing of ambiguity, and finally a theory and method for tracking decolonial agency. Chicana/Latina FCS shares affinities with other Latino critical and critical race theories and perspectives (see Elenes and Delgado Bernal, 2010; Yosso, 2006). Research informed by these intersecting perspectives probe Latinas/os' education and schooling experiences (Delgado-Bernal, 2001, 2002; Solórzano, 1998; Villalpando, 2003; Yosso, 2005, 2006), explore liberatory spaces of teaching and learning (see Elenes, 2001; Cammarrota, 2007; Trinidad Galván, 2006; and Dyrness, 2008 among others), and articulate complex Latina/o subjectivities. Such research also documents how Latina/o youths, parents, teachers and adult learners create, interpret and appropriate knowledge, culture and language (see Delgado-Gaitan, 1994, 2001; Gonzalez, 2001; Guerra, 1998; Gutierrez and Rogoff, 2003; Zentella, 1997 among many others). To be sure, the field of Latina/o education includes a vibrant community of scholars and scholar-activists who are producing a rich body of knowledge aimed at transforming inequitable social conditions (Villenas and Foley, 2002; Irizarry and Nieto, 2010; Zarate and Conchas, 2010). This research, most often interdisciplinary, is informed by the geopolitics of *la frontera* (the border), inflected with borderlands sensibilities and consciously activated within histories of struggles (Villenas and Foley, 2002). And yet, the systematic articulation of Chicana/Latina FCS with the field of education and Latino education specifically, has been very sparse (see Elenes, 2002).

A post-1980s second generation of Chicana/Latina feminist-oriented scholars/researchers brought with them to the academy an engagement with the Chicana/Latina literature, art and critical writings that exploded in the previous decade. Our paths to both the academy and Chicana/Latina feminist thought had been paved by first wave Chicana/Latina feminists and other Latino/a scholars. However, in the social sciences, and specifically in the field of education, we did not have examples for how to systematically think about education through the lens of Chicana/Latina FCS. Certainly, as Elenes (1997) states, the impact of postcolonialism, postmodernism, poststructuralism, ethnic studies and third world feminisms, made it possible for the concept of borderlands and borders to take hold in critical educational thought. Elenes (1997) argued early on that the discourse of the Borderlands as a contribution of Chicana/o scholarship, and particularly from the pen of Chicana feminists such as Gloria Anzaldúa, served as a theoretical framework to advance educational theory. Elenes identified its affinities and disjunctures with the border pedagogies articulated by critical theorists Henry Giroux and Peter McLaren. As one of the few scholars thinking education through Chicana/Latina feminist cultural studies, Elenes (2001, 2002) went on to conceptualize a border/transformative critical pedagogy from Chicana feminist perspectives. For Elenes, border transformative pedagogies recognize "that the borderlands characteristics of Chicanas/os are paradigmatic of the subject positions of people of color in the United States" (2001, p. 255).

Recently, Chicana/Latina feminist thought has been deployed as theory and method to probe Latinas/Chicanas' educational experiences, and ways of knowing, teaching, learning and doing research (see Delgado Bernal, Elenes, Godinez, and Villenas, 2006; Delgado Bernal, 2001; Dyrness, 2008; González, 2001; Revilla, 2004; Burciaga, 2007; Cuádraz, 2005). With the publication of the first special issue on Chicana/Latina education in the *International Journal of Qualitative Studies in Education* (see Elenes et al., 2001), and a subsequent edited volume, *Chicana/Latina Education in Everyday Life* (Delgado Bernal et al., 2006), my colleagues and I were interested in first, re-framing Latina spaces of teaching and learning as educational sites, and second, conceptualizing Latinas' educational experiences from high school age to mature adulthood through Chicana/Latina feminist perspectives (Villenas, Godinez, Delgado Bernal and Elenes, 2006).

An examination of the pedagogical characteristics and value of Latina spaces of teaching and learning in current and past literature yielded a wealth of de-colonizing modes of agency. These include pedagogies of the home (Delgado Bernal, 2006), pedagogies of the brown body (Cindy Cruz, 2006), *convivencia* or the praxis of conviviality (Carrillo, 2006; Dyrness, 2008; Trinidad Galván, 2006), *sobrevivencia* (agency beyond mere survival) (Trinidad Galván, 2006) , *la facultad* or intuitive knowing (Anzaldúa, 1987), *humor casero* (womanist humor) (Carrillo, 2006), *consejos y historias* (narrative advice and stories) (Delgado-Gaitan, 1994), and to *valerse por si misma* or to be self-reliant (Villenas and Moreno, 2001), to name a few. This scholarship also operationalized Anzaldúa's now oft-cited mestiza consciousness and borderlands (Anzaldua, 1987) in order to explore, for example, how high school and college age women negotiate multiple identities and navigate institutional barriers (see Knight et al., 2006; Godinez, 2006; Delgado Bernal, 2006; Burciaga and Tavares, 2006; Revilla, 2004). The above scholarship, then, points to the influence that Chicana/Latina feminist thought has had in conceptualizing women's agency and subjectivities in diverse education contexts. Its praxical effort involves fostering Latinas' educational success, and in turn, the education and welfare of children and their communities. Yet, this scholarship *by* Latinas who are severely under-represented in the academy, *about* Latinas who are marginalized in the larger society, and that utilizes a subalternized set of theoretical tools – Chicana/Latina feminist cultural studies – undoubtedly runs the risk of theoretical/conceptual isolation and invisibility. In returning to Anzaldúa (1987) and Sandoval (2000) who model how decolonizing methodologies may be enacted by all people seeking a more just society, it is appropriate to ask how we might articulate key issues in education, specifically Latina/o education, through Chicana/Latina feminist perspectives. In what follows, I re-read the theme of Latino-immigrant/diaspora education, and specifically the problematic of assimilation and Americanization, through the lens of Chicana/Latina feminist cultural studies.

LATINO IMMIGRANT/DIASPORA EDUCATION

From the lens of Chicana/Latina FCS, a discussion of Latina/o immigrant and diaspora education cannot help but begin with a hemispheric Amerindian sensibility of both place and movement as part of a millennium-old process. In this sense and as I have written elsewhere (Villenas, 2007), Latinas/os have long challenged the ahistoricism of the category "immigrant" when we are inspired to think of ourselves as belonging to these Americas, despite the creation and maintenance of nation-state borders (Villenas, 2007). Further, a diasporic orientation enables an interrogation of nation and all that nationalisms erase such as indigeneity and Black identities, diverse sexualities and genders, and processes of racialization. It enables a reconceptualization of diasporic and postnational subjectivities. Pérez (1999) explains how Anzaldua's (1987) *Borderlands/La Frontera* issued "a 'new' postnational project in which *la nueva mestiza*, the mixed-race woman, is the privileged subject of an interstitial space that was formerly a nation and is now without borders, without boundaries" (p. 25). Pérez reads the new mestiza as the always gendered transformative diasporic subject who is "not only here and there, is not only Mexican or American, or Mexican American, or Chicano/a, but more, much more" (1999, p. 79). Following suit, this section focuses on how such modes of living diasporic subjectivities are not to be neither understated nor over-determined as assimilation and Americanization. Specifically, I examine this focus through discussions on Latino school achievement and youth inter-group relations, young women's racialized gender and class experiences, parents' cultural practices, and family and community resilience. Through the lens of Chicana/Latina FCS, I examine literature that explores how both Latino parents and youths remake their cultural and linguistic practices across generations and borders in multiple and contradictory ways. I read these practices of teaching and learning, knowledge production and resilience alongside a Chicana/Latina feminist orientation to theory building from the margins.

Assimilation and Americanization

Chicana/Latina FCS challenges the usefulness of the notions of Americanization and assimilation including both its negative connotation on the part of Latino critical scholars and activists, and its positive connotations in mainstream discourses of difference. To return to the first tenet of Chicana/Latina FCS, intersectionality points to how people carve out their lives along the faultlines of race, class, gender, sexuality, nation, and language. It highlights complex and contradictory subjectivities formed at the crossroads and in the borderlands. Most importantly, operationalizing the tenets of dismantling dualisms and embracing ambiguity requires differently reading Latino subjectivities outside such binaries as activist/sellout, assimilated/resistor or Americanized/ethnicized. Chicana/Latina FCS offers a perspective for excavating complex negotiations of multiple identities and contexts, and to privileging the "interstial moves for survival" (Pérez, 1999) in all their contradictions, tensions and ambiguities.

An attempt at differently reading Latina/o diaspora subjectivities does well to begin with Richard Rodriguez's (1982) now canonical yet controversial autobiography, *Hunger of Memory*, in which the author argues against bilingual education and race-based affirmative action. From a Chicana/Latina FCS perspective, how might it be fruitful to read Rodriguez's autobiography as involving contradictory moves for survival within the interstices of power? In moving against binaries of assimilation, a close examination of Richard Rodriguez's autobiography and call for assimilation might reveal those ambiguous spaces and tensions from which people fashion identities, actions and decisions in the borderlands. Rodriguez describes the pain of moving towards English-only in the home, and the silence and disconnection that ensued, particularly between father and son. Rodriguez's parents' decision to not speak Spanish to their children may be viewed as complex negotiations within structures of inequality where Mexicanness and the Spanish language are devalued. Rodriguez writes of his father: "In Spanish, he expressed ideas and feelings he rarely revealed in English. With firm Spanish sounds, he conveyed confidence and authority English would never allow him" (1982, p. 24). And yet, in the same breath, Rodriguez decries middle class Hispanics' calls for bilingual education and their rejection of assimilation. At this moment however, the binaries of Americanized/sell-out, assimilated/clinging-to-culture and assimilated/resistor lose their meanings. These binaries signal static and linear conceptualizations of identity and agency which deny Rodriguez's profoundly ambiguous role as cultural interpreter and queer Latino man. These binaries deny the deep concessions that are his and his parents' responses to disambiguating life in the borderlands, as González (2001) so aptly puts it. In this sense, such dualistic paradigms belie people's complex and contradictory responses to the structural forces of coloniality that are still lived as social and economic disenfranchisement. The negative and positive uses of assimilation and its related binaries in both critical and mainstream discourse do little but endorse simplistic interpretations of parenting, youth identities and Latino educational achievement.

Latino Youths: Integration, Inter-Group Relations and School Achievement

I read the field of Latino education with its borderlands and trans-border sensibilities as moving against binarisms and dualistic paradigms in concert with research that further complicates the notion of assimilation and Americanization. A sensibility toward a perspective of borderlands intersectionality can be seen in the research concerning the differences in Latino educational achievement among youths of different generations in the U.S. and along the intersecting axes of race, class and gender. Nancy Lopez (2003) describes the dominant approach for studying the second generation as the ethnicity paradigm. With this framework, the focus is on uncovering "the cultural characteristics of a given immigrant group and examining whether the values of a given ethnic group have facilitated or stunted their process of becoming 'American' via assimilation" (p. 4). In other words, losing one's ethnic distinctiveness or cultural practices – that is, assimilation – is assumed necessary for intergenerational upward mobility. In contrast, as Lopez explains, segmented assimilation theory emerged to account for the different trajectories or multiple ways in which the children of post-1965 immigrants have been incorporated into different segments of U.S. society. These trajectories include upward incorporation into white mainstream middle class, downward into racially stigmatized low-income groups, or through an alternative route of claiming their own ethnic distinctiveness while also experiencing upward mobility (see Portes and Zhou, 1993). An ethnic group's mode of incorporation, its color, its place of residence, social networks and the cultural capital of each community influence the type of assimilation (Portes and Zou, 1993, cited in Lopez, 2003).

From the lens of Chicana/Latina FCS and in agreement with Lopez (2003), the segmented assimilation theory is an important and positive move because it posits cultural and ethnic distinctiveness as an alternative and important route for social mobility in the U.S. It complicates "assimilation" by referring instead to multiple modes of incorporation. However, the notion of "assimilation" remains an unchallenged category and a binarism that does not seem to account for how people disperse/remake their cultural and linguistic practices over time and space in multiple and contradictory ways. With a Chicana/Latina feminist view of both the local specificity and domestic/global dimensions of intersectionality and a decolonial agency that is activated within the interstices of difference, we might in addition highlight the hybrid cultural practices and political possibilities between stigmatized racialized groups. For example, Chicanas/Latinas' connections to other U.S. Women of Color as explored in Moraga and Anzaldua's (1983) *This Bridge Called My Back* or Anzaldúa and Keating's (2002) *This Bridge We Call Home* is pivotal theory-making for understanding the diverse ways in which women of color are racialized and how they collectively challenge racial, class, gender, and heterosexual oppression.

In a similar vein, Kasinitz, Mollenkopf and Waters (2002) explore how the experiences of the Latino diaspora's second generation in majority minority immigrant gateways such as New York City further complicate the notion of "assimilation," whether linear, segmented or otherwise. They highlight the positive outcomes of immigrant youths' identifications and socialization with native minority youths in terms of education, jobs and identity formation. They also highlight the vibrant youth culture created through immigrant - native minority relationships and how these youths are living difference in remarkably creative ways. As Kasinitz, Mollenkopf and Waters assert, these youths are creating a vibrant youth culture that is neither "immigrant" nor "middle American" but something new (2002, p. 1022, also cited in Villenas, 2007). This study of Latinos/as in New York City is an account of new kinds of consciousness at the crossroads. Importantly, it leads us to consider the complex relationships and politics that divide, but also the political and social possibilities between different generations of Latino/a diaspora students (see Bejarano, 2005; Valenzuela, 1999; Gibson, Gandara and Koyama, 2004).

The complex schooling experiences and relationships between first generation immigrant and second-generation youths are also documented in qualitative and ethnographic studies of Latino youths in high school contexts. Bejarano (2005) and Valenzuela (1999) for example studied the relationships between U.S. identified and Mexican-identified students and the differences in their school achievement and school involvement. These authors complicate formulaic notions of cultural assimilation for school success. Instead, they highlight identity-making practices that divide and sometimes unite immigrant and U.S.-born Latinas/os, and of schools that racialize, alienate, and "subtract" their cultural and linguistic resources. Both Bejarano (2005) and Valenzuela (1999) situate their students' identity-making and schooling practices within the specific cultural and social politics of the U.S./Mexican-Latin American border – a border which as Bejarano (2005) writes, "provides legitimacy for some over others and reinforces the vestiges of colonialism that saturate the region and the entire country for 'brown people'" (p. 33). Bejarano goes on to underscore how "colonialism and Latina/o youths' internalization of colonialism has permeated their lives and poisoned their relationships with other Latinas/os by causing friction between first-, second-, and third-generation people" (2005, p. 33). She attributes these conflicts to youths' understandings of themselves through the prism of dominant society's non-valuing of Latinos, and "how they are viewed in a country driven by nationalist rhetoric about becoming 'American'" (Bejarano, 2005, p. 33). Similarly, Valenzuela (1999) comes to the conclusion that negative and at best ambiguous views about immigrants and Latinos, along with the centrality of cultural/linguistic assimilation as a requirement for school success, all play a role in fracturing Latino students' relationships and undermining collaborative possibilities for educational achievement. For instance, the sharing of important social networks and Mexican national students' counter-narratives about the positive cultural value of Mexicanness are made difficult via a school system and a society that devalue Latinos' diverse worldviews and cultural resources.

Both Bejarano (2005) and Valenzuela (1999) are influenced by a Chicana feminist borderlands perspective (Anzaldúa, 1987) as they emphasize bicultural, hybrid, ambiguous and contradictory youth practices. From the lens of Chicana/Latina FCS, border youths are cultural survivors and cultural translators who are fashioning their subjecthood within the geopolitics of the border. To say yes to English only or to reject their Mexican- or Latin American-born peers, does not mean that these youths lived comfortably with racism, sexism and discrimination, as Ruiz (1998) emphasized in her history of Mexican American women. The possibilities for a new consciousness at the crossroads are always already there in the narratives of border youths who articulated the intersectionality of their experiences and the tensions of coalition-building (see also Cammarrota, 2008).

Young Women's Racialized Gender and Class Experiences

An operating perspective of intersectionality in conversations about assimilation and Americanization also produces queries about young Latinas' racialized gender experiences and home-grown feminisms rooted in trans-national histories (Lopez, 2003; Rolón-Dow, 2004; Miranda, 2003). Lopez (2003) puts in motion an operating perspective of intersectionality in her research with second-generation Dominican, Haitian and Anglophone West Indian youths. She argues that the segmented assimilation theory, while important and positive in many respects, still treats race and gender as static categories and ignores how "the second generation is treated like racialized and gendered bodies" in U.S. society (p. 5). Lopez points to how place of residence, social networks and cultural capital are all racialized and gendered. She then puts to work a race-gender experience framework developed from race theories and critical race and women of color feminisms to explain the race and gender disparities in urban education. She asks why it is that racialized women attend college at a higher rate than their male counterparts. She goes on to complicate the assimilationist explanation for young women's educational attainment and independence. As Lopez explains, young women develop a home-grown feminism in their desire for independence and higher education precisely through a sense of being rooted within a history of women kin – mothers, grandmothers, aunts – who have worked and sacrificed for their daughters to have a better life. This contextualization and connection to the history, memory and geographies of women is at the core of Anzaldúa's "new mestiza" politics and Saldívar-Hull's "feminism on the border." As Saldívar-Hull (2000) so eloquently states, Chicana/Latina feminisms articulate because of its genesis in the lives and brown bodies of our mothers.

Bettie (2000, 2003), Rolón-Dow (2004) and Miranda (2003) also explore intersecting oppressions as well as emerging modes of consciousness at the crossroads. Importantly, they do so in ways that debunk categorical binaries of assimilation equating school success with dominant class, race, gender and heteronormative performances. Bettie (2000) gives credit to third world feminist thought to argue the perspective that such categories are not a-priori but historically composed and socially performed as intersecting hierarchies (see Mohanty, 1991 and Anzaldúa, 1987). For example, the Mexican American high-school women in Bettie's study performed gender in ways that were "shaped by a nascent knowledge of racial/ethnic and class hierarchies" (2000, p. 4). Bettie argues that the enactments of femininity on the part of las chicas (Latina "girls") and las cholas (Latina "girls" in gangs) – utilizing varying markers of tight clothing, dark make-up – were not about romance and boys per se, but were as much about enactments of class and race. Similarly, the Puerto Rican girls in Rolón-Dow's (2004) study were described by high school staff as "oozing" with sexuality. Rolón-Dow explored the racialized and class overlay in the discourse surrounding Puerto Rican high school women's sexuality, and how it was dichotomized from their intellectual development.

Yet even for the young Latinas in Bettie's study who experienced school success, "assimilation" and Americanization were complicated in the web of race-gender-class hierarchies. College-bound U.S.-born Latinas were subject to the Americanization process that Olsen (1998) identifies for immigrant students, mainly that they must find their place in the U.S. racial order. These Mexican American young women worked to find their place (while also working against this very task) by creating ties with their non-college-bound Latina peers as ways to merge or reconcile identities of school success and ethnicity-race-class. Unfortunately, college-bound Latinas were offered few discursive tools from which to articulate the effects and their responses to such historically composed intersecting hierarchies.

Notwithstanding, Latina and Latino youths – including the Mexican American, Puerto Rican and Dominican young women in these studies – do create their own tools for living out the ambituities of the borderlands. Miranda's (2003, p. 3) study of "girls in gangs speaking on behalf of themselves" implicitly operationalized "Chela Sandoval's (2000) analysis of the processes and products by which women of color respond to their objectification: the 'methodology of the oppressed'" (Miranda, 2003, p. 6). In their own video production of themselves and in public forums, the Latina girls in gangs represented themselves, their gang and identity practices, and their relationships with each other in complex and nuanced ways. They shattered simplistic and dichotomous interpretations of gang life; for example the stereotype that girl gang members fight over boys obscures the close-knit and romantic friendships between the young women (p. 95). In this way, Miranda's book is a self-reflective ethnography of the multiple clashing and colluding representations by and about girls in gangs. Sandoval (2007) writes that in order to create liberatory knowledge, we need to be "self-conscious, self-reflective about how our produced knowledge may be positioned inside power" (p. 75).

The aforementioned studies concerning Latinas' racialized gender experiences, their home-grown feminisms and their methodologies of the oppressed (Sandoval, 2000), exemplify affinities with Chicana/Latina FCS. This research emphasizes how young Latinas carve out their lives along the fault lines of race, class, gender and sexuality in relation to school success, and how they represent themselves in the process. For educators to differently read Latina subjectivities outside the binaries of assimilation and Americanization – including those equating school success with "good girl" race-gender-class-sexuality performances – is to move towards creating authentically engaging spaces of teaching and learning.

Latino Parents

As we have seen, attention to the hybrid cultural practices of second-generation youth has been central to the field of Latino education (Cammarota, 2008; Lopez, 2003; Rolón-Dow, 2004; Miranda, 2003; Valenzuela, 1999). Yet, it has been equally important to consider the same for the immigrant/diaspora parent (see for example Vasquez, Pease-Alvarez and Shannon, 1994; Delgado-Gaitan, 2001; González, 2008; Villenas, 2001, 2002; Stanton-Salazar, 2001). Most often, an assimilation and Americanization model assumes the first generation to be the originators of a particular Latino culture. In the Americanization narrative, cultural change is linear; parents replace their native language with English and adopt dominant cultural practices in order to be fully integrated into an ideal mainstream U.S. society (Ngo, 2008). Similarly, the "culture clash" perspective on immigrant parent–U.S.-born child relationships assumes parents to be static in their traditions and cultural practices (Ngo, 2008). However, parents are also figuring out their identities as mestizo, indigenous, white, or Afro-Latin American nationals (maybe becoming more indigenous Ecuadorian in the U.S. than in Ecuador). They are figuring out their responses to their gendered racialization as "immigrants" and global/transnational workers. They are working out what it means to be a parent and a "citizen" (authorized or not) in the U.S. as they engage in practices of community building and socialization vis-à-vis their children and members of their social networks (Villenas, 2007; see Dyrness, 2008; Vasquez, Pease-Alvarez and Shannon, 1994; Gonzalez, 2001, 2008; Stanton-Salazar, 2001). Undoubtedly, parents are engaging in their own theorizing of the self at the crossroads.

Research in education concerning Latino parents is often dominated by the issue of parental involvement in K-12 schools. However, what most often is missing from the dominant discourse on parent involvement are discussions of Latino parents' own hybrid cultural practices as teachers and learners in their families and communities. The question at hand is how parents sustain the contradictions and ambivalence of raising children in new and old borderlands, indeed how they turn the ambivalence into something else (Pérez, 2007a). My research with Latino parents in North Carolina during its transformation as a new Latino destination in the mid 1990s, revealed the struggles and hopes for both tradition and change (Villenas, 2002; Villenas and Moreno, 2001). Parents critiqued what they viewed as lax social norms or *libertinaje* in the United States, and espoused their own family education as a rich resource from which to impart important life lessons of *una buena educacion* (a good education) to their children (Villenas 2002). However, parents also were engaged in rethinking their own upbringing and who they had become as a result of their own childhood experiences and the trials of labor, migration, settlement and parenting in a new diaspora town. In rethinking selves at the crossroads, parents expressed their desires for different and better relations with their children (Villenas, 2002). At the same time, I heard mothers talk about teaching *sobrevivencia* (survival and beyond) to their daughters through *consejos* (advice), *cuentos* (stories) and *la experiencia* (experience) (Villenas and Moreno, 2001). Similar to Ruiz's (1998) history of Mexican American women, these lessons of creative survival were a contradictory mix of acquiescence and rebellion to prescribed gender and heteronormative roles in a racialized landscape.

Almost fifteen years later in a new diaspora suburban town in Pennsylvania, Mexicanos/as are responding to dominant narratives of immigrant assimilation with an ambivalence from which they re-create stories of self, family and community in transnational spaces (see also Lukose, 2007). As part of a larger study about emerging models of identity in this new Mexican diaspora community (see Wortham, Allard and Mortimer, 2006), I participated in conversations with one of the first Latino extended families to settle in the town. Extended members of this entrepreneurial and modestly successful family mobilized the immigrant and assimilation narrative in contradictory and ambivalent ways. They simultaneously critiqued the inhumane practices of U.S. immigration policies, framed success in terms of the dominant assimilation framework, and honoured their own unique cultural, linguistic and familial practices (Villenas, 2009). Clearly, when one considers parents' "doubling" (Pérez, 1999) and "emergent practices" (O'Leary, González and Valdez-Gardea, 2008) as part of living transnational lives, what does it mean then to assimilate? Like their children, parents too represent fluid, contradictory and ambivalent lives. They creatively survive and are always in process of constructing viable identities and parenting practices in the borderlands and at the crossroads (González, 2001). From a Chicana/Latina FCS sensibility, dichotomies are refuted, ambivalence is mined, and hemispheric and global solidarities of emotion and pragmatics across borders and difference are explored.

CONCLUSION: TOWARDS DECOLONIAL POSSIBILITIES

Laura Pérez (2007a) has discussed how Chicana artists mined the ambivalence of intersectionality and turned it into art, power, resource, resilience. The same can be said for the vast funds of knowledge and cultural wealth of a community (Gonzalez, Moll and Amanti, 2005; Yosso, 2006). In the field of Latino/a education, scholars/educators have worked to excavate and name the knowledge and cultural practices which have long sustained Latino communities in the U.S. For instance, González, Moll and Amanti (2005) argue that a community's intellectual, material, social and emotional resources are historically accumulated knowledge which enable families to deal with changing and often difficult social and economic circumstances. Similarly, Yosso (2006) describes the cultural wealth of communities in terms of their bilingual/multilingual assets, familial support, social networks, strategies to navigate often unfriendly institutions and parents' aspirations for their children. These modes of knowing and living in the borderlands with all their ambiguities and contradictions are the stuff from which decolonial possibilities emerge. Latina/Chicana FCS articulates youths' and parents' funds of knowledge and cultural wealth including the knowledge or meta-awareness of how power works in everyday life. It articulates the struggles to own language and culture via the dismantling of entrenched dichotomies. It articulates how youth and parents embrace the ambiguities of straddling worlds. And while divisions and conflict are certainly rife, cross-generational and hemispheric/global solidarities are also at work. We see these possibilities in families' and youths' transnational practices as they live and exchange information across borders (see Sánchez and Machado-Casas, 2009). We see them in the activist work of the second generation bilingual youth and young adults who are translating, bridging worlds and advocating for immigration, health and education rights on behalf of their parents and diaspora communities. Bilingual Latina/o teachers and paraprofessionals too are doing incredible work as advocates for Latino bilingual children (Monzo & Rueda, 2001; Jackson, 2009; Prieto, 2009). To be sure, there is much work to be done. Challenging such dualistic categories as assimilation and Americanization that have worked to define who Latinas/os are, who Latinas/os can be and what Latinas/os can do is one point of entry. This chapter has merely scratched the surface in exploring how Chicana/Latina feminist cultural studies can guide re-imaginings of Latino education and community uplift.

REFERENCES

Alarcón, N. (2006). Chicana feminism: In the tracks of "the" native woman. In A. Chabram-Dernersesian (Ed.), *The Chicana/o cultural studies reader* (pp. 183–190). New York: Routledge, Taylor and Francis Group.

Aldama, A. J. (2002). Millenial anxieties: Borders, violence, and the sruggle for Chicana and Chicano subjectivities. In A. J. Aldama & N. H. Quiñonez (Eds.), *Decolonial voices: Chicana and Chicano cultural studies in the 21st century* (pp. 11–29). Bloomington, IN: Indiana University Press.

Aldama, A. J., & Quiñonez, N. H. (2002). Introduction: ¡Peligro! Subversive subjects: Chicana and Chicano cultural studies in the 21st century. In A. J. Aldama & N. H. Quiñonez (Eds.), *Decolonial voices: Chicana and Chicano cultural studies in the 21st century* (pp. 1–7). Bloomington, IN: Indiana University Press.

Anzaldúa, G. (1987). *Borderlands/la frontera: The new mestiza.* San Francisco: Aunt Lute Books.

Anzaldúa, G. (author), & Keating, A. (Ed.). (2000). *Gloria E. Anzaldúa: Interviews/entrevistas.* New York: Routledge.

Anzaldúa, G., & Keating, A. (Eds.). (2002). *This bridge we call home: Radical visions for transformation.* New York: Routledge.

Ashcroft, B., Griffiths, G., & Tiffin, H. (1989/2002). *The empire writes back: Theory and practice in postcolonial literatures.* New York: Routledge.

Bejarano, C. L. (2005). *¿Qué onda? Urban youth culture and border identity.* Tucson, AZ: University of Arizona Press.

Bettie, J. (2000, autumn). Women without class: Chicas, cholas, trash, and the presence/absence of class identity. *Signs: Journal of Women in Culture and Society, 26*(1), 1–35.

Bettie, J. (2003). *Women without class: Girls, race and identity.* Berkeley, CA: University of California Press.

Blea, I. (1997). *U.S. Chicanas and Latinas within a global context. Women of color at the fourth World women's conference.* Westport, CT: Praeger.

Brady, M. P. (2007). Mary Pat Brady. In A. Chabram-Dernersesian (Ed.), *The Chicana/o cultural studies forum: Critical and ethnographic practices* (pp. 38–40). New York: New York University Press.

Brown, S., & Souto-Manning, M. (2008). "Culture is the way they live here": Young Latin@s and parents navigate linguistic and cultural borderlands in U.S. schools. *Journal of Latinos and Education, 7*(1), 25–42.

Burciaga, R. (2007). *Chicana Ph.D. students living nepantla: Educación and aspirations beyond the doctorate*. Unpublished doctoral dissertation, University of California, Los Angeles.

Burciaga, R., & Tavares, A. (2006). Our pedagogy of sisterhood: A testimonio. In D. Delgado Bernal, C. A. Elenes, F. E. Godinez, & S. Villenas (Eds.), *Chicana/Latina education in everyday life: Feminista perspectives on pedagogy and epistemology* (pp. 133–142). Albany, NY: State University of New York Press.

Cammarota, J. (2008). The cultural organizing of youth ethnographers: Formalizing a praxis-based pedagogy. *Anthropology & Education Quarterly, 39*(1), 45–58.

Carrillo, R. (2006). Humor casero mujerista – Womanist humor of the home: Laughing all the way to greater cultural understandings and social relations. In D. Delgado Bernal, C. A. Elenes, F. E. Godinez, & S. Villenas (Eds.), *Chicana/Latina education in everyday life: Feminista perspectives on pedagogy and epistemology* (pp. 181–196). Albany, NY: State University of New York Press.

Castillo, A. (1994). *Massacre of the dreamers: Essays on Xicanisma*. New York: Plume/Penguin Books.

Chabram-Dernersesian, A. (2006a). Chicana/o cultural studies: Marking the conjuncture within an institutional context. In A. Chabram-Dernersesian (Ed.), *The Chicana/o cultural studies reader* (pp. 39–46). New York: Routledge, Taylor and Francis Group.

Chabram-Dernersesian, A. (Ed.). (2006b). *The Chicana/o cultural studies reader*. New York: Routledge, Taylor and Francis Group.

Chabram-Dernersesian, A. (Ed.). (2007). *The Chicana/o cultural studies forum: Critical and ethnographic practices*. New York: New York University Press.

Cisneros, S. (1991). *The house on Mango street*. New York: Vintage.

Cisneros, S. (1992). *Woman hollering creek and other stories*. New York: Random House Vintage.

Cruz, C. (2006). Toward an epistemology of a brown body. In D. Delgado Bernal, C. A. Elenes, F. E. Godinez, & S. Villenas (Eds.), *Chicana/Latina education in everyday life: Feminista perspectives on pedagogy and epistemology* (pp. 59–76). Albany, NY: State University of New York Press.

Cuádraz, G. H. (2005). Chicanas and higher education: Three decades of literature and thought. *Journal of Hispanic Higher Education, 4*(3), 215–234.

Delgado-Gaitan, C. (2001). *The power of community: Mobilizing for family and schooling*. Lanham, MD: Rowman and Littlefield Publishers, Inc.

Delgago-Gaitan, C. (1994). "Consejos": The power of cultural narratives. *Anthropology & Education Quarterly, 25*(3), 298–316.

Delgado Bernal, D., Elenes, C. A., Godinez, F. E., & Villenas, S. (Eds.). (2006). *Chicana/Latina education in everyday life: Feminista perspectives on pedagogy and epistemology*. Albany, NY: State University of New York Press.

Delgado Bernal, D. (2006). Learning and living pedagogies of the home: The mestiza consciousness of Chicana students. In D. Delgado Bernal, C. A. Elenes, F. E. Godinez, & S. Villenas (Eds.), *Chicana/Latina education in everyday life: Feminista perspectives on pedagogy and epistemology* (pp. 113–132). Albany, NY: State University of New York Press.

Delgado Bernal, D. (2002). Critical race theory, LatCrit theory, and critical raced-gendered epistemologies: Recognizing students of color as holders and creators of knowledge. *Qualitative Inquiry, 8*(1), 105–126.

Delgado Bernal, D. (2001). Living and learning pedagogies of the home: The mestiza consciousness of Chicana students. *International Journal of Qualitative Studies in Education, 14*(5), 623–639.

Dyrness, A. (2008). Research for change versus research as change: Lessons from a mujerista participatory research team. *Anthropology & Education Quarterly, 39*(1), 45–58.

Elenes, C. A. (1997). Reclaiming the borderlands: Chicana/o identity, difference, and critical pedagogy. *Educational Theory, 47*(3), 359–375.

Elenes, C. A. (2002). Border/transformative pedagogies at the end of the millennium: Chicana/o cultural studies and education. In A. J. Aldama & N. H. Quiñonez (Eds.), *Decolonial voices: Chicana and Chicano cultural studies in the 21st century* (pp. 245–261). Bloomington, IN: Indiana University Press.

Elenes, C. A. (2001). Transformando fronteras: Chicana feminist transformative pedagogies. *International Journal of Qualitative Studies in Education, 14*(5), 703–710.

Elenes, C. A., & Delgado Bernal, D. (2010). Latina/o education and the reciprocal relationship between theory and practice: Four theories informed by the experiential knowledge of marginalized communities. In E. Murillo Jr., S. Villenas, R. Trinidad Galván, C. Martinez, J. Muñoz, & M. Machado-Casas (Eds.), *Handbook of Latinos and education: Theory, research and practice.* (pp. 63–89). New York: Routledge and Taylor Francis Group.

Monzo, L., & Rueda, R. (2001). Professional roles, caring and scaffolds: Latino teachers' and paraeducators' interactions with Latino students. *American Journal of Education, 109*(4), 438–471.

Fregoso, R. L. (2003). *Mexicana encounters: The making of social identities on the borderlands.* Berkeley, CA: University of California Press.

Garcia, A. (Ed.). (1997). *Chicana feminist thought: The basic historical writings.* New York: Routledge.

Garza-Falcón, L. M. (1998). *A borderlands response to the rhetoric of dominance.* Austin, TX: University of Texas Press.

Godinez, F. E. Hacienda quehacer: Braiding cultural knowledge into educational practices and policies. In D. Delgado Bernal, C. A. Elenes, F. E. Godinez, & S. Villenas (Eds.), *Chicana/Latina education in everyday life: Feminista perspectives on pedagogy and epistemology* (pp. 25–38). Albany, NY: State University of New York Press.

Gómez, A., Moraga, C., & Romo-Carmona, M. (1983). *Cuentos: Stories by Latinas.* New York: Kitchen Table/Women of Color Press.

González, N. (2001). *I am my language: Discourses of women and children in the borderlands.* Tucson, AZ: University of Arizona Press.

Gibson, M. A., Gándara, P., & Koyama, J. P. (Eds.). (2004). *School connections: U.S. Mexican youth, peers, and school achievement.* New York: Teachers College Press.

González, N., Moll, L. C., & Amanti, C. (Eds). (2005). *Funds of knowledge: Theorizing practices in households, communities and classrooms.* Mahwah, NJ: Lawrence Erlbaum Associates, Inc.Guerra, J. (1998). *Close to home: Oral and literate practices in a transnational mexicano community.* New York: Teachers College Pres.

Gutierrez, K. D., & Rogoff, B. (2003). Cultural ways of learning: Individual traits or repertoires of practice. *Educational Researcher, 32*(5), 19–25.

Irizarry, J., & Nieto, S. (2010). Latino/a theoretical contributions to educational praxis: Abriendo Caminos, Construyendo Puentes. In E. Murillo Jr., S. Villenas, R. Trinidad Galván, C. Martinez, J. Muñoz, & M. Machado-Casas (Eds.), *Handbook of Latinos and education: Theory, research and practice* (pp. 108–124). New York: Routledge and Taylor Francis Group.

Jackson, L. G. (2009). *Becoming an activist Chicana teacher: A story of identity-making of a Mexican American bilingual educator in Texas.* Unpublished Dissertation, The University of Texas at Austin.

Johnson, R. (1986/1987, Winter). What is cultural studies anyway? *Social Text, 16*, 38–80.

Kasinitz, P., Mollenkopf, J., & Waters, M. C. (2002). Becoming American/becoming New Yorkers: Immigrant incorporation in a majority minority city. *The International Migration Review, 36*(4), 1020–1036.

Knight, M., Dixon, I., N. Norton, & C. Bentley (2006). Critical literacies as feminist affirmations and interventions: Contextualizing Latina youths' construction of their college-bound identities. In D. Delgado Bernal, C. A. Elenes, F. E. Godinez, & S. Villenas (Eds.), *Chicana/Latina education in everyday life: Feminista perspectives on pedagogy and epistemology* (pp. 39-58). Albany, NY: State University of New York Press.

The Latina Feminist Group. (2001). *Telling to live: Latina feminist testimonios.* Durham, NC: Duke University Press.

Levinson, B. A., & Holland, D. (1996). The cultural production of the educated person: An introduction. In B. A. Levinson, D. Foley, & D. Holland (Eds.), *The cultural production of the educated person: Critical ethnographies of schooling and local practice* (pp. 1–54). Albany, NY: State University of New York Press.

Lopez, N. (2003). *Hopeful girls, troubled boys: Race and gender disparity in urban education*. New York: Routledge.

Lukose, R. (2007). The difference that diaspora makes: Thinking through the anthropology of immigrant education in the United States. *Anthropology & Education Quarterly, 38*(4), 405–418.

Mignolo, W. (2000). *Local histories/global designs: Coloniality, subaltern knowledges and border thinking*. Princeton, NJ: Princeton University Press.

Miranda, M. (2003). *Homegirls in the public sphere*. Austin, TX: University of Texas Press.

Mohanty, C. T. (1991). Introduction: Cartographies of struggle. In C. Mohanty, A. Russo, & L. Torres (Eds.), *Third world women and the politics of feminism* (pp. 1–47). Bloomington, IN: University of Indiana Press.

Moraga, C. (1983). *Loving in the war years*. Boston: South End Press.

Moraga, C., & Anzaldúa, G. (Eds.). (1983). *This bridge called my back: Writings by radical women of color*. New York: Kitchen Table Women of Color Press.

Ngo, B. (2008). Beyond "culture clash:" Understandings of immigrant experiences. *Theory into practice, 47*(1), 4–11.

Ochoa O'Leary, A., González, N., & Valdez-Gardea, G. C. (2008). Latinas' practices of emergence: Between cultural narratives and globalization on the U.S.-Mexico Border. *Journal of Latinos and Education, 7*(3), 206–226.

Olsen, L. (1998). *Made in America: Immigrant students in our public schools*. New York: The New Press.

Ortega, E. & Saporta Sternbach, N. (1989). At the threshold of the unnamed: Latina literary discourse in the eighties. In A. Horno-Delgado, E. Ortega, N. M. Scott, & NSaporta Sternbach (Eds.),*Breaking boundaries: Latina writing and critical readings* (pp. 2–23). Amherst, MA: University of Massachusetts Press.

Pérez, E. (1999). *The decolonial imaginary: Writing Chicanas into history*. Bloomington, IN: Indiana University Press.

Pérez, L. E. (2007a). *Chicana art: The politics of spiritual and aesthetic alterities*. Durham, NC: Duke University Press.

Pérez, L. E. (2007b). Maestrapeace: Picturing the power of women's histories of creativity. *Chicana/Latina Studies: The Journal of Mujeres Activas en Letras y Cambio Social, 6*(2), 56–66.

Portes, A., & Zhou, M. (1993). The new generation: Segmented assimilation and its variants. *Annals of the American Academy of Political and Social Science, 530*, 74–96.

Prieto, L. (2009). *Maestra perspectives on teaching in bilingual education classrooms*. Unpublished Dissertation, The University of Texas at Austin.

Quiñonez, N. (2002). Re(riting) the Chicana postcolonial: From traitor to interpreter. In A. J. Aldama & N. H. Quiñonez (Eds.), *Decolonial voices: Chicana and Chicano cultural studies in the 21st century* (pp. 129–151). Bloomington, IN: Indiana University Press.

Revilla, A. T. (2004). Muxerista pedagogy: Raza womyn teaching social justice through student activism. *The High School Journal, 87*(4), 80–94.

Rodriguez, R. (1982). *Hunger of memory: The education of Richard Rodriguez*. Boston: David R. Godine Publisher.

Rolón-Dow, R. (2004). Seduced by images: Identity and schooling in the lives of Puerto Rican girls. *Anthropology & Education Quarterly, 35*(1), 8–29.

Ruiz, V. L. (1998). *From out of the shadows: Mexican women in twentieth century America*. New York: Oxford University Press.

Ruiz, V. (2007). Vicki Ruiz. In A. Chabram-Dernersesian (Ed.), *The Chicana/o cultural studies forum: Critical and ethnographic practices* (pp. 96–101). New York: New York University Press.

Saldívar, J. D. (1997). *Border matters: Remapping American cultural studies.* Berkeley, CA: University of California Press.

Saldívar-Hull, S. (2000). *Feminism on the border: Chicana gender politics and literature.* Berkeley, CA: University of California Press.

Sánchez, P. & Machado-Casas, M. (2009). At the intersection of transnationalism, Latina/o immigrants, and education. *The High School Journal, 92*(4), 3–15.

Sandoval, C. (2000). *Methodology of the oppressed.* Minneapolis, MN: University of Minnesota.

Sandoval, C. (2007). Chela Sandoval. In A. Chabram-Dernersesian (Ed.), *The Chicana/o cultural studies reader* (pp. 24–26, 73–76). New York: Routledge, Taylor and Francis Group.

Stanton-Salazar, R. (2001). *Manufacturing hope and despair: The school and kin support networks of U.S.-Mexican Youth.* New York: Teachers College Press.

Tapia, R. C. (2001). What's love got to do with it? Consciousness, politics and knowledge production in Chela Sandoval's Methodology of the oppressed. *American Quarterly, 53*(4), 733–743.

Trinidad Galván, R. (2006). Campesina epistemologies and pedagogies of the spirit: Examining women's sobrevivencia. In D. Delgado Bernal, C. A. Elenes, F. E. Godinez, & S. Villenas (Eds.), *Chicana/Latina education in everyday life: Feminista perspectives on pedagogy and epistemology* (pp. 161–179). Albany, NY: State University of New York Press.

Valenzuela, A. (1999). *Subtractive schooling: U.S.-Mexican youth and the politics of caring.* Albany, NY: State University of New York Press.

Vasquez, O., Pease-Alvarez, L., & Shannon, S. (1994). *Pushing boundaries: Language and culture in Mexicano community.* Cambridge, UK: Cambridge University Press.

Vélez-Ibañez, C. (1997). *Border visions: Mexican cultures of the Southwest United States.* Tucson, AZ: University of Arizona Press.

Vigil, A. E. (2008). *At a time of war: U.S. Latina/o cultural production and the Central American revolutions.* Unpublished doctoral dissertation, Cornell University.

Villalpando, O. (2003). Self-segregation or self-preservation? A crtical race theory and Latina/o critical theory analysis of a study of Chicana/o college students. *International Journal of Qualitative Studies in Education, 16*(5), 619–628.

Villenas, S. (2001). Latina mothers and small-town racism. Creating narratives of dignity and moral education in North Carolina. *Anthropology and Education Quarterly, 32*(1), 3–28.

Villenas, S. (2002). Reinventing educacion in new Latino communities: Pedagogies of change and continuity in North Carolina. In S. Wortham, E. G. Murillo Jr., & E. Hamann (Eds.), *Education in the new Latino diaspora: Policy and the politics of identity* (pp. 17–35). Westport, CT: Ablex Publishing.

Villenas, S. (2006). Latina feminist postcolonialities: Perspectives on un/tracking educational actors' interventions. *The International Journal of Qualitative Studies in Education, 19*(5), 659–672.

Villenas, S. (2007). Diaspora and the anthropology of Latino education. *Anthropology & Education Quarterly, 38*(4), 419–425.

Villenas, S. (2009). Diaspora and the anthropology of Latino education: Challenges, affinities and intersections. Reprint. In R. Sintos Coloma (Ed.), *Postcolonial challenges in education.* New York: Peter Lang Publishers.

Villenas, S., & Foley, D. (2002). Chicano/Latino critical ethnography of education: Cultural productions from la frontera. In R. Valencia (Ed.), *Chicano school failure and success: Past, present and future* (pp. 195–226). London & New York: RoutledgeFalmer, Taylor & Francis Group.

Villenas, S., & Moreno, M. (2001). To valerse por si misma (to be self-reliant) between race capitalism and patriarchy: Latina mother-daughter pedagogies in North Carolina. *International Journal of Qualitative Studies in Education, 14*(5), 671–687.

Villenas, S., Godinez, F. E., Delgado Bernal, D., & Elenes, C. A. (2006). Chicanas/Latinas building bridges: An introduction. In D. Delgado Bernal, C. A. Elenes, F. E. Godinez, & S. Villenas (Eds.), *Chicana/Latina education in everyday life: Feminista perspectives on pedagogy and epistemology* (pp. 1–9). Albany, NY: State University of New York Press.

Viramontes, H. M. (1985/1995). *The moths and other stories.* Houston, TX: Arte Público Press.

Viramontes, H. M. (2007). *Their dogs came with them.* New York: Atria Books.

Walsh, C. (2007). Shifting the geopolitics of critical knowledge: Decolonial thought and cultural studies "others" in the Andes. *Cultural Studies, 21*(2/3), 224–239.

Willis, P. (1977). *Learning to labour: How working class kids get working class jobs.* Farborough, UK: Saxon House.

Wortham, S., Allard, E., & Mortimer, K. (2006). *Chronicles of change: Models of Mexican immigrant identity in suburban community narratives.* Paper presented at the annual meeting of the American Educational Research Association, San Francisco.

Yarbro-Bejarano, Y. (2006). Gloria Anzaldúa's Borderlands/La Frontera: Cultural studies, "difference," and the non-unitary subject. In A. Chabram-Dernersesian (Ed.), *The Chicana/o cultural studies reader* (pp. 81–92). New York: Routledge, Taylor and Francis Group.

Yosso, T. (2005). *Critical race counterstories along the Chicana/Chicano pipeline.* New York: Routledge.

Yosso, T. (2006). Whose culture has capital? A critical race theory discussion of community cultural wealth. In A. D. Dixson & C. K Rousseau (Eds.), *Critical race theory in education: All God's children got a song* (pp. 167–190). New York: Routledge, Taylor and Francis Group.

Zarate, M. E., & Conchas, G. (2010). Contemporary and critical methodological shifts in Latino educational research. In E. Murillo Jr., S. Villenas, R. Trinidad Galván, C. Martinez, J. Muñoz, & M. Machado-Casas (Eds.), *Handbook of Latinos and education: Theory, research and practice* (pp. 90–107). New York: Routledge and Taylor Francis Group.

Zentella, A. C. (1997). *Growing up bilingual: Puerto Rican children in New York.* Malden, MA: Blackwell Publishers Inc.

Sofia A. Villenas
Department of Education and the Latino/a Studies Program
Cornell University

JACKSON KATZ

21. IT'S THE MASCULINITY, STUPID

A Cultural Studies Analysis of Media, the Presidency and Pedagogy

INTRODUCTION

A revealing story made its way around Washington political circles early in the new century about the first – and fateful – meeting of Karl Rove and George W. Bush. It was 1973 and Rove, a 22-year-old aide at the Republican National Committee, was asked by chairman George H.W. Bush to go to Union Station to meet his son and give him the keys to the family car. As Rove describes the encounter, reported in Newsweek magazine (Fineman, 2004) – he was blown away by his first impression of the then-27-year-old Bush. "I'm there with the keys and this guy comes striding in wearing jeans, cowboy boots, and a bomber jacket. He had this aura," Rove remembered.

What Rove saw in Bush as he walked through a train station lobby was something the incipient conservative king-maker later packaged and sold with great skill: an aristocratic white man with an affected blue collar Texas swagger who possessed in the force of his personality the raw material for electoral success in the U.S. at the end of the 20th century and the beginning of the 21st. As a young Republican activist just out of college, Rove seemed to know intuitively what many professional political consultants – especially those who work for Democrats – have only recently begun to figure out, that the "aura" he felt from George W. Bush was the stuff of political power in the media era. With historically fateful consequences, he helped turn that insight – and that aura – into 62 million votes.

In this chapter, I provide a general introduction to the importance of masculinity studies in education and cultural theory. Specifically, I intend to sketch out some of the key elements of a multiperspectival cultural studies analysis of the central role in contemporary U.S. culture and politics played by media-driven constructions of presidential masculinity. Over the past few years, researchers and theorists in political science, women's studies, communication, sociology and other academic disciplines, along with journalists and bloggers, have begun to pay closer attention to the ways in which gender functions in presidential politics. Not surprisingly, much of the pioneering work in this area has been done by feminists, whose main area of interest has been women as candidates and voters, and the changes in U.S. politics occasioned by women's increasing political activity and electoral participation. Feminist theorists have examined such issues as cultural barriers to the acceptance of women's executive-level leadership, and the role of national

Z. Leonardo (ed.), Handbook of Cultural Politics and Education, 477–507.

security in shaping public expectations about the qualities necessary in a president. (Han and Heldman, 2007; Norris, 1997). In addition, feminist standpoint theory maintains that initiating research into the social world from women's lives yields a wealth of otherwise inaccessible insight. Because women are "outsiders" to dominant institutions such as politics and media, "thinking up" from women's lives provides a lens through which to observe the myriad ways the presidency is gendered masculine, many of which remain invisible to men and male journalists and social theorists, "whose life patterns and ways of thinking fit all too closely the dominant institutions and conceptual schemes" (Harding, 1991). Because my study concerns the way presidential *masculinities* are constructed in media culture, feminist scholarship that examines how women are forced to navigate the complex cultural expectations around women's leadership in the political realm is especially revealing not only of the extent to which the presidency has always been a masculine institution, but of some of the mechanisms through which this is achieved.

Building on current and earlier feminist scholarship, scholars and activists inside and outside the academy have recently turned their attention to the gendered aspects of *men's* candidacies and gendered voting patterns. For example, it is now common to read in mainstream journalism about the problem Democrats have had for several decades in attracting white working-class male voters. (Brownstein, 2003, Kuhn, 2007, Teixeira and Rogers, 2000). Notably, however, few of the books, articles, op-ed columns and blog postings that discuss this issue offer much analysis of media culture and its relationship to gender and presidential politics. Those studies that do address this subject tend to highlight topics such as coverage about women candidates' hairstyles and clothing, although some scrutinize representations and discourse about men as well. (Han and Heldman, 2007). Occasionally an analysis manages to combine insights about both women candidates and male voters. In an astute op-ed about Hillary Clinton in *The New York Times*, Susan Faludi argued that Clinton's tenacity and fighting spirit that emerged in the 2008 Democratic primaries was attractive to white male working-class voters, who could relate to the new kind of masculinized femininity that she seemed to embody. "Her new no-holds-barred pugnacity and gleeful perseverance have revamped her image in the eyes of begrudging white male voters," she wrote, "who previously saw her as the sanctioning 'sivilizer,' a political Aunt Polly whose goody-goody directives made them want to head for the hills" (Faludi, 2008).

To date, feminists who have analyzed media content typically have focused on the role of media culture in the construction of various types of femininities. Consider the pioneering feminist media literacy work of Jean Kilbourne (1979), the work of Naomi Wolf (1991) on western constructions of female beauty, the work of bell hooks (1992) on race and representation, or the work of Susan Bordo (1994) on women's bodies and media. As these and other feminist theorists and activists have long maintained, images of women's bodies as represented in advertising and other contemporary media are much thinner, more waifish, whiter and younger than women's bodies in the real world. These portrayals of the "feminine ideal" function in the symbolic realm as a means of taking power away from women, because thin, waifish women literally take up less space in the world, and hence are less threatening. Not coincidentally, these images have flooded the visual landscape at a time when women have been challenging traditional male power in various areas of economic, social and political life.

For the past two decades, profeminist men's studies scholars and queer theorists have increasingly turned their attention to media representations of masculinities. This focus has been part of an outpouring of scholarship – and to some extent popular discussion – in recent years about various aspects of multicultural masculinities. This work has contributed to the long-term feminist project of shining the spotlight not only on women as the subordinated sex-class, but on men as the dominant one. The idea is not to push women aside and put men back on center stage, but to understand the myriad and complex ways that male dominance functions in the hope that this understanding can hasten the process of breaking down deeply rooted structures of gender and sexual inequality.

The role of media culture in the construction of presidential masculinity – and other aspects of U.S. political culture – is a crucial but barely explored topic in cultural studies. In fact, prior to Hillary Clinton's campaign for the Democratic nomination for president in 2008, there had been little discussion of the gendered nature of media coverage of presidential campaigns, and prior to Barack Obama's campaign the whiteness of major party nominees was simply assumed and rarely deconstructed. For centuries, the gendered and racialized character of the presidency was largely invisible, as white masculinity was the unquestioned norm. Through the 2004 election, every single U.S. president was a white man, and 42 of 43 were Protestant Christians.

One of the chief goals of a cultural studies approach to this subject is to make visible some of the processes by which white masculinity maintains its dominant social position – especially the role of media culture. This line of inquiry raises a number of questions about both the political and pedagogical impact of corporate and alternative media in the 21st century: to what extent are voters' electoral choices shaped by the televisual performance of candidates and politicians? How does paid political advertising on television – by far the biggest expenditure of funds in presidential campaigns – shape voters' perceptions of the relative "manliness" of candidates? How does this advertising influence political discourse in "unpaid" media? What are the similarities and differences between how women and men ascertain whether male political figures measure up to the "masculine ideal" that is circulating in media culture at a given historical moment? To what extent do issues of race and ethnicity factor into the construction of this ideal? Which mediated (white) masculine styles or archetypes have been politically successful over the past fifty years, and why? Which feminine styles or archetypes have been politically successful in recent years, and which might be successful at the presidential level in coming years? In a long political campaign that was also an unprecedented media spectacle, how did Barack Obama successfully navigate not only the racial but the masculinity politics in order to become the first African American president of the United States? What types of gendered language about leadership do journalists and other media commentators use, and how do those language choices affect who is seen as a credible – or electable – candidate? What role does conservative talk radio play for its listeners in the establishment or maintenance of prevailing opinion about what personal characteristics are considered "masculine," and hence expected in a potential "commander-in-chief "? How do new media and information technologies – including the increasingly ubiquitous *You Tube* and other streaming video – contribute either to the reinforcement or subversion of traditional constructions of presidential masculinity? Indeed, these are many questions, some of which I hope to illuminate in this chapter.

HEGEMONIC MASCULINITY AND PRESIDENTIAL PEDAGOGY

The presidency plays an important pedagogical function in the gender order, especially in the establishment and maintenance of masculine norms. Specifically, presidential masculinity as represented in media culture embodies, and thus helps to define, key characteristics of hegemonic masculinity in the U.S. Hegemonic masculinity is a sociological concept that provides a way to comprehend complex social relations and shifting hierarchies within the gender order on a local, regional, national and international level. According to Connell (1987), within a given society at a given moment in history, there is an idealized and dominant (hegemonic) form of masculinity, which in our culture is white, Christian, middle and upper-class, and heterosexual, and is further characterized as aggressive and competitive. It is an ideal that represents a social position rather than a description of specific individuals, although individuals such as sports stars, corporate CEO's, or national heroes such as astronauts may be its exemplars. At the same time, there are a series of subordinated masculinities, all competing with each other and vying for social position vis-a-vis the hegemonic masculinity. In our society these include ethnic, racial and religious minorities, poor and working-class men, as well as gay and bisexual men and others. It is important to note that both *hegemonic masculinity*, and its corollary, *emphasized femininity*, are fluid concepts that are continually subject to counter-hegemonic pressures and adaptation to ever-shifting economic, social and political landscapes.

In the U.S. constitutional system, the president wields enormous material power. For example, (he) commands the armed forces, he appoints Supreme Court justices, and he sets budgetary and legislative priorities for the federal government. But the president also possesses enormous symbolic power, in part because he is under the glare of worldwide media 24/7, to a degree perhaps unmatched in the world. On top of that, the U.S. presidency is a political office that serves a multitude of ceremonial and ritualistic functions, both formal and informal. For example, the president is the "mourner-in-chief" when tragedy strikes or beloved Americans die. The president and (his) wife and children literally comprise the "First Family." Their home, the White House, is regarded as the nation's home, and so forth. As presidential historian Forrest McDonald describes the special role of the American chief executive:

> ...in addition to the powers and responsibilities vested in the presidential office by the Constitution and those acquired over the years, the office inherently had the ceremonial, ritualistic, and symbolic duties of a king-surrogate.

> Whether as warrior-leader, father of his people, or protector, the president is during his tenure the living embodiment of the nation. (Han & Heldman, 2007, p. 49.)

The president is also – or has been – arguably the embodiment of hegemonic (white) masculinity in his era. Who he is and how he carries himself – and how his "manhood" is represented and constructed in media – has enormous influence in the fashioning of social norms and expectations of what it means to be a "real man."

To the extent that a single person can at once embody characteristics of the dominant gender, race, class, religion, and sexual orientation, while he literally and figuratively serves as a stand-in for the entire nation in its dealings with other nations, the president is as close to the hegemonic ideal as possible. In that sense, the presidency itself can be understood as a type of public pedagogy (see Giroux, this volume), with the president as a kind of pedagogue-in-chief. He literally teaches – by example – what one highly influential version of dominant masculinity looks like. Henry Giroux maintains that the relevance of pedagogy to cultural studies is that "it illuminates how knowledge and social identities are produced in a variety of sites... Pedagogy, in this sense, offers an articulatory concept for understanding how power and knowledge configure in the production, reception, and transformation of subject positions" (Giroux, 1994, p. 132). In a critique of the Hollywood movie *Fight Club,* Giroux argues that certain Hollywood films play a role as teaching machines. "A far cry from simple entertainment, such films function as public pedagogies by articulating knowledge to effects, purposely attempting to influence how and what knowledge and identities can be produced within a limited range of social relations" (Giroux, 2001). The presidency *as it is constructed in media culture* plays a similar function, especially insofar as it defines the hegemonic masculine ideal, and thus serves to model for boys and men the most socially acceptable and validated qualities of manhood at a given cultural moment. But until now, the public pedagogical role of the presidency has been under-theorized in cultural studies scholarship.

Although the focus of this chapter is on campaigns since the advent of television, the pedagogical role of the presidency in reinforcing the characteristics of hegemonic masculinity is not itself a product of the era of mass media. In fact, the founders of the American republic in the late eighteenth century were quite explicit about their desire to have a great and heroic man in the presidency who could model "independent manhood:"

> His (the President's) public exhibition of manly prowess heightened the other men's awareness of their own masculine shortcomings and encouraged them to strive for male maturity. His manly language and masterful deeds provided criteria by which most men could measure, judge and rate one another. His public persona as a self-disciplined man who transcended personal prejudices, parochial loyalties, and factional politics fostered a sense of fraternal solidarity and national pride that bound men together (Han & Heldman, p. 97).

Historical circumstances vary, and in political terms presidents can be more or less successful. Douglas Kellner (2003), in referring to the presidency in terms of a narrative and cinematic spectacle, might just as well have been talking about presidential narratives of manhood: "...successful presidencies presented good movies that were effective and entertaining in selling the presidency to the public. Failed presidencies, by contrast, can be characterized as bad movies, which fashioned a negative image that bombed with the public and left behind disparaging or indifferent impressions and reviews" (p. 160). Similarly, the degree to which presidents are politically successful has an effect on the extent of their cultural influence as masculine exemplars. Compare, for example, the enduring hagiography surrounding Ronald Reagan, the cowboy hero who in the words of Margaret Thatcher "won the Cold War without firing a shot," to the much more disparaging commentary that emerged about another faux cowboy, George W. Bush, whose failures of leadership in the Iraq War led to historically low public approval ratings. To this day Reagan, who left office relatively popular, is revered by millions of Americans as the pinnacle of twentieth century white American manhood, while Bush – who wore cowboy hats and mimicked such Reaganesque theatrics as brush-clearing photo-ops on his ranch, is regularly described as bungling and incompetent, his attempts at masculine image-making routinely mocked by late night comedians as an overgrown boy playing dress-up.

Campaigns are fertile ground for the dissemination of and competition between various cultural and political ideologies. And just as the presidency itself plays an important role in the gender order, campaigns for the presidency can be understood as struggles between competing versions of what can be considered the hegemonic masculine ideal. To put it another way, presidential elections are in a sense quadrennial referenda on what sort of "masculine" qualities a majority of the voting public admires and expects in the person who seeks to ascend to the position of highest status man.

The masculinity of various candidates – especially as seen through the filters of a 24/7 corporate media culture in paid and unpaid media – both reflects and simultaneously helps to produce and reproduce masculine norms. For example, what does it mean for a candidate to be considered "presidential?" Which masculine characteristics must a man running for office possess, or at the very least be able to perform, before he passes the threshold for this consideration? To what extent are these qualities expected of all dominant white men? Men of color? To what extent are they now and will they be in future elections expected of women? Is it possible for a man to achieve and then successfully wield political power if he does not conform to certain masculine conventions of "strength" and stoicism that can effectively be conveyed by televisual performance? Is it possible for a woman to achieve and then successfully wield political power if *she* does not conform to certain "masculine" conventions of strength and stoicism that are similarly performative?

The cultural lessons about manhood embodied in the persona of the president are not solely a product of the creativity of the president's media consultants and stage managers, or the choices of producers, editors and commentators in the news media.

For example, the way entertainment media critique or caricature presidents surely influences how many people see the president; from "hard news" to comedy and drama, the pedagogical impact of the presidency is pervasive and wide-ranging. It has become a cliché to note that many young Americans today get more information about politics from fake news show like *The Daily Show* or *The Colbert Report* than from traditional news programs. Other notable examples of entertainment culture's influence on popular perceptions about a president's masculinity in recent decades include Dana Carvey's emasculating sketches of George H.W. Bush on *Saturday Night Live* in the late 1980s; late night comedians' jokes about Bill Clinton as a hen-pecked husband (before the Monica Lewinsky scandal, when the jokes switched to playful jabs at his "player" status); and short animated features, posters, magnets, bumper stickers and editorial cartoons over the past decade of George W. Bush as a swaggering and semi-literate cowboy. Women presidential and vice-presidential candidates are now fair game for satirical attacks. In the 2008 campaign, Tina Fey's portrayal on *Saturday Night Live* of the Republican vice-presidential candidate Sarah Palin as a provincial simpleton in over her head likely contributed to a sharp decline in her popularity after an initial surge of favorable media coverage following the first-term Alaska governor's surprising selection as John McCain's running mate.

THE MALE SIDE OF THE GENDER GAP

It has been well-documented and often discussed that gender differences in voting patterns have been pronounced over the past few presidential elections. (Center for American Women and Politics, 2004). Consider: in 2004, George W. Bush won 55% of the total male vote, to John F. Kerry's 44%. Kerry actually beat Bush among all female voters 51% to 48% (although he lost 55% to 44% among white women). In 2008, Barack Obama won the men's vote by 49% to 48%, but among women he won 56% to 43%. These gender disparities offer clues to some of the differences between women and men's political priorities. They highlight differences in women and men's perceptions of the world. But these perceptions are not genetically predetermined, nor are they formed in a vacuum. What is considered "common sense" in a given society at a specific time in history is actually transmitted through various institutional, cultural and individual practices that are not fixed and immutable. And dominant ideologies, however powerful, are always subject to contestation and resistance. Thus precisely because media is the great pedagogical force of our time, it should go without saying that any serious discussion about gendered patterns in political beliefs and electoral choices – and strategies for changing them – needs to account for the breadth and depth of media's enormous influence.

Most analyses of the gender gap have focused on women – how their gendered identities impact their political choices, and how their voting habits are changing the face of U.S. politics. Only recently have political scientists and journalists begun to look at the male side of the gender gap, in order to understand how men's gendered identities and sense of themselves *as men* impact their political choices.

It is equally important to recognize that in addition to gender, there are significant racial and ethnic dimensions to political identities and voters' preferences. It is worth noting that men of color, especially African Americans and Latinos, are much more liberal and Democratic than white men. It is quite possible that for them, the masculine discourse of politics – or the masculinity of specific candidates – is less important than racial/ethnic issues, identities, and politics.

One way to frame the debate about the gender gap is to ask not why do women tend to support Democrats, but why do (white) men in such great numbers support Republicans? There are, of course, many possible explanations for this electoral gender gap. For example, Lakoff (2004) has theorized that Republican ideology embodies an authoritarian "strict father" perspective, while the Democrats are better characterized by the values of "nurturant parents." In political shorthand, this means the G.O.P. is perceived as the "daddy party," and the Democrats the "mommy party." In addition, since at least 1972, when the Democratic presidential nominee was the liberal Senator George McGovern, a former World War II fighter pilot who opposed the Vietnam War, polls have consistently shown that a majority of voters believe the Republican party to be more trustworthy on "national security" (Griffith, 2005). One way to interpret this belief is that – for whatever reasons of substance or style – the GOP is perceived to be the party that is "tougher" on communism/terrorism, which translates to mean more willing to increase military spending and resort to military force to project strength and defend US interests around the world. Because violence is seen as a masculine prerogative (Katz, 2003), the Republican party attracts a greater percentage of votes from men, who are more likely than women to prioritize "foreign policy" as an issue that determines their vote for president. Other factors contributing to the electoral gender gap include the decline in recent decades of organized labor's political influence, white male opposition to gender and race-based affirmative action policies championed by Democrats, and single-issue voting on issues such as gun control.

A further reason for performing a cultural studies analysis of how media conventions influence the political views not only of white male voters but *working-class* white male voters, is that their voting patterns over the past quarter-century confound the traditional assumption among liberal and progressive economists and political strategists that people are likely to vote their "pocketbooks," i.e. their economic/class interests. Millions of (mostly) non-union blue-collar white men have for the past couple of decades voted for the presidential nominees of the Republican Party, which favors tax cuts for the wealthy and reduced federal spending on education and health care programs that serve middle and working-class families. Consider: in 2000, George W. Bush won the support of 63% of white men without a college degree, a stunning 29 point margin over Al Gore. Pundits and writers inside and outside of academia have for years sought to understand this phenomenon. Why do so many non-wealthy white voters – men and women – consistently vote against their own (economic) interests? One of the most popular political books of the past decade, *What's The Matter With Kansas?: How Conservatives Won the Heart of America,* (2004), by Thomas Frank, directly addresses this question. Frank argues that the conservative movement has convinced millions of working-class whites that their true enemies are liberal "elites" who have contempt for good old-fashioned American values, and that the solution to cultural decline is to elect conservative Republicans. The tragedy for these working people, however, is that the economic policies pursued by these same Republicans are designed to ease the tax burden on big business and to steadily erode both the rights of workers and the social safety net that protects them from the harsh realities of economic and social inequality.

Interestingly, Frank and many others neglect to explore in any depth the role of media culture in this critical process. Kellner (1997) argues that a critical cultural studies must go beyond textual deconstruction and ask questions about the political economy of cultural production. For example, corporate media play a powerful role in promulgating constructions of presidential masculinity on cable TV and talk radio programs that are largely marketed to working and middle-class white male voters. What are the class interests and biases that frame the content of these programs?

For a long time, television advertising has been the single biggest campaign expenditure in presidential races. The 2004 presidential race was at the time the most expensive in history. *USA Today* reported that the Bush and Kerry campaigns, along with "independent" groups, spent approximately $1.6 billion dollars in the 2004 race, more than double the $771 million spent in 2000 (*Memmot*, 2004). It is estimated that in the "battleground" states alone, there were 675,000 television commercials broadcast (Anderson, 2004). Estimates of the money spent on the presidential race in 2008 put the total at over $2.4 billion, with advertising and other expenditures shattering all previous records (Schouten, 2008, Schneider, 2007). And that doesn't even begin to measure all of the *unpaid* media – the many thousands of hours of political news and talk shows on cable TV, radio, newspapers, magazines and the Internet.

In light of these facts, it is stunning that relatively little attention has been paid – in scholarship or journalism – to the relationship between white men's voting habits and media-driven constructions of masculinities (and femininities). It would seem that researchers and political writers – as well as campaign consultants – might want to seek answers to a number of questions: how have Republicans since the Reagan years used media in their marketing outreach to white men? How have Democrats attempted to do likewise? What are some of the visual cues and advertising themes that convey manly strength in a politician running for office? What are the gendered implications of positive and negative political advertising (e.g. what effect – if any – is there on the masculine "street cred" of a male candidate who is attacked in ads by his rival or a surrogate, and does not immediately "fight back")? What are the ideological biases inherent in representations that appear in "free" media, including putatively "objective" news coverage? How much influence do cartoonishly hypermasculine talk radio hosts and television news commentators like Rush Limbaugh and Bill O'Reilly have in shaping public impressions of the relative "manliness" of candidates? What are the semiotic meanings of some of the symbols (e.g. the American eagle, the Oval Office, Air Force One) that are mobilized in the service of establishing presidential manhood? How does mainstream discourse about "strength" and "leadership" and the need for a candidate to *appear* "presidential" impact voters' reading of the visual images?

Moreover, how does public discourse around violence affect people's perceptions about what sort of leadership is required in these times – and what sort of man embodies those qualities? An example of this was the minor political firestorm that erupted in the 2008 campaign when Barack Obama said that he would consider meeting with our official enemies. He was widely ridiculed by conservative pundits for being "naïve and inexperienced." In this context, that sort of language can be read as coded language for "He's not man enough to be entrusted with projecting U.S. military power around the world; our enemies will recognize his weakness and play him – and us – for soft and emasculated fools."

Entertainment Media and Presidential Masculinities

Entertainment media play an important role in the construction and critique of presidential masculinity, especially in the context of a media culture where the lines between entertainment, news and opinion blurred long ago. In today's 24/7 media environment, broadband technology and advances in digital editing have made it possible for satirists and partisans to use video in unprecedented ways to reveal the constructed nature of political candidates' gendered appeals. Consider Comedy Central's *The Daily Show with Jon Stewart,* arguably one of the most politically influential programs on television. A 2008 study by the Pew Research Center's Project for Excellence in Journalism concluded that "*The Daily Show* is clearly impacting American dialogue" and "getting people to think critically about the public square" (Kakutani, M. 2008). But while few discussions of *The Daily Show's* impact on presidential politics offer any sort of explicit gender analysis, arguably one of the show's signature features is its host's embodiment of a kind of "oppositional masculinity" that questions traditional authority and skewers the pretensions of powerful men. For example, Stewart might show a clip of a male politician making a forceful public declaration that is intended to bolster his image as a take-charge leader. Then Stewart, with a knowing smile and a well-timed sarcastic comment, runs a clip of the same man contradicting himself on the same subject in a different setting, which has the effect of completely undermining the power of the staged performance. The juxtaposition, shown to raucous laughter by the New York studio audience, uncovers the performative and phony aspects of presidential posturing with unprecedented speed and transforms a staged photo-op into an object of satirical humor. For the past decade *The Daily Show* has been a major source of news and has helped to shape a certain kind of generational sensibility for millions of college students and other young viewers. Individual skits from the popular Comedy Central program are perennial favorites online; at this writing there were more than 44,000 videos related to *The Daily Show* posted on *You Tube*.

Throughout Bush's presidency, but particularly after the Iraq war began to go poorly, repeated satirical treatment on *The Daily Show* punctured the hyper-masculine bravado of George W. Bush, and arguably did serious damage – especially with young viewers – to his masculine credibility. Although Bush provided plenty of material to hold himself up as an object of ridicule, such as his ill-fated "Mission Accomplished" speech on the aircraft carrier U.S.S. Abraham Lincoln in May of 2003, *The Daily Show* regularly trained a spotlight on Bush's seemingly insatiable need to prove his manhood. One recurring skit on the show was a cartoon video entitled "The Decider," which had its origins in a televised statement Bush made in 2006 to the effect that he was "the decider." The Decider is a superhero spoof with Bush in the lead role. The cartoon, which was only aired a few times but has a life of its own online, ridicules the simplicity of Bush's Manichean worldview as it mocks his narcissism and his seeming need to be in – or appear to be in – control at all times.

During the years of George W. Bush's presidency, the reach of the Internet increased exponentially. The availability of broadband technology also expanded rapidly, enabling millions of homes to receive streaming video. In addition, over the past decade "liberal" cable TV programs that make frequent use of video clips have proliferated, such as Comedy Central's *The Daily Show* and *The Colbert Report*, MSNBC's *Countdown with Keith Olberman* and HBO's *Real Time with Bill Maher*. As a result, Bush was the object of an unprecedented outpouring of ridicule that used his own staged performances against him. As noted above, previous presidents in the mass media era had their masculinity lampooned in media, such as George W. Bush's father, who was skewered by Dana Carvey in *Saturday Night Live* skits as an effete, feminized aristocrat. But in the late 1980s-early 1990s, those skits were only broadcast once and then repeated later that year, and unlike today, they did not achieve a second life on *You Tube*, effectively globalizing them. In addition, camcorders and other video equipment became much more widely available in the 1990s, as did the digital editing technologies that facilitate rapid video production. In light of the way George W. Bush in the current media era was the target of relentless ridicule, it is interesting to speculate about whether or not Ronald Reagan's stage-managers would have been as successful in heroicizing him in the 1980s if programs like *The Daily Show* were around to run replays of his numerous gaffes, factual misstatements, and inarticulate ramblings.

MEN'S STUDIES AND CULTURAL STUDIES

Men's studies scholarship contributes many rich veins of insight, theory and research to this topic, in particular by helping to put contemporary debates about masculinities and "men's roles" in historical context. Consider the following examples:

Michael Kimmel's cultural history *Manhood In America* (1996) documents how through the centuries, common-sense ideas about what is considered "manly" have been anything but static. Rather, they are continuously negotiated and subject to a multitude of economic, social, and political pressures. Throughout U.S. history, presidential masculinity has both reflected and helped to produce broader cultural shifts in the notion of what it means to be a man. Kimmel describes the election of

1840 as "a political masterpiece of gendered speech" (Kimmel, p. 36). This campaign, which pitted the "self-made man of the people," Willam Henry Harrison, against the incumbent Martin Van Buren, featured blistering attacks by Harrison's Whig party on Van Buren's aristocratic and European tastes and effete manhood. The strategy paid off for Harrison; Van Buren was defeated. But according to Kimmel, the strategy set a dubious precedent: "Since 1840 the president's manhood has always been a question, his manly resolve, firmness, courage, and power equated with the capacity of violence, military virtues, and a plain-living style that avoided refinement and civility" (ibid. p. 38). Notably, Kimmel's study was published four years before the aristocrat George W. Bush reached the White House after successfully presenting himself as a "regular guy," and almost a decade before he won reelection against John Kerry, whose war hero status failed to insulate him from the same sort of attack that Van Buren sustained, even down to the similarity between the attacks by Van Buren's populist opponents, who asserted that his "French cooks" furnished the president's table in "massive gold plate and French sterling silver," and those of Kerry's detractors, such as conservative talk radio icon Rush Limbaugh, who derisively referred to the senator from Massachusetts as "Looks French" Kerry (ibid, p. 37).

James William Gibson's *Warrior Dreams: Violence and Manhood in Post-Vietnam America* (1994) analyzes the class, race and especially gender-based insecurity and compensatory hyper-masculinity that characterizes the male supremacist and highly militaristic far Right-wing in U. S. politics over the past generation. In the aftermath of the devastating U.S. defeat in Vietnam, he writes: "American men – lacking confidence in the government and the economy, troubled by the changing relations between the sexes, uncertain of their identity or their future – began to *dream*, to fantasize about the powers and features of another kind of man who could retake and reorder the world. And the hero of all these dreams was the paramilitary warrior" (p.11). Gibson argues that Ronald Reagan was politically successful in part because he tapped into these anxieties and offered a salve: "He was a shaman of sorts who wanted to restore and build upon America's fundamental creation myths through presidential performances" (ibid, p. 268). This is not just a complaint by one of Reagan's legion of progressive detractors. Members of Reagan's own administration were candid about the degree to which the president actively performed his role. Reagan chief of staff Kenneth Duberstein said in 1987 that for the Reagan White House to function effectively, there had to be "a very strong stage manager-producer-director" and "very good technical men and sound men." As Gibson put it, under Reagan "the White House was a movie set, a sound stage" (ibid, p. 269).

Stephen Ducat's *The Wimp Factor: Gender Gaps, Holy Wars, and the Politics of Anxious Masculinity* (2004) is a psychologically-oriented study of "femophobia" and its deep-seated influence on men's psyches, and hence in contemporary U.S. politics. He writes "Until the gender subtext of contemporary politics is understood as an unconscious as well as a conscious phenomenon, and debated openly and widely, men's fear of the feminine will continue to be central among the various motives that drive electoral campaigns" (p. 23).

Because the president is elected to the position of commander-in-chief of the armed forces, his decisions about where and when to use military force are – at least in theory – supposed to be made in the best interests of the American people. But there is a gender dynamic at work. In a chapter on the psychodynamics of the gender gap in political attitudes, Ducat references a Gallup survey on men and women's differing rationales for the use of U.S. military force. The survey showed that men were substantially more concerned with "U.S. credibility" as a reason to justify military action. Men have:

> …a particular identification with the American nation state not shared (to the same degree) by women, one that is personified as an individual warrior whose honor (read: "phallic manhood") is on the line in any potential conflict. This interpretation is consistent with the findings of my own research on the nature of men's psychological investment in the outcome of a war. In other words, a military intervention in which one's country might assert manly dominance over another is an opportunity to achieve (or fail to achieve) a vicarious sense of personal worthiness and efficacy, which in phallic terms is expressed as potency. (Ducat 2004, p. 184)

Based on this reasoning, it makes sense that men would be more invested than women in candidates who in their physical person, military credentials, or campaign rhetoric seem willing or eager to use military force to "defeat our enemies," because men's *identities* are involved in their political beliefs. This might also help to explain the psychology underlying conservative hostility to multilateral organizations such as the United Nations, who are often characterized by conservative commentators as attempting to "tie our hands" in military engagements where nothing less than our national masculinity is at stake.

Sports Metaphors and Violent Masculinity

Sports metaphors are a ubiquitous part of political speech and journalism in the United States in the 21st century. Metaphors are not merely figures of speech. According to the cognitive scientists and philosophers George Lakoff and Mark Johnson (1980), human thought processes themselves are largely metaphorical. Our brains use them to organize and make sense of the world. According to Lakoff and Johnson:

> Our ordinary conceptual system, in terms of which we both think and act, is fundamentally metaphorical in nature…The concepts that govern our thought are not just matters of the intellect. They also govern our everyday functioning, down to the most mundane details. Our concepts structure what we perceive, how we get around in the world, and how we relate to other people. Our conceptual system thus plays a central role in defining our everyday realities…the way we think, what we experience, and what we do every day is very much a matter of metaphor. (p. 6)

This raises a series of questions about sports metaphors in U.S. presidential discourse: What effect does it have on our political system when mainstream commentary about politics is infused with the kind of language one hears every day on ESPN, in sports bars and in locker rooms? To what extent can bitter partisanship in the two-party system be understood as a political manifestation of the sort of quasi-tribalism that is routinely on display in sports rivalries? What are the particularly gendered features of sports/political discourse, and how do those influence which qualities in potential leaders are regarded as important? For example, presidential debates are routinely covered by the mainstream media as if they were boxing matches. Does this subtly – or not so subtly – influence voters' perceptions of various candidates? Can a male political figure who does not embody certain traditionally masculine qualities – such as being pugnacious enough to credibly go "toe-to-toe" with our official enemies, succeed in such an environment? Can a woman? Will we get any closer to finding solutions to complex 21st century problems when political commentary focuses not on what candidates say or stand for, but on the fact that the "frontrunner" failed to deliver a "knockout punch"?

U.S. political discourse is infused with metaphors from a range of sports. From former Central Intelligence Agency director George Tenet's infamous assertion that the presence of weapons of mass destruction in Iraq was a "slam dunk," to the criticism that some journalists are known to ask "softball" questions during presidential press conferences, to United States Supreme Court Chief Justice John Robert's assertion during his confirmation hearings that "Judges are like umpires…They make sure everybody plays by the rules," (Roberts, 2005), to then-presidential candidate Barack Obama's statement that "A nuclear Iran would be a game-changing situation not just in the Middle East but around the world," (Zeleny, 2008), everyday speech by and about politics and politicians routinely contains sports terminology whose meaning resonates with a large number of voters.

But while metaphors from sports such as basketball and baseball regularly surface in political speech, arguably the two most metaphorically influential sports in presidential campaign rhetoric are boxing and football. Not coincidentally, they are both violent sports, and they attract a disproportionate percentage of male participants and fans. It is not within the scope of this chapter to estimate how much of the white male vote is determined by impressions about the relative "manliness" or "toughness" of candidates or political parties. But there is no doubt that for several decades violence – both our individual and collective vulnerability to it, and questions about when and how to use the violent power of the state to protect the "national interest," has been an ominous and omnipresent factor in numerous foreign policy and domestic political issues (e.g. the Cold War, Vietnam, the "War on Terror," and the invasion of Iraq, as well as gun control, and executive, legislative and judicial responses to violent crime). The frequent use of boxing and football metaphors in political discourse did not cause violence to become such an important force in our politics, but this usage is one measure of how presidential campaigns in the mass media era are less about policy differences and complex political agendas than they are about the selling of a certain kind of executive masculinity, embodied (prior to Obama) in a particular white man whom the public comes to know largely through television and other technologies of mass communication. What follows is a brief discussion of the role of boxing and football metaphors in this process.

BOXING METAPHORS

Boxing metaphors help to construct presidential campaigns as the ultimate arena for masculine competition. Boxing is a prototypical working-class or poor man's (or more recently, woman's) sport that strips the notion of physical combat to its barest essence: man against man in a fight to the finish. Through the campaign of 2004, the (almost exclusively) white male candidates who have vied at the highest level for the presidency have in effect been competing to be their party's *champion*, who, if victorious, becomes the champion of the entire country, the man who stands in for the home team in international political competition against the champions of other countries (e.g. Saddam Hussein, Hugo Chavez, etc.).

For many decades, newspapers have covered presidential debates with language taken directly from coverage of title bouts, complete with "Tale of the Tape" features that quantify a candidate's strengths and weaknesses. To this day, the political fortunes of various candidates are in part determined by whether or not political and media elites describe them as "heavyweights." Anyone who follows contemporary U.S. politics even superficially knows that politicians and journalists constantly use boxing metaphors to describe political machinations. Before his first debate with Ronald Reagan in 1984, Walter Mondale was urged by Tip O'Neill to "come out slugging and come out fighting." (cited in Howe, 1988,) *The Los Angeles Times*, during the presidential primary season in 2000, ran an article about a dramatic speech by Arizona Senator John McCain under the headline "McCain Delivers Hard Left to Christian Right" (Miller and Brownstein, 2000). And in a lead-in to a jocular and substantive exchange on National Public Radio with commentator Michael Eric Dyson about the first George W. Bush – John Kerry debate in 2004, host Tavis Smiley stated: "Once the lights and cameras are off, media pundits and voters are still left to decide which punches actually landed, which political jabs will be felt throughout the rest of the campaign" (Smiley, 2004). Later in the discussion Dyson, commenting on a previous debate performance by Kerry, said "I ain't saying he was dancing like Ali, but at least he wasn't plodding like some ham-fisted contender for the crown" (Dyson, 2004).

Boxing has historically been a male bastion, and it remains so in the 21st century. But women's boxing now occupies a small – but highly visible – cultural space. It is probably too early to tell how the increased popularity of women's boxing has affected the power of masculine symbolism associated with the sport. In any case, the 2008 political season broke new linguistic ground, at first because the presence of Hillary Clinton in the ranks of political "heavyweights" complicated the boxing metaphors. Politicians and political commentators had to choose whether or not to use language that had men metaphorically hitting a woman (and vice versa). Republican Sarah Palin's entry into the race as her party's vice-presidential nominee and the second woman on a major party ticket provided another watershed cultural moment. In her first nationally televised speech, at the Republican National Convention in early September, Palin sharply attacked Barack Obama's character and record. A typical headline in the media coverage read "Defiant Sarah Palin Comes Out Swinging," (Barabak, 2008), and the *New York Times* editorialized that Palin's rallies had become "spectacles of anger and insult" (*New York Times*, 2008). One of Palin's most-quoted lines on the campaign trail in the fall of 2008 was "The heels are on, the gloves are off," which she typically delivered to wild cheers of approval. In coming years, when this historic campaign and those yet to come are analyzed, it will be particularly interesting to see how female and male voters respond to language where a woman throws the "knockout punch." Does this masculinize and thus help to make them more credible as potential commanders-in-chief? Or do women who are seen as "too-aggressive" – even if only in a metaphorical sense – turn voters off? What are the differences between how the sexes view a woman "throwing punches" if she's a conservative (like Palin) or a liberal feminist (like Hillary Clinton?).

FOOTBALL METAPHORS

Football is a hugely popular sport across the United States, and it provides a wealth of metaphors in contemporary American politics. Journalists wonder whether a politician will do an "end run" around his/her opposition in the legislature. TV pundits preface their remarks about a candidate's debate performance by apologizing for doing a little "Monday-morning quarterbacking." Newly energized campaign volunteers claim to have been inspired to "get off the sidelines" and join the political battle. An op-ed in *USA Today* runs under the headline "Don't punt on Iran: U.S. shouldn't throw bombs or play a soft defense." (Schweizer, 2007). And interestingly, the general election campaign season – when political ads increase exponentially and political talk fills the airwaves – corresponds to the main part of the football season. In fact, Election Day is the first Tuesday in November, right in the heart of the fall football schedule. This means that it is likely a common experience for men and women who watch football on television to be watching a game at one moment, then watching a political ad during a commercial break, followed by a panel of experts analyzing the game, and perhaps moments later watching a panel of experts analyzing the political ad, with much of the rhetoric about football and politics overlapping and interchangeable.

Since football is a violent sport, football metaphors bring violent language and imagery to political discourse. They also subtly and overtly link politics to warfare. As Howe (1988) puts it, "The element of physical conflict in football...makes football metaphors effective...because it establishes that politics is a violent exercise of power with clear winners and losers" (p. 92). Football metaphors with military analogues that are used commonly by sportscasters and sportswriters, such as "throwing the bomb," "penetrating the zone," and "air game vs. ground game," ensure that the language of football and the language of war cross-reference each other. Establishment politicians – men and women – who use this sort of language can thus prove their mastery, or at least familiarity, with two important masculine domains: football and the military. As Reagan and many others have proven, this can be an effective way for wealthy candidates to show blue-collar males that they're one of the guys (especially if they're a man) – whether or not their economic program addresses working people's concerns or represents their interests.

It is certainly not difficult to find examples of football metaphors in the speech of contemporary politicians. During the 2004 Republican National Convention in New York City, Rudy Giuliani praised George W. Bush as a "great president" because "he turned around the ship of state from being solely on defense against terrorism to being on offense as well" (Giuliani, 2004). Speaking to reporters about the Iraq war several years later, Secretary of Defense Robert Gates made a similar point, with even more explicit football terminology, when he said "It's important to defend this country on the extremists' 10-yard line, and not on our 10-yard line" (Richter, 2007). Republican Senator Richard Lugar compared the Bush plan for a "surge" in Iraq to "…a draw play on third down with 20 yards to go in the first quarter. The play does have a chance of working if everything goes perfectly, but it is more likely to gain a few yards and set up a punt on the next down" (Lugar, 2007).

No discussion of football metaphors in politics would be complete without mention of former Virginia Senator George Allen. Allen, a former college quarterback and the son of the late Washington Redskins coach, has taken the political use of football metaphors to a new level. As reported by Dana Milbank in the Washington Post, Allen filters nearly everything political through a football lens. He once said that critics of former secretary of state Condoleezza Rice "have used some bump-and-run defenses and tactics against her." A couple of years ago, when the Republicans won a Senate seat in Louisiana, he said it "was like a double-reverse flea-flicker and a lateral." As head of Senate Republicans' campaign efforts in 2004, he called his candidates in the southern states the "RNC South." (Milbank, 2005)

According to Milbank, "In Allen's world, primaries are 'intrasquad scrimmages,' his Senate staff is the 'A-team,' Senate recess is 'halftime' and opponents are flagged for 'pass interference.'" Allen accused the Democrats of "Constant delay of game, constant holding, constant pass interference and, once in a while, even piling on." Years without elections are the "offseason." Primaries are the "preseason." Senate Republicans are President Bush's "teammates." Big political donors join a "Quarterback Club" or a "Special Teams" committee (ibid, p. C01). It is important to note that Allen's near-obsessive use of football metaphors did not hurt him politically. In fact, while his football language was the object of ridicule in some quarters of mainstream journalism and also the blogosphere, until late in 2006 he was a major star in conservative Republican circles. Interestingly, new media contributed to the demise of George Allen's political career, which was cut short when his use of an alleged ethnic slur was caught on a hand-held video camera and broadcast widely on *You Tube*, an incident that tarnished his reputation and contributed to the loss of his senate seat.

George Allen's precipitous fall was a reminder that race and ethnicity remain central issues in presidential politics, and will likely remain so for years to come. As increasing numbers of men and women of color enter U.S. politics, including presidential politics, it is interesting to speculate about what affect race – and racism – will have on the way sports metaphors are used, and discussed. For example, if an African American male politician used football metaphors as promiscuously as does former Senator George Allen, would people find it humorous, perhaps a little "goofy," but still an indication that he's a "man's man"? Or is it possible that his stature would be questioned, as African Americans constantly have to fight the stereotype that they're "natural" athletes who lack intellectual heft? Barack Obama is a good basketball player, and often played pick-up games on the campaign trail for exercise. Basketball is a highly popular sport in this country, yet players at the elite level in college and the pros are overwhelmingly African American. Do Obama's hoop skills reinforce his "otherness" to the white majority, his *black* masculinity? Is it overdrawn to suggest that in its own minor way, this might have been one of the reasons – along with his poor bowling performance on the campaign trail in Pennsylvania – why he was slow to win the votes of working-class whites in the Democratic primaries? Furthermore, playing pick-up basketball has not traditionally been seen as "presidential" behavior. Could this have contributed to the perception among some white voters that he was young and inexperienced, and therefore not ready for the highest office in the land?

THE POPULIST APPEAL OF SPORTS METAPHORS

With some variation, certain sports are identified not only with men, but with men from specific social classes. For example, racquetball in the U.S. is largely viewed as a sport primarily for middle and upper-class men in health and fitness clubs, whereas boxing and football are considered more blue-collar (although their fan base draws heavily from the middle and upper-class as well). The "masculinity" of a given sport thus has a class dimension. As Nicholas Howe (1988) points out, American politicians, "especially those of patrician background, have long appreciated that the use of sports metaphors allows them to affect a common touch or forge a bond with average voters" (p. 89). By making references to sports that are popular with working-class men, sports metaphors and other references are surefire ways to demonstrate populist appeal. A famous example from the pre-television era is the aristocrat Teddy Roosevelt's use of boxing metaphors. More recent examples include Richard Nixon's frequent references to baseball and football, or Ronald Reagan's close identification with football.

Reagan's football credentials were enhanced by his having been a college football player, and from his movie role as George Gipp in the 1940 film about a famous football coach, *Knute Rockne: All-American* (The source of the famous line, "Win one for the Gipper," which became part of Reagan lore). Reagan also effortlessly employed gridiron metaphors, such as when he stated in 1981 that European opponents of the neutron bomb were "carrying the propaganda ball for the Soviet Union," (ibid, p. 92) or when he said, in 1984, "Isn't it good to see the

American team, instead of punting on third down, scoring touchdowns again?" (ibid, p. 90). Reagan's ability to talk the populist language of football while cutting programs that served working-class families and pursuing an economic policy that redistributed income upward is one of the reasons he earned the nickname the "Great Communicator."

On the other hand, politicians who get the class politics wrong – or who are characterized by their opponents as getting them wrong – run the risk of revealing themselves as elitist, out of touch, or aristocratic in a way that is not read as manly by millions of working and middle-class male voters. For example, during former Massachusetts governor Michael Dukakis's run for the White House in 1988, he repeatedly referred to his campaign as a "marathon," invoking his Greek heritage. The political wisdom of this description was questionable because while many Americans admire and in some ways are in awe of marathon runners, marathon running is not seen in the dominant U.S. culture as a "masculine" endeavor. Additionally, Dukakis's penchant for "power-walking" with the TV cameras rolling did not help bolster his masculine image, as this form of exercise is more often the object of ridicule than emulation in traditional male culture.

In the 2004 presidential campaign, news commentators and conservative media personalities had a field day with footage of John Kerry skiing and snowboarding in Sun Valley, Idaho, and windsurfing off Nantucket Island. While these visuals showed him to be athletic and adventurous, and symbolically reinforced Kerry's similarities and identification with fellow Massachusetts senator and former president John F. Kennedy, they also accentuated the idea that his sports passions were upper-class in nature. (The class and cultural imagery surrounding the Democratic and Republican parties in the early 21st century have changed dramatically since the Kennedy era. Hence widely circulated images of Kennedy engaged in upper-class pastimes in the early 1960s played out very differently – and much less negatively – for him and his political persona). This placed Kerry's constructed masculine image in sharp contrast with his opponent and fellow aristocrat George W. Bush's carefully stage-managed image as an average guy who rides in pickup trucks and loves baseball, as someone with whom plain folks could identify and with whom one could have a beer. The windsurfing photos also served as another kind of sports metaphor: they were the perfect visual illustration of the Republican theme of John Kerry as a "flip-flopper" who did not stand for anything and would just blow with the prevailing winds.

RECENT HISTORY

There is widespread agreement that the 1960 race between Richard M. Nixon and John F. Kennedy was the first presidential campaign where television played a substantial and even decisive role. Constructed and mediated images of presidential masculinity had long been important in presidential races, even before the mass media technologies of the 20th century. But since the invention of television, and particularly since 1960, the way a candidate for president is constructed in the representational system has not merely been an important part of his "electability;" it has arguably been the most important part. And especially since the landslide election of the former Hollywood actor Ronald Reagan in1980, effective televisual performance – including the ability to project "manly" strength, has become the sine qua non of success at the presidential level. The 1980 election was a watershed year in American politics for many reasons, not least of which is that Reagan's performance of presidential masculinity continues to loom large in contemporary presidential politics.

A former governor of California, Reagan grew up in the Midwest but was marketed to the public as a leader who embodied one of the enduring masculine myths of the United States: the strong, unwavering, moral cowboy riding in from the west to save the day. After the economic crises of Jimmy Carter's presidency, and especially after the Iranian Hostage Crisis prompted criticism from some quarters that the U.S. had become an "impotent giant," the electorate was ready to turn the government over to a man who positively radiated a belief in old-fashioned American military supremacy. It is important to note that Reagan's racial politics were inseparable from his projection of white masculine strength. For almost two decades he had been one of the most prominent opponents of the civil rights movement, opposing virtually every major piece of civil rights legislation. Also, since the mid-1960s Reagan – and many other conservative white male (and some female) politicians – played to white anxieties and fears of Black crime by promising to get "tough on crime," a phrase that reinforced not only their whiteness but also their masculine credentials.

The Republican Party has understood since at least 1972, when Richard Nixon won re-election in a landslide over Senator George McGovern (D-South Dakota), that the key to winning working class and middle-class white male votes (to complement the party's huge historic advantage with wealthy white men) is two-fold: 1) appeal to the racial resentments of white voters by coded references to the Democrats as the party of Blacks and other racial minorities, and the G.O.P. as the party who is on "your" side; and 2) frame politics, especially presidential politics, in terms of a contest about manhood, where the Republican side represents the true home of red-blooded, flag-waving, red-meat eating, heterosexual "real men." The Republican Party has been fabulously successful with this strategy, as Jimmy Carter in the post-Watergate election of 1976 and Bill Clinton, in a three-way race in 1992 with the weak incumbent George H.W. Bush and the independent and eccentric candidacy of H. Ross Perot, were the only two Democrats before Barack Obama to be elected president in the past 36 years. There are clearly other factors that contribute to this domination at the presidential level, including various macroeconomic shifts, the Democratic Party's championing of civil rights legislation in the 1960s, the continuing decline of trade unionism, the Democratic Party's retreat from social democratic principles as corporate influence increased in the party, the political emergence of the women's movement and its rapid assimilation – in electoral politics – by the Democratic Party, and other factors. But while the exact sources of the G.O.P.'s growing strength in recent decades with white male voters (especially but not exclusively in the south) is a subject of debate, the facts are not in dispute. For example, in 2004, even though women voted in significantly greater numbers than men, George W. Bush's margin among men – in particular white men – was great enough to offset and overcome his disadvantage among women.

GEORGE W. BUSH: "DON'T MESS WITH TEXAS"

The single most expensive ad of the 2004 race was a Bush TV commercial entitled "Ashley's Story" or "The Hug." It featured Bush embracing a 15-year-old girl who had lost her mother in the World Trade Center attacks on 9/11. The most memorable line of the piece was Ashley's: "He's the most powerful man in the world, and all he wants to do is make sure I'm safe, that I'm OK." In the hotly contested state of Ohio alone, this classic "president as protector" spot ran *seven thousand times* (Faludi, 2007). And this was only the "paid media." Incalculable amounts of TV and radio time were devoted to discussions of "The Hug" and other ads from the campaign. For example, the Swift Boat Veterans For Truth, an "independent" 527 group with reputed informal ties to long-time Bush adviser and political consultant Karl Rove, ran ads in several battleground states, but the free media coverage of the controversy they created amounted to tens of millions of dollars in free anti-Kerry publicity for the (largely unproven) charges they raised.

With all of this money spent on political advertising, and a considerable amount of space in the nation's newspapers and in broadcast journalism devoted to a discussion of the role of advertising (and media more generally) in contemporary presidential politics, it is notable but perhaps not surprising that the conversation was generally superficial (e.g. did Kerry help or hurt himself by doing a duck-hunting photo-op in Iowa, designed to show hunters that he would not take away their guns?)

The 2004 election – a contest between two upper-class white men – was also rich with the politics of gender. When George W. Bush launched his campaign for the Republican presidential nomination in 1999, he had several distinct advantages. As the son of a former president who shared his father's name, he already had widespread name recognition. He had his father's, and his own, ties to wealthy oilmen and other rich Republican campaign contributors. He had served two terms as governor of one of the nation's largest states. But in terms of political currency in the realm of masculine iconography, he had the enormous advantage of his identification with the state of Texas. Although Bush is the scion of a blue-blooded aristocratic family from Connecticut and Maine who was educated at such bastions of the old Republican establishment as Andover, Yale, and Harvard Business School, the imagery surrounding him – carefully constructed by Rove and company – was largely about his "just folks" cowboy masculinity and his Texas roots. He and his wife Laura purchased their Crawford, Texas ranch in 1999 – just before the campaign began – presumably to provide a visual backdrop (a Hollywood prop?) for thousands of subsequent photo ops that showed Bush as a down-home cowboy who, in the Ronald Reagan mode, liked to wear blue jeans, clear brush on his ranch and ride in pick-up trucks.

In fact, it is critical to understand the enduring power of the constructed image of the cowboy as embodying all that is right with white American masculinity in order to understand George W. Bush's electoral success. European editorialists often mocked Bush's "cowboy" persona as immature, unsophisticated and reckless, but as the 2004 election proved, for tens of millions of Americans the virtues of the cowboy outweigh the shortcomings – especially in a dangerous world. Jane Tomkins offers an explanation of this in *West of Everything* (1992), her study of the 20th century popularity of the western in both its novelistic and cinematic forms (westerns are the most popular genre in U.S. film in the 20th century). According to Tomkins, the popularity of westerns can be understood in part as a response by men to the challenges posed to (white) male power and privilege by the emergence of a women's movement in the mid-to-late 19th century. Westerns became a fictional space within which men could assert masculine power without apology, and where "feminine" traits such as empathy and compassion were seen as shortcomings in men who had to tame a wild frontier, fend off hostile natives, and enforce social codes of honor and decorum. Three of the key issues of women's reform were whiskey, gambling and prostitution. Given the enormous publicity and fervor of the Women's Christian Temperance Union crusade, Tomkins asks, can it be an accident that the characteristic indoor setting for westerns – which were written almost exclusively by men for a largely male readership and audience – is the saloon? (Tomkins, p. 45).

Tomkins examines another familiar plot-line in westerns. A lone bad guy or a band of criminals is menacing the town; the official authorities are ineffectual at responding to the threat. There is a scene set at the burial ceremony of someone killed by the bad guys, where the preacher inveighs against sin and bemoans the injustice of the killing. But of course all this talk means nothing to the criminals, who look on contemptuously from a distance. The only language they understand is the language of violence. In this way religion is feminized, because it is equated with language and passivity. Nothing changes – nothing can change – until a taciturn man of action rides into town (e.g, John Wayne or Clint Eastwood) and gets the job done with a burst of cathartic violence. In other words, talk is feminized, and action is masculinized.

The overarching issues in the 2004 presidential election were 9/11, the "war on terror," and the U.S. attack on Iraq. The Bush team and their allies in the corporate media successfully conflated the three, so that millions of Americans mistakenly believed that attacking Saddam Hussein, who led a secular fascist government, was tantamount to striking back against Islamist terrorism. Many of Bush's photo ops and paid commercials aimed to burnish his credentials as a man of few words but decisive actions – just the kind of man we need in a world where bad men with dark skin speaking a strange language are trying to kill us (Osama Bin laden and al Qaeda). At the same time, Bush's negative ads, and those devised by his political allies, sought to describe John Kerry as an indecisive "flip-flopper," just the type of rudderless, cautious politician whose "nuanced" style of leadership would put us at greater risk in perilous times.

Initially, Kerry posed a problem for the Bush reelection team, because he had the formal masculine credentials – as a decorated veteran of military combat – that could give working-class and middle-class white men who had deserted the party in recent decades cover to vote once again for a Democrat. These credentials were the most important factor when the Democratic primary electorate judged him to be the most "electable" candidate in a general election against Bush, who after all was a war-time president and leader of a party that had marketed itself for the past thirty years as the masculine party. Because one of the pillars of Republican electoral strategy since the 1980 election of Reagan had been to secure a large percentage of white male voters, Rove and company had somehow to discredit Kerry's masculinity. They were surely aware that Kerry, in his several successful campaigns for the U.S. Senate in Massachusetts, had received a strong majority of white working-class male votes in blue collar cities across the state. The aristocratic Kerry was able to escape the fate of other Democrats who had been smeared by Republican operatives and right-wing media voices as "elitist" snobs, largely because of his Vietnam War service. Kerry often appeared in campaign photo ops with fellow Vietnam veterans, blue collar as well as white collar, and he also appeared frequently with members of the fire fighters union, further reinforcing his identification with traditionally masculine blue-collar white men.

A signature campaign tactic of Rove's was to attack his opponent's strongest suit. Since Kerry's best asset in a campaign during wartime was his record as a decorated war veteran, Rove knew that the Bush campaign had to cast doubt on the credibility of Kerry's war hero status. (Rove was reputed to have strong Texas ties to one or more of the key architects of the Swift Boat Veterans for Truth group). The Swift Boat ads hit hard at Kerry's carefully constructed image as a warrior whose battle credentials earned him the respect of his "band of brothers." Although the men with whom he served directly almost all strongly supported him, right-wing activists opposed to Kerry were able to locate a significant number of Navy veterans who served on swift boats near or contemporaneous with Kerry who were willing to suggest or allege that Kerry was a poseur who exaggerated his own credentials and would say or do anything to get elected. Kerry himself contributed to this image by waiting weeks to respond forcefully to the ads, and by employing a cautious campaign strategy and failing to delineate sharp differences with Bush's policy in Iraq until the late stages of the campaign.

There are clearly a number of reasons why George W. Bush – who many progressive and even establishment historians have labelled the worst president in modern times, and whose first term earned the title of "A Failed Presidency" by the *Los Angeles Times* in an editorial endorsing his opponent – nonetheless won reelection by a popular vote margin of some three million votes. George W. Bush got the most votes – up to that time – of any presidential candidate in U.S. history. (Kerry received the second most). There will be debate about how this happened for many years to come. Part of this debate needs to focus on the televisual performance of presidential candidates, and the discourses about masculinities, femininities and power in the 24/7 media environment within which 21st century presidential campaigns are largely fought.

Obama vs. McCain

There are many binary categories that have been used to characterize the 2008 race between John McCain and Barack Obama: old vs. new, experience vs. change, the warrior vs. the orator, conservative vs. liberal. But the 2008 presidential campaign was also a competition between two styles (and ideologies) of masculinity, and in that sense this election was like every other one. The key difference – a dramatic difference – is that Obama is not a white man, which meant that for the first time in U.S. history a presidential race featured a competition between one version of white masculinity and one version of Black masculinity.

After Obama won the Democratic nomination in a protracted and historic primary struggle with Hillary Clinton, conservative activists and Republican partisans in the media began to attack him using the same strategy they had used on Democrats for almost four decades: they accused him of being insufficiently manly for the job. The right-wing talk radio icon Rush Limbaugh led the charge; some of his most cutting criticisms of Obama concerned the Illinois senator's manhood. One line he repeated frequently on his radio program was "I don't think Barack Obama is half the man Sarah Palin is." Earlier in the year Limbaugh said of Obama "He can't take a punch, he's weak, and he whines. I'm sure some women find that attractive because they would look at him as a little boy and would want to protect him...But it embarrasses me as a man" (Brownstein, 2008, p. 58). Presumably Limbaugh is unembarrassed – as a man – that while he mercilessly ridicules liberal men as "linguini-spined," emasculated wimps, the uber-hawk talker avoided military service in Vietnam by claiming an anal boil rendered him unfit for service (Greenwald, 2008, p. 110).

After Obama defeated Hillary Clinton in the 2008 Democratic primaries, commentary about gender tended to skip over the men in order to focus on Sarah Palin, the only woman on a major party ticket. But masculinity remained a crucial subtext of the political discourse in the Obama vs. McCain match-up – even if few in mainstream media identified a contest between two men explicitly as a struggle about gender. One revealing headline on the cover of *Time* magazine read "Why Obama Is Tougher Than He Looks." Perhaps responding to relentless right-wing criticism of Obama's readiness to lead the armed forces as commander-in-chief, the authors of the article stated that "you don't rise in Chicago politics or come this far this fast in a national race by being soft, naïve, or scared of a fight." They claimed that Obama's "...mild manner belies fierce self-control. The frequent self-mocking conceals a stubborn self-confidence. He not only plays hard; he plays to win, rubs it in sometimes if he does and takes losses hard" (Duffy and Gibbs, 2008, p. 36).

In the last several elections, presidential masculinity has been discussed in class-coded language, such as when right-wing commentators tried to portray Obama as an "elitist." The elitist tag has long been a smear tactic conservative activists have used to attract working-class white voters – especially men – in part by impugning the manhood of Democrats and liberals, and even moderate Republicans. The sentiment goes something like this: "'Real men' work with their hands (and vote Republican), not like those wimpy upper-class types who drive Volvos, sip lattes and listen to

National Public Radio." Initially, John McCain hoped that his war hero status and image as a "maverick" politician would be enough to win a wide margin among white male voters against the cerebral (and Black) Obama, who had no military record and scant foreign policy credentials. But unlike the election of 2004, when the Bush campaign exploited the fear of terrorism to help win an electoral majority, in 2008 the election's focus was squarely back on the domestic economy – where millions of white men (and women) feared for the loss of their jobs and the shrinkage of their retirement accounts. And after the sub-prime mortgage crisis precipitated a Wall Street collapse in the early part of the general election campaign, and the economy became the dominant campaign issue, Obama was able to project an image of competence and stability in the face of crisis, as the terms of debate shifted about the "masculine" qualities necessary in a president.

One of the more remarkable developments in American political history was the emergence of a Black man as a reassuring presidential presence at a time of great national anxiety. Barack Obama won the presidency by building an energized electoral coalition of young voters, first-time voters, and an overwhelming majority of voters of color, especially African Americans. Like every Democratic presidential candidate for the past three decades, he lost the white vote. Still, he won a landslide victory among all women. And while he failed to capture the white male vote, he did much better with white men than John Kerry did in 2004. Kerry lost among white males by twenty-five points; Obama lost by only sixteen. As a result, he won the overall men's vote, however slightly. While this election will be analyzed for many years, at this point it is reasonable to infer that Obama did better among men than any Democrat in nearly thirty years in part because he performed so well in a high pressure environment. In so doing, it is possible that he ushered in – or reintroduced – a new masculine presidential archetype. As Jewel Woods (2008) wrote near the start of the general election campaign:

> ...The key to Senator Obama's appeal among men is not solely his intelligence or his elocution, but his smooth and unflappable character, or simply his 'coolness.' Obama has become the embodiment of smooth. He is like one of the agents in the Matrix trilogy who moves so fast you can't tell he's dodging bullets. He possesses a 'grace under fire' that men have always found intoxicating. Similar to a "Black Frank Sinatra," Obama possesses a Billy Dee Williams type of cool. The result is that he...has accomplished what men like John Kerry and the former Al Gore were not able to accomplish – he has brought sexy back to white-collar masculinity. (p. 3)

It remains to be seen whether Obama's more cerebral, conciliatory and less aggressive masculine style will ultimately help or hinder his ability to govern. Early in his presidency, particularly in the health care debate, many of his own supporters and others in media questioned his "toughness" in terms of his willingness to stand firm against right-wing attacks on his progressive program. It seems likely, however, that if Obama maintains his "cool" and has a successful presidency, he will have a profound influence on the next generation of (male and female) political leaders, as well as men in general.

MEDIA AND INFORMATION TECHNOLOGY, PRESIDENTIAL MASCULINITIES, AND PEDAGOGY

New media and information technologies are in the process of changing how presidential masculinities are represented and contested, due to the fact that fragmentation and segmentation of audiences in the new media environment provides the preconditions for more diverse representations, interpretations and contestations. This distinguishes the present era from the media environment as late as the 1980s, when a handful of television broadcast networks dominated media coverage of politics. In today's ubiquitous digital media landscape, ever-growing legions of bloggers can weigh in with their assessments of candidates, and not merely have to accept the frames and conclusions of the gate-keeping image-makers in the corporate media. Wikis, bulletin boards, list serves and social networking sites such as *Facebook* provide unprecedented opportunities for like-minded or oppositional individuals and groups to share information and perceptions about candidates and political developments that might run counter to conventions of mainstream commentary. New media and information technologies (MITs) have also created new avenues and opportunities for public pedagogy about a wide range of social and political issues and themes. In addition, *YouTube* provides the platform for the democratization of televisual images: one short video of Will Ferrell playing George W. Bush as a bumbling, narcissistic frat boy trying to read the cue cards correctly for a campaign commercial paints a thousand words, as did a widely viewed campaign commercial spoof of John McCain by Paris Hilton, where she responded to his campaign's derisive use of her in an attack ad against Barack Obama by referring to McCain as "that wrinkly white-haired guy." My intent is to discuss some of the implications for constructions and representations of presidential masculinities occasioned by the growth of the Internet and World Wide Web and the new forms of online activism and community-building they enable.

There is an ongoing debate among communication and information studies scholars about the potentially transformative powers of media and information technologies on the theory and practice of political communication. This debate is part of a much larger shift underway in how to theorize "mass communication." As Leah Lievrouw writes:

> The technological convergence of MITs, in parallel with the social and cultural blending of entertainment, education, work, civic life, and interpersonal interaction, requires a complete rethinking of people's relationships with and understanding of communication media...Mediated communication processes have become thoroughly transactional and interactive; it is no longer easy to separate producers from consumers, senders from receivers...mediated communication is both form and content, the means and ends of culture and expression. (Lievrouw, 2008, p. 12)

This epochal shift has implications for political communication both in terms of challenging the primacy of "top-down" and exclusivist control of images by corporate media and in the campaigns themselves, whose hierarchical organization and ability to control the distribution and reception of their messages has been challenged by grassroots counter-organizing using meetups and social network software (Lievrouw, 2008, p. 21). The Internet in particular has become an increasingly important force in contemporary politics; a survey by the Pew Internet and American Life Project reported that although over three-quarters of Americans said that television was their main source of news about the 1994 elections, 52% of Internet users surveyed sought news about the 2004 elections online (ibid. p. 21). Kahn and Kellner (2005) argue that the Howard Dean presidential campaign's use of the Internet in 2004 showed that it could generate political enthusiasm among the youth, connect people around issues and articulate with struggles in the real world. The Dean experiment further demonstrated that "Internet politics was not just a matter of circulating discourse in a self-contained cybersphere but that it was a force that could intervene in the political battles of the contemporary era of media culture" (ibid, p. 79).

The relevance for my study of this shift toward more interactivity in media and information technology is that there are now more means available to resist hegemonic constructions of presidential masculinities. For example, feminist and profeminist netroots activists can challenge and contest the masculine mythification processes that often characterize coverage of U.S. presidents in the mainstream media, especially during wartime. There is also more space on the Internet and Web for positive representations of "alternative" masculinities, such as anti-war, profeminist and queer masculinities, all of which are marginalized and confined – if not openly ridiculed and dismissed – in corporate media discourse. This is by no means to say that the democratization of image-making will necessarily result in the triumph of counterhegemonic constructions of presidential masculinities. Right-wing individuals and groups with an ideological investment in the maintenance of traditional patriarchal power and the public pedagogies that help to sustain it, have access to the same technologies.

Consider the episode, reported by the author and star blogger Glenn Greenwald, where a 2007 news item about Democratic presidential candidate John Edwards' $400 haircut posted on the popular news site *The Politico* led to repeated coverage on network and cable television news, as well as multiple mentions in stories in the *Washington Post* and *New York Times* – not to mention incalculable mentions on talk radio and conservative blogs and web sites. The original "news story" posting linked to a widely disseminated video from the 2004 campaign, where Edwards brushes his hair in front of a mirror for thirty to forty seconds. According to Greenwald, that video was "endlessly deployed by right-wing pundits and bloggers to mock Edwards during the campaign as an effeminate girly-man obsessed with his hair" (Greenwald, 2008, p. 58). The version of the video that *The Politico* piece linked to had the song "I Feel Pretty" blaring in the background, which alone has been viewed over one million times on YouTube (ibid, p. 59).

Conclusion

While the focus of this chapter has been on matters related specifically to presidential masculinities and pedagogy, it is only a slight exaggeration to state that a critical media literacy movement is a necessary precondition for the maintenance of a democratic society in the 21st century. As Kellner and Share (2007) put it,

> Individuals are often not aware that they are being educated and constructed by media culture, as its pedagogy is frequently invisible and unconscious. This situation calls for critical approaches that make us aware of how media construct meanings, influence and educate audiences, and impose their messages and values. Critical media literacy involves cultivating skills in analyzing media codes and conventions, abilities to criticize stereotypes, dominant values, and ideologies, and competencies to interpret the multiple meanings and messages generated by media texts. (p. 372)

Perhaps nowhere is the need for media literacy skills more directly tied to the future of democratic practice than in the area of politics. Political campaigns have become media spectacles where political parties representing elite interests spend literally billions of dollars to convince voters to ratify their continued hegemony. As New York advertising executive and talk show host Donny Deutsch said, "the selling of a candidate is no different from the smart media buying for toothpaste and automobiles, especially as people fragment their media habits" (Seelye, 2004).

In mainstream media in recent years, some attention has been paid to the power of media culture in shaping political discourse and hence influencing electoral outcomes. But the analysis is typically superficial. For example, there are campaign ad watch features in various newspapers – including The New York Times and Boston Globe – which feature discussions about factual claims made in ads, such as whether a candidate's economic program would result in deficits or would require increased taxes to fund. While minimally informative, these analyses rarely deconstruct the images presented, or analyze the way that various representations tap into (or subvert) hegemonic ideals of masculine power or presidential leadership. In fact, in my careful reading of the mainstream political coverage on television, talk radio, the Internet, newspapers and in newsmagazines, I have seen or read very little – if any – mention of basic media literacy concepts that should be taught in elementary school. In one sense, this is not surprising, because corporate media is part of a capitalist political economy whose stability is ensured in part through systems of ideological indoctrination that remain invisible by passing for common sense.

Counterhegemonic analyses are unwelcome guests in this highly profitable home. On a material level, revenue from political ads has emerged in recent decades as a major profit center for network and cable television; they would be loathe to criticize this cash cow as long as it sustains them. By contrast, one of the chief goals of many campaign finance reform initiatives at the federal and state level is to diminish the need for presidential campaigns to spend so much money on television advertising.

There was some discussion throughout the 2004 campaign of images of presidential masculinity, as both major candidates put on costumes and appeared in numerous photo ops designed to create a working-class masculine image. But notably, the discussion about the respective Vietnam-era experiences of Bush and Kerry were rarely presented in gendered terms. One Newsweek cover story, which featured grainy photos of Kerry and Bush in their twenties in the late 1960s, did not once mention the word "masculinity," although the entire article can be read primarily as a discussion of the masculine credibility attaching to military service, or the avoidance of it, and – in Kerry's case – the damage to his reputation as "one of the guys" when in testimony to a congressional panel he made reference to atrocities committed by U.S. troops in Vietnam. By contrast, I would read the Vietnam-era images (and personae) of the candidates that played such a central role in the 2004 campaign not as a discourse about a war that has been over for a third of a century, but as part of a cutting-edge, 21st century debate about what it means to be a strong man and an effective national leader.

Because media play an indisputably central role in contemporary politics, political media literacy should be seen as an essential part of civics and citizen education in the 21st century. The basic rationale for the development of a political media literacy movement is that education for democracy in the 21st century requires citizens to be media literate. In this era, media is the single most important source of political information and persuasion. In order for voters to make informed choices about which parties and candidates to support, they must have the critical media literacy skills 1) to discern the underlying ideologies and class interests that shape political discourse in a 24/7 media culture dominated by corporate media, and 2) to deconstruct, read critically and contest hegemonic images of embodied power, especially white male power. There is little hope for a truly progressive politics emerging in the U.S. in the 21st century unless we address the narrow and deeply conservative ways that corporate media, in its dominance of political discourse, simultaneously reinforces hegemonic notions of "manhood," places significant obstacles in the path of women's political leadership, and frames the electoral choices available to voters.

The teaching of political media literacy in middle school and high school should be seen as a fundamental component of a revitalized push for 21st century civics/government/social studies education, and the integration of media literacy into political science curricula at the post-secondary and graduate level needs to be understood as a critical piece of a much larger progressive media reform project in the coming decade. Finally, as discussed above, political media literacy initiatives in the 21st century need to include an emphasis on new media and information technologies, and the implications of those technologies for civic engagement, electoral campaigns, and the very nature of democratic institutions.

REFERENCES

Barabak, M. (2008, September 4). Defiant Sarah Palin comes out swinging. *Los Angeles Times*.

Bordo, S. (1994). *Unbearable weight: Feminism, western culture and the body*. Berkeley, CA: University of California Press.

Brownstein, R. (2003). For 2004, Bush has strength in the white male numbers. *Los Angeles Times*, p. 1.

Brownstein, R. (2008, September). Reconcilable differences. *The Atlantic*, p. 58.

Center for American Women and Politics. (2004, November 5). Rutgers, NJ. Retrieved from http://www.rci.rutgers.edu/~cawp/Facts/Elections/GG2004Facts.pdf

Connell, R. W. (1987). *Gender and power*. Stanford, CA: Stanford University Press.

Ducat, S. (2004). *The wimp factor: Gender gaps, holy wars, and the politics of anxious masculinity*. Boston: Beacon Press.

Duffy, M., & Gibbs, N. (2008, March 17). The long way home. *Time magazine*, p. 36.

Dyson, M. E. (2004, September 30). The Tavis Smiley Show. *National Public Radio*. Retrieved from www.npr.org, http://www.npr.org/templates/story/story.php?storyId=4054526
Faludi, S. (2007). *The terror dream: Fear and fantasy in post-9/11 America*. New York: Metropolitan Books.
Faludi, S. (2008, May 9). The Fight Stuff. *The New York Times*.
Fineman, H. (2004). Rove unleashed. *Newsweek Magazine*, p. 23.
Gibson, J. (1994). *Warrior dreams: Violence and manhood in post-Vietnam America*. New York: Hill and Wang.
Giroux, H. (1994). *Disturbing pleasures: Learning popular culture*. New York: Routledge.
Giroux, H. (2001, Winter). Private satisfactions and public disorders: Fight club, patriarchy, and the politics of masculine violence. *JAC, 21*(1), 1–31.
Giuliani, R. (2004, August 31). *www.CNN.com*. http://www.cnn.com/2004/ALLPOLITICS/08/30/giuliani.transcript/index.html
Greenwald, G. (2008). *Great American hypocrites: Toppling the big myths of Republican politics*. New York: Crown Publishers.
Griffith, L. (2005, May). *Where we went wrong: How the public lost faith in Democrats' ability to protect our national security, and how to stage a comeback*. The Truman National Security Project. Retrieved from http://www.trumanproject.org/trumanpaper3.html
Han, L., & Heldman, C. (2007). *Rethinking madam president: Are we ready for a woman in the White House*? Boulder, CO: Lynne Reinner Publishers.
Harding, S. (1991). *Whose science? Whose knowledge?: Thinking from women's lives*. Ithaca, NY: Cornell University Press.
hooks, b. (1992). *Black looks: Race and representation*. Boston: South End Press.
Jamieson, K. (1993). *Dirty politics: Deception, distraction and democracy*. Oxford: Oxford University Press.
Jhally, S. (1984). The Spectacle of accumulation: Material and cultural factors in the evolution of the sports/media complex. *Insurgent Sociologist, 12*(3), 41.
Kahn, R., & Kellner, D. (2005). Oppositional politics and the Internet: A critical/reconstructive approach. *Cultural Politics, 1*(1), 79.
Kakutani, M. (2008, August 15). Is Jon Stewart the most trusted man in America? *The New York Times*.
Katz, J. (2003). Advertising and the construction of violent white masculinity: From Eminem to Clinique for Men. In G. Dines & J. Humez (Eds.), *Gender, race and class in media: A text reader* (2nd ed.). Thousand Oaks, CA: Sage Publications.
Kellner, D. (1995). *Media culture: Cultural studies, identity and politics between the modern and the post-modern*. London: Routledge.
Kellner, D. (1997). *Communications versus cultural studies: Overcoming the divide*. Retrieved from www.gseis.ucla.edu/faculty/kellner/kellner.html
Kellner, D., & Share, J. (2006). *Toward critical media literacy: Core concepts, debates, organizations and policy*. Retrieved June 20, 2008, from http://www.gseis.ucla.edu/faculty/kellner/index.html
Kimmel, M. (1996). *Manhood in America: A cultural history*. New York: Free Press.
Kuhn, D. P. (2007). *The neglected voter: White men and the democratic dilemma*. New York: Palgrave MacMillan.
Lakoff, G., & Johnson, M. (1980). *Metaphors we live by*. Chicago: University of Chicago Press.
Lievrouw, L. (2008). Technology in/as applied communication research. In L. Frey (Ed.), *Handbook of applied communication*. New York: Routledge.
Milbank, D. (2005, February 6). Mixing politics, pigskins: When Allen talks, football jargon flows. *Washington Post*, p. C01.
Miller, T. C., & Brownstein, R. (2000, February 9). McCain delivers hard left to Christian right. *Los Angeles Times*, p. 1.
New York Times. (2008, October 8). Politics of attack. p. 24.
Norris, P. (Ed.). (1997). *Women, media and politics*. New York: Oxford University Press.

Schneider, W. (2007, July 6). Presidential fundraising hits record pace. *CNN.Com*. Retrieved from http://politicalticker.blogs.cnn.com/2007/07/06/schneider-why-are-dems-winning-the-money-race/#more-729

Schouten, F. (2008, October. 23). Political spending races toward record $5.3 billion. *USA Today*, p. 1.

Schweizer, P. (2007). Don't punt on Iran. *USA Today*, p. 13A.

Seelye, K. (2004). How to sell a candidate to a Porsche-driving, Leno-loving Nascar fan. *New York Times.com*.

Teixeira, R., & Rogers, J. (2000). *America's forgotten majority: Why the white working class still matters*. New York: Basic Books.

Tomkins, J. (1994). *West of everything: The inner life of westerns*. New York: Oxford University Press.

Wolf, N. (1992). *The beauty myth: How images of beauty are used against women*. New York: Anchor Books.

Woods, J. (2008, September 11). Bringing sexy back: Barack Obama and the triumph of white-collar masculinity. *The Black Commentator, 290*. Retrieved November 17, 2008, from www.blackcommentator.com

Zeleny, J. (2008, July 24). Obama meets with Israeli and Palestinian leaders. *The New York Times*, p. A16.

Jackson Katz
Graduate School of Education & Information Studies
University of California
Los Angeles

READING FORMATIONS

DIANA SILBERMAN-KELLER

22. THE IM-PERSONATED AND PERFORMATIVE PEDAGOGIES OF SOCIAL CHANGE

Informal Education's Ever-Varying Tropes

INTRODUCTION

Informal Education refers to a theoretical and practical framework encompassing the entire spectrum of initiatives and activities promoted by informal educational organizations (Bertrand & Houssaye, 1999; Houssaye, 1993). Informal Education organizations have been considered as composed by "by-pass organizations" (e.g. political, social, ideological activist organizations, youth movements, museums, after-school clubs or programs, community centers, etc.) (Silberman-Keller, 1987). In the realm of Informal Education, "by-pass organizations" complement and sometimes contradict formal national education systems (Bock and Papagianis; 1983; Coombs & Ahmed 1974; Lamm, 1975). The two- formal and informal education systems- together configure a semiotically significant system active in the fields of cultural politics.

More than socially established education systems, informal education systems – when compared to the school system – create public spheres that culturally perform[1] and im-personate[2] vivid pedagogical[3] and political stages. Informal education and learning organizations reflect and are reflected in cultural politics because they are responsible for a growing field of cultural activities addressed to a variety of publics.

This chapter adopts the Michael Parenti (1999)[4] approach, which is based on Antonio Gramsci's[5] (1971) consideration of culture as representative of more than a society's customs and mores, its language, art, laws and religion. Parenti stresses that the state is only the "outer ditch behind which there [stands] a powerful system of fortresses and earthworks" (p. #), a network of cultural values and institutions not normally thought of as political. From this point of view, culture is anything but neutral. What we call "our culture" is largely reflective of existing hegemonic arrangements within the social order, strongly favoring some interests over others.

Against this background, the chapter centers on a description and analysis of Informal Education's differing and deferred[6] tropes vis-à-vis its History and the horizons of its "*a venir*". The chapter especially stresses the influence of the actual and general context on Informal Education tropes as signs of the cultural politics engaged in during this era of globalization, individuation and radical techno-cultural change.

Z. Leonardo (ed.), Handbook of Cultural Politics and Education, 511–526.

THE POLITICS OF INFORMAL EDUCATION

As compared to Formal Education, which is usually conformed politically through the state's dominance of the educational scene, the political spaces of Informal Education are dispersed among a variety of social, political, cultural and economic agencies and institutions. Even though states and international agencies have intercepted the effectiveness of creating Informal Education agencies in the last fifty years, the majority of these institutions remain linked to dependent on the voluntary participation motivated by their publics' interests and needs.

Moreover, the flexibility of the Informal Education System results in the relatively rapid creation and re-creation of educational, cultural, political and social agencies. This pace does not always make opportunities available for defining what Informal Education is. What are its main purposes and aims? How does it work and who works with whom?

To this volatility, composed of the alternating definitions characteristic of Informal Education, we can add that since the 1980s, with its privatization and limitation of state intervention in the supply of social, educational and cultural services, the considerable growth of the Informal Education field. New Informal Education agencies have appeared as NGOs, some as state agencies, but many more as private and public agencies supplying educational services to social, educational, political and cultural institutions.

These vivid, energetic processes have composed a semiotic field allowing the interception and observance of how the different and differing meanings of Informal Education constitute and are constituted. It is in this field that we can observe the changing tropes of Informal Education in their essence as an ever-changing repertoire of educational, cultural, social and political activities that sometimes bridge between the deficiencies of formal and informal education and sometimes propose radical alternatives to institutionalized education.

I have chosen to introduce some Informal Education tropes as they emerge during current activities in the field of practice. These tropes do not mark a hierarchy of Informal Education agencies; instead, they combine some of their rhetorical and thematic characteristics while performing and impersonating any of their salient functions.For instance, Informal Education is considered to be a bridge between traditional and modern societies, allowing temporariness and its practices to create zones where renovation and continuity can meet. The trope of "Social Change", one of the slogans adopted by some activist and radical organizations belonging to Modern Informal Education, also motivates and justifies their very existence. This same slogan grants license to the activities of a variety of Informal Institutions throughout the world while maintaining the ideological flavor of one highly salient social functions of Informal Education.

Informal Education is one of the traditional bridges for the absorption and transformation of technological change. For instance, developing countries have enlisted Informal Education to introduce new technological practices in Agriculture and Industry. Nevertheless, the Techno-Cultural Informal Learning trope nowadays underwrites the adoption of modalities unprecedented in their scope. Indeed, the trope may represent the only strategy able to deal with these new technologies and link them to cultural practices.

This chapter will center on introducing and discussing Informal Education tropes as exemplifying practices common to the field of practice. It does so by commenting critically on their shared and differing points as they delineate the "invaginated space"[7] of Informal Education's ways of generating and regenerating its position in the world.

INFORMAL EDUCATION-CHANGING TROPES

The "Between Tradition and Modernity" Informal Learning Trope

The "Between Tradition and Modernity" informal learning trope[8] includes the idea of sustaining idealized learning patterns from the past on the one hand, and the tendency to transport these patterns into modern public spheres where learning is not generally supposed to take place on the other.

The "Between Tradition and Modernity" informal learning trope is extant in informal educational frameworks such as youth movements that, by celebrating "nature," devolve learning from school classrooms to the family yard by creating "second homes" as learning places. It is from there, from those "second homes," that learning can be translated to any place where the "we" of the respective group gather (Silberman-Keller, 2006).

Guides in museums, or in after school programs, youth movements and clubs have become as close as family members and family members have sometimes become guides in these informal learning places. These added layers are revealed from the study of conversations between the family members, children and youth visiting museums of every kind.[9]

The transmission of researchers' critical attitudes toward modern society transpires – as revealed by the study of cultural learning strategies – through mourning and remembrance inscriptions to disappearing and idealized ways of learning on the one hand and when they elaborate transformative strategies for actualizing informal learning in traditional societies in voluntary organizations, interactive museums and collaborative schools in middle-class US communities on the other (Rogoff et al., 2003).

It is through the Socio-Cultural Research Stream of informal learning research that we can obtain traces of informal learning (and teaching) in traditional societies. Maynard and Greenfield (2006), for instance, have characterized cultural teaching and learning as exhibiting five features: observation, contextualized talk, scaffolding, guiding the body and multiple teachers. All these are characterized by the absence of direct praise – or criticism – directed toward the learner.

Other research on informal learning in traditional societies points to similar characteristics. Lave and Wenger (1991) illustrate their theory with observations taken from different apprenticeships (Yucatec midwives, Vai and Gola tailors, US Navy quartermasters, meat-cutters and non-drinking alcoholics in Alcoholics Anonymous).

According to Lave and Wenger, people who join communities initially learn at the periphery. As they become more competent, they move toward the 'centre' of the particular community. Informal learning is therefore not seen as acquisition of knowledge by individuals so much as a process of *social* participation. The nature of the *situation* impacts significantly on the process. McDermott (1999) has stressed the importance of learning traditionally that, in his view, is how learning progresses, that is, through relationships between people. Learning is embedded in the conditions that bring people together; it establishes a point of contact that allows pieces of information to acquire relevance. According to McDermott, without these points of contact, without the system of relevancies, there is no learning and little memory. Learning does not belong to individual persons but to the various conversations in which they take part.

Rogoff et al. (2003) have studied how people learn through actively observing and "listening-in" on on-going conversations during shared endeavors. Keen observation and listening-in are especially valued in some cultural communities where children participate in mature communal activities. According to Rogoff et al., this type of intentional participation also occurs in some settings (such as early language learning in the family) within communities that routinely segregate children from the full range of adult activities.

Most of the work cited here compare informal learning in traditional societies with formal education in modern societies as a point of departure when tracing the origins of the (dis)continuation of informal learning patterns. Significantly, these comparisons accentuate the changes suffered by informal learning in traditional communities subsequent to contact with modern society through school assistance and participation, television and economic changes. In this way, for instance, informal learning tropes construct traditional informal learning memorials parallel to the idea of dispersing traditional informal learning in schools and outside school walls.

This trope is widely celebrated in most of the pedagogies that accompany Informal Education History.[10] It reflects an attempt to bypass the temporality of education history by juxtaposing alternative developments to the conversion of the modern industrialized and industrializing school into the core educational institution of modern society.

Culturally speaking, it is as if in the same "blink of an eye," the comparison effectuated by juxtaposing traditional and modern models of learning as two polar movements, was activated in the same field. Stated differently, a situation was created where formal and informal educational settings *critique* one another at the same time that they complement one another by providing what is "missing."

From the location of the school, educational organizations ensure the perpetual return of traditional informal settings. By impersonating educational role-takers, informal education educators preserve "the family" figuration of traditional family roles in informal education. Nevertheless, these performances and impersonations are enacted from a site located in the social and cultural contexts that constantly attempt to actualize by differentiating and deferring these very traditional performances and impersonations, one from the other.

THE SOCIAL CHANGE TROPE

Social change is one of the most celebrated motifs in the overt – and covert – ideological platforms expounded by informal education organizations. Daniel Schugurensky (2006) demonstrates this assertion by tracking the long tradition linking the idea that the very act of participating in deliberation and decision making –through dialogue – has high pedagogic potential. He quotes Carole Pateman (1970/1988) from her classic book on participatory democracy in noting that the central function of participation in Rousseau's theory is an educative one, using the term 'education' in the same broad sense that permeates Freirean thought. Schugurensky cites Pateman's judgment that Rousseau's ideal system is designed to generate responsible, individual social and political action through the effect of the participatory process itself. Along the same lines, J.S. Mill also identified the educative function of participation in local governance. Following Rousseau and his proponents, Schugurensky (2006), argues that the existence of representative institutions at national levels is insufficient for true democracy. He contends that other spheres, aimed at nurturing political socialization (what he calls "social training"), are necessary for the development of those individual attitudes and psychological qualities needed for good quality participation. These additional spheres need to be created and invigorated.

As an example of the implementation of Pateman's ideas, Schugurensky (2006) refers to the participatory budget of Porto Alegre, Brazil. This project, which allows ordinary citizens to make decisions on a portion of the municipal government's budget, has been continuously elaborated since its inception in 1989. Its institutional features have been discussed extensively in the literature (see for example Abers 1998; Baierle 2000; Genro 1999; Schugurensky 2002). Schugurensky reports that the participatory budget has served as an informal school for citizenship training. It provides broad opportunities for political and democratic learning and is enjoyed by the many people who take as full advantage as possible of the program's potential. As a result, political capital, understood as the capacity to influence political decisions, is more equitably redistributed, meaning that it is no longer a monopoly of professional politicians and so-called "professional citizens".

Schugurensky (2006) concludes his research by pointing out that the development of a sense of political efficacy is only part of participation's educative effect. Other effects include the broadening of perspectives, the awareness of the linkage between private and public interests, the familiarity with democratic procedures, the concern for improving the urban landscape and quality of life in addition to the development of democratic political skills and attitudes.

His idea of a school for citizenship implies learning how to practice democracy between elections:

> ...We are not born democrats, and often we are not raised to be active democratic citizens. So, democracy is something that we can learn everyday, and the more democratic the enabling structures that nurture the deliberation process, the more significant the democratic learning will be. Most political forums today, be they right, center or left, are not characterized by dialogue

> but by monologues and confrontation. Participatory democracy, with all its flows, at least allows for listening, which is a precondition for learning. In sum, we need new ways of doing politics, and we need to create a multiplicity of healthy democratic spaces… (Schugurensky 2006, p. 180).

Conceptually close to Schugurensky's study is Kahane's (1975, 1997), elaboration of the Informal code – based on Tocqueville's (1840) analysis of America as a developing democratic society – as the generative motif of informal education. Kahane concludes that the more a society is populated by informal behaviors and institutions, the more this society will develop democratic regimes. Kahane stresses that democracy is rooted in the most basic social structures of society, such as the family. He bases his argument on Tocqueville, who pointed out that "the several members of the family stand upon an entirely new footing toward each other, that the distance which formerly separated a father from his sons has been lessened; and that paternal authority, if not destroyed, is at least impaired…" (Kahane 1997, p. 180).

Kahane had extracted from Tocqueville a structural component of the Informal code that he named *symmetry,* and to which he assigns the behavior that generates and reflects informality. He defines Symmetry as "a balanced reciprocal relationship based on equivalence of resources and mutual coordination of principles and expectations, in which no party can impose his or her rules on another" (p. 27).

While Schugurensky's recognition that democracy was not a fact of nature, fed his idea of the necessity for continual informal learning to foster participative democracy, Kahane's veiled presumption was that *asymmetry* is what characterizes most human relationships. However, his ideal type of informality – as performed and im-personated in youth movements – was what would change social reality or at least secure democratic social patterns of behavior. From his perspective, the phenomenon of informal organizations or culture is quite common in the postmodern world. It represented a fluid response to the rapid change and complexity that increased the probability of living in a meaningful civic world.

From a phenomenological point of view, says Kahane, (1997, p. 35), informal structures provide a context in which young people can freely invent and construct their concepts of reality (sometimes in a naïve way). Rational, authentic decision making is most likely to emerge in informal settings because there it can be relatively free of internal inhibitions and external constraints. Kahane goes still further with his ideal type model of informality by claiming that informal institutions provide an open setting in which individuals can interpret a wide range of experiences according to their own interests and construct their own views of reality. In that sense, informal settings are interpretive institutions where experiences gain meaning and value preferences (Kahane, 1997, p. 35).

A more dramatic function of informal learning in relation to social change is implicated by a group of social activists and researchers in Argentina, "Fundared," headed by Elinora Dabas (1995). As of 1989, Fundared, an NGO, has dedicated itself to supporting and researching social network creation as a response to the damage and destruction suffered by social institutions in Argentinean society. Dabas considers development of social networks as making great contributions to the social capital that plays so important a role in informal education and learning settings. She links the evolution of the term "social capital" to the work done by Pierre Bourdieu (1991), and Robert D. Putnam (2000).

Learning from Putman, Dabas asserts that interaction enables people to build communities, commit themselves to each other and knit social webs. The sense of belonging and concrete experience of social networks (together with the trust and tolerance that can be involved), she argues, can greatly benefit people. It follows that informal educators should work to enable people to join groups and in this way encourage the associational life that makes so significantly differentiates the experience of belonging to different communities.

The second point Dabas raises refers to informal education's longstanding concern with association and the quality of associational life, experiences that can make a direct and important contribution to the development of social networks and the strengthening of democracy. Informal educators' interest in dialogue and conversation as well as the cultivation of environments in which people can work together takes us to the heart of what is required to strengthen and develop social capital. Following Putnam while stressing the difference between Latin American societies and those where Putnam developed his theories, Dabas advises informal educators to work across communities, particularly for the purpose of sustaining the commitment and capacities already present in community organizations and interest groups together with encouraging those on the cusp to become actively involved.

Every education fosters some attitudes toward social change. Some forms of education are conservative, others are progressive; radical pedagogies may even foster radical social change. These ideological trends likewise exist in the field of informal education. However, what we learn from the social change trope performing and im-personated in informal learning programs and institutions, is the belief in informal educational activities as potentially capable of effectuating social change, beyond representing an attitude toward change.

This unique characteristic of informal education seems to represent a cultural system that implements gradual or even rapid social change as part of a general cultural system of education. This implies a division of labor between formal and informal education that could eventually result in maintaining social structures, á la Bourdieu, through social reproduction by means of the formal system. Another system, the informal system, would complement the formal education system's cultural function by sustaining atomized educational places. Atomized informal education sites would then transform social and cultural reproduction into a reproductive mechanism containing the social change trope, implemented through an economy of negotiation between the two systems as they converse in the public space. What emerges from this possibility of considering the educational system as composed by at least two differentiated ways of working and semiotic signifying, is that social change will enter the world of practice through its marginal corridors (Silberman-Keller, 2006). This implies that social change will become viable through the two educational systems that, in the final count, are cultural institutions destined to, sustain, preserve and conserve society.

THE TECHNO-CULTURAL INFORMAL LEARNING TROPE

Technological and vocational learning has been one of informal education's most traditional objectives. These learning domains bear the usual techno-cultural informal learning trope. Traditional societies use them to transfer the knowledge, usually mediated by technologies, needed in order to maintain material and social life from one generation to the other. Such transfers are completed by applying informal learning strategies, such as agriculture, construction and clothing manufacture, to name just some basic human technological fields through which humans have learned to survive. In some countries and societies, these domains are fed especially by the knowledge and skills transmitted through informal learning.

Nowadays, vocational training is especially encouraged through informal learning in large countries and continents such as India, China, Brazil and Africa because due to their size, they face difficulties in developing formal education systems. They have chosen to develop informal education and learning settings instead (Coombs & Ahmed, 1974).[11]

Informal vocational training, as carried out in Europe, is considered to be the trend in informal education for validating the knowledge and skills learned. Michael Eraut (2000) has observed that different kinds of knowledge are acquired by a combination of learning from books, learning from people and learning from personal experience. In recognition of these modes Eraut proposes specific ways of developing professional knowledge and competence.

The current attitude toward the relationship between culture and technology as a trope characterizing informal learning has been adopted by a variety of theoreticians and researchers. Along with the distinction between formal and informal education, the trope demonstrates how lifelong learning changes a particular domain from an enclosed environment to a totality of open learning events while attempting, at the same time, to change the participating individuals into self-organizing learners.[12]

This tendency is mediated mainly by Digital Media platforms, considered as significant new learning facilitator modes. For instance, Burbules (2006) focuses on self-educating communities (e-mail lists, news groups, Web-rings, blogs and ever-emerging new platforms) developed through Digital Media. According to Burbules, a self-educating community is an experiment in synergetic collective intelligence. But how can the wisdom of the whole be more that the sum of its parts? He asserts that in a real sense, the knowledge of such groups is distributed and any specific thought or belief only inheres in individual minds yet, to the extent that something is known, it is often known by the group interacting as a group.

Although Burbules asserts that the epistemology of distributed knowledge depends on the same processes of evidence, testing, argument and confirmation that are part of any epistemology, he stresses that these are not simple Baconian criteria:

> ...rather, they are inquiry processes embedded in social networks, and therefore inseparable from the social dynamics with a tacit (or openly acknowledged) commitment to enhancing the knowledge and understanding

> of all its members, and so approaches these epistemological processes with less of a sense of competition, intolerance, or hierarchy (although these certainly might remain present), and more of a sense of inclusion and patience with disagreements at least among members within that community... (Burbules 2006, pp. 277–278).

Moreover, Burbules points to a certain ethics that develops among self-educating communities. He claims that an epistemology of distributed knowledge highlights the collective processes of circulating and questioning claims, juxtaposing alternatives as an approach to problem solving, offering arguments and sharing evidence as opposed to simply making assertions. Success in persuading others may be an understandable motivation for certain individuals but, because of a sense that such things properly belong to the group, and that the group as a whole (including one's self) benefits most from the fullest and widest engagement with all the evidence, experiences; its members' perspectives can become topics of common concern. Hence, adds Burbules, the vitality and success of any self-educating community depends on the exercise of certain "civic" virtues (most notably, perhaps, generosity) directed at the interests and concerns of the group as a whole (Burbules 2006, p. 280).

Video and computer games represent a variety of platforms fomenting play and game that are also expanding in today's developing field of informal learning. Paul Gee (2003) has culled 36 principles of good learning from gaming. He illustrates these principles by considering humans as terrible at learning when given lots of verbal information in advance but outside the context where that information can be applied. Alternatively, games give verbal information "just in time," when and where it can be used, and "on demand," as the player realizes that he or she needs it.

Such activities play a role in more than persuading others to respect one's view. According to Gee (2003), good games stay inside but at the outer edge of the player's growing competence, challenging, but "doable". This creates a sense of pleasurable frustration. Good games, according to Gee, create what has been called a "cycle of expertise" by giving players well-designed problems on the basis of which they can form good strategies. Games let players practice these strategies sufficiently to routinize them, then throw new problems at them that force them to undo their now routinized strategies and think again before, through more practice, generating new and higher-order routinized skills. Good games repeat this cycle again and again. It's the process by which experts are produced in any domain.

Good games, continues Gee, also solve the motivation problem that he believes is actually a biological effect. While playing a computerized game you activate a character and, in this way, manipulate something at a distance (a virtual distance in this case), much like operating a robot but in so refined a manner that humans feel that their bodies and minds have actually been expanded into or entered that distant space. Good games make use of this effect by attaching a virtual identity to this expanded self; the player then begins to care about it in a powerful way. This identity can then become a hook for freeing people to think and learn in new ways, including learning – or at least contemplating – new values, belief systems and worldviews.

DISCUSSION: INFORMAL EDUCATION POLITICS

The notion of teaching and learning in informal education settings, as projected by its tropes, implies that these processes take place through and within comprehensive phenomena that reflect a reality in which participants are perceived as integral to the teaching-learning experience. Informal education practices are therefore more performed and im-personated than theorized. A similar approach has been recommended by numerous radical theoreticians (Foucault, 1980; Giroux, 1980; Popkewitz & Fendler, 1999). It can therefore be said that the practices associated with informal education have promoted development of a unique attitude toward knowledge and information, an attitude that has developed parallel to theoretical developments in educational theories inspired primarily by the critical philosophical works belonging to Marxist or deconstructionist streams. Yet, these theories are not openly espoused by informal education. Instead, they can be discerned as practices adopted by hegemonic as well as counter-hegemonic social agencies.

This proximity between educational practices and critical attitudes as embodied by informal education creates a place for the constant revision of educational practices. It is now possible to conjure prescriptive theories centered on future radical amelioration of the view of education as indirectly influenced by the educational scene. These theories enhance processes of ideological inclusion that include a comprehensive critical attitude toward hegemonic practices. States that have absorbed this critique within their hegemonic stance, as happens in some developing countries, have established ministries and informal education departments as mechanisms for combating the most basic problems of their societies.

Contrary to these trends, the tendency to include informal learning in cooperative programs conducted in formal and informal settings has flowered widely, especially in the Anglo-Saxon world. For instance, in the United States, informal science education – which promotes the understanding of science, mathematics, and engineering through voluntary, self-directed and life-long learning opportunities via the media (e.g., print, film, television) and informal organizations (e.g., museums, parks, zoos, libraries, community groups) – has been thought to increase its efforts to bring quality science, mathematics and engineering education to under-represented groups and under-served areas. Also on the informal education agenda is the forging of collaboration between informal and formal science education institutions, promoting parental involvement, advancing public understanding of the processes and results of current research, and expanding applied research that identifies and disseminates effective strategies for public communication.

Smith reports that in Great Britain, for example, the desire to raise educational standards has led to narrowing the educational focus of classroom teachers, particularly as they deal with increased workloads and a revised national curriculum. Teachers are now encouraged to ensure that school life is marked by reasonable behavior and attractiveness to potential students and their parents. To support these institutional goals, a range of government and local initiatives have arisen to introduce informal educators and support staff into schools (Smith, 2006).

It can be argued that the motivation for including informal education settings into the schools or integrating formal and informal education settings through school, museum or after-school cooperative programs marks the meeting of two compensating motivations. On the one hand, governments are interested in fostering variegated ways of learning in order to maintain what is considered an adequate intellectual level of society. This is considered a necessity especially in association with policies aimed at the inclusion of immigrants or marginal populations in national cultures. The other motivation comes from the populations themselves. Having emigrated from what are considered un-developed to developed countries, newcomers have recognized education to be crucial for entry into the socio-economic fabric of their adopted country.

The theoretical framework for the merging of formal with informal educational settings is being elaborated by the socio-cultural stream of research represented by several groups. For instance, the integration of informal and formal settings merging has been approached, as we have seen, though analysis and conceptualization of educational practices in traditional societies, viewed as material to be adapted for the betterment of current formal (i.e., school) educational practices (Rogoff et al., 2003). That is, cultural "learning and teaching" strategies in traditional societies, like apprenticeship, have been described and inscribed epistemologically, suggesting possible alternatives to contemporary ways of teaching and learning.

A comparison of modern informal learning with "cultural teaching and learning" in traditional societies should center on at least two specific points. First, albeit developing repetitive activities, contemporary informal education organizations are not directly based on either traditional cultural or religious rituals alone. Instead, they are established and justified by political, social or cultural ideologies that in many ways generate the means of knowledge and information elaboration — including its organizational setting — in a specific way and toward a specific objective. Historically, tailors and weavers were, however, able to develop more abstract skills, such as being citizens in a democratic society, within the apprenticeship situation, an event to be emulated today. Furthermore, despite implementing *situated learning* in the sense of making learned contents and activities closer and more relevant to the learners' habitat, this kind of learning still occurs in differentiated institutions such as those examined for the purposes of this essay. Such institutions adopt the style of a "second familial house" or a feeling of "being at home" (Silberman-Keller, 2006). These institutions can be conjured as implying and fomenting a kind of "retro", placebo-like attitude toward traditional frameworks, indicated by installing patterns of group participation reminiscent of the original family. However, it should remain clear that these frameworks are modern institutions that have profoundly revised traditional situated learning and created places exhibiting alternative family structures. These institutions should remind us that participation in a community is not limited to learning how to perform specific daily activities; instead, it rests on espousing ideals and values and adopting a vision of reality as preliminary to participation in political, social and cultural life.

CLOSING REMARKS

As observed in the changing tropes of informal education, the future of cultural politics is captured by two main tendencies. The one is the formalization and institutionalization of informal educational systems through the edification of departments, ministries and programs that foment informal education in various settings, the result of which is a kind of pedagogic and didactic pluralism of ways of learning. Accompanying this movement is the standardization of informal educational practices and their instrumentalization for the purpose of sustaining transmission of centralized curricula. By doing so, the characteristic tropes of informal education, its way of being in the world are transformed, as we have seen, into tactics of learning to a greater extent than ever.

A second tendency, opposed to the first, is taking place through the introduction of new technologies that inspire creation of new subcultures and social groups. According to Thomas Frey (2007), new technologies will foster transformations such as teacher-centric to learning-centric pedagogies, classroom-based teaching to anyplace and anytime learning, compulsory mass courses to hyper-individualized learning, a general population of student consumers to a growing population of student producers.

Frey (2007) also predicts that most of today's learning impediments will eventually disappear and that significant changes in cultural attitudes toward learning will take place. The latter in particular will significantly increase learning speed and comprehension, ultimately resulting in a dramatic change in learning motivation.

New educational theories, as those exposed in this chapter – see the examples of learning and techno-cultural mediating functions through "self-educating communities" or "videogames" – open new vistas of learning still further. Consider "mobile learning,"[13] now appearing on the cultural scene after being introduced, for instance, in an interview with the Finish entrepreneur Teemu Arina:

> Robin Good: *What about mobile learning? What is it? Is it coming?*
>
> Teemu Arina: Some years ago, Finland was very strong on the mobile side yet people where laughing at the idea of *mobile learning*. But I think it's coming. I think it's integrating with the *informal learning* space because **being mobile means that the context is around you**.
>
> You are not saying things in a classroom out of context, you are not sitting in a formal course within an organization but you are actually there, where you need to be. You need to apply the context to the context itself. I think that's what *mobile learning* does: it enables us to utilize the context in a better way....(Arina, 2006, p. #).

In this way, informal education continues to perform from the place apparently left free from the cooptation of political critique by formal educational systems. Merging formal and informal educational settings has resulted in the transformation of what was considered avant-garde educational practices as well as the impersonation and performance of an entire ongoing critique into mainstream cultural practice, causing it to lose its traditional function. It might be that the emerging techno-cultural contexts will either influence the critical discourse on education or propose an extreme new culture in order to continue maintaining the traditional place of informal education as a performed cultural critique. In either case, it is worth closely following the cultural politics that accompanies the new informal learning contexts motivated by techno-cultural figures for, as Zizek has written: "How, then, are we to revolutionize an order whose very principle is constant self-revolutionizing" (Zizek, 2004, p. 213)?

NOTES

[1] Learning through Informal Education is performative since engaging in practices is what basically characterizes informal learning. This view of Informal Education is inspired by Judith Butler's definition of "the performative". There is no alternative to the way of learning practiced in Informal Education settings since only by participation and role acquisition does one enter the educational scene. See: Butler (1990) and Rogoff, B., Paradise, R., Mejía Arauz, R., Correa-Chávez, M., and Angelillo, C. (2003).

[2] Jane Gallop deconstructs and constructs the term *im-personation* as an alternative to the Bourdieu and Passeron term *reproduction* in the sphere of education. She attributes different meanings – such as ventriloquism, role playing, in-voicing identities – to the term. I adopt im-personation to conceptualize personal participation in informal education settings. These settings, more than school, allow participants in educational activities to "wear" and "un-wear" roles in relatively flexible and permissive ways. See: Gallop (1995) and Silberman-Keller (2006b).

[3] "Every spoken word is a pedagogical action" says Derrida in a conversation with Jean Blain when referring to the formative function of philosophy. Based on this insight, it is possible to assert that those cultural spheres where cultural, social and educational activities take place have pedagogical potentialities and impacts. See: Derrida (1994) and Lave and Wenger (1991).

[4] Parenti (1999).

[5] See: Gramsci (1971, 238).

[6] This means that Informal Education tropes result from a constant interplay of different practices and meanings as explained by Derrida's different way of working: The first consequence to be drawn [from Saussure and the arbitrariness of the sign and the constitution of meaning by différance] is that the signified concept is never present in and of itself sufficiently to refer only to itself. Essentially (that is, of its being) and lawfully, every concept is inscribed in a chain or system within which it refers to the other, to other concepts, by means of the systematic play of differences. See: Derrida (1982).

[7] According to Derrida the law of genre "is precisely a principle of contamination, a law of impurity, a parasitical economy. In the code of set theories, if I may use it at least figuratively, I would speak of a sort of participation without belonging – a taking part in without dividing of the trait that makes membership, the boundary of the set comes to form, by **invagination** [emphasis added], an internal pocket larger than the whole: and the outcome of this division and of this abounding remains as singular as it is limitless". The invaginated space is, in my view and interpreting Derrida as the place where culture is generated, degenerated and re-generated. See: Derrida, J. (1980), The law of genre. (trans Avital Ronell) *Critical Inquiry* (Autumn).

[8] A trope is any literary or rhetorical device that consists in the use of words in other than their literal sense. In the case of Informal Education, the idea is that Informal Education has different, often unnamed meanings, implicitly included in the way it is publicly conceptualized.

[9] See: Hohensten (2006), http://www.exploratorium.edu/cils/research/conversation.html.

[10] See: http://www.infed.org/thinkers/et-hist.htm.

[11] See: Overwien (2000).
[12] On informal learning validation see: http://www.euracademy.org/euro-validation/rep_poland.pd and Tuschling & Engemann, (2006).
[13] See for example: http://www.iadis.org/ml2006/.

REFERENCES

Abers, R. (2000). *Inventing local democracy: Grassroots politics in Brazil.* Boulder, CO: Lynne Rienner.

Arina, T. (2006). *The future of learning is informal and mobile: A video interview with Temmu Arina.* Retrieved from http://www.masternewmedia.org/news/2007/04/12/the_future_of_learning_is.htm

Baiele. (2000). The explosion of experience: The emergence of a new ethical-political principle in popular movements in Porto Alegre, Brazil. In S. Alvarez, E. Daguino, & A. Escobar (Eds.), *Culture of politics, politics of culture* (pp. 38–118). Boulder, CO: Westview.

Betrand, Y., & Houssaye, J. (1999). Pedagogie and Didactique: An incestuous relationship. *Instructional Science, 27*, 33–51.

Bock, X., & Papagianis, Y. (1983). Some alternatives on the role of non-formal education. In X. Bock & Y. Papagianis (Eds.), *National development* (pp. 250–268). New York: Praeger.

Boud, D., & Garrick, J. (Eds.). (1999). *Understanding learning at work.* London: Routledge and Harvard University Press.

Bourdieu, P. (1991). Political representation: Elements for a theory of the political field. In *Pierre Bourdieu: Language and symbolic power* (pp. 171–220). Cambridge, MA: Harvard University Press.

Burbules, N. A. (2006). Self-educating communities: Collaboration and learning. In Z. Bekerman, N. C. Burbules, & D. Silberman-Keller (Eds.), *Learning in places: The informal education reader* (pp. 273–284). New York: Peter Lang.

Butler, J. (1990). *Gender trouble: Feminism and the subversion of identity.* New York: Routledge.

Coombs, P. H., & Ahmed, M. (1974). *Attacking rural poverty: How non-formal education can help.* Baltimore: John Hopkins University Press.

Dabas, E. N. (1995). *Red de redes.* Buenos Aires: Editorial Paidos.

Dabas, E. N. (2002). *Redes, el lenguaje de los vinculos.* Buenos Aires: Editorial Paidos.

Derrida, J. (1982). *Differance* (A. Bass, Trans.). *Margins of philosophy* (pp. 3–27). Chicago: University of Chicago Press.

Derrida, J. (1994). Toute prise de parole est un acte pédagogique, entretien avec Jean Blain. *Lire.* Retrieved from http://www.jacquesderrida.com.ar/frances/lire.htm

Eraut. (2000). Non-formal learning, implicit learning and tacit knowledge in professional work. In F. Coffield (Ed.), *The necessity of informal learning* (pp. 12–32). London: Policy Press.

Foucault, M. (1980). *Power and knowledge: Selected interviews and other writings, 1972–1977.* New York: Pantheon Books.

Frey, T. (2007). *The future of education.* Retrieved from http://www.davinciinstitute.com/page.php?ID=170

Gallop, J. (Ed.). (1995). *Pedagogy: The question of impersonation.* Bloomington, IN and Indianapolis, IN: Indiana University Press.

Gee, J. P. (2003). *What video games have to teach us about learning and literacy.* New York: Palgrave Macmillan.

Genro, T. (2001, January 25). A better world is already possible here. *Zero Hora, 3.*

Giroux, H. A. (1980). Beyond the limits of radical educational reform: Toward a critical theory of education. *Journal of Curriculum Theorizing, 2*(1), 20–46.

Gramsci, A. (1971). *Selections from the prison notebooks.* New York: International Publishers.

Hohensten, J. (2006). *Discussing the role of conversation in learning at informal science institutions*. Retrieved from http://www.exploratorium.edu/cils/research/conversation.html

Houssaye, J. (Ed.). (1993). *La pedagogie: Une encyclopedie pour aujourd'hui*. Paris: ESF.

Kahane, R. (1975). A number of assumptions on the structure and function of non-formal educational systems in modern society. In Y. Miuhas (Ed.), *Complementary education* (pp. 45–53). Jerusalem: Ministry of Education and Culture. (Hebrew)

Kahane, R. (1997). *The origins of postmodern youth: Informal youth movements in a comparative perspective*. Berlin: De Gruyte.

Lamm, Z. (1975). Complementary education in the theory of changing the educational institution. In Y. Miuhas (Ed.), *Complementary education* (pp. 38–44). Jerusalem: Ministry of Education and Culture. (Hebrew)

Lave, J., & Wenger, E. (1991). *Situated learning: Legitimate peripheral participation*. New York: Cambridge University Press.

Maynard, A., & Greenfield, P. (2006). Cultural teaching and learning: Process, effects, and development of apprenticeship skills. In Z. Bekerman, N. C. Burbules, & D. Silberman-Keller (Eds.), *Learning in places: The informal education reader* (pp. 139–162). New York: Peter Lang.

McDermott, R. P. (1999). Acquisition of a child with a learning disability. In S. Chaiklin & J. Lave (Eds.), *Understanding practice* (pp. 269–305). New York: Cambridge University Press.

Mill, J. S. (1963). *Essays on politics and culture* (G. Himmlefarb, Ed.). New York: Doubleday.

Noam, G. (2002). *After-school education: Approaches to an emerging field*. Cambridge, MA: Harvard Education Press.

Overwien, B. (2000). Informal learning and the role of social movements. *International Review of Education, 46*(6), 621–640.

Parenti, M. (1999). *Reflections on the politics of culture*. Retrieved from http://www.monthlyreview.org/299pare.htm

Pateman, C. (1988). *Participation and democratic theory*. New York: Cambridge University Press. (Original work published in 1970)

Popkewitz, T. S., & Fendler, L. (1999). *Critical theories in education: Changing terrains of knowledge and politics*. New York: Routledge.

Putnam, R. D. (2000). *Bowling alone: The collapse and revival of American community*. New York: Simon and Schuster.

Rogoff, B., Paradise, R., Mejía Arauz, R., Correa-Chávez, M., & Angelillo, C. (2003). First-hand learning through intent participation. *Annual Review of Psychology, 54*, 175–203.

Schugurensky, D. (2002). Transformative learning and transformative politics: The pedagogical dimension of participatory democracy and social action; Essays on theory and praxis. In E. O'Sullivan, A. Morrell, & M. A. O'Connor (Eds.), *Expanding the boundaries of transformative learning* (pp. 59–76). New York: Palgrave.

Schugurensky, D. (2006). This is our school of citizenship: Informal learning in local democracy. In Z. Bekerman, N. C. Burbules, & D. Silberman-Keller (Eds.), *Learning in places: The informal education reader* (pp. 163–182). New York: Peter Lang.

Silberman-Keller, D. (1987). *By-pass systems: Repetition or redundancy?* Unpublished M.A. Thesis. Jerusalem: The Hebrew University. (Hebrew)

Silberman-Keller, D. (2006a). Images of place and time in non-formal pedagogy. In Z. Bekerman, N. C. Burbules, & D. Silberman-Keller (Eds.), *Learning in places: The informal education reader* (pp. 251–272). New York: Peter Lang.

Silberman-Keller, D. (2006b). The game of non-formal pedagogy. *Educational Practice and Theory, 28*(1), 37–54.

Smith, M. K. (2006). Beyond the curriculum: Fostering associational life in schools. In Z. Bekerman, N. C. Burbules, & D. Silberman-Keller (Eds.), *Learning in places: The informal education reader* (pp. 9–34). New York: Peter Lang.

Torres, C. A (1990). *The politics of Non-Formal education in Latin America*. New York: Praeger.

Tuschling, A., & Engemann, C. (2006). From education to lifelong learning: The emerging regime of learning in the European Union. *Educational Philosophy and Theory, 38*(4), 451–469.

Zizek, S. (2004). *Organs without bodies: On Deleuze and consequences*. New York & London: Routledge. Retrieved from http://www.infed.org

Diana Silberman-Keller
School for Multidisciplinary Studies
Beit Berl Academic College

KORINA JOCSON AND TAKEO RIVERA

23. TOWARD A THEORY OF POEMNESS

Cultural Politics and Transformative Pedagogies

The treatment of poetry as transformative reflects a literary movement attentive to larger struggles over signs and meanings. It emphasizes textual play and seeks to alter the social, cultural, and institutional relations in which meanings are generated. It builds on the power of words as a form of social action. Central to conceiving poetry as transformative is asking in what ways poetic texts shape discourses and vice versa. In this chapter we turn to Mikhail Bakhtin as a departure point to explore the politics of writing and, in particular, to offer what we are calling a "theory of poemness" in contemporary youth poetry movements. Embedded are the values of intertextuality, aesthetics, and pleasure. For many poets with whom we have interacted, writing becomes a form of negotiation with positionality, a medium of expression to identify one's politics of difference through politics of representation (Hall, 1992). By "representation," we refer not only to what forms and signs are being represented but also who is creating them, for whom and for what purposes. This raises questions of power that reside "in the specific deployment of subjectivity in the artifacts of the formal and informal culture" (McCarthy, 1993, p. 295). Within education, for example, differences of gender, sexuality, class, and language add to differences by racial background and are key to treating young people's experiences not as homogeneous or fixed, but as occurring in sites of contestation in particular historical moments. These differences, structured within cultural spaces, are located beyond binaries and oppositional frameworks such as male/female, straight/queer, rich/poor, English/non-English, among others. Asymmetrical relations of power based on politics of difference are made explicit.

DIALOGISM AND NOVELNESS

Integral to poetry as a medium of expression is the notion of utterance and heteroglossia. In *The Dialogic Imagination,* Bakhtin (1981) defines heteroglossia as "multiple social discourses" or ways of seeing the world made up of alien words, "shared thoughts," and "points of view" that weave "in and out of complex interrelationships, merges with some, recoils from others" (p. 276). The word, for Bakhtin, is a concrete living utterance shaped by various historical moments in dialogically agitated social environments. Directly related to the formulation of one's language, this notion of utterance explains how alien words become appropriated, adapted, and owned. It shifts away from formalism to give attention

Z. Leonardo (ed.), Handbook of Cultural Politics and Education, 527–540.

to the way words are born in social context and also extends structuralism's linguistic model, particularly Saussure's, to emphasize that there exists a relationship between individual speakers and texts. According to Bakhtin,

> The word in language is someone else's. It becomes "one's own" only when the speaker populates it with his own intention, his own accent, when he appropriates the word, adapting it to his own semantic and expressive intention. Prior to this moment of appropriation, the word does not exist in a neutral and impersonal language (it is not, after all, out of a dictionary that the speaker gets his words!), but rather it exists in other people's mouths, in other people's contexts, serving other people's intentions: it is from there that one must take the word, and make it one's own. (1981, pp. 293–294)

This articulation of owning one's words, a social yet private act of the speaking subject, is useful to understanding how authoring through dialogic interaction takes place. It emphasizes the dialogic nature of language use by recognizing the role of others from whom speakers or writers have learned the words or the anticipatory language of those whom they are addressing or answering in particular social spaces (Bakhtin, 1986, 1990). The synchronic (vs. diachronic) dimension characterizes the complexity of their similarities and differences in the exchange. At the intersection where subject, addressee, and context meet are the ambivalent elements where words as textual units are absorbed and transformed, which according to Jakobson (1982, 1985) consistent with his analysis of the code/message relationship is a linguistic function with contrastive or distinctive features, even at the level of phonemes. As such, the interplay between textual and social spaces is deemed central to the process of becoming literate, to manipulate language and other signs, in ways that reveal the different social interests (Volosinov, 1973) and ideological becomings of individuals in their environments (Bakhtin/Medvedev, 1978; also see Freedman & Ball, 2004). Ideology in this sense is at the heart of the struggle over signs and meanings. Embedded is the orchestration of language as a medium of ideology through which social constructions of the ruling class reign over those without power. Here, words as dynamic social sign systems are treated as situated within historical contexts, thereby rendering utterances as intricately shaped by existing social relations. Individuals' social interests and ideological becomings reflect the class struggles present in communities as they share words, cultural symbols and values to extend possibilities for communication, learning, and development. They underscore the multiaccentual elements of truths, or partial truths, that emphasize the social nature of interaction among participants. In her work in education and literacy studies, Dyson (1997) asserts the importance of official and unofficial spaces where children as ideological beings learn to author selves through social play, writing superheroes, and engaging popular media. Authoring is one means to understand their surroundings and construct social meanings.

To distinguish between authoring in two genres of literature, Bakhtin (1981) argues that there is a presence of double-voicedness in the novel and ambiguity in poetry. The former consists of internal dialogism through characters with double to multiple voices, thus laden with multiple meanings, whereas the latter, arguably, consists of only a unitary voice that uses tropes (such as symbols and metaphors) to capture precise feelings that represent multiple meanings contained in it (p. 327). For Bakhtin, the principal difference between novel and poetry is apparent in the variety of speaking person(s) in the former and the author in the latter. The novel is dependent on intertextuality, a plurality of relations— "social, historical, personal, discursive, textual"—that shapes its existence (Holquist, p. 89). It primarily references other texts through a transposition of one or more systems of signs into another, a point which Kristeva (1980, 1984) develops in her application of Bakhtin's theory on literature and art. The intertextual is not simply a matter of influence but rather a permutation or new articulation of texts, a process through which "several utterances, taken from other texts, intersect and neutralize one another" (Kristeva, 1980, p. 36). The novel as text becomes a semiotic canvas with synthesized patterns of utterances. However, as we will illustrate, what had been described as distinct only to the novel becomes blurred.

In Bakhtin's view, the nature of the novel—or novelness—represents three concepts related to dialogism: polyphony, chronotope, and carnival. The first, polyphony (or multiple sounds), relates to heteroglossia and utterance as shaped by specific historical moments. The second, chronotope, refers to time and space, the axial ground essential for concretizing events, giving material form to representation, and "permitting the power of art to do its work" (Bakhtin, 1981, p. 250). The intrinsic connectedness between time and space is laden with emotions and values to allow the flesh of narrative events in the represented work to enter the world of the reader or listener and thereby participate in the creation and renewal of the text. This connectedness also binds the novel as literary work to its temporal and spatial relationship with actual reality, or what Bakhtin calls the continual mutual interaction between the real and represented worlds. The third concept of novelness, carnival, emphasizes the embodiment of otherness. Carnival represents a historical phenomenon as in carnival events and, in literary form, is associated with breaking form in the spirit of free thinking. In *Rabelais and His World*, Bakhtin (1984b) draws a parallel between the novel and the body. He describes the body as a living entity, as becoming, as grotesque, as different, and as continually created or re-created by the world, similar to the novel as intertextual and conceived from a web of relationships with the world. The novel in this light is said to be carnivaleseque as it attempts to make the familiar strange, while also distinguishing itself as original from larger bodies of literary work.

Bakhtin extensively elaborates on these multiple dimensions of dialogism in his collective work. It is worthwhile to mention his earlier works on ethics and aesthetics in such titles as *Toward a Philosophy of the Act* (1993) where he discussed Kantian principles of morality and the architectronic model of the human psyche, including "I-for-the-other," which borders Lacanian's (1991, 1998) mirror stage of Other/other and psychoanalytic theorization of the three orders (imaginary, symbolic, real). Other titles include *Problems of Dostoevky's Art* expanded later into *Problems of Dostoevky's Poetics* (1984a) where he addressed unfinalizability to explain characters' voices and interactions with one another in what would be dialogism-related terms such as polyphony and carnival, respectively. Although many of his writings were produced in the 1920s and 1930s, Bakhtin's collective works did not gain ground until after his death in the 1970s through contributions to literary theory by the likes of Kristeva and Todorov. The latter's undertaking of the fantastic, that is, the uncanny and the marvelous (Todorov, 1975), arguably echoing Bakhtin's notion of the carnival and the importance of genres. Indeed, Bakhtin's scholarly range has shaped various traditions and disciplines. Most salient to us are the literary tendencies that relate to dialogism or specifically the construction of words and meanings through dialogic encounters. As we will point out in the next section, poems produced by youth, inclusive of spoken word performances, are influenced by others' voices and writing styles, with some utterances drawn directly from existing literary texts. The poems demonstrate the nature of novelness and push the bounds of dialogism toward "poemness"—works of poetry that are also polyphonic, chronotopic, and carnivalesque. Outside the scope of this chapter is an extensive discussion of each feature or a full treatment of Bakhtin's novelness (see Bruhn & Lundquist, 2001; Kristeva, 1980; Morson & Emerson, 1990). For the purposes of our argument, we rely on poems themselves to illustrate multi-voicedness, temporalities, and politics of difference congealing into new(er) forms of textual play.

According to Aristotle's (1994) *Poetics,* mimesis (imitation) is speculated representation created by an enactment of tragedy, established in literary form through the distance between the poet and the reality s/he speaks about. Mimesis or imitation in poetry surfaces through its *medium* (rhythm, language, melody), its *object* (admirable and inferior agents), and its *mode* (drama). For Aristotle, they differ in other artistic forms such as epics and comedies, but remain not as easily distinguishable from each other given the history and development of tragedy in poetry. In this chapter we consider mimesis as we build on what Bakhtin theorized as "ventriloquating" others' words –in short, reflecting a unique speech experience that is in continuous interaction with others to create something new. Examining poems by youth poets reveals sources of meanings used at face value or explicit social dramas from prior texts. The poems contain direct or indirect quotation, recognizable phrasing, and/or language forms that echo certain ways of communicating, techniques of intertextuality "that represent the words and utterances of others" (Bazerman, 2004, p. 88). The following is a look at nuances in writing and the dialogic encounters in the production of new(er) texts.

ILLUSTRATIONS OF YOUTH POETRY

Elizabeth Acevedo is a youth slam poet from New York City. At the time of her interview in the summer of 2007, she was nineteen and had just finished her freshman year at Georgetown University. In her high school years, she learned the art of spoken word poetry through the organization Urban Word NYC, which provides free workshops, performance venues, and learning opportunities to youth in New York City. She continues writing in college, but she credits Urban Word and the community it has generated for her success in writing and performing in the genre. She is one of many Urban Word success stories, as Urban Word utilizes principles of poemness in their pedagogical techniques, stressing such principles as openness, uncensored learning, and the utilization of contemporary youth culture (hip hop especially) into its pedagogy. In her interview, Acevedo shares the following poem:

I stand in between worlds
attempting to curve my tongue accordingly
like
the get-getting shot sometimes
I bleed monthly
original gangster
no questions but answers I
look like a warrior
and I walk like a dancer
no frontin
I heard that where I'm from
girly girls hold Gilettes under their tongues
but I was raised to use my tongue as a razor blade
cuz sometimes it be more brave
to use your words than your wisdom
instead of fists to hit them
but don't get it twisted cuz
If I gotta scrape knuckles then knuckles will scrape got
pacifist visions
but mama ain't raised no punk
cuz where I'm from
hood's kings birth hood teens
so hood dreams
grow hoodwinked
blink
and life has passed them by
answers aren't in textbooks so
they learn to read the sky
they don't know there's a difference between
breathing and being alive
too many that I know are
being eaten alive
and the blocks' belly
is bottomless
they sing gunshot lullabies
forsake their livelihoods so they can
live in in a lively hood
so
I learned to sling rap like crack rocks
have heads inhaling my line

they try to hustle fake hapiness
I'm tryin to hustle my mind
you need a poem? let me know
I'll reach into my magic dime bag of rhymes
and on my block they try to peg me like
that's that school poet
but they don't know me cuz
I'm a hustler
I'm a- I'm a hustler, homie
and at school they try to peg me
like that's that hood poet
but they don't know me cuz
just like their daddies
I'm a hustler
I'm a- I'm a hustler, homie
I stand in between worlds
attempting to curve my tongue accordingly
like
it is difficult to reconcile
languages and hypocrisies
to
pick and choose words as to
not misinterpret or misrepresent
I was not raised reading Whitman
lucky to have been raised reading
I do not speak in classroom
where knocked in on the street
both because it is pompous
and reason for exclusion
I find out I am languageless un
able to speak to my community because
my diction is not recognized
it puts me in the box of the educated
therefore traitor
unable to speak to them because my ghetto accent
created laces itself between exchanges
and you cannot see past my hoodness to the meaning
this
codeswitching is tricky business
I stand in this no-man's-land of slanglish
caught in between press and express
chain of thoughts translations lost
I do not know what they have stolen
I do not know what I have lost
both by learning and remembering

I only know I am mute by default
hypocrite by nurture
Firstly by the language I use to write this poem
Secondly because the streets where I grew up
will not ever read it
And the school I attend will never hear it
It is difficult to reconcile languages and hypocrises
When you're the product
of Shakespeare and Tupac

Acevedo's piece deftly exhibits many qualities common to youth spoken word poetry that parallel Bakhtin's notion of novelness. First, Acevedo exhibits intertexuality, making casual references not only to William Shakespeare and Tupac Shakur, but her repetition of "I'm a hustler/ I'm a – I'm a hustler, homie" is a direct quotation from the chorus of rapper Cassidy's song "I'm a Hustler." The piece is by all means a socially-generated one that relies on in-group comprehension, even though the content of her poem describes the dilemma of being betwixt and between two societies. The fact that she references "I'm a Hustler" in the rhythm of the song without further explanation presupposes that the audience understands the reference she is making (and when performed live to an audience in another night, the line evoked a chuckle from the onlookers).

Both the content and form of this poem also point to the complex relationship that Acevedo has to her identity in society. The poem presents a narrative of occupying a difficult liminal space between an academic, high-brow community of practice and the community of her low-income neighborhood, and the language she uses reflects this dialogic tension. At the risk of employing a problematic description, Acevedo embodies a hybrid identity, as she herself expresses a dialogic notion of selfhood. She also therefore invokes the carnivalesque, embodying a perpetual *other* to all dimensions of selfhood. Furthermore, her emphasis on performance (i.e., that her poem must be performed with a particular cadence and sound in order for its full meaning to be conveyed) ties the poem inextricably to the chronotope, to time and space. Simply, the performance of this poem literally occupies time and space. Its embodiment exists not just mentally but in the physical dimensions of the performance hall and in the visceral physicality of sound.

Youth poetry, however, encompasses a very broad diversity of styles and cadences, yet poemness appears to remain consistent. Gloria Alvarez, youth poet from San Pablo, CA, worked with Rivera (co-author) in the summer of 2006 as a member of an experimental spoken word program. In the course of the summer, 17-year-old Alvarez wrote a series of poems, some of which on her own, some of which tailored to Rivera's exercises. One such poem is "Boxed Voice," below:

I'm told to be myself, to step out of the box.
But how can I do that
If every time I'm myself,
People judge me.
If every time I step out of the box,

People seem to put me in another one.
I want my voice to be heard.
My ideas to captivate your mind
And make you question who you are.
I want my words to cut you like a thousand swords
So you can find the healing power within you.
I want my thoughts to be intertwined with yours only to create better ones.

But all you hear is my whiny little voice with barely a trace of a Hispanic accent,
And you begin to judge me,
You begin to put me in a box
Because I learned how to make french toast before learning how to make tamales
Because I decide to make my eggs
Into omelets instead of making them revueltos con frijoles y arroz.

You put me in a box
Because you hardly hear me speak my native language.
Let me tell you something,
I can roll my 'R's perfectly,
Say the Spanish alphabet in less than 30 seconds,
And talk so fast,
You'll for sure know I'm Mexican.

You put me in a box
Because I don't mix my English with my Spanish,
Not because I don't know how
Porque mira let me tell you que lo se hacer real good.
But because I choose not to.

You dare to tell me I've forgotten my roots
Because I'm not longer catholic,
Because every time there's a Pedro Infante movie on Univision,
I flip the channel to Lifetime.
Because every time the radio plays Banda El Recodo,
I decide to listen to Green Day.
Because at my quinceañera there wasn't any alcohol,
And the only music to rock that night was Christian.

Who are you to tell me what I've forgotten if you don't even know what I learned?
I learned how to count to 100…in Spanish
I learned how to read and write…in Spanish
I learned what sex was…in Spanish
I learned how to say I love you…in Spanish

I learned how to say fuck you too bitch…in Spanish
I learned how to speak English…in Spanish
I learned that Mexico is composed of 32 states
And a Federal District,
Where I was born,
That's right,
Mexicana al 100%

You would have known that if only you would have listened to me,
But all you hear,
Is my whiny little voice with barely a trace of a Hispanic accent,
And you begin to put me in a box
As I watch my voice being judged,
Not heard.

Stylistically, Alvarez's work differs dramatically from Acevedo's, being more concise and somewhat less stage-oriented or stage-dependent, since the piece is less reliant on a particular cadence or rhythm. Yet, Alvarez touches on similar themes and employs the same principles of poemness. Alvarez, like Acevedo, speaks to the issue of otherness, primarily dealing with the issue of cultural authenticity, that in spite of the fact that she has some preferences for the American mainstream, she can still perform her Mexicana identity with equal competence. While at the outset, her otherness exists in regards to her ethnicity, there is also an implied counter-hegemonic message—she resents being placed in the box as an assimilationist precisely because she understands the importance of preserving one's native culture. The poem makes a complex argument: that it is possible to engage the dominant culture without "selling out," as long as the individual is still capable of performing cultural heritage; that is, performances of different cultural pratices are not mutually exclusive.

Her references to Univision, Pedro Infante, Lifetime, and Green Day exhibit a bicultural literacy that exhibit her ability to navigate multilayered cultural complexities. Again, like Acevedo, she is at once marginal and in-group, clearly expressing this to an audience of peers even though the topic is about not belonging. Thus, in addition to exhibiting multivoicedness, her references simultaneously exhibit chronotope, placing her work in the conceptual sphere of the in-group at this particular, contemporary point.

While not every youth poem is about conflicted biculturalism, the three features of novelness (and by extension poemness)—polyphony, chronotope, and carnival—arise in one way or another quite frequently. This phenomenon is encouraged both by the social phenomena of youth poetry venues (like open mics and slams) and by classrooms and workshops. As blurred lines between oral and written forms continue to be debated, it is important to recognize performance as a dimension of poetry in relation to poemness. The spoken becomes an embodied text.

THE SPOKEN WORD: EMBODYING POEMNESS

A key trend of youth poetry is that these poets are not just creating works for the page, but for the stage. The youth poetry movement is not just one of writing; it is one of sound, rhythm, choreography—in short, embodiment. In the writing of these works, youth poets concern themselves not only with the standalone aesthetics of the text, but the audience reaction of when the poet recites her self-authored work before a crowd of peers. It is thus informative to examine this phenomenon of performance within the framework of poemness, as it is a key illustration of poemness' pedagogical efficacy. In short, poetry performance is the physical manifestation of poemness.

Performance illustrates all three of the main components of poemness. First, it allows for multivoiced intertextuality not only through written references, but through song and dance; it is frequent practice for youth poets to begin introductions of poems with refrains of popular songs. In this regard, performance not only allows for intertextuality, but cross-genre textuality. The verbal content is only one dimension of the textuality of spoken word; sometimes one must be familiar with particular melodies or dance moves to fully understand what the poet is trying to convey. Furthermore, the practice of the literal multi-voice poem (the collaborative, poem, or "collabo"), in which two or more poets co-write then co-perform one poem, is a common one, particularly in the realm of poetry slam. It is common practice for the contemporary slam team—be it in high school, college, or professional—to employ multivoiced poems in order to be competitive. iLL-Literacy, a poetry collective of four artists that originated at University of California, Davis, is a fantastic example of a group that employs this technique regularly (www.ILL-literacy.com).

Second, poetry performance illustrates the dimension of chronotope, of time and space. The practice of viewing the poet's performance replaces the practice of reading the poem off the page. It is worth reiterating that viewership is indeed a *practice*; there is no active-passive hierarchy that contains the audience-speaker relationship. Members of the audience are expected to react audibly in the middle of a poem to indicate how much they like it. The recitation of a poem, for the youth poet, is therefore a social event. Fisher (2003), describing the Mahogany, a spoken word open mic venue in Sacramento, CA, explains that "embedded in all of the rules [of the open mic] was the expectation that everyone present would be a participant in some way, whether by active listening, sharing poetry on stage, giving verbal feedback and support, or providing the audience information about goings on in the community" (p. 368).

Consequently, as youth poets engage in this realm, a socially-generated aesthetic emerges. This aesthetic dialogues with the third dimension of poemness: carnival or newness. A strong youth poet must make contemporary references in her work in order to appeal to her peers. The socially-generated aesthetic demands originality, both in content and form. Rivera (2008) notes the importance the youth poet places on originality and the changing of perspective. Of course, like "authenticity," originality is not absolute, but a concept constructed by its observers. "Originality" is relative to the audience, as some youth are seeking not necessarily originality, but non-normative or counterhegemonic works. Rivera also points out that many poets—particularly ones who are newer to the form and its community—prefer works that are non-normative in the broader sense, as in, perceived to be deviant from the mainstream media opinion (for example, poems that criticize "the government," sometimes overgenerally). More experienced poets indicate a preference of originality from the norm of spoken word as a whole; messages once considered counterhegemonic become cliché unless they are probed at from a unique angle; one that alters perspective, so to speak. Regardless, in both instances, there is an anti-conformist desire, even if this, at times, paradoxically produces conformity, and the process of seeking originality consolidates the aspiring poet's identity as a spoken word artist. In order to have self-respect within this group of youth poets, the poet must learn to stand out originally, with that originality defined by her/his own terms.

The performance of a poem, therefore, is a crucial expression of poemness. The implications are many. The intersection of performance and poemness suggests an intersection between the pedagogical and ontological. If we understand performance not just as the staged act of performing a poem, but as a performance of identity, the importance of poemness therefore becomes far more apparent. In regards to the performance of identity, we turn to Goffman (1973) who, in *The Presentation of Everyday Life,* identifies that the routine actions of banal lifestyle are themselves a performance that he calls a "front." Goffman writes that "'front' [is] that part of the individual's performance which regularly functions in a general and fixed fashion to define the situation for those who observe the performance. Front, then, is the expressive equipment of a standard kind intentionally or unwittingly employed by the individual during his performance." Goffman's "front" refers to the amalgam of behaviors, ritualisms, and understandings that are performed day-to-day, but what is most important to note is that the "front" is socially generated by the practitioner and the society. This parallels the same way that the youth poet, the author, co-creates the aesthetic of the spoken word poem through a social setting. Furthermore, both "front" and spoken word recitation can be understood as expressions of identity. The primary difference between the "front" and poetry performance is that "front" is understood to be largely unconscious, while poetry performance is intentional and controlled.

It is then possible to understand that poetry performance among youth poets, whose aesthetic is defined by the aspects of poemness, is a form of theatrically staged recitation of the "front." But as the "front" can be understood as a projection of identity, so too can the manifestation of poemness, poetry performance. Poemness therefore is about both expression and being, and more broadly, *becoming* through *performing.* It is the process of translating the unconscious identity performance of the "front" into the conscious performance of the poem. And in doing so, the youth poet develops her identity not in a vacuum, but in relation to the social nature of being human with socioeconomic, political, philosophical, religious, and intimate perspectives, among others. The effect of engaging in poemness is literacy on the individual level (agentive) and literacy on the societal level (associative) – that is, one's ability to engage both for various purposes. In this chapter, we have focused on the particularities of literacy on the individual level without discounting the latter. Poemness in this regard provides different possibilities across contexts.

POEMNESS IN AND OUT OF THE CLASSROOM

The salience of Bakhtin's dialogism moves previous theorization about novelness toward what we have illustrated as poemness. By this, we mean paying attention to features of novelness—*polyphony* (multivoicedness), *chronotope* (time and space), and *carnival* (newness and difference)—in the treatment of poetry in and outside of classrooms. Youth poets utilized the power of words to participate in various sociocultural, historical, and political discourses. Their poems as forms of dialogic critique offered alternative possibilities to effect change. Poemness in this regard provides insights into the what, why, and how in the politics of writing. First, poemness consists of multiple voices and levels of intertextuality influenced by an array of authors, styles, aesthetics, and experiences. Such influence stems from the explicit inclusion of multicultural literature in teaching and learning that resonates with students and connects with their prior knowledge. Second, poemness is about time and space, representative of youth's experiences and what is taking place in their social worlds. The merging of these experiences underscores the centrality of writing and writing development in the classroom. It affirms the importance of holding in-class writing conferences or advocating for student-led writing workshops outside of school for sharing relevant experiences and discussing student work. And third, poemness is about creating something different, something that stands out or breaks form. It emphasizes the changing nature of writing in new media times and the possibilities of digital writing through the use of multimedia tools. It also draws attention to youth popular culture, inclusive of various artistic genres and media forms, and treats literacy learning as fluid happening both in and out of schools. Poemness is about expression—owning it and taking pleasure in it.

The poems above exhibit the nature of dialogism and demonstrate the possibilities of writing as a form of cultural politics. What surfaced in youth poetry is the use of different styles, languages, and media. According to Giroux (1992), any lived relation of difference

> ruptures the dominant order symbolically and refuses to narrate *with* permission…It not only challenges the dominant order's attempt to suppress all differences through a discourse that asserts the homogeneity of the social domain but presents the possibility of a social imaginary in which a politics of democratic difference offers up forms of resistance in which it becomes possible to rewrite, rework, recreate, and reestablish new discourses and cultural spaces that revitalize rather than degrade public life. (p. 191)

Though we are not suggesting that poetry is limited to the notion of difference, it is important to note its symbolic value to young people from historically disenfranchised communities who use poetry as a means to challenge the "homogeneity of the social domain" that often times marginalizes their experiences. Engaging in the "politics of democratic difference" by reading, writing, and performing poems has shaped the way that these young people see themselves in relation to the sociocultural contexts they occupy. Consistent in their poems were sub-topics that name and challenge certain notions about race, ethnicity, gender, sexuality, class, language, and ability, among others. They represent relations of power as a result of larger struggles over signs and meanings. Individual and collective acts of inscribing poems contribute to complex processes of self- and social empowerment (Jocson, 2008).

For educators and other youth advocates, the shift toward poemness begins with being open to non-traditional (commonly accepted) multicultural literature and making available a multitude of resources in the classroom. It means collectively learning with and from students about what it is like to live in a complex multicultural world, whether or not they are from the same ethnic background as their students. It means stepping out of bounds, trying out new approaches, and incorporating new media technologies and youth popular culture into the curriculum. It means rethinking the teaching profession's social responsibility to transform the face of literature beyond interpretation and meaning and on to real world actions. It means moving toward democratic difference and participation with young people as part of the stewardship in twenty-first century learning environments. With this in mind, it is just as important to continue to question what it means to be pedagogically inclusive and experimental. For example, is openness to ideas enough? What if approaches do not work? How does one confront multiculturalism and youth agency beyond the name of progressive education? In what ways does writing as a form of cultural politics matter both in and out of the classroom? What considerations should be made? What is at stake when complacency to normative practices in rhetoric and writing instruction takes hold? As we have highlighted above, youth poetry in its various forms – written, spoken, and embodied – represents a call to action. The shift toward poemness demands that we do.

REFERENCES

Acevedo, E. (2007, July 28). *Personal interview*.

Alvarez, G. (2006, August). Meant to survive. *Poem*.

Aristotle. (1996). *Poetics* (M. Heath, Trans.). New York: Penguin.

Bakhtin, M. (1935/1981). *The dialogic imagination: Four essays by M. Bakhtin*. Austin, TX: University of Texas Press.

Bakhtin, M. (1984a). *Problems of Dostoevky's poetics* (C. Emerson, Ed. & Trans.). Minneapolis, MN: University of Minnesota Press.

Bakhtin, M. (1984b). *Rabelais and his world*. Bloomington, IN: Indiana University Press.

Bakhtin, M. (1986). *Speech genres and other late essays*. Austin, TX: University of Texas Press.

Bakhtin, M. (1990). *Art and answerability: Early philosophical essays*. Austin, TX: University of Texas Press.

Bakhtin, M. (1993). *Toward a philosophy of the act* (V. Liapunov, Trans.). Austin, TX: University of Texas Press.

Bakhtin, M./Medvedev, P. (1978). *The formal method in literary scholarship: A critical introduction to sociological poetics*. Cambridge, MA: Harvard University Press.

Bazerman, C. (2004). Intertextuality: How texts rely on other texts. In C. Bazerman & P. Prior (Eds.), *What writing does and how it does it: An introduction to analyzing texts and textual practices* (pp. 83–96). Mahwah, NJ: Lawrence Erlbaum.

Bleich, D. (1978). *Subjective criticism*. Baltimore: Johns Hopkins University Press.

Bruhn, J., & Lundquist, J. (Eds.). (2001). *The novelness of Bakhtin: Perspective and possibilities*. Copenhagen, Denmark: Museum Tuscalanum Press.

Burn, A., & Parker, D. (2003). *Analyzing media texts*. London: Contiuum.
Fisher, M. (2003). Open mics and open minds: Spoken word poetry in African diaspora participatory literacy communities. *Harvard Educational Review, 73*(3), 362–389.
Freedman, S., & Ball, A. (2004). Ideological becoming: Bakhtinian concepts to guide the study of language, literacy, and learning. In Freedman & Ball (Eds.), *Bakhtinian perpectives on language, literacy, and learning*. Cambridge, UK: Cambridge University Press.
Giroux, H. (1992). *Border crossings: Cultural workers and the politics of education*. New York: Routledge.
Goffman, E. (1973). *The presentation of self in everyday life*. Woodstock: The Overlook Press.
Hall, S. (1998). What is this 'black' in black popular culture? In G. Dent (Ed.), *Black popular culture* (pp. 21–33). New York: The New Press.
Holquist, M. (1990). *Dialogism: Bakhtin and his world*. New York: Routledge.
Jakobson, R. (1982). *Selected writings* (Vols. I–VI). Amsterdam, Netherlands: Mouton.
Jakobson, R. (1985). *Verbal art, verbal sign, verbal time*. Minneapolis, MN: University of Minnesota Press.
Jocson, K. M. (2008). *Youth poets: Empowering literacies in and out of schools*. New York: Peter Lang.
Kristeva, J. (1980). *Desire in language: A semiotic approach to literature and art*. New York: Columbia University Press.
Kristeva, J. (1984). *Revolution in poetic language*. New York: Columbia University Press.
Lacan, J. (1991). *The ego in Freud's theory and in the technique of psychoanalysis, 1954–1955* (S. Tomaselli, Trans.). New York: Norton.
Lacan, J. (1998). *The four fundamental principles of psychoanalysis* (A. Sheridan, Trans.). New York: Norton.
McCarthy, C. (1993). After the canon: Knowledge and ideological representation in the multicultural discourse on curriculum reform. In C. McCarthy & W. Crichlow (Eds.), *Race, identity, and representation in education* (pp. 289–314). New York: Routledge.
Morson, G., & Emerson, C. (1990). *Mikhail Bakhtin: A creation of a prosaics*. Stanford, CA: Stanford University Press.
Rivera, T. (2008). *The language you live in: Youth poets and the staging of self*. Unpublished thesis, Stanford University.
Todorov, E. (1975). *The fantastic: A structural approach to literary genre*. Ithaca, NY: Cornell University Press.
Volosinov, V. N. (1973). *Marxism and the philosophy of language*. New York: Seminar.

Korina Jocson
Department of Education
Washington University in St. Louis

Takeo Rivera
Modern Thought and Literature
Stanford University

KALERVO N. GULSON

24. SPACE, CULTURAL POLITICS AND EDUCATION

> [Cultural politics] involve the very nature of the connections between cultural visions and differential power.
>
> Apple (2004, p. 185)

> Space is fundamental in any form of communal life. Space is fundamental in any exercise of power.
>
> Foucault (1994, p. 361)

> [C]ultural studies must move from a temporal to a spatial logic of power.
>
> Grossberg (1993, p. 94)

This chapter provides an overview of the connections between space, cultural politics and education. Cultural politics variously involves contestation over defining official knowledge and "visions of the family, the government, identity, and the economy [that] are to be realized in our institutions and in our daily life" (Apple, 1996, p. 21). To enact, and analyse, a cultural politics of education is to be cognisant of both time and space. The aim of this chapter is to bring the spatial to the fore without jettisoning the historical. This incomplete overview is fraught with conceptual tensions, as I cast a wide net over Neo-Marxist, postmodern and poststructural geographies. Nonetheless, this chapter aims to have a heuristic function to tease out the potential of spatial concepts for understanding the cultural politics of education in the late twentieth and early twenty first century.

The chapter commences with a brief introduction to the spatial turn in education. Second, it highlights some of the spatial images and orderings in the cultural politics of the school. Third, it explores some of the possibilities and limitations of spatial theories, with a focus on metaphors, in relation to issues of identity, specifically hybridity and 'race'. The chapter concludes with a consideration of how spatial concepts might allow for different thinking about the cultural politics of education.

THE SPATIAL TURN AND EDUCATION

Foucault (1986) suggests that whereas the nineteenth century had focused on history, or time, "the present epoch will perhaps above all be the epoch of space" (p. 22). In the late twentieth century this prediction was vindicated with a spatial turn in social and cultural theory closely linked to developments in postmodern and feminist theory. This followed earlier turns including those towards Euclidian mathematics and spatial science (Gupta & Ferguson, 1997; Peters, 1996). Spatial

Z. Leonardo (ed.), Handbook of Cultural Politics and Education, 541–553.

concepts, seemingly unchained to disciplines, now traversed social and cultural theory and were "implicated in myriad topographies of power and knowledge" (Gregory, 1994, p. 11). The spatial turn thus has some relevance for analyses in, and of, the cultural politics of education. The political was a focus for critical geographers in the 1990s who proposed that "space, place, and scale are both the object and medium of political struggle.... Political struggle still unfolds in place, and across space, but these geographies...can themselves be manipulated to facilitate or constrain particular outcomes" (Thiem, 2007, p. 18). Noting the latest assertion of space, in the 1990s Peters called for a similar spatial turn in education.

> Educational theory is dominated by theories of time, by historically oriented theories, by temporal metaphors, by notions of change and progress.... Most of the sociological or anthropological theories that educationalists use as explanatory frameworks or paradigms are variants of European strands of thought that are heavily imbued with nineteenth-century historicist assumptions. In short, 'modern' educational theory has all but ignored questions of space, of geography, of architecture (1996, p. 93).

Since Peters' call there has been an increasing spatial emphasis in educational studies, with sociology of education in particular drawing on the social constructivist aspects of space following Lefebvre (1991). While Ruitenberg (2007) identifies Plato's "Allegory of the Cave" as an example of how spatial metaphors have long represented processes of education, the recent spatial emphasis has been in response to, and as a way of understanding, the "spatialization of education" (Rizvi, 2007). This spatialisation was brought about, in part, by the reconfiguring of economic and political relations through globalization. Related work addresses the intersection of education, inequality and urban renewal (Dillabough, Wang, & Kennelly, 2005; Lipman, 2007), education, changing political formations and technology (Robertson, 2007), and the practices of research (Lingard, 2007).

Nonetheless, despite an increasing focus on the spatial in the social sciences, including education, "the academy still clearly neglects the problematic nature of spatiality despite 'space' becoming increasingly central to social and cultural studies" (Keith & Pile, 1993, p. 223). Massey (1993) suggests the proliferation of space and the spatial evokes disquiet not because these terms have prominence in social and political debates, rather this "concern about what the term 'space' is meant to mean arises simply from the multiplicity of definitions adopted" (p. 141). More pertinently space and meaning are divorced, and space invoked without referents. One strand of educational scholarship that attempts to reconnect meaning and space, and deal with the problematic nature of space, has focused on the politics of the school.

THE CULTURAL POLITICS OF THE SCHOOL

The school is an obvious site to explore a spatialised cultural politics of education. Arnot and Dillabough (2006) point to a "culturalist theory of schooling," where "schools, as sites of struggles over the meaning of democracy, take on a mediational role in both the construction and articulation of diverse political issues in the polity" (p. 172). These issues are as varied as identifying the spatial ordering and design of power relations in schools (McGregor, 2004), to contestation over the meaning and purpose of schools in relation to surrounding areas and social class (Reay, 2000). Architecturally and symbolically, then, the school is replete with spatial imagery and orderings (see Thomas, 2006). The most influential theorist in work on these imageries and orderings has been Foucault. His ideas have informed critical conceptualisations of the constraints and possibilities of educational space and school sites (King, 1980; Markus, 1993; McGregor, 2004). One of the key contributions is the constitution of the school as a disciplinary site. Foucault draws on Bentham's Panapticon design of the prison in analyses of schools, among other institutions, as disciplinary sites, and connections to surveillance (Foucault, 1977). Foucault elucidates how history and space are central to everyday life including life within schools (Symes & Preston, 1997). After undertaking a cultural studies analysis of school architecture and issues of mobility within schools, Symes and Preston (1997), informed by Foucault, argue that:

> [f]ar from being a benign element in the schooling process, then, space is a significant force in the structuration of the school's everyday life, part of its capillary network, through which the social relations and divisions which are a central part of that life are constantly recreated and via which corporate control over the school population is established. (p. 197)

Thus, in schools the division of space between administrators, teachers and students results in "a differential allocation of spatial privileges. As with everything else within the school, the power relationship where space is concerned is asymmetrical" (Symes & Preston, 1997, p. 212).

Struggles over the school are also expressions of struggle over material and discursive space. Staiger (2005), also drawing on Foucault, examines the politics of walls in a Los Angeles school. This politics is centred on a seemingly mundane and benign occurrence, the repainting of graffiti covered school walls. Each day the painter employed by the school identifies walls and other sites that have been "defaced" by graffti "tags." These "tags" are associated with gangs, the artists and members who may or may not be students. Each day these walls are repainted in school colours. The painting and tagging are unrelenting and by the following morning tags have reappeared. Staiger asserts material space, primarily walls, but also desks, toilet doors, and tattoos on bodies, provide a site of contestation over what are legitimate cultural representations within the school. Staiger (2005) suggests:

> [m]aybe the best way to understand the microphysics of power of these school colors and tags is by looking at their interface as a contested space where such walls are 'defaced'... The previously innocuous school colors on the wall, which has become increasingly covered with illicit markings, become prominent once the wall is repainted. Erasing illicit markings allows the school to reassert its legitimate hegemony and foreground itself through a fresh coat of paint. (p. 567–8)

In addition to the school, or walls, as a site of contestation, the school is also a site to be resisted, opposed, or co-opted. Thiem's work on homeschooling shows how home-schoolers practice a spatial politics that aims to legitimate the home as both like and unlike the school. Following Apple's (2001) outlining of the privatising of public life, Thiem (2007) suggests "[h]omeschooling further resonates with other forms of spatial separatism that pervade contemporary cultural politics" (p. 26). This separatism links family and privacy to construct the home as a legitimate learning space in opposition to state-run schooling. The home becomes the ultimate localised expression of a cultural politics of (non)schooling. The school as material and symbolic space is construed as a public space that fails to complement the home and family, in fact it is constituted in opposition to the home and family. Thiem (2007) argues that homeschoolers:

> [b]y targeting the state-level in early struggles, and later developing institutions that can lithely traverse this still-fragmented regulatory terrain home-schoolers... demonstrated a spatial flexibility. They...strategically worked within received geographies, transformed them, and built infrastructures that exceed or outflank them. (p. 31)

This is a spatial politics that creates networks of like-minded parents operating to reify the home whilst creating alliances, mostly via the Internet, to challenge the state. It is also a spatial politics reminiscent of the establishment of public schooling in Australia in the late nineteenth century. Rural parents, mostly on farms, resisted sending their children to newly created public schools on the basis that the home was an equally important site of economic generation, cultural values and identity formation (Vick, 1990).

IDENTITY SPACES: ON METAPHOR AND MATERIALITY

> ...all spatialities are political because they are the (covert) medium and (disguised) expression of asymmetrical relations of power. There can be no simple celebration or condemnation of transgression – the movement from one (political) place to another (political) place. Instead, there must be a commitment to the continual questioning of location, movement and direction – to challenging hegemonic constructions of place, of politics and of identity (Keith & Pile, 1993, p. 220).

The constitution and contestation of identity is an important aspect of cultural politics. Identities can also be understood as spatial, where "the language of space, perhaps because it is linked so palpably to experience, is imbued with the sense of inclusion and exclusion as individuals and groups move through, in, and out of communities" (Gulson & Symes, 2007, p. 2). For Soja and Hooper (1993), this is an explicitly postmodern discourse of spatiality that newly imagines the connections between social space and the cultural politics of difference. Cultural identities provide a fruitful example of the productive complexities of spatiality, for "spatialities represent both the spaces between multiple identities and the contradictions within identities" (Keith & Pile, 1993, p. 225). In the following I look at metaphors, hybridity and race to discern how identity is often spatially articulated in multiple and sometimes contradictory fashions.

Hybridity

Despite its social Darwinist lineage, contemporary invocations of hybridity draw attention to cultural tensions and collisions that "open [sic] up the space for the study of cultural negotiations, conflicts, and struggles against the backdrop of contemporary globalization" (Valdivia, 2005, p. 310). Hybridity is seen as a dominant, logical, yet not always desirable outcome of a globalising, postcolonial world. Scholars mobilise a spatial vocabulary, referring to both real and imaginary geographies, to articulate hybridity as concept and descriptor. According to Grossberg (1993), hybridity is simultaneously an inhabited place and a border, a liminal space, where:

> the subaltern are different from the identities on either side of the border, but they are not simply the fragments of both. The subaltern exists as different from either alternative, in the place between the colonizer and the (imagined) precolonial subject. (p. 97)

As Grossberg points out, this liminal space is what Bhabha (1994) calls "Third Space," which disrupts the homogeneity of representations of culture, an assertion that cultural politics demands no tenable claims to a purity of culture, to stable origins. Third Space, for Bhabha, is predicated on cultural hybridity that allows an "*inter*national culture" (p. 56; original emphasis) to be conceived. Spatiality as the possibility of something different is important in this conception of an "*inter*national culture" for:

> it is the "inter" – the cutting edge of translation and negotiation, the inbetween space – that carries the burden of the meaning of culture. It makes it possible to begin envisaging national, anti-nationalist histories of the "people". And by exploring this Third Space, we may elude the politics of polarity and emerge as the others of our selves (Bhabha, 1994, p. 56: original emphasis).

Higher education provides a fruitful area of study in which to examine the links between space and hybridity. Sidhu (2004), in a study of the international education sector in Australia, looks at the connection between globalization, spatialisation and higher education, and the interplay of multiculturalism and hybridity. Sidhu argues that Australian international education providers have invoked a benign form of cultural hybridity to promote Australia as a safe, multicultural study destination. However, Sidhu suggests a spatial analysis of the global and local as mutually constitutive results in a necessary reading of cultural hybridity as both "progressive and desirable," and as including more unpalatable practices such as "ethnocultural fundamentalisms" (p. 51). This ambiguity is also apparent in Behdad's (1993) work on the postcolonial diasporic academic who is characterised by an inherent itinerancy. This itinerancy leads diasporic academics to reflect on, describe and theorise their hybrid position in a new social space. These embodied spatialities of postcoloniality involve considerations of both discursive displacement and the materiality of immigration and exile. However, Behdad notes these spatialities are problematic as they fail to specify the "socioeconomic conditions that privilege some forms of mobility and render others oppressive" (p. 42).

These possibilities and ambiguities of hybridity are implicit in the plethora of spatial metaphors relating to cultural politics: surveillance, borderlands and margins. For example, Soja and Hooper (1993) argue bell hooks' selection of marginality as a subject position is simultaneously a political and geographical act, it is a re-appropriation of the centre and periphery of colonialism and modernity, and repositions the cultural politics of difference and human geography. Thus, spatial metaphors are replete with possibility and agency. These metaphors provide ways of making familiar binaries strange, to create a "'thirdspace' of political choice, containing more than simple combinations of the original dualities" (Soja & Hooper, 1993, p. 192). Spatial metaphors also assist to conceptualise power relations, where "[e]ndeavouring… to decipher discourse through the use of spatial, strategic metaphors enables one to grasp precisely the points at which discourses are transformed in, through and on the basis of relations of power" (Foucault, 1980, pp. 69–70).

However, Pile and Thrift note tensions between the material and discursive mobilisations of space and contend that spatial imagery:

> neglects the crucial importance of different *places* – performed spaces in which psychical and social boundaries are only too clear, in which resources are clearly available to some and not others, in which physical force makes contact – in fostering difference by generalising different places into in/[sic] different spatial figures. In other words, in the process of metaphorisation ground is lost. We index space, but we become lost in it (Pile & Thrift, 1995, p. 374; original emphasis).

Being "lost" has resonance with another conception of thirdspace implicit in the frightening proliferation of "spaces of the exception", such as refugee camps in the Australian desert and Camp X-Ray, Guantánamo Bay, Cuba (Gregory, 2004, following Agamben, 1998). Gregory (2004) contends that "[a]s these zones of indistinction multiply around the world, so it becomes clear that 'third spaces' or 'paradoxical spaces' are not always and everywhere the emancipatory formations that some writers have taken them to be" (p. 258). Smith and Katz (1993) argue for a spatial politics that distinguishes and relates representation and materiality, that "comprehend[s] the interconnectedness of material and metaphorical space" (p. 68).

Race/Racism

Nonetheless, linking material and metaphorical space can lead to disturbing, but significant conclusions, such as in reference to race/racism. Part of this is to recognise that while, as the result of diffuse and dispersed cultures, there is an emphasis "on globalized sensibilities and hybridized identities and identifications," there are also local referents to identity formation (Kenway, Kraack, & Hickey-Moody, 2006, p. 26). Similarly, M.P. Smith (2001) asserts "it is necessary to question all abstractions that tend to ignore the historically specific conditions of cultural production as these become *localized*, *interrelated* and *mutually constitutive* in particular places at particular times" (p. 139' original emphasis). The importance of this questioning is evident in Pugliese's (2007) caution against a-historical mobilisations of terms such as hybridity. Pugliese asserts de-historicised hybrid identities often support policy processes and practices that create destructive inbetween spaces, particularly in White settler societies like Australia and Canada. Pugliese (2007) refers to the construction of Aboriginal people during the twentieth century as "hybrids"; a liminal space between black and white that meant some Aboriginal people were neither Black nor White and were consequently targeted to become White. Through a policy of colonial assimilation mixed ancestry meant the invalidation of Aboriginality. Pugliese (2007) remarks, "[m]ore disturbing still, it was under the power of this policy that 'hybrid' children were forcibly removed from their Aboriginal parents and placed within state institutions designed to obliterate any traces of their Aboriginality and reinvent them as 'white'" (p. 29). Ergo, it is possible to delineate hybridity as an ideological re-ordering of identity that is at times driven and spatially enacted, and understood, through race/racism.

There is therefore a symbiosis between race and geography - not only is race produced by space, and space by race (Mitchell, 2000; Razack, 2002), but as Delaney (2002) notes "race – in all of its complexity and ambiguity, as ideology and identity – is what it is and does what it does precisely because of *how* it is given spatial expression" (p. 7, original emphasis). The spatial expression of race is clear not only in settler societies like Australia, but also in countries like the United States. This is evident through Critical Race Theory (see Delgado, 1995), and its application in education. Critical Race Theory is based on three interrelated propositions: that race continues to contribute to inequality; that property rights underpin the United States; and that the intersection of property and race create a frame of analysis to examine inequity (Ladson-Billings & Tate, 2006). Critical race theory recognises the spatial expression of race with its emphasis on property rights, and their relationship to social and educational inequality. In work outside of Critical Race Theory, this has been clearly demonstrated in the connection between housing and education[1]. As Anyon (2005) notes, there is a racial dimension to the lack of affordable housing in US cities. The predominance of low-income people of colour in sub-standard housing, primarily in inner city areas, results in segregated, sub-par schools. In the United States "federal housing policies that concentrate low-income residents in urban neighbourhoods contribute to the effects on education that prove in many cases to be overwhelming barriers to high quality schools" (Anyon, 2005, p. 95).

While acknowledging the problems with metaphor, discursive practices are nonetheless an important focus for work on "race" and space. Cultural geography has an increasing emphasis on "the deconstruction of the, often conflicting, representational strategies that surround particular racialized places and events"

(Bonnett & Nayak, 2003, p. 303). Related education scholarship looks at how "racialised places" are implicated in contestation over educational policy decisions involving school closures and provision of schooling for inner city children (Gulson, 2006). The significance and ambiguities of these spatial interrelations is pointed to by Lipman (2007) who notes, following Haymes (1995), that Black urban spaces, particularly in Chicago, have simultaneously been positioned as dangerous spaces by "white supremacist ideology" and drawn upon by Black communities for purposes of resistance. Lipman (2007) suggests that:

> [i]n Black urban communities, place making, and therefore the production of Black public spaces, is linked with day-to-day survival through collective support, affirmation of one's humanity, and resistance in contexts of racial terror. Thus, the dispossession of African-American working-class communities erases historically constituted spaces of collective identity and cultural resistance. (p. 167)

Aside from this manifestation of a spatialised "strategic essentialism" (see Anderson, 1993), Lipman's work identifies how space and place have been in mutually constitutive relationships. Most notably this focuses on neoliberal globalization and the enactment and re-inscription of racism implicit in gentrification and associated educational reforms. Lipman's work points to the way in which "race", racism and space are connected to the struggles for social justice in Chicago inner city schools.

CONCLUSION: SPACE, POLITICS AND PROXIMITY

This chapter aimed to fulfil a heuristic function, aspects of space and the cultural politics of education. Through necessity it only touched on selected aspects that I think are important ambiguities and conceptual clarifications. Ambiguities included the various readings of hybridity as a productive spatial intercession into binary thinking, such as the idea of Third Spaces (e.g., Bhabha, 1994), whilst also being a spatial ordering that created and maintained racial hierarchies through the removal of Aboriginal children in Australia (e.g. Pugliese, 2007). Conceptual clarifications included reiterating calls for precision in the use of space, expounded in relation to metaphors. This follows Crang and Thrift's (2000) assertion that space "is used with such abandon that its meanings run into each other before they have properly been interrogated" (p. 1). Similarly, Smith and Katz (1993), whilst supporting the use of metaphor, point out that one of the problems with spatial metaphors is that they draw on a notion of absolute space – universal and fixed. Space is reinscribed as familiar, an empty container, in a similar way to education as an empty container in which cultural politics plays out. The use of spatial metaphors, for the most part, fails to acknowledge the myriad ways in which space can be understood. Smith and Katz suggest spatial metaphors have such purchase due to the "radical questioning of all else, a decentring and destabilization of previously fixed realities and assumptions; space is largely exempted from such sceptical scrutiny precisely so it can be held constant to provide some semblance of order for an otherwise floating world of ideas" (p. 80). Thus space needs to be subject to scepticism as well as markers such as culture, identity and truth. In work on the cultural politics of education this could include challenging the conflation of space and place, terms that are often used as euphemisms for local and global. The danger in using place and space as both irredeemably distinct and conflated with the local and global comes when politics are involved. Massey (2005) contends that this leads to the idea of the global as divorced from the concrete, "reinforced by imaginations of place, or of the local, as victims of global space: the association...of place, the local and vulnerability on one hand, and space, capital and agency on the other" (p. 185). Yet, for Pile (1997) the local and the global are not essential scales, "but formed precisely out of the struggles that seemingly they only contain" (p. 13). Similarly Massey (2005) points out the global and the local are inseparable if one takes seriously the relational and mutually constitutive nature of space and place.

Additionally, in this chapter I wanted to consider what might be done differently in analyses of, and for, cultural politics of education if an explicitly spatial frame were to be adopted. In reflecting on this task I am challenged by N. Smith's contention that:

> [t[here is a crucial question of the extent to which this "spatial turn" has been more than skin deep…Put most crudely, perhaps, why space? Why *should* our analysis of social difference and political possibility be rewritten in the language of space? (2004, p. 13: original emphasis).

To conclude this chapter I offer two responses. The first relates to Keith and Pile's (1993) assertion that "cultural theory makes geography's familiar appear strange, just as geography can and should prompt cultural studies to reflect on its common sense spatialized vocabulary" (p. 223). Massey (2005) argues that it is not enough to propose that there is no politics without space, but that thinking about space as relational means that politics can be thought differently. To my mind, this is clearest in what Armstrong (2007) posits as the notion of a spatial counter-perspectives. Armstrong examines how concepts of space and place can modify understandings of social and educational exclusion and inclusion, and is particularly interested in what is possible, what can be thought differently. The possibilities of spatial concepts lie as stimuli "for thinking creatively about movements between policies, processes, and instances of inclusion and exclusion in a fresh light, from different vantage points, to provide a counter-perspective of social life as a process of change" (p. 108). Different vantage points mean that educational sites such as the school are arenas of spatial politics that create not only constraints but possibilities. Thomson (2007), in work on the politics and practices of school exclusion, focuses on geographies of exclusion, and poses three alternatives to exclusion – resistance and conformity, changes in place, and the construction of counter-public spaces, including those within schools. Thomson concludes that these alternatives "offer possibilities for young people to experience, through changed spatial relations, new opportunities for building identity and agency" (p. 126).

The second response to Smith's contention, and one I think shows some promise for connecting space, place, cultural politics and education, is based on re-thinking the notion of proximity in relation to justice, care, and ethics. Massey (2005) observes that responsibility for others seems to come about from the inside out, a responsibility to those closest before considering those further away. This can be understood in some part by Massey's refrain of Berger's claim that "[i]t is now space rather than time that hides consequences from us" (cited in Massey, 2005, p. 185). For example, people in the "Global North" lose sight of the consequences of driving cars, or consuming brand name clothing made by people paid a pittance, until that which is far away becomes close – such as pollution, climate change, consumer boycotts, and so forth. In arguing for a rethinking of proximity Massey (2005) posits spatial politics that challenges the idea of care connected to "closeness," when she suggests:

> [t]here is...a localisation of ethical commitment at the very moment of increasingly geographically expansive interconnectedness. It raises the question of whether, in a relational and globalised spatiality, "groundedness", and the search for a situated ethics, must remain tied to notions of the local. If places pose, in a highly variable form, the question of our living together in the sense of juxtaposition (throwntogetherness), there is also the question of the negotiation of those, equally varied, wider relations within which they are constituted (Massey, 2005, p. 187).

As just one example, Novelli's (2007) ethnographic work on worker and community action to successfully resist the privatisation of Colombia's state-owned utilities demonstrates how a spatial, pedagogically-based, politics of resistance and justice worked to challenge the idea of labour as local and global as capital. Colombian workers and activists used what Novelli calls "strategic pedagogy" to make connections with trade unions, social organisations and human rights groups across the globe. Novelli's work substantiates what Massey (2005) contends. If care is not just about proximity but about grounded interconnectedness then returning to the enclosures is not a viable alternative. Place cannot be caught up with nostalgia and desire to return to a safer, more comforting past (Massey, 1994).

Nonetheless, rejecting nostalgia is not rejecting history. While this chapter gave primacy to space it was not aimed at jettisoning historical analysis of the cultural politics of education. Apple (1996) posits that the cultural politics of education involves acts of challenging "existing relations, to defend those counterhegemonic forms that now exist, or to bring new forms into existence" (p. 21). Space and time are crucial to these projects. Massey (1993), in positing the notion of "space-time," asserts that "the spatial is integral to the production of history, and thus to the possibility of politics, just as the temporal is to geography" (p. 159). Paying close attention to both the historical and the spatial may conceivably inform proximal but interconnected analyses of the cultural politics of education.

NOTES

1 With thanks to an anonymous reviewer for this example.

REFERENCES

Anderson, K. J. (1993). Constructing geographies: 'Race', place and the making of Sydney's aboriginal redfern. In P. Jackson & J. Penrose (Eds.), *Constructions of race, place and nation* (pp. 81–99). London: UCL Press.

Anyon, J. (2005). *Radical possibilities: Public policy, urban education, and a new social movement*. New York: Routledge.

Apple, M. W. (1996). *Cultural politics and education*. New York: Teachers College Press.

Apple, M. W. (2001). *Educating the 'right' way: Markets, standards, god and inequality*. London: RoutledgeFalmer.

Apple, M. W. (2004). Cultural politics and the text. In S. J. Ball (Ed.), *The RoutledgeFalmer reader in sociology of education* (pp. 179–195). London: RoutledgeFalmer.

Armstrong, F. (2007). Disability, education, and space: Some critical reflections. In K. N. Gulson & C. Symes (Eds.), *Spatial theories of education: Policy and geography matters* (pp. 95–110). New York: Routledge.

Arnot, M., & Dillabough, J. (2006). Feminist politics and democratic values in education. In H. Lauder, P. Brown, J. Dillabough, & A. H. Halsey (Eds.), *Education, globalization and social change* (pp. 161–178). Oxford: Oxford University Press.

Behdad, A. (1993). Traveling to teach: Postcolonial critics in the American academy. In C. McCarthy & W. Crichlow (Eds.), *Race, identity and representation in education* (pp. 40–49). New York: Routledge.

Bhabha, H. K. (1994). *The location of culture*. London: Routledge.

Bonnett, A., & Nayak, A. (2003). Cultural geographies of racialisation - the territory of race. In K. Anderson, M. Domash, S. Pile, & N. Thrift (Eds.), *Handbook of cultural geography* (pp. 300–312). London: SAGE Publications.

Crang, M., & Thrift, N. (2000). Introduction. In M. Crang & N. Thrift (Eds.), *Thinking space* (pp. 1–30). London: Routledge.

Delaney, D. (2002). The space that race makes. *The Professional Geographer, 54*(1), 6–14.

Delgado, R. (Ed.). (1995). *Critical race theory: The cutting edge*. Philadelphia: Temple University Press.

Dillabough, J., Wang, G., & Kennelly, J. (2005). 'Ginas,' 'Thugs' and 'Gangstas': Young people's struggles to 'become somebody' in working-class urban Canada. *Journal of Curriculum Theorizing, 21*(2), 83–108.

Foucault, M. (1977). *Discipline and punish: The birth of the prison*. London: Penguin Books.

Foucault, M. (1980). *Power/knowledge: Selected interviews and other writings 1972–1977* (C. Gordon, Ed., Vol. 1). Brighton, Sussex: The Harvester Press.

Foucault, M. (1986). Of other spaces. *Diacritics*, (16), 22–27.

Foucault, M. (1994). *Power: Essential works of Foucault 1954–1984* (J. Faubion, Ed., Vol. 3). London: Penguin.

Gregory, D. (1994). *Geographical imaginations*. Oxford: Blackwell.

Gregory, D. (2004). *The colonial present*. Oxford: Blackwell.

Grossberg, L. (1993). Cultural studies and/in new worlds. In C. McCarthy & W. Crichlow (Eds.), *Race, identity and representation in education* (pp. 89–105). New York: Routledge.

Gulson, K. N. (2006). A white veneer: Education policy, space and 'race' in the inner city. *Discourse: studies in the cultural politics of education, 27*(2), 251–266.

Gulson, K. N., & Symes, C. (2007). Knowing one's place: Educational theory, policy and the spatial turn. In K. N. Gulson & C. Symes (Eds.), *Spatial theories of education: Policy and geography matters* (pp. 1–16). New York: Routledge.

Gupta, A., & Ferguson, J. (1997). Beyond 'culture': Space, identity, and the politics of difference. In A. Gupta & J. Ferguson (Eds.), *Culture, power, place: Explorations in critical anthropology* (pp. 33–51). Durham, NC: Duke University Press.

Keith, M., & Pile, S. (1993). Conclusion: Towards new radical geographies. In M. Keith & S. Pile (Eds.), *Place and the politics of identity* (pp. 220–226). London: Routledge.

Kenway, J., Kraack, A., & Hickey-Moody, A. (2006). *Maculinity beyond the metropolis*. Basingstoke: PalgraveMacmillan.

King, A. (Ed.). (1980). *Buildings and society: Essays on the social development of the built environment*. London: Routledge & Kegan Paul.

Ladson-Billings, G., & Tate, W. F. (2006). Toward a critical race theory of education. In H. Lauder, P. Brown, J. Dillabough, & A. H. Halsey (Eds.), *Education, globalization, and social change* (pp. 570–585). Oxford: Oxford University Press.

Lefebvre, H. (1991). *The production of space*. Oxford: Blackwell.

Lingard, B. (2007). Deparochializing the study of education: Globalization and the research imagination. In K. N. Gulson & C. Symes (Eds.), *Spatial theories of education: Policy and geography matters* (pp. 233–250). New York: Routledge.

Lipman, P. (2007). Education and the spatialization of urban inequality: A case study of Chicago's Renaissance 2010. In K. N. Gulson & C. Symes (Eds.), *Spatial theories of education: Policy and geography matters* (pp. 155–174). New York: Routledge.

Markus, T. (1993). *Buildings and power: Freedom and control in the origin of modern building types*. London: Routledge.

Massey, D. (1993). Politics and space/time. In M. Keith & S. Pile (Eds.), *Place and the politics of identity* (pp. 141–161). London: Routledge.

Massey, D. (1994). Double articulation: A place in the world. In A. Bammer (Ed.), *Displacements: cultural identities in question* (pp. 110–121). Bloomington, IN: Indiana University Press.

Massey, D. (2005). *For space*. London: SAGE Publications.

McGregor, J. (2004). Space, power and the classroom. *Forum: for promoting 3–19 comprehensive education*, *46*(1), 13–18.

Mitchell, D. (2000). *Cultural geography: A critical introduction*. Oxford: Blackwell.

Novelli, M. (2007). Trade unions, strategic pedagogy and new spaces of engagement: Counter-knowledge economy insights from Columbia. In K. N. Gulson & C. Symes (Eds.), *Spatial theories of education: Policy and geography matters* (pp. 251–272). New York: Routledge.

Peters, M. A. (1996). *Poststructuralism, politics and education*. Westport, CT: Bergin & Garvey.

Pile, S. (1997). Introduction: Opposition, political identities and spaces of resistance. In S. Pile & M. Keith (Eds.), *Geographies of resistance* (pp. 1–32). London: Routledge.

Pile, S., & Thrift, N. (1995). Conclusions: Spacing and the subject. In S. Pile & N. Thrift (Eds.), *Mapping the subject: Geographies of cultural transformation* (pp. 371–380). London: Routledge.

Pugliese, J. (2007). Diasporic architecture, whiteness and the cultural politics of space: In the footsteps of the Italian Forum. In S. Dasgupta (Ed.), *Constellations of the transnational: Modernity, culture, critique* (pp. 23–50). Amsterdam: Rodopi.

Razack, S. H. (2002). When place becomes race. In S. H. Razack (Ed.), *Race, space and the law* (pp. 1–20). Toronto: Between the lines.

Reay, D. (2000). 'I don't really like it here but I don't want to be anywhere else': Children and inner city council estates. *Antipode*, *32*(4), 410–428.

Rizvi, F. (2007). Personal communication.

Robertson, S. (2007). Public-private partnerships, digital firms, and the production of a neoliberal education space at the European scale. In K. N. Gulson & C. Symes (Eds.), *Spatial theories of education: Policy and geography matters* (pp. 215–232). New York: Routledge.

Ruitenberg, C. W. (2007). Here be dragons: Exploring cartography in educational theory and research. *Complicity: An International Journal of Complexity and Education*, *4*(1), 7–24.

Sidhu, R. (2004). Governing international education in Australia. *Globalisation, Societies and Education*, *2*(1), 1–33.

Smith, M. P. (2001). *Transnational urbanism: Locating globalisation*. Oxford: Blackwell.

Smith, N. (2004). Space and substance in geography. In P. Cloke, P. Crang, & M. Goodwin (Eds.), *Envisioning human geographies* (pp. 11–29). London: Arnold.

Smith, N., & Katz, C. (1993). Grounding metaphor: Towards a spatialized politics. In M. Keith & S. Pile (Eds.), *Place and the politics of identity* (pp. 67–83). London: Routledge.

Soja, E. W., & Hooper, B. (1993). The spaces that difference makes: some notes on the geographical margins of the new cultural politics. In M. Keith & S. Pile (Eds.), *Place and the politics of identity* (pp. 183–205). London: Routledge.

Staiger, A. (2005). School walls as battle grounds: Technologies of power, space and identity. *Paedagogica Historica, 41*(4), 555–569.

Symes, C., & Preston, N. (1997). *Schools and classrooms: A cultural studies analysis of education* (2nd ed.). Melbourne: Longman.

Thiem, C. (2007). The spatial politics of educational privatization: Re-reading the US homeschooling movement. In K. N. Gulson & C. Symes (Eds.), *Spatial theories of education: Policy and geography matters* (pp. 17–36). New York: Routledge.

Thomas, G. E. (2006). From our house to the 'big house': Architectural design as visible metaphor in the school buildings of Philadelphia. *Journal of Planning History, 5*(3), 218–240.

Thomson, P. (2007). Working the in/visible geographies of school exclusion. In K. N. Gulson & C. Symes (Eds.), *Spatial theories of education: Policy and geography matters* (pp. 111–130). New York: Routledge.

Valdivia, A. N. (2005). Geographies of Latinidad: deployments of radical hybridity in the mainstream. In C. McCarthy, W. Crichlow, G. Dimitriadis, & N. Dolby (Eds.), *Race, identity, and representation in education* (2nd ed., pp. 307–317). New York: Routledge.

Vick, M. (1990). 'Their paramount duty': Parents and schooling in the mid-nineteenth century. In M. Theobold & R. J. W. Selleck (Eds.), *Family, school and state in Australian history* (pp. 177–195). Sydney: Allen and Unwin.

Kalervo N. Gulson
Faculty of Arts & Social Sciences
University of New South Wales

DOUGLAS KELLNER

25. TECHNOLOGICAL TRANSFORMATION, NEW LITERACIES AND DEMOCRACY

Toward a Reconstruction of Education

New digital technologies involve the dramatic multiplication of computer, information, communication, and multimedia technologies that have been changing everything from the ways people work and consume and produce culture, to the ways they communicate with each other and spend their leisure time. This technological revolution is often interpreted as the beginnings of a knowledge or information society, and therefore ascribes education a central role in every aspect of life. It poses tremendous challenges to educators to rethink their basic tenets, to deploy the new technologies in creative and productive ways, and to restructure schooling to respond constructively and progressively to the technological and social changes currently underway and emergent forms of culture and communication, so as to promote democracy.[1]

At the same time, important demographic and socio-political changes are taking place throughout the world. Immigration patterns have created the challenge of providing people from diverse races, classes, and backgrounds with the tools and competencies to enable them to succeed and participate in an ever more complex and changing world. I argue that educators need to cultivate multiple literacies for contemporary technological and multicultural societies, that teachers need to develop new literacies of diverse sorts, including a more fundamental importance for print literacy, to meet the challenge of restructuring education for a hi-tech, multicultural society, and global culture. In a period of dramatic technological and social change, education needs to help produce a variety of types of literacies to make current pedagogy relevant to the demands of the contemporary era.

Radical pedagogy is an important element of a cultural politics aiming at democratic social transformation and in this chapter, I sketch aspects of a critical theory of education, technology and pedagogy, and democracy.[2] I will discuss the fundamental transformations in the world economy, politics, and culture in a dialectical framework that distinguishes between progressive and emancipatory features and oppressive and negative attributes and how a radical pedagogy and new technoliteracies are essential for democratic social transformation and justice. Hence, following John Dewey and Paulo Freire, I will call for a reconstruction of education to make it more responsive to the challenges of a democratic and multicultural society.

Z. Leonardo (ed.), Handbook of Cultural Politics and Education, 555–570.

NEW TECHNOLOGIES, NEW LITERACIES IN A CHANGING WORLD

Technological innovations, expansion of global media empires, an explosion of new media and cultural forms, and the unrestricted commercial targeting of children have all contributed to an environment where today's youth are growing up in a mediated world far different than any previous generation. While technological advancements have created new possibilities for the free flow of information, social networking and global activism, there is also the potential for corporations and governments to increase their control over media, restrict the flow of information, and appropriate these new tools for profit and control at the expense of free expression and democracy.

Most children born in the United States in this millennium have never known a time without the Internet, cellular phones or television.[3] Over 98% of US households have at least one television set and about one third of young children live in households where the TV is on "always" or "most of the time" (Rideout, Vandewater & Wartella, 2003, p. 4). Before most children are six years of age, they spend about two hours per day with screen media,[4] something that doubles by age eight, and before they are 18 they spend approximately 6½ hours daily with all types of media (Rideout, Roberts & Foehr, 2005).[5] It is also estimated that nearly all young children in the US, "have products—clothes, toys, and the like—based on characters from TV shows or movies" (Rideout *et al.*, 2003, p. 4). Since television programs, cellular phones, video games, music, and even toys have become major transmitters of culture, tellers as well as sellers of the stories of our time, it is now more than ever necessary that children need to learn how to critically question the messages that surround them and how to use the vast array of new tools available to express their own ideas and participate fully.

Likewise, computers, multimedia technologies and culture, and social networking are becoming a part of everyday life. Victoria Carrington (2005) writes that the emergence of new media texts, "situate contemporary children in global flows of consumption, identity and information in ways unheard of in earlier generations..." (p. 22). In the context of continuously expanding technological and economic transformation, critical media and technoliteracies are an imperative for participatory democracy because new information communication technologies and a market-based media culture have fragmented, connected, converged, diversified, homogenized, flattened, broadened, and reshaped the world.[6] These changes have been reframing the way people think and restructuring societies at local and global levels (Castells, 1996; Jenkins, 2006).

Put in historical perspective, it is now possible to see modern education as preparation for industrial civilization and minimal citizenship in a passive representative democracy. Modern education, in short, emphasizes submission to authority, rote memorization, and what Freire called the "banking concept" of education in which learned teachers deposit knowledge into passive students, inculcating conformity, subordination, and normalization. Today, these traits are somewhat undercut in certain sectors of the global postindustrial and networked society with its demands for new skills for the workplace, participation in emergent social and political environs, and interaction within novel forms of culture and everyday life.

A more flexible economy, based on an ever-evolving technological infrastructure and more multicultural work force demands a more technically literate, interactive, culturally sensitive, and educated work force, while revitalizing democracy requires the participation of informed citizens.[7] Yet, while on one hand, the demands of the expanding global economy, culture, and polity require a more informed, participatory, and active workforce and citizenship, on the other hand, a docile workforce and service industry is still the norm in many sectors of work, society, and culture. Although for a time, ideologues of technocapitalism argued that information and communication technology would of themselves dramatically reorganize and democratize the workplace, schooling, the polity, and everyday life (Gates, 1995; Kelly, 1995, 1999), it is by now clear the supposed liberating effects of new technologies were greatly exaggerated. But while globalization and technological development have highly contradictory and ambiguous effects (Best and Kellner, 2001; Kellner, 2002), they provide educational reformers with the challenge of whether education will be restructured to promote democracy and human needs, or whether education will be transformed primarily to serve the needs of business and the global economy.

To some extent, accelerating technological transformation renders necessary the sort of thorough restructuring of education that radicals have demanded since the Enlightenment of Rousseau and Wollstonecraft through Dewey, all of whom saw the progressive reconstruction of education as the key to democracy. Today, however, intense pressures for change now come directly from technology and the economy and not ideology or educational reformist ideas, with an expanding global economy and novel technologies demanding innovative skills, competencies, literacies, and practices.

It is therefore a burning question as to what sort of restructuring of education and society will take place, in whose interests, and for what ends. More than ever, we need philosophical reflection on the ends and purposes of education, on what we are doing and trying to achieve in our educational practices and institutions. In this situation, it may be instructive to return to Dewey and see the connections between education and democracy, the need for the reconstruction of education and society, and the value of experimental pedagogy to seek solutions to the problems of education in the present day. A progressive reconstruction of education will urge that it be done in the interests of democratization, ensuring access to information and communication technologies for all, helping to overcome the so-called digital divide and divisions of the haves and have nots, so that education is placed, as Dewey (1997/1916) and Freire (1972, 1998) propose, in the service of democracy and social justice.

Yet we should be more aware than Dewey of the obduracy of divisions of class, gender, and race, and work self-consciously for multicultural democracy and education. This task suggests that we valorize difference and cultural specificity, as well as equality and shared universal Deweyan values such as freedom, equality, individualism, and participation. Theorizing a democratic and multicultural reconstruction of education forces us to confront the digital divide, that there are divisions between information and technology have and have nots, just as there are class, gender, and race divisions in every sphere of the existing constellations of society and culture. The latest surveys of the digital divide, however, indicate that the key indicators are class and education, as well as race and gender, hence the often-circulated argument that new technologies merely reinforce the hegemony of upper class white males must be questioned, at least for some contemporary societies.[8]

Rob Shields (2001) has argued that the concept of the "digital divide" serves as a marketing device for the benefit of technology disseminators and that on the whole the development of new technologies helps increase the divide between haves and have nots. While no doubt hi-tech corporations and affiliated government institutions have promoted the notion of a digital divide, the concept points to some serious problems and challenges. It is clear by now that providing access and computers alone without proper training and pedagogy does not advance education or social justice. Thus, more broadly conceived, the notion of a digital divide points to disparities in terms of access, training, skills, and the actual use of technologies to improve education and promote social justice.

With the proper resources, policies, pedagogies, and practices, educators can work to reduce the (unfortunately growing) gap between haves and have nots by promoting broad training in information and computer literacy, that embraces a wide range of projects from providing technical skills to engaging students in the production of media projects. Indeed, teaching critical media literacy through production is an efficacious way of teaching students and citizens the codes and forms of media culture and new media and using these new cultural forms to provide for a diversity of voices and to promote progressive cultural change (see Kellner, 1995; Hammer, 1995, 1996; Hammer and Kellner, 2001).

Clearly, technology alone will not suffice to democratize and adequately reconstruct education, yet providing proper access and training can improve education if it is connected with critical pedagogy and aids to give voices to producers to enable them to participate in their society (see Kellner and Kim, 2009).[9] That is, technology itself does not necessarily improve teaching and learning, and will certainly not of itself overcome acute socio-economic divisions. Indeed, without proper re-visioning of education and without adequate resources, pedagogy, and educational practices, technology could be an obstacle or burden to genuine learning and will probably increase rather than overcome existing divisions of power, cultural capital, and wealth.

In the following reflections, I focus on the role of computers and information technology in contemporary education and the need for new pedagogies and an expanded concept of literacy to respond to the importance of information and communication technologies (ICTs) in every aspect of life. I propose some ways that ICTs and new literacies can serve as efficacious learning tools that will contribute to producing a more democratic and egalitarian society, and not just provide skills and tools to privileged individuals and groups that will improve their cultural capital and social power at the expense of others. How, indeed, can education be re-visioned and reconstructed to provide individuals and groups with the tools, the competencies, the literacies and social practices, to overcome the class, gender, and racial divides that bifurcate our society and at least in terms of economic indicators seem to be growing rather than diminishing?

Many changes in the last couple of decades have contributed greatly to the need for critical media and technolitericies and the reconstruction of education. New critical pedagogies for new media literacy education is now necessary because of the rapid growth of information communication technology, the expansion of free market global capitalism, and the escalating and vanishing linguistic and cultural diversity that is changing social environments at local as well as global levels.

Looking at the impact of globalization on identity, Manuel Castells (1996) asserts that people's lives are being shaped by the forces of the network society. He suggests that the interconnections between technology, economics, culture and identity are challenging, conflicting and impacting upon each other on a global scale.

Already in the 1960s, Marshall McLuhan argued that many of the characteristics of premodern oral culture will again rise up in importance as the instantaneous and continuous electronic age proves to be more similar to oral cultures of the ancient past than the last five centuries of typographic literacy. He wrote these ideas before the existence of cellular phones, the Internet, HDTV, iPads, and social networking, yet today as the World Wide Web and wireless communication become common place in most "First World" countries, as well as in many parts of the "Developing World," his words ring more true today than when he first wrote them a half century ago.

According to McLuhan (1964), before print literacy, humans were hunters and gatherers living in oral societies with tribal cultures that were unified, inclusive, auditory, organic, and had high levels of participation. With the invention of the phonetic alphabet, a new era began. Literacy caused the eye to replace the ear and the cosmic culture became fragmented and separated by a new system of repeatability and uniformity. In the fifteenth century these changes exploded with the invention of Gutenberg's printing press. McLuhan calls this the "mechanical age" and attributes the arrival of individualism, rationalism and nationalism to this new literate culture of homogeneity and lineal organization.

The next great change for humanity, according to McLuhan, came with the discovery of electricity and the invention of the telegraph. The new electronic age has and continues to cause an implosion within society that is returning humans to their earlier oral roots. This latest age of automation and cybernation takes us back to a more participatory, integral, decentralized and inclusive way of living. McLuhan asserts that electricity, with its speed and constancy, is the medium that created simultaneity, it is an extension of our central nervous system, "instantly interrelating every human experience" (p. 358). He suggests that all media are extensions of ourselves; the print is an extension of the eye as the wheel is an extension of the foot.

Now more than ever, we are seeing the transformation of societies into what McLuhan coined, the "global village," and the electronic age that he spoke of is in full force, reshaping societies and identities across the globe. For today's literate society to keep pace with the age of information, education must let go of curriculum that is separated by subjects and "changeover to an interrelation in knowledge," asserts McLuhan (p. 35). He asks, "Would it not seem natural and necessary that the young be provided with at least as much training of perception in this graphic and photographic world as they get in the typographic? In fact, they need more training in graphics, because the art of casting and arranging actors in ads is both complex and forcefully insidious" (p. 230).

Adding economic and technological determinist perspectives to McLuhan's technological determinism, Thomas Friedman (2005) argues that at the turn of this millennium, humans entered the third major shift in globalizing change. He writes that the first great era of globalization began in 1492 when Columbus opened trade between the New World and the Old. During what Friedman calls Globalization 1.0, imperialism and religion drove global integration through brute force as colonizing countries deployed the labor power of exploited peoples until about 1800. The second era, Globalization 2.0, ran from about 1800–2000 and involved multinational companies expanding their markets and labor forces as industrialization reshaped the world. This second era benefited first from the decrease in transportation costs and later from the decrease in telecommunication costs, and was marked by the inventions of new hardware. Yet in the 21st century, Friedman claims that Globalization 3.0 is driven by innovative software and a global fiber-optic network, and asserts that the unique character of this era is "the newfound power for *individuals* to collaborate and compete globally" (p. 10).

Friedman's claim that the world is now less hierarchical with a more level playing field than ever before is overly ideological and optimistic; Friedman is too uncritical of inequalities and injustices of neo-liberal globalization (Klein, 2007). However, his assertion that "the world has been flattened by the convergence of ten major political events, innovations, and companies" (p. 48) is highly provocative and highlights many recent changes in society that are having a global impact. I do not agree, however, with his utopian conclusion that the world is now flat and there is more equal opportunity, since one-third of the world's population still lives without electricity. Yet, Friedman's discussion of the major forces which have changed the world in just the last couple of decades, makes it clear that the 21st century is a different world and will continue to change due to the influences of new ICTs and global economic systems. The examples he describes of transformations in technology, society, and economy provide strong reasons for the need to change education and especially literacy practices. In my view, the type of changes that would best accommodate a globalized world perpetually transformed by technology include multiple literacies, of which critical media and technoliteracies are essential, as argued below.

The diversity of ideas and people is increasing in countries, cities and classrooms as escalating amounts of information become available and larger numbers of people travel and immigrate across the globe. At the same time there is a reduction of diversity as cultural colonialization and commercial homogenization spreads throughout the global markets with the ease of new information communication technologies (ICTs). One example of the loss of diversity can be seen in UNESCO's warning that, "Over 50% of the world's 6000 languages are endangered" with one disappearing almost every other week.[10] Joseph Lo Bianco (2000) states, "During this and the next decade there will be the greatest collapse of language diversity in all history." (p. 94). He attributes these changes to an emerging global system being generated by three principal forces: "The first is the almost universal phenomenon of market deregulation; the second is the advanced integration of international financial markets; and the third is the critical facilitating force of instantaneous communications" (p. 93).

One of the common themes running through many analyses of the changes in the relationship between media and society is a high degree of *convergence* that is occurring in numerous ways (Considine, 2003; Gutiérrez, 2003; Luke, 2006, Jenkins, 2006). Henry Jenkins (2006) insists that we are now living in a *convergence culture*, in which our socio-cultural practices are changing because of the influences of technology and economics, and convergence of old and new media. He explains, "Media convergence is more than simply a technological shift. Convergence alters the relationship between existing technologies, industries, markets, genres, and audiences" (p. 15).

Jenkins highlights two major and often contradictory trends, one in which large media corporations threaten democracy by their concentration of ownership, giving less people a greater ability to push and amplify their limited content out to the masses while new media technologies have made it easier on a grassroots level for more people to pull, create and distribute much more diverse media content, thereby offering new opportunities for democracy. This dynamic push and pull of media is a key aspect of convergence and something Jenkins states, "represents a paradigm shift – a move from medium-specific content toward content that flows across multiple media channels, toward the increased interdependence of communications systems, toward multiple ways of accessing media content, and toward ever more complex relations between top-down corporate media and bottom-up participatory culture" (p. 243).

These changes in technology and society are shaping the way people think and relate to media. Jenkins asserts that the larger problem for educators today is not the old notion of a digital divide that separates people based on limited access to the tools of communication, since more people have access today than ever before, but the larger problem today is a *participation gap*, "the unequal access to the opportunities, experiences, skills, and knowledge that will prepare youth for full participation in the world of tomorrow." (Jenkins *et al.*, 2007, p. 3). Jenkins writes, "We need to rethink the goals of media education so that young people can come to think of themselves as cultural producers and participants and not simply as consumers, critical or otherwise" (2006, p. 259).

Framing the changes in technological and social terms, Carmen Luke (2006) argues for an expanded form of media literacy because of three increasingly growing levels of media convergence. One level of convergence is the functional ability of hardware devices to perform multiple tasks, such as a cell phone that can take and send pictures (still and moving images), play music, send and receive text messages, upload and download content online, play games, and can still be used for chatting. A second level of media convergence entails provider convergence which has been greatly enhanced by deregulations of media ownership and the numerous mergers and acquisitions of multinational media corporations. The horizontal and vertical integration of media companies allows fewer corporations the ability to control more different types of services and content (Bagdikian, 1997; McChesney, 2004). The ability of ICTs to perform more functions and the integration of media providers are creating what Marsha Kinder (1991) labels *transmedia intertextuality*.

According to Luke, the third level of media convergence is a consequence of the two previously mentioned that have had the effect of creating "a much tighter synergy between previously disparate industries, between knowledge and information, consumerism, popular culture, entertainment, communication, and education" (2006, p. 5). As politics, news and entertainment converge into new forms of media, an entire spectator culture is evolving. Spectacle itself is becoming one of the organizing principles of the economy, polity, society, and everyday life (Kellner, 2003a, 2003b, 2005, 2008). In order to grab larger audiences and increase profit and power, the culture industries aggressively create and promote a synthesized spectacle-centered media culture.

James Paul Gee (2000) suggests that technological innovations and hyper-competitive global "fast capitalism" are creating a new type of individual whom he calls the "portfolio person" (p. 43). Gee explains that the idea of 'expertise' has moved "away from 'disciplinary' or academic expertise to a broader notion more compatible with the new capitalist world view" (p. 48). He writes that this business orientation, much like Friedman's flat world perspective, emphasizes "efficient problem solving, productivity, innovation, adaptation, and non-authoritarian distributed systems...In the new capitalism, it is not really important what individuals know on their own, but rather what that they can do with others collaboratively to effectively add 'value' to the enterprise" (p. 49). A problem with this education of the portfolio person is that it is based on a cognitive notion of knowledge workers who have the facility of "higher order thinking" but lack the ability to think *critiquely*. Gee describes critiquely as the ability "to understand and critique systems of power and injustice" (p. 62). The inability to understand or empathize with marginalized, poor and oppressed people is a major problem of this fast capitalism epistemology.

Another problem with the model that creates the portfolio person is that it advantages most the children from dominant positions in society (ie. white, male, middle or upper class), who have easier access to this expertise and "school language" based on their lifeworld experiences and privileges. It is much easier to bridge the home culture to the public school domain for students who have been exposed to white middle class values such as reading children's literature from an early age or visiting museums and art galleries. The common deficit thinking approach that many educators internalize, undervalues the cultural assets that minority and poor students bring to school and often frame those resources as problems to be overcome (Valencia & Solorzano, 2004). Gee writes, "We rarely build on their experiences and on their very real distinctive lifeworld knowledge.

In fact, they are often asked, in the process of being exposed to specialist domains, to deny the value of their lifeworlds and their communities in reference to those of more advantaged children (p. 66).

To counteract the problems of inequality and lack of social critique, Gee promotes a Bill of Rights for all students that includes four pedagogical principles: situated practices, overt instruction, critical framing and transformative practice. He writes, "These principles seek to produce people who can function in the new capitalism, but in a much more meta-aware and political fashion than forms of new-capitalist-complicit schooling" (p. 67). The situated practice can help value the different cultural capital (Bourdieu, 1986) students bring into the classroom as child-centered experiential practices allow students to discover connections between their lifeworlds and school. A major aspect of these principles is a metacognitive awareness about the interconnections of thinking, knowledge and power relations. The need for some overt instruction and critical framing assures that students will engage with texts critiquely to understand the interconnections and systems of power.

The fourth principle of transformed practice suggests that education must involve acting on learning and empower students to use and transform knowledge. When Gee's fourth principle of transformative practice is built on critical framing, then Jenkins' goal of bridging the participation gap can become a reconstruction of education promoting critical media literacy. In a report funded by the MacArthur Foundation, Jenkins and others assert the need for teaching "new media literacies: a set of cultural competencies and social skills that young people need in the new media landscape. Participatory culture shifts the focus of literacy from one of individual expression to social practice and community involvement. The new literacies almost all involve social skills developed through collaboration and networking. These skills build on the foundation of traditional literacy, research skills, technical skills, and critical analysis skills taught in the classroom" (Jenkins *et al.*, 2007, p. 4).

TECHNOLOGY, LITERACY, AND TECHNOLITERACY

Upon first consideration, seeking a suitable definition of "technology" itself appears to be overly technical. Surely, in discussions concerning technology, it is rare indeed that people need to pause so as to ask for a clarification of the term. In a given context, if it is suggested that technology is either causing problems or alleviating them, people generally know what sort of thing is due for blame or praise.

Yet, the popular meaning of "technology" is problematically insufficient in at least two ways. First, it narrowly equates technological artifacts with "high-tech," such as those scientific machines used in medical and biotechnology, modern industrial apparatuses, and digital components like computers, ICTs, and other electronic media. This reductive view fails to recognize, for instance, that indigenous artifacts are themselves technologies in their own right, as well as other cultural objects that may once have represented the leading-edge of technological inventiveness during previous historical eras, such as books, hand tools, or even clothing. Secondly, popular conceptions of technology today make the additional error of construing technology as being merely object-oriented, identifying it as only the sort of machined products that arise through industry. In fact, from the first, technology has always meant far more; and this is reflected in recent definitions of technology as "a seamless web or network combining artifacts, people, organizations, cultural meanings and knowledge" (Wajcman 2004, p. 106) or that which "comprises the entire system of people and organizations, knowledge, processes, and devices that go into creating and operating technological artifacts, as well as the artifacts themselves" (Pearson and Young, 2002).

These broader definitions of technology are supported by the important insights of John Dewey. For Dewey, technology is central to humanity and girds human inquiry and practice in its totality (Hickman, 2001). In Dewey's his view, technology is evidenced in all manner of creative experience and problem-solving. It should extend beyond the sciences proper, as it encompasses not only the arts and humanities, but the professions, and the practices of our everyday lives. In this account, technology is inherently political and historical and in Dewey's philosophy, it is strongly tied to notions of democracy and education, which are considered technologies that intend social progress and greater freedom for the future.

Dewey's view is hardly naïve, but it is unabashedly optimistic and hopeful to assume that if people are sufficiently educated so as to be able to understand the problems which they face, that people can experimentally produce and deploy a wide range of technologies so as to solve those problems accordingly. Although in the spirit of Dewey one may recognize that the present age is beset by the unprecedented problem of globalized technological oppressions in many forms and contexts, it is too optimistic to assume that the solution can be achieved through education alone.

To this end, the insights of radical social critic and technology theorist Ivan Illich remain important (Kahn and Kellner, 2008). Specifically, Illich's notion of "tools" mirrors the broad humanistic understanding of technology outlined above, while it additionally distinguishes "rationally designed devices, be they artifacts or rules, codes or operators...from other things such as food or implements, which in a given culture are not deemed to be subject to rationalization" (Illich, 1973, p. 22). Consequently, Illich polemicizes for "tools for conviviality," which are technologies mindfully rationed to work within the balances of both cultural and natural limits and that can be employed by individuals and social movements to produce a more ecologically viable society that is more just and convivial. In view of the technological revolution we need to imagine how technologies can be deployed to promote progressive social change and the sort of 21st century technoliteracy necessary to meet the demands of a sustainable and ecumenical world.

Marshall McLuhan (1964) also provides a rationale for education to cultivate new literacies in his argument that new media produce new environments in which people live and navigate. For instance, electricity produced entirely new urban and living spaces as well as new sciences that contributed to the development of contemporary physics and new technologies like television and the Internet. Just as print culture for McLuhan placed literacies of reading and writing in the center of education, so do new electronic mediarequire new literacies and to developing multiple technoliteracies in order to properly perceive, navigate, and act in the new technological environment (see Kahn and Kellner 2006).

"Literacy" is often used by educators and policy makers, but in a variety of ways and for a broad array of purposes. In modern education in industrial societies, basic literacy was connected to vocational proficiency with language and numbers such that individuals could function at work and in society. Thus, even at the start of the 20th century, literacy largely meant the ability to write one's name and decode popular print-based texts, with the additional goal of written self-expression only emerging over the following decades. Street (1984) identifies these attributes as typical of an autonomous model of literacy that is politically conservative in that it is primarily economistic, individualistic, and is driven by a deficit theory of learning. On the other hand, Street characterizes these ideological models of literacy as prefiguring positive notions of collective empowerment, social context, and the encoding and decoding of non-print-based and print-based texts, as well as a progressive commitment to critical thinking-oriented skills.

In this conception, "literacy" is not a singular set of abilities but is multiple and comprises gaining competencies involved in effectively using socially constructed forms of communication and representation to function effectively in a given society. Learning literacies requires attaining competencies in practices and in contexts that are governed by rules and conventions. Thus, literacies are socially constructed in educational and cultural practices involving various institutional discourses and pedagogies. Against the autonomous view that posits literacy as static, one should see literacies as continuously evolving and shifting in response to social and cultural changes, as well as the interests of the elites who control hegemonic institutions and social movement seeking transformation and justice. Further, it is a crucial part of the literacy process that people come to understand hegemonic codes as furthering the interests of the established society and ruling elites.

This expanded conception of literacy follows Freire and Macedo (1987) in conceiving literacy as connected to issues of power. As they note, literacy is a cultural politics that "promotes democratic and emancipatory change" (p. viii) and it should be interpreted widely as the ability to engage in a variety of forms of problem-posing and dialectical analyses of self and society.

Based on these definitions of "technology" and "literacy" it should be obvious that, holistically conceived, literacies are themselves technologies that serve to facilitate and regulate technological systems. In this respect, to speak of "technoliteracies" may seem inherently tautological. On the other hand, however, the concept helps to highlight the constructed and potentially reconstructive nature of literacies, as well as the educative, social, and political nature of technologies and need for new literacies as technology and society evolves. Further, more than ever, we need philosophical reflection on the ends and purposes of education and on what we are doing and trying to achieve in our educational practices and institutions, which require new technoliteracies to participate in and transform contemporary societies.

For a progressive cultural politics, new technoliteracies can be seen as involved with the need to comprehend and make use of proliferating new technologies and media, and the political economy that drives them, towards furthering radical democratic understandings and transformations of our worlds. In a society inexorably undergoing processes of globalization and technological transformation, we cannot advocate a policy of clean hands and purity, in which people shield themselves from new technologies and their transnational proliferation. Instead, technoliteracies must be deployed and promoted that allow for popular interventions into the ongoing (often anti-democratic) economic and technological revolutions taking place, thereby potentially deflecting these forces for progressive ends like social justice and ecological well-being.

In this context, technoliteracies encompass computer, information, critical media, multimedia, and new media literacies presently theorized under the concept "multiliteracies" (Cope and Kalantzis, 2000; Luke, 1997, 2000; Rassool, 1999; New London Group, 1996). But whereas multiliteracies theory often remains focused upon digital technologies, with an implicit thrust towards providing new media job skills for the Internet age, I would explicitly highlight the social and cultural appropriateness of technologies and provide a critique of the emergent media economy as technocapitalist (Best and Kellner, 2001; Kellner, 1989), while acknowledging its progressive potentials. Thus, we draw upon the language of "multiple literacies" (Lonsdale and McCurry, 2004; Kellner, 1998) to augment a critical theory of technoliteracies to understand, decode, and intervene in media and digital culture (for examples, see Kellner 1995 and 1998; Kahn and Kellner 2006; and Kellner and Share 2005).[11]

TOWARD THE RECONSTRUCTION OF EDUCATION

Critical technoliteracies in this conception are tied to the project of radical democracy and are concerned to develop skills that will enhance democratization and civic participation. Teachers are cultural workers who are either participating in a transformative cultural politics, attempting to reconstruct education and society in a progressive direction, or they are involved in cultural reproduction and what Freire calls the "banking" system of education. A radical and transformative pedagogy should thus be seen as a cultural politics that takes a comprehensive approach that teaches critical skills and how to use media and technology as instruments of social communication and change. The new forms of culture and technologies of communication are becoming more and more accessible to young people and ordinary citizens, and can be used to promote education, democratic self-expression, and social justice – as well as consumerism, narcissism, and worse. Technologies like television, the Internet, and social networking that could help produce the end of democracy could generate the acceleration of participatory democracy. Critical education today should thus conceive of how to use new media and technologies to reconstruct education and help create a more democratic and just society.

NOTES

1 This chapter is indebted to collaborative work with Jeff Share on critical media literacies and with Richard Kahn on technoliteracies, as well as to members of my technology and education seminars at UCLA over the past years and discussions with colleagues to numerous to list.

2 On a critical theory of education, see Kellner 2006 and on the critical theory of technology, see Feenberg 1991, 1995, 1999 and Best and Kellner 2001; and Kellner 2002.

3 While all people born in this millennium have been alive since the invention of the Internet, cellular phones and television, this does not mean that everyone can access this technology. Since approximately one third (about two billion) of the world's population still live without electricity, it is important to remember that billions of people are being left behind the so-called technological revolution.

4 This data is based on random telephone interviews in 2003 with 1,065 parents of children between six months and six years of age. "Screen media" refers to watching TV, watching videos/DVDs, using a computer and playing video games. This research was reported in the Kaiser Family Foundation *Zero to Six* study available on-line at http://www.kff.org/entmedia/3378.cfm (accessed October 4, 2009). For graphic documentation of the growing time and involvement of youth and new media, see the PBS *Frontline* documentaries *Growing_Up_Online* (2008) and *Digital Nation* (2010), both available online at http://www.pbs.org/wgbh/pages/frontline/view/ (accessed on April 14, 2010).

5 The number of hours spent with media is based on questionnaires from a 2004 national sample of 2,032 students between 8 – 18 years of age, as well as 694 media-use diaries, as reported in the Kaiser Family Foundation *Generation M* study available on-line at http://www.kff.org/entmedia/entmedia 030905pkg.cfm (accessed on October 4, 2009). The figure of 6½ hours per day, includes ¼ of that time spent multitasking with several different media at the same time, thereby increasing media exposure to an estimated 8½ hours per day.

6 For an articulation of the concept of technoliteracies that this paper draws upon see Kahn and Kellner 2006.

7 Studies reveal that women, minorities, and immigrants now constitute roughly 85 percent of the growth in the labor force, while these groups represent about 60 percent of all workers; see Duderstadt 1999-2000: 38. In the past decade, the number of Hispanics in the United States increased by 35 percent and Asians by more than 40 percent. Since 1991, California has had no single ethnic or racial minority and almost half of the high school students in the state are African-American or Latino. Meanwhile, a "tidal wave" of children of baby boomers are about to enter college; see Atkinson 1999–2000: 49–50. Obviously, I am writing this study from a U.S. perspective, but would suggest that my arguments have broader reference in an increasingly globalized society marked by a networked economy, increasing migration and multiculturalism, and a proliferating Internet-based cyberculture. There is by now a tremendous amount of books and articles on the global economy, technological revolution, new cultural spaces, and the implications for every aspect of life from education to war. See, for example, the monumental studies by Castells 1996, 1997, and 1998, and the analyses of the restructuring of capital, technological revolution, and the postmodern turn in Best and Kellner, 2001.

8 The "digital divide" has emerged as the buzzword for perceived divisions between information technology have and have nots in the current economy and society. A U.S. Department of Commerce report released in July 1999 claimed that digital divide in relation to race is dramatically escalating and the Clinton administration and media picked up on this theme (See the report "Americans in the Information Age: Falling Through the Net" at http://www.ntia.doc.gov/ntiahome/ digitaldivide/ (accessed October 4, 2009). A critique of the data involved in the report emerged, however, claiming that it was outdated; subsequent studies by Stanford University, Cheskin Research, ACNielson, and the Forester Institute claim that education and class are more significant factors than race in constructing the divide (see http://www.clickz.com/stats/big_picture/demo graphics/ (accessed October 4, 2009) for a collection of reports and statistics on the divide; see also http://nces.ed.gov/pubsearch/pubsinfo.asp?pubid=2004011 (accessed October 4, 2009). Earlier and more recent research both make clear that there is a gaping division between information technology haves and have nots, that this is a major challenge to developing an egalitarian and democratic society, and that something needs to be done about the problem. My contribution involves the argument that empowering the have nots requires the dissemination of new literacies and thus

empowering groups and individuals previously excluded from economic opportunities and socio-political participation.

9 See the Ph.D. dissertations by two of my UCLA students, Jennifer Janofsky Rawls 2000 and Roy Zimmermann 2000 who argue that without proper training technology does not improve education. See also Bernard Warner, "Computers for Youth: Spreading the Net," *The Standard*, March 27, 2000 which reports: "A study conducted recently by Denver-based Quality Education Data showed school districts across the country spent $6.7 billion on technology in the 1998-1999 school year, up almost 25 percent from the previous year. But the same study revealed that an equally crucial funding component – computer training for teachers – was startlingly low, rising just 5.2 percent over the same period." In June 2000, however, President Bill Clinton argued for increased funding for teaching training to use new technologies so while there was growing recognition of the problem in the Clinton era, the issue seems to have disappeared in the Bush administration.

10 The quote was found on the official UNESCO web site. Retrieved October 23, 2006, from: http://portal.unesco.org/culture/en/ev.php-URL_ID=8270&URL_DO=DO_TOPIC&URL_SECTION=201.html (accessed October 4, 2009).

11 For three recent examples of studies that propose how new technoliteries can deploy media and technologies to promote social transformation and justice, see Share 2009; Kahn 2009; and Kim 2010.

REFERENCES

Aronowitz, S. (1985, May). Why Should Johnny read? *The village voice literary supplement, 13.*

Best, S., & Kellner, D. (2001). *The postmodern adventure: Science, technology, and cultural studies at the tird millennium.* New York and London: Guilford Press and Routledge.

Bourdieu, P. (1986). The forms of capital. In J. Richardson (Ed.), *Handbook of theory and research for the sociology of education* (pp. 241–258). New York: Greenwood Press.

Carrington, V. (2005). New textual landscapes, information and early literacy. In J. Marsh (Ed.), *Popular culture, new media and digital literacy in early childhood* (pp. 13–17). London: Routledge Falmer.

Castells, M. (1996). *The information age: Economy, society and culture Vol. I: The rise of the network society.* Cambridge, MA: Blackwell Publishers.

Considine, D. (2003). Weapons of mass destruction? Media literacy, social studies & citizenship. In B. Dunca & K. Tyner (Eds.), *Visions / revisions: Moving forward with media education* (pp. 24–45). Madison, WI: National Telemedia Council.

Cope, B., & Kalantzis, M. (Eds.). (2000). *Multiliteracies: Literacy learning and the design of social futures.* New York: Routledge.

Dewey, J. (1997 [1916]). *Democracy and education: An introduction to the philosophy of education.* Carbondale, IL and Edwardsville, IL: Southern Illinois University Press.

Feenberg, A. (1991). *Critical theory of technology.* New York: Oxford University Press.

Feenberg, A. (1995). *Alternative Modernity.* Berkeley, CA: University of California Press.

Feenberg, A. (1999). *Questioning technology.* New York and London: Routledge.

Friedman, T. (1999). *The lexus and the olive tree.* New York: Farrar Straus Giroux.

Friedman, T. (2005). *The world is flat.* New York: Farrar, Straus and Giroux.

Freire, P. (1972). *Pedagogy of the oppressed.* New York: Herder & Herder.

Freire, P., & Macedo, D. (1987). *Literacy: Reading the word and the world.* Westport, CT: Bergin & Garvey.

Gardner, H. (1983). *Frames of mind.* New York: Basic Books Inc.

Gee, J. P. (2000). New people in new worlds: Networks, the new capitalism and schools. In B. Cope & M. Kalantzis (Eds.), *Multiliteracies: Literacy, learning & the design of social futures* (pp. 43–68). Melbourne, Australia: Macmillan.

Gutiérrez Martín, A. (2003). Multimedia authoring as a fundamental principle of literacy and teacher training in the information age. In B. Duncan & K. Tyner (Eds.), *Visions / revisions: Moving forward with media education* (pp. 12–22). Madison, WI: National Telemedia Council.

Hammer, R. (1995). Strategies for media literacy. In R. Peter McLaren, Hammer, D. Sholle, & S. Reilly, (Eds.), *Rethinking media literacy: A critical pedagogy of representation* (pp. 225–235). New York: Peter Lang.

Hammer, R. (2006). Teaching critical media literacies: Theory, praxis and empowerment. *InterActions: UCLA Journal of Education and Information Studies*, *2*(1), Article 6. Retrieved from http://repositories.cdlib.org/gseis/interactions/vol2/iss1/6

Hammer, R., & Kellner, D. (2001). Multimedia pedagogy and multicultural education for the new millennium. *Current Issues in Education*, *4*(2). Retrieved from http://cie.ed.asu.edu/volume4/number2/

Harding, S. (Ed.). (2004). *The feminist standpoint theory reader: Intellectual and political controversies*. New York and London: Routledge.

Hickman, L. (2001). *Philosophical tools for technological culture*. Bloomington, IN: Indiana University Press.

Illich, I. (1973). *Tools for conviviality*. New York: Harper and Row.

Jegede, O. (2002). "An Integrated ICT-Support for

Kahn, R. (2010) *Critical pedagogy, ecoliteracy & planetary crisis. The ecopedagogy movement.* New York: Peter Lang

Kahn, R., & Kellner, D. (2006). Reconstructing technoliteracy: A multiple literacies approach. In J. R. Dakers (Ed.), *Defining technological literacy* (pp. 253–274). New York and England: Palgrave Macmillan.

Kahn, R., & Kellner, D. (2008). Paulo Freire and Ivan Illich: Technology, politics, and the reconstruction of education. In C. Torres (Ed.), *Paulo Freire and the possible dream*. Urbana, IL: University of Illinois Press.

Kellner, D. (1989). *Critical theory, marxism and modernity*. Baltimore: Johns Hopkins University Press.

Kellner, D. (1995). *Media culture: Identity and politics between the modern and the postmodern*. New York: Routledge.

Kellner, D. (1998). Multiple literacies and critical pedagogy in a multicultural society. *Educational Theory*, *48*, 103–122.

Kellner, D. (2002, November). Theorizing globalization. *Sociological theory*, *20*(3), 285–305.

Kellner, D. (2003a). *Media spectacle*. London and New York: Routledge.

Kellner, D. (2003b). *From 9/11 to terror war: The dangers of the bush legacy*. Lanham, MD: Rowman & Littlefield.

Kellner, D. (2005). *Media spectacle and The crisis of democracy: Terrorism, war, and election battles*. Boulder, CO: Paradigm Publishers.

Kellner, D. (2007). Toward a critical theory of education. Critical theory and critical pedagogy today. In I. Gur-Ze'ev (Ed.), *Toward a new critical language in education* (pp. 49–69). University of Haifa, Studies in Education.

Kellner, D. (2008) *Guys and Guns Amok: Domestic Terrorism and School Shootings from the Oklahoma City Bombings to the Virginia Tech Massacre*. Boulder, Col.: Paradigm Press.

Kellner, D., & Kim, G. (2009). YouTube, politics and pedagogy: Some critical reflections. In R. Hammer & D. Kellner (Eds.), *Media/cultural studies: Critical approaches* (pp. 615–635). New York: Peter Lang Publishing.

Kellner, D., & Share, J. (2005). Toward critical media literacy: Core concepts, debates, organizations and policies. *Discourse: Studies in the cultural politics of education*. The University of Queensland, Australia: Routledge.

Kelly, K. (1995). *Out of control. The new biology of machines, social systems, and the economic world.* New York: Addison, Wesley.

Kelly, K. (1998). *New rules for the new economy*. London: Fourth Estate.

Kim, G. (2010*). The Popular as the Political: Introduction to Critical Media Pedagogy as a Condition for Grassroots Collective Action Mobilization via YouTube Videos*. Ph.D. Dissertation: Graduate School of Education & Information Studies, University of California – Los Angeles

Klein, N. (2007). *The shock doctrine. The rise of disaster capitalism*. New York: Metropolitan Books.

Lo Bianco, J. (2000). Multiliteracies and Multilingualism. In B. Cope & M. Kalantzis (Eds.), *Multiliteracies: Literacy, learning & the design of social futures* (pp. 92–105). Melbourne, Australia: Macmillan.

Lonsdale, M., & McCurry, D. (2004). *Literacy in the new millennium*. Adelaide, Australia: NCVER.

Luke, C. (1997). *Technological literacy*. Melbourne, Australia: National Languages & Literacy Institute. Adult Literacy Network.

Luke, C. (2000). Cyber-schooling and technological change: Multiliteracies for new times. In B. Cope & M. Kalantzis (Eds.), *Multiliteracies: Literacy, learning, and the design of social futures* (pp. 69–105). South Yarra, Australia: Macmillan.

Luke, C. (2006). *As seen on TV or was that my phone? New media literacy*. Unpublished manuscript, University of Queensland: Centre for Critical and Cultural Studies.

Luke, A., & Luke, C. (2002). Adolescence lost/childhood regained: On early intervention and the emergence of the techno-subject. *Journal of Early Childhood Literacy, 1*(1), 91–120.

McChesney, R. (2004). *The problem of the media: U.S. communication politics in the 21st century*. New York: Monthly Review Press.

McLuhan, M. (1964). *Understanding media: The extensions of man*. New York: Signet Books.

National Commission on Excellence in Education. (1983). *A nation at risk: The imperative for educational reform*. Washington, DC: U.S. Government Printing Office.

National Telecommunications & Information Administration. (2002). *A nation online: How Americans are expanding their use of the internet*. Retrieved from http://www.ntia.doc.gov/ntiahome/dn/nation online_020502.htm

New London Group. (1996). A pedagogy of multiliteracies: Designing social futures. *Harvard Educational Review, 66*, 60–92.

Ó Tuathail, G., & McCormack, D. (1999). The technoliteracy challenge: Teaching globalization using the internet *Journal of Geography in Higher Education, 22*, 347–361.

Park, L. S.-H., & Pellow, D. N. (2004). Racial formation, environmental racism, and the emergence of Silicon Valley. *Ethnicities, 4*(3), 403–424.

Pearson, G., & Thomas Young, A. (2002). *Technically speaking: Why all Americans need to know more about technology*. Washington, DC: National Academies Press.

Plotnick, E. (1999). *Information literacy*. ERIC Clearinghouse on Information and Technology, Syracuse University. ED-427777.

Rassool, N. (1999). *Literacy for sustainable development in the age of information*. London, UK: Multilingual Matters Ltd.

Rawls, J. J. (2000). *The role of micropolitics in school-site technology efforts: A case study of the relationship between teachers and the technology movement at their school*. Ph.D. Dissertation, Graduate School of Education & Information Studies, University of California – Los Angeles

Rideout, V. J., Vandewater, E. A., & Wartella, E. A. (2005). *Zero to six: Electronic media in the lives of infants, toddlers and preschoolers*. Washington, DC: Kaiser Family Foundation.

Share, J. (2009) *Media Literacy is Elementary. Teaching Youth to Critically Read and Create Media* New York: Peter Lang

Shields, R. (2003). *The virtual*. London and New York: Routledge.

Zimmerman, R. (2000). *The intersection of technology and teachers: Challenges and problems*. PhD Dissertation, Graduate School of Education & Information Studies, University of California – Los Angeles

Douglas Kellner
Graduate School of Education & Information Studies
University of California
Los Angeles

NOTES ON CONTRIBUTORS

Michael W. Apple is John Bascom Professor of Curriculum and Instruction and Educational Policy Studies at the University of Wisconsin, USA and Professor of Educational Policy Studies at the Institute of Education, University of London, UK. He has written extensively on the relationship among power, knowledge, and education and on understanding and interrupting dominant models of educational reform. Among his recent books are *Educating the "Right" Way: Markets, Standards, God, and Inequality* (2nd ed., 2006), *The Routledge International Handbook of Critical Education* (2009), and *Global Crises, Social Justice, and Education* (2010).

Gert Biesta is Professor of Education at the Stirling Institute of Education, University of Stirling, UK and Visiting Professor for Education and Democratic Citizenship at Mälardalen University, Sweden. He conducts theoretical and empirical research and is particularly interested in the relationships between education, democracy and democratization. He takes inspiration from pragmatism and Continental philosophy and educational theory. His books include: *Derrida & Education* (co-edited with Denise Egéa Kuehne; Routledge 2001); *Pragmatism and Educational Research* (with Nicholas C. Burbules; Rowman & Littlefield 2003); *Beyond Learning: Democratic Education for a Human Future* (Paradigm Publishers 2006); *Democracy, Education and the Moral Life* (co-edited with Michael Katz and Susan Verducci; Springer 2008); *Derrida, Deconstruction and the Politics of Pedagogy* (with Michael A. Peters; Peter Lang 2008); *Good Education in an Age of Measurement: Ethics, Politics, Democracy* (Paradigm Publishers, 2010); *Jacques Rancière: Education, Truth, Emancipation* (with Charles Bingham; Continuum 2010). His website is at *www.gertbiesta.com.*

Rodrigo G. Britez is a doctoral student in Educational Policy at the University of Illinois, Urbana-Champaign, USA. His major research interests include: globalisation and education policy, higher education policy in South America, and networks of governance in higher education policy. He is currently working on issues relating to social networks and the role of transnational agencies in policy processes in higher education.

Alicia A. Broderick is an Assistant Professor in the Elementary Inclusive Education Program in the Department of Curriculum and Teaching at Teachers College, Columbia University, USA. She adopts a broad definition of inclusive schooling, in keeping with international discourses that seek to resist and redress the many ways in which students experience marginalization and exclusion in schools. Thus, she argues that inclusive education is not just about students with labeled disabilities, but is fundamentally about all students, and more significantly, about the cultural practices of schooling. To that end, her work seeks intersections among a variety of criticalist discourses, including critical disability studies and critical race theory, in engaging in cultural critique of schooling practices and dis/ability constructs. She has a particular interest in the construct of autism and is committed to working collaboratively with autistic colleagues in academic and political endeavors.

Ergin Bulut is a doctoral student at the University of Illinois, Urbana-Champaign, USA. He earned his B.A and M.A degrees at Bogazici University in Turkey, in the departments of Translation Studies and History of Modern Turkey respectively and wrote his thesis based on a field work on the issue of the transformation of vocational training in Turkey. His research interests include social theory, social class and reproduction, working class youth and culture.

Kristen L. Buras is Assistant Professor of Multicultural Urban Education and Reform in the Division of Educational Studies at Emory University, USA. She is author of *Rightist Multiculturalism* and co–editor of *The Subaltern Speak* as well as *Pedagogy and Policy in the Privatized City*. Her forthcoming book is entitled *Schooling, Race, and Urban Space: Where the Market Meets Grassroots Resistance*.

Dennis Carlson is Professor of Curriculum Studies and Cultural Foundations of education in the Department of Educational Leadership at Miami University, USA. He is the author of *Teachers and Crisis: Urban School Reform and Teachers' Work Culture* (1992), *Making Progress: Education and Culture in New Times* (1997), and *Leaving Save Harbors: Toward a New Progressivism in American Education and Public Life* (2003). He has also co-edited a number of books in education, including most recently (with C. P. Gause) *Keeping the Promise: Essays on Leadership, Democracy, and Education* (2007). Carlson has also published in major educational journals and is completing a memoir of serving in the Peace Corps in Libya.

Seehwa Cho is Associate Professor in the School of Education at the University of St. Thomas in Minnesota, USA. She teaches in the areas of critical theory, Marxist theory, critical pedagogy, sociology of education, and philosophy of education. Her past research projects include education reform in the USA, globalization and its impacts on education in South Korea, and the relationships between labor, gender, and schooling. Her recent research focuses on the political economic analysis of critical theories and critical pedagogy.

Noah De Lissovoy is Assistant Professor in Curriculum Studies in the Department of Curriculum and Instruction at the University of Texas at Austin, USA. His research centers on critical approaches to curriculum, pedagogy, and educational theory, with a particular focus on cultural studies, globalization, and contemporary social movements. He is the author of *Power, Crisis, and Education for Liberation: Rethinking Critical Pedagogy* (Palgrave Macmillan, 2008). His work has been published in a number of journals and edited collections, including the *Review of*

Education, Pedagogy, and Cultural Studies, the *Journal of Education Policy*, and *Cultural Studies/ Critical Methodologies*.

Greg Dimitriadis is Professor of Sociology of Education at the University at Buffalo, The State University of New York, USA. He is the author of *Performing Identity/Performing Culture: Hip Hop as Text, Pedagogy, and Lived Practice* (Peter Lang, 2nd ed., 2009), *Friendship, Cliques, and Gangs: Young Black Men Coming of Age in Urban America* (Teachers College Press), and *Studying Urban Youth Culture* (Peter Lang). He is co-author of *Reading and Teaching the Postcolonial: From Baldwin to Basquiat and Beyond* (Teachers College Press), *On Qualitative Inquiry* (Teachers College Press), and *Theory for Education* (Routledge). He is also co-editor of *Promises to Keep: Cultural Studies, Democratic Education, and Public Life* (Routledge), *Learning to Labor in New Times* (Routledge), *Race, Identity, and Representation in Education* (Second Edition) (Routledge), and *Ideology, Curriculum, and the New Sociology of Education* (Routledge).

Michael J. Dumas is Assistant Professor of Social and Cultural Analysis of Education, and also teaches in the doctoral program in Educational Leadership at California State University, Long Beach, USA. His research focuses on the cultural politics of Black education, redistributive justice, and urban educational policy discourse. A graduate of the Ph.D. Program in Urban Education at The Graduate Center of The City University of New York, he received a Spencer Foundation dissertation fellowship to study the Black cultural politics of school desegregation in Seattle. In all of his work, he is interested less in contributing to the literature (although that has its place), and more in inspiring a radical and joyful imagination of education in Black life.

Benjamin Frymer is Assistant Professor of Sociology in the Hutchins School of Liberal Studies, Sonoma State University, USA and Director of Project Censored. He works in the areas of critical theory, youth, education, media, and cultural studies focusing on contemporary alienation and ideology. His publications include co-editing the book *Cultural Studies, Education, and Youth: Beyond Schools* (Forthcoming, Lexington Books), a co-edited book on Hollywood films and education, and several essays on the Columbine shootings. He will soon be directing the Center For the Study of Media in a Global Society at Sonoma State.

David Gillborn is Professor of Critical Race Studies in Education at the Institute of Education, University of London, UK. Recently described as 'one of Britain's leading race theorists', David is the author of numerous books and articles, including *Racism and Education: Coincidence or Conspiracy?* (2008) the first major application of 'critical race theory' to the English education system and winner of "Book of the Year" from the UK Society for Educational Studies, and *Rationing Education* (2000, with Deborah Youdell) which won "Best Book in Education," also from the Society for Educational Studies. He is recognized internationally as a leading writer in the field and was recently honoured for his work "Promoting Multicultural Education" by the American Educational Research Association (AERA) special interest group on the Critical Examination of Race, Ethnicity, Class and Gender in Education. David's writing spans both quantitative and qualitative research. He is founding editor of the international journal *Race Ethnicity and Education* and co-editor (with Ed Taylor and Gloria Ladson-Billings) of *Foundations of Critical Race Theory in Education* (2009), the first collection to bring together key texts in legal and educational CRT.

Henry A. Giroux currently holds the Global TV Network Chair Professorship at McMaster University, Canada in the English and Cultural Studies Department. He has published numerous books and articles and his most recent books include: *The University in Chains: Confronting the Military-Industrial-Academic Complex* (2007); *Against the Terror of Neoliberalism* (2008); and *Youth in a Suspect Society: Democracy or Disposability?* (2009).

Kalervo N. Gulson is Senior Lecturer in the Faculty of Arts and Social Sciences at the University of New South Wales, Australia. His research is in critical policy studies and urban studies. It focuses on how education policy, notably that relating to education markets in K-12 schooling, reflects and constitutes the changing nature of cities. Using theories of space and place, this work includes examining the connections between education policy, gentrification, and social inequality, with a focus on race and ethnicity, in inner city areas of Sydney, London and Vancouver. His work has been recently published in *Race Ethnicity & Education*, *Journal of Education Policy*, and *Urban Studies.*

Sandra Harding is a philosopher who teaches in the Graduate School of Education and Department of Women's Studies at the University of California, Los Angeles, USA. She is the author or editor of 15 books, including *Sciences From Below: Feminisms, Postcolonialities, and Modernities* (2008); *Science and Social Inequality* (2006); and *The Feminist Standpoint Theory Reader* (2004). She co-edited *Signs: Journal of Women in Culture and Society* between 2000–2005.

Sherick Hughes is Assistant Professor of Education, University of Maryland, College Park, USA. He earned a BA from UNC-Wilmington, MA from Wake Forest University, and MPA and Ph.D. from UNC-Chapel Hill. He teaches several graduate courses in the Department of Curriculum and Instruction including: Introductory and Advanced Qualitative Research Methods; Power, Privilege, and Diversity in Teaching; and Urban Education. He has developed a new undergraduate research course focused upon global education studies in marginalization and interdependence. He serves as on the editorial boards of the *Urban Review*, *Educational Studies*, and *Educational Foundations.* His research generally involves: (1) Black education and family pedagogy of hope; applied critical theory, research methods, and analytic frameworks; critical race pedagogy and urban teacher education/professional development; and global marginalization and interdependence. He has published numerous articles, book chapters, and two books including the 2007 AESA Critics' Choice Award-Winning title, *Black Hands in the Biscuits Not in the*

Classrooms: Unveiling Hope in a Struggle for Brown's Promise. Dr. Hughes is currently completing a co-edited book for Hampton Press with Dr. Thea Berry, which centers living, learning, and teaching the new cultural politics of race in education.

Korina Jocson is Assistant Professor of Education in the College of Arts & Sciences at Washington University in St. Louis, USA. Her research and teaching interests include literacy, youth, and cultural studies in education. For the past decade, she has collaborated with university programs, schools, and community-based organizations to promote literacy development. She has published in various scholarly journals and is the author of *Youth Poets: Empowering Literacies In and Out of Schools.*

Jackson Katz, Ph.D., is an educator, cultural critic, filmmaker and Huffington Post blogger whose main areas of research and activism are gender violence, media, sports culture and contemporary U.S. political discourse. He is co-founder of the Mentors in Violence Prevention (MVP) program, the most widely utilized sexual and domestic violence prevention initiative in college and professional athletics. He is the creator of popular educational videos including *Tough Guise: Violence, Media and the Crisis in Masculinity.* He is the author of *The Macho Paradox: Why Some Men Hurt Women and How All Men Can Help.* He lectures widely in the U.S. and around the world on violence, media and multiracial/multiethnic masculinities.

Douglas Kellner is George Kneller Chair in the Philosophy of Education at University of California, Los Angeles, USA and is the author of many books on social theory, politics, history, and culture, including *Camera Politica: The Politics and Ideology of Contemporary Hollywood Film*, co-authored with Michael Ryan and an *Emile de Antonio Reader* co-edited with Dan Streible. Other works include *Critical Theory, Marxism, and Modernity*; *Jean Baudrillard: From Marxism to Postmodernism and Beyond*; works in cultural studies such as *Media Culture* and *Media Spectacle*; a trilogy of books on postmodern theory with Steve Best; and a trilogy of books on the media and the Bush administration, encompassing *Grand Theft 2000*, *From 9/11 to Terror War*, and *Media Spectacle and the Crisis of Democracy*. Author of *Herbert Marcuse and the Crisis of Marxism*, Kellner is editing collected papers of Herbert Marcuse, four volumes of which have appeared with Routledge. Kellner's *Guys and Guns Amok: Domestic Terrorism and School Shootings from the Oklahoma City Bombings to the Virginia Tech Massacre* won the 2008 AESA award as the best book on education. Forthcoming in 2009 with Blackwell is Kellner's *Cinema Wars: Hollywood Film and Politics in the Bush/ Cheney Era.* His website is at http://www. gseis.ucla.edu/faculty/kellner/kellner. html

Zeus Leonardo is Associate Professor of Social and Cultural Studies in the Graduate School of Education and Affiliated Faculty of the Critical Theory Designated Emphasis at the University of California, Berkeley, USA. Leonardo has published many articles and book chapters on race, class and educational theory. His books include *Ideology, Discourse, and School Reform* (Praeger) and he is editor of *Critical Pedagogy and Race* (Blackwell), His articles have appeared in *Educational Researcher*; *Race, Ethnicity & Education*; and *Educational Philosophy and Theory*. Some of his essays include: "The Souls of White Folk," "Critical Social Theory and Transformative Knowledge," and "The Unhappy Marriage between Marxism and Race Critique." His recent book is *Race, Whiteness, and Education* (Routledge).

Jennifer Logue is an Assistant Professor of Educational Foundations in the Department of Educational Leadership at Southern Illinois University, Edwardsville, USA. Her dissertation is entitled, "The Unbelievable Truth and the Dilemmas of Ignorance: Rethinking Student Resistance in Social Justice Education." She has published in the areas of Cultural Studies in Education, Gender and Women's Studies, and Philosophy of Education.

Cameron McCarthy is Communication Scholar and University Scholar in the Department of Educational Policy Studies and the Institute of Communication Research at the University of Illinois, Urbana-Champaign, USA. He is the author or co-author of several books including *The Uses of Culture: Education and the Limits of Ethnic Affiliation*; *Reading and Teaching the Postcolonial; Globalizing Cultural Studies: Ethnographic Interventions in Theory, Method and Policy;* and *Transnational Perspectives on Culture, Policy, and Education: Redirecting Cultural Studies in Neoliberal Times.*

Peter McLaren is a Professor in the Division of Urban Schooling, Graduate School of Education and Information Studies, University of California, Los Angeles, USA. He is the author and editor of 45 books on critical pedagogy, Marxist humanist theory and philosophy, and the political sociology of education. His writings have been translated in twenty languages. His work has been the topic of two edited books, *Teaching Peter McLaren*, edited by Marc Pruyn and Luis Huerta-Charles, and *Peter McLaren, Education and the Politics of Liberation*, edited by Mustafa Eryaman.

Michael A. Peters is Professor of Education in the Department of Educational Policy Studies at the University of Illinois, Urbana-Champaign, USA and Royal Melbourne Institute of Technology (School of Art), Australia. He held joint professorial positions at the Universities of Auckland, NZ and Glasgow, UK. He was elected Academic Vice-President of the New Zealand Association of University Teachers and elected an inaugural Fellow of the NZ Academy of Humanities. He is the executive editor of *Educational Philosophy and Theory* (Wiley-Blackwell) and editor of two international ejournals, *Policy Futures in Education* and *E-Learning* (Symposium). His interests focus broadly on education, philosophy and social theory and he has written some fifty books and many academic papers, including most recently: *Governmentality Studies in Education* (Sense, 2009 forthcoming);

Neoliberalism and Intellectual Life (Sense, 2009); *Showing and Doing: Wittgenstein as a Pedagogical Philosopher* (Paradigm, 2008) with Nick Burbules and Paul Smeyers; *Global Knowledge Cultures* (Sense) with Cushla Kapitizke; *Subjectivity and Truth: Foucault, Education and The Culture of Self* (Peter Lang, 2008) with Tina Besley; *Why Foucault? New Directions in Educational Research* (Peter Lang, 2007) with Tina Besley; *Knowledge Economy, Development and the Future of the University* (Sense, 2007); *Building Knowledge Cultures: Educational and Development in the Age of Knowledge Capitalism* (Rowman & Littlefield, 2006), with Tina Besley. Currently, he is writing a trilogy published by Peter Lang: *Creativity and the Global Knowledge Economy* (2009), *Global Creation: Space, Mobility and Synchrony in the Age of the Knowledge Economy* (2009), and *Imagination: Three Models of Imagination in the Age of the Knowledge Economy* (2010) with Simon Marginson and Peter Murphy.

Takeo Rivera holds an MA in Modern Thought & Literature and a BA in Comparative Studies from Race and Ethnicity, both from Stanford University, USA. He is primarily invested in the intersection of the arts, the community, and the academy, exploring these issues through scholarship, performance poetry, and playwriting. His work as a poet and playwright has been recognized by the John F. Kennedy Center for the Performing Arts and by San Francisco's Kearny Street Workshop, and has won him Third Place in the New Works of Merit Playwriting Contest in New York City. He currently works as an educator and rape crisis advocate at the YWCA of Silicon Valley. He intends to pursue a Ph.D.

Jen Sandler is Visiting Assistant Professor of Education at Bates College, USA. She studies how individuals and institutions conceptualize and attempt to shape social and educational reform in community and policy contexts. Her current projects involve epistemic social and political movements, as well as ongoing studies of the relationships between community organizing, elites, and educational reform. Jen received her Ph.D. in Educational Policy Studies from the University of Wisconsin, Madison.

Valerie Scatamburlo-D'Annibale is an Associate Professor in the Department of Communication, Media and Film and Chair of the Graduate Program in Communication and Social Justice at the University of Windsor, Windsor, Ontario, Canada. Her various works have been published in the *International Journal of Progressive Education*, *Educational Philosophy and Theory*, *Cultural Studies/ Critical Methodologies*, and *Public Resistance*.

Diana Silberman-Keller was Professor and Dean of the School of Multi-disciplinary Studies, Beit Berl College, Israel, where she was previously Head of the Non-Formal Education Department. She wrote widely in the areas of ideologies in education, literary theory and semiotics in education, non-formal education, and learning. Before her death in 2009, she published (with Schirmacher) *Mirrors Triptych Technology: Remediation and Translation Figures* and co-edited (with Bekerman, Giroux, and Burbules) *Mirror Images: Popular Culture and Education*.

Sofia A. Villenas is Associate Professor of Education and Director of the Latino/a Studies Program at Cornell University. A former Spanish bilingual elementary school teacher and adult educator in Latino communities, Dr. Villenas is now a teacher educator and a researcher who explores education through the lens of culture, language, race, class, gender and migration. She is currently involved in three projects. They include a service learning ethnographic study of how diverse families and youths experience inclusion and exclusion in a college town school district, a study of Latino family education as it intersects with schools and other sites of education in new Latino destinations, and a conceptual project of thinking with the knowledge and organic theories of Latina/Chicana feminist thought as a way to perceive transformative modes of teaching, learning and social movement. Dr. Villenas has published in journals such as *Harvard Educational Review*, *Anthropology and Education Quarterly* and the *International Journal of Qualitative Studies in Education.* She has been co-editor of the *Anthropology and Education Quarterly* and is currently associate editor of the *Journal of Latinos and Education.* Her co-edited books include *Race is ... Race isn't: Critical Race Theory and Qualitative Studies in Education*; *Chicana/Latina Education in Everyday Life: Feminista Perspectives on Pedagogy and Epistemology*; and forthcoming, the *Handbook of Latinos and Education: Theory, Research and Practice*.

Deborah Youdell is Professor of Education at the Institute of Education, University of London. Her work is located in the Sociology of Education and is concerned with educational inequalities in relation to race, gender, sexuality, religion, social class, ability and disability and the way these are connected to student subjectivities and everyday life in schools. Deborah is co-author of the award-winning *Rationing Education: Policy, Practice, Reform and Equity* and author of *Impossible Bodies, Impossible Selves: Exclusions and Student Subjectivities*. Her latest book, *School Trouble: Identity, Power and Politics in Education,* will be published in early 2010. She is Regional Editor of the *International Journal of Qualitative Studies in Education* and is on the Editorial Boards of the *British Journal of Sociology of Education*, *Race Ethnicity Education*, and *Critical Studies in Education*.

CPSIA information can be obtained at www.ICGtesting.com
Printed in the USA
LVOW09s0830140915

453967LV00022B/339/P